STEPHEN GARDINER

FROM ONE OF THE PORTRAITS BELONGING TO TRINITY HALL, CAMBRIDGE

Reproduced from "Historical Portraits," through the courtesy of Mr. Emery Walker and the Clarendon Press.

STEPHEN GARDINER
AND THE TUDOR REACTION

THE MACMILLAN COMPANY
NEW YORK · BOSTON · CHICAGO · DALLAS
ATLANTA · SAN FRANCISCO

MACMILLAN & CO., Limited
LONDON · BOMBAY · CALCUTTA
MELBOURNE

THE MACMILLAN CO. OF CANADA, Ltd.
TORONTO

STEPHEN GARDINER

AND

THE TUDOR REACTION

BY

JAMES ARTHUR MULLER, Ph.D.

PROFESSOR OF CHURCH HISTORY
EPISCOPAL THEOLOGICAL SCHOOL
CAMBRIDGE, MASSACHUSETTS

New York

THE MACMILLAN COMPANY

1926

Few have risen higher by mere dint of abilities, few suffered greater changes of fortune, few have been more magnified or commended, few more invidiously and outrageously treated, than this famous prelate, in his lifetime and since his decease; yet for any tolerable account of him there is none.—*Biographia Britannica.* Article, "Gardiner."

Although I go not about to prove myself a saint, for I have made no such outward visage of hypocrisy, yet it shall appear I am not utterly a devil.— GARDINER to PAGET, November 5, 1545.

My word is *vana salus hominis.*—GARDINER to SOMERSET, October 14, 1547.

TO THE READER

That the biography of Gardiner has not before been written is the excuse for this volume—if any excuse be needed for the study of the career of one who, as Bishop of Winchester, Master of Trinity Hall, Chancellor of Cambridge University, Privy Councillor to Henry VIII, and Lord Chancellor of the realm under Queen Mary, led the conservative forces in Church and State for the quarter of a century from the fall of Cardinal Wolsey to the return of Cardinal Pole.

I have profited much from the work of historians and biographers of the Tudor period, but my chief study has been of the letters and books of Gardiner himself, the books and letters of his contemporaries, the State papers, statutes, chronicles, and ecclesiastical, academic, and social records of his day.

To achieve even a passing acquaintance with the mass of this contemporary literature has been the work of several years. I can only say that I have tried to examine it with care and, on the many vexed questions which the career of Gardiner presents, to weigh the evidence with impartiality. That the reader may not be without material from which to form his own judgement I have quoted from the writings of Gardiner and his contemporaries in as full a measure as the scope of this volume permits.

I came to this study without any desire to prove anything; I leave it not without sympathy for that "proud and glorious" prelate whom John Foxe delighted to call "Wily Winchester."

ACKNOWLEDGMENTS

The documentary material for this study has been gathered during two residences in England, in 1913 and 1923, the first made possible by the award to me of the Alexander Viets Griswold Allen Fellowship in Ecclesiastical History from the Episcopal Theological School, Cambridge, Massachusetts.

A portion of the finished work was presented in 1915 in partial fulfilment of the requirements for the degree of Doctor of Philosophy in the Department of History at Princeton University.

I am indebted for courtesy and assistance to those in charge of many libraries and collections—to the librarians at Harvard, Columbia, Princeton, and Cambridge Universities, and at the British Museum and the Public Record Office; and in particular to Mr. J. P. Gilson of the British Museum, to Mr. R. H. Brodie and Mr. A. E. Stamp of the Public Record Office, to Sir Geoffrey Butler and Mr. E. A. G. Robinson of Corpus Christi College, Cambridge, to Professor Claude Jenkins of Lambeth Palace Library, to the Reverend T. P. Stevens of Southwalk Cathedral, to the Hon. Philip P. Cary, York Herald, of the College of Arms, to Dr. Charles R. Gillett of Union Theological Seminary, and to all the other members of the unfailingly gracious staff of the library of that institution.

My thanks are due to my former teacher Professor John Howell Westcott of Princeton, my former pupil the Reverend DuBose Murphy, and my recent colleagues, Professors Irville F. Davidson and James A. Wilson of St. Stephen's College, for helpful suggestions in the translation of difficult passages of sixteenth-century French and Latin.

My brother, the late Robert H. Muller, Esq., of Philadelphia, contributed many hours of painstaking labour to the preparation of my manuscript.

The Master and Fellows of Trinity Hall, Cambridge, have graciously granted me permission to reproduce as frontispiece one of the portraits of Gardiner in their possession, and Mr. Emery Walker and his publishers, the Clarendon Press, have no less graciously permitted me to use a reproduction of his photograph of this portrait.

To the historian of Trinity Hall and editor of Gardiner's Episcopal Register, Mr. H. E. Malden, I am indebted for a generous use of time and knowledge in answering queries concerning Gardiner's diocesan and college activities, and for placing at my disposal copious notes on his Register.

The care and accuracy of Miss D. M. Page of London in transcribing for me several of Gardiner's unpublished letters has appreciably lightened my labours.

For criticism, suggestion, and encouragement I am under especial obligations to Professors Paul van Dyke and William Starr Myers of Princeton, and to Miss E. Jeffries Davis of University College, London, who have read portions of the manuscript, and to Professor Roger B. Merriman of Harvard, who has read the proof.

The extent of my indebtedness to editors of sixteenth-century collections and historians of the Tudor period will appear in my frequent citations from their works.

NOTE ON SOURCES

The sources for much in Gardiner's life are the sources for the history of the reigns of Henry VIII, Edward VI, and Mary. They are adequately enumerated in the *Cambridge Modern History* and the *Political History of England*.

The three chief groups of source material specifically for Gardiner are his works, his letters, and the records of his trial.

The titles and editions of his works and the libraries where copies may be found, together with the titles of works written in confutation of them, are given in Appendix II.

With a few exceptions, noted in Appendix III, his letters during the reign of Henry VIII are printed in abstract with varying degrees of fulness in the *Letters and Papers of the Reign of Henry VIII*. Many of them for this and subsequent periods are printed in full in such collections as those of Pocock, Burnet, Strype, Ellis, Foxe, Lamb, and the *State Papers of Henry VIII*. Over a score of his letters, written during the reigns of Edward VI and Mary, some of great length and of peculiar importance for his biography, have never been published. Considerable portions of them are quoted in this volume, and a calendar including both published and unpublished letters in the reigns of Edward VI and Mary is given in Appendix III.

The records of his trial have been preserved by Foxe (*see* Chapter XXV, n. 2), who also gives much other information of diverse value about him, including the accounts of his examinations of the reformers in 1555 (*see* Chapter XXXII, n. 8). No little acquaintance with Foxe has led me to the following conclusions concerning his worth: (1) When he quotes letters, documents, books, or pamphlets, he usually does so with honesty and a fair degree of accuracy. (2) When he retails a rumour or a story based on hearsay, he usually indicates that it is such, which should be a warning to the student to apply to it the canons of historical criticism. (3) His animus towards Gardiner and his admiration for the reformers are so frank and obvious that they may readily be discounted. He remains, therefore, for those who use him with judgement and historical knowledge, an invaluable collection of material for Tudor history. The best edition of Foxe, and that cited in this volume, is the edition in the *Church Historians of England* series, where mistakes in editing, such as Maitland pointed out in the earlier of the modern editions, have been corrected, and valuable addenda and appendices added. The pagination is the same as that in other modern editions. When the early editions, *e.g.*, 1563, 1570, have been cited, the date is given with the citation.

For the last two years of Gardiner's life a good deal of our information is supplied by the dispatches of foreign representatives at Mary's court. While the ambassador of Venice appears to have observed events with a discerning and impartial eye, his knowledge of some of them was not so intimate as that of the French and Imperial ambassadors, especially the latter. Yet both French and Imperial diplomatic correspondence must be used with caution where Gardiner is concerned. His opposition to the Spanish marriage on the one hand, and to the French intrigues with English rebels on the other, caused both Frenchmen and Imperialists to regard him with distrust. Their comments on his actions and motives are coloured accordingly.

Sketches of Gardiner's life appear in many histories, biographical dictionaries, and encyclopædias. One of the longest, and one which undertakes impartially to estimate his character, is that in the *Biographia Britannica* of 1750, signed "E." Thanks to the source material since made available, this is now far from adequate. That by Mr. J. Bass Mullinger in the *Dictionary of National Biography* uses some of the new material, but often imperfectly and sometimes carelessly. Its inaccuracies are pointed out as occasion offers in the notes in this volume. Mr. H. E. Malden has an interesting chapter on Gardiner in his history of Trinity Hall. The most careful, though brief, account of Gardiner, based on intimate knowledge of the sources, is that by Mr. James Gairdner. This has appeared in three forms, substantially alike—in *A Dictionary of English Church History*, in the *Encyclopædia Britannica*, 11th edition, and in *Typical English Churchmen*, Series II. Mr. Gairdner also treats phases of Gardiner's career in his *Lollardy and the Reformation*. In an unpublished doctor's thesis in the Harvard Library there is a life of Gardiner of some length. To 1547 it is based, frankly, on secondary writers; after that on such sources only as were available at Harvard. It repeats, therefore, many of the old errors and adds little of importance.

NOTE

In quotations from sixteenth-century books and documents the spelling, except of obsolete or unusual words, is modernized.

Dates are given in modern computation.

For explanation of abbreviations used in the notes and the appendices for the citation of authorities, *see* p. 338.

ERRATA

p. 9, line 3 from bottom, for "Terrence" read "Terence."

p. 14, line 20 from bottom, for "Baalam" read "Balaam."

p. 64, line 21 from top, for "wordly" read "worldly."

p. 90, line 3, for "this fall" read "his fall."

p. 93, last line, for "principl" read "principle."

p. 96, line 8 from top, for "according the" read "according to."

p. 185, line 22 from top, period after "added" should be comma.

p. 256, line 3 from bottom, for "mort" read "more."

p. 276, line 10 from bottom, for "as war" read "at war."

p. 282, line 20 from bottom, for "or Augsburg" read "nor Augsburg."

p. 288, line 5 from top, comma after "unshaken" should be period.

p. 300, line 15 from bottom, for "apostacy" read "apostasy."

p. 300, last line, for "dissention" read "dissension."

p. 306, line 25 from top, for "1597" read "1497."

p. 342, note 3, for "archdeaconal" read "archidiaconal."

CONTENTS

STEPHEN GARDINER
AND THE TUDOR REACTION

I

A SALAD FOR ERASMUS

"In the name of God, Amen.

I, John Gardiner, of Bury St. Edmunds, cloth-maker, with an whole and good mind, being at Bury aforesaid the 18th of January, in the year of Our Lord God 1507, make my testament and last will in manner and form following."

Thus begins the earliest record of Stephen Gardiner. It is the will of his father.

The first bequests therein give us a glimpse of the unquestioning piety of a successful fifteenth-century burgher, of his affection for the parish church, of his implicit faith in the efficacy of good deeds done by proxy and paid for by legacy.

"First, I bequeath my soul to Almighty God, to Our Lady St. Mary, and to all his saints, and my body to be buried in the north aisle of St. James' Church, afore the Salutation of Our Lady, standing by a glass window in the same aisle.

Item, I bequeath to the high altar in the same church, for my tithes and offerings forgotten and negligently paid, 20s.

Item, I bequeath to the St. Mary priest of the same church to pray for my soul, 3s. 4d."

A cope of the value of £10 is left to the church for the use of the priest of Candlemas Gild; a stipend of £10 13s. 4d. is provided for "an honest priest" to pray for the soul of the testator and the souls of all his good friends that he is "in debt or bound to, by the space and term of two whole years;" "a new Salutation of Our Lady" is to replace the old one near his tomb; and a dole of "10s. in bread to poor folks" is to be distributed for eight years at the anniversary of his "earthtide." Should his minor children die before coming to age, their patrimony is to go to the Church of St. James.

Despite the changes which the years have brought to Bury, one may still share John Gardiner's enthusiasm for St. James' Church. It is all simplicity and clarity—nine arches long, a broad, glowing window at the west, the slender Gothic columns crowned with a ribbon of clerestory sunlight and the finest of open timber roofs.

It is here that Stephen must have been baptized,[1] here that he received those first indelible impressions of childhood—of silences and singings, colours and lights and incense, figures robed and softly moving, and the resonance of bells.

It is of the child Stephen that John Gardiner, after disposing of his own resting-place and the repose of his soul, first thinks.

"I bequeath to Stephen my son 20 marks [2] of lawful money of England to his exhibition to find him to school, to be paid him as he shall need it honestly.

Item, I bequeath to the said Stephen, when he cometh to the full age of 21 years, a silver salt with a covertill, parcel gilt, weighing 13 ounces, 1 mazer with 3 feet, silver and gilt, 6 silver spoons knopped with lions, weighing together 7 ounces and a half.

Item, I bequeath to the said Stephen £4 to be paid him by Agnes my wife when he shall take commencement in the school at the university. . . .

Item, I bequeath to the said Stephen 1 feather bed, 1 bolster, 1 red coverlet of damask work, wrought with 5 Jesus thereon, 1 pair blankets, and 1 pair sheets."

It is plain that Stephen was destined for what was practically the only learned profession then open to the children of the middle classes—the priesthood.

From the further bequests we learn that he was one of five children. One sister, Rose, was to enter a nunnery, the other, Joan, though not yet of age, was evidently regarded as marriageable, for she was to come into her heritage of money and jewels, feather beds and bolsters, at twenty, or as soon before as she married. Brother John, though still a minor, was, it seems, to succeed, on coming of age, to his father's business, inheriting scales, weights, shears, and market stalls. Another brother, William, was grown and had already set up for himself as a cloth-maker.

John Gardiner made his wife Agnes his executrix, trusting in her piety "to do good deeds of charity" for the health of his soul, and in her ability to oversee the business until his son John came of age. That is all we know of her.

The will tells us of the comfortable circumstances of the Gardiner family. The money bequests amount to £90 at a time when money had perhaps fifteen times its present purchasing power. Beside this there is silverware, jewellery, bedding, business equipment, and some real estate.

Within a year of the making of the will John Gardiner died.[3] How old Stephen was at the time is uncertain. The language of the will suggests that he was still a small boy. This is in accordance with his later reference to himself as a lad in the spring of 1511, with his entrance at Cambridge in the autumn of that year, and with his reception of the degree of Bachelor of Laws in 1518. The usual age of boys entering the university in his day was thirteen or fourteen, that of bachelors of law, twenty. "About" 1497 is as close as we may safely come to the date of his birth.[4]

Of his early boyhood we know nothing, except that it was spent in Bury, a narrow-streeted, bustling town where the Linnet flows into the Lark. It was a growing centre of the wool trade, with "about 3,000 houseling persons" (*i.e.,* communicants, representing perhaps 9,000 inhabitants), when the eighth Henry ascended the throne. It was shadowed, dominated, hallowed by the holy Edmund, around whose shrine had grown the powerful Benedictine abbey, with broad lands, towering gateways, "long-drawn arches, cloisters, sounding aisles." The abbot was a mitred abbot who sat with the peers in Parliament. Without the walls were fields, boroughs, tenants under his sway; within were eighty monks and a hundred servants.

"The sun does not shine," wrote Gardiner's contemporary Leland, "on a town more prettily situated—so delicately does it hang on a gentle slope, with a little stream flowing to the east—nor on an abbey more famous."[5] Notable was the abbey in the time of Henry II and Richard of the lion heart, when Samson the sub-sacrist, eulogized in the thirteenth century by Jocelyn and in the nineteenth by Carlyle, came to be abbot. It was at the high altar of the abbey church that the barons, in the presence of Stephen Langton, had sworn to take the field against John.

When the leaves began to turn and the harvests were safe within the barns, came the Bury Fair, with its jugglers and minstrels, mountebanks and tumblers, its wonderland of booths lining the avenues up to the abbot's palace. Here glittered the wares of jeweller and silversmith, silk-mercer and toy-man. The neighbouring nobility came with music and gay-coated retainers, the knights tilted in the lists. Three days before the feast of St. Matthew did the merriment begin, and not till three days after did it end, and all the while the tables of the abbey were spread and the doors open to all who came.[6]

Two months later, when the days grew short and winter was in the air, the festival of St. Edmund was kept with Masses and processions, while the Church of St. Margaret, where rested the body of the martyr King, glowed with a hundred and fifty candles.

The abbey, like its monks, the town, like its cloth merchants, was prosperous, contented, untroubled.

It may have been in the ancient grammar school, established before the days of Cnut, endowed and given a house in Schoolhill Street

by Abbot Samson himself, that Gardiner was "found to school."ᵀ
It was doubtless in the shallow, easy-flowing Lark that, as a boy,
he learned to swim, an art for which, even when he became a bishop,
he was noted.⁸

When a lad of, perhaps, fourteen, he was taken to Paris, in the
household of an Englishman named Eden, in all likelihood either
Thomas or Richard Eden, "gentlemen," friends of his father, in
whose will they are named as trustees for the children.⁹ We should
know nothing of this visit to Paris, had it not been made memorable
to Gardiner by his meeting Erasmus, then a guest of Mr. Eden,
and serving him daily with a favourite salad. This was in the spring
of 1511. Sixteen years later he wrote to the great scholar recalling
the Paris days:

> "When others vie in writing from England, should that
> Stephen alone be silent who, as often as men talk of Erasmus,
> boasts with some pride that he was once Erasmus' cook—doing
> so, forsooth, to establish among his hearers a confidence in his
> learning, just as do those who would fain be known as saints
> boast that they once visited the Holy Land. . . .
>
> If I may recall a trifling incident of other days to that memory
> of yours, devoted as it is to the most careful preservation of
> the best things, do you remember sixteen years ago when you
> were a guest in the house of a certain Eden, an Englishman,
> then living in Paris in the Street of St. John? It was the time
> that you first published your *Folly,* if I am not mistaken, and
> even then you had acquired a mass of Greek and Latin books
> for your own use. Do you remember that there was then with
> Eden a certain small boy whom you daily ordered to prepare
> lettuce for you, dressed with butter and sour wine, and you
> said that you had never had this dish more daintily served than
> by him?
>
> I am that very boy, Stephen Gardiner, heartily attached to
> you, and though absent from you, maintaining my loyalty to
> you.
>
> For some time past I have been so drawn away from you by
> the business of State that though I am permitted still to love
> you, as I do, I fear that I shall not for a long while be per-
> mitted to enjoy that intimacy with your works which is so
> delightful. I was certainly unfortunate in not taking that
> opportunity you offered me through Gerard, the Cambridge
> bookseller—if he did not lie to me—of entering your service,
> and in the place of your silent, written words, of which I have
> indeed some knowledge, I might have lived with the power of
> your personality as my guide. But I am a fool to complain of
> what cannot be altered. . . .

So farewell, most learned Erasmus, and may you consider that Stephen—whom you formerly thought a cook not unskilful in preparing lettuce to your taste—a friend not unfaithful if by any chance he can aid you. . . ." [10]

Erasmus replied, with renewed praise of the salad:

"It was most agreeable to me, my dear Stephen, to have my memory refreshed by your letter. There was no need of so many reminders. That image of you in Paris has remained so vivid in my mind that I could almost paint it in colours. I recognize the same cleverness in scholarship and in affairs of importance that you showed at Paris in household matters. Nor was a letter written by you less refreshing to my spirit than was the lettuce dressed by you delicious to my taste. . . ." [11]

These two letters tell us all we know of Gardiner's youthful sojourn in the French capital. It must have been at this time that he began to acquire that proficiency in the French tongue for which he was afterward conspicuous. It is just possible that while there he attended some lectures at the University of Paris, and so formed the opinion he later expressed, that it was "a university most plenteously furnished and occupied with great, learned men;" indeed one which he was tempted to call "the head university of the world." [12]

II

A DOCTOR OF BOTH LAWS

Although the mother university of north Europe might be named the head university of the world, her English children were not far behind her. Thomas More, who visited Paris and Louvain in 1508, found them in nowise superior to Oxford and Cambridge; and Erasmus, eight years later, declared that the advance in scholarship in a single generation at Cambridge had been so notable that that university might vie with the first schools of the age.[1]

Within a few months after leaving Paris and Gardiner's salads, Erasmus was in Cambridge, where he remained for the next three years teaching Greek and finishing his edition of the New Testament. His arrival in this town where, in the language of Parliament, "many worshipful men's children be put to learning and study," must have been almost coincident with that of Gardiner who entered Trinity Hall in 1511, after his return from Paris.[2]

Gardiner remained at the university as student and teacher for thirteen years.

Cambridge in his day was not so delightful a place as it is now. It was "very sore decayed in paving, and the high streets and lanes within the same town exceedingly noyed with filth and mire lying there in great heaps and broad plashes"—a condition which a meliorating Parliament censured as "not only noisome and cumberous," but "also very perilous and tedious."[3] This was typical of many communities of the time, and what the legislators objected to in the streets, Erasmus found equally objectionable in the houses. He complained that the windows admitted light, but no air, and that the bottom layer of the rushes on the clay floors was "left undisturbed sometimes for twenty years, harbouring expectorations, vomitings, the leakage of dogs and men, ale droppings, scraps of fish, and other abominations not fit to be mentioned."[4] It is not surprising that during Gardiner's years of residence in Cambridge the plague broke out four times.[5]

Cambridge today has such an air of antiquity that it is hard to believe that since Gardiner's time almost every college has been rebuilt or remodelled out of all recognition. Queen's and the old court of Corpus Christi give us, perhaps, the best impression of things as they were. The fine first court of St. John's, and King's Chapel, the glory of Cambridge, were a-building when Gardiner studied. His own college, Trinity Hall, has been quite made over.

The site is the same, with its pleasant, quiet garden running back to the river, but fire and the "elegance" of the eighteenth century have given the buildings a new fashion, without and within. The little early Gothic church of St. Edward, however, in the town, used in Gardiner's time as a chapel by both Trinity Hall and its neighbour Clare, retains its original appearance. According to David Loggan's engraving [6] the early college consisted of an enclosed court with a few adjacent buildings, the whole rather stolid and heavy, with much wall and few windows.

Then, as now, the college was a small one. The master, ten fellows, and perhaps thirty students made up its membership.[7] Among them Gardiner found a place at the long tables in the stone-paved, rush-strewn hall, "very gloomy and dark," its oak-beam ceiling "black and dismal" from the charcoal fire burning in the centre—for the smoke found its way but imperfectly through the awkward cupola above. On a dais at one end sat the fellows, and from the single oriel came the voice of the reader, droning the Latin chapter at the meals.[8]

We are so prone to think of Gardiner as an ecclesiastic and a humanist, that it is surprising to learn from the Cambridge Grace Books that his principal study at the university was neither arts nor theology, but law. That some of his time was devoted to classical studies may be inferred from his knowledge of Greek and Latin. Indeed, before entering the university he must have learned sufficient Latin to understand lectures in it, and he himself became a lecturer; his later use of it as a vehicle of literary expression is easy if not altogether transparent. Moreover, we know that at some time in his life he acquired an acquaintance with, and an appreciation for, Latin literature, for he brightened the long days of his imprisonment in the Tower, in the reign of Edward VI, by filling almost two hundred pages of a note-book with Latin proverbs, extracts from Martial, Juvenal, and Virgil, and Latin verses of his own composition.[9] Of Greek he knew sufficient to translate the Gospels of Luke and John for a proposed edition of the New Testament in 1535.[10] Yet he took neither a full course nor a degree in Arts.[11] Theology he was required to study as a minor subject for a degree in Canon Law,[12] but this major study was law, and it was pre-eminently as a legist that he became known to his contemporaries, especially in the early years of his public career. Cranmer might be called "theologus," but Gardiner was "jurisconsultus." [13] His enemies dubbed him "popish lawyer;" [14] his friends likened him to Cicero in the clarity and eloquence with which he argued his cases.[15]

Trinity Hall had been founded as a college for law students, and it was to the study of law, not English or Common Law, but Civil and Canon Law, that its fellows and scholars devoted themselves.

Canon Law was the law of the Church. It consisted of the decrees of councils and the rescripts of Popes. It claimed jurisdiction over the clergy in all questions of doctrine and practice, and in all cases criminal and civil; likewise over all suits in which the clergy were parties or where Church property was involved. It controlled the belief and morals of the laity. Heresy, marriage, wills, contracts, oaths—all came within its sphere. That Churchmen should study it was not only natural but necessary. Ecclesiastical judges and advocates must be trained. Bishop's chancellors, vicars general, commissaries, archdeacons and their officials, scribes and registrars must all be lawyers.

Civil Law was the law of the Roman Empire. The study of it had been revived in the universities during the twelfth century. From it the Canon Law drew its forms and phraseology as well as the procedure of its courts. Its study, moreover, was the natural preparation for the diplomatic service, for it was, in the sixteenth century, already becoming the foundation of international law; ambassadors had to be skilled civilians. "We are sure ye are not ignorant," wrote Somerset to Ridley in 1549, "how necessary a study that study of Civil Law is to all treaties with foreign princes." [16]

Besides the diplomatic service and the Church court there was still another field of activity open to the ecclesiastical lawyer—that of adviser to the king. On the all-important questions of the relation of nation to nation, of Church to State, of the king to the law, the judgement of canonist and civilian could not lightly be passed over. Moreover, the law of the Church and the law of the Roman Empire supplied those principles of equity on which the decisions of the Court of Chancery were based.

Hence in the fifteenth and sixteenth centuries the study of Canon and Civil Law was a study of immediate and practical value. One of the clauses in the foundation instrument of Trinity Hall has a peculiarly modern ring—a college was to be established "for the advantage, rule, and direction of the commonwealth." [17]

Advocate, judge, ambassador, royal counsellor, Lord Chancellor—Gardiner became each of these. His studies foreshadowed his career. They did more; they determined the fashion of his thinking. They gave him, or at least strengthened in him, that legal temper of conservatism which even his enthusiasm for humanistic studies did not destroy. While the revival of learning made sceptics or reformers of the theologians, the study of things classical caused the ecclesiastical lawyers merely to transfer allegiance from Pope to king, to clothe the king in the garments of the Roman emperor, and thus to magnify the Civil at the expense of the Canon Law; but the legal habit of thought was unchanged—the shrinking from innovation, the demand for order and for submission to existing conditions, the spirit which asks what is, rather than what ought to be.

When we come to judge of Gardiner's aims and actions we dare not forget that for thirteen years he was a student and a teacher of law.

After his first seven years of study, upon payment of 20d. "commons," and delivery to the proctors of a caution or pledge to fulfil the duties of a newly made Bachelor of Civil Law, Gardiner was admitted to that degree in 1518.[18] The chief of these duties was to give elementary instruction in the subject, extending, if the bachelor purposed proceeding to the doctor's degree, over a period of three years. Such instruction, together with further hearing of lectures and frequent disputations with students and teachers, was the necessary training for the doctorate, which Gardiner attained in the allotted time, becoming Doctor of Civil Law in 1521—the only doctor in that faculty graduated at Cambridge that year.[19]

The next year, 1522, he proceeded Doctor of Canon Law.[20] This meant that he had been studying that subject concurrently with Civil Law for some years, and had spent the last year intensively upon it.

In his day the winning of a doctor's degree did not end a man's active relation to the university. There were at the time no permanent professorships of law at Cambridge; every doctor of Civil or Canon Law, on receiving his degree, was sworn to remain at the university to lecture for two years in his subject. This lecturing consisted of reading the law books to the students and commenting upon them paragraph by paragraph, for which the lecturer would receive the fees of his hearers—3s. for reading the digest and 2s. for the code. If he failed to complete his courses within the time set by statute, the students could recover their fees.[21] Were the lecturer a fellow of one of the colleges, he also received a stipend from that source.

Gardiner, who was, in all probability, a fellow of Trinity Hall,[22] lectured in Civil Law during the college year 1521-2, in Canon Law, 1522-3, and in both, 1523-4.[23] His admirer, John Leland, praised him for reforming the study of law and teaching that the arid comments of the glossators were worthless and misleading.[24]

At the end of the academic year 1521 he was one of the auditors of the university accounts. In 1523-4 he was appointed university examiner in both Civil and Canon Law for the next four years. In the same year he was one of a committee of three to draw up statutes governing the lectureships in Terrence, philosophy, and logic, endowed by Sir Robert Rede, and, in the summer of 1523, was the representative of the university on a mission to Wolsey.[25]

The Cardinal was not blind to ability, nor tardy in securing it for his own purposes. In the autumn of the next year, 1524, Gardiner was in his service. [26]

The university continued to look upon him as its advocate, and when there were letters and business for Wolsey there were letters and business for Gardiner, and likewise gifts. [27] Nor did his own college fail to recognize the advantage of having one pledged to its interest in places of influence. In 1525 Gardiner was elected to the mastership of Trinity Hall. [28] This office, the yearly income of whose holder was but £6 13s. 4d., offered little to attract anyone but a quiet scholar desiring to live in Cambridge, yet Gardiner held it, except for a brief period of deprivation in Edward's reign, until his death. His motive for doing so would seem to have been the simple, natural one of affection for his college, which, he told Somerset in 1548, he valued almost as highly as his bishopric. [29] In the next century Archbishop Williams remarked that although Gardiner gave forty better preferments to others, he would never give up the mastership of Trinity Hall, "but said often, *If all his palaces were blown down by iniquity, he would creep honestly into that shell.*" [30]

There can be little doubt that when Gardiner held the wealthiest see in England his interest in his college took substantial form, as it did in his will. It was during his mastership and doubtless through his influence that Trinity Hall acquired additional grounds, rounding out its possessions to practically their present extent. As the historian of the college says, "there was an advantage in having as master a bishop whose income was counted in thousands." [31]

That life at Trinity Hall during the first eager stirrings of the Reformation was not all serious is made clear in a later reference by Gardiner to an hour of play which lived in his memory for years. When in Bruges on a difficult mission of diplomacy in 1545, he recalled it. England was then at war with France and Scotland, and at enmity with Rome; the Protestant Princes in Germany were suspicious, the Emperor uncertain. Gardiner contrasted the perplexity in which he and his correspondent, Sir William Paget, and the Lord Chancellor, Sir Thomas Wriothesley, had fallen, to the ease with which they had once outwitted the braggart captain in Plautus' rollicking comedy, *Miles Gloriosus*:

"We be now," he writes to his old friend, "in a world where reason prevaileth not, learning prevaileth not, covenants be not so regarded but the least pretense sufficeth to avoid the observation of them. This is another manner of matter than when I played Periplectomenus, you Meliphidippa, and my Lord Chancellor Palestrio, and yet our parts be in this tragedy that now is in hand. If we three should now sit together and take counsel what might be done, as we did in the comedy, we should not be a little troubled, and Palestrio fain to muse longer for compassing of this matter and seding of it, as the poet calls it, than we did there." [32]

The part played by Gardiner was that of a wealthy old bachelor—agreeable, leisure-loving, polished, a hospitable guest and a knowing man of the world. Paget was the clever maid—he must have just come up to the university—and Wriothesley the facile, inventive servant who has a way out of every difficulty. Leland the poet saw the play and some years later complimented Gardiner on his delivery and histrionic grace, declaring that his acting had so impressed him that he would never forget the performance. [33]

Gardiner was about ten years the senior of Paget and Wriothesley. They probably entered Trinity Hall when he was lecturing. Both were later admitted to his household. [34] They were by no means the only men of future prominence whom he knew at Cambridge. Thomas Cranmer of Jesus College was graduated Bachelor of Divinity the year Gardiner became Doctor of Civil Law; the year of his Canon Law doctorate Nicholas Heath proceeded M.A., Nicholas Ridley, B.A.; the year following Robert Barnes, the Austin friar, was graduated D.D., and a year later Hugh Latimer, B.D., and Matthew Parker, B.A. The vituperative George Joye and the virulent John Bale were both students at Cambridge during portions of Gardiner's university career. Richard Sampson of Trinity Hall, later Bishop of Chichester, was one of his teachers, the martyr John Frith of King's College (B.A. 1525) one of his pupils. The brilliant Edward Fox, also of King's (M.A. 1520), was perhaps his best friend.

The likable, good humoured Thomas Thirlby, destined to be the first and last bishop of Henry VIII's diocese of Westminster, was a member of Trinity Hall, and, as he was graduated Bachelor of Civil Law at the time Gardiner became a doctor in that faculty, he must certainly have been his pupil as well as his friend. He lived to be an executor of his will. Another Trinity Hall man, a contemporary of Thirlby, and doubtless also a pupil of Gardiner's, was the intense, overly conscientious Thomas Bilney, who soon forsook law for theology—an exceptional type for Trinity Hall. He was the centre of the little group of Cambridge reformers. Three of his companions, Barnes, Lambert, and Latimer, perished at the stake, and he himself was burned in 1531, the first and gentlest martyr of them all. John Foxe, with surpassing beauty, describes him at the university,

"preaching at the lazar cots, wrapping them in sheets, helping them of that they wanted, if they would convert to Christ; laborious and painful to the desperates; a preacher to the prisoners and comfortless; a great doer in Cambridge."

The contrast between Bilney and Thirlby is amusingly epitomized in Foxe's illustration of Bilney's feeling that music was a "mockery with God," for "when Dr. Thirlby, bishop after, then scholar, lying in the chamber underneath him, would play upon his recorder, as he would often do," Bilney "would resort straight to his prayer." [35]

One imagines that in this controversy on the mockery of music, Gardiner was on the side of the jovial Thirlby and his flute.

There is something prophetic in the appearance of the four names, Gardiner, Cranmer, Thirlby, Bilney, on the degree lists of the same year; and over the page is a fifth, Martin Luther, at the burning of whose books in the Easter Term of 1521 the proctor laconically records an outlay for drink and other expenses of two shillings.

It has often been remarked how many of the leaders of both reform and reaction came from Cambridge, how few from Oxford. Of those from Cambridge no mean number were there as students or teachers in Gardiner's day. They were, to recapitulate, the future Archbishops Cranmer, Heath, Parker, and May, the future Bishops Latimer, Ridley, Sampson, Shaxton, Bale, Capon, Fox, Day, and Thirlby, Lords Paget and Wriothesley, the Henrician martyrs Frith, Bilney, Barnes, and Lambert, the controversialist Joye, the translator Coverdale, the poet Leland, the court physician Dr. Butts, [36] and the most illustrious scholar of the age, Erasmus.

It was indeed no empty boast of Gardiner when he said, "almost all that have been notable have been of my special acquaintance" [37]— an acquaintance beginning in his college days.

III

THE HERESY OF FRIAR BARNES

On the death of Abbot Bere, in February 1525, the monks of Glastonbury placed in Cardinal Wolsey's hands the choice of his successor. On March 3, in the chapel at York Place, and in the presence of a notary and four witnesses, among whom were Thomas More and Stephen Gardiner, the Cardinal named Richard Whiting for the place.[1] This witnessing of the election of the last abbot of Glastonbury is the first incident recorded in Gardiner's career after his entry into the Cardinal's service.

In the summer of the same year, we find him penning, under the direction of the Cardinal, the treaty between France and England at More Park; penning it so skilfully that he won the approbation of King Henry VIII.[2]

His next appearance in the public records is in the following February (1526), when, as Archdeacon of Taunton, he is named as one of the assistants to his ordinary, Bishop Clerk of Bath and Wells, in the examination of some German Hanse merchants for heresy, in the Chapter House at Westminster.[3]

These Stilyard men were docile heretics who confessed to having eaten meat on Friday, to the reading of Luther's books, to some indistinctly unorthodox opinions on the Sacrament and the Pope. They submitted to correction.

On the day they left the court room for the Fleet, there to await their public penance, an Augustinian friar from Cambridge entered. This was Robert Barnes. He described himself as a "poor simple worm and not able to kill a cat." Yet with the superb egotism of humility declared:

> "To burn me or to destroy me cannot so greatly profit them. For when I am dead the sun and the moon, the stars and the element, water and fire, yea and also stones shall defend this cause against them, rather than the verity should perish." [4]

The examiners found the case of this emotional, impressionable, confident, obstinate reformer far different from that of the easily silenced Easterlings.

The examination of Barnes is significant in a study of Gardiner: it illuminates his attitude toward heresy; it exemplifies his relation to the heretic; it introduces us to his struggle with the cause which was to be his lifelong antagonist.

13

The accounts of the examination and of the occurrences leading up to it are exceptionally full. We have Barnes' own story published six years later;[5] we have Gardiner's statement written in 1545;[6] we have the narrative of John Foxe which is apparently independent of both.[7]

> "Barnes, whom I knew first at Cambridge," says Gardiner, "was a trim minion friar Augustine, one of a merry scoffing wit, friarlike, and as a good fellow in company was beloved by many. A doctor of divinity he was, but never like to have proved to be either martyr or confessor in Christ's religion; and yet he began there to exercise railing (which among such as newly profess Christ is a great piece of cunning, and a great forwardness to reputation, specially if he rail of bishops as Barnes began, and to please such of the lower sort as envieth ever authority) chiefly against my Lord Cardinal, then, under the King's Majesty, having the high administration of the realm."

The railing to which Gardiner refers reached its climax in a sermon preached in St. Edward's Church, Cambridge, Christmas Eve, 1525. From the twenty-five articles, "either heretical, seditious, contentious, blasphemous, or else *piis auribus offensivus*," taken by Barnes' enemies from this sermon, we find that he denounced the observance of holy days, the temporal possessions and the secular jurisdiction of the Church. The only Apostle followed by the bishops, he said, was Judas; the only prophet, Baalam. Holy orders, Church hallowings, and pardons were sold "as openly as a cow and an ox." It was the teaching of St. Paul, he averred, that no bishop should be bishop of more than one city. He did not pray to our Lady, nor for the souls in purgatory. He affirmed that it was not lawful for one Christian to sue another.[8]

Not without justice Barnes complained that in these articles his words were wrested from their context and appeared worse than he really intended. "But nevertheless I do grant," he said, "that here be many of my words and also a great many of my sentences that I did speak;" and he went about to prove their truth quite as much as to explain their context.

The sermon created a stir in the university. Barnes was at once examined, but when the proceedings against him were twice interrupted by a mob of his favourers he was taken to London.

> "At the time of this accusation of Barnes, I was," says Gardiner, "in service with my Lord Cardinal, of acquaintance with Barnes, and not accompted his enemy, and yet I thank God I never favoured such strange opinions as he and some other wantonly began to set forth; but because there was not then

in them malice, and they maintained communication having some
savour of learning, I was familiar with such sort of men, and
was then sorry for Barnes, and glad to help him, so far as might
stand with my duty to my Lord, my master."

Barnes arrived in the city Tuesday, February 6, 1526.[9] He
waited all day Wednesday for an audience with Wolsey. "Then,"
says Foxe, "by reason of Dr. Gardiner, secretary to the Cardinal (of
whose familiar acquaintance he had been before) and Master
[Edward] Fox, Master of the Wards, he spake the same night with
the Cardinal."

As Barnes and his two friends entered Wolsey's gallery at Westminster, the Cardinal asked, "Is this Dr. Barnes your man that is
accused of heresy?"

"Yea, an't please your Grace," they answered, "and we trust you
shall find him reformable, for he is both well learned and wise." [10]

Then, writes Barnes, the Cardinal "read all my articles quietly."
He paused to explain what St. Paul meant about having a bishop in
every city, but read the rest without comment, till, near the end, he
came to this: "They have also pillars and pole axes and other
ceremonies, which, no doubt, be but trifles and things of naught."

Thereupon followed that memorable conversation in which Wolsey
asked: "Were it better for me, being in the honour and dignity that
I am, to coin my pillars and pole axes and to give the money to five
or six beggars, than for to maintain the commonwealth by them as
I do? Do you not reckon the commonwealth better than five or six
beggars?"

Barnes had the courage—or the effrontery—to answer that the
coining of them might be for the salvation of the Cardinal's soul,
and as for the commonwealth it "did not hang on them, for as his
Grace knew, the commonwealth was afore his Grace and must be
when his Grace is gone." Barnes added, by way of explanation,
"Alonely, I damned in my sermon the gorgeous pomp and pride of
all exterior ornaments."

Not without a touch of humour Wolsey replied, "Well, you say
very well." [11] Then turning to Barnes' sponsors he exclaimed: "Lo
Master Doctors! here is the learned, wise man that you told me of!"

Gardiner and Fox kneeled down and said, "We desire your Grace
to be good unto him for he will be reformable."

"Stand you up!" answered the Cardinal, "for your sakes and the
university we will be good unto him." He then tried to persuade
Barnes to recant, but Barnes insisted on a trial, "and forthwith he
should have gone to the Tower but that Gardiner and Fox became
his sureties that night." [12]

The next day, February 8, Barnes appeared before the examiners.
During the proceedings Bishop Fisher of Rochester, Chancellor of

the University, entered. He saw no heresy in Barnes' attack on holy days but "it was foolishly done (quod he) to preach this before the butchers of Cambridge." [13]

The examination lasted three days, Barnes defending his views by quotations from the Fathers and Scriptures until, on Saturday, the Bishop of Bath summarily ordered him to read the recantation prepared, or to burn. Said Barnes, "Jesus have mercy on me, I will surely not read it." His friends, fearing that he would stick to his resolution, assailed him once more with entreaties to recant. Finally, by "reason of their good words and piteous," says Barnes, "I granted to read the roll."

The recantation seems to have covered all or most of the statements which Barnes had been charged with uttering. He felt, however, that his condemnation was wholly due to his attack on the Cardinal. Gardiner, who was on the inside of the proceedings, gives a different reason. He speaks of Barnes' railing at his master, but adds, "that railing in a friar had been easily pardoned if Barnes had not fondly persisted in the Anabaptists' opinion denying suits to be lawful among Christian men." The exact words attributed to Barnes were:

> "These laws, these lawyers, these justiciaries, that say that a man may lawfully ask his own afore a judge and contend in judgement, have destroyed all patience, devotion, and faith in Christian people.
> This pleading in judgement is manifestly against the Gospel and contrary to St. Paul."

Barnes' defence is quite as characteristic of the mental and emotional processes of the non-legal reformer, as is Gardiner's comment typical of the juristic mind. Barnes says he did not mean to indict all law and all lawyers. He was not thinking in general terms at all. He had been stirred by a particular case of crying injustice. A poor man in Cambridge willed a kettle worth two and four pence to one of the churches. He was not, apparently, in possession of the kettle; he merely left instructions in his will that his executor should purchase it for the church. The executor, also a poor man, failed to do this and, in his necessity, seems to have applied the two and four pence to other uses. He "desired the church warden of longer respite, but he could not be heard, for the church warden would have the uttermost of the law," and sued the poor man and caused his condemnation to prison, "where," says Barnes, "he lay, and neither was able to pay his debt nor to help his wife and children," who had "not one bite of bread towards their food."

The enormity of the proceeding aroused the indignation of Barnes; he pleaded with the warden for mercy, but in vain. Then on Christmas Eve in the midst of his sermon he spied him sitting smugly there in the congregation. He could not contain himself; he passed from the superficial and perhaps flippant criticism of ecclesiastical formality to an arraignment of the prevailing injustice. Spurred by this satisfied respectability, this pious Pharisaism, he struck more deeply than he knew. He was inflamed by that sense of a twofold justice—one law for the rich and another for the poor; that feeling as old and as new as society, made articulate by Amos in his parables and by Galsworthy in his plays. He lashed with a fine scorn those who "undo a whole household for a naughty, lewd kettle." It was but a step to the condemnation of suits at law. He found words of St. Paul and Athanasius and Jerome to support him.

To Gardiner the individual case of injustice was an incident, magnified out of all importance by Barnes. To him the law was the law no matter whether the debtor were rich or poor. Barnes' teaching, he felt, would knock the bottom out of organized society. "Barnes began," he says, "at the lewdest opinion of the Anabaptists, whereby to extinct the order of justice." All Barnes' attacks on sin and ceremonial, on Church dignitary and Church day, could have been "easily pardoned," but not that which destroyed the very essence of the State. Gardiner's attitude toward Barnes has much in common with that of ancient Rome toward Christianity; it is the inevitable attitude of the legist in all ages towards the reformer. Moreover, the atrocities of contemporary peasant risings in Germany, connected, as they were, in the minds of European statesmen with Anabaptist principles, appeared to many as a conclusive argument on the side of the legist. It was such an extinction of the order of justice that haunted Gardiner.

He heartily desired, however, to get Barnes out of trouble.

"I laboured with Barnes secretly," he tells us, "to bring that [opinion concerning law suits] out of his head, wherein he yielded to me upon the showing to him of a saying of St. Austin expounding the Scriptures where Barnes took his error; so as afterwards Barnes was content to abjure that opinion, with crosses, staves, and mitres, and all his jesting matter, and all this time took me for his friend, as I was in deed, his folly set apart, and had showed him, as I thought, a friendly turn."

Barnes' penance consisted of bearing a faggot the next day, which was Quinquagesima Sunday, in procession at St. Paul's in company with the repentant Germans, marching with it thrice around a blazing pile of heretical books and then flinging it into the flames. Bishop Fisher preached the sermon, and the Cardinal himself, mitred and in purple, sat "enthronized" upon a scaffolding with "his chaplains and spiritual doctors," and "six and thirty abbots, mitred priors, and bishops." [14]

Barnes was not the only one of Gardiner's university acquaintances whom he had need to befriend. George Joye, that abusive reformer, who later assailed Gardiner most malevolently, had the grace to acknowledge his help on two occasions. The first was during a search for heretical books at Cambridge, possibly that of 1521, when they were both at the university. Joye had some translations by Œcolampadius, which were in danger of confiscation, and Gardiner, as Joye said, standing by the searchers "at the cup-board in Peter College aula did speak for me and for my books," and Joye was allowed to keep them. The second time he profited by Gardiner's assistance was in 1527, when Bilney and another Cambridge man, Thomas Arthur,[15] were summoned before the Cardinal on the charge of heresy. Joye was sent for at the same time, but arrived in London after the examination of the others had begun. Not being closely watched, he fled to the Continent, and gave Gardiner the credit for it. "It was showed me," he wrote afterwards, "what good words and good counsel ye gave me; and even after it I did, and so escaped the Cardinal's and the bishops' hands. . . . I thank God for your good premonition and counsel."

Joye also credited Gardiner with assisting another Cambridge man, George Stafford, who was reported to Wolsey as having said some unorthodox things in his lectures on the Epistle to the Romans. Gardiner gave him warning and "showed him how he should temper his lection in uttering the truth, and excuse himself." Gardiner likewise, according to Joye, wrote at the same time to a "Mr. Chikes," possibly John Cheke, the Greek scholar, some favourable letters "concerning the cause of the Gospel then in growing."

All this Joye recalled many years later, when Gardiner had become the leader of the anti-reforming party. He cited these kindly acts to Cambridge friends as evidence of inconsistency or degeneration. In the old days, said Joye, "ye defended the truth against this papistry which ye now maintain."[16] But there is no reason to believe that Gardiner was ever attracted by the doctrinal aspect of the Reformation. He did his best to save his friends from the stake by warning them of their danger or by persuading them to change their views.

As he said himself, "I have loved the men, and ever hated the naughty opinion."[17]

IV

"WHEN DOCTOR STEPHENS CAME TO ORVIETO"

Besides the trial of Barnes, we have little information about Gardiner in 1526. His master the Cardinal was absorbed in the double effort to keep England out of entanglement on the Continent, and to make her the arbiter of its peace. How far Gardiner was entrusted with even the secretarial duties which this work involved is a matter of conjecture. We find him busied about indentures with the silversmith for Wolsey's plate.[1]

In 1527, however, he steps into prominence. Whether he had any part in the making of the peace with France, which was celebrated by the pageants at Greenwich early in May, we are not told, but at the end of the month he acted with Sir Thomas More as commissioner for England in drawing up a supplementary treaty, arranging for Wolsey's visit to France and providing for the support of an army in Italy.[2]

Shortly before signing this treaty, he was one of the few persons present at the collusive divorce proceedings when the King was secretly summoned to appear before Wolsey, as Papal legate, in his house in Westminster, to answer the charge of living for eighteen years with his deceased brother's wife. After a few sittings the project was abandoned, for, in spite of the utmost secrecy, Catherine learned of what was happening, and her nephew, the Emperor Charles V, was informed.[3]

Charles was, at the moment, supreme in Italy, for his armies had just sacked Rome and shut the Pope in the Castle of St. Angelo. It was futile to hope for Papal confirmation of a sentence passed in England, until the English-French alliance was strong enough to outweigh the influence of the Emperor at the court of Rome. Hence Wolsey's visit to France.

On July 3, with a train of nine hundred horse, the Cardinal began his journey from Westminster, passing through all London, upon his crimson-saddled mule, with his crosses and pillars, the great seal of England, and his Cardinal's hat before him. Gardiner accompanied him as secretary.[4] At the first night's halt near Dartford, they were met by Warham, Archbishop of Canterbury, an old man, who promised to follow Wolsey's instructions, should Catherine ask counsel concerning the divorce. The next night at Rochester, Bishop Fisher, who was sounded on the same topic, agreed to do nothing contrary to the King's pleasure. That Gardiner was privy to the purport of these secret conversations, is evident from the fact that Wolsey's letter to the King describing them was written by him.[5] He was, indeed, the only man among Wolsey's helpers who thoroughly understood the "King's matter."

The journey through France was one long ovation. Wolsey amusingly excused his inability to describe to Henry the "three goodly pagents" given in Boulogne, because of the obstinacy of his mule, which, he said, "by the terrible noise of the gunshot was driven to such a melancholy that I had enough to do to keep myself upon her back." After this, Gardiner was commissioned to observe and describe the performances.[6]

On August 4 they were met by the French King, Francis I, near Amiens. Then followed five consecutive days of conference, in the midst of which came this request from Henry's secretary, Knight:

> "the King's pleasure is that your Grace do send hither imme-diately Mr. Doctor Stephens, for his Highness desires to com-municate and confer divers things with him which cannot so readily follow the pen as they should."

"Mr. Doctor Stephens" was none other than Gardiner, "Stephens" or "Stevens" being colloquial versions of *Stephanus,* the Latin form of his first name.[7]

If the King's request shows a growing recognition of Gardiner's discretion, the Cardinal's reply reveals a conviction that his devotion and ability were not to be replaced. Wolsey asked Henry "to for-bear the sending of the said Master Stephens," until he had heard what was being done for the advancement of his "secret matter," for in this, said the Cardinal,

> "I have none other help or instrument, but the said Master Stevens, and if I should send him with diligence to your Grace, he shall be in no little danger and peril of life, for both he and I, by the excessive heats which be now here, and our continual travail, be not only put from our sleep and appetite, but mar-vellously weaked and altered in our bodies."[8]

Gardiner remained with the Cardinal.

At the conclusion of the negotiations a perpetual peace was sworn on Sunday, August 18. Wolsey had not yet broached the matter of the divorce to Francis. He would defer this, he said, till his departure, and then only speak of it in "cloudy and dark" hints, but he began correspondence with Rome about it. At the end of Sep-tember he returned to England.[9]

Meanwhile, Henry, growing impatient, despatched his secretary, Knight, to the Pope with instructions concealed even from Wolsey.

But Wolsey, becoming aware of them, and of certain diplomatic blunders which Henry had committed, was placed once more in charge of the negotiations. What the King wanted was a commission from Pope Clement VII empowering Wolsey, or some other favourably minded prelate, to pronounce invalid the dispensation of a previous Pope, Julius II, sanctioning Henry's marriage with Catherine, his deceased brother's wife—a marriage forbidden by the law of the Old Testament. During the early part of the negotiations with Rome, the validity of Julius II's dispensation was called in question on certain technical grounds, among which were the facts that it had been issued when Henry was only twelve years old, without his knowledge or desire, and that on reaching the age of fourteen he had formally renounced any intention of marrying Catherine. Hence, it was argued, his subsequent marriage to her should have been sanctioned by a new dispensation.[10] It was not until after the failure of the legatine court to pass judgement on the case in 1529, that it was urged that since marriage with a deceased brother's wife was forbidden by divine law, no Pope had a right to permit it under any circumstances.

Knight secured a commission, which does not appear now to exist, probably enabling Wolsey to pass upon the validity of the dispensation, but certainly reserving the right of final judgement to the Pope. Hence its value in the eyes of the King was negligible.[11] If Henry's case against the Emperor's aunt were to succeed, the judgement given in England must be final. To wring from the Pope his consent to this, the most skilful, wary, tenacious, resourceful diplomat was needed. Gardiner was chosen for the mission, and Wolsey, in a letter to Pope Clement, announcing his coming, paid him the singular tribute of calling him "my other half."[12]

The difficulties to be overcome were political rather than moral. Though divorce as we know it was unknown to the laws of the Church, separation by pronouncing the marriage invalid was by no means infrequent.[13] Clement had, it seems, little moral objection to Henry's repudiation of Catherine; according to the Canon Law there was much in favour of Henry's contention; but, unfortunately for Henry, the nephew of Catherine, Charles V, happened to be ruler at once of Spain, Netherlands, Germany, Austria, and most of Italy. His armies, supported by the gold of America, had recently terrorized Rome, and crushed his only continental opponent, Francis I. To induce the Pope to say that Catherine had never been Queen of England, and that her daughter Mary was a bastard, was, in the face of the opposite assertion of the Emperor, an impossibility. To persuade him to delegate his authority to a legate in England, who was sure to pronounce a like judgement, was scarcely less difficult. This was the task before Gardiner. With him was associated Edward Fox, whom he had known at Cambridge, with whom he had stood sponsor for Barnes, and whom Wolsey spoke of as Gardiner's dearest friend.[14] This friendship was strengthened by Fox's frank recognition of Gardiner's superior ability, and cemented by his willingness to play the second rôle even where formal etiquette gave him precedence, for he was now in the King's service, and, as royal secretary, was expected to act as ceremonial head of the embassy, though Gardiner was entrusted with its actual direction. They agreed between themselves, however, that "the pre-eminence of place, speech, and utterance" be always given to Gardiner, "without altercation or variance, as our old amity and fast friendship doth require."[15]

There was no question among observers about Gardiner's preeminence. A year after the embassy, members of the Papal court spoke of the time "when Dr. Stephens came to Orvieto."[16]

The two friends were dispatched early in February 1528. At Hever they delivered to Anne Boleyn a letter from the King, commending them to his "own sweetheart," and explaining that they were sent "with as many things to compass our matter . . . as our wits could imagine or devise."[17]

Arriving at Dover, Tuesday the 11th, they set sail on the morrow for Calais, but were compelled "by contrarious wind" to turn back and wait till Saturday, when they embarked again at two in the morning. This time there was so little wind that they "travelled the seas all that day and night following," and on Sunday morning found themselves five miles from their destination; but "tempestuous weather so suddenly arose and in so terrible manner," that they could approach no nearer than two miles from the harbour. It was "the greatest tempest," they wrote, "as the mariners said, that hath been seen, who were all brought to utter desperation of our and their lives, putting more trust in prayer than man's help." The anchor hold failed; they were driven up the coast toward Flanders—territory of the Emperor—and fearing that their dispatches might be seized, "concluded to make some adventure" to reach less perilous land. They set out with two of their servants in the ship's boat, and "by the miracle of God" made a landing near Gravelines, "being," as they wrote, "marvellously weak and feeble, as well for long abstinence, having neither eaten ne drunken two days and two nights before," as for "the fear we were in, and sickness of the seas, which was to us both marvellous extreme."[18]

During a two days' rest in Calais, Gardiner was so impressed with the defenceless condition of the town, then English territory, that he wrote to Wolsey urging immediate succour, which came within a week.[19] From Calais he and his companion rode post to Paris where they dined and supped with Thomas Winter, Wolsey's son, a lad whom they found studying "very diligently" under Lupset the

grammarian.[20]   At St. Germain they explained their mission to
Francis I, who promised to write to the Pope in Henry's favour—a
promise which he fulfilled.[21]

They rode post again through Nevers, Roanne, Lyons, to Genoa;
thence they passed by sea to Lucca, and again by land to Florence
and Orvieto, whither the Pope had fled the previous December from
the Imperialists at Rome.   They travelled "evermore from before
day till it was within the night."   Of all the cities passed through,
Lucca, "a city of marvellous quietness," pleased them most.   There
they tarried a day to rest, and the citizens honoured them by a gift,
with which they were so delighted that they took pains to describe it
in their letters.   There were great fish in basins of silver, "bread
made in toasts and dry, being a very dainty thing," goodly march-
panes and great boxes full of confections and comfits, "candles of
virgin wax," and "forty gallon bottles with sundry wines, and of
all sorts."   It is small wonder that they added, "We could be contented to dwell here at Lucca." [22]

The goal of their journey, Orvieto, a town near the Tiber, a little
more than half way from Florence to Rome, was far less attractive.
They reached it March 20, after a wetting in a near-by river that
caused the death of one of their attendants.   Having left their
baggage at Calais in order to make greater speed, they had no coats
but those they rode in, and were forced to tarry two days before
seeing the Pope, while their "garments were at the making."

The city, they said,

> "may well be called *Urbs vetus,* for every man in all languages
> at his entry would give it none other name.   We cannot well
> tell how the Pope should be noted in liberty, being here where
> hunger, scarcity, ill-favoured lodging, ill air, and many other
> incommodities, keep him and all his as straitly as he was ever
> kept in Castle Angel. . . .   The Pope lieth in an old palace
> of the bishops of this city, ruinous and decayed, where, or we
> come to his privy bed chamber, we pass three chambers, all
> naked and unhanged, the roofs fallen down, and, as we can
> guess, thirty persons, rif raf and other, standing in the cham-
> bers for a garnishment.   And as for the Pope's bed chamber, all
> the apparel in it was not worth twenty nobles, bed and all." [23]

As soon as their garments were ready they "were with his Holiness every day three or four hours, consulting and debating." [24]

Besides endeavouring to induce him to remedy the defects in the
commission granted to Knight, they were to request the appointment
of a legate to act with Wolsey—thus removing the complaint of
Catherine that an English court would be partial—and, if possible,
to secure for this office the Cardinal Campeggio, who was receiving

a large income from an English bishopric. They were to convey to the Pope Wolsey's assurance that the King's desire for the divorce was due to the urgent need of a male heir, so that the realm might be freed from the dangers of a disputed succession, and not to infatuation for Anne Boleyn. They were, however, to dilate on that gentlewoman's "constant virginity, her maidenly and womanly pudicity," her "apparent aptness to procreation of children." They were to present to the Pope a book of arguments against the validity of the King's marriage, and to urge Henry's attachment to the See of Rome, but to intimate that if no remedy was there given, one would be sought elsewhere.[25]

Clement protested affection for Henry, commended the book of arguments for the divorce, and listened with patience to Gardiner's demands. "In this matter," said Gardiner, "were two things to be considered. First, the law, if the fact be true; and second, to know whether the fact be true or no." The question of law here mooted was not whether the Pope had power to dispense with the ordinances of the Old Testament, but whether the irregularities in the dispensation of Julius II and in the circumstances under which it was granted, were sufficient to invalidate it. The question of fact was that of the existence of these irregularities. Gardiner asked for a decretal commission, that is, a commission to examine the question of fact in England, embodying a decretal, or definite pronouncement by the Pope, settling the question of law. He also asked that a clause be inserted preventing appeal to Rome, and presented a specimen commission in the exact form desired. This Clement referred to his legal advisers, who tried to persuade the Englishmen to accept a general commission, with a promise that the Pope would ratify the decision given in England.

"On Passion Sunday at after dinner," Gardiner told Clement that the matter resolved itself to two questions: Was he willing to grant the commission? If he was willing, did he have the power to do so? His good will was manifest, and as for his power, they had been promised that if they accepted a general commission he would confirm the sentence given under it, "which promise," said Gardiner, "if it be to be trusted unto, is a plain confession that our cause is good"—hence the objection to the decretal commission was merely one of form, which when the King understood, he would use a remedy of his own.

"When I had thus spoken," he writes, "every man looked on other and so stayed." Finally the Pope "perceiving that our words were somewhat plainer than they had been," consented to waive the question as to the form of the commission, provided there were just cause in the law for a divorce, a matter which again had to be referred to the cardinals.

After the disputation, the Pope inquired of the health of the

English bishops, especially Richard Nyx, of Norwich, who had been a member of Trinity Hall many college generations before Gardiner. In reply, his Holiness was told

> "a merry tale of the Bishop of Norwich's good heart, and how being above fourscore years old, he would have a chamber devised near the ground, without any stairs, to lie in twenty years hence, when he knew well he should be somewhat feeble."

By the end of the first week's negotiations, the Englishmen had come to the conclusion that fear of the Emperor was the chief motive for the refusal of their demands, that Clement, because of this fear, wished to escape all responsibility for the divorce, and that his policy was to be one of delay. "His Holiness," they wrote "is *cunctator maximus*." Finally, they saw that, in spite of "marvellous good words," it would be impossible to get the decretal commission.²⁶

On the Friday before Palm Sunday the discussion "waxed hot," and at the end of it Gardiner desired them "to note and ponder such words" as he should say "of duty and obedience towards the See Apostolic." He broke into a brief, vigorous arraignment of the shiftiness and dissimulation of the Papal court, concluding that the King and nobles of England would be forced to the inference that Papal laws which were clear to neither the Pope himself nor his advisers might well be given to the flames. "To my words thus spoken," he says, "no man answered."

Having lost all hope of the decretal commission, Gardiner submitted a form for a general one, which, after the cardinals had considered it, he found revised out of all recognition. "Trusting by importunity" to obtain his purpose, he debated with Pope and cardinals, on the Tuesday after Palm Sunday, from six in the evening until one in the morning, and then had to retire unanswered.

One wonders quite as much at the endurance of Clement as at the insistence and intrepidity of Gardiner. Nor was the Papal endurance without a touch of humour; at the end of the long discussion the Friday before, the Pope had remarked that although all laws were locked within his breast, God had never given him the key!

After another day's wrangling, agreement was reached on all but two words enabling one of the legates appointed to act without the other. Postponement till the next morning was again suggested, but the English complained that they were deluded and scorned, and Gardiner told the Pope that he "handled the King's Highness as though he had been the most ingrate man and of mean sort," whereupon "the said Holiness said nothing but sighed and wiped his eyes." Gardiner added that when this was related in England the Pope would lose the favour of the only prince who really supported him, and the chair of Peter, already tottering, would tumble to pieces, with the consent and applause of everybody.

It was again an hour after midnight. The tired, fearful, hesitating Clement at last gave way. At the allusion to the tottering chair of Peter, "the Pope's Holiness," says Gardiner, "casting his arms abroad, bade us put in the words we varied for, and therewith walked up and down the chamber, casting now and then his arms abroad, we standing in great silence." [27]

The commission thus granted empowered Wolsey and Campeggio to examine the validity of the dispensation of Julius II, and to give sentence accordingly as to the lawfulness or nullity of Henry's marriage with Catherine. There was a clause enabling either legate to act if the other were disabled or unwilling to do so, and one forbidding appeal. It did not exclude objection to the place of trial nor to the persons of the judges, nor did it contain any pronouncement by the Pope determining the law on the points at issue. [28]

Although Gardiner had not received all he had demanded, he had made the best of a bad situation. Incidentally he had proved himself—what a libellous detractor later conceded him to be—"a good lawyer and a Ciceronian rhetorician, bold and eloquent." [29]

It was decided that Fox return immediately with the news, and Gardiner repair to Rome to find Campeggio and hurry him off to England.

Wolsey "seemed marvellously perplexed" when Fox first showed him the commission, but next morning, after reading Gardiner's letters, he was persuaded, or, making the best of it, pretended to be persuaded, that nothing better could have been devised. Fox's reports of his friend's "fidelity, diligence," "learning and vehemency," were so glowing that Anne Boleyn spoke of "large recompense" for Gardiner; all the doctors of law joined in extolling his "wisdom, dexterity, and right excellent good conducting of this cause;" and the King and the Cardinal took every occasion to commend his ability, exclaiming that he was an invaluable treasure and the pearl of the realm.

Wolsey, however, felt that it was essential to get the Pope's pronouncement on the law in question before the trial began, hence he instructed Fox to write Gardiner to use "all kinds of persuasions" which possibly by his "wisdom or rhetoric" he could "devise and excogitate," to secure the decretal commission, which he promised would be kept secret from every one but the King. [30]

During the month after Fox's departure, Gardiner encountered so many "contrived delays" in the sending of Campeggio, and, after the receipt of the instructions to obtain the secret decretal, so many "great difficulties pretended," that he seems to have despaired of obtaining either object.

We do not have his letters to England, but we know the impression they created from one of Fox's replies, which tells how the joy of the King and Wolsey on receiving the first commission "is now expelled, made cold, and almost extinct;" and what, says Fox, "grieveth me" is that they seem "secretly to arrect and impute unto you blame herein." [31]

Thanks to some successes of the French army in Italy, and the consequent diminution of Imperial prestige, Gardiner finally succeeded in getting Campeggio started from Rome, and in securing from Clement, who had, early in June, moved to Viterbo, a promise to send a decretal commission with Campeggio. He wrote to the King telling of his success, and defending his former expressions of despair, being determined, he said, "to say and write unto your Majesty the truth . . . whether the same shall delight and please for the time or otherwise." [32]

At the end of June, or beginning of July, he went to Venice, to urge the restoration to the Pope, of Cervia and Ravenna, Papal cities which the Venetians had seized.[33] The recovery of these places was the prime object of Clement's policy. The Hildebrandine vision of Papal control of Europe had long since dwindled into contentment with a petty Italian Kingdom. Even this had now been shaken. Clement vacillated between Charles and Henry as either held out the hope of effecting a restitution of its broken pieces. So delighted was he with the prospect of recovering these towns, that he declared that though he had always loved Gardiner for his virtue and scholarship, he now loved him all the more for his diligence at Venice.[34] The word *"amo"* sounds strange in the mouth of one whom Gardiner had literally worried into acquiescence. Gardiner gained nothing but fair words from the Venetians, and, having fallen "sore sick in the flux," decided to depart. He was in England in the beginning of September.[35]

It is noteworthy that on this long mission Gardiner gave no indication of reverence for the Papacy, certainly none for Clement the Pope. Nor does he seem to have doubted the justice of the King's cause. Perhaps his attitude towards that would be best described by saying that he did not think of it under the categories of just and unjust. He was convinced of its legality. He was an advocate straining every faculty for his client, a client who could be lavish of preferment and praise.

V

THE PRINCIPAL SECRETARY

While at the Papal court Gardiner had laid before Clement the reasons why monastic endowments should be converted to Wolsey's newly founded colleges at Ipswich and Oxford. During the three weeks after his return to England, in September 1528, he was busy with their affairs. He was placed by the Cardinal on a commission to revise their statutes; he went, with Dr. Rowland Lee and Thomas Cromwell, to furnish the chapel and induct priests, clerks, and children at Ipswich; he sat as judge for the suppression of the priories of Felixstowe, Rumburgh, and Bromhill, turning their property over to the Ipswich college. In these proceedings he is called Archdeacon of Worcester—an office which was perhaps a reward for his recent diplomatic services.[1]

On October 8 Campeggio arrived in London. Since he had left Italy, the collapse of the French siege of Naples removed all hope of any but Imperial power dominating the peninsula for the time. Hence he received implicit instructions to delay the trial and pronounce no judgement without new orders from the Pope.[2] Gout enforced quiescence for two weeks; a third was consumed in fruitless attempts to persuade Henry to abandon his intention and Catherine to enter a nunnery. Campeggio refused, moreover, to put the secret decretal which he bore, in Wolsey's hands.

Action was further delayed by Catherine's production of a copy of what was claimed to be a brief from Julius II, remedying all the defects in the bull of dispensation from the same pontiff, and permitting Henry to marry her even if her marriage with Arthur had been consummated. The original of this brief was said to be in Spain. If it were genuine, the whole of Henry's case, which rested on the defects in the bull of dispensation, fell to the ground. Hence, at the end of November, Sir Francis Brian and Peter Vannes were dispatched to Rome to secure evidence of its falsity. Such was the impatience of Wolsey and the King, that Brian and Vannes were soon followed by William Knight and William Benet, and finally by Gardiner, who embarked for Calais January 22, 1529.[3]

It must have been a day or two before this that he wrote this pleasant good-by greeting to Thomas Arundell, then one of the gentlemen of Wolsey's privy chamber:

28

"Gentle Master Arundel, by these letters I shall take you by the hand, and bid you most heartily farewell, . . . but though I depart from you in body, I depart not in mind and soul, which, considering it may be where I list, ye may be well assured it shall be ever where you be during my life, wheresoever this body shall fortune to wander. . . .

Entirely your own,
STEVEN GARDYNER." [4]

Gardiner made all haste in his journey. On January 30 he reached Lyons. Thence to Alessandria, where he arrived February 6, he had "good fortune in his voyage . . . except that he had one jeopardous and perilous fall." From Alessandria "he intended the same day to ride twenty miles, accompanied with a number of men of war, because he would be continually for that space in dread and fear of the Spaniards." On February 15 he arrived, despite robber-infested highways, safely at Rome,[5] whither the Pope had returned in the autumn of the previous year. Clement was seriously ill and the city in confusion.

News had reached England that he was dead. Immediately royal instructions to use every effort to secure the election of Wolsey to the Papacy were dispatched to Gardiner. These were accompanied by a note from Wolsey "to the person whom I most entirely do trust," urging him to stretch every nerve for his election, as the only means of preserving the authority of the Church in England.[6] Clement recovered, and Gardiner's labour was spared.

Difficult as the task of securing Wolsey's election to the Papacy would have been, that of obtaining a favourable solution of the King's matter from the convalescing Clement was no whit easier. Gardiner was at Rome almost a month before the Pope was well enough to be seen, and even then he could be seen only for a few minutes. The first interview of any length, which appears to have been on April 1, was not encouraging. Gardiner's letters to the King are characterized by a contemporary as written with "desperation."[7] The King and Wolsey, nevertheless, ceased not to urge renewed efforts. In "the King's great and weighty cause of matrimony," wrote Wolsey, Gardiner was "for no earthly cause to suffer or tolerate tract or delay, in what case soever the Pope's Holiness be of amendment or danger of life." If all other methods failed, he was to be "plain and round with the Pope's Holiness," threatening the loss of England and her ally France to the Papal See.

Threats, however, were futile, and on April 21, the Pope wrote to Henry regretting that he could not pronounce the brief a forgery without hearing both sides.[8]

On the same day Gardiner also wrote to the King. He had seen the Pope privately and had said such things as "ought to fear the

Pope's said Holiness . . . using all ways possible to enforce him to do somewhat, being a man of such nature, as he never resolveth anything, but by some violent affection compelled thereunto." Clement cared little, thought Gardiner, how the case was settled as long as he himself was not responsible. He would be glad if it were determined in England, and then if the Emperor objected he would serve him as he had served Henry—with delays and excuses. Gardiner advised Henry to begin the trial, and "I would trust," he added, "being there with such consultations as I should bring from hence, to say somewhat to this brief there, . . . for from hence shall come nothing but delays." He thought that the words "weighing carefully the justice of the cause," with which Clement had begun a written promise, made the previous summer, not to revoke the commission and to confirm the legates' decision, committed the Pope as completely as did the decretal commission, which Campeggio refused to show to anyone but the King. This promise, which for some reason had not been sent to England when granted, was now sent, and, as Gardiner said, Henry could show it to anyone in justification of his course.[9]

The promise was not so unconditional as desired, hence Wolsey suggested that Gardiner get it amplified in this ingenious fashion: he was to tell the Pope that it had been so wet in transmission as to be illegible, and that he would devise a duplicate as nearly as he could remember. This would give him the chance to insert "as many of the new and other pregnant, fat, and available words as is possible." Gardiner followed this advice, but Clement was not to be tricked, nor was a new promise granted.[10]

Meanwhile, Mai, the clever and able ambassador of the Emperor at the Papal court, had been exerting all his powers, not only to thwart Gardiner, but to persuade the Pope to revoke the case. Sometime late in April, or early in May, he and the "lawyer ambassador," as he called Gardiner, debated the question of revocation before the Pope in full consistory. Brian reported that Gardiner, "like a wise man and a true servant" of the King, "made the Pope ashamed of his own deeds." Mai said his Holiness had been very much provoked by the Englishmen.[11]

Gardiner saw clearly that further effort was useless.

"All jointly, and I myself apart," he said, "applying all my poor wit and learning to attain at the Pope's hand some part of the accomplishment of your Highness' desires, finally have nothing prevailed; but now see it called in question whether the authority given to the legates there should be revoked or no."

Under such discouraging circumstances it was perhaps excusable that he should have addressed the King in words of flattery, fulsome beyond his wont.

"Your Highness," he said, "hath so much virtue in you, whereof God is to be thanked, as may suffice to convert other men's faults into goodness." [12]

Before this letter reached England, Wolsey and the King had decided to push the case there. Campeggio had now been in England seven months without proceeding to trial. No aid was to be expected from the Pope; much hindrance was feared from the Emperor. It was better, as Gardiner had suggested, to settle the case in England on the chance of Clement's acquiescence, than to wait till he called it to Rome. Wolsey therefore notified Gardiner that the King willed him to return "with diligence," and explained that if it had not been for his absence the trial would have been begun before Whitsuntide;

"but because his Grace would have you here present, as well for the forming of the said process, and for such things as he trusted that ye shall obtain and bring with you, as also for the better knowledge to be had in sundry matters, wherein you may be the better riped and informed, . . . his Highness will somewhat the longer defer the commencement of the said process, and respite the same, only for your coming." [13]

Gardiner arrived in London June 22,[14] having missed only the first two sittings of the court, which had opened on the 18th. He was in good time to assume the duties of "chief scribe" at the trial.[15] Just what the pertinent "somewhat" was, which he had promised to say concerning the brief, is not recorded, but the French ambassador was given to understand that he brought an expression of the Pope's personal opinion that the brief was spurious. This is highly probable, for Clement had written to Campeggio authorizing him to reject evidence in behalf of the brief "as an evident forgery." [16]

Gardiner's knowledge and skill availed little, except to insure him the favour of the King, for Campeggio, in accordance with his instructions, did all he could to delay the proceedings. Despite the frequent sittings of the court, he succeeded in staving off the evil day until July 23. Then, when everyone was expecting a decision, he rose and declared the court, according to the Roman custom, prorogued for vacation until October.

Five days later, July 28, 1529, Gardiner entered upon the position of Principal Secretary to Henry VIII.[17]

The holder of this post lived in attendance on the King, expressed with his pen the royal wishes, and, in some cases, saw to the execution of them. This gave him an intimate knowledge of royal affairs, foreign as well as domestic, and enabled him to exert no little influence on the business of state. With Gardiner, the principal secretaryship began to be the administrative centre of the diplomatic service.

It was perhaps at this turn in his fortune that Leland addressed to him the encomium of which we have already spoken. The poet praised his acting, his eloquence, his teaching, and declared that he had achieved a success beyond any he had ever known, in combining the skill of jurist and advocate, the knowledge of canonist and civilian. He concluded his verses with the prophesy that a bishop's mitre would one day crown Gardiner's head.[18]

VI

THE FALL OF THE CARDINAL

"What the future has in store I know not; I take up my residence at court today. You will, as I hope, shortly see an advance in my fortunes." [1] So wrote Gardiner, July 28, 1529, announcing his promotion, to his Italian friend Peter Vannes, who had assisted him on his recent embassy to Rome, and who had previously acted as Latin secretary to both Wolsey and Henry VIII.

It was a letter to Vannes written in the previous month, June 25, which Gardiner closed with the master phrase, "Yours assuredly to my little power."

In that letter he had urged Vannes and his colleagues at the Papal court to prevent the calling of the King's case to Rome. If the Pope, said Gardiner, "as God forbid," should summon the action thither,

> "not only thereby the King's Grace and all his nobles should decline from the Pope and See Apostolic, but also the same should redound to my Lord Cardinal's, our common master's, utter undoing." [2]

Gardiner's forecast was prophetic. On July 13 Clement decided to revoke the case. Although Wolsey remained for the time at the head of the Government, his opponents, the Dukes of Norfolk and Suffolk and the Boleyns, rejoicing at the royal disfavour into which this revocation of the case and the failure of the legatine court to pronounce judgement had brought him, did all in their power to prevent his personal access to the King. During August and September Henry and Anne Boleyn toured the country as far as Woodstock and Buckingham, hunting and making merry. [3] Gardiner accompanied them. Through him, Henry's wishes were communicated to the Cardinal. We have no less than eighteen letters from Gardiner to Wolsey from the end of July to the beginning of October 1529. [4] The first of these, written on the day Gardiner took up his residence with the King, throws an interesting side-light on Henry's character. After telling of the royal satisfaction with Campeggio's promise not to give anyone an extra-judicial opinion on the divorce, Gardiner writes:

> "I should have come unto your Grace to have declared this by mouth, but that his Highness, having before my coming appointed me a chamber and spoken for mine allowance, gave

me special commandment not to depart hence, with this addition, *nescitis neque diem neque horam* [you know not the day nor the hour]. So as looking this night that his Highness will call for me *ut experiatur et cognoscat* [in order to find out] how I will follow his Grace's commandment in that behalf, I dare not depart hence." [5]

Two days after this, Brian Tuke, Treasurer of the Chamber, came upon Henry, Gardiner, and Anne's father, Lord Rocheford, conversing about continental politics.[6] A month later he found Rocheford and Gardiner the only persons admitted to secret conference with the King. At the same time he gave this pertinent characterization of Gardiner, possibly in answer to a query from the Cardinal:

"In the residue of my communications with Mr. Stephens, I assure your Grace I found him such one as towards your Grace he should be; and a man neither minded to meddle with many things, but to deal with one thing, such as he shall fortune to be appointed unto, ne minded to write more in his letters to your Grace than shall be to the purpose, thinking that, like a wise man, to be the best way." [7]

Gardiner's letters to Wolsey exemplify this business-like precision. There is hardly an intimate reference in them. He ends one note in a hasty, tired scrawl, saying, "I have been forth from morn to night a-hunting by the King's Highness' commandment." [8] For the rest, the letters deal strictly with politics. The possible citation of the King to Rome, and the Treaty of Cambray are the chief topics. Wolsey was exhorted to prevent the citation as an indignity not to be suffered by the nation. He succeeded in persuading Catherine not to press for it, for which he received, through Gardiner, the King's hearty thanks. As for the recent treaty of Cambray between Francis I and Charles V, Wolsey felt that by it France had broken the pledge made to England at Amiens. When Henry heard this his wrath was stirred against the French, and Gardiner ventured to disagree with his old master in order to keep Henry from foolishly breaking with France.

"If your Grace had been here," wrote Gardiner, "and seen how the King's Highness took it, you would rather have studied how by some benign interpretation to have made the best of that which is past remedy, than to have persisted in the blaming of non-observation of covenants on the French part." [9]

Sometime in September Wolsey, alive to the danger of continued absence from the King, asked for a personal interview. He was put off at the time, but his chance came when Campeggio took leave of the King, Sunday, September 19. He was then received so graciously by Henry at Grafton that, in the words of his devoted servitor, Cavendish, "to behold the countenance of those that had made their wagers to the contrary, it would have made you to smile." In the evening the Cardinal went by torchlight to a house three miles from Grafton, where, says Cavendish,

> "he had to supper with him divers of his friends of the court; and sitting at supper, in came to him Doctor Stephens, the Secretary, late ambassador unto Rome, but to what intent he came I know not; howbeit my Lord took it that he came to dissemble a certain obedience and love towards him, or else to espy his behaviour and to hear his communication at supper. Notwithstanding, my Lord bade him welcome, and commanded him to sit down at the table."

They spoke of Gardiner's greyhounds, of "hunting and like disports,"

> "and after supper my Lord and he talked secretly together, till it was midnight or they departed." [10]

The next morning Wolsey returned to the King. Thomas Alward, one of his attendants, wrote to Cromwell, telling how his master sat with the King's Council all that day, and how Suffolk, Rocheford, Tuke, and Gardiner

> "did as gently behave themselves, with as much observance and humility to my Lord's Grace as ever I saw them do at any time tofore. What they bear in their hearts I know not. Of the premises I have seen with mine eyes." [11]

This was the last time Wolsey saw the King. Three weeks had not passed before he was indicted for præmunire, and within a month he had surrendered the great seal.

Many years later Gardiner confessed that he had never been able to see the justice of the indictment although it was entirely in accord with English law. Wolsey had, he said, been appointed Papal Legate at the King's request,

> "yet because it was against the laws of the realm the judges concluded the offence of the præmunire; which conclusion I bear away and take it for a law of the realm, because the lawyers so said, but my reason digested it not." [12]

Gardiner's relation to the Cardinal's fall is not entirely clear. Cavendish, as we have seen, attributed to Wolsey a suspicion of Gardiner's sincerity. Cavendish wrote some years after the Cardinal's death, and his estimate of his master's feelings may be no more than a conjecture; it does, however, show what Cavendish himself thought. Just before Wolsey's final interview with the

King, the French ambassador, Du Bellay, wrote that he felt sure that some of the Cardinal's protégés—hinting perhaps at Gardiner and Tuke, although he named none—had betrayed him.[13] Of modern historians Mr. Brewer remarks that it is not easy to decide whether or not Gardiner helped in the designs of the Norfolk-Boleyn party to estrange the King from Wolsey.[14] Professor Busch, using the sources Mr. Brewer made available, calls Gardiner a veritable Judas.[15] Mr. Friedmann asserts that Anne, her adherents, and Gardiner formed an alliance to bring Wolsey down,[16] but he gives no evidence for his inclusion of Gardiner in the alliance.

Anne and her adherents believed Wolsey in large part responsible for Henry's failure to obtain the divorce, and it is true that when the subject was first broached, the Cardinal's ideas as to who should be Henry's second queen differed from those of Anne; but he came clearly to see that his own supremacy depended on his securing the divorce and furthering Anne's marriage. Nor can there be the least shadow of doubt that Gardiner threw every energy into the attempt to help Wolsey attain these ends. He had cajoled, besought, threatened, manœuvred, to wring from Clement that which would not only have satisfied Anne and Henry but also have assured, if anything could have assured, the Cardinal's position. That the fiasco of the trial in the legatine court and the revocation of the case to Rome discredited Wolsey and not Gardiner, was due to the obvious fact that Wolsey was a Papal legate and one of the judges empowered to give sentence; it had been he, moreover, who had persuaded Henry to apply to the Pope for a solution of the difficulty rather than settle it in an English court; it had been his foreign policy which had proven insufficient to counterbalance the influence of the Emperor in Italy. With the least show of royal displeasure the long accumulating hatred of the old nobility for the upstart Cardinal was bound to break over him. That it needed plot or perfidy on the part of Gardiner to bring him down is a gratuitous assumption. That Gardiner had, for perhaps a year before the Cardinal's disgrace, sought to ingratiate himself with both Henry and Anne, is at most evidence that, foreseeing the inevitable ruin of his master if the divorce were not obtained, he thus prepared a shelter into which he might step when the storm broke.

On Sunday, October 17, (1529) he was, with Norfolk, Suffolk, Fitzwilliam the Treasurer, and Dr. Taylor, Master of the Rolls, present at Wolsey's surrender of the great seal in the gallery of his house at Westminster. It was Gardiner who locked and retained the key of the casket in which the seal was placed. He was also present at Windsor, when, three days later, the King took the seal out and used it.[17] Mr. Friedmann hazards the suggestion that if Anne Boleyn had had her way, Gardiner, not Thomas More, would have received the chancellorship,[18] an hypothesis possible, but not demonstrable. DuBellay, writing of Wolsey's fall, on October 22, said that "Mademoiselle Anne" was supreme, and her uncle, the Duke of Norfolk, chief of the Council. Gardiner, he expected, would have a large share in the management of affairs, "especially," he added—in reference to the increasing hostility to the clergy—"if he will throw off his gown."[19] To one who had observed Gardiner's career up to this point, it might well seem that he was ready to throw off his clerical gown, but we have no hint that he ever had the least intention of doing so.

Wolsey retired to Esher in the diocese of Winchester, where he remained in an ill-furnished house throughout the winter, plying Cromwell and Gardiner with requests for assistance. His goods at York Place were seized for the King's use, and Fitzwilliam and Gardiner appointed to see that nothing was embezzled.[20]

On October 22 he made a complete submission, surrendered all his possessions and offices, and threw himself on the King's mercy, having been promised—with how much definiteness it is impossible to say—that if he gave up everything, he would receive back the revenues of Winchester and St. Albans. He asked Cromwell to remind Norfolk, Suffolk, and Gardiner of this, and mentioned it more than once to Gardiner; at one time saying, "ye with other my lords showed me that I should otherwise be furnished and seen unto. Ye know in your learning and conscience whether I should forfeit my spiritualities of Winchester or no." Half a year later he seems to have instructed his chaplain, Thomas Runcorn, to remind Gardiner "that he, and only he, was privy how and with what hope and trust" he committed himself and all his goods unto the King.[21]

Gardiner promised to "do his best"[22]—a promise which one person at least did not think he fulfilled.

> "In mine opinion," wrote Ralph Sadler, Cromwell's servant, "the said Mr. Secretary will do little or nothing that shall be to the avail or profit of my Lord his Grace, . . . more than he may not choose for very shame, considering the advancements and promotion that he hath had at my Lord his hands."[23]

Thomas Arundell, on the contrary, wrote to the Cardinal:

> "As to Master Secretary, I assure your Grace I do not perceive but that he is glad to do your Grace pleasure, always regarding that by means of setting forth your Grace's suits he be not preferred too much on your part."[24]

When, at the end of January or beginning of February 1530, Wolsey heard that the King had declared his intention of pardoning him and of considering in Council how he should be treated, he wrote to Gardiner, at once hopefully and pathetically:

"I . . . thank God that ye have occasion given unto you to be a solicitor and setter forth of such things as do and shall concern my said end; in the making and componing whereof mine assured trust is, that ye will show the love and affection which ye have and bear towards me, your old lover and friend."[25]

What Gardiner advised we do not know, but on February 12, 1530 Wolsey received a full pardon. Two days later he was restored to the archbishopric of York with all its possessions, except York Place in Westminster, and was granted money, clothing, provisions, and horses, valued together at over £6,000. He was not allowed to retain Winchester or St. Albans, but was to receive a yearly pension of 1,000 marks.[26]

In anticipation of his removing to York he asked Gardiner to secure letters from the King commending him to the nobility of the North, and to pen them as favourably as possible—a request which was heartily granted, if we may judge from one such letter which is still extant. Cromwell's plan of gaining friends at court for Wolsey and, incidentally, for himself, by advising him to grant them fees and annuities out of his ecclesiastical revenues, was seconded by Gardiner, and it was Gardiner to whom, it seems, Cromwell frequently went for information and advice concerning his master's affairs.[27] To Gardiner, Wolsey entrusted the future of his son, Thomas Winter, and Gardiner brought the youth to the King, who promised to be gracious to him and accepted him "as his poor orator and scholar." Two years later Winter spoke in the highest terms of Gardiner's "virtue, faith, probity, and humanity." [28]

After his pardon and restitution to the see of York, Wolsey was in continual financial difficulty. What with debts, and repairs of long-neglected dwellings, he complained to Gardiner again and again of his "poor estate." [29] In the summer of 1530 he sent his chaplain, Thomas Runcorn, to tell him that the 1,000 marks he had for his journey to the north were almost all used in paying debts before starting, and that he had to "shift and borrow" to pay his servants. Gardiner said that he was ready to do everything possible for Wolsey, and acknowledged that he was in such favour with the King that he had access to him at all times, and could, as occasion offered, "speak a good word for his friends; yet he had not with him such a trade . . . that he might in all causes deduce his Grace to his purpose." If Wolsey had not enough to live on, said Gardiner, it was his own fault, for he might have kept enough with the King's consent, but he would not, "so that the show might be the greater when it should be presented to the King's sight." Further, he had concealed so many of his debts that the King had "paid four times double more than was thought he should;" hence, said Gardiner, it would do Wolsey more harm than good if he broached the subject to the King.[30] Wolsey's apologist, Mr. Brewer, remarks that in Gardiner's reply to Runcorn there was "probably more truth than grace."[31]

Though finances were the source of much anxiety, the objects of Wolsey's "vehement and entire care" were his colleges. The King threatened to dissolve them and appropriate their lands and revenues. "Good Master Secretary," wrote Wolsey, "I beseech you to be good master and patron to the said colleges."[32]

Gardiner did everything possible to save them. William Capon, dean of Ipswich, reported that "Doctor Stephens hath spoken and done the best he can to the King, that the said college should continue, but the King will in no wise hear him."[33] He had better success with the college at Oxford. He urged its preservation on the King, and aided John Higden, the dean, in securing immunity from visitation by the royal commissioners.[34] Thomas More told the representatives from Oxford that Gardiner "was singularly and effectuously good for the continuance and establishment" of their college;[35] and Arundell wrote to Wolsey:

> "I do not see but that he favoureth more your college than any other one, [and] hath now lately spoken to the King that I have sure knowledge of, whereby the King hath spoken to his judges and Council to devise for the surety of the college."[36]

This letter, written October 17, 1530, completes the contemporary references to Gardiner's dealings with his fallen master.

On November 29, 1530, the Cardinal died.

Gardiner had profited by his fall, and had accepted the profit without protest. It is clear from his letter to Vannes, quoted at the opening of this chapter, that from the moment Gardiner entered the King's service he looked for speedy advancement, but there is hardly sufficient evidence for concluding that he achieved his desire at the price of treachery. The dominant powers at court, coupled with the failure of the legates to settle the question of the marriage, were enough to bring Wolsey to the ground. Gardiner's ability, and the singleness of his devotion to the King's cause, were sufficient, without perfidy, to put him in the position of a favourite. The clearest judgement upon him was perhaps that which declared him willing to help the Cardinal so long as he did not hinder himself, and the most lifelike description, that which pictured him as not minded to meddle with many things but to deal with the one thing, to which he might fortune to be appointed.

VII

THE RIGHT HAND OF THE KING

During the period of the Cardinal's disgrace and the year following his death, Gardiner became increasingly influential in the counsels of the King.

Soon after his entry into residence at court in 1529, he advised the King to have his illegitimate son, the Duke of Richmond, educated in Greek and Latin.[1] In October, when the departing Campeggio complained of rough treatment at the hands of Customs officials at Dover, it seems to have been Gardiner who composed the King's caustic reply.[2] As the King's Chief Secretary he sat in the Parliament that assembled in November 1529, and was the first named of a committee of three to receive petitions for the redress of grievances from Gascony and parts beyond sea.[3] In the Convocation, meeting at the same time, he sat by the double right of his two archdeaconries, Taunton and Worcester.[4]

Though the settlement of the marriage question had been withdrawn from England by the Pope, it did not cease to be the chief care of the King and his counsellors. It entered now upon what has been called the second stage of its solution—the collection of the opinions of the universities of Christendom that the dispensation of Julius II had been invalid, not because of its technical irregularities (as Gardiner had argued at the Papal court), but because the Old Testament prohibition of marriage with a deceased brother's wife was divine law and could not be dispensed with, even by the Pope.

The idea of consulting the universities originated with Cranmer. He had, in the summer of 1529, retired from Cambridge, because of the plague, to the home of two of his scholars at Waltham, The King, as we recall, was then upon his pleasure-journey, and, coming to Waltham early in August, it chanced that Gardiner and his friend Fox, "the great and only chief doers of the King's said cause at that time," were lodged in the same house with Cranmer. "By means whereof all they three, being of old acquaintance and meeting together the first night at supper, had familiar talk concerning the estate of the university," and "the King's divorcement." Cranmer suggested that the best way to determine the truth of the King's case was to consult the theological faculties of the universities. His listeners "liked well his counsel," and two days later Fox mentioned it to the King, who, after his return to Greenwich in November, bade them summon Cranmer to him.[5]

Cranmer was thereupon commissioned to write a book in favour of the King's cause, which was circulated among the doctors and masters of Cambridge in preparation for the coming of Gardiner and Fox, in February 1530, to secure their official opinion.[6] Cambridge was pretty evenly divided on the question, and on Gardiner's arrival the opposition organized itself. "As we assembled, they assembled," he wrote; "as we made friends, they made friends." The doctors of theology discussed until "dark night," but came to no decision. Next day, "by labour of friends to cause some to depart the house which were against it," Gardiner and Fox succeeded in getting a grace or decree passed, naming a committee of twenty-nine to decide the question for the university by a two-thirds vote. Sixteen of those named were already of the King's opinion; of four others Gardiner had "good hope."

After a public discussion in which he and Fox and two of the Cambridge doctors upheld the King's side, Gardiner answering all questions of Canon Law, the committee reached the unanimous decision that to marry a deceased brother's wife was forbidden by both divine and natural law.[7]

Fox soon after secured the favourable opinion of Oxford and Paris, and when four other French universities and a few in Italy had added their decisions in the King's favour, a letter, signed by a number of nobility and clergy, including Gardiner as a "doctor in Parliament," was sent to the Pope informing him of this consensus of learned opinion.[8] The judgement of the university theologians had been sought, however, not so much to impress the Pope, as to justify in the eyes of Europe any action Henry might see fit to take apart from the Papacy.

As a member of the King's Council and Principal Secretary, Gardiner was engaged in a multitude of diverse matters during the years 1530 and 1531. Before his activity at Cambridge he had, in February 1530, taken part in the deliberations leading to Wolsey's pardon,[9] and at about the same time had arranged with the French ambassadors for the delivery of the far-famed *Fleur de Lis,* a jewel which Henry held in pawn from the Emperor, and for the restitution of which the French, now in the Emperor's debt, agreed to pay.[10] In May of this year he acted with Warham, More, Tunstall, and other "chief learned men," in examining and condemning certain books "containing many detestable errors and damnable opinions," including the translation of Scripture "corrupted by William Tyndale."[11] In September he discussed the divorce with the Papal Nuncio, Baron del Borgho; in October and November he treated with the French for the conversion of their yearly tribute of salt into a money payment; and in January 1531 he was present at the consultations of Chapuys, the Imperial ambassador, with the Duke of Norfolk.[12]

At the end of the following May he was one of the leaders of the group of nobles and ecclesiastics who tried to shake the resolution of the Queen. To her assertion that her marriage with Prince Arthur had never been consummated, he replied that the fact that she had married and lived with him was presumption sufficient in the law; to which she answered with spirit that she was proceeding on a truth, not a presumption, "and as for his presumptions and his laws, he could go and ventilate them at Rome."[13] In July the King consulted him before sending a bitter answer to her request to say good-by before he left her for the last time;[14] and sometime before August he wrote a reply—much praised by the French lawyers to whom his friend Fox showed it—to the objections of Catherine's counsel at Rome to Henry's "excusator," Sir Edward Carne, who had been sent to convince the Pope that the King of England could not appear, even by deputy, in a foreign court of law.[15]

When Gardiner was away on a brief embassy to France in 1532, Henry was "pestered with business," and complained that there was no one "to rid ne depeche the same." "His absence," exclaimed the King, "is the lack of my right hand."[16]

Gardiner's varied services did not go unrewarded. Sometime in 1529 he had been made Archdeacon of Norfolk;[17] in the summer of 1530 the King granted him the rent of the manor of Hanworth, and the reversion of its lands on expiration of the lease of the possessor;[18] in March 1531 he received the archdeaconry of Leicester,[19] and in September of the same year he was elected—that is, appointed by the King—Bishop of Winchester.[20] The University of Oxford hastened to confer upon him the honorary degree of Doctor of Laws.[21] His election to Winchester received Papal confirmation October 20;[22] he was consecrated December 3;[23] the King bestowed the temporalities on him December 5;[24] he was installed December 27.[25]

Winchester was the wealthiest diocese in England, worth, at Gardiner's accession, £4,000 a year.[26] For the "restitution of the temporalities," as the bestowal of the sources of revenue was called, Gardiner paid the King £366 13s. 4d.,[27] though he complained to Cromwell that he received from the see £1,300 less a year than did Richard Foxe (Bishop from 1501 to 1528), and owed twice as much as Foxe was worth when he died. Moreover, he would be put to great expense to replenish "the implements of the bishopric," for, he added, "I find in no place a pan." "I would be glad," he said, "to pay nothing if it were remitted unto me, and the less I pay the better." Still he did not want to be "seem to huck of or stick to pay" his duty, since the King had given him the bishopric, without his asking for it.[28]

Henry, in a letter to his ambassadors at Rome, justifying the prohibition of the payment of annates or first-fruits for the Papal bulls necessary to obtain a bishopric, said that they were so large in Gardiner's case that he had to borrow money to pay for them. It seems to have been Cromwell from whom he borrowed it.[29]

Though the costs of accepting Winchester were great, they in no-wise deterred Gardiner from accepting it; nor was the financial pressure more than temporary. Thereafter he became the "princely prelate," whose magnificence was only less than Wolsey's. His critics accused him of extravagance.

If Winchester was the wealthiest of dioceses it was also, next to Canterbury, the most important. The present diocese of Southwark had not yet been cut from it, and Winchester House, the Bishop's palace, lay in a wooded park on the south bank of the Thames, just over London Bridge. Park and palace have long given place to the dusty warehouses of Greater London, but the neighbouring Church of St. Mary Overies,[30] now Southwark Cathedral, has, after much change and dilapidation, been restored to something of the semblance it wore when Gardiner celebrated Mass at its high altar. The proximity of the diocese to the court made it peculiarly attractive to statesmen-bishops. John of Stratford, William of Wykeham, Cardinal Beaufort had all held it. Richard Foxe, Lord Privy Seal to Henry VII and to the young Henry VIII, was Bishop of Winchester for twenty-seven years. On his death, in 1528, Wolsey asked the King for the diocese, in order, he said, "to be in the service of your Highness, nearer unto my spiritual cure."[31]

The little town of Winchester, once the capital of England, the city of Alfred and Athelstan and Cnut, was the ecclesiastical centre of the see. Here was the cathedral with its well knit Norman transepts and the finest of Gothic naves; here the goodly priory of St. Swithin, and Wolvesey, the Bishop's house—a "palace well towered"—and the college of Wykeham, and the slender-pillared hall of Henry III. Of all the places with which Gardiner was connected, Winchester, for all its changes, has changed least since he knew it.

But his permanent residence was not there, nor at his other palace at Esher, a few miles from Hampton Court, nor at his house at Farnham, but at Winchester House in Southwark. Here, in sight of the single spire of old St. Paul's and the battlements of London Tower, he gathered round him a group of younger contemporaries—scholars and diplomats—of whom Paget and Wriothesley were chief. Leland called it the home of eloquence and the muses.[32]

Out from Winchester House, out over London Bridge, past St. Paul's, down the Fleet and the Strand to Westminster, would ride the Bishop "in his velvets and satin, aloft upon his mule trapped with velvet with gilden stirrups and bridle, with his gentlemen bare head, chained with gold, before and after him. Who will not say," adds his observer, not without irony, "but he rideth a princely prelate, a glorious bishop to orne [*i.e.*, adorn] and honour a whole realm? See what a cleanly sort of tall man he hath about him; what costly liveries giveth he, what a many idle bellies daily feedeth he!" [33]

Another contemporary speaks of the "great number of gentlemen's sons, knights' sons, and lords' sons with him in service at one time;" [34] and Jacques Wingfield, one of his lifelong servitors, later testified that his household numbered "seven score and odd." They were, he said, "as quiet and well ordered company" as he had ever known. [35]

We have seen how Gardiner told Cromwell that the King gave him Winchester without his asking for it. After Henry's death, in a letter to Somerset, he added this detail of the giving:

"When he gave me the bishopric of Winchester he said he had often squared with me, but he loved me never the worse, and for a token thereof gave me the bishopric."

In the same letter Gardiner gives an illuminating analysis of his own and Henry's character and of their relations to each other. When it was reported to Henry that Gardiner "stooped not and was stubborn," Henry commended to him "certain men's gentle nature (as he called it) that wept at every of his words," and not infrequently wrote a sharp letter calling it a "whetting,"

"which was not all the most pleasant unto me at all times; yet when I saw in my doings was no hurt, and sometimes by the occasion thereof the matter amended, I was not so coy as always to reverse my argument, nor, so that his affairs went well, did I ever trouble myself, whether he made me a wanton or not. . . . I esteemed him, as he was, a wise prince; and whatsoever he wrote or said for the present, he would after consider the matter as wisely as any man, and neither hurt nor inwardly disfavour him that had been bold with him; whereof I serve for a proof, for no man could do me hurt during his life. . . . And once when he had been vehement with me in the presence of the Earl of Wiltshire [father of Anne Boleyn] and saw me dismayed with it, he took me apart into his bed chamber and comforted me, and said that his displeasure was not so much to me as I did take it, but he misliked the matter, and he durst more boldly direct his speech to me than to the Earl of Wiltshire. And from that day foreward he could not put me out of courage. . . ." [36]

Gardiner's first important duty after receiving the bishopric was a mission to France. The year 1531 was not closing any too hopefully for Henry. The Pope had decided that the cause must proceed at Rome; the Emperor was all powerful in Italy; former supporters of the divorce in England began to cool. Although Henry

had begun to tighten his grip upon the English clergy, he still hesitated to defy the Pope, for Scotland, always waiting its chance to
attack England, had been making overtures of alliance to France,
and Charles V seemed on the point of coming to terms with the
Protestant princes of Germany. Gardiner was hurried off to France
to prevent French alliance with Scotland, to urge France to encourage the German princes against Charles, and to secure a definite
agreement that France would assist England offensively against
Charles, should any of the English territories be invaded.

After presenting Henry with a golden candlestick as a New Year's
gift, Gardiner rode post to Dover on the Feast of St. Thomas à
Becket, December 29—two days after his installation at Winchester
—stopping scant long enough to drink or warm himself while changing horses in the city of Becket's martyrdom.[37]

The French showed themselves none too eager to enter an offensive league against the Emperor, nor give up the proposed alliance
with the Scot. Moreover, the situation was aggravated by the
English seizure of a packet of Scotch dispatches on their way to
France. Gardiner had to use "dolce and pleasant words" to calm
the French resentment at this act,[38] but in the end he was successful.
An agreement was formally ratified in April 1532, a month after
his return to England, providing for mutual naval and military
assistance in the event of a Spanish invasion of either country.[39]

While in France, the royal instructions to the English ambassadors
with the Emperor and the Pope passed through Gardiner's hands.
The fact that the King asked him to add to them anything he thought
proper,[40] shows to what extent Henry had become dependent upon
him in the conduct of foreign affairs.

At home, however, Cromwell, whom Gardiner—if we can trust
expressions in their correspondence—still regarded as his friend,
was aiding if not inaugurating a policy revolutionary to all that
Gardiner regarded as the essence of stability and order.

VIII

THE LIBERTIES OF THE CHURCH

On March 6, 1532 Gardiner arrived in London on his return from France.[1] Convocation was in session, and at the meeting of April 12, 1532, Archbishop Warham presented for consideration the document known as the Supplication of the Commons against the Ordinaries (*i.e.*, ecclesiastical judges, such as bishops, archdeacons, and their deputies). This was a petition from the lower house of Parliament to the King, asking him to reform certain evils in the Church. It was one of the many manifestations of a growing hostility of the more prosperous laity to the clergy— skilfully used by the court. It repeated the stock complaints against simony, nepotism, and the taking of fees for Sacraments. Saints' days, it averred, were too numerous, and trials in Church courts tedious, vexatious, and expensive; heresy examinations were unfairly conducted. The chief blow, however, was aimed at the independent legislative power of the Church. To make laws in Convocation without consent of the King or laity was declared to be a derogation of the prerogative royal and a damage to the King's subjects.[2]

To Gardiner was intrusted the framing of a reply, which was adopted by Convocation and in the hands of the King before the end of the month. In it the ordinaries pointed out that the Supplication was full of sweeping general charges unsupported by a single specific instance. If there were corruption in the Church, the bishops were not only sorry but ready to punish the offenders. As for heresy trials, the ordinaries would be glad if God would discharge them from conducting them, for they were "full of trouble and business, without any fruit, pleasure, or commodity worldly, but a continual conflict and vexation." The reform of the court system, already begun by Archbishop Warham, was noted; and the King was reminded of the "high service" which doctors of Civil Law, trained in the Church courts, had done him and his progenitors "concerning treaties, truces, confederations, and leagues, drawn, devised, and concluded with outward princes." On the main question at issue, the reply declared that the authority of Convocation for making laws for the maintenance of faith and virtue was "grounded upon the Scripture of God and the determination of Holy Church." The clergy dared not submit, it said, to the King's assent the execution of a "duty certainly prescribed by God."

The King delivered this answer to Thomas Audley, Speaker of Commons, April 30, saying, "We think their answer will smally please you, for it seemeth to us very slender." He also let Convocation know that their answer did not suit him concerning his "own particular interest, specially in that point that concerneth laws." Whereupon they drew up a second reply—a vigorous, brief defense of the right of Convocation to make laws, conceding, however, to the King the privilege of publishing or confirming them, and granting him a limited veto power. This answer was no more satisfactory than the first, and on May 10 Henry sent Edward Fox, his almoner, to lay before Convocation the demand that it abdicate the right to legislate without royal approval, submit all existing canons to revision by a committee of the King's appointment, and recognize the need of his assent for the retention of any of them. The next day he conveniently discovered—or Cromwell discovered for him—that the higher clergy, because of their oath to the Pope, were only half his subjects, and reported his discovery to Commons.

Meanwhile he tried to get measures through Parliament embodying his demands upon Convocation. They were passed by Commons but were defeated in the Lords by the clerical opposition led by Gardiner and Thomas More, the Chancellor. The King, wrote Chapuys on May 13, "is very angry, especially with the Chancellor and the Bishop of Winchester." On the 14th Parliament was prorogued, and Gardiner retired to his country place at Esher, deep in the royal displeasure. Two days later, Convocation, fearful of what consequences the King's recent discovery might lead to, made a full submission. On the same day More resigned the chancellorship.[3]

Sometime during this conflict the King let Gardiner know, through his friend Edward Fox, what he thought of his actions. The manliness, the vigour, the adroitness of Gardiner's letter to Henry, upon receipt of this message, made it worthy, in the eyes of Convocation, of a place upon its journal. He was greatly troubled, he said, to hear what opinion the King had conceived of him, but was comforted by the remembrance of his Highness's goodness, and the knowledge that with him truth always conquered. As for the answer concerning the right of Convocation to legislate, he believed it to be true, because so great a number of learned men had so precisely affirmed it to be so. Indeed, the King's own book against Luther approved it; the book written in the King's cause allowed it; the Council of Constance, condemning the articles of Wyclif, manifestly decreed it. Perhaps the King had discovered some proofs to the contrary, but Gardiner, who had not yet heard them, could hardly be blamed for not accepting them; nor was he, he acknowledged, with a hint at his legal training, learned in divinity. When he heard these proofs perhaps he would change his mind. It would indeed be pitiful if the clergy invoked God's name merely to uphold a position displeasing to the King, but on the other hand, he said, "if it be God's authority to us allotted, though we cannot use it condignly, yet we cannot give it away." He was most desirous of pleasing the King and "appliable to learn the truth," but trusted that the King would take it in good part that he continued to consider that true for which, he said, "I have so good grounds and authorities, until I have stronger grounds and reasons to the contrary." [4]

Edward Fox, doubtless out of consideration for his friend, wrote to Benet, in Italy, that gout was the reason for Gardiner's absence from Court, but Chapuys knew that the real cause was the anger of the King. By the end of May, however, Henry was urging Gardiner to return and conduct the correspondence with Rome. [5]

Although he was thus rapidly restored to favour, or at least to a service in which he was indispensable, there can be little doubt that his opposition to the King cost him the primacy of England. Archbishop Warham died within three months. [6] Reginald Pole, who might well have been considered for the place, had already declined the archbishopric of York and gone into voluntary exile on the Continent. Gardiner was the outstanding Churchman in England. But Henry now knew that Gardiner, once in the chair of St. Augustine, would not lightly regard the restriction of clerical power and privilege. A candidate more favourable to Henry's plans was sought, and found in Cranmer. It is perhaps with justice that historians have felt that Gardiner's lifelong opposition to the reforming Archbishop was intensified by the bitterness of personal disappointment.

Gardiner's stand against the King in 1532 is significant as showing us—and one might almost say, as showing Gardiner himself—what his attitude was to be in the impending struggle between the laity and the Church. Up to this moment he had evinced no other motive than faithfulness in his duties and ambition for his career. The Supplication of the Commons and the activities of the King and the Boleyn party against the Church made the issue of his life plain. That he adhered to the policy of conservatism and supported the immemorial rights of Church and clergy was, in the light of his training and office, natural. That he supported them against the opposition of an all-powerful King, whose good will he desired to retain, indicates elements of strength not to be explained merely in terms of his legal habits of thought.

IX

THE END OF THE KING'S MATTER

During the year 1532 occasional rumours reached the ears of the Imperialists that Gardiner had changed his opinion on the divorce.[1] It is difficult to appraise the worth of these reports. He was at this time undoubtedly aware that the success of the Boleyn party meant innovation in religion and destruction of Church privilege, and hence may have hoped for some course which might satisfy the King and defeat the Boleyns; but there is no evidence that he had any serious intention of aiding Catherine.

Immediately upon his return to court he was active in cementing the French alliance, whose only object was to put such pressure upon the Pope that Henry's desires would be granted, or, in default of that, so to strengthen Henry that he might act for himself. On Sunday, September 1, 1532, he stood beside the King at Windsor and read the patent creating Anne Boleyn Marchioness of Pembroke, while she knelt before them, "in a surcoat of crimson velvet." He then celebrated Mass, after which Henry and the French ambassador came to the altar to swear to the alliance.[2]

Six weeks later he accompanied Henry to the Continent for a personal but spectacular interview with Francis I.[3] After an initial conference at Boulogne, the Kings were received at Calais "with great melody, what with guns and all other instruments," and Francis "danced a dance or two" with Anne Boleyn. The diplomatic discussions with the French were conducted by Norfolk, Suffolk, and Gardiner.[4] Henry was well pleased with the interview, for Francis sent two cardinals to the Pope to plead Henry's cause as if it were his own, and behaved with such friendliness that Henry was heartened to proceed decisively with the divorce after his return to England in November.[5]

In the following January, 1533, Cranmer was elected Archbishop of Canterbury; on March 30 he was consecrated. Henry's next step was to see that his Archbishop's decision should be final, and for this end he secured the passage of an act of Parliament forbidding appeals to Rome. He then induced Convocation to assent to two propositions: first, that the prohibition of marriage with a deceased brother's wife was a divine ordinance from which the Pope could not dispense; second, that the consummation of Catherine's marriage with Arthur had been adequately proven. More than a month before Convocation met, Henry had asked the two Archbishops,

and the Bishops of London, Lincoln, and Winchester to subscribe a
similar declaration. Gardiner and Lee, Archbishop of York, refused
to sign it,[6] probably because of some legal irregularity in the proceeding rather than from sympathy for Catherine. When the matter was brought up in Convocation, in April, the question of Papal
dispensation was submitted to the theologians, that of the consummation of the marriage to the canonists. Gardiner, as a canonist, voted
that the consummation had been adequately proven, and, as proxy
for three absent bishops, cast like votes for them.[7]

Cranmer's task was now simple; he had merely to apply the decisions of Convocation. On May 10, 1533 he opened court at Dun-
stable, a few miles from Catherine's residence. The diocesan, John
Longland, Bishop of Lincoln, assisted him upon the bench, while
Gardiner acted as chief counsel for the King.[8] Catherine ignored the
summons to appear, and, on May 23, Cranmer pronounced her marriage with Henry null and void from the beginning. One of Cromwell's correspondents, who reported to him the progress of the trial,
said that Gardiner was studying most diligently "to cause everything
to be handled so as it may be most consonant to the law, as far as
the matter will suffer"[9]—a sentence which epitomizes Gardiner's
relation to the King. His services were peculiarly those of a legal
adviser. Legality was his touchstone for royal righteousness;
whether the King's actions were right or wrong, they must at least
be "consonant to the law." As Mr. James Gairdner says, "it was a
good deal to give honest advice even from such a point of view."[10]

There is a paragraph in one of Gardiner's letters to Somerset,
written after Henry's death, which gives us, in dramatic setting,
Gardiner's theory of the relation of the king to the law:

> "The Lord Cromwell had once put in the King our late
> Sovereign Lord's head to take upon him to have his will and
> pleasure regarded for a law; for that, he said, was to be a very
> king; and thereupon I was called for at Hampton Court. And
> as the Lord Cromwell was very stout, 'Come on, my Lord of
> Winchester,' quoth he (for that conceit he had, whatsoever
> he talked with me, he knew ever as much as I, Greek or Latin,
> and all), 'answer the King here,' quoth he, 'but speak plainly
> and directly, and shrink not, man! Is not that,' quoth he, 'that
> pleaseth the King, a law? Have ye not there, in the civil laws,'
> quoth he, *'quod principi placuit,* and so forth?' quoth he, 'I have
> somewhat forgotten it now.' I stood still and wondered in
> my mind to what conclusion this would tend. The King saw
> me musing, and with earnest gentleness said, 'Answer him
> whether it be so or no.' I would not answer my Lord Crom-
> well, but delivered my speech to the King, and told him, I had
> read indeed of kings that had their will always received for a

law, but, I told him, the form of his reign, to make the laws
his will, was more sure and quiet; 'and by this form of government ye be established,' quoth I, 'and it agreeable with the
nature of your people.' " [11]

It was Cromwell, whose policy Gardiner thus describes, who was,
in 1533, supplanting him in the royal favour.   Though Gardiner
retained for the time the chief secretaryship, Chapuys noted in May
that Cromwell was managing all the King's affairs. [12]   Gardiner,
however, deemed it expedient to bide his time, and for the present
to work side by side with both Cromwell and Cranmer; nor did he
fail to sanction by his presence the ascendancy of Anne Boleyn.

Five days after Henry's marriage with Catherine had been pronounced void, Cranmer gave sentence that his marriage with Anne
was valid. [13]   The next day, May 29, began Anne's coronation festivities, culminating at the high altar of the Abbey on Whitsunday, June 1.   On the Thursday before, Gardiner had been one
of those who, with the King, had received her at the Tower when
she came up the river from Greenwich, and there can be little doubt
that he was among the bishops riding two and two before her litter
in the triumphal procession Saturday afternoon from the Tower to
Westminster.   On Sunday morning when "this gorgeous lady," as
Cavendish called her, walked with archbishops, bishops, and abbots
from Westminster Hall to the Abbey, she was, in the words of
Cranmer, "sustained" on each side by Bishops Stokesley and Gardiner.   In the phrase of the chronicler Hall, "the Bishops of London
and Winchester bare up the laps of the Queen's robe." [14]

Cranmer's judgement on the marriage of Catherine was given
while the case was still pending at Rome.   If Clement wished to retain
an ounce of self-respect, to say nothing of the respect of Europe
and the friendship of the Emperor, he could not pass it over in
silence.   On July 11 he declared both the divorce from Catherine
and the marriage with Anne null, and pronounced Henry to have
incurred the greater excommunication, suspending, however, the
declaration of it for three months, [15] in the hope that he would
repent.

Meanwhile Francis I was arranging an interview with Clement
at Marseilles.   Henry at first protested against this, but seeing that
his protests were unavailing, decided to use the occasion to serve
notice on the Pope that he appealed from his judgement to that of
a general council.   To do this, Gardiner was dispatched, September
3, 1533.   With him went Sir Francis Brian and Sir John Wallop;
Edmund Bonner, late ambassador at Rome, was instructed to assist
him. [16]   On October 5 Gardiner wrote from Marseilles to Lord
Lisle, who had been their host at Calais.   We are, he said, "abiding
here with evil wines the Pope's coming as a hawk prieth for her

prey. . . . We would ye had part of the wines we drink here and then we doubt not ye would pity us." [17]

Clement arrived on the 11th. After a month of fruitless conference Gardiner instructed Bonner to intimate to him in person the appeal, or rather the two appeals which Henry had previously made in Gardiner's presence, and which were probably of Gardiner's composition. This Bonner did on November 7, while the listening Clement "was continually folding up and unwinding of his handkerchief, which he never doth but when he is tickled to the very heart with great choler." After consultation with the cardinals, he rejected the appeals as "frivolous, forbidden, and unlawful," and on November 12 left Marseilles. [18]

Francis was highly indignant with the English ambassadors. They would not have dared to do such a thing at Rome; to do it at Marseilles was a violation of his hospitality. Besides, it hindered reconciliation between England and Rome, which, he flattered himself, he could have effected. In a lively conversation with him Gardiner tersely defended the English action. Francis therefore requested Henry to recall the Bishop of Winchester, whom he found "not possessed of good will." [19] The Bishop returned to England.

Clement's refusal to entertain the King's appeal was quite as much to Henry's purpose as his acceptance of it would have been. It put him in the position of one who feared the judgement of Christendom upon his actions.

Gardiner was never to be entirely free from the "trouble and business" of heresy trials. At the meeting of Convocation in 1532, when he had opposed the King, he was one of the bishops before whom Hugh Latimer confessed errors in discretion and doctrine. [20] In 1533, in the month of Anne Boleyn's coronation, he took part in the examination of John Frith. Latimer had been absolved, but the trial of Frith was not to end so happily. Frith was a young man of exceptional ability; he had been one of Gardiner's scholars at Cambridge, and had been taken by Wolsey to his college at Oxford; here he incurred suspicion of heresy and escaped to the Continent. On his return he was put in the Tower through the efforts—if we may believe Foxe—of Sir Thomas More, some of whose writings he had refuted with a moderation surprising in a controversialist of his time. The King appointed Cranmer, Gardiner, Stokesley, the Lords of Suffolk and Wiltshire, and Audley, the Chancellor, to examine him. They found his opinion, in the words of Cranmer, "so notably erroneous" that they could not release him, but were "fain to leave him to the determination of his ordinary," [21]

Stokesley, Bishop of London, who, assisted by Gardiner and Longland of Lincoln, examined him again at St. Paul's, June 20, 1533.

Frith did not believe in transubstantiation or purgatory, but claimed that neither belief nor disbelief in these things should be obligatory.

Germain Gardiner, a member of the Bishop's household and possibly a kinsman, has left us some account of Frith's latter days. "My Lord, my master," says Germain, ". . . bearing a special love and affection toward this young man, because that once he was his scholar, sent for him unto his house, and there began to enter communication with him," hoping to convert him. When, to prove a point, Frith cited a line from Isaiah, the Bishop opened a Bible and showed him that if he had completed the verse instead of stopping in the midst of it, the meaning would have been quite different. Thereupon Frith,

> "being confounded, would no more dispute of anything, but said, except my Lord were touched with the same spirit wherewithal he was himself, it should not avail to dispute with him. Whereunto my Lord answered, 'If I should say likewise to you, and every man to other, then should no man labour to bring in again him that once were out of the right way. . . . If your cause be better why should ye not think to win me?'"

Frith finally said he would acknowledge as true what could plainly be shown to have been the teaching of the Fathers; whereupon Gardiner tried "very diligently and earnestly" to convince him, out of the Fathers, of his error. One passage from Chrysostom so impressed the young scholar that the Bishop left him, hopeful of his conversion; but next day Frith said he had prayed most of the night and believed God had answered by revealing to him that Chrysostom was wrong. It appears that the only authority he found himself ready to acknowledge was that of personal conviction, which was precisely what none of his examiners would countenance. His appeal for toleration seemed to them a request for license to spread divisive opinions. Moreover, they, like most men of their time, believed that heresy tended not only to the dividing of the Church, but also, in the words of Germain Gardiner, to "the pulling down of all power, and utter subversion of all commonwealths."

Inevitable as his condemnation was, it was given with reluctance. Germain tells "how fatherly" all the examiners "laboured and travailed for the amendment of that ungracious child." He had at least one opportunity to escape, which he refused. On July 3 Stokesley delivered him to the civil powers to be burned. With him suffered one of his disciples, a simple tailor's apprentice, who, to the bishops' questions, answered simply that he believed as Master Frith did, nor would he, for all their persuasions, say otherwise.[22]

X

THE ROYAL SUPREMACY

In the Convocation which met early in 1531, Gardiner had voted with the majority of the lower house, in which he then sat, to acknowledge the King as Supreme Head of the English Church.[1] The clause which qualified Henry's headship "as far as the law of Christ allows," doubtless satisfied him if he had harboured any scruples concerning the title. Moreover, the declaration of Henry's supremacy in the Church in England by no means completed the separation from Rome; it did not necessarily deny the supremacy of the Pope over the Church Universal.

When the year 1534 opened there was doubtless a hope lingering in many minds that a reconciliation with Rome was not impossible, for it was not until March 23 of that year that the Pope, seven years after the trial had begun, gave sentence that Henry's marriage with Catherine had been valid. This decision created no excitement in England, and little in Europe; the universal unconcern with which it was received showed the utter helplessness of the Papacy.

Meanwhile Henry was proceeding rapidly toward a complete separation from Rome. There might be murmurings at home and threats abroad, but he knew well that his enemies were, in neither place, united, and were therefore powerless. In the session of Parliament which met from January to March 1534, a new act forbidding the payment of annates was passed; another stopped the payment of Peter's pence; a second act of appeals not merely confirmed the abolition of appeals to Rome, but ordained that an appeal in England lay from the archbishop's court to chancery, thus placing a lay court at the summit of ecclesiastical jurisdiction. This act also embodied the submission of the clergy concerning their law-making powers, made by Convocation in 1532, which at that time had been defeated in the House of Lords by the activities of More and Gardiner.[2] Finally, the succession to the throne was settled by Parliament upon the offspring of Henry and Anne in an act to be enforced by an oath, which, it seems, was intended to be administered to every male of years of discretion in the kingdom. It was the refusal to swear to maintain this act, the preamble of which denied the Papal authority, that occasioned the imprisonment of Fisher and More. Gardiner, as an active member of the House of Lords, was among the first to whom the oath was administered.[3]

The report that he had resisted "these new opinions" concerning the Church was current in France,[4] and was true in the sense that he had opposed the anti-clerical and anti-Papal measures in Parliament up to the point of their adoption. After that he acquiesced. We have no immediately contemporary record of his activities in the Parliament of 1534, but his friend Thirlby later testified that Gardiner had been "earnest against alterations as well concerning the Bishop of Rome as other orders in religion," until these matters "were established and set forth by the acts, statutes, and laws of the realm." [5]

Despite his acceptance of the King's measures after they had passed Parliament, his previous resistance to them resulted in a complete loss of royal favour during the year 1534. His name drops almost entirely out of the public records.[6] On April 6 we read, "my Lord of Winchester is gone to his diocese, and is not to return till the King sends for him;" on April 15, "my Lord of Winchester is out of the secretaryship," Cromwell being put in his place; a week later, "the Bishops of Durham, Winchester, and York have been sent for. Some think they will be committed to the Tower." [7] This last was but a rumour; Gardiner was permitted to reside unmolested in his diocese, which he did for almost a year and a half.

Shortly before retiring to his diocese he had acted with Cranmer, Cromwell, Audley, and the two chief justices in settling a dispute between the clergy of London and their parishioners concerning tithes;[8] and at about the same time he decided, in conference with Cranmer, Stokesley, and Longland, to prohibit in his diocese, as they would in theirs, all preaching except by those who received new licences, and to instruct the recipients in no way to bring in doubt "the Catholic and received doctrine," nor to discuss the King's marriage and succession.[9]

On April 29 he received the King's commission for taking the oaths to the act of succession, and on May 4 called before him in the great hall of the Castle at Winchester all the "abbots, priors, wardens of friars . . . with all the curates of all the other churches and chapels in the shire." They took the oath "very obediently," and handed in lists of their male parishioners above the age of fourteen, to each of whom the commissioners were to administer the oath, which, wrote Gardiner, "is a long work and will require a long tract of time." [10]

His absence from court was the opportunity for his registrar, John Cooke, to air certain grievances against him to persons in authority, and to accuse him of withholding his salary. The complaints were believed, and the Duke of Richmond wrote to Gardiner in Cooke's behalf. Gardiner replied that there was not "one true sentence" in the whole story, and was compelled to seek the aid of his all-powerful rival, Cromwell, through whom he succeeded in getting his defence brought before the King.[11] At the same time he sought Cromwell's advice on how he should conduct himself when the King made his progress to Guildford, in the diocese of Winchester. He was likely to irritate Henry if he received him personally, he was likely to offend him if he did not.

"I am in no little perplexity of mind," he wrote, "how to use myself. . . . In effect, Master Cromwell, I mean that I would, as I have heretofore written unto you, *abstinere ab omni specie mala* [abstain from all appearance of evil], and in all occasions show myself so as I might appear a true subject and a faithful servant. . . . I have now recourse unto you as to mine especial friend, and desire your counsel what I shall do. . . . Thus amongst other your great matters, I trouble you with mine, but I shall say to you as a poor man said once to my Lord of Norfolk in like case, my small matter, quod he, is the greatest matter that I have. I pray you, good Master Secretary, that I may shortly hear from you."[12]

We do not have Cromwell's reply.

Of Gardiner's activities during the rest of the year 1534 there are but two scant notices. He was present August 2, when Henry ratified a treaty with Scotland at Blackfriars, and on October 30 he attended an assay of silver in the Star Chamber.[13] But if the records of his public life are meagre, there is one private letter of interest. It is a note to his hostess at Calais, the wife of Lord Lisle, Deputy there, asking her help for an unnamed widow. It is one of the few letters we have of Gardiner's addressed to a woman; it shows that he was not inept in the art of gracious and subtle compliment.

"Madame, after my most hearty commendations, knowing how effectually your Ladyship is accustomed to solicit your friend's cause, and nothing doubting of your special love and friendship toward me, I am so bold to recommend this widow's cause, bearer hereof, unto your good Ladyship, heartily desiring and praying you to regard it as it were mine own. I write neither to my good Lord, your husband, unto whom I beseech you make my most hearty commendations, ne to any other herein, knowing that your Ladyship may stand in stead sufficient in this matter, wherein is only required justice at the marshall's hands, which by your good means I know well shall be attained; whereby your Ladyship shall bind me more and more to do that shall lie in my little power, in any such matter of your friends as shall occur here.

Thus my good Lady most heartily fare ye well.
From London, the 20th day of June.
Your Ladyships to my little power,
STE. WINTON.
To my singular good Lady, my Lady Lisle."[14]

At the November session of Parliament in 1534 the royal supremacy, acknowledged by Convocation in 1531, was made the law of the land, but the law makers did not restrict the King's headship by the qualifying phrase upon which the clergy had insisted. The King was declared to be "the only Supreme Head in earth of the Church of England," and empowered to repress and reform all errors and abuses in religion. In the following months the bishops were required to renounce obedience to Rome. The first to do so were the two Archbishops and Gardiner, all upon the same day, February 10, 1535. Gardiner signed a renunciation of the jurisdiction of the Papal See, declaring that the Papacy was not ordained by God, but set up by men, and pledging himself to obey all the laws of England made for the suppression thereof. "The Pope," read the promise, "only ought to be called Bishop of Rome and fellow brother . . . ; this I shall to my power openly maintain and defend." A similar promise was given by the other bishops. Thus, in the phrase of Foxe, was the Pope "abolished, eradicated, and exploded out of this land."[15]

Cromwell soon discovered that the doctrine of supreme headship might be used against his rivals. According to the report of Chapuys, the Imperial ambassador, he did

> "not cease to harass the bishops, even the good ones like Winchester and some others, whom he called lately before the Council to ask them if the King could not make and unmake bishops at pleasure; who were obliged to say Yes, else they should have been deprived of their dignities; as the said Cromwell told a person, who reported it to me, and said the Council had been summoned only to entrap the bishops." [16]

This testimony concerning Cromwell's attitude toward Gardiner, though given by Chapuys at second-hand, receives confirmation in that of John Mores, receiver of the monastery of Sion, in Middlesex, just over the border of Gardiner's diocese. The monks of Sion had offered a hesitating resistance to the King's supremacy, and Gardiner seems to have written Henry that he was successfully using his influence to bring them to a better mind. Mores reported to Henry in person on April 26. We have neither the words of Mores on this occasion nor the letter of Gardiner, but Henry, after listening to Mores, wrote to Cromwell saying, "We may well perceive" that Gardiner boasted "to have done more than indeed he hath, and a coloured doubleness either to be in him or in Mores, or in both; Mores not answering directly to diverse introgates by us to him ministered." Mores was sent to Cromwell for examination. He was closely questioned: What had Gardiner said to him concerning the primacy of Rome? Had Gardiner expressed any evil opinion of the new statutes? What conversation had passed between them touching the King's marriage and succession?

Mores replied that Gardiner had shown him

> "that the primacy of the Bishop of Rome began by the policy of man, and since then clerks have applied Scripture, to make it appear that the primacy had the beginning of God, which he thought could not be truly maintained."

When Mores had suggested that a general council had confirmed the Papal primacy, which could therefore be recognized without offense to conscience, Gardiner gave a characteristically English reply: "that he thought the act of Parliament discharged his conscience, and that of all the King's subjects;" and he desired Mores to declare this to the brethren of Sion. Mores had never heard Gardiner say anything contrary to the statutes of the realm, and as for the King's marriage and succession, he did not mention them. Mores was especially impressed with Gardiner's refutation of Rome, because he had heard Cromwell say "that the Bishop was much affectionate to the Papacy."[17] There was nothing in the answer to incriminate or entrap the Bishop of Winchester.

The same session of Parliament which enacted the royal supremacy granted to the King the first fruits and tenths of all the sees and benefices in England; and on January 30, 1535 commissions were appointed in each county to ascertain the value of ecclesiastical income. Gardiner headed the Commission for Hants, and Fitzwilliam, the Treasurer, conducted the assessment in Surrey, the two counties included in the diocese of Winchester. Gardiner reported in May that the work was progressing quietly and without causing discontent. It was also done promptly, for the completed returns of the whole diocese were in the hands of Chancellor Audley in September, when he was complaining of the negligence of other commissioners. The income of the bishropric was estimated at £3,885. In a letter to Cromwell, Gardiner says:

> "Ye shall see in the valuation of my bishopric a good portion; but whereof I shall not receive now very little above the one-half to mine own use. I am in some men's judgement too strait in charging myself, but I will have mine own will therein, that I may be called self-willed for some things."[18]

In the summer of the same year Gardiner and Fitzwilliam were sent to examine into the state of Chertsey Abbey, which lay in Winchester diocese, but their report that all was well there was not, it seems, what was wanted; Thomas Legh, a minion of Cromwell's, proceeded thereafter to make a different one.[19]

While the valuation of Church revenue was going on, Cranmer was conducting a visitation of the dioceses in the province of

Canterbury. Graciously as Gardiner had fulfilled the royal commands in the valuation of his see, he endeavoured to thwart the Archbishop's visitation of it. In this he doubtless had the support of his clergy, for the payment of fees attendant upon such a visitation was sufficient to make it unpopular. Moreover, less than five years had elapsed since Archbishop Warham had visited the diocese. Gardiner lodged a protest with the King, claiming that Cranmer's title, Primate of all England, by virtue of which he was making the visitation, was derogatory to the King's authority as Supreme Head. As Mr. A. F. Pollard has aptly said, Gardiner thought that all bishops should be equal under the crown—as long as Cranmer was Archbishop.[20] Cranmer, to whom Cromwell forwarded Gardiner's protest in May, replied to Cromwell that he could not see how a primate under the royal supremacy detracted any more from the King's power than he did under the old arrangement from the Pope's.

> "I suppose that to make his cause good," said Cranmer, Gardiner "doth mix it with the King's cause, (as ye know the man lacketh neither learning in the law, neither witty invention, ne craft to set forth his matters to the best). . . ."[21]

The visitation was held.

The royal supremacy had been established by Parliament; the bishops had renounced the jurisdiction of the Pope; it remained to persuade the people of the wisdom of these changes. So, early in June 1535, Henry issued a proclamation to the bishops commanding each of them in his "own proper person" to preach every Sunday and high feast day, not only "the sincere word of God," but also the validity of the King's title of Supreme Head, and to instruct the clergy and schoolmasters in their dioceses to preach and teach the same.

Gardiner accordingly sent the necessary instructions throughout his diocese and caused verses "extolling the King's supremacy" to be learned by the scholars of Winchester College. He had so devised the words to be spoken by his clergy that, he wrote to Cromwell, his tongue was really speaking in every pulpit. There was hardly need for him to preach himself;

> "yet will I preach also," he said, "omitting all other respects of myself, rather than I should be otherwise taken than I am; that is to say, openly to swear one thing, and privily to work, say, or do otherwise, whereof I was never guilty. Nevertheless, I have as great cause as any man to desire rest and quiet, for the health of my body . . . and to abstain from books and writing, having finished the translation of St. Luke and St. John wherein I have spent a great labour."

Besides this work of translation which had grown out of a reso-
lusion of Convocation in December 1534 to have the Bible put into
English by approved scholars (but which was never published),
Gardiner was also at the moment looking forward to the duties
awaiting him in superintending the collection of a subsidy, and
presiding over the work of two Commissions of Sewers,[22] and one
for Musters. In short, he concluded, "I seem to be here *in otio,*
and I was never more busied."[23]

While he was thus for over seventeen months engaged in diocesan
and county business,[24] a new international situation had arisen in
which Henry needed at once an advocate and a diplomat. Since
Gardiner had shown himself constant in his support of the royal
supremacy, he was drawn once more into the King's service. Clement
VII died September 26, 1534. His successor, Paul III, made
Bishop Fisher a cardinal while in prison for refusing to take the
oath to the Act of Succession. Henry was enraged, and declared
he would send Fisher's head to Rome for the cardinal's hat. With
the aid of parliamentary enactment, which made it treasonable to
deny the royal supremacy, it was not difficult to trap both Fisher
and More into condemnatory statements. Fisher, moreover, had
been guilty of treasonable communication with Charles V. He was
executed June 22, More, July 6, 1535.

Twenty days later Paul III wrote to Francis I that he felt bound
to deprive Henry of his kingdom, and urged him to stand ready
to execute justice upon him.[25] Francis had no intention of attempting so hazardous a venture, but he was not averse to using
the Papal brief as diplomatic blackmail with which to secure material support for his designs in Italy. When his envoy, the Bailly
of Troyes, arrived in England about the middle of September with
the brief, and asked what answer could be made to it, the Council,
if we may believe Chapuys' informant, "were quite astonished without knowing where to begin, until the Bishop of Winchester came."
To him was entrusted the composition of a reply, defending the
execution of Fisher as a traitor.[26] This may not have been an altogether pleasant task; still, he had the lawyer's consolation that Fisher
had been found guilty according to law.

At the same time Gardiner had been engaged in other literary
composition. On September 26, when he sent to Cromwell the draft
of his answer to the Papal brief, he said he had already completed
and "polished" his "oration," which he would deliver to Bartlet,
the London printer.[27] This was his defence of the royal supremacy,
De Vera Obedientia Oratio (An Oration on True Obedience), his
first volume to be published, and the one destined to be the most
frequently republished of all his writings.

XI

THE ORATION ON TRUE OBEDIENCE

To obey truly is to obey truth. God is truth. Therefore true obedience is obedience to God and to those whom God appoints to represent him. The Bible, which is the true word of God, recognizes kings as God's representatives on earth. Hence the king should be obeyed in matters religious as well as in matters secular. This is also in accord with reason, for the people who compose the Church are the same as those who compose the Realm; and to deny the king's authority over them in one capacity and not in the other is an absurdity. Further, Scripture sets no limits whatever to a subject's obedience to his king. If royal commands are contrary to God's will, it is the king giving them, not the subject obeying them, who will be judged of God.

The royal supremacy is no new thing. The kings of Israel exercised it; so did the Roman emperors; so did the ancient kings of England. To call the king Supreme Head in Earth of the Church of England is merely expressing an existing right in plain words.

The claim of the Bishop of Rome to supremacy in Church and State is no where sanctioned in Scripture. In the Old Testament the high priest was subject to the king; in the New, Christ expressly renounced all claim to earthly rule. Peter was chief among the Apostles because he was the foremost preacher and teacher; he was supreme in defence of the truth. If the supremacy of the Bishop of Rome means a like leadership in virtue and religion, there is no objection to it. In early days the Bishop of Rome was reverenced because he maintained such a leadership; but worldly power, usurped and asserted by one no longer in the moral van of Christendom, is not to be tolerated.

Such, in outline, is the argument of the "right notable learned oration," *De Vera Obedientia Oratio,* which Gardiner wrote in defense of the royal supremacy. It was prepared, not for oral delivery, but for publication. It covers seventy-five pages of modern print.[1]

The doctrine of the divine right of kings is the author's starting point. This doctrine was the peculiar contribution of the New Learning to political and ecclesiastical theory. The men of the

Renaissance found in the Roman Law the emperor as the source
of all jurisdiction, ecclesiastical as well as secular; they discovered in the Old Testament that kings were the Lord's anointed;
they read in St. Paul an unqualified approval of the civil power.
Thus law and religion became the handmaid of the new national
consciousness.

Gardiner, despite his loyalty to the Church, his leanings toward
the Papacy, and his adherence to things established, was a student
of the Civil Law, a disciple of the new classical learning, and a
thorough Englishman. Hence it could not have been with any
great strain upon his conscience that, having accepted the royal
supremacy, he found arguments in its favour. Indeed, the book may
well have been written quite as much to clarify his own opinions
as to retain the good will of the King.

He is but echoing the all but universal dictum of the sixteenth
century when he says that the king, "though he be an infidel, repre-
senteth, as it were, the image of God upon earth." God, he continues, has made kings his vice-regents, and to them subjects owe
obedience as unto God himself. God would have kings

> "reputed in the supreme and most high room, and to excel
> among all other human creatures. . . . By me, saith God, kings
> reign; in so much that, after Paul's saying, whosoever resisteth
> power, resisteth the ordinance of God."
>
> "Princes ought to be obeyed by the commandment of God;
> yea, and to be obeyed without exception." [2]

The transition to the royal control of the Church is easy:

> "The Church of England is nothing else but the congregation
> of men and women, of the clergy and of the laity, united in
> Christ's profession."
>
> "Surely I see no cause why any man should be offended that
> the king is called the head of the Church of England, rather
> than the head of the Realm of England, . . . and seeing the
> Church of England consisteth of the same sorts of people at this
> day that are comprised in this word Realm, of which the king is
> called the head, shall he not, being called the head of the Realm
> of England, be also the head of the same men when they are
> named the Church of England?"
>
> "The king, say they, is head of the Realm but not of the
> Church. O what an absurd and foolish saying is that! As
> though, because the people beginneth now to believe in God,
> it were a just cause why they should be no more in subjection
> to the king, God's lieutenant."

The Apostles and their successors, to whom is committed the
government of the Church, exercise a jurisdiction subordinate to

that of the king. Their chief duty is to teach and to administer the Sacraments. The distinction between temporal and spiritual power is "a blind distinction and full of darkness," invented by Churchmen to prevent the king from punishing them for their sins. To restrict the king's control over the clergy "is the most speedy way to mar all, and far contrary from his office that occupieth God's room in earth."

Gardiner admits that "Christ only is head of the Church," but says that this is beside the question, for the doctrine of the royal supremacy merely asserts that the king is head of the Church "in earth," and not of the whole Church in earth, but of the Church "of England." [3]

Concerning the general acquiescence in the Papal control of the Church in the past, he puts this question:

> "Because men have used to ask the Bishop of Rome counsel in governing the Church, is it not lawful, therefore, to do anything without his counsel? And because princes have suffered their subjects to ask his counsel, did they by that means give over their own authority? . . . Let the matters that have in times past been made a mingle mangle, be called again to the true square of God's word."

Applying the test of God's word, he finds that the Papal contention amounts to this: that although Christ

> "never sought authority among men, he gave it, notwithstanding, to the Bishop of Rome, to use as his vicar,"

which is blasphemous.

As for the Roman Bishop's claim to be a successor of Peter, Gardiner curtly remarks, "I would he were!" and shows that Peter's supremacy consisted in a more plenteous endowment of grace, that he might be "the ringleader in virtue," and "fight like a tall fellow for the defense of the truth."

> "Because he was bidden to confirm his brethren in faith, was it given him to bear rule over his brethren?" [4]

Gardiner frankly admits that the early Bishops of Rome did maintain a moral and spiritual pre-eminence which was gladly recognized by the world, but which gave them no more right to political power or to power over the Church than the pre-eminence of a physician gives him the right to rule the commonwealth or even to dictate to others of his own profession. Moreover, the physician retains his pre-eminence only so long as he surpasses all other physicians in learning and skill. The Roman claim to supremacy is like the claim of a lame man to be a champion runner because his ancestors were.

In times past the Church of Rome was supreme in preaching God's word, "in the cure and charge of advancing of Christ's name," "in prompt valiantness of mind to defend the truth, and to keep the faith of Christ from heresies."

"The Bishops of Rome, yea, almost none but they, at the first beginning of the spring of the Church, were diligent to heal the furor of tyrants raging against Christian people."

"No man ought, I say, to think it any marvel though the glorious name of the Church of Rome, being at that time famous in excellent virtue, drawing and alluring almost all parts of the world into admiration of it for virtue's sake . . . knit all men to it, and caused that Church, whom all men might see so notably virtuous, to be reverenced as the chief and principal church among other."

If the Bishops of Rome today sought this kind of supremacy, there is not, says Gardiner, a Christian prince but would do them honour.

"I do not so much contend about the supremacy so they rack it out no further than it appeareth to be meant from the beginning. But this I utterly deny, that God ordained the Bishop of Rome to be the chief, as touching any absolute wordly power; of this is the question; in this point the whole cause consisteth."

"Well," he concludes, "all sorts of people are agreed upon this point, with most steadfast consent, learned and unlearned, both men and women, that no manner person born and brought up in England hath aught to do with Rome." [5]

In the early part of the book he touches incidentally on the divorce as an illustration of obedience, saying that Henry, in putting away Catherine according to the commands of Scripture, had "obeyed God and obeyed truly." [6]

He ends with an answer to the charge that he has broken his oath to the Pope, pointing out that it is a recognized principle of both Civil and Canon Law "that no man is bounden to perform an unlawful oath." He was sincere, he says, in taking the oath, but since he has been convinced of its unlawfulness, he can hardly be urged to keep it, "unless we must be persuaded that constancy is commendable in naughty and perverse matters." [7]

The book was completed by September 26, 1535. [8] At least a dozen copies were through the press by November 19, when Cromwell sent that number to Gardiner, then in France, for distribution. Copies were given to foreign ambassadors in England as well as to prominent persons abroad. One was sent to Reginald Pole as a hint of the line which Henry expected him to follow. [9]

It was regarded by anti-Papal Churchmen in England and on the Continent as the ablest vindication of the royal supremacy then written. The year following its appearance in London, it was published at Hamburg, with an introduction by Bonner, under the direction, it seems, of the North German princes, and at Strassburg by the reformers Capito, Hedio, and Bucer, who prefaced it with a highly commendatory letter. Cardinal Contarini, to whom Pole forwarded a copy, admitted that it was written with the highest art, and Pole agreed, quoting a proverb about dice—the better the player the worse the man. Both Pole and Contarini naturally thought the arguments weak, and Pole boasted that there was nothing in them which a man of moderate understanding could not answer.[10]

Continental supporters of the Papacy began to call Gardiner hard names. The Admiral of France said he was *"un gran poltrone"*—a great big good for nothing. Dr. Ortiz, Catherine's proctor at Rome, wrote that while Gardiner was formerly accounted among the good, he was now one of the worst. The Bishop of Faenza, Papal Nuncio in France, called him a rascal unabashed (*scoperto ribalissimo*). The Pope said he was a scoundrel.[11]

Some months after the publication of the *De Vera,* the Bishop of Faenza wrote to the Papal secretary that Gardiner was "most desirous of his king's returning to the right road, and he made his book under compulsion, not having the strength to suffer death patiently." [12] Faenza does not say where he gathered this information. It is possible that it reached him with Gardiner's knowledge and intention, but that need not lead us to regard it as anything more than a diplomatic blind. At the moment Faenza spoke of Gardiner's desire to bring England back to the Papal fold, Gardiner was endeavouring to induce the French King to renounce the Papacy on condition of English aid against the Emperor. At the same time he was assuring the Imperial ambassador at the French court that England had no intention whatever of helping Francis against Charles![13] Statements of this sort were Gardiner's stock in trade as a diplomat, and cannot be taken too seriously. He had no hesitation in defending his opinions on the royal supremacy in debate with a certain Friar Pallavicino at the French court in December, 1535,[14] and the next year he seems to have been the source of a suggestion made to Henry VIII that Papal bulls which were to be kept in force be passed by a royal grant without mention of the Bishop of Rome, in order to avoid even a hint that his authority had ever been respected in England.[15]

XII

THREE YEARS IN FRANCE

By accepting the royal policies and defending them, in his answer to the Papal brief and his *Oration on True Obedience,* Gardiner had so convinced the King of his "wisdom and discretion" that he was appointed ambassador to France at the end of September 1535. He reached Calais October 24 in company with his friend Edward Fox, who was starting on an embassy to the German princes.[1] Just one month before, on Sunday, September 26, Fox had been consecrated Bishop of Hereford in Winchester Cathedral, Gardiner and Shaxton assisting Archbishop Cranmer in the consecration.[2] When the two friends took their several ways from Calais they said good-by for the last time, for when, three years later, Gardiner returned to England, Fox had been for some months in his grave.[3]

During Gardiner's three-years' residence in France much of importance happened in England. Catherine died; Princess Mary acknowledged the royal supremacy; Anne Boleyn was executed; Jane Seymour became Queen, gave birth to Edward VI, died; the dissolution of the monasteries was begun and almost completed; the only formidable insurrection during Henry's reign was thoroughly crushed; the Ten Articles were passed by Convocation, marking the first doctrinal gain, though a slight one, by the reformers; a royal proclamation called for an English Bible in every parish church; *The Institution of a Christian Man* or *Bishops' Book,* incorporating the teaching of the Ten Articles, was published; the destruction of images began, and the shrine of St. Thomas à Becket was dismantled. Cromwell remained supreme.

There can be slight wonder that Gardiner, after a year in France, heartily desired his recall. Both Henry and Cromwell kept holding out hopes that he would be replaced, but when he was on the point of returning, commanded him to stay, on the ground that it was unwise to change ambassadors in "this troublous time."[4] It was rumoured that he "was kept abroad for a purpose," for if he were at home "many things would be brought to pass otherwise."[5]

There were, however, some things at home on which his advice was asked and others on which he volunteered it.

On Christmas Day 1535 the princes at Schmalkald presented to Fox a number of propositions as the basis for a league with England. Henry was, among other things, to promote the Gospel as set forth by the Augsburg Confession; to become an associate to

66

the league of German princes under the title of Protector; to contribute to their defence; and, after agreeing to all this, to receive German ambassadors who were to confer with him "upon the articles of Christ's doctrine and the ceremonies . . . to be changed, ordered, and reformed." These propositions were sent to Gardiner, February 4, 1536, Henry desiring his opinion "touching every part of the same." [6]

Gardiner replied that such an alliance would put the English Church about as effectively under German control as it had been under Papal control, and that it would give away the case for the royal supremacy; for the supreme authority in Germany was the Emperor, not the princes.

> "How shall they," asked Gardiner, "without the consent of the head of their Church, which is the Emperor, establish with us the agreement upon their religion; or how shall we, without derogating the King's cause of his prerogative and supremacy, covenant with them in that behalf . . . ?"

If England accepts the proposition concerning the Augsburg Confession, "then shall the King's Highness be bound to the Church of Germany, and without their consent may not do that the word of God shall permit." It is beneath the dignity of England to be merely an "associate" in a league of German princes; and as for the articles concerning mutual defence and money, they "be very good for the said princes."

> "Where they desire to have all things agreed unto before they send an ambassador to the King's Highness, they speak therein wisely for their own commodity. . . . They shall then send unto us not to learn of us but to instruct and teach us; not to sue to us but to direct our Church." "I would rather advise the King's highness to give them money . . . than to enter any league. . . . To hear their ambassadors . . . were very good, but upon the word of God to make a new knot, whereof the one end shall be in Germany, shall declare rather a change of a bond of dependence, than a riddance thereof." [7]

No alliance was made.

At the same time Gardiner incidentally expressed himself on the death of Catherine. The Germans, he said, should be urged to agree with Henry "upon his cause of matrimony wherein God hath given sentence for the most part by the death of the Dowager." [8]

On June 9 of this year (1536) Bishop Latimer preached at the opening of Convocation. Grandfather Devil, father World and mother Hypocrisy, he said, have begotten "a great sort of bishops and prelates"—a majority, he feared, of the members of Convocation, which during the last seven years and more had done nothing for the glory of Christ. He attacked vigorously the abuses connected with images, relics, pilgrimages, ceremonies, purgatory, holidays, and Church courts, all of which, he said, needed drastic reformation, if not abolition.[9] When Gardiner received a report of this discourse, he wrote in protest to Cromwell, and composed an answer to it, which we do not have, but which, we may well believe with one of Cromwell's correspondents, showed that he loved Latimer "never a dele." [10]

The next happening in England to draw forth his comment was the rising in the north, known as the Pilgrimage of Grace, in the latter part of 1536. This was aimed chiefly at the restoration of the suppressed abbeys whose social and economic service to the commonwealth was deemed by the rebels indispensable. Prominent among their other demands was that for the restoration of the supremacy to the Pope, although they were willing to see considerable curtailment of Papal authority in England, and were not entirely averse to the King's title of Supreme Head if it were limited to such matters as did not affect the cure of souls and the administration of the sacraments. They desired an autonomous English Church within the larger unity represented by Papal supremacy in things purely spiritual [11]—an ideal which has seldom lacked Anglican advocates. It appears that when Gardiner heard of the extent and force of the rising, he wrote confidentially to Henry, counselling acquiescence in this and perhaps other demands of the rebels. We have only Henry's reply, not Gardiner's letter. Wrote Henry:

> "We might conceive [from your advice] that either your old opinion is not utterly mortified in you, or else that you have had some advertisement from some persons of that faction that would put you in fear of things to win you again to their naughty opinion. But . . . we may not approve that counsel that would have us yield to our subjects." [12]

This was written February 17, 1537, when Henry had succeeded, by craft, in dispersing the rebels. That he may not, a few weeks earlier, have looked on the suggestion with so much disdain, is indicated by a sentence in Gardiner's sermon of December 2, 1554, on reunion with Rome:

> "When the tumult was in the north, in the time of King Henry VIII, I am sure the King was determined to have given over the supremacy again to the Pope, but the hour was not then come, and therefore it went not forward, lest some would have said that he did it for fear." [13]

The last matter of domestic concern on which we have record of

Gardiner's expressing an opinion is the *Bishop's Book*. This was an exposition of doctrine composed in the spring and early summer of 1537 by a special Convocation of bishops and divines, and published the same year. A request for royal approval, printed over the names of the members of Convocation, served in lieu of a preface. Among these names was that of Gardiner, although he knew nothing of the book till a published copy, sent by Cromwell, reached him at Lyons. He "disliked many things in it," especially the unauthorized use of his name. He wrote, he says, to the King in protest "even the first night that ever I received the book," spending the "whole night in that matter." What his objections were in detail we do not know, since his letter to the King is lost. In a later reference to it he says that the book in his judgement resembled

> "a common storehouse where every man laid up in store such ware as he liked, and could tell where to find to serve his purpose;"

an opinion which he declares was confirmed when, on his return to England, he learned that much of it had been the result of compromise between his old friend Bishop Fox, who had imbibed Lutheran ideas in Germany, and Bishop Stokesley, exponent of conservative opinion.[14]

That Gardiner's protest was not without weight may be inferred from the fact that although the King had sanctioned the publication of the book he never gave it official approval.

Gardiner had arrived in Paris November 3, 1535, and there had occasion to pay twenty shilling overplus on a "girdle of the best fashion" for his hostess at Calais, Lady Lisle. More than once during his stay in France he received from her a gift of sprats which he ate "merrily;" and he interested himself in the education of her son by a former marriage, James Basset, a lad of about twelve years of age at the close of the embassy, and at that time admitted to the Bishop's household.[15]

The French court was at Dijon where Gardiner arrived on or a little before November 21; a few days later he had "a gentle and familiar conference" with the King.[16] In his negotiations he was assisted by the resident ambassador in France, Sir John Wallop, an old soldier, whom he called the "dean and most ancient of ambassadors."[17]

The occasion of Gardiner's mission was, as we have seen, the coming of the Bailly of Troyes to England with the Papal brief, intimating that the Pope was ready to deprive Henry of his kingdom. This was a hint that, although France might not desire to enforce the Pope's wishes, the Emperor might intend to do so, and therefore it would be to the advantage of England if France kept the

Emperor busy on the Continent by an attempt to regain from him
her Italian possessions—Milan, Genoa, and Aste. This would be of
such advantage to England, said France, that England should be
willing to contribute at least one-third of the expense of the
venture.[18]

That war between France and the Empire would free England
from all anxiety concerning the attitude of either of these orthodox
children of the Papacy, was clear to Henry. That he should have
to pay for it as heavily as the French suggested was neither so
manifest nor so desirable. Gardiner was to stir France up to war
with the Emperor, on the promise of English aid, which, however,
was to be dependent on French support of England against the
Papacy. He was to be ever egging Francis on to follow Henry's
example toward Rome and not to assent to the calling of a general
council. In all this he was to proceed in such a manner that the
French would think everything was "done altogether for their benefit and no whit for ours."[19] Indeed, Henry boasted in his letters
to Gardiner that the Papal sentence depriving him of his kingdom
was "as much to be regarded as if one should stand afar off and spit
so towards another as the violence of the wind against him should
turn his despite again into his own teeth."[20] As long as England
could count on the mutual jealousy of France and the Empire, such
boasting was not vain. Gardiner's task was to foment this jealousy.

The death of Catherine, on January 7, 1536, abolished, as Cromwell, speaking for Henry, expressed it, "the only matter of un-
kindness" betwixt Henry and Charles; and Gardiner was instructed
to keep himself "the more aloof and be the more froyt and cold in
relenting to any their overtures." In order to impress the French
with the renewed friendship between England and the Empire, as
well as to sound the truth of the rumour that Charles and Francis
were about to compose their difficulties amicably, Gardiner invited
the Imperial ambassador at the French court to supper in his garden, "made familiar cheer with him" at Wallop's lodging, and, accompanied by Wallop, ostentatiously went off into the country with
his wife.[21]

Within two months of Catherine's death the armies of France
began to advance through the neutral territory of Savoy. Gardiner,
writing March 9, 1536, from Lyons, whither he had followed the
French court, described the situation to Lord Lisle in a homely
simile:

> "We can write you no tidings, but after such sort as one an-
> swered his friend that asked him whether it should rain or no
> that night. In good faith, quod he, the weather is much over-
> cast and very cloudy. Nay, quod he, I see that myself, but I
> ask you whether it will rain or no. The other answered, In

good faith, quod he, I doubt thereof as well as ye. And in that case be we here, whether there shall be war or peace." [22]

He had not long to wait for the rain.

Before the end of March Francis was master of Savoy; by April 12 all Piedmont had fallen into his hands; by June 10 the Imperial armies had entered Piedmont and won their first successes against the French. This was exactly the situation which Henry desired. It must have contributed no little to the sense of his own importance to find not only France seeking his assistance, but also to receive overtures from Charles V in which that monarch expressed a willingness to forget his indignation at the treatment of Catherine if only Henry would give the Princess Mary some legitimate standing, and come to his aid against the French. Any contribution Henry made for this purpose was, said the Emperor, equivalent to aiding a crusade against the Turk! [23]

Meanwhile Henry stiffened the conditions on which he would consider an offensive alliance with France. Gardiner was instructed to propose that France, in return for English aid, should undertake to defend England against all potentates in all causes, to be the enemy of the Papacy unless all Papal processes against Henry were annulled, not to agree to a general council without England's consent, and to make no peace with the Emperor without this same consent and unless the Emperor agreed to repute all Papal proceedings against England void. [24] Henry could hardly have expected the French to agree to these terms, but their refusal to do so would at least give him an excuse to prolong negotiations without committing himself to either side.

On August 19, 1536 he proclaimed his neutrality. At the same time there began a series of negotiations concerning the marriage of Princess Mary to the third son of Francis, which neither side seems to have taken seriously; yet when Gardiner, feeling that the main objects of English diplomacy had been attained, requested his recall, Henry replied that he "must remain for the present, especially for this matter of the marriage." The matter of the marriage was discussed sporadically for two years, but nothing came of it. [25]

That Gardiner's description of these negotiations and of the attitude of France towards England during the latter part of 1536 was sombre, we may infer from a letter from the Duke of Norfolk to the Council in December of that year. Despite Norfolk's "desperate" accounts of the northern rebellion, he hopes ever to have the royal favour,

"though my fortune," he adds, "be not to find no good ink to write withal, as my Lord of Winchester cannot do in France.

Surely we be both much like of one nature, very wilful to write the truth as we hear and see." [26]

Though Gardiner "found no good ink to write withal," there was no doubt as to the position of advantage in which the turn of continental politics had placed England. Both Francis and Charles were ready to do Henry's bidding, as appeared in the affair of Reginald Pole. The insurrection in England, the promise of Scotch aid, and the possibility of peace between France and the Empire, combined to make the Pope feel that the moment for winning England back to the Roman allegiance had come. Hence, on February 7, 1537, Pole, who had been made cardinal the previous December, was commissioned as Legate to England to encourage the insurgents by his presence, and to aid them with money. The Most Catholic Monarch, Francis I, notified Henry of the purpose of Pole's coming! [27]

Pole reached Paris April 10, while Francis was in Picardy pushing the war. Henry demanded the delivery of Pole, according to treaty agreements, as a traitor to England, in spite of his safe conduct; and the Papal Nuncio in France wrote that "this ribald Winchester has done against the Legate those offices which one can expect from devils." [28] It seems, however, that Gardiner, with more humanity than obedience, told Francis that it would be enough to command Pole to avoid the realm. [29] This was done, and Pole, without having had an audience with the King, started for the Imperial territory of Flanders. Here he was refused admission, also as the result of Henry's insistence, and compelled to linger almost two months in the neutral border territory of Cambray. To have a Papal legate driven from one pro-Papal country and refused admission into another, was nothing less than a triumph for Henry.

Another notable visitor to Paris was James V of Scotland who, on New Year's day 1537, married Magdalen, daughter of Francis I. Henry, who was uneasy as to the attitude of Scotland toward the northern rebellion, and who had never seen his nephew James, asked his ambassadors to note his "nature and qualities." What they replied to the King we do not know, but we have their impressions of James in three letters to Lord Lisle. "He is a man of the fewest words that may be. . . ." wrote Gardiner. "His wife shall temper him well, for she can speak; and if she spake as little as he, the house should be very quiet." Wallop said that James was universally praised as very gentle, but added, "My Lord of Winchester and I feel little thereof. . . . His manner of using himself . . . is after the northern fashion . . . now looking over one shoulder, and now over the other, with a beck to one and a beck to another, and unto us nothing." Later he admitted that they "found him in his words as sober and discreet as might be, and very firm in opinion." The wedding was "very triumphant." Gardiner and Wallop walked immediately behind James and Francis in the procession to Notre Dame, and at the banquet that night the ladies were so richly gowned that Wallop thought "the King of Scots never saw no such sight." [30]

The death of Jane Seymour, October 24, 1537, left Henry with matrimonial possibilities of diplomatic advantage. Gardiner was instructed to report on the "conditions and qualities" of the French King's daughter and the Duchess of Longueville; later Francis was asked to send three or four of the noblewomen of France to Calais, that Henry might look them over in person. The King, as Gardiner put it, "would gladly see the personage with whom he should contract, before he entered a bond of so long continuance as marriage requireth." The French wondered whether Henry thought their women were horses to be trotted out for inspection! [31]

Although England had, for almost two years, been in a position successfully to maintain a nice balance between France and the Empire, it became increasingly clear during the latter part of 1537 that peace was "brewing" between them. Personally Gardiner was not averse to it. He wrote to Norfolk: "It is a good rent the King, our master, has of France, and it were better to have them agree than to help one to overrun the other." [32] The failure of the rebellion in England and the continual threat of the Turks on the borders of the Empire made the possibility of English conflict with any continental power remote, even if Charles and Francis came to terms, and Gardiner was well enough acquainted with continental politics to know that Charles and Francis could not long remain friends on any terms. Still, Henry was uneasy at the prospect of the Pope's acting as peacemaker, and securing the consent of Frenchmen and Imperialists to a general council.

On January 11, 1538 a six-months' truce was made, and thereafter the object of English diplomacy was not to prevent peace but to have England included as one of the principal parties to it, to prevent the acceptance of the Pope as arbiter, and to keep France from assenting to a general council. Henry not only offered his services as arbiter to both Charles and Francis, but went so far as to write to his representative at the Imperial court that Francis would be glad to have him act as peacemaker if Charles consented, and to instruct Gardiner to tell Francis that Charles wanted Henry as arbiter if Francis would approve! Francis warily answered that if Charles could be induced to tell him this directly, he would consent, and pointed out that since Henry had not aided France with a single penny in the war, he had little right to dictate on what terms and by whom peace was to be made. [33]

From the beginning of 1538 Gardiner had seen the futility of his negotiations. He wrote home "bitterly," saying:

"This troubleth me that any man should think we had need of their promises. Me thinketh it were possible they should depend of us. And then the King's Highness, as he is emperor in deed in his realm, so he should in deed *imperare* through and over all, and himself no further to care what other men do, but all they to care what he doth. In that me thinketh were quietness ; and I am weary of travail, and specially in writing such displeasant matter. I must ever write as truth requireth." [34]

When, early in March, Gardiner was informed that the French King was really going to Nice for a conference with the Emperor, his countenance, said Montmorency, "was the most piteous and astonished one ever saw." [35]

Wallop had been recalled from France in the spring of 1537. Thereafter Gardiner's chief associate was Sir Francis Brian, poet, courtier, royal favourite, popularly known as the "vicar of hell," who made three short trips to France during the last year and a half of Gardiner's stay there. On the last of these, beginning April 1538, he was accompanied by Gardiner's college friend Thomas Thirlby. All three followed the French court southward toward Nice, but owing to an anticipated lack of accommodation, and doubtless a fear of being ignored, Gardiner and Thirlby stopped at Aix while Brian alone went on. [36] At Nice the French and Imperial courts met, the Pope acted as arbiter, and on June 18, 1538 a ten-years' truce was concluded. A month later Charles paid Francis a friendly visit at Aigues Mortes on the south coast of France.

Henry openly expressed dissatisfaction with his ambassadors in France, and Cromwell laid the blame for the failure of the English diplomacy on the irritability and clumsiness of Gardiner. [37] Indeed, the relations between Gardiner and Cromwell during Gardiner's residence in France had been none too cordial. In 1536 Gardiner had reluctantly granted a pension of £100 a year from the revenues of Winchester to Sir Francis Brian, and with equal reluctance had, a year later, ceded his estate at Esher, the property of his see, to the King. He felt that Cromwell had inspired the King to request these gifts, and when Cromwell advised him to yield with good grace, Gardiner replied that he might keep his advice to himself, and as for his promise of assistance, he would thank him for "the deed when it is done and not for the promise of good will in the mean [time]." [38]

In July 1538 Gardiner, Thirlby, and Brian were recalled, and replaced by Bonner, [39] Archdeacon of Leicester, ambassador with the Emperor, and, at that time, a protégé of Cromwell. Under these circumstances it was perhaps to be expected that when Gardiner was met by Bonner near Lyons, his temper, aggravated by Bonner's flippancy, was none too gracious.

Bonner wrote a long letter to Cromwell enumerating the things for which he "misliked" Gardiner.

"I mislike in the Bishop of Winchester," he began, "that when any man is sent in the King's affairs, and by his Highness' commandment, the Bishop, unless he be the only and chief inventor and setter forth of the person, he will not only use many cavillations, but also use great strangeness in countenance and cheer to the person that is sent."

In proof of this Bonner told how, when they talked together of the King's request that Gardiner supply his successor with equipment, Gardiner replied that he needed his mules himself, that since their trappings were marked with his own arms they were unmeet for Bonner, that his raiment, being that of a bishop, Bonner could not wear, and that table linen was unnecessary for it was not used in France. He assured Bonner, however, that Thirlby was prepared to turn his equipment over to him. Bonner caustically answered that he would then thank Thirlby. Gardiner explained that his refusal to give his own stuff was because he could not spare it, not because he did not want to give it. This he reiterated several times, and Bonner, on his own admission, pertly replied each time that this would not help him on his journey, and if he was to get nothing, he would thank him for nothing, and provide for himself. If it were Bonner's intention to rouse Gardiner's temper, he certainly succeeded, for finally, in vast irritation, Gardiner answered: "Dirt in your teeth! provide as ye will."

"Bishop-like spoken!" retorted Bonner.

Then followed a fruitless altercation in which Gardiner's temper did not improve, and the flesh of his cheek, says Bonner, "began to swell and tremble, and he looked upon me as he would have run me through; and I came and stood even by him and said, 'Trow you my Lord that I fear your great looks?'"

Later that same day, however, Gardiner "very gently put off his bonnet" to receive Bonner, and told him that, lest the royal honour suffer from his lack of equipment, he would see that everything was provided, and trust to repayment from the King.

All this Bonner adduced as proof of the "hard heart and cankered malicious stomach" of the Bishop who, he said, in malice and disdain "may be compared to the devil in hell, not giving place to him in pride at all." [40]

It is small wonder that when Gardiner, shortly after this, heard that the bishopric of Hereford, left vacant by the untimely death of his friend Edward Fox, had been bestowed by Cromwell on Bonner, he "cast down his head, making a plaicemouth with his lip." [41] Nevertheless he took pains to write out for Bonner a long account of the matters under negotiation between France and England, adding thereto some pertinent advice concerning the behaviour of an ambassador:

> "Be neither in communication too sharp, whereby you should exasperate them, nor duller in language than the case shall require."

Ambassadors are the best sources of information for they be commonly men of experience. "Wise they be, and without great familiarity they will go about to know what they can, and say themself as little as they may. . . . With all sorts I have used to commune, and of divers tales have picked out that [which] hath been likely; but among ambassadors a truth is to be known. . . . Insinuate yourself into their friendship, . . . not pretending to search tidings at their hands," but "induce them indirectly to that which apertly they would refuse. . . . For one thing the world laboureth now chiefly in, to make by secrecy all things uncertain."

Be not over sanguine. It is better to fear the worst than be over confident of the best, "for, as the old proverb of England is, the best will save itself, the worst had need of provision." [42]

Of Gardiner's manner of living in France we get a glimpse in Bonner's letter of complaint.

> "The said Bishop," he writes, "hath a great number of servants in their velvets and silks, with their chains about their necks, and keepeth a costly table with excessive fare, and exceeding expenses many other ways." [43]

After Bonner's arrival Gardiner proceeded slowly homewards. On September 27, 1538 Thomas Wriothesley, formerly a member of his household, but now a satellite of Cromwell, starting on a mission to Flanders, encountered him between Sittingbourn and Rochester, and wrote to Cromwell immediately thereafter describing the meeting. Gardiner's train, said Wriothesley,

> "is very gallant; he hath five mulets and two carts made of the nonce, all covered with cloths of his colours, with his arms in garters embroidered on the same; a number of lackeys, I ween above a dozen, a fresh sort of gentlemen, in gay apparel of velvet cheyney, cloaks turned down with capes of velvet, large; and thereunto he hath a good number of yeomen, with sundry of his servants and officers. . . . At our meeting he did off his hat, and I in like manner mine. I told him I was glad to see him in health; he told me he was glad of mine. I showed him the King's Majesty was at Greenwich; he said he heard so."

A few brief questions concerning Wriothesley's journey were then asked and answered.

> "This," says Wriothesley, "is the whole effect of our communication, which was strange, and with much courtesy, for his hat was ever off as soon as mine, or before."

Thirlby rode back a little way with Wriothesley who asked what Gardiner thought of "our doings here," with reference, it seems, to the dismantling of shrines, especially Becket's. Thirlby answered that Gardiner had

> "said he misliked not the doing at Canterbury, but rather seemed to like it, saying that if he had been at home he would have given his counsel to the doing thereof, and wished that the like were done at Winchester."

Wriothesley continues, giving Thirlby's estimate of Gardiner's prudence:

> "I asked Mr. Thirlby what he thought of my Lord's [i.e. Gardiner's] disposition. He commended unto me his wisdom, and said that he hath sundry times told him that he would go with the King's Highness, and as far as he, but he would never go before, nor enter any dangerous matters, not knowing certain, by himself, whether his Grace would after allow them or no. And here he told me how my Lord had seen the new injunctions [issued by Cromwell, September 5] and in appearance liked them well; noting specially one point, where it is appointed that curates should advise their parishioners, in confession, to learn their *Believe* and other things there mentioned, in English, and saying upon the same, 'Ha! I see the King's Majesty will not yet leave this auricular confession; me think I smell the King in this point.'
>
> Mr. Thirlby also told me that he was a man of great forecast, and hath many times said to him that his study hath been how to answer men in the parts where he hath been for the King's estimation, who, he said, would not be left alone, but would be a king still. . . . He showed me further, upon my questions, that my Lord would say many times, he would not be compassed to enter into dangerous things by any man, before the King; but as is before written he would go with and follow. And he told me that the tragedy between him and the elect of Hereford [i.e. Bonner] was very ill handled on [his] side; for at the first meeting my Lord of Winchester called him fool." ⁴⁴

That Bonner had been instructed by Cromwell to spy on Gardiner and, if possible, to get evidence of some misdoing, if not disloyalty, on his part, was asserted shortly after by Sir Thomas Wyatt; ⁴⁵ but the Bishop's lavish table and loss of temper, as described by Bonner, could hardly be construed as treasonable. The less scrupulous Sir Francis Brian, however, did not, it seems, hesitate to bring more serious charges against him. We do not know what these charges were, but it is probable that the investigation of Gardiner's conduct, to which Gardiner himself referred many years later, occurred at this time.

> "Once the Lord Cromwell," wrote Gardiner in 1550, "caused one day and a half to be spent in a matter between Sir Francis Brian and me; which was ended and I declared an honest man; which the King's Majesty . . . set forth with his familiarity to me incontinently [*i.e.* immediately]." [46]

Certainly the Lord Cromwell must have viewed the return of the ablest conservative with no little apprehension, and although he was unable to secure any damaging evidence against him, he contrived to keep him from court for several months.

Gardiner arrived in London September 28, 1538,[47] and probably retired at once to his diocese, for his name appears but infrequently in the public records during the rest of the year. On November 16 he took a minor part in the trial of John Lambert for heresy at York Place,[48] and some time, presumably near the New Year, he first saw the baby Prince Edward and presented to him a silver cup on which was engraved the motto *Sequere justitiam et invenies vitam.*[49]

On his first visit to his see city the pupils of Winchester College met him with greetings and verses, saying: "Welcome home, great counsellor of the realm and purger of the faith." [50]

XIII

THE END OF THE VICAR GENERAL AND THE FATE OF FRIAR BARNES

It had been Cromwell who, shortly after the fall of Wolsey, stepped into that position of influence with the King which Gardiner had hoped to occupy. It had been Cromwell who from that time onward was the chief mover in the subordination of the Church to royal authority and the appropriation of ecclesiastical revenues to royal uses. It was Cromwell who, for the accomplishment of these ends, favoured the reformers, or, as Gardiner deemed them, the heretics. Finally, it was Cromwell whose foreign policy, actuated by the fear of a Papal combination against England, was directed to an alliance with the Protestant princes of Germany.

It is small wonder therefore that Gardiner, once more in England, bent every energy to the accomplishment of Cromwell's overthrow.

Although out of favour for some months after his return from France in the fall of 1538, Gardiner lost no opportunity to thwart his rival. Early in 1539 he ejected a married parson from the parish of Bentworth, despite Cromwell's support of the man, and permitted another cleric, whom Cromwell's henchmen had jailed for "suspect preaching," to speak in Winchester Cathedral.[1] In the spring he opposed Cromwell's candidates for Parliament in Hampshire and Surrey, but without much success. Fitzwilliam, Earl of Southampton, toured these constituencies in Cromwell's interest, and although he expressed fears that Gardiner's candidates would be chosen at Farnham, he appears to have been able to secure the election of Cromwell's nominees in other places. Thomas Wriothesley and one Worsley were elected in Hampshire in spite of Gardiner's opposition.[2]

Cromwell's foreign policy seemed to be justified when, in January, 1539, Charles and Francis, through their representatives at Toledo, agreed to make no new alliance with England without each other's consent. The possibility of a match between Henry and Anne of Cleves was now broached.[3]

Charles and Francis, however, soon made it clear that they had no wish to break with England; and Henry, desiring at once to disarm domestic discontent and to remove all pretext for French or Imperial hostility by convincing Catholic Europe of his entire orthodoxy,

urged Parliament, on May 5, to take such action as would banish all
diversity of religious opinion from the realm.

The result was the passage of the Act of the Six Articles, which
declared: (1) that in the Sacrament of the Altar "no substance of
bread or wine" remained after consecration, but only "the natural
body and blood of our Saviour;" (2) that Communion in both kinds
was not necessary; (3) that the marriage of priests was contrary to
God's law; (4) that vows of chastity ought, by the law of God, to be
observed; (5) that private Masses were agreeable to God's law and
ought to be continued; (6) that auricular confession was expedient
and necessary to be retained. Anyone who denied the first article
was to forfeit his property and suffer death by burning, even if he
were willing to abjure—a provision of greater severity than any in
earlier heresy laws. Those who taught or maintained publicly
anything contrary to the other five articles were to suffer loss of
goods and death as a felon; those who wrote or privately professed
such opinions were to suffer loss of goods for the first offense and
a felon's death for the second.[4]

There has been much discussion among historians over the question of who was to blame for this ferocious act. Mr. Froude says
the bishops; Canon Dixon and Mr. Gairdner, the laity. As a matter
of fact it appears that everyone—King, Parliament, and people,
laity and clergy alike, with the exception of a handful of reformers,
favoured it. In Parliament Cranmer and five reforming bishops
argued against it, but they had no support, lay or clerical. The King
came in person into Parliament to refute them. As for the lay
lords, "we of the temporality," wrote one of them, "have been all
of one opinion"—that of complete approval of the act.[5] So over-
whelming was the sentiment that Cromwell discreetly refrained
from opposition. When the articles were presented to Convocation
the entire body of clergy in the lower house, with but two exceptions, voted in their favour.[6] The French ambassador observed that
the people made great demonstration of joy, being "much more inclined to the old religion than to the new."[7]

There may have been much anti-Papal and anti-clerical feeling in
England, but as yet there was little desire for doctrinal change. The
prosperous middle class, who had profited by the restriction of clerical trading and the abolition of clerical privilege, and the gentry
and nobility, who had been enriched by monastic lands, supported
the royal ecclesiastical policy, but neither they nor their royal master
desired any new theology. Still less did the common people. Cromwell had used his influence for the advancement of clergy of reforming ideas because they could sincerely support his attack on
the wealth and power of the Church, but the doctrinal influence of
these clergymen had at this time only spread far enough to alarm
their countrymen. Englishmen looked with apprehension at the

disintegration and disorder which the Reformation in Germany appeared to be fostering; they were shocked by what they regarded as the irreverence or the excesses of the reformers; they were aroused by a policy which was filling the bench of bishops with men in favour of doctrinal innovation. One reformer, lamenting the unwillingness of Englishmen to accept the new ideas, said, in the summer of 1539:

> "Who is there, almost, that will have a Bible, but he must be compelled thereto? How loth be our priests to teach the commandments, th' articles of the faith, and the *Pater Noster* in English! Again, how unwilling be the people to learn it! Yea, they jest at it, calling it the new *Pater Noster* and the New Learning." [8]

Another reformer, some time after this, described how the "inordinate rich, stiffnecked citizens" of London went in procession through the streets in times of epidemic, calling upon the saints with *"ora pro nobis."* They would not have the New Testament in their houses, "nor suffer their servants to read it, neither yet gladly read it, or hear it read." [9]

That the penalties for the breach of the act were extreme, is but an indication of the fear men felt that the new doctrines made for "the pulling down of all power and the utter subversion of all commonwealths." There can be little doubt that most Englishmen agreed with the arguments in favour of the act which John Foxe puts in the mouth of Gardiner—that "civil tumults and commotions" were especially to be feared "by reason of innovation of religion," considering "what a dangerous matter in a commonwealth it is to attempt new alterations in anything, but especially of religion." [10]

The part Gardiner played in framing the articles is a matter of inference. He was not a member of the committee first chosen to consider the banishment of diverse opinions. Conservative and reforming ideas were so equally represented by the bishops on this committee that after ten days' discussion they had reached no agreement. Hence, on May 16 the Duke of Norfolk moved that the matter be settled in full Parliament, and presented for consideration six articles which became the basis of the act. [11] The fact that Norfolk, who was no theologian, and who in most things was Gardiner's ally, presented the articles, goes a long way to confirm the truth of the view current among reformers that Gardiner was the author of them. They were dubbed "Gardiner's Gospel." [12] He was one of the half dozen bishops conspicuous for their advocacy of the articles in the House of Lords. [13] He was also a member of one of two committees appointed to draw up suggestions for the penal portions of the act, and it appears that the suggestions brought in by the committee on which he acted were those accepted. [14]

The articles became law on June 28, 1539. Immediately thereafter a barber-surgeon, a soldier, and two priests, suspected of erroneous views on the Sacrament, were examined in London. They
were all from Calais, where, said Lord Lisle, "their naughty and
abominable fashions" had "done much to move sedition." Their
chief examiners were Bishops Cranmer, Sampson, and Repps. Gardiner was present at the examination of the soldier, Ralph Hare, at
Lambeth, July 6. When Hare was told that if he defended the
opinions with which he was charged, it would cost him his life, the
poor man was thoroughly frightened, and Gardiner, seeing his
plight, said to him:

> "Ralph Hare! Ralph Hare! by my troth I pity thee much.
> For in good faith, I think thee to be a good simple man, and
> of thyself wouldest mean well enough, but that thou hast had
> shrewd and subtle schoolmasters. . . . It were indeed pity
> that thou shouldest be burned, for thou art a good fellow, a
> tall man, and hast served the King right well in his wars. I
> have heard thee well commended, and thou art yet able to do
> the King as good service as ever thou wast. . . . Thou
> knowest my Lord of Canterbury's Grace here is a good gentle
> lord, and would be loth thou shouldest be cast away. Tell me,
> canst thou be content to submit thyself unto him . . . ?"

Whereupon Hare fell on his knees, shed tears, and submitted.
Neither he nor any of the others from Calais were burnt.[15]

Thus what appears to have been the first examination after the
passage of the Act of the Six Articles resulted, as the authors of
the act undoubtedly hoped it would, in frightening the heretics into
submission without compelling their examiners to proceed to ex-
tremities.

Early in July, Shaxton and Latimer, the two most advanced reformers on the bench of bishops, resigned their bishoprics;[16] and a
London grand jury, acting under the statute, indicted, in a wave of
anti-reforming hysteria, over five hundred citizens for heresy within
two weeks. Infrequent church attendance or failure to perform
customary acts of reverence at the Mass were deemed by this jury
sufficient grounds for an indictment.[17]

At the moment, however, of this apparent conservative success,
the face of European politics began again to change. It appeared
highly probable that the Emperor intended paying a friendly visit
to France; hence it behooved Henry to do nothing more to alienate
the German princes. The five hundred indicted Londoners were
freed by a general pardon; further enforcement of the articles was
stayed; and Gardiner was excluded from the Council, on the ground
so it was reported, that he had objected to Cromwell's employment
of a heretic as an ambassador.[18]

This heretic was none other than Robert Barnes, the one-time Augustinian Friar of Cambridge, whom Gardiner, fourteen years before, had befriended and persuaded to recant when he was in danger of burning. At that time Gardiner had, according to Foxe, urged upon Barnes, with unconscious irony, the consideration that if he recanted and lived "he should do more in time to come." After his recantation he had been placed in the custody of his own order, whence, probably in 1528, he escaped to Germany and made friends of Luther, Melancthon, and other reformers.[19] There, it seems, he wrote his *Supplication to King Henry VIII,* in which he defended most of the opinions he had recanted, and arraigned the "delicious living" and "sumptuous palaces" which the bishops maintained "by false feigned holiness in deceiving and robbing the people." This was not calculated to bring him into favour with the bishops, but other things in his book made it clear that he might be useful to the King. He had devoted much space to an uncompromising defense of the royal supremacy, and had referred to Becket as "a stinking martyr." If laws against lay control of the clergy "be not of the devil," he exclaimed, "tell me what is of the devil!"[20]

He returned to England, and, according to Foxe, was shielded by Cromwell when Thomas More, then Chancellor, sought his arrest.[21] This must have been in 1531 or early in 1532; and soon thereafter Gardiner happened to meet him at Hampton Court and taxed him with having published a falsehood. Barnes had, at Cambridge, as we recall, denounced law suits as unchristian, and Gardiner had induced him to give up this opinion by showing him a passage from St. Augustine. Barnes, according to Gardiner, later printed a statement that Gardiner had withheld a part of the passage which supported Barnes' view. Hence at Hampton Court, in the presence of Cranmer,

> "I laid that misreport of me to his charge," says Gardiner, "and there showed him the book to see St. Austin's words which in the first part and also last part condemned his Anabaptistical opinion. Whereupon Barnes fell down on his knees and asked me instantly forgiveness, with promise to write a book to the world wherein to declare that he had belied me. Upon which reconciliation I had Barnes home to my house that night and made him the best cheer I could."

The promised book was not forthcoming; nevertheless

> "after this Barnes returned freely into England and lived here triumphantly."[22]

He was employed by Cromwell on missions of State to Protestant powers on the Continent in 1534, 1535, and 1536, and again in 1539; in June 1538 he had, at Henry's appointment, acted on the side of the German envoys in their conference with English divines in an

endeavour to reach a common basis of doctrine, and in October of
the same year was appointed by the King to act with Cranmer,
Stokesley, and others on a commission to proceed against Anabaptists.[23]

Although he maintained a sufficiently orthodox position on the
Sacrament of the Altar, he had published much in defence of such
Protestant doctrines as these: that faith alone justifieth, that the
free will of man of its own strength can do nothing but sin, that
it is lawful for priests to marry, that auricular confession is not
necessary to salvation, that saints should not be invoked as mediators, that "the holy Church of Christ is nothing else but that congregation that is sanctified in spirit." He had, moreover, maintained
a position which some of his contemporaries thought subversive of
social order, namely, that civil laws "which are not grounded in
Scripture bind not the conscience of man." [24]

On his last mission to the Continent in the spring of 1539 he had
so far convinced the King of Denmark and the Elector of Saxony
of the desirability of an alliance with England that they were on
the point of sending ambassadors to conclude it when news of the
Six Articles gave them pause. Barnes returned in the summer "very
sad," and "had licence because of his weariness to depart" without
seeing the King until he should be sent for.[25] It must have been
shortly after this that Gardiner objected to him, as one who was
"defamed of heresy, and who had done penance for it."

There can be no doubt that Gardiner was heartily opposed to
Barnes' opinions, but it seems equally certain that his objection to
Barnes at this time was primarily an objection to his patron. He
judged the moment had come to strike at Cromwell and saw that
Cromwell's most vulnerable point was his support of radical reformers. It was, however, at this juncture that the continental situation, as we have seen, shifted in Cromwell's favour, and Gardiner
was excluded from the Council. The Duke of Cleves, fearful lest
the Emperor seize Gelderland, welcomed the prospect of an alliance
with England. The treaty for the marriage of his sister Anne with
Henry was signed October 4, 1539. The wedding took place January 6, 1540.

Cromwell had shown his appreciation of Barnes by giving him
the prebend of Llanboidy in the diocese of St. David's sometime
before the middle of December 1539, and early in January an
English reformer at Basle received a letter from "brethren" in
England telling how "the word" was "powerfully preached" by
Barnes and his fellows.[26]

The political situation, however, which had saved Cromwell and
brought about the marriage with Anne, was altering again. The
Emperor had, indeed, spent the New Year's season in Paris, but he
evinced no willingness to return Milan to the French. Henry, who

had little liking for the German alliance, less for his German wife, and none for German theology, sent Norfolk to France in February with the express purpose of sowing dissention between Charles and Francis.[27] Moreover, if Charles were, as it seemed, about to seize Gelderland, Henry, if he adhered to the German alliance, might be called on to undertake the unprofitable task of aiding his brother-in-law. In spite of Cromwell's apparent ascendancy, Henry, in the Spring of 1540, was watching for a chance to repudiate his foreign policy.

Utterly failing to perceive the direction in which events were moving,[28] Barnes recklessly involved himself, early in March, in a ruinous controversy with Gardiner, and thereby gave the conservatives an excellent pretext for the attainder of Cromwell. One sign of the times which Barnes failed to read was that Gardiner had been asked to preach before the King every Friday in Lent.[29] Another was that Barnes himself, who had been appointed to preach at Paul's Cross on the first Sunday in Lent, February 15, 1540, was compelled to give place to Gardiner. On the day before, Gardiner had sent his chaplain to secure this pulpit for him for some Sunday in Lent. What followed may be read in Gardiner's own words:

"When I had done my business at Lambeth, which ended not afore five of the clock that Saturday, my chaplain, then waiting for me, told me he had been so bold over me to appoint me to preach the next day at Paul's Cross, adding how he thought better to disappoint Barnes on the morrow than some other Catholic man appointed on other Sundays. Whereupon I gathered my wits to me, called for grace, and determined to declare the Gospel of that Sunday, containing the devil's three temptations, the matter whereof seemed to be very apt to be applied to the time, and good occasion to note the abuse of Scripture among some, as the devil abused it to Christ, which matter indeed I touched somewhat plainly and, in my judgement, truly. And alluding to the temptation of the devil to Christ to cast himself downward, alleging Scripture that he should take no hurt, I said, nowadays the devil tempteth the world and biddeth them cast themself backward. There is no foreward in the new teaching, but all backward. Now the devil teacheth, come back from fasting, come back from praying, come back from confession, come back from weeping for thy sins. . . . And all, I said, is turned backward.

And amongst other things noted the devil's craft, what shift he useth to deceive man whose felicity he envieth, and therefore coveteth to have man idle, and void of good works, . . . and for that purpose procured out pardons from Rome, wherein heaven was sold for a little money, and for to retail that merchandise the devil used friars for his ministers. Now they be gone with all their trumpery, but the devil is not yet gone. And now he perceiveth it can no longer be borne to buy and sell heaven. . . . The devil hath excogitate to offer heaven without works. . . . To be in heaven needs no works at all, but only belief, only, only, nothing else. And to set forth this the devil's craft, there were, I said, ministers but no mo friars. Fie on the name and the garment; but now they be called by an English name 'brethren,' and go apparelled like other men, amonges whom be some of those that were friars. . . . But if the King's Majesty, as he hath banished friars by the French name, would also banish these that call themself brethren in English, the devil should be greatly discomforted. . . .

This my sermon was thought to some very plain, and Barnes, as he confessed after, and as appeared by that he did, could not digest it, but was persuaded and comforted to handle me somewhat rudely, which he did the Sunday fortnight after, in the same place, where he took to intreat the same text of the Gospel that I had declared, and left the Scripture of the Sunday he preached on, which had not been seen in that place before. There he began to call for me to come forth to answer him. He termed me to be a fighting cock and he was another and one of the game; he said I had no spurs and that he would show. And after he had pleased himself in the allegory of a cock fight, then upon a foolish conclusion, he cast me openly his glove, and, not content therewith, he called me forth by my name Gardiner, and opposed me in my grammar rules, and said if I had answered him in the school as I had there preached at the Cross he would have given me five stripes, and raged after such a sort as the like hath not been heard done in a pulpit (ordered to declare the word of God in, and not to touch any particular man), as he railed of me by name, alluding to my name Gardiner, what evil herbs I set in the garden of Scripture, so far beyond the terms of honesty as all men wondered at it, to hear a bishop of the realm as I was so reviled, and by such one openly." [30]

Gardiner complained to the King, who summoned Barnes and lectured him for his folly, in the presence of Fitzwilliam, Sir Anthony Browne, Dr. Cox, Dr. Robinson, and Gardiner himself.[31] "One notable thing was done in the hearing of the matter," says Gardiner. When Barnes offered to yield to the King,

" 'I am,' quoth his Majesty, 'a mortal man,' and therewith rising and turning to the Sacrament and putting off his bonnet said, 'yonder is the master of us all, author of truth; yield in truth to Him, and I shall,' saith the King's Majesty, 'defend the truth. And otherwise, Barnes,' quoth the King's Majesty, 'yield not to me.' "

Gardiner then suggested that Barnes and he be permitted to discuss the new doctrines together. To this Henry agreed, and appointed Drs. Cox and Robinson and two others "to be indifferent hearers." They met that evening, which was the Friday after Barnes' sermon (March 5), and when Barnes asked that he might be given the night to think over Gardiner's arguments, Gardiner assented. Next morning they spent two hours in debate "very quietly and patiently."

> "And suddenly," says Gardiner, "beyond all our expectations, when it was Barnes' part to have spoken, he fell on both knees and desired me to have pity upon him, good Bishop, and spake so many words to my glory and in praise of my learning as I was ashamed to hear them. . . . Barnes granted himself overcome and desired he might be my scholar. . . . I took him up from kneeling, I remembered old familiar knowledge, assured him of me; I refused to be his schoolmaster, but being, as I perceived he was, minded to fall from error, I would communicate to him some honest portion of my living, and named £40 a year, and he to live fellowlike with me in my house. And this I rehearse because it was told abroad afterward how I offered him £40 a year to leave his opinion, but he would not. (It is hard meddling with such manner of men; if a man procure their punishment as they deserve, there followeth defamation of cruelty; if a man would do them good, it is slandered as corruption or flattery.) But to Barnes again—he would needs be my scholar for aught I could do, and said God had given a gift to me wherewith to do much good."

Hence, with the King's consent, Barnes came for Gardiner's instruction on the following Monday.

Barnes was an impressionable individual, and there is no reason to doubt the sincerity of his action in this instance. As Gardiner says, "If Barnes counterfeited in that submission, he deceived mo as well as me." But as he was convinced of his error while he was with Gardiner, so when he returned to his friends he was strengthened in his former opinions; and he undoubtedly expected protection from Cromwell. Hence—to continue Gardiner's account:

> "When Master Barnes had gone to school two days, he waxed weary of that humility and came the third day and signified to me that if I would take him as one that came to confer he would come still, but else he would no more come. I perceived from whence the change came and told him, seeing he had once yielded himself to me as a scholar, I would so use him till I saw him

better learned, able to be my fellow, which he had not yet attained since Saturday."

Barnes refused to come again under these conditions, and so, says Gardiner, "was I rid of my wayward scholar." [32]

Barnes had doubtless been encouraged both in his own opinions and in his hope of protection from those in authority by the fact that on the Sunday after his sermon, the very day after he had agreed to go to school to Gardiner, the preacher at Paul's Cross was William Jerome, vicar of Stepney, a preacher of the new doctrines, who did not hesitate to proclaim them in his sermon.

Both Barnes and Jerome, however, as well as Thomas Garret, rector of All Saints, Honey Lane, a protégé of Cranmer,[33] were summoned before the King, to whom they promised to recant. This, says Gardiner, was "not at my suit, persecution, or prosecution," and there is no reason to doubt him, for although Henry had permitted Cromwell to encourage the new theologians, he himself never had any liking for the new theology, and at this moment he had little need of either, for Norfolk had recently returned from France well satisfied with the success of his mission.[34] Moreover, Henry took no little pride in his own theological attainments and welcomed occasions to display them. As Norfolk said:

"Never prince with more affection and with more charitable dexterity hath and daily doth persecute such ungracious persons as do preach and teach ill learnings." Barnes, Garret, and Jerome have "recanted from their lewd opinions. And, to be plain, his Highness is of such sort that I think all Christendom shall shortly say the King of England is the only perfect of good faith. God save him!" [35]

Jerome preached a recantation sermon Monday in Easter week, March 29, Barnes on Tuesday, and Garret on Wednesday.[36] Gardiner was present at Barnes' sermon and gives this account of it:

"When Barnes right solemnly and formally had made his recantation in the former part of his sermon, at the end of that he cried out to me and asked me forgiveness with a marvellous circumstance, as though the world should think I had need of such a public obtestation, and needs I must hold up my hand in token of a grant, and where I, encombered with shamefastness, did not by and by as he required, he called for it again and bade me hold up my hand. So it liked him with a courage to play with me and to blind the other submission done secretly as though it had been of none other sort, and therewith to boast his own charity and bring mine in doubt. And when he had in the pulpit played these two parts, to recant his opinion as he was appointed, and ask me forgiveness, which he did of wantoness, then after the prayer he beginneth a process of a matter and plainly and directly preacheth the contrary of that he had recanted, so evidently as the Mayor of himself asked whether he should from the pulpit send him to ward. . . . But Barnes was not stayed ne spoken to, whiles Jerome and Garret had both preached and followed the same trade. . . . One that favoured them had written to his friend at the court how gaily they had all handled the matter, both to satisfy the recantation and also in the same sermons to utter out the truth, . . . and this letter by negligence came to light, whereupon, and report of the sermons, they were all apprehended and by the secret Council (to which company I had then none access, ne had not almost a year before, ne had not after, so long as Cromwell's time lasted) sent to the Tower, and thereupon ensued further process by the whole realm, whereunto I was privy, but among the rest." [37]

The royal interest in Barnes' heresies was ominous for Cromwell. His biographer, Mr. Merriman, concludes that there is "every internal evidence" that Cromwell at this time apologized to Gardiner. Certain it is that sometime near the end of March he dined with Gardiner, on which occasion, as Norfolk learned from Wriothesley, they were together

"more than four hours, and opened their hearts, and so concluded that, and there be truth or honesty in them, not only all displeasures be forgotten, but also in their hearts be now perfect, entire friends."

"In order to maintain his very precarious position," says Mr. Merriman, "Cromwell had been forced to grovel before a man whom two years before he could have ordered about to his heart's content." [38]

At the same time Wriothesley was reconciled to his old master. [39] He remained an adherent of the conservative cause for the rest of his days.

On April 3, the Saturday following the inadequate recantation sermons, Barnes and his companions were sent to the Tower. [40] The next day, in the chapel of London House, Gardiner, assisted by Bishops Sampson and Skip, consecrated Bonner Bishop of London, and Heath Bishop of Rochester. [41] Bonner had, like Wriothesley, made his peace with Gardiner, [42] and thereafter remained a staunch conservative. Heath was likewise an addition to the conservative forces. Six days after the consecration, Marillac, the French ambassador, observed that Cranmer and Cromwell "do not know where they are," and that Cromwell was "tottering," for the King had summoned Gardiner and Tunstall to the Privy Council. [43]

But Cromwell found means to maintain his position for two months longer, and Gardiner remained out of the Privy Council till this fall.[44] Cromwell's brief continued ascendency was no doubt due to his activities in the King's behalf in the session of Parliament which opened April 12, a session which voted the King an unusually large subsidy, and enacted the suppression of the wealthy order of Knights of St. John of Jerusalem. Moreover, the report, which reached England early in April, that Francis I was fortifying Ardres,[45] a town on the border of the English territory in France, may have given Henry pause in his determination to break with the Germans. On April 17 Cromwell was created Earl of Essex. On the 24th Marillac wrote that he was in as much credit with the King as ever, "from which he was near being shaken by the Bishop of Winchester." [46]

This apparent restitution of Cromwell to favour evidently encouraged religious extremists among the people to rash utterances, while conservative officials, confident of the ultimate success of their faction at court, pressed examinations under the Six Articles and brought three obscure persons to the stake in Southwark early in May for heresy on the Sacrament.[47] This was in the diocese of Winchester, and although the Bishop does not appear to have had any part in the examinations, he could hardly have been unaware of the proceedings.

Pretexts, on the other hand, were found for attacking some of Gardiner's prominent partisans. His friend Lord Lisle, Deputy of Calais, was sent to the Tower, May 19, charged with complicity in a plot to deliver Calais to Cardinal Pole. From the shock of this misfortune Lady Lisle "fell distraught of mind, and so continued many years after." [48] Lisle was followed to the Tower by Bishop Sampson, Gardiner's former teacher, and Dr. Nicholas Wilson, both noted adherents of the old religion, accused of "relieving certain traitorous persons who denied the King's supremacy." [49]

Marillac wrote, June 1:

"Things are brought to such a pass that either Cromwell's party or that of the Bishop of Winchester must succumb. Although both are in great authority and favour of the King their master, still the course of things seems to incline to Cromwell's side, as Winchester's chief friend, the said dean of the chapel [Sampson], is down, and the Bishop of Canterbury, his chief adversary, appointed in his place preacher and reader at St. Paul's, where he has begun to put forward the contrary of what Winchester preached there in Lent last. Moreover, Dr. Barnes, heretofore made prisoner, is, it is said, at the letters of some German lords, to be soon released." [50]

The day before this was written Henry had dismissed with a non-committal answer the ambassadors of Cleves, who came to ask his advice concerning the Emperor's demand for Gelderland.[51] He had now received from Parliament everything which Cromwell's clever manipulation could get him, and as the fortification of Ardres had been followed by no other unfriendly act on the part of France, the situation was favourable for the repudiation of the German alliance and of the councillor who had effected it.

Meanwhile Gardiner had been making opportunity for Henry to meet the vivacious niece of the Duke of Norfolk, Catherine Howard, at dinners and entertainments in his house in Southwark.[52]

Within ten days after Marillac had written that things were inclining in Cromwell's favour, Cromwell had been sent to the Tower on the charge of supporting preachers of Lutheran opinions and working to overthrow "the mean, indifferent, true, and virtuous" religion established by the King. On June 17 his attainder was introduced in the House of Lords. In it he was declared not only a traitor, but "a detestable heretic," who had furthered the spread of heretical books, advanced heretical preachers, released imprisoned heretics, "terribly rebuked" those who accused them, affirmed Robert Barnes' preaching to be good, and sworn to defend it even against the King.[53]

Cromwell had probably done all these things, except the last, but he had done them with the King's tacit consent and in the interests of the King's polity; but Henry was not the man to protect an unpopular minister who was no longer of use to him, especially when that minister had led him into a marriage with a lady for whom, as he was about to reveal, he had a decided aversion.

On June 23, Marillac wrote that people said that if a vicar general were to be appointed in Cromwell's place, it would be Gardiner,[54] but no vicar general was appointed. From this time on Henry was his own vicar general. Yet it was Gardiner in whom he found the ablest exponent of his theological views. Rumour had it that he called him "his own bishop." [55]

The overthrow of Cromwell was speedily followed by the rejection of Anne. In this, as in an earlier divorce case, Gardiner was the King's chief counsel. He prepared a complete scheme of procedure, noting the points on which evidence should be secured and suggesting the examination of Cromwell, who testified, perhaps with some faint hope of pardon, that Henry had loathed his bride from the first and never consummated the marriage. Gardiner was one of the committee who, on July 6, persuaded Anne, at Richmond, to consent to the determination of the case by the clergy; the same night he hurried back to London to explain to Convocation on the morrow the reasons for the nullity of the marriage; on July 9 he signed, with the other members of Convocation, the judgement declaring the marriage null. He appears to have composed the letter sent by Anne to her brother, saying she was well satisfied with the judgement and the King's liberality—a letter she was evidently able to send in all sincerity, for one month later Marillac wrote that she was as joyous as ever and wore new dresses every day! [56]

Before the end of July Catherine Howard had become Henry's fifth wife.[57]

Parliament was dissolved July 24. Two days before this, Barnes, Garret, and Jerome were attainted for heresy.[58] On the 28th Cromwell was executed. On the 30th three noted Papists were hanged as traitors for denying the royal supremacy, and on the same day Barnes and his fellows were burned.[59]

They had not been convicted under the Act of the Six Articles nor were they charged with violation of it. They were sentenced without a hearing, by a vote of Parliament, as Cromwell had been;[60] nor were the heresies for which they were condemned specified. They had been so closely connected with Cromwell that their fate was inevitably involved in his. After Parliament had made the support of Barnes' teachings one of the chief charges against Cromwell, it could hardly let Barnes off with any lesser punishment. At the same time there were elements in his teaching which were believed by the conservatives to be a menace to the national life.

His principal dogma, that of justification by faith only, with its emphasis on Christian liberty and its discount of good works, appeared to Gardiner to tend directly to licence and evil works. In his discussion six years later with George Joye, the defender of Barnes' doctrines, Gardiner stated clearly what he believed to be the social results of this tenet:

> "Ye flatter the world with licentious doctrine, and offer them to pull from their necks all such yokes as ye think did at any time let [*i.e.*, hinder] or impeach them either in thought or deed. Ye promise them liberty of all thing[s] and then to rid them out of debt ye translate St. Paul thus, that we owe nothing to no man but love. Ye flatter the covetous master with pulling away holy days that he may have the more work done him for his year's wages. Ye flatter again the servant with pulling away all opinion of fast by abstinence from any meat, either in Lent or otherwise. Ye offer priests wives to wit and they can win them to you. Ye rid all of confession and weeping for sin. Ye take away distinction and difference of apparel, days, times, and places. Ye take away ceremonies which in deed do much let [hinder] good cheer in assemblies of good fellows. Ye give women courage and liberty to talk at their pleasure so it be of God's word, and to make the husband amends for that encombrye ye teach men secretly . . . that they may have as lawfully two wives at once as one"—

which was what Luther and Melancthon sanctioned in the case of

Philip of Hesse in 1540, and what the more radical Anabaptists openly advocated.[61] (It had also been one of the solutions for Henry VIII's difficulties proposed by Clement VII,[62] who could hardly have been accused of sharing Barnes' views.) In short, said Gardiner, "ye conspire *adversus dominum et adversus christum eius,*" and he added this significant marginal note, evidently taking the word *christum* in its literal sense as "anointed one," saying, "the English of this Latin *dominum et christum* is God and the king." [63]

No less destructive of civil and social life did Gardiner find the teaching concerning predestination and election which was bound up with Barnes' doctrine that man of his own free choice could do no good thing. This belief made inevitably, thought Gardiner, for the conviction that

> "all things come to pass by an absolute necessity, and so man's life, death, manners, behaviour, state, condition, and everything is fixed and fastened in his place appointed, with nails riveted, and clenched with mere necessity."

This, he said, doth

> "not only impugn the whole process of Scripture, but also subverteth all stay of good direction and endeavour either to Godly exercise or politic [*i.e.,* political or civil] behaviour. It is the extremity of all mischief to say that a man cannot choose whether he will use God's gifts or no." [64]

Mischievous as these doctrines appeared, Barnes' teaching that civil laws were not necessarily binding on the conscience appeared more mischievous still.

In mediæval times the Church had represented the ultimate unity of life. Conscience and the king were both, in the last resort, subject to the Church. But the renewed study of Biblical and Roman antiquity led the scholars of the Renaissance to conclude that the king was superior to both conscience and the Church. Men as widely divergent in other matters as were Cranmer and Gardiner found common ground in their support of the royal supremacy. By a strange irony the new learning fathered a second principle which became the mortal foe of this one, a principle latent in the words of St. Paul and of his greater Master, namely, that the individual conscience is superior to Church and king—a principle which the settled, conservative forces of society have, from that age to this, found dangerous; and today, when most men have given up even the dream that either Church or king should represent our supreme sanction, we are still striving to co-ordinate conscience with social organization, and seeking an arbiter between them.

The reformers were not unaware of the perils of the new principl, and many of them set up the Scriptures as the ultimate umpire; yet whenever a question as to the interpretation of Scripture arose, its weakness as a final authority appeared. Barnes appealed to Scripture, but assumed the right of the enlightened individual to interpret it. His chief difficulty lay in reconciling the rights of conscience with the authority of princes, for he also had accepted the thesis that the king, no matter how wicked, ought to be obeyed. It was easy enough to maintain this principle when it served his argument against Pope or bishop, but when the king issued ordinances against what Barnes considered true religion it was another matter. He solved the problem thus:

> "If the king forbid the New Testament or any of Christ's Sacraments or the preaching of the word of God or any other thing that is against Christ,"

subjects should make "diligent intercession" to the king to withdraw his command.

> "If he will not do it, they shall keep their Testament with all other ordinance of Christ, and let the king exercise his tyranny, if they cannot flee, and in no wise, under pain of damnation, shall they withstand him with violence," but "leave the vengeance of it unto their heavenly Father." [65]

This is an admirable statement of the doctrine of non-resistance, but it is hardly in accord with the theory that to the king, as to the Lord's anointed, is due obedience without question. It is not surprising that sixteenth-century statesmen felt Barnes' teaching to be subversive of the State. In comment on William Jerome's preaching of the same doctrine, Gardiner remarked that it made "obedience to princes an outward behaviour only, which is a play, either for fear or manners' sake." [66]

The official Tudor view is well put in the recantation which Barnes, Garret, and Jerome were compelled to sign:

> "I do also confess with my heart that laws and ordinances made by Christian rulers ought to be obeyed by the inferiors and subjects not only for fear but also for conscience; for whoso breaketh them breaketh God's commandments." [67]

XIV

A LETTER FROM THE POPE

The fall of Cromwell, the repudiation of Anne of Cleves, and the reaction in religion opened the way for closer relations between England and the Empire. Hence Gardiner, after a few busy months supervising the collection of the subsidy granted by the recent Parliament, and attending to the varied business of the Privy Council, now at London, now at Windsor,[1] set out in the middle of November 1540 on an embassy extraordinary to the Emperor.

He was accompanied by Sir Henry Knyvet, "a young man of very good qualities and towardness," who was to remain at the Imperial court after the Bishop's return. The embassy partook of something of the magnificence of the days of Wolsey, Gardiner's train consisting of more than a hundred horsemen "all in grey velvet with great gold chains on their necks," a circumstance which Marillac observed was intended to impress Europe with the fact that the Church in England was "not so despoiled as might be thought." [2]

Gardiner arrived at Calais in the end of November. The Emperor was at the time in Flanders but was about to start for Bavaria to meet the Diet at Ratisbon (Regensburg), where an attempt was to be made to bring the Catholic and Protestant princes of his realm into agreement. As the Imperial departure was delayed, Gardiner lingered a while at Calais, then moved on to Mons, and finally "went to his Majesty with great pomp," on Christmas Day at Namur. The next two months were spent in a leisurely progress to Ratisbon, by way of Luxemburg, Spires, and Nuremberg.[3]

At Nuremberg the reformer Osiander was introduced to the English ambassadors by an old friend whom he found in attendance upon Knyvet. He dined with them and discussed theology with Gardiner for three hours. They agreed that Faith was the hand that grasped God's gift of justification, but disagreed when Gardiner wished to add Love as another hand.

Osiander, writing to Justus Jonas, described Gardiner as a man adept in all courtly usages, and a most accomplished dialectician, his dialectics, however, being those of a jurist, not those of a theologian or a philosopher. His body, said Osiander, was well proportioned and vigorous, poised and alert, his complexion somewhat unwholesome—if this last be the right interpretation of Osiander's difficult phrase *"virulentiam quandam in colore preferens,"* by which he may perhaps have meant that a flush of high colour or some unpleasant trick of facial expression in Gardiner indicated a quick and vehement disposition.[4]

It was likewise at Nuremberg that Granvelle, the Imperial prime minister, suggested to Gardiner that Charles V was ready to mediate between England and the Papacy, and urged Gardiner to think it over carefully, for this was, he said, Gardiner's business, now that God had removed the sinister Cromwell who was the cause of all the evil. Gardiner, according the Granvelle's account of the interview, "seemed to allow all that, but said it was a capital offense to move such practices to his king."[5] That he did, however, report the interview to Henry is clear from the fact that six weeks later, at the end of March 1541, he received at Ratisbon instructions from Henry to thank Granvelle for his offer. Then, or sometime thereafter, he seems to have assured Granvelle that if the German princes could be induced to recognize the Papal primacy, of which Granvelle had high hopes, Henry would permit the Emperor to undertake England's reconciliation with Rome.[6]

It is possible that Gardiner felt the time was ripe for such reconciliation; it is possible that Henry, having heard from Gardiner, just before the opening of the Diet, that the chances of agreement between Catholics and Protestants were favourable,[7] concluded that reunion with Rome might become a political necessity; it is possible that by thanking Granvelle for his offers and holding out some hope that they might be acceptable, he was merely engaging in such diplomatic courtesy as would facilitate closer political relations with Charles.[8] Fourteen years later, after England under Queen Mary had become reconciled to Rome, Gardiner said in a sermon: "Master Knyvet and I were sent ambassadors unto the Emperor to desire him that he would be a mean between the Pope's Holiness and the King, to bring the King to the obedience of the See of Rome."[9] But at that time Gardiner was speaking under circumstances which made it natural for him to picture as the objective of this mission what may have been one of several diplomatic alternatives.

However that may be, we do know that Gardiner, while at Ratisbon, received a letter from the Pope. What the letter contained or how it was answered, if it were answered, we do not know. Indeed the fact that it had been received would have remained a secret had not an accident brought the fact to the astonished attention of Knyvet, who had been kept in the dark concerning possible relations with Rome. This is how he came to know it: When the Papal Legate, Cardinal Contarini, left Ratisbon, he asked an Italian merchant, named Ludovico, to go to the English ambassador and request him to send an answer by the next courier to the letter which he had received from the Pope. Ludovico, deeming one English ambassador as good as another, gave this message to a member of Knyvet's household who reported it to Knyvet. Knyvet sent for Ludovico. The merchant confirmed the message, explaining, however, that the ambassador for whom it was intended was a bishop. He was then directed to Gardiner's dwelling. Knyvet, having carefully secured witnesses to Ludovico's statement, wrote an account of it to Henry.

Two of these witnesses, members of Knyvet's household, gave sworn testimony to this effect in 1551, five years after Knyvet's death. One of them stated further that as soon as Gardiner learned that the Cardinal's message had reached Knyvet, he induced Granvelle to commit Ludovico to the keeping of one of the Emperor's marshalls and informed Knyvet that the merchant had evidently been "suborned to be his destruction." When Knyvet suggested that Ludovico be examined before both himself and Gardiner, the latter replied that the Emperor's council would examine him. Knyvet protested against thus turning the matter over to foreigners, and had a falling out with the Bishop "till at last by letters from the King's Majesty both the Bishop and Sir Henry [Knyvet] were commanded to lay all things under foot, and to cease that matter, joining together in service as before. And so they did, without further outward demonstration of any grudge or variance." [10]

Foxe cites this incident as one which led Henry to suspect Gardiner's "fidelity toward his godly proceedings in religion," [11] but there is not the slightest reason to believe that the King was not fully aware of Gardiner's doings at Ratisbon. The summary way in which the Bishop was said to have silenced Ludovico and kept Knyvet from further knowledge of the affair was—if truly reported —due to a desire, not to keep the King in ignorance of it, but to prevent its coming to the ears of the reforming party in England. Had Gardiner admitted holding correspondence with the Pope, even with the King's consent, his enemies might well have made it the basis of an accusation of treason, as indeed they tried to do some years later.

The Diet, which opened April 5, 1541, drew to Ratisbon men of note from all quarters of Germany as well as a few from beyond its borders. There was the liberal Cardinal Contarini who was working for a reform of the Church from within, and who hoped for reunion with the Lutherans; there were the moderate Catholic theologians Gropper and Von Pflug, and the less compromising Eck, Luther's noted opponent. Albrecht of Brandenburg, Cardinal Archbishop of Mainz, Primate of Germany, notorious for the dealings in indulgences which had provoked Luther's protests, was there; and Peter Faber, friend and disciple of Loyola. The Protestant spokesmen were Melancthon, Bucer, and Pistorius; Cruciger also was present, as was Alexander Alesius, the cosmopolitan Scot. Most of the German princes of prominence, with the exception of the

Elector of Saxony, attended the Diet, and, according to the Venetian ambassador, did nothing but banquet daily. Before it closed the Emperor's brother, Ferdinand, Archduke of Austria and King of the Romans, arrived.

The observing ambassador of Venice noted that although Gardiner was opposed to the interests of the Pope he was with the Catholics in other matters and defended them stoutly.[12]

He conferred with Bucer, at the request of Bucer himself, although he suggested that a discussion might be fruitless since they acknowledged no common authority. To Bucer's contention that Scripture was authority sufficient, he answered that since both sides would apply "their own interpretation and therein stand obstinately," he preferred to "use Socrates' manner of disputing;" to which Bucer agreed. To begin the discussion Bucer said he thought it cruel to forbid priests to marry on pain of death. Gardiner said the penalty to him seemed merciful since its very extremity kept men from danger by fear of it. Bucer then asked what right the King had to forbid clerical marriage. Gardiner answered by a series of Socratic questions on the fifth commandment, leading Bucer to admit that the King had the same right to command his subjects as a father to command his children. Then said Gardiner:

"By St. Paul the father may order some of his childer not to marry. Ergo, the prince, may order some of his subjects not to marry."

Bucer denied the minor premise. Gardiner turned to I Cor. vii. 36-38, where St. Paul, after advising men and women not to marry, says that although a father sins not in giving his daughter in marriage, he does well if he keep her unmarried, concluding that "he that giveth her in marriage doeth well; but he that giveth her not in marriage doeth better."

"At the which text," says Gardiner, "Bucer so stumbled and stayed, much contrary to my expectation, as though he had never read it before. And because Alesius, the Scot, was by and hitherto spake nothing, Bucer took the book to Alesius and bade him speak his mind, whereunto Alesius went to the first part of the chapter, out of our purpose, which the said Alesius understood so foolishly that thereupon rose a new communication in which were interlaced many matters which Bucer and I afterwards intreated by writing."[13]

Bucer, in his account of the conference, says that he maintained "this undoubted principle of Holy Scripture, that the father can have no power to keep his daughter except he perceive it to be for her profit." He also says that when, in the discussion, Gardiner became excited, and especially when the Scotchman Alesius said anything that misliked him, "his very veins in his hands shook and trembled, which I never saw in all my life time in any man before." [14]

Gardiner said that never in his life had he met so big a fool discussing theology as Alesius. [15]

The debate with Bucer was continued at first by correspondence and, in subsequent years, in an acrimonious war of treatises on clerical celibacy. [16]

Gardiner's opinion of the Protestants was not, apparently, made more favourable by what he saw of them at Ratisbon. There is in the Public Record Office a copy of the Emperor's opening address at the Diet, on the margin of which is a note in Gardiner's handwriting in which he says that he had seen another copy made by the Protestants in which a statement not in the original had been inserted, and concludes: "these Protestants will say nothing truly, be it divine or human." [17]

At the end of May, when the Diet was drawing to a close and it became increasingly clear that no agreement between Catholics and Protestants would be reached, the Venetian ambassador was impressed by the frequency of Gardiner's interviews with Granvelle and the Emperor, and wrote that negotiations between them seemed to become closer hourly. [18] The result of these negotiations was that Charles expressed his willingness to enter a treaty of friendship with England, to be made within ten months, provided that neither party should meanwhile treat to the prejudice of the other —an arrangement to which Henry assented with a very good will. [19]

Gardiner received leave to return at midsummer and, if the Venetian ambassador's forecast was correct, left Ratisbon about July 15. [20] Bishop Morone, Papal Nuncio at the Diet, wrote that Gardiner on his recall feared for his life, for persuading the King to return to the Church, and the Queen of Navarre is reported to have said that he was in disgrace and would sooner flee to Rome than return to England. [21] It is easy to see how rumours of this sort arose from the affair of the merchant Ludovico, and how the Queen of Navarre might make political capital of them when boasting of Henry's attachment to France and estrangement from the Empire, but we have no evidence that Gardiner had any fears for his safety or that he was out of favour with the King.

On his homeward journey he passed through Louvain, whither he came, says Driander, who was in the city at the time, "with a great rout and bravery, and was there, at a private man's house called Jeremy's, most honourably entertained and received; where the faculty of divines, for honour's sake, presented him wine in the name of the whole university." But someone remembered that he was the author of a book on True Obedience, a copy of which was, it seems, found in the university. When the learned doctors had perused it "they did not only repent them for attributing such their honour unto him," but "boldly enterprised to dispute with him concerning the Pope's supremacy."

"The Bishop stoutly defended his said oration. The divines, contrary, did stiffly maintain their opinion, and divers times openly, with exclamation, called the said Bishop an excommunicate person, and a schismatic, to the no little reproach and infamy of the English nation. . . . The Bishop, not long after, minding to say Mass in St. Peter's Church, they did deny unto him, as to an excommunicate person, the ornaments and vestments meet for the same; wherewith being highly offended, he suddenly hastened his journey from thence." [22]

On his way from Dover Gardiner stopped at Canterbury to hear Mass, then went on to London, whence, on October 7 (1541), he departed for the north to meet the King, who was on his way back from York. He found him at Collyweston, was well received, and on October 16 resumed his seat in the Privy Council,[23] no whit lower in the royal esteem because of his negotiations with the Pope.

While at Canterbury he had conversed with one of the prebendaries about Cranmer's new preachers—a conversation of which we shall speak later [24]—and had inquired about "the ordinances in the choir" and the statutes, which were doubtless of interest to him since his own cathedral at Winchester had, like Canterbury, been recently converted from a monastic to a secular foundation. This was a change which, in all probability, he had furthered himself, in order to get as good terms as possible. Certainly the terms were favourable, for on May 1, 1541 the chapter of the Cathedral Church of the Holy Trinity, as it was now called, had been re-endowed by the King with almost all the lands it had held as the Benedictine Priory of St. Swithen, plus considerable additions from the estates of other suppressed houses.[25]

Gardiner's London church, the Priory Church of St. Mary Overies, Southwark, after dissolution in October 1539, had, in 1540, been acquired by the united parishes of St. Mary Magdalene and St. Margaret, and been called the Church of St. Saviour, "which church," wrote the chronicler Wriothesley,

"the inhabitants of the said church borough had bought of the King, with the bells of the same, to their great charges, which now is the largest and fairest church about London; the good Bishop of Winchester . . . putting to his helping hand to the redeeming of the same." [26]

XV

THE BISHOP OF WINCHESTER BENDS HIS BOW

Within a month of Gardiner's return from the Continent he was called upon to deal once again with Henry's matrimonial difficulties. On November 2, 1541 Cranmer revealed to Henry information he had received concerning Catherine Howard's premarital indiscretions—a revelation which seems to have genuinely grieved the King. That Catherine had been guilty of misconduct before marriage and had put herself into compromising positions thereafter, is reasonably clear. The charges against her were not partisan inventions. But the fact that Cranmer, when he first heard of her shortcomings, conferred with Edward Seymour and Chancellor Audley as to what he should do about it, may indicate a hope on the part of the reformers that Catherine's fall would involve a setback for the conservatives. It undoubtedly did cause Norfolk, several of whose relatives were involved in the affair, considerable uneasiness,[1] but Gardiner's position remained unchanged. Upon the discovery of Catherine's misdemeanours the Council met at his house for a day and a night, and he himself guided their proceedings.[2]

Indeed, in the following spring Henry appears in some way to have explicitly designated him as his chief minister. As Gardiner himself put it in a letter to Cranmer early in the next reign,

"In the same Lent [1542] the King's Majesty accepted me to be with him in credit as Granvelle was with the Emperor, by the same terms, which was kept secret, but many there be living that knew it to be true."

So busy was he with affairs of State that his friends marvelled, he said, to hear him preach once that year in the King's Chapel.[3]

On February 13, 1542, after attainder by Parliament, the unhappy Catherine Howard was executed. The ambassador of Cleves suggested that Henry should receive Anne as his wife again, to which Gardiner replied with indignation that her separation was founded on great reason, and that the King would never take her back.[4]

Despite the tragic end of Henry's Catholic bride, Henry had no intention of encouraging Protestantism or renewing the German connection. Norfolk favoured an alliance with France and heartily supported the French proposal, revived early in 1542, for the marriage of the Duke of Orleans to Princess Mary. This was discussed for almost a year by a committee of the Council, of which Norfolk and Gardiner were chief, but it came to nothing.[5] In consequence, Francis I "spake vehemently and in terms of great indignation" of Gardiner to Paget, then ambassador in France, to whom Cardinal Tournon likewise complained, saying, "there is the Bishop of Winchester, he is our mortal enemy, as his Highness told you the other day, and yet in all our negotiations together is always appointed to be one, which we think *iniquum.*"

"Yea, this is your ambassador's [Marillac's] report, . . ." retorted Paget. "He is somewhat glorious, and by all likelihood ever cocking with my Lord of Winchester in matters of learning, wherein your ambassador is not to be compared with him, . . . therefore he is a great mote in his eye, and by his report in yours. You must know that Monsr. de Winchester is too wise to take upon him to govern the King our master." [6]

Paget's observations, like most diplomatic assurances, were but half truths. Marillac may have been a coxcomb, but Gardiner was imbued with a settled distrust of France, epitomized later in his advice to Protector Somerset to take it for a rule that the French were so wanton they would do well only so long as they feared a scourging.[7] He was, moreover, convinced that both politically and ecclesiastically an alliance with the Empire was essential.

Hence, while he had been thwarting the advances of France and the plans of his ally Norfolk, he was busy smoothing the way for the completion of friendlier relations with Charles V, inaugurated by the journey to Ratisbon. The ten months' engagement between Charles and Henry, arranged at Ratisbon, expired at the end of April 1542. On May 2 Charles commissioned Chapuys, his ambassador in London, to treat for an alliance with England.[8] Before this commission reached England, Gardiner, evidently in some anxiety lest Charles should no longer desire the alliance, went, on May 11, to live in a little house in the fields, in Stepney, near Chapuys' lodging, on the pretext of escaping the sweating sickness in London, but in reality to sound the Imperial ambassador. The way he contrived to make Chapuys believe that their meeting was a lucky accident pleased him so much that he described it in detail to the King:

"Yesternight, after mine arrival at Stepney, I . . . sent unto him this message, that by chance I was his neighbour for a season, and having been three years in France, I had there learned a lesson to be bold to send for wine wheresoever I thought the best to be, and much more if my friend had it; whereupon I sent now unto him for some wine to my supper; for that manner of France, I said, liked me, and many of their other conditions I liked not very well, for I was a Frenchman only in that point. The ambassador liked the message very well, and specially that I said I was a Frenchman only in that point, and thereupon sent his secretary unto me to desire me to dine with him the next day. . . . And so we came together rather of his provocation than of mine, as he taketh it; and I have so fashioned myself in our communication all this forenoon, that he sueth unto me to be a mean to your Majesty that he may repair unto the same, . . . for he knoweth by his own wisdom that your Majesty may be the stay of Christendom . . . and that without your Majesty there can be nothing stable . . ." [9]

When Paget said that Gardiner was too wise to try to govern the King, he was correct. Gardiner was much too wise to insist on any policy which did not have the King's approval, but the concluding phrases of the letter last quoted make it clear that he did not hesitate to try to win that approval, nor was he ignorant of the surest way of doing so. Indeed, while he thus assured Henry of the Imperial conviction that the King of England was indispensable to the stability of Europe, he advised Chapuys, if he would gain Henry's favour for the alliance, to persuade him, not that it was advantageous or necessary, but that it would enable him to fulfil his virtuous and magnanimous desire to remedy the ills of Christendom! [10]

After the first meeting at Stepney, daily conferences between Gardiner and Chapuys followed; [11] but nothing was concluded before war broke out between France and the Empire in July 1542, which gave Henry an excellent opportunity for settling affairs with Scotland. To Gardiner fell the oversight of the provisioning of the army that marched against the Scots, [12] and negotiations with the Empire were dropped during the summer. They were resumed in the autumn, and on February 11, 1543 a treaty was concluded providing for mutual aid in case of actual invasion of either monarch's territories, and for a joint expedition against France within the next two years. [13]

Meanwhile, in the end of November 1542, the Scotch had been completely routed at Solway Moss. A fortnight later their King, James V, died, of chagrin, it was said, at the defeat. Henry was so elated that Chapuys thought he might even marry again, a prophecy which came true on July 12, 1543, when Gardiner performed the wedding ceremony of the King and his sixth and last wife, Catherine Parr, already twice a widow—a woman, as one of the courtiers expressed it, "for virtue, wisdom, and gentleness most meet for his Highness." [14]

In June 1543 Gardiner acted with five other Privy Councillors in concluding two treaties with the Scotch, one for peace and one for the marriage of Prince Edward to the infant Mary, Queen of Scots;[15] and on the last day of the year, as one of a committee of eight members of the Privy Council, he signed an agreement with the representatives of the Empire in pursuance of the treaty already made, pledging Henry and Charles jointly to invade France in person before June 20, 1544.[16]

Side by side with the diplomatic negotiations of 1542 and 1543, which confirmed the reversal of Cromwell's foreign policy, went Gardiner's attempt effectually to nullify the doctrinal consequences of Cromwell's ecclesiastical régime. Convictions under the Act of the Six Articles had been few, but they had been reasonably effective in stopping the mouths of the extremists or frightening them into exile; yet the knowledge that the primate of all England was in sympathy with German opinions, and retained the friendship of the King, gave encouragement to the reformers. Hence, while Gardiner was engaged in cementing the Imperial alliance, he was no less active in forwarding plans for anchoring the Church in England to the tenets of Catholic theology and for extirpating heresy in high places.

In the Convocation of 1542 Cranmer, after announcing that the King desired the clergy to consider the correction of the English Bible, asked each member individually if he thought the Great Bible (essentially the work of the reformers Tyndale and Coverdale)[17] could be retained without offence to the faithful. The majority answered that it could not, unless it were carefully revised and made to accord with the Bible commonly read in the English Church, that is, the Vulgate. Thereupon committees were appointed to examine the Old and New Testaments. Tunstall and Gardiner headed the New Testament committee, and to Gardiner in particular was assigned the Gospel of Luke, one of the two books he had previously translated.

On February 17 he read in Convocation a list of ninety-nine Latin words and phrases from the Vulgate which, he said, because of their peculiar significance and the importance of their content should, in any translation of the New Testament, either be retained in their Latin form or rendered in English as nearly like the original as possible. These were such words as *Christus, Dominus, Spiritus Sanctus, ecclesia, apostolus, episcopus, presbyter, martyr, sacramentum, religio, poenitentia, impositio manum, confessio, gratia, justificare, charitas, parabola, mysterium.*[18]

It is easy to see how men for whom Latin was the living language of learning and religion feared to desecrate words fraught with the sacred associations of centuries, by turning them into the homely phrases of a speech which, in the sixteenth century, was still a "vulgar" tongue. Gardiner undoubtedly expressed the feeling of many a scholar of his day when he remarked, as he did some years later, that while Latin and Greek had been the vehicles of religion for fifteen hundred years, English "hath not continued in one form of understanding two hundred years; and without God's work and special miracles it shall hardly contain religion long when it cannot last itself." [19]

Moreover, the translators of the Great Bible had already put the matter of Bible translation into the realm of theological controversy by so rendering some of the words on Gardiner's list as to turn subjects in dispute into foregone conclusions. Thus *ecclesia* had become "congregation" and *sacramentum,* "secret." It could hardly have been expected that the champions of orthodoxy would accept this without challenge. Gardiner felt, as he said to Cranmer five years later, that the Great Bible was "contaminate, sometime . . . with the malice of the translator, . . . sometime by ignorance, and sometime by negligence." He recalled the pains taken to correct it,

> "and how his Highness . . . at a Shrovetide feasted us all, and after dinner told us how gladly he would have that done and how he would be at the cost to have it printed again. Whereupon there was used a marvellous diligence, and at my cost a Bible divided into quires in the Convocation House by your Grace's direction. The faults were found in a marvellous number and very dangerous as cannot be denied." [20]

The whole subject of a Bible translation was, however, taken out of the hands of Convocation as soon as that body set about to produce one. The King, through Cranmer, announced on March 10 that the matter was to be referred to the universities. All the bishops except Cranmer, Goodrich, and Barlow protested against this, saying that the learning of the land was chiefly in Convocation, while the universities were in the hands of young men of immature judgement. Two days later a patent granting the sole right to print the Bible in English during the next four years was given to a London haberdasher, Anthony Marler, who appears to have bought up Grafton's stock of Great Bibles after that printer had been committed to the Fleet for publishing Melancthon's letter against the Six Articles. [21] Mr. Gairdner suggests that the King's announced intention to submit the matter to the universities was merely a pretext to stop the work of Convocation in order to protect vested interests. [22] Certainly we have no record of the universities doing anything about it, or even being asked to.

The version of the Scriptures made by reformers thus remained the authorized version, but the Catholic party succeeded, in the Parliament of 1543, in passing an act forbidding anyone to read or expound the Bible in church or other assembly without permission from the authorities. The upper classes might read it in private, but a month's imprisonment awaited any of "the lower sort" who read it at all. The controversial annotations of the existing editions were to be excised.[23]

Indeed, the year 1543, the year in which the alliance with the Empire was completed, was a period marked by especial efforts to uphold the ancient faith. The observant Chapuys wrote early in April that Parliament seemed bent on the extirpation of heresy, and that

> "the principal man at the head of this reformation, and who is now trying with all his might to bring it on, is the Bishop of Winchester, who happens to be at this moment most in favour with this King, to the great regret, annoyance, and disgust of the Lutherans, and also of the French, who hate him like poison." [24]

From the middle of March to the middle of May the minutes of the Privy Council record unusual activity in connection with religion.[25] Citizens of London who ate flesh in Lent, translators, printers and sellers of unlawful books, "licentious" players, heretics from Calais,[26] heretics from Windsor, rumours of heresy at Canterbury, all came within the purview of the busy Council; and on May 5 "the Book of Religion was read in the Council chamber before the nobility of the realm."

This Book of Religion was none other than *A Necessary Doctrine and Erudition for Any Christian Man*, which came to be known as the *King's Book*, since it was issued by the authority of the King and with a preface written by him. It was an exposition, on the basis of the traditional theology, of the Creed, the seven Sacraments, the Commandments, and the Lord's Prayer. The reformers attributed it to Gardiner. In this they were both right and wrong; wrong if they meant that Gardiner was the author of it in the sense that he was the author of the *Oration on True Obedience*, for large portions of the *King's Book* were taken over without change from the *Bishops' Book*, which had been issued in 1537 while Gardiner was in France; they were right if they meant that he was the dominant member of the committee which prepared the *King's Book*, and that in the composition of some parts of it he undoubtedly had a hand. The chief matters of controversy with the reformers—the Sacrament of the Altar, justification, good works, freedom of the will—are much more fully treated in the *King's Book* than in the earlier formulary, and it is here that we find a close resemblance to Gardiner's theological writings.[27]

It is, said George Joye, in one of his assaults on Gardiner, "a book belike penned by you, for it savoureth everywhere of your damnable doctrine." [28] "The *King's Book* is of your making, as every man can tell that hath heard you preach or hath read your writings," wrote William Turner.[29] Cranmer's secretary, Morice, later told how, when the book was in preparation, "the whole rabblement," whom Cranmer

> "took to be his friends, being commissioners with him, forsook him and his opinion in doctrine, and so, leaving him post alone, revolted alltogethers on the part of Stephen Gardiner." [30]

Early in the next reign Cranmer himself wrote to Gardiner expressing his disapproval of the book and intimating that Gardiner had been responsible for it. We do not have Cranmer's letter, but Gardiner replied:

> "It grieveth me much to read written from your Grace . . . how the King our late Sovereign was seduced, and that he knew by whom he was compassed in that I call the King's Majesty's Book; which is not his book because I call it so, but because it was indeed so acknowledged by the whole Parliament, and acknowledged so by your Grace then and all his life." [31]

Gardiner, despite his own part in the book, was right. It was the King's book; it was also the Parliament's book, and the clergy's book, and the people's book, for it expressed the prevailing theology in England at the time. It represents the most successful attempt in the Reformation age—perhaps in any age—to set forth a doctrinal exposition of anti-Papal Catholicism.

It containeth, said Gardiner four years later, "a true, resolute doctrine, passed by mature deliberation, confirmed by acceptation and use." [32]

It was published May 29, 1543.

Gardiner was not, however, satisfied with the mere publication, official though it was, of an extended instruction on the theology of the Six Articles; he was resolved that this theology should no longer be flouted by those who, through archiepiscopal or royal connection, felt themselves secure in contemning the law of the land. The activities of the Council, already referred to, make this clear. As Foxe put it:

> "The gospellers were so quailed that the best of them all looked every hour to be clapped in the neck; for the saying went abroad that the Bishop [of Winchester] had bent his bow to shoot at some of the head deer." [33]

"The head deer" were to be found in the King's household and the Archbishop's diocese. A fortnight before the *King's Book* was read in the Council Chamber, three gentlemen of the royal house-

hold were committed to the Fleet for maintaining Anthony Peerson,[34]
a preacher of Windsor, whence three other heretics were summoned
for examination at the same time. It was suspected that a group
of gentlemen of the King's Chamber and their ladies were actively
supporting reform propaganda at Windsor.

The evidence for this had, according to Foxe, come to Gardiner
from William Simons, a Windsor lawyer, and Dr. John London,
Warden of New College, Oxford, and, since 1540, a prebendary of
Windsor. London had been active in the suppression of the monasteries, and, it seems, did not hesitate to use the same unscrupulous
methods in gathering evidence against persons suspected of heresy
as he had previously used in securing the surrender of monastic
houses. It does not appear, however, that Gardiner in the first
instance sought out or employed him for this work, but rather that
he, seeing how things were going at court, gathered matter against
the Windsor heretics and brought it to the attention of Gardiner
and the King. After he had thus begun, he was encouraged by
both the King and Gardiner to go further. As a result five men
were apprehended: Peerson the preacher; Bennet, a lawyer; Filmer,
a tailor and one-time church warden; Testwood, a chorister; and
John Marbeck, organist of the Royal Chapel, a composer whose
music is still played in England and America. At least three of
them appear to have had preliminary examinations before the Privy
Council, and some, perhaps all, were further examined by a commission consisting of Bishops Capon, Skip, and Goodrich. Finally,
in July, four of the accused were brought to trial before a jury and
justices at Windsor, convicted of having spoken or written against
the Sacrament of the Altar, and sentenced to death under the Act
of the Six Articles. As soon as Gardiner heard of the sentence,
he secured the pardon of Marbeck, the organist; and, shortly after,
Bennet, who had not been brought to trial because of illness, was
released, as a result, it would seem, of a letter from Bishop Capon to
Gardiner in his behalf. The other three were burned at the stake
July 28, 1543.[35]

After the initial appearance of the Windsor heretics before the
Privy Council, there is no record of Gardiner's having taken part
in the examination of any of them except Marbeck, and from his
dealings with him, of which Marbeck himself wrote an account,
it is clear that his interest in the case arose, not from a desire to
secure the punishment of these lesser men, but from the hope that,
through them, evidence might be secured against the "head deer."
Immediately upon Marbeck's commitment to the Marshalsea, Gardiner sent him a promise of pardon if he would reveal the heretics
with whom he was acquainted; he later questioned him in person
at Winchester House in Southwark about the leaders of the sect,
and permitted his wife to visit him in prison, urging her to counsel

him "to utter such naughty fellows as he knoweth," adding, "I do fancy him for his art, wherein he has pleased me as well as any man." [36] Marbeck steadfastly maintained that he knew of none whom he could accuse, and, as we have seen, secured his pardon nevertheless.

There is a revealing passage in Gardiner's examination of Marbeck. Among the papers discovered at Windsor was a manuscript of the first half of an English concordance to the Bible which Marbeck had been preparing. When this was first seen by the Council, Gardiner explained to the laity present what a concordance was, and that one existed in Latin, adding, with characteristic solicitude for that language, "if such a book should go forth in English it would destroy the Latin tongue." When he talked again with Marbeck he reverted to the concordance, asking:

"What a devil made thee meddle with the Scriptures? Thy vocation was another way, wherein thou hast a goodly gift, if thou didst esteem it. . . . I do not discommend thy diligence, but why shouldest thou meddle with that thing which pertained not to thee?" [37]

Although no one had been implicated by Marbeck, the activity of Dr. London brought to light the heresies of no less than eleven members of the King's household. [38]

Meanwhile the search for heresy went on apace in other quarters. Early in July three adherents of the new doctrines made public recantations at Paul's Cross in London. Two of these, Robert Wisdom and Thomas Becon, were preachers of some note, Becon being likewise a voluminous writer. Both lived to receive preferment under Edward and Elizabeth. According to Wisdom, his recantation, in which he extolled "the most perfect Christian doctrine now set forth by the King's Majesty," and acknowledged that "this is a realm of justice and of no persecution of them that be good," was penned by Gardiner. [39]

London and Windsor were not, however, the only or the chief centres of the new doctrines. It was well known that the Archbishop sympathized with much that continental reformers taught. His chief representative at Canterbury, his Commissary, Dr. Nevinson, openly favoured preachers of the new learning, had invited Anthony Peerson to expound the Bible at Canterbury, and was thought to have exceeded the royal injunctions in the destruction of images. Although Cranmer only succeeded in placing one reformer, Dr. Nicholas Ridley, later bishop and martyr, among the twelve prebendaries of his cathedral, he did secure the King's permission to appoint six cathedral preachers, three of the new learning and three of the old, "that they might between them try out the truth of doctrine." The prebendaries vainly protested that this would cause dissension.

This state of affairs had been known to Gardiner for at least two years. On his return from Ratisbon in 1541 he stopped at Canterbury, as we recall, to hear Mass, after which he spoke to one of the prebendaries, a certain William Gardiner, taking him by the hand and asking "how they did in Canterbury, meaning as to the quietness of Christ's religion." The prebendary replied that sometimes they did not agree in preaching. "So do I hear," replied the Bishop. The prebendary then described the preaching of the most outspoken reformers.

"This is not well," said the Bishop. "My Lord of Canterbury will look upon this, I doubt not, or else such preaching will grow into an evil inconvenience."

"I am much marked in my sermons," said the prebendary, "I pray your good Lordship of your counsel what were best for me to do." The Bishop told him to write his sermon in a book, adding:

> "When you go into the pulpit deliver your book unto the chiefest man there that can read, and let him take heed of your book while you do preach; and say no more but that you have written and studied for, and I warrant you shall do well enough. And when you do hear any man preach otherwise than well, hold you contented and meddle not; so shall you do best." [40]

It had been clear to the Bishop in 1541 that the time was not ripe for meddling in Cranmer's diocese, but in the spring of 1543 the alliance with the Emperor had been concluded, the *King's Book* had been completed, the King himself, as Dr. London put it, "was astonied and wonder angry" at the "abominable heresies" which had been brought to light at Windsor. Accordingly, Dr. London was "set a-work by the King" in the examination of conditions at Canterbury.

Now Prebendary Gardiner and others of the Catholic party at Canterbury had been gathering evidence of heresy in Kent sometime before Dr. London took up the matter, and one of the Canterbury preachers, Robert Serles, met Dr. London in the metropolis and gave him a "book of articles" on Palm Sunday, March 18, 1543. As Serles was out of favour with the Archbishop he did not subscribe the articles himself, lest they should seem to be presented from ill will; but he and Dr. London persuaded Dr. Willoughby, a royal chaplain from Chilham, in Kent, to assume responsibility for them, though Willoughby could testify to nothing except on hearsay. "Then," in the words of Serles, "Dr. London began to pen them very sore to make the matter the more pithy than they were written in mine exemplar." According to Willoughby, Dr. London made additions of his own "to bring the matter into the justices' hand and certain of the spirituality." The articles were then sent to Bishop Gardiner, and Willoughby was sent back to Kent to tell the justices of the peace that it was their duty to inform against heretics. On Easter Eve at Canterbury Willoughby received another set of articles to be delivered to Bishop Gardiner, this time specifically against Cranmer, drawn up by Prebendary Gardiner and a petty canon named Coxon.

On St. George's Day, April 23, Prebendary Gardiner and two other Canterbury clergymen were interviewed in London by Sir John Baker, of the Privy Council, to whom the King had committed the matter. Baker instructed them to revise certain articles and go on gathering information, fearing "no man but God and the King." They then took their revised book of articles to Bishop Gardiner, who, after counselling the omission of certain items for which there was but a single witness, said "it was well enough," and bade them "go again to Mr. Baker, and tell him that he said so." Still another set of articles, drawn up by Canon Coxon, containing many items "not perfectly proved" was submitted to Bishop Gardiner in the latter part of May, but he sent it back "because it was unperfect."

It appears that while the Bishop sought to exclude charges not based on sufficient or reliable evidence, Dr. London, on the contrary, tried to make legal accusations out of every morsel of hearsay. As Shether, one of the Canterbury preachers, said, "he showed me the manner of making his book, which was a great thing, and had articles I had not before heard of." But however much Dr. London may have garnished the evidence, it is indubitable, from the long and exhaustive records we have of the subsequent examinations at Canterbury, that preaching contrary to established doctrines had received official encouragement in the primate's see.[41]

As early as May 4, 1543, the Privy Council had gone on record that a commission, to be appointed by the King, ought to be sent into Kent to examine "all abuses and enormities of religion." That such a commission was not sent at the time was doubtless due to the fact that all the charges against Cranmer and his Canterbury officials were not yet in Gardiner's hands. When, in the course of the following months, the case against the Archbishop was completed, it only remained for Henry to name a commission with Gardiner at the head, to insure the conservative triumph.

XVI

BOULOGNE

"My Lord of Canterbury is too old a truant for us twain!" exclaimed Henry when he and Gardiner had together been defending against Cranmer the proposition that the Canons of the Apostles were of as good authority as the four Evangelists.[1]

In the summer of 1543 it was the King who proved himself too old a truant for Gardiner. When all the accusations against Cranmer were in his hands, Henry, to the amazement of every one, turned them over to Cranmer himself and committed the investigation of them to him and such as he should appoint.[2]

No matter how desirable it was to uphold the faith, Henry could not afford to sacrifice a prelate of Cranmer's learning and piety, whose convictions concerning the royal supremacy so sincerely coincided with his own. Moreover, Cranmer was one of the few men, if not the only one, for whom Henry harboured a genuine and lasting affection.

The natural result of the King's unexpected action was, as Morice says, that "everyone that had meddled in those detections shrunk back and gave over their hold." Gardiner was disgusted at the way in which the Catholic preachers at Canterbury backed down before Cranmer's examiners. He said to Shether's servant: "Your master seemeth to be a child. He wept before my lords when he should have answered. Bid him not weep for shame, but answer like a man." And when the servant told "how men were handled for setting forth of the truth," Gardiner answered: "My Lord of Canterbury cannot kill them, let them suffer; for all this makes against himself. Ye shall see what will come of it. Bid them be merry."[3]

Gardiner was, evidently, pretty sure of his case even under Cranmer's examiners.[4] Indeed the examination went on for some six weeks, and in spite of the prebendaries' attempts each to escape responsibility for the beginning of their movement, there was much straightforward testimony which was anything but favourable to Cranmer and his preachers. Then Dr. Thomas Legh, a one-time monastic visitor like Dr. London, and no whit more scrupulous, was sent down to Canterbury on Cranmer's behalf, and by his summary methods "all the confederacy was utterly known and disclosed."[5] Thus was the attempt of the conservatives to check the spread of the new doctrines turned into a "plot" against the Archbishop. The plotters, however, were treated leniently. A few of the cathedral clergy suffered temporary durance, but a general pardon was soon granted them, and no one appears to have lost any preferment.

Meanwhile the credit of Dr. London and Simons, the Windsor lawyer, had been shaken, and they were adjudged perjurers, on exactly what counts we do not know, but apparently in connection with the accusations of heresy brought against the gentlemen of the King's household. These gentlemen, warned of their danger by one of the Queen's men who had been in Windsor during the trial of the heretics, succeeded in intercepting the clerk of the court who was bearing indictments against them to Gardiner. They immediately laid their case before the King, who "of his special goodness" gave them "his gracious pardon." [6]

In the next session of Parliament, which began in January 1544, the Act of the Six Articles was so amended that while hitherto only two witnesses were required for a prosecution, now no one could be arraigned except on the oath of twelve accusers.

The "head deer" had not only escaped, they had slackened if not snapped Winchester's bow string. Having done so, they planned a counter attack. On March 7, 1544 Germain Gardiner, secretary to the Bishop and for many years a member of his household, was executed, with five others, for denying the royal supremacy.[7] The "head deer" then endeavoured to persuade the King to have the Bishop sent to the Tower and there examined concerning his relations with his secretary;[8] but the Bishop, in the phrase of Foxe, conducted himself "in such sort that (I cannot tell how) he still kept in with the King."[9] If Henry could not afford to abandon Cranmer, no more could he dispense with Gardiner. Now that he was about to embark on a joint enterprise with the Emperor, a bishop who combined in his person unquestioned orthodoxy and unrivalled knowledge of continental diplomacy was more necessary to him than ever.

Before England could give its attention to this joint enterprise, Scotland again proved troublesome. On December 11, 1543 the Scotch Parliament declared the peace with England at an end and renewed the French alliance. Henry's capable brother-in-law, Edward Seymour, Earl of Hertford, was put in command of the army against Scotland, and Gardiner was made Purveyor (or, in modern phrase, Quartermaster) General, an office which he had held in the Scotch campaign of 1542 and in which he continued throughout the wars with Scotland and France, which occupied much of the remaining years of the reign. Everything from the tonnage of transports to the price of biscuits and beer came under his scrutiny. In 1547 he observed with some merriment that for the past five years he had been "a continual purveyor of cheese, butter, herrings, and stockfish." [10] "Stephen Stockfish" he was nicknamed by his enemies,[11] one of whom sarcastically scored his many non-episcopal activities, saying, "Ye will teach Cambridge men to pronounce Greek, brewers to make beer, tailors to make garments, cooks to dress meat." [12]

After Hertford had thoroughly crippled the Scots by the burning of Edinburgh and Leith in May 1544, the energies of England were turned to the expedition to France which the King was to lead in person. For this venture Gardiner was expected to supply 100 horsemen, 200 foot soldiers, and £1,000 as a "loan" to the King.[13] He had not accompanied the army to Scotland, but he crossed from Dover to Calais July 2, one day ahead of Suffolk, and two weeks ahead of the King, in order that they, at their coming, might "find things the more ripe." [14] Norfolk was already besieging Montreuil and Suffolk proceeded to invest Boulogne. Henry crossed the Channel, July 14. Just two months later, September 14, 1544, Boulogne surrendered.

Five days before this, ambassadors from Francis I arrived at Hardelot and began negotiations for peace with an English commission led by Gardiner, who on one occasion so triumphantly outargued Jean du Bellay, Cardinal Archbishop of Paris, that the latter lost his temper and became abusive. Nothing was concluded, and the Frenchmen departed September 25.[15] On the 30th Henry embarked for England, leaving Norfolk, Suffolk, Gardiner, and some others of the Council at Boulogne.[16] Meanwhile the Emperor had advanced on the way to Paris as far as Chateau Thierry, but, seeing that no help was to be expected from Henry, made peace with France at Crespy, September 18, 1544. In a moment of overconfidence at Boulogne Henry had told the Imperial envoy that he had no objection to Charles making a separate peace.[17]

At the Emperor's instance France renewed negotiations with England early in October, and Henry commissioned Gardiner and four other councillors to treat with both the French and Imperial ambassadors at Calais.[18] The English demands, that France give up her alliance with Scotland and acquiesce in the English possession of Boulogne, were flatly refused as intolerable. The English commissioners then advised a special mission to the Emperor at Brussels to induce him to put pressure on the French. Henry thought the advice good, and appointed for this mission Hertford and Gardiner, who had expressed his willingness to undertake it. They rode post, reaching Brussels October 26, within sixty hours after leaving Calais.[19]

Charles received them most cordially, "being," as Gardiner said, "very diligent, at every time we put off our caps, to cause us to put on the same again." They tried to persuade him that according to his treaty with Henry he was now bound to declare France again his enemy, since France had refused the English demands and continued the war. Charles professed every intention of fulfilling his obligations, but left to his counsellors the question of how the treaty bound him to act. Then began a series of lengthy discussions with Granvelle and others, and occasional conferences with Charles him-self, who was suffering severely from gout, "his legs wrapped in a black cloth and laid forth as high as his body."

Gardiner reported the proceedings in great detail to Henry, admitting, after three weeks in Brussels, that his letters were "of many words and small purpose," yet adding that "undoubtedly" the Emperor and his advisers "be greatly troubled with our matter, and by all likelihood would be clearly rid of it."

Charles finally repeated his promise to observe his treaty "in every point," but asked that he be not pressed to take any definite action for the next ten weeks, manifestly hoping that matters would right themselves without his having to act at all; he showed, however, a genuine desire to retain the friendship of Henry. Being able to secure no more favourable answer, Hertford and Gardiner left Brussels November 22, 1544, and returned to England.[20]

Charles thereupon sent two ambassadors to explain his position to Henry, who appointed Hertford, Gardiner, and Paget to confer with them.[21] The ten weeks elapsed and the situation remained unchanged; ambassadors, councillors, and monarchs argued the matter in England and the Empire for another year, while England continued at war with France and Scotland.

The holding of Boulogne was a costly enterprise, and many and devious were the ways used to fill the empty coffers of the King— loans from the Fuggers, a new benevolence, a new subsidy, the dissolution of chantries and hospitals, the rigorous exaction of old debts due the crown, and the debasement of the currency. Gardiner sat on several commissions for the ingathering of these moneys,[22] but there is no evidence that he was responsible for the policy of debasing the coinage, although Ponet later charged him with it.[23]

To offset the scarcity of provisions caused by the war, Gardiner, by virtue of his position as Purveyor General, appears to have instituted both meatless and wineless days, for in a letter to Hertford in the beginning of Edward's reign he recalled his war-time measures, saying, "When I was purveyor for the seas, what an exclamation was there, as your Grace showed me, of the bishops' fasting-day as they called Wednesday," and he went on to cite a popular ballad whose burden was:

"Winchester, Winchester, grand mercy for your wine;
I beshrew your heart for your water!"[24]

In the Summer of 1545 Francis I expressed his willingness to treat with Henry through the mediation of the German Protestants, but nothing was accomplished by the German envoys who came to England for this purpose. One of them, Sleidan, the celebrated historian of the Reformation, tried in vain to convince Gardiner that the Protestant cause was justified because of the Emperor's inability to crush it.[25]

Charles had no desire to see England, France, and his own Protestant subjects become too intimate. Hence he himself undertook the rôle of mediator and induced Francis I to promise to send the Admiral of France to the Imperial court in Flanders, and suggested that Henry send a person of like dignity to confer with him. On October 15, 1545 Henry announced Gardiner's appointment to this mission, and instructed him not only to treat for peace with France, but also to secure such a renovation of the existing treaty with the Empire that its interpretation could no longer be a matter of dispute. He was to be assisted by his old friend Thirlby, resident ambassador with the Emperor, and Sir Edward Carne, ambassador to Flanders.[26]

The leisurely journey of three weeks, from October 18, the day he left London, until his "familiar and gentle" reception by the Emperor at Bruges, November 4,[27] was, despite some illness, employed in literary composition of which we shall speak in a subsequent chapter.[28]

Soon after his arrival at the Imperial court, he heard from Paget that French ambassadors were also to go to Calais to treat there for peace with England, again through the mediation of the German Protestants, and that Paget himself was likely to be sent thither to meet them.[29] "God send us a good end of our Protestants!" replied Gardiner. He would thank them, he said, if they brought peace, but it would be an evil thing if they only succeeded in defaming England, as a nation which agreed with their opinions. Their defiance of their sovereign, the Emperor, showed how they regarded obedience to princes.

> "I never saw that the King's Highness of himself had any affection to them, but hath ever wisely weighed and considered the natures of them, and understandeth them as right as any man could describe them. His Highness, sometime of necessity, sometime of policy, hath wisely used them, and sometime I know hath been informed and told many greater things of them than have followed."

> "They trouble the world as promoters of God's quarrel. . . . They cannot continue ne prosper, but wrangle to trouble themself and other."

If they become mediators between princes,

> "then they begin to join worldly authority to their gospel and play the Bishop of Rome's part; which, if they do as faithfully

as he did, by bearing in hand, then hath they his office upsy down." [30]

On November 10 Gardiner had his first conference with the representatives of France—d'Annebaut the Admiral, Olivier the Chancellor, and Bayard, Secretary of State. The next day he sent an eighteen-page report of it to the King,[31] and a shorter letter to Paget. In the latter, dated 4 P. M., he said that except for a little sleep he had "not ceased talking and writing since yesterday three of the clock," and was "yet fasting." He was pleased with himself that he had not lost his temper with the French Chancellor.

> "I knew him sometime for a Lutheran," he wrote, "and was well acquainted with him in France, and now and then disputed together, and if I had fallen out with him now he would have said it had been for that. But how constantly he affirmed a lie for a true tale, and how fain I would [have] talked with him as I have done, upon like occasion, with the Cardinal of Bellaye! But I refrained and ever avoided the giving check, and gave only a bare mate without any check; wherein I pleased myself, and the Emperor's Council marvelled. . . ."

He had a better opinion of Bayard, recognizing in him qualities like his own. Indeed his picture of him might well do for a self-portrait:

> "He is very wise, very sober. . . . He is choleric and in his anger . . . very stout . . . but I think they have no man can speak more ne better in their affairs than he can."
> "Because I spake to them plainly I was noted an enemy. . . . Bayard said he loved me the better for my plainness, for he said that was his nature. . . ." [32]

The French demanded the immediate restitution of Boulogne and the comprehension of the Scots in the peace, nor would they listen to any of the compromises suggested by the Emperor's counsellors. They did indeed offer money compensation for Boulogne, but since France, with treasury depleted, was already, under former treaty arrangements, in England's debt to the amount of 450,000 crowns, to say nothing of at least a million more due on arrearages of a pension to Henry VIII, such an offer was little more than a mockery. The situation looked black to Gardiner. Peace at almost any price, he felt, was necessary for England at the moment,

> "for unless we have a good companion in war it will be from henceforth very fashious; and whose company were worth the war I know not. Trust is sore decayed in the world." [33]

But such a peace as France offered would, he knew, be a blow to Henry's pride from which, in his present precarious state of health,

he might not recover. Then England would be open to the still
greater dangers of a child king. Everything, he wrote to Paget, must
be done to preserve Henry's repose of mind, for "prorogation of his
life till my Lord Prince may come to man's estate." He had written,
he said, vehemently for peace, noting that the worst peace was better
than the best war, yet he would rather be killed in war than die
languishing under so ill-favoured a peace as the French proposed.
He was so perplexed by the situation that when Henry expressed
a willingness to leave things to his discretion, saying, in the language
of the hunt, that he durst let him slip, Gardiner exclaimed, "I stand
amazed after which deer to run," and asked for absolute
instructions.[34]

Yet he could not help thinking that it would be best to give up
Boulogne if any reasonable terms could be secured.

> "Boulogne," he wrote, "in process may be lost many ways;
> the name, fame, honour, and renown gotten by it can never
> decay. . . . They say an Englishman in all feats excelleth,
> if he could leave when it is well." [35]
>
> "There was a good fellow in Cambridge, well learned, that
> for his pleasure maintained in communication this paradox, that
> increase of worldly things make men poor and not rich, be-
> cause every worldly thing hath a need annexed to it."

He had, he said, discovered the truth of this himself after he received the bishopric of Winchester, so that he could write, "as
they do upon medicines, *Probatum est*," and added that if some in
England read this they might say that it was well to make bishops
rich! Boulogne, he concluded, was such a worldly thing, and the
keeping of it like to make England poor.[36]

The French refused all compromises, and, on November 25, departed from Antwerp, whither the court had moved.[37] The situation was not, however, so desperate for England as the failure to
make peace with France might indicate. Although Charles was unwilling to re-enter the war against France in England's behalf, he
had no wish to lose England's friendship; so Gardiner remained at
the Imperial court at Antwerp until the end of November, then
at Utrecht, whither he arrived after a difficult journey over winter
roads on December 10.[38] After much discussion with Charles and
his ministers, an agreement was reached January 16, 1546, clearing
up ambiguities in the treaty of 1543, and defining more precisely the
conditions under which mutual assistance was to be given. The
ratifications of this Treaty of Utrecht by the two monarchs were
exchanged by Gardiner and Scepperus, one of the Imperial counsellors, on February 13, at Bois-le-Duc in Brabant.[39]

On Sunday morning, March 21, Gardiner arrived once more in
London, and was immediately received by the King who had just

recovered from a three weeks' illness which, from the traces left upon his face, appeared to have been more severe than he admitted. Gardiner went on to Greenwich the same day and resumed attendance at the Privy Council.[40]

We have over sixty letters, many of great length, written by Gardiner during this mission.[41] Those to the King were usually sent in the names of both himself and his colleagues, and contain matter-of-fact accounts of negotiations; those to Paget, from a few of which we have quoted, are enlivened by observations upon situations and men, and were doubtless sent with the knowledge that the King would see them, for Gardiner well knew Henry's interest in the human side of diplomacy. "I was wont to write to our late Sovereign Lord," he said after Henry's death, "when I was ambassador, refreshing myself sometimes with a merry tale in a sad matter."[42]

Among the letters to Paget there is one long one entirely devoted to an account of the meetings of the Order of the Golden Fleece at New Year's time 1546 in Utrecht. It reveals the Bishop's delight in pageantry, as well as an interest in ceremonies which, as Prelate of the Order of the Garter (a title held by virtue of his bishopric), he might naturally be expected to show. He tells how the church was "magnifiquely garnished" with rich arras, how the arms of the knights were hung in the choir and their stalls decked with crimson, "a very gorgeous show to the eye." He describes the Emperor and his companions "all apparelled in crimson velvet, both kirtles and robes, with hoods of the same, as the knights of the Garter have." On the third day of the feast they came in black, to mourn departed members, and on the fourth "all in white damask, with their garments girt, and their hoods of crimson velvet on their heads, which was a very good sight." The Mass for the departed impressed him. Fifty candles were lighted on the high altar, one for each member of the order, and when the herald came to the name of one who had died during the past year, he added *"Il est morte,"* and the pursuivant blew out a candle.

> "The lamentable words, *'Il est morte,'* with the putting out of the candle, was a good representation of our estate, how weak it is indeed."
>
> "And I may say a circumstance also, for there was experimented the conclusion that want of measure destroyeth the effect, for when he blew too much the candle went not out."
>
> "If ye know any," he concludes, "that loveth no ceremonies, give him this letter to read for special news!"[43]

Within a month after Gardiner's return, negotiations were reopened with France, this time without the mediation of either the Emperor or the Protestant princes. Paget and John Dudley, who had succeeded to the title of his stepfather, Gardiner's old friend, Lord Lisle, were the chief English negotiators.[44]   There were many anxious moments before peace was concluded, and on the very eve of the final agreement the outlook was so dubious that Gardiner and his friend Sir Anthony Browne were dispatched to the Continent to confer with Hertford on the defense of Boulogne, should the parleys come to nothing; but on June 7, the very day they sent home their recommendations for new fortifications, the treaty was signed.   France agreed to pay England two million crowns by 1554, and England was to retain Boulogne until the payment was completed.   Gardiner and Brown returned immediately thereafter.[45]

The increasing prominence at this time of Hertford, uncle of Prince Edward, is worthy of note.   His activities, however, were still chiefly military; the conduct of civil and diplomatic business remained in the hands of Gardiner and his two protégés and one-time scholars, Paget and Wriothesley.   Paget had been one of the Principal Secretaries since 1543, and Wriothesley, Lord Chancellor since 1544.   In the summer of 1545 the Imperial ambassadors said unhesitatingly that Gardiner and Paget were "the King's most influential ministers," and a year later named them and Wriothesley as the leaders of the Council.[46]

XVII

GREEK AT CAMBRIDGE

When, in October 1545, Gardiner passed through Canterbury on the first stage of his journey to the Imperial court, the Mayor and aldermen made complaint to him of the recent misconduct of a band of soldiers on their way to Boulogne. One of the aldermen remarked that some of these disorderly warriors were so clever at stealing they must surely have been "scholars of Cambridge," at which the Bishop could not repress a smile to think how, unawares, the alderman touched him as Chancellor of that university.[1]

He had been elected Chancellor to succeed Cromwell on the latter's fall in 1540,[2] and one of his first official acts had been the appointment of Norfolk as Steward of the university.[3]

His next activity as Chancellor, of which we have record, was in 1542, when, from May to October, he carried on, in occasional letters, a discussion about the pronunciation of Greek with two of the younger teachers at Cambridge—John Cheke, afterward tutor to Prince Edward and Secretary of State in his reign, and Thomas Smith, Secretary of State and Privy Councillor in the reigns of both Edward and Elizabeth.

The men of the Renaissance had learned Greek from Byzantine Greeks who pronounced their language as do Greeks today. Early in the sixteenth century certain scholars began to doubt whether this pronunciation was that of the ancients, for in contemporary Greek several vowels and diphthongs were given the same sound, that of the Italian *i*. Erasmus, in 1528, published a dialogue setting forth what he believed to have been the ancient pronunciation, although he seems to have continued to use the current pronunciation himself. About 1535 his theories began to be practised at Cambridge by Smith and Cheke, then at the ages of twenty-two and twenty-one respectively. Smith was, at the time, lecturing on Greek, and sought occasionally and somewhat furtively to accustom his hearers to the new, or, as he believed it, the ancient pronunciation. He went abroad in 1540 to study Civil Law, and the newly founded Regius Professorship of Greek was given to Cheke, to whose enthusiasm Roger Ascham, then a fellow of Cheke's college, St. John's, attributed the unprecedented ardour for classical studies at the university. Smith returned late in 1541 or early in 1542 as Regius Professor of Civil Law, and supported Cheke in his efforts to spread the new ideas about Greek.

When Gardiner learned of this movement he wrote to Cheke, asking him not to insist on introducing his theories. Gardiner admitted that the modern pronunciation doubtless differed from the ancient, but said that it was sheer arrogance to assume such a knowledge of the ancient manner of speech as to warrant setting up an authoritative standard for it. Moreover, it would encourage presumption and insubordination on the part of the younger scholars to the older. This he followed by an edict on May 15, 1542, upholding the modern pronunciation and providing that members of the university senate who used Cheke's method were to be excluded from that body, candidates for degrees who did so were not to be graduated, refractory scholars were to forfeit the advantages of their scholarships, and other undergraduates were to be birched. Both Cheke and Smith protested against this ruling in lengthy Latin treatises, and the Bishop replied in Latin letters of no small compass. He maintained that usage was the best guide to pronunciation, and that a pronunciation peculiar to Cambridge would isolate that university from the Greek-speaking scholars of Christendom. He did not say that the modern pronunciation should be used because it was right, but because it was used it was right to use it. His main contention, however, was—characteristically—that novelty and innovation on the part of young teachers fostered rashness and vanity in the youth whom they taught.

The question of Greek pronunciation has exercised the abilities of philologists from that day to this. Although the majority of modern scholars, other than the Greeks themselves, appear to favour a reconstructed ancient pronunciation, scholars in the sixteenth century of no less repute than Reuchlin, Melancthon, and Dr. Caius used the current pronunciation, which had the manifest advantage of enabling them to speak a living language to living men. Smith admitted that the one Greek he had met was unable to understand his Greek conversation and told him in French that Erasmus was an ass for introducing the new method.

Roger Ascham humorously remarked that after Gardiner's decree all the Greek vowels were said in such a slender fashion that they sounded like the peeping of a sparrow or the hissing of a snake. His statement that the decree almost extinguished all zeal for classical learning at Cambridge can hardly be taken seriously, for in the same letter in which he said this he also told of the interest and ardour with which Greek and Latin authors were being studied. He lamented the decree the more, he said, since one so famous for prudence and wisdom as Gardiner had issued it.

Sometime during the controversy Smith discussed the matter in person with Gardiner, an occasion which he recalls in his defense of the new pronunciation addressed to the Bishop. His words must contain some measure of truth despite their freight of compliment.

"Great was the pleasure," he says, "I took in your discourse with me when I was the other day at Hampton Court to wait upon you. . . . For that which I had before learned by fame only and hearsay of your wisdom, being then present I understood by experience; and that your Lordship was endued not only with very great skill and insight in the weighty affairs of State, but also in these light and literary controversies with an incredible sharpness, and an excellent facility and plenty, joined with a wonderful obligingness while you are disputing and arguing." [4]

That Gardiner's decree was not fully obeyed appears from references to it in his subsequent correspondence with the university about other matters. On May 15, 1543 he had occasion to instruct Dr. Edmonds, the Vice-Chancellor, to punish members of the university who had "very dissolutely used themselves in eating flesh" in Lent. He counselled moderation in dealing with offenders, suggesting that they be spoken to privately and made to pay a fine, "without further publishing of their names," but if they remained obdurate he would insist on a public examination.

"I will not suffer the university," he said, "with these dissolute manners to be corrupt. Lands have not been given, ne lectures founded for any such evil purposes."

At the same time he reminded the Vice-Chancellor of the order he had given concerning Greek, saying, "I did it seriously and will maintain it."

"The King's Majesty," he added, "hath, by the inspiration of the Holy Ghost, composed all matters of religion; which uniformity I pray God it may in that and in all other things extend unto us. . . . But I will withstand fancies even in pronunciation and fight with the enemy of quiet at the first entry." [5]

In Lent 1545 he again found it needful to fight with the enemy of quiet, this time in the shape of a play called *Pammachius* which had been acted in Christ's College, and which, according to reports he had received, was "so pestiferous as were intolerable." This was a Latin tragedy written by Thomas Kirchmeyer, a German Calvinist, in which Pammachius, an imaginary Pope of the fourth century, transfers his allegiance from Christ to Satan, deposes the Roman Emperor, and finally comes into conflict with St. Paul, who revisits the earth. The subject gave wide scope for invective against Catholic practises, including, of course, those still retained in England.[6]

Gardiner wrote to Matthew Parker, who had been elected Vice-

Chancellor early in the year, to examine carefully into the matter, saying:

> "If I could have leisure to come myself I would not spare to come thither for this purpose. . . . As wild wanton liberty sometime bresteth out in youth to their reproach, so let soberness and gravity appear in us requisite for the execution of our charge. . . . If learning should now be an instrument to stir up dissention and trouble the common quietness, their opinion should be confirmed which not many years past have laboured to prove in books, printed in English, that the universities be the corruption of the realm. Oxford liveth quietly with fewer priveleges than we have; there be that would we had as few as they."

He looked on the affair, he said, as a breach of obedience to the King and treated it as such, not touching the truth or falsity of the views expressed in the play, "because the capacity of the offenders seemeth to stretch no farther; and he that regardeth not his obedience to his prince regardeth not much his obedience to God."

Parker sent a copy of the play to Gardiner who found in it "so many abominable and detestable lies. . . . as no Christian ears should patiently hear," and forthwith procured an order from the Privy Council that "no such matter either in play or earnest . . . be moved or meddled with." Those who took part in it were to be admonished "to employ their wits and studies in knowledge that is good, true, and wholesome," and all were to "practise rest and quietness."

In this correspondence with Parker, Gardiner again referred to his edict on Greek pronunciation, saying that he heard it was not obeyed, and directing Parker to enforce it.

> "I was chosen Chancellor," he says, "to be so honoured (although above my deserts) . . . and I have given no cause to be despised. I will do that I can for the maintenance of virtue and good order there, and challenge again, of duty, to be regarded after the proportion, not of my qualities, but mine office." [7]

Cheke's method prevailed in Edward's reign, and although Gardiner renewed his prohibition of it under Mary,[8] Cheke's followers in subsequent times carried on his ideas, which by some process of degeneration resulted in the nineteenth century English academic pronunciation—utterly unlike anything ever spoken by any Greek, ancient or modern.

XVIII

THE DEVIL'S SOPHISTRY

During the years from 1543 to 1546 while, as Henry's chief counsellor, Gardiner was busied with finances, wars, and diplomacy, he found time to write and publish five books of theological controversy—two slender volumes in Latin against Bucer, one in English against William Turner, another against George Joye, and a third against the devil!

His discussion with Bucer at Ratisbon in 1541 had been continued in subsequent correspondence;[1] and in 1544 Bucer, in a published debate on theology with Bartholomäus Latomus, a Catholic counsellor of Trier, gratuitously brought Gardiner's name into the discussion and so quoted, or, as Gardiner maintained, misquoted him on the use of a passage in St. Paul on celibacy (I Cor. vii. 36-38), as to draw forth his "Complaint against Bucer for his shameless mendacity" (*ad Martinum Bucerum De Impudente eiusdem Pseudologia Conquestio*). This was written and published in the summer of 1544. On Bucer's failure to reply, Gardiner republished it in 1545, and on December 12 of the same year dated the completion of a second book against him (*ad Martinum Bucerum Epistola*), published 1546, challenging him to answer. In this he not only defended the traditional position against clerical marriage but went on to speak briefly of the Sacrament of the Altar, free will, and justification. He voiced contempt for Bucer's learning and called him, in the plainest possible Latin, a liar. Paget, though approving the substance of the book, expressed his regret that Gardiner had not "contained himself a *maladicentia*."[2] Gardiner admitted that he wrote sharply, but said that Bucer was so thick-skinned that the only way to make any impression upon him was to smite vehemently.[3] Bucer did not reply until 1548, when Gardiner wrote an immediate rejoinder.[4] But this is taking us ahead of our story.

In the years when Gardiner was disputing with, and writing his early books against, Bucer, he was, as leader of the conservative reaction, the butt of literary libels in England. The Act of the Six Articles, in its stern insistence upon clerical celibacy, had called forth, in 1541, *The defence of the Marriage of Priests, against Steven Gardiner, Bishop of Winchester, William Repps, Bishop of Norwich, and against all the bishops and priests of that false popish sect,* by a certain James Sawtry, who roundly denounced "these venomous, virulent vipers, Winchester with his advouterous [*i.e.* adulterous] generation." Winchester made no reply. Two years later, in 1543, William Turner, botanist, physician, and reformer of extreme Puritan type, published, under the pseudonym of William Wraghton, a spirited attack on the whole Henrician establishment, entitled: *The hunting and finding out of the Romish fox, which more than seven years hath been hid among the bishops of England.* He assailed images, holy water, communion in one kind, prayers to saints, lent, clerical celibacy, the Canon Law, services in Latin, "vestments and copes, incense and altars, organs and descant in the church." His line of attack—a favourite one with later Puritans—was that, since these things had been originated or enjoined or sanctioned or used by the Popes, they were of the devil. The Canon Law was the Pope's law, the Church's services were the Pope's ceremonies, the teachings of the Church were the Pope's doctrines, Latin was the Pope's mother tongue. And chief among the bishops who were the secret servants of the Papacy was Gardiner, "the noble waterer of the Pope's garden," the "lying limb of the devil."

This drew a reply from the Bishop, called *The Examination of the Hunter,* of which no copy appears now to exist, but of which considerable portions are quoted in another book of Turner's in answer to it.

No man of sense, said Gardiner, ever supposed

"that all that which was taught either by the Bishop of Rome or under his authority was his own doctrine and to be cast away."

That which was good was

"to be retained and kept, not because it was his, but because it was good. Shall we not confess Christ the Son of God because the devil said the same?"

Turner was like that factious Florentine who, when asked for his opinion on a matter under discussion,

"looked about and, espying out one of his enemies, said, whatsoever such a man would say, pointing to his enemy, he was of the contrary opinion."

"The King's Majesty . . . hath rejected the Bishop of Rome so far as he swerveth from the truth. And, so far as the truth will bear, his Majesty agreeth with all the world."

It was almost in the terms of modern psychology that the Bishop defended the practices of the Church:

"These men," he said, referring to the reformers, "speak much of preaching; but note well this, they would we should see nothing in remembrance of Christ, and therefore can they not abide images. They would we should smell nothing in memory of Christ, and therefore speak they against anointing and holy water. They would we should taste nothing in memory of Christ, and therefore they cannot away with salt and holy bread. . . . Finally they would have all in talking they speak so much of preaching, so as all the gates of our senses and ways to man's understanding should be shut up saving the ear alone."

The Bishop went on to answer Turner in detail, but by the time he reached the latter part of his book he lost patience with what he deemed Turner's presumption.

"Who," he asked, "shall answer him that thinketh no man hath wit but himself, . . . as this proud, arrogant, presumptious fool doth in this little book." [5]

Turner replied in *The second course of the hunter at the Romish fox and his advocate and sworn patron, Steven Gardiner, doctor and defender of the Pope's Canon Law and his ungodly ceremonies.* This failed to draw fire from the Bishop who "contemned," as he said, "the jolly hunter and other janglers, wisely in my friends opinions." [6]

While Turner was assailing the ecclesiastical establishment, Henry Brinklow, ex-friar and mercer of London, was impugning Henry's entire political and economic régime, under the pseudonym of Roderick Mors. Enclosures, exorbitant rents, misuse of monastic property, delays of the law, maltreatment of prisoners, the corruption of Parliament, as well as the sins of bishops and clergy, came within his view; and, like Turner, he singled out the Bishop of Winchester as the chief obstacle to "godly redress." [7]

In November 1545 Gardiner, at Bruges, received from Paget a copy of one of Mors' books. "How many books and scrolls have been cast abroad in London within this year and the offender never found out!" exclaimed the Bishop, and this one he pronounced a "most abominable book," tending to bring the King and his government into contempt; but he followed Paget's advice and took no further notice of it. The author, he supposed, was George Joye, because Mors everywhere printed the word "Joy" with a capital letter. He expressed regret that "a knave lurking in a corner, as Joye doth at Antwerp" should be permitted to trouble the realm thus, and, if he may believe Joye, sought his apprehension, but without success. [8]

In supposing Joye to be the author of Mors' *Lamentation* Gardiner was mistaken, but Joye had, in 1543, published under his own name an abusive attack on Gardiner, charging him with Barnes' death and seeking to refute certain doctrinal statements which Gardiner had explained to Barnes when the latter "had gone to school" to him in 1540.

On November 5, 1545 Gardiner wrote from the Imperial court at Bruges to Paget that he had completed a reply to this book by Joye.

> "Although," he said, "I go not about to prove myself a saint, for I have made no such outward visage of hypocrisy, yet it shall appear I am not utterly a devil, and if I be a devil I am not of that kind of devils that he noteth me of . . . I never wrote so much in a month as I have done in this; and I look so lustily, thanks be to God, that I talk shamefastly of any sickness by the way. God make all that be sick, either in body or soul, whole." [9]

This reply to Joye, published before Easter 1546, as *A Declaration of such true articles as George Joye hath gone about to confute as false,* is peculiarly important in a study of Gardiner; first, because it contains more autobiographical matter than any other of his books, a preface of thirty-five pages being devoted to an account of his dealings with Barnes; and second, because it gives us a summary of Gardiner's views on three of the principal questions in controversy at the Reformation—predestination, the right of private judgement, especially in the interpretation of Scripture, and justification by faith.

Much of the autobiographical preface has already been quoted. A few paragraphs from the remainder of the volume may help us to understand Gardiner's theological position.

The emphasis on predestination by the new teachers, he said, resulted in the belief "that men be saved by predestination," and this, in his view, was but the natural outcome of their doctrines, for

> "When men have so long striven to attain knowledge of the truth, and babbled of faith and works without attaining either of both, then as men do that be weary of all together, they resort to the idle reasoning, as the Greeks call it: 'that shall be, shall be,' and 'as God hath appointed so must it be,' and 'God knoweth who be his, and he will lose none of them.' "
>
> "They will ask me, 'Thou papish bishop and foolish lawyer, dost thou deny predestination?' "
>
> "I acknowledge God's predestination, as whereof I am most certainly assured by Scripture;" but "the holy men of our religion, such as have travailed in the expounding of Scripture, do specially note that no Scripture may be thought right unstanded whereby to take away man's free choice, and thereby to confirm compulsion or absolute necessity."

Predestination, said Gardiner, is "God's high secrecy," and yet these new preachers profess to know all about it. It was an unsolved mystery even to St. Paul, as is shown by his perplexity over the fate of the Jews, yet St. Paul concluded that if the Jews were rejected by God it was their own fault. Much of the difficulty seemed to Gardiner to arise from the inadequacy of human speech, and he quoted with approval the Greek philosopher who said,

"It is hard to know God throughly, but impossible to express God in language."

"We ought," he continued, "not be ashamed to learn and confess ignorance in these high mysteries, wherein an arrogant, proud, curious wit should clearly be put to silence; and yet nevertheless a sober, humble spirit by a devout search and consideration may learn somewhat."

"It is a more shame, confusion, and rebuke to us to be noted in an error of blustering knowledge than to be accompted in the number of simple ignorants."

He concluded that no matter what predestination is, we may with surety say

"to any man particularly, Thou mayest be damned by thine own sin, and likewise to every particular man, Thou mayest be saved by God's mercy."

Some men, he observed, do "not fear to say of God blasphemously that he is the author of evil," to which he replied,

"God is the superior cause without which nothing worketh,
. . . but man's free choice and the devil add the mischief to every act where any is."

The errors of the new preachers seemed to him to arise from their misuse of Scripture. They ignored the texts which made against their doctrines and stressed those which they thought supported them, and these they interpreted as they liked, without regard to the traditions of the Church. "There was never heretic," he exclaimed, "but boasted Scripture."

"Scripture is a sweet pure flower whereof spiders gather poison and bees honey. . . . Go thither instructed with wholesome doctrine and there thou shalt see it confirmed. Go thither infect with malicious opinions and there thou shalt writhe out matter wherewith to maintain them."

He made this straightforward confession about his own use of the Bible:

"I protest openly and take God to record that I never yet durst be so bold to gather any sense of Scripture but such as

I have read gathered already in good authors, whose spirit I durst better trust than mine own. I knowledge and confess mine own poverty therein. I know none opinion of mine own finding in Scripture, and whatsoever gift other have, Scripture is to me over dark to understand it alone."

The result, he said, of the individual interpretation of Scripture is that "each one man" becomes "a Church alone." Each one fasts alone—"if he fast at all." Each one prays alone—"if he prayeth at all." And so each is "alone, alone, alone, mine own self all alone."

"And such men lay their hand on their breast and say they spake as their conscience serveth them, or tell how they have prayed for grace and cannot believe the contrary; some lift up their eyes and wish that the truth may spread abroad that hath been long hidden. And thus as they would have it they will have it, and be clearly deaf to any other teaching."

Incidentally he defended the custom of praying to the saints to pray for us.

"We say, 'God and our Lady help us,' wherein God giveth the help and our Lady prayeth for it, which is a help to obtain help. . . . God's honour is nothing diminished by addition of his servant to wait upon him. . . . But ye call his servants, the saints departed, dead men, and for spite cut off their ears and say they cannot hear because they want their bodies."

He admitted that in this matter "among the rude people by misunderstanding there hath grown superstition . . . and the reformation therein hath been expedient."

In discussing the central teaching of the reformers, justification by faith, he began by agreeing that the passion of Christ was the "only sufficient sacrifice for the sin of all the world." The question is, he said, on what conditions men receive the benefits of Christ's passion. Barnes had maintained that faith was the only condition. Gardiner said there were others, such as the forgiveness of our neighbours, "incorporation into Christ by baptism," "returning to Christ by penance," and "perseverance in virtue." All these—the outgoings of man in affection to God and his neighbour—Gardiner included in the word love or charity. Hence while Luther and his followers taught that man was justified by faith only, Gardiner said "to the attainment of justification is required faith and charity." He quoted with approval the words of St. Augustine, "to believe in God is by loving to go unto him."

"The effect of faith," he said, "is, properly, to illuminate the understanding and of charity to warm and kindle man's cold and earthly affections. Now if the justification of man implied only the expulsion of darkness from man's understanding, the effect of faith would suffice, but, seeing God in justification moveth man's heart and kindleth love in it, why may not these two virtues, with their two effects, by God's working, concur in man's justification?"

"As the promise of God is knit to faith, so it is knit to love; as life is promised to men believing, so it is promised to men loving. And as often as St. Paul nameth faith, not speaking of love, so often and oftener, doth St. John, in his epistles, speak of charity without mention of faith, and declareth plainly that he that loveth not is in death."

"St. Austin saith that St. Paul, speaking of faith, did ever mean such a faith as had the gift of charity with it, whereof he spake . . . to the Corinthians, 'he that hath not charity is nothing.'"

Joye, on the other hand, said that if justification was not a free gift from God, independent of any condition which man must fulfil, we could never be sure of our justification.

"Such assurance," answered Gardiner, "as ye speak of, without regard to the conditions, I have not read. Thus have I learned in Scripture; if we turn when God turneth to us, if we believe when God illuminateth us, if we love as God kindleth us, if we be baptized as God commandeth us, we shall be justified; if we walk in justification, as God by Christ taught us, and therein persevere, we shall be glorified. And I know none other English for so many ifs but to call them conditions, and works also to be done by us."

Gardiner said he never held that works justify a man or that a man of himself may merit salvation, for the impulse to love as well as that to believe comes from God. "We cannot love God unless he prepareth our heart, . . . no more can we believe God unless he giveth us the gift of belief. And so God is the author of all our wealth . . . he is the only justifier."

It is perhaps superfluous to point out that this controversy over justification—as old as St. James and St. Paul—sprang from two disparate conceptions of what faith was. To Gardiner, as to St. James, faith meant intellectual assent, and hence of itself was clearly inadequate for the attainment of virtuous life among men or vital relationship with God. To St. Paul and Luther faith was a complete self-surrendering confidence in God. When they said that a man was justified by faith they meant, in part at least, that, in his utter reliance upon God's love and care, he received a new undefeatable power for righteousness and an assurance of spiritual peace. Yet it is clear, from the controversial writings of the sixteenth century, that many of those who were loudest in their assertion of this doctrine had little understanding of its essential significance. They used the phrase as a party shibboleth and sought to establish its validity not by an appeal to spiritual experience, but to this or that text from St. Paul.

There was not a little truth in Gardiner's contention that according to some of the new preachers all a man need do to be saved was to say "only faith justifieth, and a priest is a knave, and Mass is not in Scripture, and an image is an idol." Nor can there be any doubt that the vaunted assurance of salvation was often little less than presumption, and that not a few of the "godly sort" were narrow, contentious, disagreeable folk.

> "The name and works of God," exclaimed the Bishop, "have been so familiar in our talk that the reverent fear of his majesty is almost extinct amongst many. Unhappy we be in whose time learning should be ministered to such effects."

No matter what we think of Gardiner's theology, we cannot, after reading invective such, for instance, as Joye wrote, help feeling that there was perhaps something to be said for the Bishop when he affirmed:

> "The malicious railing of you that be the masters, and the spiteful hatred without cause of them that be your scholars, daily more and more confirmeth unto me the detestable naughtiness of that ye intend. . . . Your learning cannot be good that preach so like the devil." [10]

The suggestion contained in this last sentence was elaborated in the Bishop's next book—*A Detection of the Devil's Sophistry,* also published in 1546.

"The first, chief, and principal" sophistry, he says, is that God gives wisdom to every man for the mere asking—"we might as well and better ask our bodily food without our labour." This is the root of all false doctrine, and leads men to speak with "presumptuous pride and intolerable arrogance," especially about the Sacrament of the Altar. Thus the devil leads men away "captive and thralled from the true Catholic belief" by his appeal to the senses, which tell us that the bread and wine remain bread and wine even after the consecration. But if carnal reason of this sort be applied to the mysteries of our religion, the Trinity, the Incarnation, the Resurrection are equally unbelievable. Again, the devil points out that God is incorruptible, while the Host may become mouldy or be eaten by a mouse. But why should these things seem more strange than the breaking of the Host by the priest, at which no one has ever been offended? The breaking, as the moulding, affects only the form, or outward qualities, which remain those of bread and wine, not the substance of Christ's body. "A mouse cannot devour God."

Another of the devil's sophistries is to persuade men that Christ meant something different from what He said when He said "This is my body;" so that nowadays those who have been deceived by the devil ask, as did the people of Capernaum; "How can this man give us his flesh to eat?" Another sophistry is the use of certain seeming contradictions such as, Christ is in heaven, therefore He cannot be in the Sacrament, in which the devil "causeth us to measure God's doings by our natural imbecility;" whereas Christ "tarrieth in the Host consecrate . . . to be a continual and daily food, wherewith, being nourished, we may strongly walk, till we come to the mount of God."

Still another sophistry is "the perverse, crooked, and crafty expositions" of Scripture and the Fathers. Thus into the phrase, "Do this in remembrance of me," the devil inserts the word "but," making it appear that the Sacrament is but a remembrance of Christ and nothing more; and when one of the Fathers calls the Sacrament a figure or sign, the devil's syllable turns it into "but a sign, but a figure."

Moreover, the devil tries to persuade men that death for a cause is proof of the righteousness of that cause; but recently "stubbornness mixt with vainglory" has brought many a man to death.

> "The Anabaptists and Sacramentaries have with devilish pertinacity manifested their heresies, whose wilful death in obstinacy, if it could serve for an argument to prove the truth of their opinion, the truth of God's Scriptures should be brought in much perplexity. . . . If such as lately suffered were severally considered, there may appear tokens sufficient, besides the condition of the matter they suffered for, to declare their zeal not to have proceeded of the spirit of God, but of arrogant pride and presumption and the spirit of the devil."

When the devil cannot answer the arguments brought forward from the Fathers he says they were only men, which is true, but they lived in days of faith, charity, and devotion, "when God's word dwelt in men's hearts and came never abroad to walk in men's tongues, . . . whereas now, jesters, railers, rimers, players, janglers, prattlers, and simpering parrots take upon them to be the administrators and officers to set forth God's word." The devil persuades men to think that everyone is competent to interpret Scripture, and quotes Christ on hiding things from the wise and revealing them to "younglings." He likewise says that the word "Mass" is not in Scripture, so that rude ignorants now speak of the "Lord's Supper" instead of the "Mass," but "what the word 'Mass' meaneth they cannot tell."

The devil likewise persuades men that fasting is superstitious, so that soberness and moderation "be clearly banished and exiled." He aims "to diminish and extinct prayer, with temptation of attaining knowledge by study and sermons. So as now among many the house of God, which Christ called the house of prayer, hath (as many practise it) changed the name with the thing. For many, if they come to church, either it is to hear one talk and rail after their fancy in a pulpit, which they call a sermon, and learn only thereby other men's faults and care nothing for their own, or else in reading or musing of that [which] they understand not but would learn, they spend all the time they tarry there."

Indeed the devil's sophistry concerning God's mercy "with only faith and only saviour and omnisufficient saviour, serveth to make men forget God's justice and wax wantons."

Finally, the sophistry that certain single acts or ceremonies are unessential tends, by assailing them one by one, to impugn religion itself. The devil takes the words of the Mass separately and asks, is it this one, or this which produces the miracle? and "by sophistry in division wipes out all." He asks:

"Shall forbearing of meats save a man? The answer must be, No. And then, Ergo, eat all day long. Doth watching bring a man to heaven? Nay. Ergo, sleep and spare not. Is the place cause why a man's prayer is good? . . . Nay. And what needest thou come to church then? . . . And thus by these subtle questions the devil robbeth simple men even of the substance by degrees of true religion."

As rich young men, persuaded by parasites that this and that small expenditure is of no consequence, are "suddenly brought to naught and made very beggars," so by the devil's persuasions "the substance of our religion is among many prodigal children wasted and consumed." [11]

This volume called forth immediate replies from two reformers, John Hooper, later bishop and martyr, and Anthony Gilby, that "fast and furious stickler against Church discipline," as Fuller called him, who became notorious for his assaults on the Elizabethan settlement. Hooper, whose book was singularly free from personal invective, dedicated it to Gardiner "to declare," as he said, "that it is against your cause and opinion that I write, and not against you." Gilby did not exercise such restraint. He dubbed Gardiner "a soldier of Satan," and a "blasphemous messenger of the proud Sennacherib," but he paid his book the tribute of saying that of all others he esteemed it "most perilous and poisonful, both for the authority of the author and the subtle handling of the matter;" and noted that it was "spread everywhere, and received in many places more reverently than the blessed Bible." [12]

XIX

THE LAST STAND OF THE CONSERVATIVES

In January 1546, while Gardiner was on the Continent endeavouring to put the alliance with the Emperor on a stabler basis, Cranmer seized the opportunity offered by his absence "somewhat to further the reformation of the corrupt religion." He proposed, not without encouragement from the King, that the vigil of All Hallows, with its all night bell ringing, the veiling of images in Lent, the kneeling to the cross on Palm Sunday and at other times, and the creeping to it on Good Friday, be abolished. He drafted a letter for the King to send him, enjoining these reforms, but Henry, when he received it at the hand of Sir Anthony Denny, said:

> "I am now otherwise resolved. Send my Lord of Canterbury word that since I spake with him about these matters, I have received letters from my Lord of Winchester . . . and he writeth plainly unto us that the league will not prosper nor go forward if we make any other innovation, change, or alteration, either in religion or ceremonies." [1]

No innovation was made, and Gardiner, as we have seen, returned to England in March 1546, having brought his negotiations with the Empire to a successful conclusion.

For the next half year the Privy Council had much to do with persons whose utterances laid them under suspicion of heresy.[2] Early in May Lord Thomas Howard was summoned because of his "disputation of Scripture matters more largely and indiscreetly than good order did permit," and he and Sir Edward Warner were admonished to reform; one Wourley, page of the Pallet Chamber, was committed to examination by Tunstall and Gardiner because of "unseemly reasoning" upon Scripture; and Dr. Crome, the popular preacher, was "examined upon his rashness and indiscreet proceedings." He had preached in Lent against purgatory and Masses for the dead, and had been enjoined to recant publicly on May 9, on which occasion he not only did not recant but told his audience that it was not his purpose to do so. The next day he was brought before the Council, and finally on June 29 made a very humble public submission.[3]

Meanwhile the Council was examining others who had "specially comforted [*i.e.* encouraged] Crome in his folly," among whom were both Latimer and Shaxton,[4] the reforming bishops who had resigned their sees after the passage of the Six Articles. Latimer at first objected to answering the interrogatories put to him, saying that he believed Gardiner "had procured this against him for malice." He cited "certain words" that once passed between them in the King's presence, as well as Gardiner's protest to Cromwell against a sermon he (Latimer) had preached in Convocation. Whereunto, says Gardiner,

> "I, the said Bishop of Winchester, made to him a true and plain answer, containing in effect, and proving by remembrance of things passed between us, that he did me much wrong; for I declared plainly how much I had loved, favoured, and done for his person, and that he had no cause to be offended with me though I were not content with his doctrine." [5]

Latimer's final answer to the interrogatories was not satisfactory; he was kept in custody until the end of the reign.

Shaxton's views on the Sacrament brought him in danger of the Six Articles, under which he was actually condemned by a commission sitting at the Guildhall, June 28, but he was persuaded to change his opinions, and, on August 1, made a public recantation,[6] in accordance with which he lived consistently until his death in 1556.

Robert Wisdom, whose recantation in 1543 Gardiner is said to have written, was again summoned before the Council, but fled to the Continent, and Dr. John Taylor, later Bishop of Lincoln, was induced to subscribe articles like those signed by Shaxton.[7]

Among the two dozen lesser persons whose heresies came to the notice of the Council at this time perhaps the best known was the ill-fated Anne Askew, a zealous student of Scripture, who in 1545 had been examined by Bonner for evil opinions on the Sacrament, and persuaded, much against her will, to sign a statement of belief in the orthodox doctrine. She was brought before the Council June 19, 1546. When asked for her view of the Sacrament she at first gave an evasive answer. Then, according to her own account of the examination,[8]

> "The Bishop of Winchester bade me make a direct answer.
> I said I would not sing a new song of the Lord in a strange land.
> Then the Bishop said I spake in parables.
> I answered, it was best for him, 'for if I show the open truth,' quoth I, 'ye will not accept it.'
> Then he said I was a parrot."

Gardiner tried the next day, together with Sir William Parr, brother of the Queen, and John Dudley, Viscount Lisle, both of whom were thought to be friendly to the new theology, to persuade her to accept the orthodox teaching, but she told Parr and Dudley that "it was a great shame for them to counsel contrary to their knowledge," and when Gardiner said he wished to speak to her familiarly she replied, "So did Judas when he unfriendly betrayed Christ." She refused to consider his further suggestion that he speak with her alone, and when he finally warned her that she was in danger of the stake, she retorted, "God will laugh your threatenings to scorn."

This is the last mention she makes of Gardiner. He evidently gave her up as an impossible person. Others continued to urge her to subscribe to the orthodox position, but in vain, so the law was allowed to take its course. With Shaxton and two others she was arraigned at the Guildhall and condemned. Shaxton, as we have seen, recanted, as did one White, but Anne, despite further persuasions, steadfastly adhered to her denial of Christ's body in the Sacrament, saying that the Mass was "the most abominable idol that is in the world." She was burned at Smithfield July 16, 1546 with three others—a tailor, an obscure priest, and a gentleman named John Lascelles.[9]

Gardiner did not hesitate to say, in a letter to Hertford some ten months later, that he believed Anne Askew had been "by the laws worthy the pains of death," for so blasphemously denying the presence of Christ's body in the Sacrament.[10]

Anne and her three fellow sufferers, together with three others condemned in Essex in May,[11] made up the tale of victims under the Act of the Six Articles in 1546. These seven deaths, the burning of heretical books,[12] the examination of suspects by the Privy Council, and the public recantations of such prominent persons as Crome, Taylor, and Shaxton, all tended to the suppression of reform propaganda. Many an extremist fled to the Continent. Nor did the common people show any more liking for innovation in religion now than formerly. John Hooper, later Bishop, at Strassburg in January 1546—the very month in which Cranmer was proposing his simplified ceremonial—heard from England that Catholic beliefs and practices "were never before held by the people in greater esteem than at the present moment;"[13] and Cranmer himself told the King that if creeping and kneeling to the cross "be taken away, it shall seem to many that be ignorant, that the honour of Christ is taken away, unless some good teaching be set forth withal to instruct them sufficiently therein." If the people be not thus instructed they would, he said, "obey with mumuration and grutching."[14]

Hooper also pointed out that the cause of the new theology at court had suffered severe loss in the recent deaths of no less than six prominent courtiers, thought to be favourers of it—the Duke of Suffolk, Lord Chancellor Audley, Sir Thomas Poynings, Captain General of Boulogne, Sir Thomas Wyatt, poet and diplomat,

Dr. Butts, the King's physician, and Sir Edward Baynton, first lord of the Queen's bedchamber.[15]

Moreover, the alliance with the Empire and the peace with France formed a political background favourable to the conservatives. The Council of Trent had begun its sessions; the Emperor was moving against the German Protestants; it was essential that England impress Europe with her orthodoxy so that the Pope would have no excuse to urge Charles and Francis to break with Henry as with a heretic. When Sir Thomas Cheyne was sent to France in June 1546 to represent Henry at the christening of the Dauphin's daughter, he was instructed by the Council strictly to observe fish days and devoutly to hear Mass, so that his behaviour might "be confusion to such as would defame this realm."[16]

Favourable as circumstances appeared for the conservatives in 1546, there was still the court influence of several adherents of reform to be reckoned with. Not a few ladies of the court, including the Queen herself, were showing increasing interest in the new ideas; and the leaders of the new nobility, in particular Edward Seymour, Earl of Hertford, uncle to the Prince, and John Dudley, Viscount Lisle, were ready to throw in their lot with the reformers if by so doing they could discredit the old nobility and those Churchmen who opposed the spoliation of the Church.

It was undoubtedly in the hope of implicating persons of prominence at court that Anne Askew had been summoned before the Council; for after her conviction, when she was examined in the Tower by Lord Chancellor Wriothesley and Sir Richard Riche, she was told that the King had been informed that she could name a great number of her sect, and she was questioned specifically about the Duchess of Suffolk, the Countesses of Hertford and Sussex, and Ladies Denny and Fitzwilliam, and was even told that certain members of the Council were known to have maintained her. She admitted that money had been sent her in prison, and that those who brought it said it was from the Countess of Hertford and Lady Denny, but further than this she could say nothing, although she was brutally tortured upon the rack.[17]

What use, if any, was made of this information we do not know, but it must have been at this time that there occurred the attempt to put an end to the influence of Queen Catherine Parr, if Foxe's story of this incident may be trusted. We do not know where Foxe found the tale, and certain elements in it are self-contradictory, yet much of it has the appearance of truth. He tells us, quite rightly, that the Queen "was very much given to the reading and study of the Holy Scriptures;" and it is altogether probable that she took occasion, as he says, to discuss theology with her royal husband and urge upon him some of the new opinions. It is also true that as Henry's illness increased, his temper, which he had never controlled very well, became more violent than ever. Foxe puts it mildly, saying, "the sharpness of the disease had sharpened the King's accustomed patience;" and, irritated by his wife's arguments, he "began to show tokens of misliking."

At one of these domestic discussions Gardiner, says Foxe, happened to be present, and after Catherine left the room, ventured to tell the King

> "that the religion by the Queen so stiffly maintained, did not only disallow and dissolve the policy and politic government of princes, but also taught the people that all things ought to be in common; so that what colour soever they pretended, their opinions were indeed so odious, and for the prince's estate so perilous . . . that the greatest subject in this land, speaking those words that she did speak, and defending those arguments that she did defend, had with indifferent justice, by law deserved death."

The argument is quite in accord with what we know of Gardiner's opinions on the political dangers of heresy, and his conclusion, in the light of the law at the time, was undoubtedly true. The King, according to Foxe, so far agreed with the Bishop that he gave "warrant to certain of them . . . to consult together about the drawing of certain articles against the Queen, wherein her life might be touched," but Foxe, in order to maintain Henry's reputation as a "loving husband," adds that he did this "closely dissembling with them, to try out the uttermost of Winchester's fetches." Yet we read on the previous page that Henry was genuinely angry at the Queen and alarmed for his own safety, should her opinions prevail.

The Queen, however, briefly to conclude Foxe's long story, got wind of this "conspiracy" against her, came to the King humbly avowing her entire agreement with his theology, and tactfully saying that she had argued against him merely "to minister talk;" whereupon she was joyfully received again into favour.[18]

After we discount Foxe's animus toward Gardiner, and his desire to put the King's proceedings in the best light possible, there is nothing inherently improbable in the story.[19] Gardiner must certainly have looked with apprehension at the growing influence of the reformers at court, and have seen clearly that so long as the Queen maintained her influence over the King, whose illness was daily growing more serious, the situation boded no good for orthodoxy in the Church or stability of the State.

Gardiner's party appears to have maintained its supremacy in the Council until early in November 1546. During September and October, while the King was away from London, Wriothesley, St. John, and Gardiner remained in the city to conduct many of the affairs of the government—a task which they found increasingly

difficult inasmuch as all the treasuries were empty and the nation
on the verge of bankruptcy.[20]   As early as the beginning of September, however, the influence of Hertford and Lisle began to be
ominous.   At that time, Van der Delft, the Imperial ambassador
in England, remarked to the three councillors in London that he
had heard that certain persons favourable to the Protestants—he
had in mind, he says, Hertford and Lisle, but did not name them—
had come into great favour with the King, and he expressed a wish
that they were as far away from court as they had been last year.
To this Gardiner and his colleagues made no reply, although the
ambassador thought they clearly understood him.   They said, with
some concern, that Henry had been credibly informed that Charles
had promised, in the event of victory over the German Protestants,
to assist the Pope against England.   Van der Delft assured them
that such a thing could never happen.[21]   It seems, however, to have
troubled the King,[22] and such misgivings as thus arose in his mind
were undoubtedly nurtured by the anti-Imperial, pro-Protestant
politicians.   Gardiner and his followers urged Van der Delft to do
everything possible to keep Henry well disposed to the Imperial
alliance, and to counteract the influence of Hertford and Lisle by
depicting to the King the dire dangers of Protestantism.[23]

With the rapidly failing health of the King both parties bent their
energies to securing the regency in the coming reign.   Sometime
near the beginning of October Lisle had a falling out with Gardiner
in the Council and so far forgot himself as to strike the Bishop a
blow.   For this incivility he found it necessary to leave court, but
within a month he was well received again and resumed his place
at the Council table.[24]   It was probably sometime after this that
such "violent and injurious words" were spoken by Lisle to Gardiner
and by Hertford to Wriothesley that the veteran Chapuys, watching the English situation from Louvain, said that he doubted if any
of the other councillors would dare longer to oppose the Hertford-
Lisle ascendancy.[25]

The final struggle in the Council must have occurred after the
end of November, for at that time Gardiner, though absent from
the court while acting on a commission in Southwark, felt himself
sufficiently secure in the royal favour to express his unwillingness
to exchange with the King certain lands which the latter desired.
It is highly unlikely that he would have done this had he not supposed his position to be as strong as ever.   To his request for permission to explain his attitude in person, Henry replied that he
would not deny him audience "at any meet time," but clearly indicated irritation and displeasure at his hesitancy to give up the
coveted lands.[26]   There can be no doubt that Gardiner's rivals did
everything in their power to magnify this difference between the
Bishop and the King.

By the middle of December it was clear how things would end. The rash words and acts of the Earl of Surrey, Norfolk's eldest son, laid the conservative cause open to sure disaster. On December 12 he and his father, the chief of the old nobility, were sent to the Tower on a charge of treason, a charge which Surrey's conduct in some degree justified. Their real offense, however, was their desire to do what Hertford and his followers were doing more successfully—secure for themselves and their party the ascendancy in the coming minority. That Gardiner was aimed at in their overthrow is evident from one of the questions put to Norfolk. What, he was asked, did he know of a letter from Gardiner to Henry outlining Granvelle's proposition in 1541 "for a way to be taken between his Majesty and the Bishop of Rome?" Norfolk declared that he knew nothing of it.[27]

On Christmas Eve Van de Delft wrote that the Council now met usually at Hertford's house; that practically all of the councillors, including those who had previously opposed Hertford and Lisle, had gone over to them; and that the members of the "perverse sects" no longer concealed their desire to see the Bishop of Winchester keeping company with Norfolk in the Tower [28]—a statement borne out by a letter from John Bourchier, an Englishman at Strassburg, who wrote to Bullinger a week later, rejoicing at the arrest of Norfolk and Surrey, and adding that the one person still wanting was Gardiner, for "unless he be also caught the evangelical truth cannot be restored." [29]

On the night after Christmas, when the King's will was revised, Gardiner's name was dropped from the council of regency therein appointed to govern during the boyhood of Prince Edward.

The circumstances attending the exclusion of Gardiner's name from Henry's will are obscure. We have the will itself,[30] which is dated December 30, 1546, and which, according to Paget, was revised by Henry, who felt himself in peril of death, on the night of December 26, in the presence of Hertford, Lisle, and a few others. We also have the depositions of four of Gardiner's opponents at his trial four years later, as well as a story which Foxe says was told to Cranmer by Sir Anthony Denny, who was one of those present at the revision of the will, and whose conversation with the Archbishop was overheard by the latter's secretary Morice, from whom Foxe got it. According to this, Sir Anthony Browne, a good friend of Gardiner's,

> "kneeled down to the King's Majesty, lying in his bed, and said, 'My Lord of Winchester, I think, by negligence is left out of your Majesty's will; who hath done your Highness most painful, long, and notable service, and one without whom the rest shall not be able to overcome your great and weighty

affairs committed unto them.' 'Hold your peace,' quoth the
King. 'I remembered him well enough, and of good purpose
have left him out; for surely if he were in my testament, and
one of you, he would cumber you all, and you should never
rule him, he is of so troublesome a nature. Marry,' quoth the
King, 'I myself could use him, and rule him to all manner of
purposes, as seemed good unto me; but so shall you never
do.' " [31]

Of the four depositions bearing on this subject made at Gardiner's
trial, two mention Sir Anthony Browne as having called the King's
attention to the omission of Gardiner; all agree that the King used
words to the effect "that the said Bishop was a troublesome man, and
that he would trouble all the rest if he were named among them." [32]

The difficulty with this evidence, despite its agreement, is that it
was given by Gardiner's opponents, the little group who were
present at the revision of the will, and undoubtedly represented the
view which that group desired to make current. It was, moreover,
given after the death of Sir Anthony Brown, the one man at
Henry's bedside who had a good word to say for the Bishop.

Whatever the circumstances of Gardiner's exclusion may have
been, the new nobility made no move against his person. This was
doubtless because they feared, on the one hand, to antagonize the
great body of conservative Churchmen who looked to him as their
leader, and because they hoped, on the other, to win his support, as
they had won that of Paget, and most of his other followers in the
Council. Moreover, the King, although he may have been willing
to have the Bishop excluded from the governing council of his son,
was not ready to consent to his ruin. "No man," said Gardiner,
with evident truth, "could do me hurt during his life." [33]

He retained his place in the Privy Council [34] and in the House
of Lords [35] until the end of the reign.

On January 28, 1547, in the early morning, Henry VIII died.
His body lay at Westminster for over a fortnight, while Gardiner,
as prelate of the Order of the Garter, assisted by Tunstall, Bonner,
and others, "continued in all manner of service and ceremonies,
dirges and Masses." On Sunday, February 13, Gardiner, vested in
black, sang a solemn requiem. Next morning the body of the King
began its grave and splendid progress to Windsor, where, on the
15th, it was received by Gardiner, who led the dirge that afternoon
in St. George's Chapel, standing at the high altar, while Cranmer
and the other executors sat "upon forms on either side of the choir
beneath the prelate." The next morning, it was Gardiner who celebrated the final requiem Mass and preached the sermon. "Blessed
are the dead who die in the Lord," was his text.

"He declared," says a contemporary, "the frailty of man, and

community of death to the high and to the low, showing the
pitiful and dolorous loss that all manner men had sustained
by the death of so gracious a King.   Yet he recomforted them
again by the resurrection in the life to come, and exhorted
them all to rejoice and give thanks to Almighty God, having
sent us so toward and virtuous a prince to reign over us,   .   .   .
desiring all men to continue in obedience and duty."

Mass ended, he proceeded with the burial office, laying his master
to rest in the choir of the chapel, beside the body of Jane Seymour.
After the *De Profundis,* King Edward VI was proclaimed, while
"the trumpets sounded with great melody and courage to the comfort of all them that were present." [36]

The nameless recorder of these events gives no hint of how
little comfort came to the chief celebrant from these melodious and
courageous trumpets.

XX

"PRINTERS, PLAYERS, AND PREACHERS TROUBLE WINCHESTER"[1]

Gardiner, writing to Paget in 1545, said he did not fear the "malicious follies" of the reformers as long as the King lived; but what, he asked, with no little apprehension, will ensue when those who are now young shall contemn religion and conceive another opinion of God than is true? Everything must be done, he urged, to preserve the King's life "till my Lord Prince may come to man's estate."[2]

My Lord Prince had come to the age of nine when Henry VIII was gathered to his fathers and the government fell into the hands of the Prince's uncle, Sir Edward Seymour, Earl of Hertford, who on the third day after the King's death, was given the title of Lord Protector by the Council and soon thereafter created Duke of Somerset.

Gardiner, as a member of the House of Lords, was present before the boy King, February 1, 1547, when the royal assent to the protectorship was announced, and on Sunday, February 20, four days after the burial of Henry VIII, he acted, on the nomination of the Protector and Council, as one of Cranmer's chief attendants at the Mass in Edward's coronation service.[3] This is his last recorded participation in a public governmental function in the reign of Edward VI. He appeared at court, however, during February to hear the sermons preached before the King, and maintained his residence in Southwark for that month.[4]

He early sought out Somerset, volunteered his advice on matters of government, and secured the Duke's permission to put his opinions in writing. They were given in no uncertain terms: Continue the Imperial alliance; distrust France; let Scots be Scots till the King comes of age; devote your energies to restoring the prosperity of England; forestall religious dissension by maintaining the ecclesiastical settlement of Henry VIII.[5]

Somerset assured him "that he would suffer no innovations in religion during the King's Majesty's young age,"[6] and was doubtless sincere in his assurance, but his overoptimistic belief that order might be maintained without recourse to Henry VIII's methods of repression encouraged the radicals to open activity. His support, moreover, came, on the one hand, from reforming Churchmen who, like the mild and scholarly Cranmer and the energetic Ridley, sincerely desired further change in religion, and, on the other, from politicians and courtiers who, like Somerset himself, had gained fortunes from the dissolution of the monasteries and who hoped to increase them by further spoliation of the Church. It was but natural that these last should seek to colour their attack on Church property by an alliance with reformers to whom ecclesiastical wealth and luxury were anathema, and it is perhaps explicable that the reformers were gullible enough often to believe their professions of zeal for the word of God.

Nor was it only those courtiers who had always been of the reforming party who now fell into line with the innovators. Sir William Paget, once Gardiner's scholar at Cambridge, later a member of his household, advanced in the service of Henry VIII through his influence, regarded by him as a friend and a staunch supporter of Catholic principles, went over completely to the new régime— indeed was instrumental in inaugurating it, for during the closing days of the last reign he had been Somerset's confidant and confederate in the plan to set up the protectorate.

It was difficult for Gardiner to believe that Paget had deserted him; we find him, on more than one occasion during the opening days of the new reign, appealing to his old friend for assistance, and, in one instance, acknowledging redress through his advice, but for what we are not told.[7] In one of his letters to Paget, written from his house in Southwark on February 5, 1547, eight days after the death of Henry VIII, he complains:

> "Tomorrow the parishioners of this parish and I have agreed to have a solemn dirge for our late Sovereign Lord and master, in earnest as becometh us. And tomorrow certain players of my Lord of Oxford's, as they say, intend on the other side, within this burgh of Southwark, to have a solemn play, to try who shall have most resort, they in game or I in earnest; which me seemeth a marvellous contention, wherein some shall profess, in the name of the commonwealth, mirth, and some sorrow at one time.
>
> Herein I follow the common determination to sorrow till our late master be buried; and what the lewd fellows should mean in the contrary I cannot tell, nor cannot reform it, and therefore write unto you, who by means of my Lord Protector may procure an uniformity in the commonwealth. . . ."[8]

We do not have Paget's reply, but we do have some further correspondence which ensued upon the determination of the Council, on February 6, that since bishops had exercised "authority of spiritual jurisdiction" by virtue of royal licence, this jurisdiction had come to an end at the death of the late King, and was to be renewed under commissions which Paget, as chief secretary, was authorized to issue.[9] Cranmer's was issued immediately,[10] but Gardiner's, owing to his strictures on the wording of the commissions, not until March 14.[11] We find him, on March 1, writing to Paget to expedite his commission favourably and objecting to the word "delegate" as applied in it to a bishop, an addition of Paget's, which, he said, he had just seen and liked not, for in fulfilling his duties as an ordinary [*i.e.*, one who had, of his own right and not by deputation, immediate jurisdiction in ecclesiastical cases] he might find he had exceeded his authority, being but a delegate of the crown.

"I have," he wrote, "been exercised on making of treaties, where words, as ye know, have been thrust in to signify somewhat at length and have then such an interpretation as might serve. And we poor bishops be not such a match as the parties be in treaties. . . .

It would be a marvellous matter if after my long service and the loss of my master [Henry VIII], I should lose that [which] he gave me by construction of a commission, and that I should offend in going about to do well, to see things well by visitation, and receiving of convicts to my charge as ordinary, and am but a delegate. And then the case would be so much the more strange if you might relieve it and did not.

Ye must grant archdeacons authority to visit or they cannot pay their tenths, for thereupon their profit doth arise; and then how shall it stand, the archdeacon to have more authority than the bishop, having in his name to be overseer and yet may not go see. And now is the time when such as have office to order the people should rather have more committed unto them than less. . . .

What are you the better if ye be called of some a pincher of the bishops, and, among them, me? It healeth no disease in you; ye sleep never the better; ye have never the better stomach. Nothing is better and somewhat is worse. Plutarch saith, he that is sixty years old and putteth forth his hand to the physician to ask how his body is, in temperance declareth himself not wise; and me thinketh the time we have lived is long enough to learn men what the state of this world is and how soon it is altered. . . .

I thank God I could skill of this philosophy when I was as ye be; and howsoever it served for men's purpose to say I was a persecutor, I was never so in deed; and me thinketh I have felt the reward of it, for no persecution hath hitherto prevailed against me. . . .

All is uncertain, and, in the uncertainty, to do a certain displeasure which remaineth in memory when benefits vanish away, hath in it small policy, and less than I would wish to be in you. . . ."

He wrote, he said, in behalf of all bishops, but specially the Bishop of London, for

> "like as the brethren have made a ballad and solace themself in it, where Bonner lamenteth the fall of Winchester, so for recompense of his lamentation I speak in his cause, with whom I perceive ye be offended. . . . But howsoever he be, I would wish ye did best for yourself, which is to love your enemies, . . . for you have passed the state of wrangling and revenging. . . . Ye need study to increase nothing but love, for in the plenty thereof is all felicity. I speak of plenty that bishops might have part, for in the opinion of some they should be served last."

Those who hold this opinion, he adds, fail to consider that the realm has never been without bishops. "And how it would do if they were away, it were a new experience."

He had even heard of one who boasted that he would willingly give his lands if it were lawful to kill the Bishop of Winchester, thinking thereby to do God "a great sacrifice." "A godly enterprise and a devout!"

> "But let him say what he will, so our commission be well written, expressing all that we shall do and denying that we shall not do, so as ye express that I may receive convicts, for that is the only case in which the judges of the realm will have me do it whether I may or I may not."

At the sessions of the past Thursday the judges informed him that he would have to pay £1,000 if he refused to receive convicts, no matter whether he had power to receive them or not;

> "which was like the bellowing of the priest, made in the north, for bringing ducks again that were lost, for he said the parishioners must bring them again, see them or see them not." [12]

Paget replied the next day, March 2, that he trusted Gardiner would think, no matter what some people "unjustly or slanderously" reported of him, that he did not mean to "nip or snatch any person." Then, after professing the most disinterested concern for the public welfare, he proceeded to the matter in question:

> "I malign not bishops, but would that both they and all other were in such order as might be most to the glory of God and the benefit of this realm; and much less I malign your Lordship, but wish ye well; and if the estate of bishops is or shall be thought meet to be reformed, I wish either that you were no bishop or that you could have such a pliable will as could well bear the reformation that shall be thought meet for the quiet of the realm."

Ominous words these, from his Majesty's Chief Secretary. He added, however, that Gardiner should have his commission in "an ampler manner" than he had it before.[13]

Despite further professions of friendship on Paget's part, Gardiner's correspondence with him appears to have ceased after this. It may be an authentic saying of the Bishop which Ponet gives us: "Let my scholar go on as he hath begun, for Gardiner cannot play the knave so."[14] Hereafter when the Bishop had aught to say concerning proposed changes in Church or State he addressed Somerset directly.

Although the anti-Papal Catholicism of Henry VIII remained the established religion of England for the first ten months of Somerset's régime, outspoken reformers whose utterances foreboded much change were appointed as court preachers. Barlow, Bishop of St. David's, laid down a platform for reform in one of his sermons in February. Just what this platform was we do not know, but Gardiner wrote immediately to Somerset urging that the great need of England was "quiet, tranquillity, unity, and concord."

> "If," he said, "my Lord of St. David's, or such others, have their head cumbered with any new platform, I would wish they were commanded, between this and the King's Majesty's full age, to draw the plat diligently, to hew the stones, dig the sand, and chop the chalk in the unseasonable time of building; and when the King's Majesty cometh to full age to present their labours to him; and in the meantime not to disturb the state of the realm. . . .
>
> You need fear nothing if quiet be preserved at home; and at home, if the beginning be resisted, the intended folly may easily be interrupted. . . .
>
> I have been oftentimes blamed for fearing overmuch, and yet I have had an inkling that they that so blamed me feared even as much as I. Being in the state that you be in, it shall ever be commendable to foresee the worst. In quiet ye be strong, in trouble ye be greatly weak. . . .
>
> I know you have authority sufficient and wisdom plenty, and yet, being entered to write, I forget for the time what ye be, and commune with you as I were talking at Brussels with you, devising of the world at large."

After this reminiscence of their joint mission to the Emperor in 1544, the Bishop goes on to give the political advice already referred to, and ends with a reference to the ill will borne him by some of the reforming party who "have burst out and wished that they might, without breach of laws, kill me; which is to me a token of a marvellous fury."[15]

In this letter, written February 28, 1547, Gardiner enclosed for Somerset's perusal a copy of a letter he had written to Dr. Ridley (soon to be made Bishop of Rochester), who had preached at court on Ash Wednesday, February 23. Ridley had denounced "the Bishop of Rome's pretended authority in government . . . and in pardons," "which two matters," wrote Gardiner, "I note to be plain and here without controversy;" but Ridley had gone on to attack the use of images and holy water, both of which practices, Gardiner argued, were of great antiquity and genuine helpfulness.

"We be assured by Scripture," he said, "that in the name of God the Church is able and strong to cast out devils," and holy water, not supposed by the intelligent to have any virtue in itself, is used to convey the effect of this invocation of God's name, just as water in baptism is a vehicle of God's grace, just as the spittle and clay conveyed Christ's healing power to the blind, just as rings of silver and gold carried abroad the King's invocation of the name of God to drive away cramp and "the falling evil."

> "For such effect as they have wrought," he adds concerning these cramp rings, "when I was in France I have been myself much honoured; and of all sorts entreated to have them, with offer of as much for them as they were double worth. . . . And our late master continued all his life the exercise of that gift of God, . . . and yet he had no Scripture especially for it, that spake of rings of silver or gold, no more than is for ashes ministered a little before you last preached."

> "When any man hath denied that water may do service because Scripture appointeth it not, that 'because' driveth away much of the rest which the Church useth."

"If holy use," he concluded, "were coupled with holy water, there should be more plenty of holiness than there is."

As for images, to maintain, as Ridley had done, that they were idols because the words image and idol originally had the same meaning, was like saying that kings were necessarily tyrants because the word tyrant was once synonymous with king. "All the matter to be feared," said Gardiner, "is excess in worshipping." The function of images is to work in us "a holy remembrance of Christ and his saints." "We kneel and bow and cense not at that the images be, but at that the images signify." The Church of Rome, on the one hand, has very precisely forbidden such adoration to images as should be given to God, and, on the other, Luther, who "pulled away all other regard for them, strove stoutly and obtained, as I have seen in divers of the churches in Germany, . . . that they should, as they do, still stand." It is as gross an error, said the Bishop, "to take an image for God" as to deny that we may "worship before them."

In illustration of his contention that there was not much super-stition in the use of them, he told, not without humour, how the sexton, going for the silver crucifix to be used in the Good Friday service, " will not be afraid to be homely and hold it under his gown whilst he drinketh a pot of ale." [16]

The attack on images was not confined to sermons at court. In the beginning of May, Gardiner, then at his house Wolvesey at Winchester, whither he had retired early in March, heard that images had been "most contemptuously pulled down and spitefully handled" in the town of Portsmouth in his own diocese. He wrote at once to the Mayor and to Edward Vaughan, captain of the gar-rison there, with whom he was acquainted, asking about the cir-cumstances of this "great and detestable innovation," and whether the movement had gone too far to be stayed by preaching.

"I would use preaching," he wrote, "as it should not be occa-sion of any further folly where a folly is begun; and to a mul-titude persuaded in the opinion of destruction of images I would never preach; for, as Scripture willeth us, we should cast no precious stones before hogs. . . .

In Germany such as maintained that opinion of destroying images were accounted the dregs cast out by Luther. . . . For the destruction of images containeth an enterprise to subvert religion and the state of the world with it."

Since "not the hundredth part of the realm" can read, the devices on the escutcheons of the nobility and the figures on the royal arms, which even the most illiterate understand, help to maintain reverence for civil authority. Why then, asked Gardiner, are not images of like utility in religion?

"If the Cross be a truth, and if it be true that Christ suffered, why may we not have a writing thereof such as all can read, that is to say, an image?"

There is no more reason for contemning images because they are made of "stocks and stones," than for despising books because they are made of "clouts and pitch." Scripture forbids not all images, but false images, just as it reproves false men. [17]

Vaughan forwarded this letter to Somerset, to whom Gardiner had also written on the subject, and Somerset replied to Gardiner, May 27, telling him that he was too fearful of innovation, since only images used idolatrously had been pulled down, but adding that it were better that all be destroyed than the people put to variance over them. Gardiner showed too much concern, said the Protector, when images were burned and too little when the English Bible received like treatment. Moreover, it was the duty of the civil

ruler to steer his course between those who feared "every reformation to be a capital enterprise against all religion and good order,"
and the rash and headlong who desired to change everything. He
admitted, however, that it was his intention to reform all ancient
errors and abuses in religion, to which task, he concluded, "your
Lordship, as a man to whom God hath given great qualities of wit,
learning, and persuasion, could bring great help and furtherance,
if it were your pleasure." [18]

In answer to this Gardiner wrote, June 6, that he had gone in
person to Portsmouth, conducted an inquiry, and could find no
evidence that the images had been idolatrously used, but a good deal
that they had been sacrilegiously treated—"an image of Christ crucified so contemptuously handled as was in my heart terrible—to
have the one eye bored out and the side pierced!" He urged that
with images as with all else in religion the *King's Book* be retained
as the standard during Edward's minority, and marvelled that
Cranmer and Tunstall should so soon forget its doctrine. Religious
innovation would, be said, play directly into the Pope's hands,
"for he wanteth not wits to beat into other princes' ears that where
his authority is abolished, there shall, at every change of governors,
be change in religion." "I know but one way of quiet: to keep and
follow such laws and orders in religion as our late Sovereign Lord
left with us."

In this letter Gardiner incidentally expressed astonishment at the
Protector's policy of restraining bishops from preaching except in
their cathedral churches, "the like whereof," he said, "hath not been
known in my time." [19]

The destruction of images and the restraint of episcopal preaching were not the most ominous signs of change. As early as May 21
(1547), the Bishop had been constrained to write to the Protector
a long letter warning him of the dangers likely to result from the
spread of heretical books and the sermons of heretical preachers.
The worst of the books he had seen were the recent publications of
John Bale on Luther and Anne Askew. [20] It was a slander on the
late King, he said, to extol as a martyr a woman like Anne Askew
who had suffered death justly under the laws.

> "Bale praiseth Luther . . . with commendation as of a saint;
> which Luther (whatsoever he was otherwise) stoutly affirmed
> the presence really of Christ's natural body in the Sacrament
> of the Altar. And yet Bale, the noble clerk, would have Anne
> Askew, blasphemously denying the presence of Christ's natural
> body, to be taken for a saint also. So as Bale's saints may
> vary in heaven if they chance not [to vary] by the way; which
> might suffice to disprove the man's credit, if thwarting talk
> were not more desired of many than the truth indeed; which

truth was supposed to have been . . . well established long before our late Lord's death. . . ."

"I cannot forget your Grace told me you would suffer no innovations," continued Gardiner, and yet

> "Certain printers, players, and preachers make a wonderment as though we knew not yet how to be justified, nor what Sacraments we should have. And if the agreement in religion made in the time of our late Sovereign Lord be of no force in their judgement, what establishment can any new agreement have? . . .
>
> Many commonwealths have continued without the Bishop of Rome's jurisdiction; but without true religion, and with such opinions as Germany maintained, no estate hath continued in the circuit of the world to us known since Christ came."

The truth of this judgement appeared at the time to be borne out by the ruinous civil strife in Germany and the recent defeat of the Protestant leader, John of Saxony.

Moreover, the growing disregard of Lent, fostered by sermons and ballads, alarmed the Bishop.

> "What rhymes be set forth to deprave Lent," he exclaimed, "and how fond and foolish! And yet people pay money for them. . . .
>
> The fishmonger will never hope to have good sale when the butcher may with flesh outface him. And fish is the great treasure of this realm and food inestimable. And these good words I give, although I love it not myself. . . .
>
> Every country hath its peculiar inclination to naughtiness: England and Germany unto the belly, the one in liquor, the other in meat; France a little beneath the belly; Italy to vanities and pleasures devised; and let an English belly have a further advancement, and nothing can stay it. . . .
>
> Lent is among Christian men a godly fast to exercise men to forbear, and in England both godly and politic."

He had heard that some of the new preachers were declaring that Christ's Lenten fast was a miracle and therefore not intended to be imitated by us. The same, he replied in words of no little beauty, might be said of Christ's love, "for all his life was miracles, and his love, that is our badge, most miraculous of all, to die for his enemies."

He closed, characteristically, in lighter vein:

> "As one asked when he saw an old philosopher dispute with another, what they talked on, and it was answered how the old man was discussing what was virtue; it was replied, 'If the

old man yet dispute of virtue when will he use it?' so it may
be said in our religion, 'If we be yet searching for it, when
shall we begin to put it in execution?' " [21]

Somerset replied, commending the Bishop's "vigilant and diligent
eye, . . . very fearful of innovation," and assuring him that the
world was never so quiet but that "printers, players, and preachers
would set forth somewhat of their own heads which the magistrates
were unawares of." But his assurances concerning Lent were not
such as to put the Bishop's mind at rest. "Lent remaineth still,"
he wrote, "and shall, God willing, till the King's Highness, with
our advice and the residue of his Grace's Council, take another
order." [22]

If another order given in the name of the boy King by a council
composed almost wholly of laymen, most of whom had little interest
in religion, could abolish the observance of Lent, Gardiner might
well fear the worst. He was reassured at the time by Somerset's
proclamation against innovations in religion,[23] but soon after disturbed again by Cranmer's proposal to set forth a book of homilies,
or instructions for the people to be read by the clergy in lieu of
sermons. It was clear that there were to be others beside "printers,
players, and preachers" to "trouble Winchester."

XXI

THE HOMILIES

When Cranmer spoke of issuing a book of homilies, he was not fathering a new plan. Such a volume had been proposed as early as 1542,[1] and at that time Gardiner had promised to assist in its composition; but the plan, lacking royal commendation, had been dropped. When Cranmer, early in June 1547, revived it and reminded Gardiner of his promised assistance, Gardiner, foreseeing that it would now mean doctrinal innovation, refused to have any part in it, and justified his refusal on the double ground that it was unwise to make any religious change during the minority, and that the need for such instruction as the Homilies had been intended to give had been adequately met by the *King's Book*.

To Cranmer some portions of the *King's Book* were not, and probably never had been, acceptable, though he had not said so during Henry's life. He now expressed to Gardiner his disapproval of the book, saying that Henry had been "seduced" into assenting to it.

> "After your Grace," replied Gardiner, "hath four years continually lived in agreement of that doctrine under our late Sovereign Lord, now so suddenly after his death to write to me that his Highness was seduced, it is, I assure you, a very strange speech. . . . And as often as your Grace shall say he was seduced you shall more touch yourself than him, in that ye told him not so in his life."

To say he was thus seduced "is either to condemn his wit and learning or his will and intent," which

> "is matter for enemies slanderously to rail with, rather than to be professed and confessed of us. . . . Is not thereby a window opened for such as dare speak to speak the like of anything that may be done now? . . . Alas! my Lord, let not us bishops be called the breakers of all authorities, and to regard no more religion but to confess of ourselves that willing, witting, and waking we lived under our late Sovereign Lord, approving a book of religion by him set forth wherein he was seduced."

Gardiner went on to express the hope that the Archbishop might spend his leisure to some better purpose than "to trouble this realm in the time of our Sovereign Lord's minority with any novelty in matters of religion; being so many other matters . . . requiring the whole endeavour of such as have charge, and silence in the people who should serve and obey without quarrelling among themselves for matters in religion, specially considering it is agreed our late Sovereign is received to God's mercy. And though some would say he had in knowledge but one eye and saw not perfectly God's truth, yet for us it were better to go to heaven with one eye after him, than to travail here for another eye with danger to lose both. There was good humanity in him that said, *Malim errare cum Platone, quam cum aliis vera sentire* [I would rather err with Plato than think correctly with others]."

"If the wall of authority which I accounted established . . . be once broken and new water let in at a little gap, the vehemency of novelty will flow farther than your Grace would admit."

This, he pointed out, had already happened in Germany in the Peasants' Revolt and in the war between the princes. That the like had not occurred in England was, he inferred, evidence that "it was a notable act of our late Sovereign Lord to reform and then moderate religion as he did."

As for homilies, if Gardiner were, for example, to write one on the perfect life, he would, he said, "take occasion to speak of faith, the gift of entry to life, and of charity, the very gift of life, which who hath not remaineth in death." But if he so wrote, his homily, in such a collection of homilies as Cranmer proposed, might encounter one which taught different doctrine, such as, he hinted, Cranmer's homily on justification by faith would be. Thus, homilies would "bring forth matter of contention and altercation, without all fruit or edification." The bishops and learned men would, he said,

"be better occupied to preach themselves . . . than to send down homilies which, being never so well made, shall work small effect when they be not handsomely uttered, as appeareth in a parish church at Cambridge where, I hear say, it is ordinary when the vicar goeth into the pulpit to read that [which] himself hath written, then the multitude of the parish goeth straight out of the church home to drink. . . . And it is contrary to the inclination of us Englishmen to be long in the state of hearers. The King's Majesty's founded lectures at Cambridge and furnished them with great learned men; at the beginning came many hearers; and within a while so few as were able to discourage any man. And even so it is in preaching, and specially where the man is not esteemed, as priests be not, and should be less if they fell a-talking, for so they would call it to rehearse an homily made by another. . . . If the priests should be universally bound to read homilies, they should read them as bachelors do the *Institutes* at Cambridge for their form, even to themselves and to the walls."

Cranmer in his presentation of the need for homilies had urged Gardiner "to consider the patience of the people that have heard so many foolish lying legends" of the saints from the *Legenda Aurea* and the *Liber Festivalis*. Gardiner answered by an amusing appraisal of the people and their attention to things theological. "Such as be most rude," he said, are

"led to good life by imitation rather than hearing. They move in the body of the church with much simplicity; and when they have heard words spoken in the pulpit they report they were good and very good and wondrous good . . . but what they were . . . they cannot tell. . . . Another sort . . . will take upon them to travail in everything they hear, . . . as the Mayor of Cambridge did, who told his wife, when she feared he would sometime oversee himself in disputing with the scholars, . . . not [to] fear him therein, for he had one thing for a ground which preserved him from all error in the Trinity, for as long as, quoth he, I say there be three Gods and one Person I care not for them all."

"Of this sort of men," adds Gardiner, "I have known a great many—I mean for their presumption in knowledge."

The multitude, he said, would as patiently suffer the legends of the saints for eight years more till the King came of age, as they had done for eight years past; and men of understanding considered it unseasonable to make any innovation in religion during the minority. As for the *Legenda Aurea* and the *Festival*,

"what they contain, I cannot tell, for I have not read them. And I think not impossible but there may be in them many foolish, lying tales; and I would wish Christ's religion cleansed and purged from all tales, but so as Christ said, as with the cockle the wheat were not pulled up by the root also."

"I was never very inquisitive to prove or reprove such stories as be received or used to be read in the Church, but of Christian simplicity think well of them till I see the high powers reprove them."

"I would wish the Church had never suffered anything to be read in it . . . but Scriptures or stories very authentic, and I abhor foolish lies. . . . But I cannot call a lie everything I know not or like not to believe."

The attempt to separate lies from the truth is, said Gardiner, "a very dangerous enterprise," since, in the process, truth is likely to be rejected by mistake and falsehood advanced by ignorance. It is an enterprise which "requireth an Hezekias present." The current English version of the Bible, he said, is full of mis-translations, some maliciously, some ignorantly, some negligently made; yet, much as he would like to see a correct translation issued, he would not advise it during the minority, lest men say,

> "we bishops went now about to fashion God's word after our own fancy, whilst we want the presence of our head that durst, could, and would control us."

True, the royal authority is now properly exercised by the Protector and Council, "and yet it is a difference, in the judgement of the people, to direct and order things established, and to make in the highest innovations."

"It is abomination indeed that Christian men should maintain lies wittingly," but lies should be removed

> "upon a sure, a solemn, approved judgement . . . and in a time where there is opportunity to entreat of such matters, which cannot be in the minority of a prince or without a solemn assembly." [2]

That Cranmer replied at some length is evident from Gardiner's well-nigh interminable rejoinder.[3] Gardiner was glad, he said, that his letter had amused the Archbishop, but added, "although I have a merry head, as your Grace writeth, yet my words be not placed idly, where I seem merriest." He then went on at great length to try to convince the Archbishop of the unwisdom of religious change and the untruth of the doctrine of justification by faith only, which Cranmer had defended in his reply. Though not without irony, the discussion was conducted in good temper. As Gardiner said, "St. Austin and St. Jerome wrote not more quietly and soberly one to another than your Grace and I do."

It appears that Cranmer had, in his letter, made a distinction between justification by faith only and justification by faith alone, saying that the King's Book, while condemning the latter, permitted the former doctrine; namely, that while faith only justified it was not alone or unaccompanied by other virtues in the act of justification. Gardiner pointed out that this was the position Cranmer had taken in the Convocation which sanctioned the King's Book, that the wording of the book was fashioned explicitly to make this position untenable, and that Henry himself had discussed it thoroughly with Cranmer and finally brought him to assent to the condemnation of "only faith." Despite the seriousness with which Gardiner regarded the matter, he could not resist a "merry tale" in illustration of his point. When Cranmer confidently questioned whether the *King's Book* really condemned justification by faith only, Gardiner was reminded of an acquaintance

"who moved among divines for a solemn doubt a matter that had no doubt at all, but he brought it in with such a circumstance that they . . . understood not . . . that [which] was evidently laid before their eyes, for he that moved the question fashioned it thus: How himself had sundry times looked upon divers authors to know, where the Gospel speaketh *de duobus filiis Zebedei* [of the two sons of Zebedee], who was those children's father. Whereunto no man would answer at that time; but within a month a good old man that had mused abroad and at large of the matter and wandered wide to find that [which] lay even before him, as one did his glove while he held it in his hand—this divine, I say, met him that asked the question a month after in Cheapside, and told him he had studied somewhat in the doubt he moved and had found who was these children's mother, but of the father he had read nothing." [4]

In reply to Gardiner's censure for dissenting from the *King's Book,* Cranmer had recalled how Gardiner had dissented from the *Bishops' Book,* to which Gardiner truthfully answered that the *Bishops' Book* had never been authoritatively sanctioned, and that he had protested against it immediately on its publication.

"If," he said, "I could have framed my conscience to agree with such a book during the King's life, I would not have written of it after his death, nor leapt into the pulpit to draw my sword which I had, all the King's life, kept in the sheath." [5]

His observation about the unwillingness of Englishmen to be long hearers evidently drew a reply from Cranmer, for Gardiner returned to the matter, with an illuminating picture of contemporary religious practice. He had not, he said, called his countrymen unwilling hearers in reproach, but rather to "extol the excellency of their wits," for

"we be accompted, next the Italians, the most ingenious people of Christendom. We will take a tale to be told ere it be half told, and by a word understand a sentence. . . . Your Grace would take an argument to the contrary from hearing of Mass and Matins. . . . It is in speech so called hearing, but indeed nothing so practised, nor never was, for in times past when men came to church more diligently than some do now, the people in the church took small heed what the priests and the clerks did in the chancel. . . .

It was never meant the people should indeed hear the Matins or the Mass, but be present there to pray themselves in silence.

. . . And good simple folk were wont so to be, and other more dissolute used to commune in the time of Matins and Mass of other matters. And I have known that after their little devotions said . . . some used to gather by the penny or twopence such money as they had lent in gross. . . .

And it is a common fashion to ask who preacheth; so as the audience increaseth by the man that preacheth and not by the matter. . . . There is in this church [at Waltham probably] good preaching and solemn singing to it, and yet of all this town there may be percase sometime not above twenty at a sermon. And I was in your Grace's church at Canterbury upon Ascension Day was twelvemonth, . . . where, I think, besides the children of the school and such as were of the house, there were but one hundred for so great a town. And yet he that preached pretended to preach mere godliness. And at another time when I was there and Mr. Ridley preached and I dined afterwards with your Grace, I thank you, there were not, for all Canterbury, many more; whereof I was not sorry because the chief part of the sermon was directed to me to set forth the bishops' fare." [6]

Gardiner concluded this long letter by saying that he took Cranmer's exhortation to obedience in good part, trusting that Cranmer himself would obey the authorized standards of doctrine. As for expressing his own mind on the plans of those in authority, he intended, he said, to do so freely, but only to those in authority and not to the people, for he would not "wrangle out of place and time, only to do hurt."

"This," he said, "is my determination: to serve God whilst I am here with all such gifts as I have received of him, which I do not so perfectly as I should, but somewhat towards it; so as though I be not perfectly good, I will not by God's grace be utterly naught; so to care for this world as if I thought to go hence, and yet to use it whilst I am here, and not to be weary of it out of reason ne despair in it without cause, as indeed I see no cause why I should." [7]

He also wrote to Somerset concerning the Homilies. That they had been brought forward in a previous Convocation was not, he said, sufficient warrant for issuing them now. "A new authority from the King's Majesty that now is" would be necessary, but in any event it were better not to issue them at all.

"For like as in a natural body, rest without trouble doth confirm and strengthen it, so it is in a commonwealth; trouble travaileth and bringeth the things to looseness. . . .

A new order engendereth a new cause of punishment against

them that offend; and punishments be not pleasant to them that
have the execution; and yet they must be, for nothing may be
contemned. And thus I travail in the matter with my Lord of
Canterbury, because he would I should weigh things. And so
I do as indifferently [*i.e.,* impartially] as ever man did for the
preservation of the ship wherein I sail myself and so many
others whose prosperity I am bound to wish. I can admit no
innovations." [8]

Despite Gardiner's protests the *First Book of Homilies* was issued
July 31, 1547, and on the same day appeared the royal injunctions
enjoining its use and that of an English translation of Erasmus'
Paraphrase of the New Testament. Thus did the Protector and the
Archbishop ignore Gardiner's contention that changes in the established religion during the minority of Edward VI were unwise and
hazardous.

Yet a few months previous, when the French ambassador had
suggested that certain Papal representatives be permitted to come
to England, Somerset replied that Henry VIII

"at his death had very expressly commanded both him and all
others of his Council to keep not only the laws but all else in
the state of the realm in such condition as he had left them,
without changing anything." [9]

Cranmer opposed the dissolution of chantries on the ground that such
a step should not be taken until the King came of age; [10] and when
his secretary, Morice, suggested to him, on the eve of the general
visitation of 1547, that this was the time to reform "certain enormities" and "vain ceremonies," the Archbishop replied:

"It was better to attempt such reformation in King Henry
VIII's days than at this time, the King being in his infancy.
For if the King's father had set forth anything for the reformation of abuses, who was he that durst gainsay it? Marry! We
are now in doubt how men will take the change or alteration of
abuses in the Church." [11]

Evidently both Somerset and Cranmer found Gardiner's position
had more to be said for it than they were willing to admit to him.
The principle of no change during the minority was a convenient one
to invoke when no change was wanted, but troublesome when "alteration of abuses" was desired.

XXII

THE FLEET

When Gardiner wrote from his diocese to Cranmer in the summer of 1547, advising against issuing the Homilies, he said he accounted it a piece of good fortune "after so many years' service . . . to arrive in this haven of quietness without loss of any notable tackle, as the mariners say." He justified Henry VIII's religious policy by the successful reign and honourable death of that monarch, pointing also to

> "myself, his poor servant, with a little flea biting of this world, conveyed to an easy estate, without diminution of my reputation." [1]

It was, however, the fact that his reputation was undiminished which threatened the haven of quietness which his diocese afforded. The position of the Protector and the Council was not so well established as to permit them to leave at large an ecclesiastic of the prominence of Gardiner, who, though ousted from the Council, might still marshall the conservative forces in Parliament.

Royal injunctions were, as we have seen, issued at the end of July 1547, enjoining the use of the *First Book of Homilies*—a collection of discourses to be read as sermons to the people—and Erasmus' *Paraphrase of the New Testament,* which was to be studied by the clergy, and placed in the churches to be read by the people if they so desired. A general visitation of the whole kingdom to enforce the injunctions was likewise decided upon.

Gardiner says that he did not hear of "the execution of the visitation" until after Somerset had departed on his campaign against Scotland, that is, some time after August 23, 1547.[2] Then, as soon as the newly printed copies of the enjoined books came to his hands, he took no sleep till he had read them. He thereupon lodged a vigorous protest with the Council against their use; for the haste with which the Council seemed bent on acting during the Protector's absence, encouraged him to believe that if action could only be checked till Somerset returned, the injunctions might be withdrawn.

> "Let no man be offended," he said later, "with the vehemency of my writing, for I wrote with a whole heart; and if I could have written it with the blood of my heart I would have

done it, to have done good, in staying the thing till it had been more maturely digested, and till your Grace's safe return." [3]

His initial protest to the Council was against the Homilies only. In the *King's Book,* he wrote, the people had been taught "a very true doctrine; that faith doth neither justify only, ne alone, but as it is coupled together with other virtues." In the Homilies they are to be taught that only faith justifies, and that whoever denies this is no true Christian,

> "which is a terrible speech and a marvellous to be published in this realm to the condemnation of our late Sovereign Lord, the condemnation of our self, and the prejudice of the truth."

The doctrine of justification by faith only is, he averred, contrary to the Scriptures, to the Fathers, and to the established standards of the English Church. It is, moreover, invariably connected with such other false doctrines as the Germans have maintained to their own confusion.

The whole matter of religious change, he added, has a bearing on international relationships, for when he was last at the Imperial court Granvelle assured him that Henry VIII's

> "resolutions in religion much moved the Emperor to withstand such persuasions as the French King, by means of a friar, used to persuade him to slip from us."

Finally, he justly complained that the Homilies had been issued

> "without any solemn assembly of us together to hear such speak with us as make these Homilies. . . . Our late Sovereign Lord made no alteration in his time without a convocation of bishops and open debating of the matter." [4]

Soon after sending this letter, it occurred to him that there was on the statute books a law passed in 1543 condemning as heretics all who taught anything contrary to the doctrines set forth in the *King's Book.* He immediately wrote a second letter reminding the Council of this law, and maintaining that anyone who, in obedience to the injunctions, read the Homilies publicly would be incurring the guilt of præmunire, since an act of Parliament was of superior authority to an injunction, even if issued in the name of the King as Supreme Head.

> "I have heard," he wrote, "the learned men of the common law say that if any, although he be deputed by the King, do, in execution of spiritual jurisdiction, extend the same contrary to any common law or act of Parliament it is a præmunire. . . . And seeing the præmunire is dangerous to all that be parties in the matter, I trust ye will take in good part that I beware of it."

"If your Lordships do not stay the matter . . . I must and will allege here, in the most quiet and humble manner I can, the said act of Parliament, and desire the benefit of it for conservation of religion, . . . and that good simple souls be not enjoined to speak in the pulpit matter against the act of Parliament, for doing whereof they were in danger to be punished by the order of the King's law."

"Beware, my Lords, of them that preach 'only faith.' . . . For that opinion . . . was the curse of Germany. . . . And all that have of late preached it ought by the act of Parliament in any wise recant. This is the law of the realm at this day." [5]

At the same time, August 30, 1547, he wrote to Sir John Mason, one of the commissioners appointed to visit his diocese, assuring him that he would be as welcome as any man of his degree in England, but warning him that at every sitting where he, as Bishop, was commanded to appear, he would make humble suit that he and his clergy might not, by an injunction, be compelled to offend an act of Parliament. He reminded Mason

"that every act of Parliament is as strong in one case as in another, and that which is today a spiritual man's case may be tomorrow a temporal man's case." [6]

This legal aspect of the question was still further discussed by him in a later letter to the Protector:

"Whether the King may command against an act of Parliament and what danger they may fall in that break a law with the King's consent, I dare say no man alive at this day hath had more experience, what judges and lawyers have said, than I."

He cited, among others, the case of his old master, Cardinal Wolsey, and that of John Voysey, Bishop of Exeter, in whose behalf, when "brought in a præmunire," in 1541, Gardiner, as he said,

"reasoned with the Lord Audley, then Chancellor, so far as he bade me hold my peace for fear of entering into a præmunire myself. Whereupon I stayed, but concluded it seemed to me strange that a man authorized by the King (as, since the King's majesty hath taken upon him the supremacy, every bishop is such a one), could fall in a præmunire."

He further told how, when he brought up the matter again in Parliament, "where was free speech without danger," Audley, knowing him to be "in some secret estimation," addressed him thus familiarly:

"Thou art a good fellow, Bishop—look at the Act of Supremacy, and there the King's doings be restrained to spiritual jurisdiction; and in another act it is provided that no spiritual law shall have place contrary to the Common Law or act of Parliament. And [*i.e.* if] this were not, you bishops would enter in with the King, and by means of his supremacy order the laity as ye listed."

He also related, how, shortly before the close of the last reign, he had occasion even at the Emperor's court to explain the English principle "that the kings of this realm were not above the order of their laws," a principle which he had learned, he said, "by hearing the common lawyers speak, whose judgements rule these matters, howsoever my reason can digest them." [7]

Mr. A. F. Pollard credits Gardiner, in this protest against the injunctions, with "the liberal contention" that "the royal authority in the Church was, or should be, limited by the same statutory and common law restrictions as in the State. The injunctions, he said, had not received parliamentary authorization and were therefore illegal"—an argument which Mr. Pollard goes on to declare unsound, because "the same might have been said of Cromwell's injunctions; but the Act of Supremacy covered both cases, unless Gardiner's further contention held good that the royal supremacy was in abeyance during the royal minority." [8]

This is not an accurate statement of Gardiner's position. He objected to the injunctions, not because they had no parliamentary authorization, but because they were in direct contradiction to parliamentary enactment. He contended that it was a principle of English law, not that everything enjoined by the Supreme Head must have the sanction of Parliament, but that nothing might be enjoined by the Supreme Head which required disobedience to an act of Parliament. Mr. Pollard justly observes that "the Act of Supremacy and subsequent legislation in Henry's reign had given the King legal authority to reform any ecclesiastical abuses he thought needed reformation;" but no act in Henry's reign empowered him to enjoin upon his subjects disobedience to a statute. Even the law of 1539, which gave to royal proclamations the force of statutes, expressly provided that these proclamations should not infringe any act of Parliament. [9] It would seem therefore that Gardiner's contention was constitutionally impeccable. Certainly the only constitutional answer which Somerset and the Council vouchsafed to give him was the repeal, in the next Parliament, of the law on which he took his stand. [10]

What Mr. Pollard calls Gardiner's further contention "that the royal supremacy was in abeyance during the royal minority" is nowhere to be found in Gardiner's writings. He merely maintained that religious changes during the minority were highly unwise because, among other reasons, they were popularly regarded as of questionable validity, and because they might, even if embodied in acts of Parliament, be annulled by Edward when he came of age. Here again his position was unassailable, for the law of 1536, empowering Henry's successor to repeal by letters patent, on coming of age, any act of Parliament passed during his young years, was still on the statute books. To this contention Somerset's answer was the essential modification of the act in the next Parliament.

Shortly after Gardiner sent his protest against the injunctions to the Council, Sir John Godsalve, one of the visitors appointed for London, Norwich, and Ely, wrote to him advising acquiescence. Gardiner's reply, says Burnet, "has more of a Christian and a bishop in it than anything I ever saw of his." [11]

"I was called to this bishopric," he wrote, "without the offence of God's law or the King's in the attaining of it. I have kept my bishopric these sixteen years, accomplished this very day that I write these my letters unto you, without offending God's law or the King's in the retaining of it, howsoever I have of frailty otherwise sinned. Now if I may play the third part well, to depart from the bishopric without the offence of God's law or the King's, I shall think the tragedy of my life well passed over; . . . for so I offend not God's law nor the King's I will no more care to see my bishopric taken from me than myself to be taken from the bishopric.

I am by nature already condemned to die, which sentence no man can pardon, ne assure me of delay in the execution of it, and so see that of necessity I shall leave my bishopric to the disposition of the crown from whence I had it, my household also to break up, and my bringing up of youth to cease, the remembrance whereof troubleth me nothing.

I made in my house at London a pleasant study that delighted me much, and yet I was glad to come into the country and leave it; and as I have left the use of somewhat so can I leave the use of all to obtain a more quiet. It is not loss to change for the better. Honesty and truth are more leefe to me than all the possessions of the realm, and in these two to say and do frankly, as I must, I never forbare yet; and in these two, honesty and truth, I take such pleasure and comfort as I will never leave them for no respect; for they will abide by a man, and so will nothing else. No man can take them away from me but myself; and if myself do them away from me, then myself do undo myself, and make myself worthy to lose my bishopric."

When the visitors come, he will, he says, make "a plain allegation" that, in accordance with "the inheritance of the King's laws due to every Englishman," he ought "not to be enjoined against an act of Parliament." Moreover, the Protector had, he said,

> "in one of such letters as he wrote unto me, willed me not to fear too much; and indeed I know him so well, and divers other of my Lords of the Council, that I cannot fear any hurt at their hands in the allegation of God's law and the King's." [12]

How far he was to fear the lords of the Council he was soon to see. On September 21, 1547 they summoned him to appear before them at Hampton Court on the following Sunday morning, September 25.[13] "I came to them," he says, "with my sleeves and bosom trussed full of books to furnish my former allegations." He admits that he "was heard very well and gently," and that the councillors used "many good words" to bring him to their opinion. When pressed to declare whether he would receive the injunctions, he answered that he would do so as far as God's law and the King's would bind him; whereupon it was intimated that unless he avowed his intention to receive them unconditionally he would be sent to the Fleet. He pointed out that although his conscience prevented his acceptance of them at the moment, the visitation of his diocese was still distant by three weeks, during which he might change his mind. He offered to dispute the matter at Oxford and abide by the decision there given, so he might say, if he yielded, that learning had overcome him. When this was refused he asked that men of learning be sent to instruct him at his house in Southwark. The reply of the Council was commitment to the Fleet.

> "I told my Lords," he says, "I thought it hard . . . to send me to prison for declaring beforehand what I minded to do, before any thing had been by me actually done to resist the visitation." [14]

Two weeks later, October 7, he was brought from prison "with some gazing of the world," to a conference with Cranmer at the deanery of St. Paul's, in which the Archbishop, in the presence of Bishop Ridley, Dr. Cox, and Dr. Ayre, endeavoured to convince him of the position on justification taken in the Homilies. Gardiner offered to yield provided he could be shown a single place in Scripture or a single quotation from the Fathers "affirming faith to exclude charity in justification." Cranmer, being unable to show such a passage, fell to arguing, says Gardiner, in order to "overcome me that am called the sophister, by sophistry."

The Archbishop, moreover, hinted broadly that if Gardiner would support the new religious policy he would be readmitted to the Council, saying he was "a man meet in his opinion to be called to the Council again." "They were worldly comfortable words," wrote

Gardiner later, but added that if he had agreed with Cranmer in order to regain his place in the Government, he were worthy

> "to be whipped in every market town in the realm, and then hanged for example, as the veriest varlet that ever was bishop."

Cranmer finally charged him with liking nothing unless he was author of it himself, a charge which he vehemently denied, exclaiming, with characteristic concern for things established, "I was never author of any one thing, either spiritual or temporal; I thank God for it."

On his failure to come to an agreement with the Archbishop, he was returned to the Fleet, which was, he caustically remarked, "one argument I could not assoil." [15] Here he remained for exactly three months more, without judicial examination or conviction, without even being charged with a breach of any existing law.

He wrote several letters to Somerset, after the latter's return from his victorious campaign in Scotland, complaining of this manifest injustice.

> "Before a law made," he said, "I have not seen such a kind of imprisonment as I sustain, humbly offering myself ready to learn. Our late Sovereign Lord . . . suffered every man to say his mind without imprisonment till the matter were established by law."

> "Howsoever your Grace be informed, I never gave advice, nor ever knew man committed to prison for disagreeing to any doctrine, unless the same doctrine were established by a law of the realm before."

He put this significant question to the Protector:

> "If your Grace would have this for a precedent, that whatsoever the King's Council for the time of a prince's minority shall send to be preached much needs be received without allegation, of what strength is the act of Parliament against the Bishop of Rome?"

> "Precedents," he added, "be dangerous, for I have seen it almost for a rule that whatsoever hath been once done may then without question be done again."

He denied the accusation that he had "spoken to others impertinent things of the King's Majesty's visitation," saying, "I never advised any man to object anything against these books, no one man, not my chaplains." [16] When he saw that his protest had not succeeded in staying the visitation he had instructed his proctors, chancellor, and clergy to receive the visitors honourably, and observe the injunctions. [17]

In spite of what his opponents said of "Winchester's faction," he had never, he averred, laboured secretly to bring others to his opinion. He had not even advised the religious measures which his protégé Wriothesley had taken as Chancellor—an office of which he had been deprived in March of this year. It was not his custom, he said, to urge any ecclesiastical policy upon anyone but the sovereign himself or those exercising the royal authority in his behalf.[18]

Although his complaints of unjust imprisonment went unheeded, he felt it his duty to continue to urge the Protector to recall the Homilies and the *Paraphrase,* in which, he said, now that he had so much leisure to study, he found daily some new fault. Justification as treated in Cranmer's *Homily of Salvation,* was, he affirmed, a question which might better be discussed at the universities than preached to the people,

> "for we all are justified in Baptism while younglings, and, falling after Baptism, we must arise by the Sacrament of Penance."
>
> "It is a terrible matter to think on, to see such a contention to rise upon a matter not necessary to be spoken of; wherein if my Lord of Canterbury will needs travail, my judgement is that he will never persuade that faith excludeth charity in justification, unless he borrow, of your Grace's authority, prisons; and then he shall percase have some agree unto it, as poor men kneel at Rome when the Bishop there goeth by; that is to say, are knocked on the head with a halbert, if they kneel not, for that is one piece of the office of the Bishop of Rome's guard."

As for the *Paraphrase,* it encouraged contempt for government, for the Sacrament, and even for morality. It had been written, he said, by Erasmus more than twenty-six years past, "when his pen was wanton," and contained things which he had unsaid in his later writings. Moreover, bad as the original Latin edition had been, the English translation now issued was worse; it was full of errors, some made through the "arrogant ignorance of the translator," some "evidently of purpose." If he could prevent its going abroad even at the expense of his life, he would be satisfied, he said, that he had done as good a deed as ever was done in the realm.

> "I have favored Erasmus' name as much as any other, but I never studied over this book till now, and now I agree with them that said, 'Erasmus laid the eggs and Luther hatched them.'"

And this "abomination" would cost the purchasers throughout the realm at least, he estimated, £20,000.

He excused the homeliness of his language to Somerset on the ground of their old friendship:

> "Though some account me a Papist, yet I cannot play the

Pope-holy, as the old term was. I dare not . . . speak of God and his truth in every second sentence, and become suddenly a prophet to your Grace . . . with whom I have been heretofore so familiarly conversant." [19]

Although he was permitted to have his cook and two servants to wait on him in the Fleet, he was straitly kept from all intercourse with friends or other members of his household.

"Here I remain," he wrote at the end of October, "without bail or mainprise, without comfort of any of my friends or servants, as one divided from the world; no chaplain to accompany me in prayer; no barber nor tailor for bodily necessaries; nor liberty to use physician for relief of disease, whereof I have need."

Two weeks later he wrote again, remarking that although the Stoics taught contempt for pain, they doubtless shrank a little when "any disease nipped them."

"And now my stomach nippeth me, which I have favoured as much as any man in England, and have laden it as light, either with meat or drink of many years. . . . as any other. And after I saw I could get no answer from your Grace for a physician, I have left off such study as I used, and given myself to continual walking for exercise."

"The world is mere vanity, which I may learn in mine own case, being now destitute of all such help as friendship, service, familiarity, or gentleness seemed to have gotten me." [20]

About the middle of November Somerset permitted Gardiner's physician to visit him and, for the first time, it seems, replied to his communications. The reply must have been a sharp one, for Gardiner says of it:

"Your Grace's letters return every word of my letters in my neck, and take my fly as it were a bee, which I thought should have stung no man."

This did not, however, prevent the Bishop from insisting that he ought to be thanked rather than blamed for his protest against the books and injunctions.

"I have a charge in the bishopric of Winchester to see the people fed with wholesome doctrine; . . . and how can it be taken for a fault to say reverently to the Council, 'My Lords! me seemeth this and this cannot stand together; either instruct me in them, or amend them.' . . . Am I worthy for so saying to be condemned to a perpetual prison?"

His objections were not, he averred, raised through captiousness.

"I do not trifle with my wit to undo myself, but travail with my honesty to preserve my country, to preserve my prince, to preserve religion."

"I adventure as much as any man hath done to save my conscience."

"And if I be not heard, my conscience telleth me I have done my duty, and therewith from travail shall apply myself to prayer."

"Why should my Lord of Canterbury so fear me as he doth, that he may not suffer me to come abroad as one that should hinder his enterprises . . .? He that feareth me must fear only truth."

"If my Lord of Canterbury think I will wax mad, he is deceived, for I wax every day better learned." [21]

The straitness of his detention was mitigated about a fortnight before Christmas, when William Medowe, the chaplain longest in his service, was permitted to come and stay with him; shortly after, James Basset, son of his old friend Lady Lisle of Calais, and other members of his household were given the like permission. [22]

Meanwhile Parliament had begun on November 4 (1547), and Gardiner suspected, not without reason, that one cause of his imprisonment was the desire of his opponents to keep both himself and those he was "used to name in the nether house" from attending. [23] His protests on this score were, however, unavailing.

In this Parliament the Act of the Six Articles and the act of 1543 giving parliamentary sanction to the *King's Book* were repealed. The act concerning laws passed during a minority was so reworded as to make it clear that although the King, on coming of age, might repeal statutes enacted during his young years, the repeal was not to be retroactive, and everything done under such statutes up to the time of their repeal was to remain valid. [24]

With his ground thus cut from under him, Gardiner was, on Sunday, January 8, 1548, two weeks after the end of the session, and fifteen from the day of his commitment, brought before the Protector and Council at Hampton Court and informed that his offences were remitted by a general pardon. "Having ministered to him a good lesson and admonition," the Council set him at liberty, not, however, until they had demanded whether he would conform to the injunctions and Homilies "and such other doctrine as should be set forth from time to time by the King's Highness and clergy of this realm; articles of part whereof touching justification were then exhibited to him to declare in the same his opinion."

He answered "that he would conform himself accordingly as other bishops did," but "touching the articles delivered to him he desired respite of answer for four or five days," which was granted him.[25] The answers he presented to the Council the following Thursday were unsatisfactory. Since he refused to subscribe to the articles as they stood, on the ground that they had as yet no official sanction, he was committed prisoner to his own house in Southwark a week later, January 19. Here he remained just one month, during which several attempts to persuade him to subscribe were made by Bishop Ridley, William Cecil, and Sir Thomas Smith. Cecil, the future Lord Burghley, was a young man of twenty-seven, rising in the favour of the Protector and acting as his private secretary; Smith, with whom Gardiner had held friendly debate on the pronunciation of Greek in 1542, was now clerk of the Council and soon to be made one of the two principal Secretaries of State. Gardiner did not subscribe, but finally produced an answer which was accepted by the Protector, February 20, and, "discharged thereof with thanks, . . . went down to Winchester as a person delivered from all trouble or travail of business."[26]

He came to Farnham on St. Matthias' Eve, and hearing from the vicar that the people were murmuring against the destruction of images and other things done in the late visitation, he preached next day on obedience, and quieted the people by telling them that it was within the power of princes to alter ceremonies. He exhorted them to conform to whatever was set forth by their superiors.[27]

On reaching Winchester he endeavoured to see that injunctions, royal proclamations, and statutes were scrupulously obeyed in his diocese, and to secure the use of the new order of Holy Communion, issued by royal authority early in March 1548, containing certain English additions to the Latin Mass and providing for the administration of wine as well as bread to the laity.[28] He continued, however, to use customary ceremonies not forbidden.

He had been at liberty in his diocese scant two weeks when he was asked by the Protector, who had succeeded him as Chancellor of Cambridge University late in 1547,[29] to surrender his old college, Trinity Hall, of which he still held the mastership, that it might be converted, with its neighbour, Clare Hall, into a new college for the study of Civil Law. This Gardiner refused to do, and the chief reason for his refusal appears to have been a fear that, when surrendered, Trinity Hall and its endowments would find their way into the pockets of the Protector and his insatiable followers ere the new foundation was effected. He prized his college, he said, almost as highly as his bishopric, to which the Protector retorted that since distance prevented his presence in both places he should let him know which he preferred to relinquish![30] His refusal to surrender the college may have had something to do with his subsequent loss of the mastership;[31] it did not deter Somerset from pursuing the plan, which was not, it seems, effectively interrupted until the insurrection and general confusion of the following year demanded his attention elsewhere.[32]

The next disturbance of the Bishop's quiet came in the shape of a summons from the Council, issued on Easter Day, April 1, to appear within a fortnight in answer to a report that some of his servants at Winchester had been "kindling up of the people's minds against things set forth by the King's Majesty's authority;" but illness secured a postponement of his journey for a time.[33]

Meanwhile on the Sunday before Easter, or perhaps the Sunday after, he preached a sermon in his cathedral church similar to the one at Farnham on obedience. In the Winchester sermon, however, he considered the problem of the man who is commanded by his sovereign to do something contrary to God's law, and his solution was strangely like that once given by Friar Barnes. In this case, he said, we ought neither to act contrary to God's law, nor to resist the command, but "suffer willingly the power of the superior to punish us."[34] The intimation that he looked upon the religious policy of the Government as likely to involve suffering for the conscientious Christian could hardly have been pleasing to the Council.

On April 12 (1548), the second Thursday after Easter, there arrived at Winchester two of the King's chaplains, Dr. Giles Ayre and a certain Dr. Tonge, who had been sent down to be prebendaries of the cathedral. They were received hospitably, but after the Bishop's sermon the next Sunday, they complained to the Protector that they had been defamed. Just what was said in the sermon is not clear; the prebendaries reported that the Bishop alluded to new preachers in his diocese (although they did not say that he named them), and exhorted his flock rather to believe the doctrine he had taught them than that preached by men they had never before seen, "than the which words," reads the official record of the Council, "none could have been spoken more perilous and seditious."[35]

A second summons to appear before the Council reached him three days before Whitsuntide. He was at the time "diseased of a fistula," so that he could not ride his mule without much pain, and was, moreover suffering from "a great rheum . . . which caused the one side of his head to be much swollen." He had himself, therefore, brought in a horse litter to the Thames at Kingston and thence in his barge to London.[36]

He came before the Council May 26, the day after his arrival in the city. The Protector not only taxed him with the defamation of the prebendaries but also with creeping to the cross on Good Friday, carrying palms on Palm Sunday, having a "solemn sepulchre"[37] at Easter, preaching that the body of Christ was really present in the Sacrament, and saying with derisive iteration in a sermon that "the Apostles went from the presence of the Council, of the Council, of the Council." (Palms, creeping to the cross, and discussion of the

Sacrament in other than Scriptural terms had been forbidden by recent proclamations.)

Gardiner replied that Somerset had been misinformed about the defamation of the prebendaries, the palms, the creeping to the cross, and the contemptuous allusion to the Council. He admitted the solemn sepulchre and other ceremonies not forbidden, and defended his use of them as obedience to the royal proclamation against unauthorized alterations. He denied that he had used the word "really" in connection with the Sacrament, but confessed that he had taught his people the "very presence" as the plain meaning of Scripture, which was no more than the Archbishop himself had done when refuting the heretic Lambert in the late reign. He concluded by declaring how much he esteemed obedience and how he had preached in his diocese that "the whole life of a Christian man consisteth in suffering properly," and that "we must either suffer the rulers' will or . . . their power to punish us."

Neither were the charges serious enough nor the evidence sufficient to warrant further procedure against him; but since the Council thought that his return to Winchester "might be a hindrance to the King's Majesty's proceedings," the Protector told him he must tarry about London and bade him write his mind on ceremonies, which he afterward did. He asked for the use of a country house near the city, such as Esher, which had formerly been the property of his see, but as this was refused, he once more took up his residence in Southwark. [38]

Despite these many disturbances to his peace of mind and body, the Bishop had, during the previous months, been engaged in literary composition. His old antagonist Bucer had at last published, early in this year, a reply to Gardiner's two books of 1544 and 1545. Bucer said he would have done so sooner had not Henry VIII asked him to defer it lest it hinder a possible concord between England and the continental reformers. [39] Gardiner charged him with waiting to renew the conflict till his opponent was downed by circumstances, and confessed that he himself was in no state of mind for theological writing. He was not, he said, one who could accept misfortune with equanimity; he was often worried even by little things, and despondent in time of trouble. Yet Bucer's impudence and shiftiness spurred him to reply. [40] On May 7, 1548 he dated the preface of his "Examination of the passages from the holy Fathers which Martin Bucer has unholily brought forth in support of his heretical opinion on the gift of celibacy" (*Exetasis testimoniorum*, etc.), [41] and hurried it off to the printer at Louvain, where, owing to further misfortunes which overtook its author, it lay unpublished till 1554. [42]

XXIII

ST. PETER'S DAY

Gardiner had hardly taken up his residence again in Southwark, when, early in June 1548, Cecil came to him with a request from Somerset that he preach before the King and submit his sermon in writing before preaching it. Cecil at the same time intimated that inasmuch as the Bishop was an offender the Protector had already shown him more favour than he deserved. The Bishop was "somewhat moved" at this, and declined to answer Cecil, and, when an audience with the Protector was denied him, sent his scholarly young chaplain, Thomas Watson,[1] to the Duke to protest against Cecil's language, saying he "was never so spoken to in all his life." Watson was also to express the Bishop's willingness to preach, but to make it clear that he would not submit his sermon in advance, as such a procedure would put him in the place of an offender, which he was not.

Somerset told Watson that Cecil had not exceeded his authority, and that, since the Bishop refused to write his sermon, certain articles would be sent him on which he would be required to preach. He added, however, that he had declined to speak with him, not for any displeasure, but because "it was thought he favoured him overmuch." If he "had followed other men's advices he should have sent him to the Tower when he was last before the Council."[2]

Within a few days Cecil brought the Bishop the articles on which he was to preach. They touched on the abrogation of Papal authority, the suppression of monasteries, shrines, chantries, and Masses satisfactory, the destruction of images, and the abolition of certain ceremonies such as the hallowing of ashes, palms, candles, water, and beads, and such children's mummeries as that of the boy bishop chosen on the feast of St. Nicholas; they called for the Bishop's acknowledgment that auricular confession was unnecessary, and for his approval of the administration of the Communion in both kinds, and of the "procession" (*i.e.* the litany) and common prayer in English. They involved, in short, an acceptance of the changes so far accomplished in the Church, and, it would seem, from the reference to common prayer in English, an approval of changes as yet only in contemplation.[3]

When Cecil presented the articles he said the Bishop would have to repeat them word for word in his sermon. This Gardiner flatly refused to do, again on the ground that so doing would put him in place of a penitent offender against the laws. Moreover, it was, he said, "like a lesson made for a child to learn." [4]

Thereupon the Protector summoned him to court Monday morning, June 18 (1548). The Bishop, coming in his barge, was admitted by a back stairs directly into Somerset's chamber, where, in the presence of William Paulet, Lord St. John, Somerset showed him the opinion of certain experts in the law, gathered by Sir Thomas Smith and Paget, at the instance of Somerset himself, that an ecclesiastical person disobeying an injunction from the King, "might, after certain circumstances and admonitions, be deprived." Gardiner said that if he could speak with these learned lawyers it would soon appear that their opinion did not touch his case, but Somerset replied that he should speak with no one, but do as he was bidden or do worse, giving him till afternoon to decide whether he would read the articles in his sermon or not. The Bishop was then taken by a secret way to Paulet's chamber where dinner was served him alone, after which Smith came to him to persuade him to read the articles as desired. Gardiner pointed out that if it were the purpose of the Council to make him appear publicly as one who read words which he did not mean in order to get himself out of trouble, their purpose would be accomplished if he obeyed, but if they really wanted to know his own opinions and have him preach for the edifying of his hearers, they would leave his sermon to his own judgement. Smith then said that it would not be necessary to rehearse the articles word for word if only he preached on the matters contained therein. This he readily consented to do, and repeated his consent when Smith brought him again into the presence of Somerset and Paulet; but he declined to give his sermon in writing, saying that he never wrote sermons, and added that he did not think it fitting to speak particularly of all the abolished ceremonies named in the articles, especially such "children's toys" as "the going about of St. Nicholas," else his audience would laugh at him and call him "a babbler of ceremonies."

> "When ceremonies were plenty, they will say, I did nothing but preach on them, and now they be gone I babble of them still."

He said he would touch the chief points, adding that he would speak of other matters also; and being given liberty to choose the day for the sermon, departed.

St. Peter's Day, June 29, which in 1548 fell on a Friday, was the day he chose, since the Gospel for that day, containing St. Peter's confession, "served well for the purpose." [5]

Thrice during the ten days preceding the sermon Cecil came to him with suggestions concerning it. On the first occasion he recalled how Gardiner had once said that a king was as much a king at one year of age as at a hundred, and said it would be well taken if this were touched on in the sermon, but on his second coming (Monday, June 25) he said that if the Bishop spoke of the King's authority during his minority he should also speak of that of the Council.

> "Whereunto," says Gardiner, "I made no answer, but shifted to other matter, without making him any promise or denial, because I would neither bind myself nor trouble myself to discuss that matter."

There was no word of this in the articles on which he had promised to preach, and although he was not averse to defending the King's authority on the basis of Scripture, he found no divine sanction for the authority of king's councillors.

On his third visit (Wednesday, June 27), which was but two days before the sermon, Cecil brought Somerset's advice that if Gardiner wished to avoid trouble, he would not speak of the Sacrament. When he saw that the Bishop did not take this very well, he added that he meant "doubtful matters," such as transubstantiation. Gardiner replied that Cecil "wist not what transubstantiation meant," and told him to tell Somerset not to meddle with matters of religion, but refer them to bishops who could understand them. As for himself, he "must and would utter the Catholic faith," if he were permitted to preach.

> "I will preach, quoth I, the very presence of Christ's most precious body and blood in the Sacrament, which is the Catholic faith, and no doubtful matter, nor yet in controversy. . . . Among the matters, quoth I, whereof I have promised to speak, I must by special words speak of the Sacrament and of the Mass also. . . . I will not forbear to utter my faith and true belief therein, which I think necessary for the King's Majesty to know; and therefore if I wist to be hanged when I came down I would speak it." [6]

The next afternoon—the afternoon before the sermon—between three and four of the clock, Gardiner received a letter from Somerset charging him, on the King's behalf, not to speak "of any matter in controversy concerning the said Sacrament." This was, as Gardiner himself said, rather short notice, seeing that Somerset knew well that he might, and supposed that he would, speak of the Sacrament. Somerset added, in reply to Gardiner's admonition not to meddle with religion, that he deemed it his duty to bring the people "from superstition to true religion," and had determined,

> "where there is a full consent of other the bishops and learned men in a truth, not to suffer you, or a few other wilful heads, to disorder all the rest."

The Bishop was "much unquieted, perplexed, and troubled" by this letter, and was for a time at a loss as to whether he ought to answer it or not. He summoned his chaplain, Watson, to take an immediate reply, but after he had written two lines he stopped and began giving him an answer to be conveyed by word of mouth. This he broke off before he had finished, and in the end said: "You shall not go, I will do well enough, I warrant you."

It was indeed, a difficult position in which the letter placed him. Although it only forbade his speaking on matters *in controversy* touching the Sacrament, it was perfectly clear that Somerset wanted him to avoid all discussion of the Sacrament, and, in particular, of the presence in it of Christ's body and blood. But it was just this which Gardiner regarded as the foundation of Christian belief. To preach a sermon in which he had promised frankly to utter his mind on the state of the Church, and to side-step this issue would not only have lost him the respect of all Catholic-minded Churchmen, but have been an intolerable violation of his own conscience. As he said of it later:

> "I might not take my Lord of Somerset's letter for an inhibition to hold my peace, when God biddeth me to speak, as he doth when the wolf cometh, and not to hide myself in silence, which is the most shameful running away of all."

He had warned Cecil the day before that he would declare his faith in the Sacrament even if he were to hang for it, and he determined to stick to his purpose despite Somerset's letter, but he took great pains so to frame his speech as to avoid a breach of the proclamation against speaking of the Sacrament otherwise than Scripture taught. If for this guarded utterance he were taken to task, he felt he had a double defense, first that Somerset's letter was signed by Somerset alone and not by the Council, and hence might be regarded as a personal request rather than an official command, second, that a simple affirmation of belief in the words "this is my body" could not justly be looked on as a discussion of matters in controversy, since it was clearly the Catholic faith, and still, officially, the faith of the Church of England. Nevertheless, Somerset's letter so disturbed him and interrupted his preparation for the sermon that, according to his own statement, supported by the testimony of his chaplains and servants, he "did neither eat, drink, nor sleep, till the next day at five o'clock at afternoon when his sermon was done; and only travailed in mind how to bring in and order what he should utter." James Bassett, who had been in his household almost a decade, said he had never seen the Bishop "in the like trouble before," for "the most part of all that night the said Bishop walked in a chamber, musing and devising of his sermon, speaking and preaching aloud thereof." [7]

It was in the new "preaching place"—an open air pulpit in the King's privy garden at Whitehall, where the preacher "might be heard of more than four times so many people as could have stood in the King's Chapel," and where Latimer had preached the first sermon a few months previous [8]—that Gardiner stood on the afternoon of St. Peter's Day 1548. [9] At a window in the gallery facing the pulpit sat the boy King and his uncle; a few favoured auditors stood "in the pulpit," that is, on the raised platform, under the canopy with the preacher; the rest of the congregation—nobility, gentry, clergy—thronged the garden, closely standing, alertly attent to orthodoxy or heresy, loyalty or treason as their interests and partisanship prompted. There was, in the words of the official minute of the Council, "such an audience as the like whereof hath not lightly been seen." [10]

One of those "in the pulpit" was Nicholas Udal, famed in the history of literature as the author of *Ralph Roister Doister,* diligently noting the words of the preacher in an effort to secure for a certain "noble personage" a verbatim report of the sermon. [11] It is not without irony that the author of the first comedy in the English tongue should have been the official reporter of the sermon whose sequel held so much of tragedy for the Bishop of Winchester.

The Bishop began by bidding his auditors pray for the King, whom he was careful to designate as "of the Church of England and Ireland, next and immediately under God, here on earth the Supreme Head." They were to pray likewise for his mother and sisters, for the Protector and Council, and for souls departed, "and among these most specially" King Henry VIII.

He then proceeded to comment on the Gospel for the day— Matthew xvi. 13-19. The diverse conjectures of the people there recorded, that Jesus was John the Baptist, or Elijah, or Jeremiah, showed, he said, how impossible it was for even well meaning men who were "out of Christ's school," not to mention those who through pride in their own opinions formed sects of their own, either to know the truth or to agree in it, whereas both knowledge of it and agreement in it were easy for disciples who partook of the obedience and simplicity of St. Peter, who, in confessing Jesus to be the Christ, spoke not only for himself but for his fellows.

This confession, "Thou art the Christ," led to the consideration of what Christ was. Christ, said the preacher, was our Messias, our Saviour, our Mediator, our Bishop, "for that was the office of a bishop to sacrifice for the sins of the people, and to make intercession for the people." He was also our Sacrifice. This led to the forbidden subject of the Mass:

"And like as his Sacrifice then made was sufficient for us, to deliver us from our sins, and to bring us in favour with God, so to continue us in the same favour of God he ordained a perpetual remembrance of himself. He ordained himself for a memory of himself at his Last Supper when he instituted the Sacrament of the Altar. Not for another redemption, as though the first had not been sufficient, nor as though the world needed a new redemption from sin; but that we might thoroughly remember his passion he instituted this Sacrament by his most holy word, saying, 'This is my body,' which word is sufficient to prove the Sacrament, and maketh sufficiently for the substance thereof. . . . And this is what we must believe of Christ, and believe it thoroughly; and therefore by your patience, as St. Peter made his confession, so will I make my confession. Wherein, by your Majesty's leave and sufferance, I will plainly declare what I think of the state of the Church of England at this day, how I like it and what I think of it."

Since the Mass is "a Sacrifice ordained to make us the more strong in the faith . . . and for commending unto God the souls of such as be dead in Christ . . . the Parliament very well ordained Mass to be kept."

"It is well done of the Parliament, for moving the people more and more with devotion, to ordain that this Sacrament should be received in both kinds. . . . I was ever of this opinion."

"The proclamation which was made, that no man should unreverently speak of the Sacrament, or otherwise speak of it than Scripture teacheth them, was well made; . . . for in Scripture is there nothing to be found that maketh anything against the Sacrament, but all maketh with it."

If the Mass has been abused in the chantries, by making it a satisfaction for sins, then it was well that the chantries were dissolved. "I, that allow Mass so well, and I, that allow praying for the dead, as indeed the dead are of Christian charity to be prayed for, yet can agree with the realm in that matter of putting down chantries." But the poor chantry priests, thus deprived of their livings, should be provided for.

"Now I will return to the text." That the Bishop of Rome should found his supremacy on Christ's words: "Thou art Peter, and upon this rock will I build my Church," is indeed a "marvellous thing," for Christ's meaning was: "Upon this confession of thy faith here, I will build my Church." Peter might perhaps "be called the head of the Church as the head of the river is called the head, because he was the first that made this confession of Christ," but "the first man is not evermore the best." That kings of England have sent to Rome for advice in religious matters is no reason for concluding that the Bishop of Rome is superior to the king. "For if a king be sick he will have the best physician; if he hath war he will have the best captain; and yet are not those the superiors but the inferiors."

"But now to go forth declaring my mind: in my time hath come many alterations. First, a great alteration it was to renounce the Bishop of Rome's authority, and I was one that stood in it. A great alteration it was that abbeys were dissolved. A great alteration it was that images were pulled down. And to all these did I condescend, and yet I have been counted a maintainer of superstition, and I have been called a master of ceremonies."

"As touching ceremonies, I esteem them all as Paul esteemeth them—things indifferent." Their purpose is "to move men to serve God, and as long as they be used for that purpose, they may well be used in the Church." When they are abused, it is in the power of the ruler either to reform or to abolish them. If they be essential to Christianity, like Baptism and preaching, they may be reformed but not abolished; if they be non-essential, like many monastic practices and the veneration of images, they may be either reformed or abolished. So the monastic orders, having fallen away from the purposes for which they were founded, have been abolished, "but one thing King Henry would not take away; that was the vow of chastity." The vow of obedience he has converted to himself; "their vow of poverty was provided for meetly well, for many of them are become poor enough."

Images likewise have been removed. "I have preached against the despisers of them, and have said that images might be suffered and used in the Church, as laymen's books. . . . But now that men be waxed wanton they are clean taken away, wherein our religion is no more touched than when books were taken away for abusing of them." "We had palms and candles taken away . . . but the religion of Christ is not in these exercises. . . . Men must in such things be conformable."

"I have told you my opinion. . . . I like well the Communion. . . . I like well the proclamation. . . . I like well the rest of the King's Majesty's proceedings concerning the Sacrament. . . . But shall I speak nothing of what I mislike? . . . I mislike that preachers which preach by the King's licence, and those readers, which by the King's permission and sufferance do read open lectures, do openly and blasphemously talk against the Mass and against the Sacrament. . . . To speak so against the Sacrament, it is the most marvellous matter that ever I saw or heard of. . . . It misliketh me that priests and men that vowed chastity should openly marry and avow it openly, which is a thing that since the beginning of the Church hath not been seen in any time."

Finally he misliked, he said, subjects "that would take upon them to rule like kings, to the diminishing of the King's dignity and the confusion of their own estate," and he pointed dramatically to the young King in the gallery, saying that he would have but one king, and he only was to be obeyed.[12]

Having been "very quietly heard," Gardiner was "merry and quiet" on the way home in his barge, and dined peacefully that night, in the conviction that he had entirely satisfied the Council. The next morning Watson, his chaplain, heard a rumour in the city that his master would be sent to the Tower, and reported it to him, but the Bishop said "it was but tales, for he thought that he never pleased the Council better in all his life." He entertained the Lady St. Leger (a niece of Archbishop Warham) and other guests at dinner, and Basset tells us that "he was never more merry" than he was at table that day, which was Saturday, June 30 (1548). He was, it seems, taken by surprise when Sir Ralph Sadler and Sir Anthony Wingfield appeared after dinner with a company of the guard, though he lost none of his wonted composure at their coming. When his secretary announced them, he said:

> " 'They are welcome. Give me my book,' and therewith put the Bible in his bosom and went to them. And . . . seeing his servants, when he came through the hall, lament and bewail, he said unto them cheerfully, 'Lament not for me, for I am a true man to my prince; and there is no cause why ye should so lament. I shall do well enough.' "[13]

Sadler explained "very soberly" that they had come because he had not obeyed Somerset's letter, and Wingfield, laying his hand on his shoulder, arrested him in the King's name for disobedience. The Bishop, as he tells us himself,

> "desired them to be suitors that he might not be forgotten in prison, as he was in the Fleet, but heard with more speed and be charitably handled in the prison; wherein they promised to be suitors."[14]

The Council entered on its records a long justification of his imprisonment. His "wilful disobedience" at the time of the general visitation, said this official minute, was "worthy most sharp punishment;" yet he had only been sequestered for a time in the Fleet, where he lived "as much at his ease as if he had been in his own house"! On his release and return to Winchester "he began forthwith to set forth such matters as bred again more strife, variance, and contention in that one small city and shire than was almost in the whole realm," and had, so the Council professed to be informed, secretly armed his servants to withstand anyone sent thither by the

Government. When summoned again before the Council and willed to remain in London, he had begun "afresh to ruffle and meddle in matters wherein he had neither commission nor authority." In his sermon he had "most arrogantly and disobediently" disregarded the King's commands, using such speech "as was very like, even there presently, to have stirred a great tumult;" and "in certain great matters touching the policy of the realm . . . showed himself an open great offender and a very seditious man." [15]

Similar accounts were sent to foreign courts, [16] and on Sunday, July 8, Dr. Cox, Chancellor of Oxford, Dean of Christ Church, and tutor to the King, "rehearsed" the sermon at Paul's Cross, showing how the Bishop had contemptuously failed to preach as he had promised, and exhorting the congregation to pray for his conversion. [17] "All those preachers that preached at Paul's Cross at that time," says the chronicler of the Grey Friars, "spake much a-gayne the Bishop of Winchester; and also Cardmaker, that read in Paul's three times a week, had more or less of him." [18]

XXIV

THE TOWER

Gardiner's premonition that he would be left in prison without a hearing proved all too true. He was taken to the Tower—"a dankish and uncomfortable house," as his servant Wingfield called it, for one "much given to rheums"—and lodged for the first month "in a place called the Garden. Tower . . . fast locked in, without coming abroad in all that space." Then because of a death from the pestilence in an adjacent chamber, he was removed to "a place in the same Tower called the King's Lodging." Here he was kept no less closely, not even being permitted to exercise in the gardens. For eleven months more he saw no one save the Lieutenant of the Tower, the jailors, a physician who came when he was sick of a fever, his chaplain, William Medowe, who was permitted to visit him once in his fever and again on Easter Day, and two servants of his household,[1] who waited on him and who were not allowed to leave the Tower confines.

When three months of imprisonment had passed, he received from Somerset, after much importunity, permission to write to him requesting a trial, but no attention was paid to his request. Six weeks later he wrote again, demanding that he be given "the benefit of the laws of the realm, like an Englishman; and not to be cast in prison without bail or mainprize, without accusation or indictment;" but this appeal was heeded no more than his first. Meanwhile James Basset, Jacques Wingfield, Francis Allen, and other gentlemen of his household made suit to Somerset and the rest of the Council in his behalf. "They divided themselves," says Basset, "and sued, some one day and some another day, because they would be continual suitors; and one to one, and some to other of the Council." As this importunity brought nothing but "fair words and promises," they drew up a petition to Parliament asking that their master's cause be heard there. Lord Chancellor Riche, through whom the petition had to be presented, referred it to the Council who pigeonholed it. Thereupon Basset, Wingfield, and the rest renewed their suits to Somerset who assured them that it was for their master's interest to be kept in the Tower, for he would, if released, surely disagree with certain laws recently passed in Parliament and thereby get himself into trouble![2]

One of the laws to which the Protector referred, in his solicitude for the Bishop, was undoubtedly that enforcing the use of the first

English Prayer Book, which had been sanctioned by Parliament in January 1549, published in March, and first used Whitsunday, June 9. A fortnight later a copy was brought to the Bishop by Riche, Paulet, and Sir William Petre.

It was now a whole year, saving one week, since the Bishop's arrest, and this was his first opportunity during that time to speak with anyone in authority. They told him that on his promise of conformity to the new book the Protector would sue on his behalf to the King for mercy. He replied that he desired justice, not mercy, adding, " 'not guilty' is and hath been a good plea for a prisoner." He refused to look at the book, saying that it was not meet for him to give an opinion on it in the Tower, lest such opinion appear constrained. Chancellor Riche then called his attention to the danger of disobeying the Act of Uniformity, but Gardiner, who had already seen a copy of the act pointed out its provision that no one was to be troubled for breach of it unless he were first indicted. Since it was the law of the land, he would, he said, honour it like an obedient subject, or willingly suffer punishment. Riche and the others finally promised to make suit that he should be heard, and said he would hear from them in two days.

No word came from them or from any other councillor for another year.[3]

During this year much of importance happened without the Tower. In the summer of 1549 the men of Cornwall and Devon rose in revolt against the recent changes in religion; and in East Anglia and practically every county in the south of England the long smouldering economic discontent, due to rapidly rising food prices, debasement of coinage, enclosure of commons, conversion of arable lands into sheep pasture, raising of rents, and eviction of tenants by the new landed gentry, flamed into open insurrection. Somerset had tried to secure legislation in behalf of the peasants in previous sessions of Parliament, but had only succeeded in making himself unpopular with the moneyed classes. The revolts were all put down with severity before the end of the summer, and Warwick, who quelled in person the most formidable of them, became the hero of gentry and nobility. When France, taking advantage of these domestic disturbances, declared war in August for the recovery of Boulogne, most of the English strongholds in Scotland had to be abandoned. Thus was Somerset's policy, foreign as well as domestic, discredited. In October Warwick, cleverly marshalling all dissatisfied factions, seized the government and sent the Protector to the Tower.

Warwick's chief ally in this *coup* was Wriothesley, who had undoubtedly been led to expect that its success would pave the way for a conservative reaction. Henry Fitzalan, Earl of Arundel, Sir John and Sir Thomas Arundell, Sir Richard and Sir Robert Southwell—all Catholics—found favour at court, and Gardiner wrote

hopefully from the Tower to Warwick, October 18, thanking God
that Warwick had become "a mean for the relief of the captivity
and thralldom of this realm from the tyrannous government of the
Duke of Somerset," and gratefully attributing to Warwick the
preservation of his life from the secret destruction intended by
others.[4] As this letter brought no reply, he wrote to the Council,
October 30:

"I have continued here in this miserable prison now one year,
one quarter, and one month, this same day that I write these,
my letters, with want of air to relieve my body, want of books to
relieve my mind, want of good company, the only solace of this
world, and finally want of a just cause why I should have come
hither at all."

The annalist Stow, who preserves this bit of correspondence, adds
that "the lords took it in good part, and laughed very merrily thereat,
saying he had a pleasant head," but did not vouchsafe a reply.[5]

After the beginning of Parliament in November 1549, the Bishop
wrote again to the Council, urging his right to a seat in the upper
house. "I am," he said, "a member in my degree called unto it by
writ, and not put from it by any fault, but only by power kept here."
Among the many things done amiss by Somerset, no one thing, he
added.

"was of worse example, ne more prejudicial to the good order of
the high court of Parliament . . . than to allow for a prec-
edent that any one man, being member thereof, might without
cause be excluded, and so letted to parle there his mind in public
matters." [6]

But Warwick had little interest in the rights and privileges of Parliament.

Although he had been helped to power by Wriothesley and the conservatives, he had also been aided by radical reformers who were
impatient of Somerset's moderation. He now found he could best
maintain his position by throwing in his lot, as far as Church affairs
went, with the radicals, for it was obvious that the continued spoliation of the Church by which he might pay for the support of the
nobility, could not go on without vigorous opposition from Catholic
leaders like Gardiner, were they restored to influence, while it might
at least cloak itself in plausible excuse if Churchmen in high places
were advocates of apostolic simplicity.

By the beginning of 1550 it was clear that not only had the conservatives nothing to hope from the new Government, but that even
the moderate reformers were to be hustled into further change by
the extremists. Early in the year the two Arundells were committed

to the Tower, Sir Richard Southwell to the Fleet, and the Earl of Arundel to his own house. On February 2 Wriothesley, who had ceased to attend the Council from illness after October 1549, was excluded from it; on the same day a committee of bishops was appointed to devise an English Ordinal; on that day also Bishop Tunstall attended the Council for the last time.

Now that Somerset's fall began to be regarded as the result of a Catholic plot, he could not well be kept longer in the Tower, especially as a move for his freedom had been made in the recent Parliament. He was, accordingly, released February 6, 1550. The next day the Council upheld Bonner's deprivation, to which he had been sentenced the previous October 1, and on February 8 summoned Bishop Heath of Worcester for refusing assent to the new Ordinal. On February 24 Ridley was named, not only as successor to Bonner in the see of London, but also to Thirlby in that of Westminster, which was to be reunited to London; while the Catholic but pliant Thirlby was gotten out of the way by translation to Norwich.[7] A month later a humiliating peace was made with France, by which Boulogne was surrendered and French ascendancy in Scotland acknowledged. This left Warwick free to pursue his aims at home. What these boded for the Church was indicated all too clearly by the offer, on April 7, 1550, of the see of Rochester to that vituperative reformer, Ponet, and of Gloucester to John Hooper, the most extreme Zwinglian of them all. Hooper thought the Communion Service in the Prayer Book in some respects "manifestly impious," and the new Ordinal a device to promote the Kingdom of Antichrist![8]

Hooper and Gardiner were not unacquainted, if we may believe Foxe, who tells us that when the former was forced to leave Oxford at the time of the Six Articles he secured a position as steward in the household of Sir Thomas Arundell, who, on discovering what his opinions were, sent him to Gardiner to learn better, but that Gardiner, after four or five days conference, sent him back unconverted.[9] He went to the Continent and, in 1547, published at Zurich an answer to Gardiner's *Detection of the Devil's Sophistry*. Returning to England in the Spring of 1549, he lectured daily to throngs in London, and in Lent 1550 preached weekly before the King.

Early in Lent Gardiner sent him from the Tower a challenge to a disputation, doubtless on the subject of the Sacrament. We would know nothing of this except for a reference to it in a letter from Hooper to Bullinger, March 26, 1550, in which Hooper says that Gardiner had sent him the challenge about a month before, that the keeper of the prison had accepted the conditions on which the disputation was to be held, that the day was fixed, but that when Gardiner learned that Hooper was not afraid to dispute with him, he backed out on the ground that he could discuss nothing unless he were at liberty.[10]

What the conditions were which the keeper of the prison accepted, and who imposed them Hooper does not say, but it is hard to believe that such a disputation could have been held under any conditions not made by the Council, and the Council was not at that time likely to make them favourable to Gardiner. It is, moreover, strange that Gardiner, whose keenness for debate was proverbial, should have challenged Hooper and then feared to meet him. It would seem rather that he had stipulated at least a temporary release from the Tower as a condition of the disputation. He could have had no desire to debate with Hooper in jail. He wanted to be heard at court.

On April 10, 1550, three days after Hooper had been offered a bishopric, Somerset was readmitted to the Council. Galling it must have been to take a place there inferior to that of Warwick, distasteful to sanction his extreme measures. As he who begins a revolution often finds himself, after a time, resisting the further innovations of his more radical comrades, so Somerset seems now to have aimed at the building up of a conservative party which would take its stand on the changes so far legally established. At any rate he was desirous of encouraging certain conservative influences and of gaining friends for himself. His plan involved the liberation of Gardiner and the Arundells from the Tower, and an understanding with the Earl of Arundel.[11] It was, evidently, at his suggestion that the Council, in Warwick's absence, decided, June 8, 1550, to offer Gardiner his freedom upon condition of his acceptance of the Prayer Book.

Somerset himself, William Parr, Marquis of Northampton, the two recently created earls, Paulet, of Wiltshire, and Russell, of Bedford, and Secretary Petre were chosen to bring this offer to the Bishop.[12] Coming to the Tower June 9, they told him they had been "specially sent to know his conformity." He assured them that he was "ready to show as much conformity as ever any subject did, which was to be contented to be ordered by justice, . . . and desired them, for the Passion of God, that he might come to some end of this matter by it." They urged him not "to stick so much to the demand of justice," but "to let all be forgotten that was by-past." He then said they might report to the King that he was always ready to observe what was set forth in the commonwealth. They asked what he thought of the Prayer Book. He objected, as he had done a year before, to giving an opinion in the Tower, not only because "in so doing he should slander himself," but also because it would "somewhat touch" the Council if "by weariness of prison" they should "fear him to it." Somerset then asked him, for his sake, to let the Council decide whether he should give his opinion in prison or out.

To this he at length assented, and as the lords showed him so much
gentleness he "was bold to tell them it was a marvellous matter to
keep one in such close prison, solitary, two years . . . unless it were
for murder, felony, or treason." "It was," he said, "such a new
diet as would purge a man." [13]

The next day the Council agreed that a copy of the Prayer Book
be sent him, and that he be permitted to walk in the garden when his
fellow prisoner, the Duke of Norfolk, was not there. [14]   On June
14 the councillors who had recently visited him went again to the
Tower, this time accompanied by Lord Cobham. Gardiner now told
them that he himself would not have made the Prayer Book in the
form in which it was, "but as it was he could with his conscience keep
it, and cause others in his diocese to keep it." He desired, however,
that they would not require him to write his opinion, or to subscribe it, when written by Secretary Petre, lest by so doing he "seem
to grant himself an offender," and they were content. He further
assured them that when he said he would keep it, he meant "every
part of it." He

> "then told them why he liked the said book, and noted unto
> them how, nothwithstanding the alteration, yet touching the
> truth of the very presence of Christ's most precious body and
> blood in the Sacrament, there was as much spoken in that book
> as might be desired; and that although the elevation was taken
> away, yet the adoration, in one special place, was indeed
> reserved, and showed it them, adding it must needs be so; affirm-
> ing also, there was never more spoken for the Sacrament than
> in that book."

He further

> "showed them how he liked the declaration of the cause of the
> change, in the end of the book, whereby appeared the Catholic
> doctrine not to be touched, but only ceremonies removed, which
> the said Bishop said, was wisely handled."

Somerset then asked him what he thought of the new service of
ordination, which had been brought to him with the Prayer Book.
This had been published separately a year later than the Prayer
Book, and had been sanctioned by Parliament in a curious piece of
anticipatory legislation, on January 31, 1550, by which a committee,
yet to be named, was to draw up an ordinal to come into use April 1.
One member of this committee, Bishop Heath of Worcester, dissented, as we have seen, from the form agreed to by the other members, and was committed to the Fleet by the Council, March 4, 1550,
for his refusal to make the committee's report unanimous! [15]   In
October of the following year he was deprived of his bishopric.

When Somerset put the question about the Ordinal to Gardiner, Heath had already been three months in jail.

Gardiner replied that he had not promised to give an opinion on this, but pointed out what he regarded as one serious defect—the omission of unction. How, he asked, could an unanointed priest administer unction in Baptism, a ceremony retained in the Prayer Book, and how could the King at his accession be anointed by an unanointed archbishop? This, he said, touched the King's dignity. The councillors made no reply to this but suggested that the Bishop "should find other faults than that" in the Ordinal. He replied that the Ordinal, like all else established by law, was either to be observed or the punishment for non-observance suffered.[16]

Having thus shown, as he thought, as much conformity as had been asked of him, he suggested that they send him home that night, but they replied that they must first speak with the Council again. He was, nevertheless, given to understand that he would shortly be released. So confident was he of this that he gave a farewell feast to the Lieutenant and Knight Marshall of the Tower, their ladies and their friends, ordered a piece of satin to be divided as a parting gift among the ladies, and sent word to two of his servants then at Farnham, to get his house in Southwark ready for him. They took horse at once and, though it was ten in the evening, others of the household joined them and, riding all night—such was their eagerness in his service—came to Southwark at seven next morning.[17]

There can be no doubt of Somerset's desire to have Gardiner now at liberty, but the plan was not to Warwick's liking. Winchester was at once too wealthy and too important a diocese in which to have a bishop who would stand stubbornly for the property and the prerogative of the Church. Cecil, who now decided to desert Somerset for Warwick, wrote to Warwick of Somerset's doings, and enclosed a set of articles prepared by himself for Gardiner's subscription. Warwick was "vehemently troubled" and even wept a few tears to show his concern that Somerset should attempt "such perilous causes." He praised Cecil highly for devising the articles.[18]

Gardiner's case was therefore dropped until Warwick's return, and no mention of his acceptance of the Prayer Book was placed in the minutes of the Council, the next entry therein concerning him, on July 8, 1550, being the barefaced assertion that his case was renewed "upon report of the lords that had been with him that his answers were ever doubtful, refusing while he were in prison to make any direct answer."[19] The Council agreed that a set of articles, undoubtedly based on those already submitted by Cecil to Warwick, be prepared for his subscription, and that a letter be sent him in the name of the King, reminding him of his "notorious and apparent contempt," despite the great favour hitherto shown him, and telling him that they desired both the world and himself to know that they delighted "more in clemency than in the strait administration of justice"!

The articles, briefly summarized were as follows:

I. The King is, by Scripture and the law of God, Supreme Head of the Church of England.

II. Holy days and fast days, such as Lent, may be appointed or dispensed with by the King.

III. The Prayer Book is a godly and Christian book and to be accepted by all the King's subjects.

IV. The King is a "full and entire King" in his minority, and all his proclamations and laws are to be obeyed as if he were forty years old.

V. The Act of the Six Articles has, for just causes, been repealed.

VI. The King has the authority to alter rites and ceremonies in so far as the alterations be not contrary to Scripture and the law of God.[20]

This did not go much beyond what Gardiner had already acknowledged. No mention was made of the Sacrament, nor of the power of the King to alter doctrine, nor of his right to enjoin disobedience to an act of Parliament. The articles, however, were prefaced by a paragraph in which Gardiner was to confess that he had been suspected as one too much favoring the Bishop of Rome and not approving the King's proceedings in religion, that in his St. Peter's Day sermon he had neither preached as he ought to have done nor as he had promised to do, that divers persons had been encouraged by his example to repine at the King's doings, and that he was "right sorry" for all this and acknowledged himself "condignly to have been punished."

On July 9 Warwick himself, accompanied by Paulet, Sir William Herbert, and Secretary Petre brought him the letter and the articles, which he received kneeling, and kissed as befitted communications from the King. He remained on his knees while he read them, although the Councillors gently urged him "to take more ease." He declared that he could not on his conscience subscribe to such a confession of guilt as the preface contained, saying, "I should sooner, if ye would bid me, tumble myself desperately into the Thames."

Warwick, seeing him "in that agony," asked if he would subscribe the articles apart from the preface, and on his reply that he would, said that he might write on the margin of the preface what he had to say to that.

"And then," says Gardiner, "my Lord of Warwick entertained me very gently, and would needs, whiles I should write, have me sit down by him; and when he saw me make somewhat strange so to do, he pulled me nearer him, and said, we had or this sat together, and trusted we should do so again."

The Bishop wrote beside the preface, "I cannot in my conscience confess the preface, knowing myself to be of that sort I am indeed and ever have been." He then subscribed the other articles.

"Thereupon," to continue in Gardiner's own words, "it pleased them to entertain me much to my comfort. And I was bold to account unto them merry tales of my misery in prison, which they seemed content to hear. And then I told them also (desiring them not to be miscontent with that [which] I should say) when I remembered each of them alone I could not think otherwise but they were my good lords; and yet when they met together I felt no remedy at their hands. 'I looked,' quoth I, 'when my Lord of Somerset was here to go out within two days, and made my farewell feast in the Tower and all; since which time there is a month past or thereabout; and I agreed with them, and now I agree with you, and I may fortune to be forgotten.'

My Lord Treasurer [Paulet] said, Nay, I should hear from them the next day. And so by their special commandment I came out of the chamber after them, that they might be seen to depart as my good lords." [21]

Warwick, however, tells us that "they left him, being sorry they could do no more good to him"! [22] The "good" which Warwick was so desirous of doing the Bishop was to induce him to sign the confession of guilt with which the articles had been prefaced. There can be no doubt that the courtesy and friendliness with which he was treated had this in view, for the Council went on record two days later (July 11) that they deemed this confession "the principallest point" to be gained, and therefore appointed Herbert and Petre to go to the Bishop again and exhort him "to look better upon it." [23] This they did on July 12, but in vain. Gardiner observed that if "he were by his own pen made a naughty man, yet then he were not the more sure to come out, but had locked himself the more surely in," adding that even if he did thus secure freedom, it would be a small pleasure to him "to have his body at liberty by their procurement, and to have his conscience in a perpetual prison by his own act."

"I require you," he concluded, "for the Passion of God, that my matter may take an end by justice." [24]

Justice was, evidently, the last thing which the Council desired to afford him. Immediately upon Herbert and Petre's report, a new confession of guilt was drawn up, followed by a new set of articles, this time twenty in number, which not only set forth all the changes so far accomplished in the Church, but interpreted them in a pronouncedly Protestant fashion.

The monasteries had been rightfully suppressed, said the articles, and by that suppression the monks were clearly released from all their "unwitty and superstitious vows." Pilgrimages, images, relics had caused "much wickedness and idolatry" and were therefore justly abolished, as was the foolish "counterfeiting of St. Nicholas" and other saints by children. Anything which prevented all men from reading the whole Bible in English was evil and damnable. Chantries, private Masses, Masses for the souls of the dead, and all Latin service books had been justly suppressed. "The Mass, that was wont to be said of priests was full of abuses," and for the most part invented by the Bishop of Rome. It was justly replaced by the Communion, which is "very godly." All Christians should receive the Sacrament in both kinds. Mass in which the priest alone receives is the invention of man and contrary to Scripture. The Sacrament should neither be elevated nor adored. The clergy are not commanded by the law of God to vow chastity or abstain from marriage, and all laws prohibiting clerical marriage have been justly repealed by Parliament. The Homilies are "godly and wholesome," and their doctrine "ought to be embraced of all men." The new ordinal is godly and in no point contrary to the Gospel. Minor orders are unnecessary. The Scriptures contain all doctrine necessary for salvation. The *Paraphrase* of Erasmus has, "upon good and godly considerations," been set up in every parish church so the people may read it. All this the Bishop was asked not only to subscribe but to declare his readiness to publish and preach as his Majesty deemed requisite.[25]

These articles were brought to Gardiner July 14 by Herbert and Petre, who, "for the more authentic proceeding with him," were accompanied by "a divine and a temporal lawyer"—Bishop Ridley and one Richard Goodrick. Gardiner, being "loth to meddle with any more articles," at first refused even to read them, but did so when urged. He then said he would in no wise subscribe to the prefatory confession of guilt, but would make answer to the articles immediately upon his deliverance from prison. He would gladly have discussed them with Ridley, but Ridley told him he had not come to dispute, adding, as Gardiner tells us, that "it was the hand of God that I was thus in prison, because I had so troubled other men in my time." Gardiner finally asked them to tell the Council that he thanked them for their offer of mercy but that he would rather have justice, "which although it were more grievous, yet it hath a commodity with it, that it endeth certainly the matter."

The Council thereupon decided to examine him "peremptorily," and, if he again refused to subscribe the articles, to sequester the revenues and possessions of his see and to warn him that if he "were not reformed within three months" he would be deprived of it entirely."[26] On Saturday, July 19 (1550), the Councillors sought the boy King's presence and secured his sanction for their next move. That afternoon, as the strains of evensong came from the chapel of the court, Gardiner was brought to the Council Chamber at Westminster. It was the first time he had been out of the Tower since his commitment over two years before.

When the articles were read, he fell upon his knees and, in his accustomed phrase, exclaimed, "For the Passion of God, my Lords, be my good lords, and let me be tried by justice." Some of the articles, he said, were laws to which he must needs assent, but some were matters of learning and of fact which might have divers interpretations, "and a subscription to them without telling and declaring what he meant were over dangerous." Somerset later testified that Gardiner promised "that as many of the said articles as were set forth by any law or proclamation, he would set forth."[27]

In order to convince the Council of his desire to conform, the Bishop further proposed that if the articles were delivered to him in prison he would make answer to each one in particular even while there, but this proposition was rejected, the Council insisting on an immediate and unconditional subscription. This he refused, and defended the refusal on the ground—again strangely like that taken by Barnes—that

> "it is taught in this realm for a doctrine of obedience that if a king command that which is contrary to the commandment of God, the subject may not do as he is commanded, but humbly suffer;[28] which is my case, who could not with my conscience do as I was required."

Then Secretary Petre read the "Sequestration and Intimation," declaring the revenues and possessions of the bishopric of Winchester committed to the receipt and custody of such persons as the King should appoint, and admonishing the Bishop to accept, within three months, on pain of deprivation, not only the articles, but also "all such other matters as be or shall be set forth by his Majesty's authority." Incidentally the document enlarged upon the King's clemency and the Bishop's disobediences which, it said, had been "so many times doubled, renewed, and aggravated," as manifestly to declare him "to be a person without all hope of recovery and plainly incorrigible."

That the Bishop had, as he himself pointed out, neither confessed to nor been convicted of anything justifying the sequestration of his benefice, was of no weight with the Council. During the three months, however, which he was given before final deprivation, his house and servants were to be maintained in their accustomed state, and the whole matter to be kept secret.[29] This was, according to the Council, in the hope that he might "be yet reconciled," but the real reason was, more probably, as Mr. Gairdner suggests,[30] to keep the public from learning too soon what action the Council intended to take.

It is hardly unfair to the Council, or at least to a majority of that body, to say that when they expressed a hope that Gardiner would be yet reconciled, they meant reconciled to making such a confession against himself as they had endeavoured to wring from him, which would have enabled them to proceed with his deprivation without more ado.

He was taken back to the Tower again the same day, and although the decree of sequestration provided that he be admonished to subscribe the articles at the end of each of the three months named therein, the months passed without such admonition. He was not even furnished a copy of the articles, and it was not until five months after his appearance before the Council that, on December 15, 1550, he was suddenly and without warning roused from his bed at seven in the morning and told by the Lieutenant of the Tower to present himself at Lambeth forthwith.[31]

XXV

THE TRIAL

After two and a half years imprisonment, Gardiner was now to be accorded at least a show of that justice for which he had repeatedly asked. In the great hall of the episcopal palace at Lambeth, whither he was hurried on the morning of December 15, 1550, sat the royal commissioners—Archbishop Cranmer; Bishops Ridley of London, Goodrich of Ely, and Holbeach of Lincoln; Secretary Petre; Sir James Hales, a justice of the Common Pleas; Griffith Leyson and John Oliver, doctors of law; and two other lawyers, Richard Goodrick and John Gosnold, designated in the commission as "esquires."

The commission, dated December 12, 1550, appointing them to their office, put them in the position of prosecutors rather than judges. It expressly informed them that the Bishop of Winchester had shown disobedience and contempt of authority in his St. Peter's Day sermon, and that by continuing in this disobedience and refusing to acknowledge the same, he had "totally abused" the "princely clemency" shown him since that time; it instructed them to remove him from his bishopric if, when called before them, he still refused to conform himself to the commands of King and Council. It incidentally made the significant admission that the religious changes against which he had protested had not been welcomed by a large section of the people, for it asserted that his sayings and doings had encouraged opposition to these changes "amongst the multitude of our subjects not yet well persuaded therein."

Despite this instruction to proceed to his deprivation, the Council felt the necessity of providing some kind of legal process to this end. Hence the commissioners were empowered to take all steps requisite to "the examination, trial, proof, and full determination" of the case.[1]

This they did in twenty-two sessions, ranging from December 15, 1550 to February 14, 1551.[2] Nine were held at Lambeth, and to these Gardiner was brought in person. One was held in his lodging in the Tower. At the others, held in the houses of bishops and lords, in the Council Chamber at Greenwich, and in London prisons, for the examination of witnesses, Gardiner was represented by his proctors.[3] His visits to Lambeth were, it seems, staged by the Government as spectacles for the multitude. An observer of one of them describes how he "was brought from the Tower to Lambeth, going by land through Southwark, with forty of the King's guard with their halberds going afore him, and threescore of the wardens of the Tower with halberds after him." [4]

He was allowed by the court the assistance of Dr. Richard Standish and Dr. William Jeffrey, advocates of the Court of Arches, as counsel, and was further aided in his defence by James Basset, Jacques Wingfield, and Thomas Somerset, members of his household, who acted as his proctors or representatives, [5] and who appear to have been skillful and tireless in his behalf.

The charge of contemptuous disobedience, made in the commission appointing his judges, was elaborated in a set of nineteen articles ministered to him at the first session of the trial. In these it was said, vaguely, that he had been "at sundry times" complained of for opposing "sundry injunctions, orders, and other proceedings" of the King, and had been "sundry times" admonished to conform, but to no purpose. Specifically, it was charged that in his St. Peter's Day sermon he had spoken of the Sacrament contrary to Somerset's order, had not extolled the King's authority during his minority, and had failed to refer to other matters contained in the articles on which he had promised to preach, thus threatening the quiet and unity of the realm; he had subsequently refused to conform to the Prayer Book or subscribe to a confession of his guilt and to twenty articles setting forth changes in religion appended thereto. He had hitherto neither "submitted, reconciled, nor reformed" himself. [6] Moreover, according to the Council's record of his original commitment to the Tower, which was now brought forward by the prosecution, he had wilfully disobeyed the injunctions of 1547, and treasonably armed his servants at Winchester. [7]

The Bishop expressed surprise that most of the matters now laid to his charge were those in which Somerset, Paulet, Russell, and Parr had, in the previous June, made such an end with him "that he verily thought never to have heard any more thereof." This statement, made "in the hearing of a great multitude of people" present at the opening of the case, so embarrassed the Government that the councillors concerned were constrained to make a formal denial, read at the next session of the trial, in which they lamented the Bishop's "impudent avowal," and expressed their regret that he should "lay the first foundation of his defence upon so false and manifest an untruth"! [8]

In answer to the charges against him, Gardiner delivered to the court a long and circumstantial account of his words and actions relating to religious changes from the establishment of the royal supremacy to the opening of his trial. [9] The accuracy of this account was vouched for, not only by the testimony of witnesses called in his behalf, but by a number of letters presented as evidence, especially his correspondence with Somerset since the beginning of Edward's reign. He frankly admitted that he had opposed most innovations up to the moment when they had become established by law; after that he had in all cases conformed and directed those in his diocese to conform. Although he might not, he said, approve of some of the recent enactments, he had as yet had no opportunity either to obey or disobey them, having spent the last two and a half years in close confinement; according to all the principles of English justice he ought not to be convicted because it was feared he might disobey the laws if set at liberty.

As for the St. Peter's Day sermon, there were the articles on which he had promised to preach, there was Somerset's letter enjoining his silence on matters in controversy touching the Sacrament, there was Nicholas Udall's verbatim report of the sermon. The whole thing should have been perfectly clear to the court, yet innumerable depositions were taken as to what this or that auditor remembered the Bishop saying two and a half years ago, and whether they deemed he had therein performed his promises. Indeed, the bulk of the testimony brought forward by the prosecution went to show that Gardiner had not preached on the King's authority during his minority, nor regarded Somerset's letter as of sufficient force to prevent his speaking on the Sacrament, both of which contentions Gardiner admitted. He pointed out that the matter of the King's minority was not among the articles submitted to him, and that when Cecil had suggested that he speak of it he had given no promise to do so, especially as Cecil desired him to extoll not only the King's authority, which he was willing to do, but also that of the Council, for which he found no Scriptural sanction.[10]

The articles, he said, required some reference to the Sacrament; and no matter how much the presence of Christ's body and blood had become a matter of controversy since the time of his sermon, it was not so then, for that very summer Cranmer had published, for use in England, a translation of a German catechism in which the presence of the very body and blood in the Sacrament was clearly taught.[11] Moreover, in December 1548, almost six months after his sermon, no less than eight bishops, in the discussion preceding the adoption of the Prayer Book, had defended the same doctrine openly in Parliament.[12]

Somerset's letter, unsigned as it was by any other councillor, was, said Gardiner, an instance of that unauthorized assumption of authority for which the Council had afterward deposed him from the protectorship, and therefore ought to have been disobeyed.

As for the omission of certain minor matters in his sermon, he had told Somerset, when he promised to preach, that he thought it unnecessary to speak in particular of all abolished ceremonies. If he had omitted anything of importance it was unintentional, and due to the fact that Somerset's letter had compelled him to revise his sermon at the last minute. His statement that it was in the power of the ruler to reform or abolish ceremonies should have been regarded as a sufficient acknowledgment of the validity of all minor changes.

His acceptance of the Prayer Book in June 1550, his subscription to the first of the two sets of articles submitted to him in July of the same year, and his expressed willingness to assent to those of the second set in so far as they spoke of things established by law, were all matters of such recent and evident a nature that they could not be denied.

He produced many and credible witnesses to the fact that the injunctions of 1547 had been scrupulously obeyed in his diocese and the visitors everywhere received with courtesy, that his household had ever been noted for its peaceable nature, and his servants never armed except when they went forth as members of the King's forces.

One line of his defence; namely, that he had been "always ready with his best endeavour, diligence, and industry" to set forth the royal supremacy and to disprove "the usurped power of the Bishop of Rome," and that in the reign of Henry VIII he "was never found faulty, nor any fault objected and proved against him, but hath always been, and yet is, a true, painful, and just servant and subject," called forth an attempt on the part of the prosecution to prove that Henry had "reputed the said Bishop for a man vehemently suspected to favour the Bishop of Rome," had misliked him, and "was much offended with him" for being ill pleased with changes in religion.[13]

In support of this contention there was brought forward, first, evidence that Gardiner had received a letter from the Pope at Ratisbon (which, as we have seen, had been known and approved by Henry);[14] second, the fact that his name had been dropped from Henry's will (the circumstances of which none but the inner ring of councillors knew, and on which they could hardly have been expected to admit anything favourable to the Bishop); third, the assertions of Paget, now Baron Paget de Beaudesert, who set about deliberately to defame his old master at the cost of truth.

Paget testified that King Henry "misliked the said Bishop ever the longer the worse," and that,

> "if the said King had lived any while longer than he did, he would have used extremity against the said Bishop, so far forth as the law would have borne; his Majesty thinking to have just and sore matter of old against the said Bishop in store, not taken away by any pardon; and at divers times asked the said Lord Paget for a certain writing touching the said Bishop, commanding him to keep it, save that he might have it when he called for it."

If this were true it would seem rather to reflect on the ingratitude of the King than on the faithlessness of Gardiner, but Paget neither ventured to produce this "certain writing" nor more fully to describe it. He proceeded, however, to affirm that he believed that the Bishop, in the latter part of Henry's reign, was the man whom the King

> "abhorred more than any man in his realm, . . . ever naming him with such terms as the said Lord Paget is sorry to name. And the said Lord Paget thinketh that divers of the gentlemen of the privy chamber are able to depose the same." [15]

None of these divers gentlemen were, however, forthcoming, and privy councillors, who might have been supposed to know something of the matter at first hand, offered the most tenuous hearsay testimony. Somerset said he had "heard say that certain of the Bishop's doings were not best liked in the King's Majesty's days that dead is;" Warwick said he had "heard" that Gardiner was "most vehemently suspected" by Henry VIII to be the chief hinderer of reform. Northampton (William Parr, brother of Henry's last Queen) said

> "that he remembereth not to have heard of the late King himself any word spoken of misliking of the said Bishop; but he hath heard of others that were wont to have more secret conference with the said late King than his Lordship was, that the said late King misliked the said Bishop, but for what cause specially his Lordship knoweth not, saving that his Majesty took him to be a wilful and heady man."

Paulet and Russell claimed to have heard Henry himself express misliking for the Bishop, but as to the Bishop's opposition to Henry's reforms they spoke of what was "commonly reported." [16]

The venerable Tunstall, on the other hand, said that "he never heard or knew that any thing was objected unto the said Bishop, but that he was always taken among the Council for a true, just, and painful man in the King's affairs."

The most discriminating testimony on this point was given by Bishop Thirlby:

> "Although the said Bishop of Winchester (very loth to condescend to any innovations) was earnest against alterations as well concerning the Bishop of Rome as other orders in religion, yet after those matters were established and set forth by the acts, statutes, and laws of this realm, and the King's Majesty's injunctions and proclamations, this deponent hath known and heard the Bishop of Winchester publish, declare, and set forth as well the supremacy or supreme authority of the King's Majesty's father of famous memory, as the abolishing of the usurped power of the Bishop of Rome."

Thirlby had never, he said, heard that King Henry had expressed misliking for Gardiner because of the latter's attitude toward established changes in religion, "but when such matters were in debating, he hath heard say, that the King that dead is, was displeased some time with the said Bishop of Winchester for his earnestness in the same." [17]

Gardiner was the last to deny this. Indeed, he had written to Somerset in 1547 describing how the late King had often "squared" with him, and used sharp speech to him, yet loved him never the worse. And this letter he presented in evidence at the trial.

He forced his opponents to admit that within a fortnight of Henry's death he had represented the Privy Council in diplomatic discussion with French, Scotch, and Imperial ambassadors; [18] that he had remained a member of the Privy Council till the end of the reign; and that he had been on such terms with King Henry that the latter had not hesitated to ask of him a favour and thank him heartily for it within a few days of that time. [19]

As evidence of his consistent advocacy of the royal supremacy he submitted a copy of his book *De Vera Obedientia*, [20] as well as a letter from Francis Driander describing his vigorous defense of this book against the Papal theologians of Louvain in 1541; [21] he produced as witnesses auditors of sermons on various occasions in which he upheld this position, and referred his judges to the recorded words of his sermon on St. Peter's Day.

Jehan Scheyfve, the Imperial ambassador in England, heard before the end of the trial that Gardiner had so ably defended himself that he had won the hearts of many, even among his enemies, and was consequently more highly esteemed than before, which was not, adds Scheyfve, to his advantage with the Government, who feared that he might become the centre of a successful opposition to it. Several persons, wrote the same observer, were watching for the spoils of his diocese, for his deprivation was a foregone conclusion, his trial a mere pretence, kept up to satisfy the people. [22]

At the twentieth session, February 3, 1551, the judges decided to "publish" the depositions of the witnesses, thus bringing to an end the taking of testimony. At the next session, February 13, at which final judgement was to be given, Gardiner formally took exception to the witnesses for the prosecution. Several members of the Council, although laymen, had been permitted to give evidence without oath, a procedure contrary to ecclesiastical law, and one which the Bishop felt more than justified in protesting, since, as he said,

"the Lord Paget hath, in his depositions, evidently and manifestly neglected honour, faith, and honesty, and showeth himself desirous, beyond the necessary answer to that was demanded of him (only of ingrate malice) to hinder, as much as in him is, the said Bishop, who was in the said Lord's youth his teacher and tutor, afterward his master, and then his beneficial master, to obtain of the King's Majesty that dead is, one of the rooms of the clerkship of the signet for him; which ingrate malice of the said Lord Paget, the said Bishop saith, in the depositions manifestly doth appear, as the said Bishop offereth himself ready to prove and show."

Further, much of the testimony of the other councillors was admittedly hearsay, much dealt in generalities, and such as was specific often lacked the necessary proof. Moreover, interrogatories had been administered to Paget by the prosecution without Gardiner's knowledge of what they were, thus introducing new matter, against which he had no chance to defend himself. And, what was "against all law, equity, and justice," the members of the Council, having been his former judges in committing him to the Tower, had been called as witnesses for the prosecution in order "to approve the justness of their own former doings." [23]

This protest was not admitted by the court, but final judgement was not given until the next morning, Saturday, February 14 (1551), at the twenty-second session. Before it was given, Gardiner presented an appeal to the King in which he briefly repeated some of his objections to the witnesses for the prosecution and charged his judges with partiality. He pointed out that Cranmer, the chief among them, had been one of those who had committed him to the Tower and kept him there; that three of the others, Hales, Goodrick, and Gosnold, had given counsel and advice concerning the same; that Cranmer, Ridley, and Holbeach

> "do, contrary to the laws ecclesiastical of this realm, teach and set forth the manifest and condemned error against the very true presence of Christ's body and blood in the Sacrament of the Altar, and because I (the said Bishop) am, and have been always, of the true Catholic faith, contrary to them . . . do show themselves unduly affected against me;"

and that Sir William Petre, having been one of the judges who, seven months previously, decreed the fruits of his bishopric sequestered, was now "judge in his own cause, concerning his own fact." Indeed all of the judges showed themselves more eager, he averred, to convict him than did the promotors, as the prosecutors in an ecclesiastical trial are called. They had not given him access to necessary documents, they had proceeded to judgement before his defence was completed, and they had afforded him insufficient opportunity to consult with his counsel before the final session.

Moreover, he had come, he said, to this session with "great travail" of his body, having been "so pestered" the day before "with the populous audience." [24]

The court, however, proceeded to the final sentence, which was read by the Archbishop, and which stated that forasmuch as Stephen, Bishop of Winchester, "remained a person much grudging, speaking, and repugning against the godly reformations of abuses in religion," and had been a "contemptuous disobeyer of sundry godly and just commandments," and continued to refuse to recognize his "notorious negligences and misbehaviours," he was, for these and "sundry other great causes"—not specified—"deprived and removed from the bishopric of Winchester."

The Bishop now made a final appeal to the King by word of mouth, but since this, like that of the day before, was virtually an appeal from the King's Council to the King's Council, nothing could be hoped from it. [25]

The next day the Council formally considered the Bishop's case, and decided that since throughout the trial he had "used himself unreverently to the King's Majesty, and very sklaunderfullie towards the Council," and had, in his appeal, "called his judges heretics and sacramentaries,"

> "he should be removed from the lodgings he hath now in the Tower to a meaner lodging, and none to wait upon him but one by the Lieutenant's appointment, in such sort as by the resort of any man to him he have not the mean to send out to any man, or to hear from any man; and likewise that his books and papers be taken from him and seen, and that from henceforth he have neither pen, ink, nor paper to write his detestable purposes, but be sequestered from all conference and from all means that may serve him to practise any way." [26]

Letters were thereupon sent to English ambassadors at foreign courts telling how Gardiner had railed upon his judges, sought to defame the whole estate of the realm and shown himself a subject utterly given to disquiet. [27]

Daniele Barbaro, Venetian envoy in England, astutely observed that Gardiner's bishopric "was perhaps his greatest sin, as it yielded him a rental of 12,000 crowns." [28] The truth of this became all too clear when Ponet, Bishop of Rochester, was, on March 8, 1551, "appointed and admitted Bishop of Winchester," [29] on condition that he surrender to the crown, in exchange for a yearly salary of 2,000 marks, all the lands of the see, which were soon thereafter regranted to the chief members of Warwick's faction. [30]

Bishop Ponet married—in ignorance, it is to be hoped—a woman who was in reality the wife of a butcher of Nottingham, and, on July 27, four months after he received the see of Winchester, was "divorced" at St. Paul's "with shame enough," as Machyn says, and adjudged to pay her husband a pension for life.[31]

Sometime thereafter, according to Sanders, a certain nobleman, gaining access to Gardiner in the Tower, asked him if he ever expected to recover his bishopric. "Why not?" replied the Bishop, "The butcher has recovered his wife!"[32]

XXVI

AN EXPLICATION OF THE FAITH

Durance brought little abatement of Gardiner's wonted energy. In the five years of his sojourn in the Tower he wrote six volumes of theological controversy,[1] and in odd moments collected Latin proverbs, made excerpts from the Latin poets, and practised the composition of original Latin verses.[2] That at least two of the six volumes of divinity were written after his trial, indicates that the order of the Council depriving him of pen and paper was not rigorously enforced.[3]

The most influential of the reformers against whom he wrote were Hooper and Cranmer.

We recall how Hooper had preached at Court during Lent 1550, and how Gardiner had, at that time, desired to dispute with him.[4] The Book of Jonah had been Hooper's text, which, on seven successive Wednesdays, he expounded in the light of contemporary conditions. He compared the ship in which Jonah sailed to the ship of State, in which, he said, there were many Jonahs—the conservative clergy not the least among them—who should be cast overboard. At the verse "the people of Nineveh believed God," he took occasion to speak of the relation of belief to the Sacraments, and devoted the best part of two sermons to exhibiting the absurdities, as he deemed them, of the doctrine of Christ's bodily presence in the Sacrament of the Altar.

In September of the same year he published these sermons with an introduction in which he advised King Edward VI not to trouble himself when evil men said that "as long as the King is in his tender years his Council should do nothing in matters of religion," and cited Josiah to the contrary. He exhorted King and Council to remove all the "leavings of papistry," saying, "as ye have taken away the Mass from the people, so take from them her feathers also: the altar, vestments, and such like." He entitled the volume: *An oversight, and deliberation upon the holy Prophet Jonas.*

Gardiner made merry over the title. The word "oversight," he said, exactly fitted the book. It was filled with oversights. He called his reply *A Discussion of Mr. Hooper's oversight where he entreateth among his other Sermons the matter of the Sacrament of the Body and Blood of Christ,* and adorned the title page with the proverb, "Answer a fool according to his folly, lest he be wise in his own conceit."

Hooper's treatment of the Sacrament had been wholly negative. He had asserted without qualification that the body of Christ was not present in it, that its purpose was to admonish us to meditate on the meaning of Christ's death, and that we might eat Christ's body, that is, apply by faith the virtue of his merits to our souls, as well without the Sacrament as with it. He concluded by a description of how he thought the Lord's Supper ought to be celebrated. If the minister, he said, "have bread, wine, a table, and a fair table cloth, let him not be solicitous nor careful for the rest." "Candles, vestments, crosses, altars," were all to be abandoned, and, to avoid the idolatrous associations of kneeling, the communicants should receive standing or sitting, "but sitting," he said, "in mine opinion were best." [5]

Here was uncompromising continental Protestantism of the Zwinglian variety preached by an English bishop, preached before King and Council, and published with the evident approval of those in authority in both Church and State. Three editions were issued in rapid succession. Gardiner might well ponder whither the Church in England was bound.

It was an easy matter for him to tear Hooper's arguments into tatters, for despite the vigour of Hooper's eloquence his reasoning was neither sound nor subtle. A great deal of what he said was, as Gardiner justly dubbed it, "rhetorique stuff." He made much, for instance, of the fact that Christ's body was in heaven. Ergo, he said, it cannot be in the Sacrament. Gardiner answered that since Christ was God, and with God nothing was impossible, the question was not whether Christ's body could be in two places at once, but whether he willed it so to be. Hooper stressed the verse "the flesh profiteth nothing," saying:

> "We must therefore lift up our minds unto heaven when we feel ourselves oppressed with the burden of sin, and there by faith apprehend and receive the body of Christ."

Gardiner pointed out that, according to Catholic teaching, the flesh received in the Sacrament was identical with the flesh of Christ's body in heaven, "which," he asked,

> "if it profiteth nothing in the Sacrament . . . how shall it profit in heaven? . . . And . . . why should Christ, after Mr. Hooper's doctrine, ordain in his Supper a figure of that [which] profiteth nothing? . . . If flesh profiteth nothing, how can the figure of flesh profit anything?"

This was answering a fool according to his folly; but Gardiner perceived that Hooper's teaching contained more than easily turned arguments against the bodily presence in the Eucharist. It implied, even if it did not express, a fundamental dissent from the whole

Catholic conception of the Church. Said Gardiner, referring further to the passage from Hooper last cited:

> "Mr. Hooper maketh here an insinuation to send every man to seek his communion in heaven, whither he will have each man take his journey when he feeleth himself oppressed with the burden of sin, without seeking any help of the ministry of the Church in earth. . . . I know Christ calleth them to him that be burdened, but yet would therewith have the ministry of the Church regarded, ordering himself to be come unto by his ministers, and by them to forgive sin, by them to purge, by them to cleanse, by them to sanctify, and by them to work the edification of his Church, which this teaching of Mr. Hooper doth plainly destroy."

In this passage is expressed more clearly perhaps than in any other writing of Gardiner his sense of the gulf between the Catholic and Protestant viewpoints. Mr. Hooper's teaching did without doubt destroy the Catholic conception of the Church and of the place and prerogative of the priesthood in it. Possibly this was what Mr. Hooper intended it to do. Certainly this result was no inconsiderable reason why his teaching found approval among the politically and economically powerful classes of his and subsequent days. Men who understood little of the subtleties of the sacramentarian controversy were ready to embrace a doctrine which, while claiming to be apostolic, tended to free life from clerical control.

In reply to Hooper's objections to altars, Gardiner admitted that an altar might properly also be called a table since at it we are fed, but to regard it as only a table was to think only of what we receive from God and to forget what we should offer to God. "In the Book of Common Prayer," he said, "it is well called both names."

He also appealed to the Prayer Book in the matter of ceremonies:

> "The Book of Common Prayer . . . giveth a good lesson to avoid Mr. Hooper's faults, which is, that some ceremonies there must needs be, and then such as be old and may be well used, be for the anciety to be the rather retained."

> "As I can well agree with the Book of Common Prayer, so me thinketh it intolerable to see such licentious arrogance in one unlearned (as Mr. Hooper is) to dare reprove in open sermons that [which] hath been consented and agreed unto."

If Hooper would really study the Scriptures, said Gardiner, he

> "should find himself such a Jonas in the tempest of this world, now travailed with opinion, as he should desire of charity to be cast out, that the tempest might assuage." [8]

In Cranmer Gardiner found an opponent less radical than Hooper and more learned, clearer headed and more skilful. Cranmer had, in 1550—the year in which Hooper's *Oversight* appeared—published *A Defence of the True and Catholic Doctrine of the Sacrament*, which to Gardiner seemed neither true nor Catholic. He wrote an immediate reply, which, unlike his book against Hooper, was not merely a refutation of his opponent's arguments, but also an exposition of his own "opinion and true belief of the Sacrament of the Altar, and of the true Catholic faith therein." This he presented at the thirteenth session of his trial, January 26, 1551, to the Commissioners at Lambeth "for part of his proof of his matter justificatory," and "offered himself to be ready, at the will and pleasure of the judges, at any time and place convenient, and before a due audience, by learning to defend the said book." [7]

Cranmer had originally held the traditional view that the bread and wine were, at consecration, changed into the real and substantial body and blood of Christ. From this point his opinions appear to have gone through two phases of development; first a phase in which he rejected transubstantiation but held to the Real Presence—a view not unlike Luther's, although he never formulated it in Luther's words; second, a phase in which he rejected everything but the spiritual presence of Christ received in the Sacrament by the believer. This was his final view and the one expressed in the volume rebutted by Gardiner. Here Cranmer approached the position of Zwingli and Hooper, with this difference—with Zwingli and Hooper the Sacrament was a service merely commemorative of Christ's death, with Cranmer it represented "our most perfect spiritual conjunction" with Christ. Christ's presence at the Sacrament, though spiritual, was nevertheless very real to Cranmer. It is, however, obvious that his teaching struck at the roots of the accepted doctrine.

The mediæval statement of that doctrine, known as transubstantiation, had arisen from the philosophical hypothesis that in every object a distinction was to be made between "substance" and "accidents," that is, between essential reality and outward appearance. Accidents, said the scholastic philosophers, were those qualities of an object such as its shape, size, weight, smell, and colour, which were perceived by the senses; substance was an inward reality, not experienced by the senses, but assumed by the reason to exist. Hence, when the mediæval theologian explained what he believed to be the change in the Sacrament, he said that while the "accidents" of the bread and wine remained the same after as before consecration, the "substance" was miraculously converted into that of the body and blood of Christ.

Cranmer trenchantly noted, in the very terms of scholasticism, the difficulties of this position.

"The Papists," he wrote, "say that in the Supper of the Lord after the words of consecration (as they call it) there is none other substance remaining but the substance of Christ's flesh and blood, so that there remaineth neither bread to be eaten nor wine to be drunken. And although there be colour of bread and wine, the savour, the smell, the bigness, the fashion, and all other (as they call them) accidents or qualities and quantities of bread and wine, yet (say they) there is no very bread nor wine, but they be turned into the flesh and blood of Christ. And this conversion they call transubstantiation, that is to say, turning of one substance into another substance. And although all the accidents, both of the bread and wine, remain still, yet (say they) these accidents be in no manner of thing, but hang alone in the air without any thing to stay them upon. For in the body and blood of Christ (say they) these accidents cannot be, nor yet in the air, for the body and blood of Christ and the air be neither of that bigness, fashion, smell nor colour that the bread and wine be. Nor in the bread and wine (say they) these accidents cannot be, for the substance of bread and wine (as they affirm) be clean gone. And so there remaineth whiteness but nothing is white; there remaineth colours but nothing is coloured therewith; there remaineth roundness but nothing is round; and there is bigness and yet nothing is big; there is sweetness without anything sweet; softness without any soft thing; breaking without any thing broken; division without any thing divided; and so other qualities and quantities without any thing to receive them. And this doctrine they teach as a necessary article of our faith."

Cranmer did not, however, rest his case on the absurdities of the mediæval teaching. His chief attack was on what he felt to be the crass materialism of it. "The gross error of the Papists," he said, "is of the carnal eating and drinking of Christ's flesh and blood with our mouths."

"As Christ is a spiritual meat, so is he spiritually eaten and digested with the spiritual part of us, and giveth us spiritual and eternal life, and is not eaten, swallowed, and digested with our teeth, tongues, throats, and bellies."

Christ's words, "this is my body," were, said Cranmer, clearly figurative, and the bread and wine of the Sacrament are figures, but "not bare and naked figures, but so pithy and effectuous that whosoever worthily eateth them, eateth spiritually Christ's flesh and blood, and hath by them everlasting life." We should

"come to this mystical bread and wine with faith, reverence, purity, and fear, as we would do if we should come to see and receive Christ himself sensibly present. For unto the faithful Christ is at his own holy table present with his mighty spirit and grace, and is of them more fruitfully received than if corporeally they should receive him bodily present."

"Figuratively he is in the bread and wine, and spiritually he is in them that worthily eat and drink the bread and wine, but really, carnally, and corporeally he is only in heaven."

The Papists, said Cranmer, err when they teach that evil men as well as good receive Christ in the Sacrament. When they say that Christ is offered daily for the remission of sins in behalf of the quick and the dead, they impiously assume that his Sacrifice on the Cross was incomplete. Their adoration of the Sacrament is idolatry. Moreover, private Masses are the result of superstition, ignorance, and the desire of priests for gain.

All this Cranmer supported by much quotation from Scripture and the Fathers, and claimed that it was the doctrine of the early Church and therefore truly Catholic.[8]

Gardiner in his reply feigned surprise that the Archbishop should be the author of this book. He would forbear, he said, to name him in his answers,

"because it may possibly be that his name is abused, wherewith to set forth the matter, . . . being a thing to me greatly to be marvelled at that such matter should now be published out of my Lord of Canterbury's pen."

It was no less to be marvelled at, he said, that this author should call his teaching Catholic, for in the whole history of the Church there were only some half dozen who had taught such doctrine— Bertram, Berengarius, Wyclif, and the contemporaries Œcolampadius, Zwingli, and Joachimus Vadianus.

"I will not reckon Peter Martyr, because such as know him saith he is not learned; nor this author, because he doth but as it were translate Peter Martyr. . . . Which matter being thus, it is a strange title of this book, to call it the true Catholic doctrine."

Moreover, it was "a matter wonderful" that the author should use the term Papist for those who believed in the real and substantial presence of Christ's body and blood in the Sacrament, for this was the faith not only of those who adhered to the Papacy but also of such leading reformers as Luther, Bucer, Melanchthon, Œpinus, Justus Jonas—whose catechism setting forth this faith had been translated and issued by Cranmer himself but two years past—and Erasmus, who, observed Gardiner, was so highly esteemed in England that his *Paraphrase of the New Testament* had been ordered to be set up in every church in the realm.

This was a telling thrust, but he went even further and pointed out how the service of the Holy Communion in the Book of Common Prayer accorded with the same doctrine, and that even the theory of transubstantiation had, some years after the repudiation of the Papacy by England, been "confessed for a truth by all the clergy of this realm in an open council," and had never been, "by any public council, or anything set forth by authority, impaired."

He was not, however, content merely to point out that Cranmer's teaching was unusual and unauthorized; he aimed to set over against it an exposition—an "explication" he called it—of what he believed to be the true Catholic faith. Christ's words, "This is my body," were, he said, literal truth, and always had been so taken by the faithful. This, indeed, involved a miracle, but if Christ be God, and God be omnipotent, why should this be impossible? True, it transcends reason and nature, but this is no obstacle to the man of faith, who humbly admits that he cannot explain the mystery.

> "I know by faith Christ to be present, but the particularity how he is present, more than I am assured he is truly present, and therefore in substance present, I cannot tell. . . . The ways and means whereof no man can tell, but humble spirits, as they be taught, must constantly believe it."

He is at pains to free the Catholic teaching from the imputation of grossness. Christ's body is so truly present, he says, that even the words carnal and corporeal may be used of it, yet these words when applied to Christ have a different significance than when applied to men, for, in the first place, he united in his body divinity with humanity, and in the second, he has ascended into heaven, and his body, albeit the same in which he lived on earth, has been spiritualized, as St. Paul says all our bodies will be at the resurrection. In the Sacrament, says Gardiner, we partake of this divine-human, glorified, spiritual body of Christ, and not of this body only, for "there is also understanded by concomitance to be present the substance of his soul, as very man, and also of the Godhead, as very God."

"Flesh profiteth nothing in itself," but "flesh in Christ is united to the divine nature," and is therefore "spirit and life" to the believing partaker.

> "As Christ is naturally in his Father, and his Father in him, so he that eateth verily the flesh of Christ, he is by nature in Christ, and Christ is naturally in him, and the worthy receiver hath life increased, augmented, and confirmed by the participation of the flesh of Christ."

> "We eat not the carnal flesh of a common man, as the letter soundeth, but the very spiritual flesh of Christ, God and man, as faith teacheth."

"We receive Christ's flesh glorified, incorruptible, very spiritual, and in a spiritual manner delivered unto us."

The words carnal and corporeal, as applied to an ordinary human body have no place, says Gardiner, in the true conception of heaven or of the Sacrament. They are used of Christ in the Sacrament to express the truth that his own very body, the same in which he lived and died, rose and ascended, and in which he sits at the right hand of the Father, is present on the altar.

He adroitly points out that while Cranmer deems the words carnal and corporeal too gross to be used of Christ's presence in the Sacrament, he does not hesitate to use them of Christ's presence in heaven. "Really, carnally, and corporeally he is only in heaven," said Cranmer.

"In such a sense," writes Gardiner, "as this author useth the terms carnal and corporeal against the Sacrament to imply a grossness, he cannot so attribute those terms to Christ's body in heaven."

Gardiner so strives to give spiritual expression to what he believes to be the truth of Christ's substantial and corporeal presence in the Sacrament that he seems at times to fall into contradictory statements. Thus in one place he affirms that "the body that suffered, . . . the body of very flesh" is present in the Sacrament, and in another that "we receive not in the Sacrament Christ's flesh that was crucified . . . but Christ's flesh glorified, incorruptible and impassable, a godly and spiritual flesh." His meaning is that, while Christ's body—now in heaven—which we receive in the Sacrament, is the same as that in which he suffered, the flesh of which it is composed has undergone a profound change. To use an analogy which Gardiner does not use, but which helps to illustrate his meaning, the body of a man of three score years is, in the commonly accepted sense of the term, the body in which he was born, yet the actual matter composing it has, since birth, changed completely several times. An even more complete change in Christ's body occurred, in Gardiner's view, at the Ascension. Hence he could say that although in the Sacrament we do not receive the flesh that was crucified, we do receive the body that suffered. "Christ's body and flesh is a spiritual body and flesh, and yet a true body and flesh."

It is obvious that Gardiner here uses the word "spiritual" in a different sense than does Cranmer. With Cranmer spiritual was the antithesis of corporeal and substantial. With Gardiner that which was corporeal and substantial might also be spiritual. In this, as in many another notable debate, the arguments of the disputants fail fairly to meet each other because of the initial failure to agree upon a common meaning of the principal term involved.

Since Christ's body in the Sacrament is substantial as well as spiritual, it is—to continue Gardiner's exposition—actually present, not figuratively, nor in the heart of the believer only, and is received by good men and evil, worthy and unworthy; but from the evil and unworthy, as from vessels unmeet to contain him, Christ immediately departs.

In teaching that the Sacrament is a sacrifice propitiatory for sin, the Church, says Gardiner, in no way derogates from the complete and perfect sacrifice of Christ upon the Cross. The Sacrament is not a repetition of that sacrifice, it is rather a representation of it, the same in essence with it, and "is daily offered for sin, not for any imperfection in the first offering, but because we daily fall." The priest celebrating the Sacrament does not, of his own power, perform the miracle; it is the exalted Christ, our invisible Priest, who performs it, working through the ministry of the visible priesthood. That which is adored in the Sacrament is the invisible presence, not the visible elements.

Cranmer's explanation of Christ's words as figures, says Gardiner, takes all the wonder out of the Sacrament; it is "a jolly easy way without any mystery or marvel at all;" but he admits that all that Cranmer says of spiritual hunger and spiritual feeding on Christ is "good teaching and wholesome exhortation;" for every Christian should learn to feed on Christ continually, without the use of the visible Sacrament; but to identify this spiritual feeding with the eating of Christ's body in the Sacrament tends to confusion. There are, he says, three ways of eating Christ's body; "one spiritual only," which is the continual feeding on Christ by the believer; another "both sacramentally and spiritually, which is when men worthily communicate in the Supper; the third is sacramentally only, which is by men unworthy, who eat and drink in the holy Supper to their condemnation." Cranmer's teaching makes the first equal to the second, which is "to diminish the effect of the institution of the Sacrament, which no Christian man ought to do."

He also observes that Cranmer's attempt to prove that evil men receive not the body and blood of Christ in the Sacrament

> "is a very superfluous matter. For if the Sacrament be only a figure, and the body and blood of Christ be there only figuratively, whereto should this author dispute of evil men's eating, when good men cannot eat Christ in the Sacrament because he is not there?"

Cranmer had begun his work by a denial of transubstantiation and from that passed on to a denial of any corporeal presence of Christ in the Sacrament. Gardiner reversed the order. He first affirmed the presence, then went on to transubstantiation. This gave him a strategic advantage, since he could appeal, as has been already indicated, to the leading Lutherans who affirmed the presence of Christ's body and blood in or with the bread and wine, although they denied transubstantiation. Moreover, Gardiner held that the order he followed was the more natural one, since the theory of transubstantiation was the logical corollary of a belief in the Real Presence.

Reason, he said, will plainly affirm that if it be the body of Christ in the Sacrament, it is not bread, "for in the rule of common reason the grant of one substance is the denial of another." Now "in every thing all is substance and accidents; but the accidents be not changed, and yet, a change there is; it must needs be then that substance is changed." This, he said, is not held by the Church because it has been so decreed by a Pope, but because it is manifest truth, as even Zwingli acknowledged when he wrote to Luther: "It must needs be true, that if the body of Christ be really in the Sacrament, there is of necessity transubstantiation also."

It is not surprising, said Gardiner, that the evidence of the senses, of which Cranmer makes so much, is untrustworthy on the substance of the Sacrament, since it may be untrustworthy on the substance of anything; for substance "as it is truly in learning understanded" is "an inward, invisible, and not palpable nature, but only perceived by understanding."

He amusingly illustrated this point by supposing that a rude, unlearned man should bring forth, in the presence of a scholar, "a piece of bread, another of cheese, and a pot of ale," and should desire the scholar "to learn him the substance of them, and show it with his finger." If the scholar explained that substance is "the inward nature," the rude man, touching the bread, would ask roundly, "Callest thou not *this* substance, this good thick piece that I handle?" To which the scholar would have to answer that substance, "as it is properly understood," cannot be handled. What we feel and see in a piece of bread, its colour, largeness, weight, and softness, are its accidents; and if, by a miracle, the substance of the bread were removed and the accidents or visible part remained, the visible part would have the appearance of bread, and might, in common speech, be called bread, but would not be bread. To this the rude man would exclaim:

> "Here is sophistry indeed, for here is substance and no substance, matter of bread and no bread, appearance of bread and no bread, called bread and no bread; this is plain juggling."

Moreover, if he asked the scholar to show him the difference between the substance of bread, cheese, and ale, the scholar could only answer:

> "I know bread is no cheese, and cheese is no ale, and of their accidental parts I can indeed show differences, but of the very substance none."

At which the rude man would laugh loudly and "would keep the accidents of his bread, cheese, and ale for himself, and give the substance to the scholar . . . as a reward for his cunning."

"And this," said Gardiner, "I write after this gross sort, to show that this matter of substance is not commonly understanded as senses exercised in learning perceive it, and how man's outward senses cannot, as this author would have it, be judges of the inward nature of substance."

"I will grant," he said, "that accidents to be without substance is against the common course of natural things, and therefore therein is a special miracle of God." To the question, what is broken in the Sacrament, he answered, neither the bread nor the body of Christ, but "the visible matter of the Sacrament, under which is present invisibly the substance of the most precious body of Christ." This may sound absurd "to the ethnic or carnal man's ears," but "that is only to be accounted for an absurdity that should repugn to the Scripture and God's will."

Gardiner was not granted opportunity to defend his book before "a due audience" as he desired, but he did succeed in having it published sometime during the year 1551, under the title *An Explication and Assertion of the True Catholic Faith Touching the Most Blessed Sacrament of the Altar.*[9]

Cranmer replied immediately in *An Answer . . . unto a Crafty and Sophistical Cavillation Devised by Stephen Gardiner,* in which there reappeared Cranmer's book of 1550, the whole of Gardiner's answer to it, and Cranmer's rejoinder to this. This volume, as reprinted by the Parker Society, is the form in which the controversy is most easily accessible. Cranmer's arguments are always vigorous and often telling, and his English surpasses Gardiner's in clarity and precision, but the reader of the volume must remember that in it Cranmer has the advantage of the last word. It was not, however, the last word in the controversy, for Gardiner published in Paris in 1552 a Latin work on the Sacrament entitled *Confutatio Cavillationum . . .,* under the pseudonym of Marcus Antonius Constantius, Theologian, of Louvain. A second edition was published under his own name at Louvain in 1554, after his release from the Tower. This is a volume of eight hundred pages, over two-thirds of which is devoted to answering two hundred and fifty-five objections to the Catholic doctrine of the Sacrament, the rest, to a discussion of other phases of the same subject.

Although it was not specifically directed against Cranmer, Cranmer began to write a reply to it when he in turn became a prisoner under Queen Mary. His chief reason, he said, for desiring to appeal his case to a general council was to gain time to finish this reply before death; and he wrote to his friend Peter Martyr saying that of all his sufferings in prison nothing distressed him more than the thought that Gardiner's book was unanswered.[10]   Cranmer did not live to finish his reply, nor was the part he had completed ever published; but in 1559, four years after both his death and Gardiner's, Peter Martyr published a Latin rejoinder, exceeding Gardiner's volume in length by a hundred pages.[11]

It is wholly beyond the scope of this biography to discuss the later phases of this well-nigh interminable controversy; nor can we give more than passing mention to the other books written by Gardiner in the Tower.   One was an answer to Peter Martyr's treatise of 1549 on the Sacrament; one an examination of certain passages from the Greek Fathers cited by the Swiss reformer Œcolampadius in a dialogue on the Sacrament published in 1530; another was a discussion of the articles which Hooper presented for subscription to the clergy of the diocese of Worcester in 1552.   Not only would an exposition of these writings take us quite out of bounds, it would be unnecessary, for Gardiner's essential views on the Sacrament appear in his book against Cranmer of 1551.

The effect of that volume on the revision of the Prayer Book is of perhaps greater import than its incitement to continued doctrinal discussion.   We recall how, on his first examination of the Prayer Book, Gardiner told Somerset and the other councillors that although he would not have made it as it was, nevertheless he liked it because it taught the Catholic faith concerning the Sacrament.   He appealed to it against Hooper.   He did so against Cranmer also. It was one of his strongest tactical positions, for the Prayer Book was largely of Cranmer's composition, and was, moreover, the official liturgy of the Church of which Cranmer was primate.

Gardiner pointed to five passages in the Communion Service which, he said, explicitly upheld Catholic doctrine.   First, the words of distribution (The body of our Lord Jesus Christ, which was given for thee . . .   The blood of our Lord Jesus Christ, which was shed for thee . . .) made clear the teaching of the Church that the body and blood were present under the form of bread and wine, and not, as Cranmer said, only in them that worthily ate and drank the bread and wine.   Second, the rubric providing for the division of each wafer into at least two pieces and explaining that "men must not think less to be received in part than in the whole, but in each of them the whole body of our Saviour," was, said Gardiner, "agreeable to the Catholic doctrine."   Third, the words in the prayer of consecration, "with thy Holy Spirit and word vouchsafe to bless and sanctify these thy gifts and creatures of bread and wine, that they may be unto us the body and blood of thy most dearly beloved Son Jesus Christ," taught that "the body of Christ is by God's omnipotency . . .   made present unto us at such time as the Church prayeth it may please him so to do." Fourth, the prayer for the whole state of Christ's Church, (which in the first Prayer Book contained petitions for dead as well as living, and was placed in immediate connection with the consecration) was consonant with the belief in the Sacrament as a sacrifice propitiatory for the sins of the world, for when Christ gives himself in the Supper as a sacrifice for our sins "it is very profitable at that time . . . to remember in prayer all estates of the Church." Fifth, in the prayer now known as the Prayer of Humble Access (which in the first Prayer Book stood after the consecration and immediately before the communion) "the adoration of Christ's flesh in the Sacrament . . . is," said Gardiner, "in my judgment, well set forth."

The holy mystery of the Sacrament, he concluded, "in the Book of Common Prayer is well termed, not distant from the Catholic faith in my judgement;" and he declared that "the effect of all celestial or worldly gifts to be obtained of God in the celebration of Christ's holy Supper . . . shall be obtained, if we devoutly, reverently, charitably, and quietly use and frequent the same, without other innovations than the order of the book prescribeth." [12]

Gardiner's arguments struck home. Although Cranmer would not admit that his interpretations of the Prayer Book were correct, he could not deny that they were possible. In the revision of the Prayer Book, which received Parliamentary sanction in the spring of 1552, every passage in which Gardiner had read a Catholic meaning was deleted or changed. The words of distribution became "Take and eat this in remembrance that Christ died for thee;" the rubric stating that the whole body was in each piece of bread was omitted; the phrase in the prayer of consecration to which Gardiner had appealed was dropped; the prayer for the whole state of Christ's Church was removed from the canon, and all reference to the dead expunged from it; and the Prayer of Humble Access was placed before the consecration. Finally, the word "altar," to which Gardiner had referred in his discussion of Hooper's *Oversight,* was no longer used.

Thus the experiment in anti-Papal Catholicism which Gardiner had championed had become, in his view, anti-Catholic as well as anti-Papal. The publication of the second Prayer Book of Edward VI must have done much to convince him that Thomas More had been right and Henry VIII wrong. [13]

XXVII

THE NEW CHANCELLOR

In the night of July 6, 1553 King Edward VI, that "godly and virtuous imp," as Foxe calls him, "yielded up the ghost, leaving a woeful kingdom behind unto his sister." [1] Thanks to the changing economic conditions, the avarice of Henry VIII, and the arrant misgovernment of Warwick, now Duke of Northumberland, the kingdom was indeed a woeful one, but it had not been the intention of the boy King to leave even this to his sister. To the ill-starred Jane Grey, daughter-in-law of Northumberland, Edward had been persuaded to bequeath his crown.

Early on July 7 Northumberland's supporters seized the Tower, and on that day, if we may believe the report that reached the Imperial ambassador, Gardiner and two of his fellow prisoners, the Duke of Norfolk and Edward Courtenay, were warned to prepare for execution.[2] Gardiner had now been in the Tower five years, Norfolk almost seven, and Courtenay, great-grandson of King Edward IV, fifteen. The report of their intended execution may not have been well founded. Certainly it was not carried out. Northumberland had more urgent matters to look to during the following fortnight. Lady Mary had eluded him by leaving London before her brother's death. Lady Jane was proclaimed Queen July 10. On the 12th news reached him that the nobility and gentry of Norfolk and Suffolk were flocking to Mary's standard; on the 13th he set out with an army to oppose her; on the 19th the Council, seeing that his cause was hopeless, had Mary proclaimed Queen in London amid the riotous rejoicings of the citizens.

Two days later, July 1, the day of Northumberland's arrest, Gardiner was offered his liberty; but he preferred not to leave the Tower except by the Queen's authority. Meanwhile the councillors in London conferred with him on affairs and, according to the Imperial ambassador, adopted his advice.[3]

He began at once to gather together the scattered property of his see. Winchester House in Southwark had come into the hands of William Parr, Marquis of Northampton, who was brought as a prisoner to the Tower, for complicity in Northumberland's conspiracy, July 26. Gardiner immediately notified the Marchioness to quit the Southwark residence, and at the same time intimated to William Herbert, now Earl of Pembroke, that he should return certain revenues to Winchester Cathedral. "Several persons," says the Imperial ambassador, "consider this unwise and too hasty, for the matter is a ticklish one, especially where Church property is concerned." [4] Thus at the very outset of the reign we hear the first murmur of what became perhaps the strongest objection to the restoration of the old religion—the ticklish question of property once belonging to the Church, now in the hands of the laity.

On August 3, 1553 Mary, in a "gown of purple velvet, French fashion," mounted on a palfrey trapped with gold embroidery down to its feet, rode for the first time as Queen into London, "all the streets by the way as her Highness rode standing so full of people shouting and crying 'Jesus save her Grace,' with weeping tears for joy, that the like was never seen before." When she came to the Tower, there upon the hill within the Tower gate, were Gardiner, Norfolk, Courtenay, and the widow of Protector Somerset, all upon their knees. In the simple and dramatic language of the chronicler, "she came to them and kissed them and said, 'These be my prisoners.'" [5]

The next day the prisoners had the Queen's pardon, and on the night of August 4, or the morning of August 5, the day Bonner was released from the Marshalsea and Tunstall from the King's Bench, Gardiner was sworn of the Privy Council. [6] He continued his residence in the Tower, however, until August 11, when he once more returned to his house in Southwark [7] and the delights of that pleasant study which he had reluctantly abandoned half a decade before. No more formal restoration to his bishopric was deemed necessary. [8] At about the same time he was reinstated as Master of Trinity Hall and Chancellor of Cambridge University. [9] On August 23 he was appointed by the Queen Lord Chancellor of England. [10]

By thus placing her ablest statesman and her chiefest Churchman in the chancellorship Mary reinvested that office with its former prestige; she also restored an ancient dignity to the Church, for until the days of Thomas More chancellors had almost invariably been Churchmen. [11] Gardiner's immediate predecessor had indeed been a Churchman, Bishop Goodrich of Ely, but he had been a mere cipher at Northumberland's council board; and the five laymen who filled the office before him had had little more weight than he in determining the policy of the Government; for, since the fall of Wolsey, the rulers of England had desired in their chancellors subservience rather than initiative. Of the five laymen, More was the only one of note. After his brief tenure came the pliant Sir Thomas Audley who held the office through the ascendancy of Cromwell and four years beyond. [12] For the last three years of Henry's reign the place was filled by Gardiner's protégé Wriothesley, who was ousted from it early in Somerset's régime. He later conspired, as we have seen, with Warwick (Northumberland) against the Protector in the hope of a Catholic revival, and died—some said of disappointment—

in 1550. After Wriothesley, Paulet, as Lord Keeper of the Great
Seal, held the office but not the title of Chancellor for seven months
in 1547. Then came Sir Richard Riche, until the early months of
Northumberland's supremacy, and finally Bishop Goodrich.[13] Both
Paulet and Riche found places in Mary's Council.

If Gardiner's recent predecessors were not men of distinction, the
office was, nevertheless, one on which some of the greatest names
in English history had shed lustre. Thomas à Becket, William
Longchamp, William of Wickham, Cardinal Beaufort, Cardinal
Bourchier, William Waynfleet, Archbishop Warham, and Cardinal
Wolsey had all been Lord Chancellors.

The difficulties which confronted the new Government of which
Gardiner was thus made the head were of two sorts—those arising
from the condition of the country, and those springing from the
clash of personalities and interests among the persons composing
the Government. The country was indeed in a distressful condition.
England has seldom been afflicted with such a corrupt, inefficient, and
thoroughly evil rule as that of Northumberland. This had, however,
fortunately been short, and cannot be held accountable for all the
ills of the time. It was Northumberland's misfortune, as well as
that of Queen Mary and her Chancellor, that their lot fell upon
days when the unrest and disintegration attendant upon two generations of social and economic revolution had reached a culmination.
And this state of affairs was infinitely complicated by religious
dissension.

Mary's Government early attempted to better the economic situation. It announced the Queen's intention to assume the debts of
Henry and Edward; it remitted the subsidy granted by the last of
Edward's Parliaments; it issued new coin of good metal; it sought
to reduce the expenditures of the crown. These measures, which
were evidently designed to win for the Government the support of
the commercial classes, and which have, with probable truth, been
credited to Gardiner,[14] were but a drop in the bucket of economic
adversity.

The religious problem was equally difficult of solution. The
Queen desired speedy reunion with Rome; the great body of Englishmen, especially in the north and west, were still strongly attached to the forms and usages of the old faith, though many of
them may have had no great love for the Pope; in London and the
counties in contact with Germany and Flanders there were thousands
who had sincerely rejoiced to see the Mass, in the vigorous phrase
of Foxe, "exploded out of all the churches." The strength of this
Protestant party, although still in the minority, lay, on the one hand,
in the energy and zeal of its religious leaders, on the other, in the
support it received from men of no religious convictions whatever,

merely because the religious simplicity preached by the reformers
gave colour and excuse for the confiscation of Church lands and
the appropriation of Church treasures. Moreover, practically all
the wealthier families in England, whether Protestant or Catholic,
had, by purchase or inheritance, become possessed of some portion
of erstwhile monastic land, and looked with alarm at any proposed
restoration of authority to the Church which might threaten the
security of their title to it.

Great as were the difficulties arising from the economic and religious situation, they might have been encountered with a good hope
had the Government presented to them a united front. But the
Government was not united. A week before Gardiner was sworn
of the Council, the Queen expressed amazement at the dissension
among her councillors,[15] and this dissension gave little sign of abating
as the reign progressed.

It has been said, truly enough, that Mary's Privy Council of over
forty members was too large. But this did not present an insuper-
able difficulty. More than half of the forty were usually absent
from Council meetings, and there soon sprang up an informal inner
council of some half dozen who conducted all the important business
of State. The difficulty lay in the fact that the Council was made
up of antagonistic factions. Mary had naturally rewarded with
places in it those gentlemen of her household who, under Northumberland, had suffered imprisonment rather than force her to
give up the Mass at his bidding. Such were Sir Robert Rochester,
Sir Francis Englefield, and Sir Edward Walgrave. But these men
had neither experience in Government nor large influence in the
realm. Hence she was glad to welcome such conservative leaders
as Gardiner, Norfolk, and Tunstall, despite their previous support
of the royal supremacy. She was, moreover, constrained to admit
Paget and Fitzalan, Earl of Arundel, who had been active in Northumberland's overthrow. Nor was it safe or possible for her to
ignore the capable Sir William Petre and the wealthy and powerful
lords of Northumberland's Council, Paulet, Marquis of Winchester,
Russell, Earl of Bedford, and Herbert, Earl of Pembroke, who could
plead that they had, albeit at the last moment, deserted Northumberland in her favour. Their presence in the Council stirred the
jealousy of those whose loyalty to Mary had never been questioned,
and the resentment of those who had suffered at their hands in the
late reign. Nor was the opposition merely one of personal pique.
The conservative bishops and the men of Mary's household stood
for a restoration of ecclesiastical power and privilege which the
lords who had grown fat on the spoils of the Church were determined to withstand. And this division of persons and policies extended to the inner council, composed of Gardiner, Rochester.
Arundel, Paget, Petre, and Thirlby.[16] Here as in the larger body

there was the Chancellor's party and the opposition. The opposition was led by Paget. He was supported by Arundel and Petre.

Henry VIII had, from the fall of Wolsey to the end of his reign, maintained of set policy a two-party Council. Although Mary had much of her father's strength of will, she had neither his experience nor his sagacity. She did not desire a two-party Council, nor could she dominate it. Circumstances had forced such a Council upon her. Hence she was, as she herself confessed, afraid and distrustful of many of her councillors,[17] and took no one of them, not even the Chancellor, into her confidence on some of the most important problems which confronted her at the opening of her reign.

It may be, as had been suggested, that Gardiner's advocacy of the divorce of her mother kept her from placing unreserved confidence in him, but we are probably nearer the truth if we say that she now sought advice elsewhere simply because she had been so doing all her life. Considering the ill-treatment she had received at the hands of Englishmen, it was but natural that she should look to her cousin the Emperor now, as she had done on many a former occasion, for advice. After God, there was no one for whom she had so much respect, she said, as for him. In advising her, Charles professed the most disinterested motives, but his eye was ever to his own advantage, and his ambassador, the adroit and proficient Simon Renard, lost no opportunity to advance his master's interests. For Renard Mary contrived interviews unknown to the Council; to Renard she confided her perplexities. Noailles, the French ambassador, observed that she was completely under Renard's thumb, and Renard himself boasted that she was so good, so inexperienced, and so easily influenced that he had things pretty much his own way.[18]

This was by no means the least of the difficulties confronting the new Chancellor.

XXVIII

TREASON AND HERESY

One piece of advice which the Emperor sent to the Queen through his ambassador was that mercy should be shown to all but the leaders of Northumberland's conspiracy—an admonition of which there was little need, said Renard, for the Queen was naturally merciful.[1] The leaders only—Northumberland, Gates, and Palmer—were executed. Gardiner even sought to save Northumberland, if we may believe the story told by the Jesuit, Robert Parsons, late in the reign of Elizabeth.

"The Duke," says Parsons, "being condemned to death, and knowing the gentle nature of the Bishop, and that he was nothing vindicative," asked to speak with him. To this the Council consented, but fearing "the Bishop's tenderness of heart," sent with him

> "another councillor to be present at their talk, who afterward recounted (and I have heard it from his own mouth) the hearty tears that the said Bishop shed at the sight and conference with the Duke."

Northumberland begged abjectly for his life, and Gardiner promised to do what he could for him, but warned him that since his adversaries were many he had better prepare for the worst. He went, nevertheless, to the Queen and entreated so earnestly for him that the Duke's enemies, apprehensive of his release, got the Emperor to write to the Queen that it was unsafe to pardon him.

This, in brief, is Parsons' story.[2] He is obviously making a case for Gardiner's "tenderness of heart," and there is at least one impossibility in his narrative. As Northumberland was condemned August 18, 1553, and executed August 22, there was not time to write to the Emperor and receive an answer between these dates. Yet the tale receives some confirmation from other sources. A contemporary French account of Northumberland's death tells how the Duke sent for Gardiner and begged for his life, saying:

> "You, although devoted to a peaceful calling, have often confronted death without fear; I, on the contrary, who as a soldier ought to despise and have so often despised every danger, lose my courage now that my sentence is shown me."[3]

Renard tells us that Gardiner comforted and sustained Northumberland at his execution;[4] and we know that the Emperor had already advised against leniency to the leaders of the conspiracy, and that Renard had urgently seconded his advice.[5]

Another topic on which the Emperor thought good to advise his cousin was that of religion. Mary's dearest desire was reunion with Rome; and Cardinal Pole, created Legate to England August 5, 1553 by Pope Julius III, urged her by letter to proceed to it at once.[6] Mary was not unaware of the opposition this would encounter in her Council, hence her messages to the Pope, asking remission of ecclesiastical censures against England, were, it seems, kept secret even from Gardiner. Renard, who fully appreciated the difficulties in the way of an immediate submission of England to the Papacy, suggested that she get her Chancellor's advice about it.[7]

What the Chancellor's advice was we do not precisely know, but from the fact that Renard, who on a certain other vital matter did not, as we shall see, think the Chancellor's advice should even be considered, suggested consulting him on this, indicates that he must have known that Gardiner's position on this question was not much different from that of the Emperor who, immediately on Mary's accession, admonished her to go slowly in making religious changes, and do nothing of importance without Parliamentary sanction.[8]

Gardiner later averred that in the matter of reunion with Rome "the Queen went before him, and that it was her own motion;" and when John Rogers, to whom this was said, replied that he could not believe it, Sir Robert Rochester and Sir John Bourne stood up and bore witness to the truth of the statement, and Bishop Aldrich of Carlisle said that all the bishops would do the same.[9]

It would seem, therefore, that Gardiner counselled a not too precipitate return to Rome. Whether he would have counselled a return to Rome at all, had the matter been wholly in his choice, is impossible to say. There can be little doubt that if Mary had desired to go no farther than the religious settlement of Henry VIII, he would have supported her heartily. As a matter of fact he supported her no less heartily in the re-establishment of Papal authority. Thus to follow his sovereign in religion was of the essence of that doctrine of royal supremacy he had so long defended. Moreover, there had been much in his experience during the past five years to convince him that Catholicism in England without the Pope was exceedingly difficult if not impossible of achievement.

However that may be, he set to work to restore the Church to the position it occupied in the latter years of Henry VIII. The first official step in this direction was in connection with Edward's funeral on August 8. Mary desired that this should be conducted according to the ancient rites, but Renard, and undoubtedly her English councillors as well, advised against it, fearing opposition in London before her position was established. She was persuaded, therefore, to satisfy her conscience by a compromise. While Cranmer said the Holy Communion and the burial service in English at the Abbey, she attended a solemn requiem in the Tower, celebrated by Gardiner, "who had on his mitre, and did all things as in times past."[10] This was August 8, but four days after he had regained his liberty. There was much murmuring, even among the Queen's bodyguard, some of whom cursed the Bishop; but he continued, nevertheless, to say Mass daily in the Tower during the rest of the week while Mary remained there.[11]

An old priest at St. Bartholomew's in Smithfield who followed his example, August 11, was almost pulled to pieces by the congregation; whereupon the Lord Mayor informed the Queen that there would be trouble if the Mass were permitted.[12] Next day she told Mayor and aldermen that, with the approval of her Council, she had determined to continue Mass at court, but would compel no one to attend, and that her subjects would be free to follow either the new religion or the old until Parliament came to some determination in the matter.[13] The rulers of the city expressed approval of this resolution, but on the morrow, Sunday, August 13, there was a riot at Paul's Cross when the preacher, Dr. Bourne, declared that Bonner had been unjustly imprisoned. "Liar!" "Papist!" shouted the auditors, and the preacher barely escaped with his life.[14]

The Council met at once and instructed the Mayor to call a common council, charge the householders with the duty of maintaining order, and inform them of what the Queen had said about compelling no one in matters of religion until Parliament had settled the question. Every clergyman holding a cure in London was to be notified that neither he nor anyone else was to preach or publicly read the Scriptures in his church without special licence from the Queen. The Mayor was further warned that if he did not feel capable of preventing tumult he must surrender his sword.

These vigorous measures, in which we are doubtless justified in discerning Gardiner's hand, met with success. The Mayor reported to the Council, August 16, that the city would henceforth be kept in order, and some half dozen persons, suspected of complicity in the recent disturbance, were arrested.[15] Among them were John Bradford and John Rogers, prominent prebendaries of St. Paul's, and Thomas Becon, with whom Gardiner had had dealings in 1543.

The day preceding these arrests, a pamphlet was scattered throughout London calling on nobles and gentlemen who favoured the word of God to withdraw themselves from the Queen because several of her councillors were hardened and detestable Papists, especially Gardiner, the great devil, who must be exorcised and, with his followers, exterminated, before he poison the people.[16]

On August 18, two days after the Mayor's report on the order of the city, the Queen's intentions concerning religion were made public in a proclamation, composed in all probability by Gardiner. Her Highness, said this manifesto, cannot hide the religion she has professed from her infancy, and as she is minded to maintain it for herself, so she would be glad if her subjects quietly and charitably embraced it. Yet she will not compel any thereto until such time as further order by common consent may be taken therein. But she does command her subjects to forbear calling each other Papist and Heretic, and bids them by their charitable and godly doings to express that hunger for God's word which by rash talk many have pretended. The rigour of the law will be used against any presuming to call an assembly of the people or otherwise to stir disorder; and those who preach, expound Scripture, print books, or play interludes without her licence will incur her indignation and displeasure.[17]

The next Sunday, August 2, the sermon at Paul's Cross was delivered by Gardiner's chaplain, Thomas Watson, without interruption, two hundred of the guard being present "to see no disquiet done."[18] On the same day, Gardiner, as Chancellor of Cambridge, was formally instructed by the Queen, in a letter which he, as her chief minister, must himself have composed, to see that the ancient statutes and foundations of the university, which had in the late reign been "almost utterly subverted," be henceforth "inviolably kept," so that the youth should no longer, as at present, be "loosely and insolently brought up." Since it is our duty, reads the letter, to see God's will truly declared to our subjects, we "have thought good for a beginning to wish that the examples hereof may first begin in our universities," so that young men, "joining godly conversation with their studies," may afterward instruct the people.[19] Thereupon Gardiner's chaplain Watson was sent "with instructions to every college."[20] Watson, a former fellow at St. John's, called by his friend, Roger Ascham, "one of the best scholars that ever St. John's College bred," was elected master of it in September 1553,[21] in accordance with Gardiner's design "to have good and discreet heads in the colleges,"[22]—a design which resulted in replacing most of the Edwardine masters by orthodox scholars.[23] The study of Canon Law was likewise revived at Cambridge at this time.[24]

Meanwhile in London on St. Bartholomew's Day (August 24), the day after Gardiner was made Lord Chancellor, Mass was begun, according to the chronicler Wriothesley, in five or six London churches, "not by commandment, but by the people's devotion," and on the following Sunday, it was sung at St. Paul's.[25] Two days later the power of licencing preachers for all cathedrals, churches, and chapels throughout the entire realm was placed by the Queen in Gardiner's hands, and its exercise left solely to his judgement.[26]

Early in September Renard wrote that news came daily to the court of the unopposed revival of the old services in various parts of the kingdom. At the same time Gardiner remarked to him with satisfaction, that without compulsion or commandment affairs were following the right course to the greater glory of God.[27]

With the act of 1552, enforcing the use of the second Prayer Book of Edward VI, still on the statute books, this revival of the Latin Mass was clearly illegal. Gardiner, like many another Government leader, before and since, was employing methods strikingly akin to those he had so resolutely denounced when in the Opposition. Yet it may fairly be said in his vindication, that while he had protested against the injunctions of 1547 on the ground that they enforced disobedience to an act of Parliament, his revival of the Mass in 1553, although in itself contrary to an act of Parliament, enforced no one to disobey that act. In other words, under Somerset the executive had, in Gardiner's view, enjoined disobedience to the law; under Mary the executive announced that the law would not be enforced, and encouraged, but did not enjoin, disobedience to it.

Mary regarded much of the ecclesiastical legislation of the previous reign as void because in conflict with the laws of Christendom. She had, during the late régime, refused to acknowledge the proceedings of Edward's Council in

> "making (as they call it) laws both clean contrary to his [Henry VIII's] proceedings and will, and also against the custom of all Christendom, and (in my conscience) against the law of God and his Church."[28]

Although Gardiner did not express himself in precisely this way, he had laid down in his St. Peter's Day sermon a similar principle. There were, he said, many things connected with the practice and organization of religion which the civil ruler might abolish; and he acknowledged his own acquiescence in the abolition of Papal supremacy, monasteries, chantries, images, palms, candles, and certain ceremonies. But there were some things, he went on to say, of the very essence of the Church, like Baptism and preaching, which, if abused, the civil ruler might reform, but not abolish. He then discussed two other things which, by implication, he placed in this category—the doctrine of the presence of Christ's body in the Sacrament, and the celibacy of the clergy.

Having thus not only avowed the principle, but explained his attitude toward two specific applications of it, he can hardly be charged with inconsistency if, when he came to power, he deprived married clergy and restored the Mass. Yet he does not appear to have deprived any priest because of marriage until after the laws permitting clerical marriage had been repealed by Parliament, nor

is there any conclusive evidence that he punished any one for ad-
hering to the Edwardine service until its use had been forbidden by
law, although he attempted to alarm extremists into abandoning it.

He does, however, seem to have questioned the validity of certain
acts of Northumberland's Government on the ground that it was an
usurpation. This we learn from conversations recorded by Richard
Bertie and John Rogers. Bertie, second husband of the Duchess of
Suffolk, was, in 1554, summoned before Gardiner and told he must
pay the Queen £4,000, due Henry VIII from the late Duke of Suffolk.

> "'Pleaseth it your Lordship,' quoth Master Bertie, 'that debt is
> estalled, and is according to that estallment truly answered.'
>
> 'Tush!' quoth the Bishop, 'the Queen will not be bound to
> estallments in the time of Kett's Government; for so I esteem
> the late Government.' " [29]

(Kett was a rebel who had set up a local government in Norfolk in
1549.)

Rogers, at his examination in 1555, maintained that he had been
illegally deprived of the revenues of his benefice during his imprisonment, to which Gardiner answered, says Rogers,

> "that Dr. Ridley that had given them me was an usurper, and
> therefore I was the unjust possessor thereof.
>
> 'Was the King then an usurper,' quod I, 'that gave Dr. Rid-
> ley the bishopric?'
>
> 'Yea,' quod he, and began to set out the wrongs that the King
> had done them [Bonner and himself] . . . 'but yet,' quod
> he, 'I misuse my terms to call the King usurper.' " [30]

Ridley had been put in Bonner's place by Northumberland.

On the other hand, in Gardiner's conversation with Judge Hales,
of which we shall shortly speak more fully, he nowhere suggested
that he deemed Edwardine legislation, even when enacted during
Northumberland's supremacy, void for any reason. He censured
Hales for enforcing it against the Queen's wishes, but admitted
that Hales had the law on his side.

It would appear, therefore, that Gardiner made a distinction between executive acts of Northumberland, whether civil or ecclesiastical, and laws passed by Parliament. Certainly he used every influence to secure Parliamentary sanction for the religious changes
desired by the Queen, and he seems to have restrained her tendency
to run before the law.

Apropos of this, Burnet tells a story which, though curious, is
certainly in keeping with all we know of Gardiner. Burnet got it,
he says, from an account written by the Earl of Leicester who, in
Queen Elizabeth's days, was told it by a certain Fleetwood, after-

ward recorder of London. According to this, a one-time minion of Cromwell's prepared "a new platform of government" by which Mary was to declare "that she, having succeeded to the crown by common law, was not at all to be limited by the statute laws, since those were only restrictions upon the kings but not on the queens." Thus "she might establish religion, set up the monasteries, . . . and rule according to her pleasure." One of the Emperor's ambassadors, a friend of the author, carried it to Mary who asked her Chancellor's opinion of it.

"It is a pity," replied Gardiner, after reading it, "that so noble and virtuous a lady should be endangered with the pernicious devices of such lewd and subtle sycophants; for the book is naught and most horrible to be thought on."

Upon this, says Burnet, she thanked him and threw the book into the fire.[31]

The case of Judge Hales, however, has been cited as an illustration of Gardiner's disregard for Edwardine legislation. Sir James Hales was a staunch adherent of the reformed theology; he had been one of a commission to enforce respect for the Prayer Book of 1549; he had been one of the judges who confirmed the deprivation of Bonner; he had been one who pronounced sentence on Gardiner. Yet to his great credit he was the only judge who had not set his hand to Northumberland's device for excluding Mary from the throne.

At the first assizes in Kent in the new reign certain priests were indicted for saying Mass, and Hales charged the jury to bring in a verdict according to the existing law—the second Edwardine act of uniformity. When, on October 6, 1553, Hales came to take his oath as judge before the Michaelmas term, Gardiner told him that the Queen, on hearing of his refusal to support Northumberland, had conceived a good opinion of him, which his recent doings had altered. Hales replied that he had merely done what the law required and if it were to do again he would do no less.

> "Why, Master Hales," replied Gardiner, "although ye had the rigour of the law on your side, yet ye might have had regard to the Queen's Highness' present doings in that case. And further, although ye seem to be more than precise in the law, yet I think ye would be very loth to yield to the extremity of such advantage as might be gathered against your proceedings in the law, as ye have sometimes taken upon you in place of justice. And if it were well tried, I believe ye should not be well able to stand honestly thereto."

This was doubtless a thrust at Hales' part in Gardiner's own trial and deprivation.

Hales answered that he was ready to maintain his doings at all costs, saying:

> "If my goods and all that I have be not able to counterpoise the case, my body shall be ready to serve the turn."
>
> "Ah, Sir!" said the Bishop, "ye be very quick and stout in your answers. But, as it should seem, that which ye did was more of a will favouring the opinion of your religion against the service now used, than for any occasion or zeal of justice, seeing the Queen's Highness doth set it forth, as yet wishing all her faithful subjects to embrace it accordingly; and where ye offer both body and goods in your trial, there is no such matter required at your hands, and yet ye shall not have your own will neither."

Hales replied that he trusted his religion was such as pleased God, and that he was ready to adventure his life for it. Gardiner thereupon told him he was "scarce worthy the place," and refused to take his oath before the Queen was informed of his opinion. Hales said he would gladly relinquish his place if such were the Queen's desire, and so departed.

A pamphlet reporting this conversation was published sometime in 1553,[32] as a score against the religious policy of the Government. It ends with Hales' departure, but Foxe, who reprints it, adds that "not many days after this" Hales was committed to the King's Bench at Gardiner's command. Elsewhere, however, he records the date of Hales' imprisonment as January 27, 1554.[33] This was two days after Wyatt took the field, and almost four months after the conversation with Gardiner, during which time the old religious practices had received parliamentary sanction.

Hales was induced to recant his theological views in prison, and thereafter tried to kill himself. On April 14, 1554, the day after Hales' attempt at self-destruction, the Chancellor in the Star Chamber referred to the new religion as "the doctrine of desperation," which drove men to suicide. This called forth a vehement protest from Hooper, entitled *A brief treatise, wherein is contained the truth that Mr. Justice Hales never hurt himself until such time as he condescended unto their papistical religion,*[34] in which he says that Hales was imprisoned because he would not conform to the "religion set forth at this time by the bishops;" and although he calls Gardiner a murderer of God's elect, and asserts that he was the chief cause of the deaths of Frith, Barnes, Garret, Jerome, Anne Askew, and Lascelles, he nowhere gives the least hint that he believes him to have ordered Hales' imprisonment. It would seem that Canon Dixon weighed the evidence correctly when he concluded that Hales was not imprisoned until a considerable time after his conversation with Gardiner, nor in consequence of his conduct as judge, nor through Gardiner's intervention.[35]

The unhappy Hales was released after his wounds healed, but succeeded in drowning himself.

Another alleged case of unlawful imprisonment by Gardiner is that of John Philpot, a Hampshire man of good family who became Archdeacon of Winchester under Ponet, "by virtue of a former advowson," so he said, given him by Gardiner. In the lower house of Mary's first Convocation, October 1553, he was the most outspoken dissenter from the doctrine of the bodily presence of Christ in the Sacrament, to which all but six members subscribed. At his instance a disputation was held, after the doctrine had been subscribed to, which, as Weston the prolocutor said, was "not to call the truth into doubt, . . . but that those gainsayers might be resolved of their arguments." Philpot proceeded to declare that the Mass "is no Sacrament at all, neither is Christ in any wise present in it," upon which he was warned by the prolocutor that such language put him in danger of jail.

In an account he wrote of his examination by the Queen's commissioners in 1555 he mentions the fact that he had been previously examined by Gardiner, and infers that he had been then imprisoned for his words in Convocation, despite the liberty promised to every man to utter his conscience there—a statement which Foxe eagerly repeats. But Philpot also tells us that he was not imprisoned until five months after the disputation, and not until he had published an account of it. This contained his own vehement denials of Christ's body in the Sacrament, and was prefaced by a statement that it was put forth in the hope that the reader might see the viciousness of the conclusions reached by Convocation. Such a publication was contrary at once to the royal proclamation against heretical books, and to the Henrician standards which had by that time been re-established by Parliament.

It bespeaks no little patience on the part of the Bishop of Winchester that for almost half a year he suffered in his diocese an archdeacon who believed, as he did not hesitate later to profess, that the one Catholic Apostolic Church was "the Church of Geneva."[36]

Still another case held up against Gardiner is that of Thomas Mowntayne. Of this, Mowntayne's own account of his troubles is our sole source of information.[37] He was parson of St. Michael's in the Tower Royal, and, on Sunday, October 8, 1553, while celebrating the Communion according to the second Prayer Book of Edward, he was rudely interrupted by one of Gardiner's serving men who called out, at the distribution of the elements, that he would be made to sing another song in a few days. The Wednesday following he was summoned before the Bishop. It is highly probable

that he had disregarded the Queen's proclamation forbidding un-
licenced preaching.

His picture of Gardiner, exaggerated though it may be, is lively
and graphic:

> "When I came into the great chamber at St. Mary Overies,
> there I found the Bishop standing at a bay window with a
> great company about him, and many suitors, both men and
> women, for he was going to the court; among whom there was
> one Mr. Sellinger [Sir Anthony St. Leger], a knight and Lord
> Deputy of Ireland, being a suitor also to my Lord. Then the
> Bishop called me unto him and said, 'Thou heretic! how darest
> thou be so bold to use that schismatical service still, of late set
> forth? seeing that God hath sent us now a Catholic Queen, whose
> laws thou hast broken, as the rest of thy fellows hath done, and
> you shall know the price of it if I do live. There is such abom-
> inable company of you as is able to poison a whole realm with
> your heresies.'
>
> 'My Lord,' said I, 'I am none heretic, for that way that you
> count heresy, so worship we the living God. . . .'
>
> 'God's Passion!' said the Bishop, 'did not I tell you, my Lord
> Deputy, how you should know an heretic? He is up with the
> "living God," as though there were a dead God. They have
> nothing in their mouths, these heretics, but "the Lord liveth,
> the living God ruleth, the Lord, the Lord," and nothing but
> "the Lord."'
>
> Here he chafed like a bishop, and, as his manner was, many
> times he put off his cap and rubbed to and fro, and up and down,
> the fore part of his head, where a lock of hair was always
> standing up, and that, as some say, was his grace."

St. Leger urged Mowntayne to submit himself, but Mowntayne
said he had never offended. Then someone discovered that he had
been involved in Northumberland's treason and exempted from the
general pardon.

> "These two," observed the Bishop, "be always linked to-
> gether, treason and heresy, and thou hast like a shameless man
> offended in both."

He then charged one of his gentlemen to take "this traitorous heretic" to the Marshalsea, for said he, "this is one of our new brochyd
brethren that speaketh against all good works."

Mowntayne protested that he never spake against good works, but
had said that no one ought to think himself justified thereby, but
count himself an unprofitable servant even when he had done his
best.

"That is true," quoth the Bishop, "indeed your fraternity was, is,

and ever will be altogether unprofitable." What good works, he
asked, were done in the days of King Henry or King Edward?
Mowntayne replied at length, enumerating the dissolution of the
monasteries, the appointment of godly masters at Cambridge and
Oxford, the erection of schools and hospitals. The Bishop, who
seems to have listened in patience quite to the end of this catalogue
of Henrician and Edwardine achievements, caustically concluded:

> "Sir, you have made a great speak; for whereas you have
> set up one beggarly house, you have pulled down an hundred
> princely houses for it, putting out godly, learned, and devout
> men that served God day and night, and thrust in their place a
> sort of scurvy and lowsy boys."

The talk then turned to the Sacrament and the Bishop asked
Mowntayne what he thought of "the holy and blessed Mass." "I
neither believe it to be holy nor yet blessed," said the latter, "but
rather to be abominable before God and man;" and with that he
knelt before the whole company and prayed aloud that God would
"shortly cast down forever, that shameful idol the Mass." It is
small wonder that Gardiner cried: "Away with him! it is the stub-
bornest knave that ever I talked with."

He was later removed to Cambridge Castle, being charged with
treason there committed; was released by the justices on bail, and
escaped to the Continent.[38]

The flight of such trouble-makers as Mowntayne was not unwelcome to the Government. Early in September the congregations of
foreign Protestants at Glastonbury and London were permitted by
the Council to depart,[39] and Peter Martyr, the most influential continental divine in England, was, despite his fears to the contrary,
given a passport under the Queen's sign manual,[40] "none being more
forward to furnish him with all things necessary for his going hence
than the new Lord Chancellor."[41] At the same time Gardiner told
Renard that he had hit upon a device for getting rid of foreign
preachers who did not willingly leave the realm: If a summons to
his house was not sufficient to alarm them into flight, they would be
told that the Emperor and the King of France were about to ask
for the extradition of their refugee subjects, which, he hoped, would
be equally effective in hastening their departure.[42]

Nor was it only foreign Protestants whose exodus the Chancellor
encouraged. When Rogers came before the Council charged with
seditious preaching, August 16, he was merely told to keep himself
prisoner in his own house, where he remained in comparative liberty
for over five months, and whence, as Foxe says, he might easily
have escaped.[43] When Hooper was sent for, August 22, he had
ample opportunity to flee, and was urged to do so by his friends.[44]

When Latimer was summoned, September 4, he received private warning six hours before the summons reached him, and when it did come the pursuivant who brought it said he was commanded not to tarry for him, by which, says Foxe, "it was manifest that they would not have him appear, but rather to have fled out of the realm." [45] Cranmer, although implicated in Northumberland's conspiracy, was left at liberty for two months, until the Council was forced to deal with him because of an outspoken attack on the Mass, in which he said that the attempt to revive that service was a work of the devil. This was naturally regarded by the Government as a seditious bill tending to occasion tumult, and he was committed to the Tower September 14. [46] Although Lawrence Saunders publicly defied the Government by preaching in Leicestershire without licence for two months, no attempt was made to apprehend him until he came up to London and there, on October 15, boldly declared "the abomination of the Mass." [47] Even in the following spring, when Dr. Rowland Taylor was summoned by Gardiner from Hadleigh in Suffolk for trying to prevent the celebration of the Mass, which at that time had become the only legal service, no constraint whatever was put upon him to obey the summons, and his friends pressed on him repeatedly the wisdom of flight. [48]

To their own everlasting credit, but none the less to the embarrassment of the Government, neither Cranmer, nor Latimer, Hooper, Rogers, Saunders, nor Taylor availed themselves of the opportunity to flee; but it was undoubtedly to the satisfaction of the Chancellor that Bishops Ponet, Bale, and Scory, Doctors Richard Cox and John Knox, and several hundred others betook themselves to the Continent. [49]

Cranmer's manifesto of September 7 on the Mass, copies of which were speedily multiplied and circulated, proved a serious setback to that quiet progress toward the restoration of the old religion on which Gardiner had remarked with approval but a few days before. Pamphlets reflecting on the Queen and the Chancellor were now scattered daily through the city, and shortly after the middle of September there was a riotous demonstration against the Mass at Greenwich. Rumours reached London of a plot to kill the Chancellor and sack his Southwark residence. The Chancellor put on a coat of mail and set a guard of a hundred men in his house. The Queen expressed fears that there might be trouble when she rode through the streets at her coming coronation. [50]

There was, however, no disturbance in London, and everything at the coronation went smoothly. On the afternoon of September 30 the Queen came from the Tower to Westminster. It was a gala procession, with gentry and noblemen in their gayest silks, judges and bishops in their best robes. Gardiner rode beside Paulet, Marquis of Winchester and Lord High Treasurer, "having the seal and the mace before them."

Through streets hung with tapestry and strewn with flowers, under arches of triumph, past conduits flowing with wine they came, now and again halting to gaze at some splendid pageant or listen to verses of salutation; and when they reached St. Paul's, there on the very top of the weather cock, waving a flag in his hand, stood an acrobat, who, "after standing on one foot, did shake his other leg, and then kneeled on his knee upon the said weather cock, to the great marvel and wondering of all the people." Thus was the populace regaled, and the procession passed to the satisfaction of everyone.

The next day, Sunday, October 1, the Queen went on foot to the Abbey, whence came to meet her the Bishop of Winchester with four-score singing men and ten bishops, mitred, "their crosier staves in their hands and rich copes upon them, every one." "Queen Mary! Queen Mary!" shouted the people as Gardiner presented her to them from a raised platform in the Abbey, built for the occasion. It was Gardiner likewise who administered the coronation oath, who anointed her, and who crowned her with three crowns. Seated upon a throne, she received the homage of her nobles, "beginning at the Bishop of Winchester and the Duke of Norfolk, and ending at Lord Paget, then youngest baron." Gardiner celebrated Mass, "the Queen kneeling throughout with great devotion." [51]

Some weeks before the coronation, Mary had sent to Cardinal Pole asking absolution for herself and Gardiner, that the ceremony might be valid; she had made a secret protestation against the title of Supreme Head which she was compelled to accept at her crowning; she had the words "just and licit" inserted before the word "laws" in her oath to obey them, thus excluding those laws on religion which she regarded as void; and she had obtained the oil with which Gardiner anointed her from the Bishop of Arras, fearing that oil blest in schismatical England would be inefficacious. [52]

In all this she ran ahead of the general feeling of the country. That feeling was fairly well expressed in the Parliament which assembled October 5. Gardiner, as Chancellor, opened the session with a speech in which, according to Henry Penning, Pole's messenger in England,

> "he treated amply of the union of religion, and that it should be resumed, without which nothing good could be done; demonstrating how many disadvantages had befallen the realm owing to its separation. He accused himself and all the bystanders as guilty of it, telling them that Parliament was assembled by her Majesty and Council to repeal many iniquitous laws made against the said union, and to enact others in favour of it." [53]

This is the only report we have of Gardiner's speech, and it is significant that although it was sent to the Pope there is no specific mention in it of the Papacy. It would seem that Gardiner so discreetly turned his words that they might be taken either to imply a desired reunion with Rome, or merely a reunion in doctrine and practice with Catholic Christendom. At any rate Parliament soon let the Queen know that there were two topics with which it would have nothing whatever to do; namely, the restitution of Church property and the restoration of Papal authority.

Even the bill legitimizing Henry VIII's marriage with Catherine made no mention of the Pope, although, according to Canon Law, the marriage had originally been regarded as lawful solely because of a Papal dispensation. Thirlby, in conversation with Renard, said that Gardiner would have liked some reference to the Pope's authority in the bill;[54] and Gardiner himself confessed in Parliament, while the bill was under discussion, that he had sued at Rome for a dissolution of the marriage in obedience to Henry and in the hope of pleasing him, and that therein he had done wrong.[55]

On the question of Catholic doctrine and practice, however, Parliament showed itself more willing to conform to the wishes of Queen and Chancellor, and, early in November, repealed, though not without much debate, the entire ecclesiastical legislation of Edward VI, re-establishing the Latin services of the latter years of Henry VIII. After December 20, 1553, no other services were to be permitted.[56]

On another matter of importance, not unrelated to the question of religion, Parliament found itself in opposition to the Queen, but in agreement with the Chancellor; which brings us to a third topic on which the Emperor had been advising his cousin.

XXIX

THE SPANISH MATCH

The inhabitants of the Low Countries were weary of war. They were beginning to suggest that a change of rulers would not be unwelcome, that even French sovereignty would be better than Spanish. Hence, from the moment of Mary's accession, Charles V aimed at her marriage with his son Philip. With England and the Netherlands under one rule France would be held perpetually in check, and the commercial prosperity of the Emperor's Dutch and Flemish subjects assured.[1] On the day after he heard of Northumberland's arrest, Charles had written to Philip asking if he would be willing to marry Mary; and long before Philip's affirmative reply was received, Charles' ambassador, Renard, was sounding the Queen as to her matrimonial intentions, urging reasons in favour of a foreign husband, and subtly suggesting that of all possible foreign husbands Philip was the paragon. Among all Renard's reasons, that which weighed most with Charles—the insurance of the Netherlands—was never mentioned to Mary. To her the marriage was depicted as the most effective means to her firm establishment on the throne and to the restoration of religion.

Even before her entry into London, she had assured Renard, in a secret interview, July 29, that she was ready to take the Emperor's advice as to the person of her husband.[2] This was a good beginning for Renard, but he found that popular opinion in England was unfavourable to a foreign, and especially to a Spanish, match, and, further, that the Lord Chancellor had a candidate of his own for the Queen's hand. This was Edward Courtenay, son of that Marquis of Exeter whom Henry VIII had beheaded in 1538, and great-grandson of Edward IV. Although the last fifteen of the twenty-seven years of his life had been spent in the Tower, he was, in the opinion of the French ambassador, "the handsomest and most agreeable gentleman in England."[3] He had formed such a friendship for Gardiner during their years of imprisonment together that he spoke of him as his father.[4]

The only other Englishman of royal ancestry whom rumour named as a possible candidate for the Queen's hand was Cardinal Pole, who, though a Churchman, was as yet in deacon's orders only, and might therefore be permitted by dispensation to marry. That he should not stand in Courtenay's way, Gardiner and Tunstall—so it was said—agreed to support him for the see of Canterbury. But Pole had no desire for matrimony.

There was undoubted truth in Renard's insinuation to the Queen that Gardiner's advocacy of Courtenay was not entirely unselfish, considering his influence over that young man. At the same time Gardiner saw clearly the folly and the danger of a match with Spain.

Renard, on the other hand, found an ally in Paget, who, he very soon discovered, was more than willing to recoup his fortunes, seriously damaged under Northumberland, by Imperial pensions, and to get himself into favour with the Queen at the expense of the Chancellor.[6]

Although Mary took the utmost precaution to keep her interviews with Renard secret from the Council, Gardiner suspected them, and, on August 31, and again the next day, had long talks with her, endeavouring to sound her, without much success, as to whether the Emperor had already proposed a husband for her. He expatiated on the virtues of Courtenay, without, however, proposing that she marry him, though she was well aware at what he was driving. He then called to his assistance Rochester, Englefield, and Walgrave, councillors whose faithfulness to the Queen had been tried in days of adversity, and whose words, therefore, might be expected to have weight with her. They all pressed on her the claims of an English husband, broadly hinting at Courtenay, but she put them off by saying that she did not wish to attend to private affairs before Parliament met.[7]

The proposal was then made by the Chancellor, backed by several of the Council, that the coronation be postponed till Parliament establish the Queen more firmly on her throne. This plan, observed Renard, was sponsored by Gardiner in order that Parliament might "bridle the Queen and prevent her marrying a foreigner." Both Renard and Paget opposed it, and Mary insisted that the original plan of holding the coronation before Parliament met be carried out. Gardiner did not, however, give up the hope of bringing the influence of Parliament to bear on the matter.

On October 10, five days after Parliament opened, Renard made a definite though confidential offer of Philip's hand to the Queen. She said she would have to consult with her Council, and conjured Renard to tell her truthfully of Philip's character, of which, it seems, she had heard some not too complimentary reports. Renard assured her that Philip was "so admirable, so virtuous, prudent, and modest as to appear too wonderful to be human." Two days later Paget talked to her at length in favour of the match, advising her to regard it as "a solemn alliance" for the good of her kingdom. Almost immediately thereafter she told Renard that he should set to work to win over her councillors, although she refrained from an outright acceptance of his offer.

Although Gardiner was probably still in the dark as to just how far Renard had gone, he scented danger and, accompanied by

Rochester, Englefield, and Walgrave, this time reinforced by Sir
Robert Southwell, he again spoke to the Queen on the subject of
matrimony, October 20. He told her that the country would never
abide a foreigner and that Courtenay was the only possible match for
her. Englefield went so far as to say that Philip's own subjects
spoke ill of him, and Walgrave added that if she married Philip,
England would soon find itself at war with France. Mary replied
that Gardiner was "somewhat open to suspicion," evidently referring
to his influence over Courtenay, but, as she afterward confessed to
Renard, she had no answer to their arguments except to talk of the
welfare of the country. She assured Renard that she had no liking
for Courtenay and that she did not believe that Philip's subjects
spoke ill of him.

A week later, October 27, after many tears and prayers, she so
far came to a decision as to tell Renard that "she believed she would
agree" to the Emperor's proposal; and on Sunday evening, October
29, she gave him her solemn promise, before the Sacrament, to wed
Philip. She had consulted Arundel and Petre, as well as Paget, and
found them favourable, but she had not broached the subject to
Gardiner. This Renard undertook to do, and asked the Chancellor
for an interview; but the Chancellor put him off for several days,
during which it became clear that he was encouraging Parliamentary
opposition to the match. Paget, who had won Mary's confidence by
his advocacy of Philip, and who, for the time, practically replaced
Gardiner as her chief minister, instructed Renard to press Gardiner
for audience till he gave a downright refusal, in which case the
Queen could then demand from him an explanation of his conduct.[8]

Renard therefore continued to importune the Chancellor who
finally gave him an interview Sunday, November 5, at daybreak,
saying that "he had had so much to do with Parliament, religious and
other affairs that he had not had time to breathe." Renard began by
assuring him that the Emperor's "only care was for the Queen's hap-
piness and the good of the realm," and that he desired to further
her inclinations in the matter of matrimony, whether her choice
were to fall on an Englishman or a foreigner. If, however, it were
to be a foreigner, his Majesty could suggest a suitable match; but
that depended on her inclinations. Could the Chancellor, perhaps,
frankly tell him if he had heard anything about them!

Gardiner replied that he had not yet gone so far in conversation
with the Queen, but agreed that Charles was right in holding that she
ought to make known her inclinations first of all, as she was the
party chiefly concerned. As for himself, "he was determined never
to attempt to persuade the Queen to choose any given person, but
only to advise her to ponder inwardly on whom her choice ought to
fall," but if his advice were asked, "he would always assure her that

it would be better for the public good, for the security of her person, and her subjects' tranquillity, that she should choose a husband in England."

If Renard desired frankness he certainly had it. Although Philip's name had not been mentioned, Gardiner drove straight to the point. It would be difficult, he said, to induce the people to consent to a foreigner, for the very name was odious to them; and they would never put up with the Spanish character. In this they would only be imitating the Emperor's own Flemish subjects who could not bear the Spaniards. The fact that neither Philip nor his attendants would be able to speak English would be a cause of continual friction, and although the Prince might intend to adapt himself to English ways, the people would fear he meant to do otherwise, and for the people, fearing something and being convinced of it were the same. Already the fear of a foreign match had been sufficient to cause several noblemen to join Northumberland's conspiracy. Moreover, "England would be marrying everlasting strife and danger from the French."

Further, it would be necessary to obtain a Papal dispensation for the marriage because Mary and Philip were second cousins; but this would have to be done secretly lest the people rise against the Pope's authority; then if children were born of the union their legitimacy would be attacked because the dispensation had not been made public. Finally, the cause of religion would be hindered rather than helped by the marriage, for it would give the ill-disposed an opportunity to declare that Philip intended to restore religion by force—the very ground on which the French King was already encouraging the heretics in England to opposition. "It was much more important to remedy religious affairs than to arrange a foreign match."

As for himself, said Gardiner, he was no politician, and felt less bound up with worldly affairs than was generally imagined; but while in prison he had thought a great deal about the troubles of Christendom, and had come to the paradoxical conclusion that the Emperor would do better to keep England's friendship than to seek a closer alliance, and that England had better remain a friend of the Emperor than become possessor of the Low Countries. The marriage would not provide a remedy both for the Emperor's affairs and religion.[9]

Seldom has clearer political foresight been displayed. Yet, a few days before, Renard had written that he had been assured—undoubtedly by Paget—that it seemed as if Gardiner's imprisonment had affected his mind![10]

The Chancellor concluded his observations to Renard by remarking that it was a dangerous matter to take a share in the marriage of princes, as Cromwell had experienced, and that he did not intend to take such a share in the Queen's as might later bring blame upon him.

Renard rebutted the Chancellor's objections at length, but could only bring him to admit that much might be said on both sides.

As soon as Gardiner reached court he spoke briefly of the interview to Mary, saying that he had told Renard that her inclinations ought to be the first consideration and the one by which he himself would be guided. Mary replied that after a week of sore affliction and prayer, she had come to the decision never to marry at all rather than marry an Englishman.

"And what," exclaimed Gardiner, "will the people say? How will they put up with a foreigner who will promise things he will not keep, once the marriage has been concluded?"

Mary replied that her mind was made up, and if he preferred the will of the people to her wishes, he was not acting towards her as he had always promised to act. For her part, she believed hers was the best course for the country.

She immediately told Paget and Renard what Gardiner had said, and informed them at the same time that the members of Parliament were importuning her for audience to speak about her marriage. It was therefore decided that before she granted the request of Parliament, she should give audience to Renard, in the presence of her chief councillors, and then express her willingness to consider a formal offer of Philip's hand, thus practically settling the matter and committing her councillors to that settlement before Parliament had a chance to interfere.[11]

Before either audience was given, Gardiner summoned Renard to another early morning conference at his house, Tuesday, November 7, between 6 and 7 A.M. What conditions, he asked, was the Emperor prepared to offer with Philip's hand? Renard assured him that the conditions would be such that everyone of his objections would be disposed of, and every other condition which seemed to him necessary would be put into the marriage treaty. Gardiner could not but reply that this was a great offer, but he cautioned Renard to take no further steps until it were seen whether the bill repealing the ecclesiastical legislation of Edward VI, which was at the moment under debate in Commons, would pass; otherwise it might encounter fresh difficulties.

Renard communicated the content of this interview at once to Paget, who said that the Queen was very angry with Gardiner for inventing this new excuse for delay, and that she wished Renard to ask Arundel to arrange for the desired audience with her. This he did, and it was set for the next day, November 8. Just before it was held, Gardiner met Renard and told him that the bill restoring religion had passed, and that he might proceed with his business.

In the presence of Gardiner, Arundel, Thirlby, Paget, and Petre, Renard addressed the Queen, after which she conferred at length with these councillors, "dissembling," says Renard, "as if she had never heard the question mentioned before." Her reply was, of course, favourable, and both she and Renard supposed the Chancellor had been won over to their view.[12]

The Chancellor, however, still seems to have hoped that an appeal from Parliament might have some weight with her. This was made November 16, when the Speaker of Commons, accompanied by a delegation from both houses, warned her, in a lengthy discourse, of the dangers of a foreign match. It would be better, he said, for her to marry one of her own subjects.

Mary, who was offended by the whole procedure, was so irritated by the word "subject" in this connection that she could not contain herself. Neglecting the customary formality by which Gardiner, as Chancellor, should have replied for her, she told the speaker that his language was neither suitable nor respectful, and that, in short, her marriage was her own business. After the interview Arundel laughed at Gardiner, saying "that he had lost his post of Chancellor that day, for the Queen had usurped it."

The Queen complained to Renard that Gardiner one day "assured her that the people would obey her and do her will with regard to religion and everything else, and the next, speaking on a matter that touched him personally, he continually harped on disobedience in the people," but for all his intrigues, she said, she would not break her promise. Nor did she hesitate to tell Gardiner himself that she suspected him of having inspired the Speaker of Commons, adding that she desired him clearly to understand that she would never marry Courtenay. Gardiner, according to Renard, replied with tears that he had not instructed the Speaker, although he had mentioned certain considerations to him, and that it was true that he had been fond of Courtenay ever since they were in prison together. Mary asked whether it was right to force her to marry a man because her Chancellor had conceived a friendship for him in prison, to which the Chancellor replied that it was not right to force her to marry anyone, and that he whom she chose would command his obedience.[13]

Renard, who now knew in detail all the objections which had been urged against the match, advised the Emperor to draw up the articles of the marriage treaty in a form so favourable to England that no opportunity would be left even for Gardiner to criticize them. Charles was wise enough to follow this advice, and when the preliminary draft was presented by Renard to the Council early in December, the few slight revisions suggested by Gardiner and his fellows were at once accepted.[14]

Gardiner, now seeing that it was futile to try further to persuade

Mary against the marriage, and that the conditions offered by the Emperor were all that could be desired under the circumstances, openly declared himself in favour of the match and used his influence to win others, who were still halting, to this view.[15] To have done otherwise would have been to play into the hands of French and Protestant interests, for France was thoroughly alarmed at the prospect of this close alliance of England with the Empire and, as Gardiner had already warned Renard, did not hesitate to encourage Protestant opposition to it in England. Noailles, the French ambassador in England, had been active in stirring parliamentary opposition to Philip, which had been by no means to Courtenay's or Gardiner's advantage, for Renard lost no opportunity to warn Mary of the French intrigues. Gardiner had, however, kept so clear of all co-operation with the French that Noailles believed him to have become a partisan of the Spanish marriage as early as September 25.[16]

At the end of December the special ambassadors who were to act with Renard for the conclusion of the marriage treaty reached England. On New Year's Day 1554 the boys of London pelted their retinue with snowballs, and when, the next day, the ambassadors themselves rode through the city, "the people, nothing rejoicing, held down their heads sorrowfully." They were, however, splendidly received at court where the Queen told them that she had committed the business of the marriage treaty to her Chancellor, as keeper of the laws of her realm. With him were associated Arundel, Rochester, Paget, and Petre. There was not much left to negotiate. Gardiner insisted on certain further safeguards against the possibility of England's having to assist the Emperor in war against France, which, he said plainly, England had no intention of doing. On January 9, after a great banquet at Winchester House, final terms were agreed on.[17] According to these, Philip was to enjoy the title of King of England, and to assist in the Government, but Mary alone was to have the disposal of all offices in Church and State, which were to be filled by Englishmen only. The laws and customs of the nation were to remain inviolate. Mary was to share all of Philip's titles and to receive a dower of £60,000 a year. The issue of the marriage was to inherit Burgundy and the Low Countries as well as England. If Don Carlos, Philip's son by his first wife, died childless, Spain and all the Spanish possessions were to go to the English heir as well. The Queen was not to be taken abroad without her own consent, nor her children without the consent of the nobility. If she died childless, Philip's connection with England was to cease. The existing treaties between England and France were to be maintained, and England was not to be involved in war between France and the Empire.[18]

On Sunday, January 14, Gardiner explained to an assembly of

nobles and gentlemen, in the presence chamber at Westminster, the advantages which the treaty brought to England. He noted particularly how it put Philip in the place of a subject rather than a ruler, and how no Spaniard should be of the Council, nor have custody of any fort or castle, nor bear rule or office either in the Queen's house or elsewhere in all England. The next day he made a similar speech to the Lord Mayor, aldermen, and chief citizens; but despite these assurances the news of the marriage was "heavily taken of sundry men, yea and thereat almost each man was abashed, looking daily for worse matters to grow shortly after."

The Chancellor at the same time took occasion to exhort Mayor and aldermen to see that the religion of the Queen, "which they had yet very slackly set forth," be so observed within the city "that they might be a spectacle to all the realm." [19] Not a fortnight before, he had summoned the churchwardens of thirty London parishes to inquire why they had not had Mass in their churches "as some of them had not. . . . And they answered that they had done what lay in them." [20] There was evidently a good deal of passive resistance in London to a return even to the religious conditions of Henry VIII.

Indeed, a clever and telling shot had been aimed at Gardiner just before the close of the old year, in the publication of an English translation of the *De Vera Obedientia,* the book he had written in defence of the royal supremacy eighteen years before. This had been well known to Churchmen in England and on the Continent, but, being in Latin, had never been read by the less learned. Now for the first time the citizens of London perceived what convincing words had been uttered against the Papacy by the man who appeared to be leading the English Church Rome-ward. The edition translated was that printed in north Germany in 1536, for which Bonner, then at Hamburg on a mission from Henry VIII, had written a commendatory preface. Thus the translator, who in all probability was the "foul mouthed Bale," was enabled at one stroke to convict, out of their own mouths, the two prelates of the metropolis of that crime which is so often regarded as the worst which public men can commit—the crime of changing their minds.

"A double-minded man is inconsistent in all his ways," is the text on the title page. The reader is admonished to "mark the notes in the margin," which consist of such comments as "Hearken to your own reason my Lord Doctor Doubleface," and "By your double sayings you are a double traitor and a very weathercock." In the translator's preface Gardiner is described as "now Lord Chancellor and common cutthroat of England;" the Catholic leaders, including the mild and ageing Tunstall, are the "lecherous litter of Romish whelps;" the Bishops of Winchester and London are "murderers of men's souls, . . . impudent maintainers of filthy and stinking whoredom, . . . covetous catchers, double-faced perjurers, . . . spoilers of poor men's patrimony, . . . builders of Satan's synagogue, merciless persecutors of Christ's flock, ravening wolves in sheep's clothing, mockers of God's glorious Gospel, servers of time, and very imps of Anti-Christ." [21]

According to a contemporary chronicle the translation appeared "about Christmas Eve," 1553.[22] That the publication of a book should be thus noted in a chronicle or record of events shows, as Canon Dixon remarks, the impression it made.[23] Three editions were issued in rapid succession.

Popular as were such attacks upon Gardiner in the capital, there is much reason to believe that, had the religious question been un-complicated by the Spanish marriage, the return to the Catholicism of Henry VIII, and perhaps even to that of the Pope, would have been accepted by the nation at large without serious protest; but as Gardiner had clearly foreseen, and had not hesitated to say, even after he had promised to support the marriage, "the marriage question was as dangerous as that of the heretics." [24]

From the moment the nation knew that Mary really intended to wed Philip, rumours of disaffection came thick and fast. On the very day the Imperial ambassadors were received in London, Sir Peter Carew was summoned to appear before the Council; but Carew was on his way to stir revolt in Devonshire. Sir James Crofts was to raise Wales. Suffolk, father of Lady Jane Grey, thankless for the Queen's clemency, was to rouse the midlands. And Sir Thomas Wyatt, son of the poet and diplomat of Henry VIII's days, was to head the rebellion in Kent. Noailles, the French ambassador, who appears to have known a good deal about the plans of the rebels, be-lieved the movement aimed at putting Elizabeth on the throne with Courtenay as King Consort. The leaders professed that they rose merely to prevent the realm from falling into the hands of Spain.

Courtenay had indeed gone so far as to hold communication with both Carew and Wyatt.[25] Gardiner sent for him and, apparently on January 21, warned him "that the company he kept was *suspecte;* that there was serious misgiving that he would forget his duty to the Queen; that if he did, it would be the worse for him." He added that the Queen wished to send him on a visit to the Emperor. Courtenay not only professed unswerving loyalty but revealed to Gardiner the whole of Carew's plot.[26] By this revelation the in-surrection, which was planned for Palm Sunday, March 18, was precipitated almost two months earlier.

The plans of Carew, Crofts, and Suffolk fell flat, but Wyatt, who took the field in Kent on January 25, 1554, met with such success that, at Dartford on the 31st, he insolently demanded from the two councillors who came to parley with him the custody of the Tower and the Queen's person, and the replacement of certain of her councillors by others of his nomination.

The Council wisely refused the aid of Imperial troops and advised the Queen to appeal in person to the citizens of London.[27] This she did in a brave speech at the Guildhall on February 1, at the end of which Gardiner cried to the people "O how happy are we to whom God hath given such a wise and learned prince!"[28] The Londoners rallied to her, and when Wyatt reached Southwark, February 3, he found the gates of London Bridge shut and the citizens armed in its defence. Although he had forbidden plunder, "divers of his company, being gentlemen (as they said) went to Winchester Place," Gardiner's house in Southwark, and made havoc of his goods,

> "not only of his victuals, whereof there was plenty, but whatsoever else, not leaving so much as one lock of a door, but the same was taken off and carried away, nor a book in his gallery or library uncut or rent into pieces, so that men might have gone up to the knees in leaves of books cut out and thrown under feet."[29]

Finding access to the city by London Bridge impossible, Wyatt left Southwark, February 6, crossed the river at Kingston, and entered London the next morning. His approach caused consternation at court; and Gardiner, who had already advised the Queen to seek safety at Windsor, now, between two and three in the morning, urged her to fly by boat. Renard, on this occasion, gave the sounder advice, saying that if she wanted to retain her kingdom she would not leave London. She decided to stay if Pembroke and Clinton, who were in command of her forces, would do their duty—which they promised to do.[30]

Wyatt got as far as Ludgate, but, as no help was given him by the citizens, returned, found himself trapped by the Queen's men at Temple Bar, and surrendered. That afternoon he was committed to the Tower.

That he came so near success, despite the handicaps to his movement resulting from Courtenay's confession, shows in what danger the Government stood. It is, moreover, significant that although he bid for the support of the reformers by talking of the intended restoration of God's word, he put the political issue in the forefront in his proclamation, showing that he expected to win more followers in opposition to the Spanish marriage than in opposition to the Mass and the Pope; showing also how sound Gardiner's conclusions had been concerning the relative unpopularity of the Queen's two projects.

XXX

"HURTFUL MEMBERS"

On February 11, the Sunday after Wyatt's surrender and the
first in Lent, Gardiner preached at court. His text was the Epistle
for the day, II Cor. vi. 1-10; but just how he connected this Scripture with his discourse is difficult to say, for the report we have
of the sermon is, on the one hand, very brief, but, on the other, indicates a surprising range of topics. He spoke, we are told, first of
free will, secondly of Lent, thirdly of good works, fourthly of the
detestable errors preached during the past seven years, and "fifthly
and lastly" of the Queen's mercy. Here he took occasion to suggest "that like as she had before-time extended her mercy particularly and privately," and since "through her lenity and gentleness
much conspiracy and open rebellion was grown," she should now
"be merciful to the body of the commonwealth and conservation
thereof, which could not be unless the rotten and hurtful members
thereof were cut off and consumed." [1]

This was the signal for severer treatment of political offenders,
and the first victims, executed the next morning, were Guildford Dudley and his youthful and sainted wife, the Lady Jane Grey. As
Mr. Gairdner has pointed out, these executions were not the result
of Gardiner's sermon; the sermon was the announcement of a previously determined policy, for the order for Lady Jane's death had been
given while the forces of Wyatt were threatening the city. [2] That
her father, the Duke of Suffolk, had been active as a leader in the
rebellion, even if he had not revived his daughter's claim to the
throne, was doubtless regarded by Mary as sufficient reason why
she should at last heed the advice which the Emperor and Renard
had long pressed upon her.

It was the Lady Elizabeth, however, not the Lady Jane, who was
the menace to Mary's safety. Although Elizabeth was canny enough
to keep clear of treasonable communication with either Wyatt or
the French, there is no shadow of doubt that the rebels regarded her
as an assured partisan in the event of their success. From the beginning of the reign, Renard lost no opportunity to advise Mary to
watch her sister carefully or shut her in the Tower, and, if we may
believe Paget, Gardiner agreed with Renard. [3] Elizabeth was, however, permitted to leave London in December 1553 for her house at
Ashbridge, whence Mary, writing to her January 26, 1554, summoned
her to return. This was the day after Wyatt's proclamation had been

issued and some five days after Courtenay's revelations to Gardiner, in the course of which Courtenay had admitted that he had been spoken to about a marriage with Elizabeth.

The evening of the next day, January 27, there was delivered to Gardiner a packet of intercepted dispatches from the French ambassador. Suspecting that France was encouraging the rebellion, he opened them. They were, he wrote to Petre,

> "such letters as in times past I durst not have opened, but now somewhat hette [*i. e.* heated] with treasons I waxed bolder, wherein I trust I shall be borne with. Wherein hap helpeth me, for they be worth the breaking up and [*i. e.* if] I could wholly decipher them. Wherein I will spare somewhat of my leisure if I can have any. But this appeareth, that the letter written from my Lady Elizabeth to the Queen's Highness now late in her excuse, is taken a matter worthy to be sent into France, for I have a copy of it in the French ambassador's packet." [4]

The letter from Elizabeth was innocent enough of intrigue. In it she excused herself for not acknowledging certain favours from the Queen, and tendered her good wishes on the coming wedding, but the fact that it was thought worth sending to France was suspicious. Moreover, the French ambassador announced in his dispatch that Elizabeth had "withdrawn thirty miles farther off than she was, . . . where, as is said, great assembly is already made of gentlemen devoted to her." Now Elizabeth had not withdrawn from Ashbridge, but the Government had, through other sources, come by the information that it was her intention to do so. This dispatch seemed to connect her intended removal with the plans of the rebels. It also named Courtenay among the conspirators. Gardiner, when he deciphered it, left a blank for the symbol that stood for Courtenay's name, but Renard, who obtained the original from the Queen, made another decipher in which Courtenay's name appeared. Gardiner, says Renard, changed colour when he saw it. Mary believed a second intercepted French packet was purposely mislaid by Gardiner in order to shield Courtenay. [5]

When the French ambassador complained to the Queen that his letters had been intercepted, she referred him to the Council, on whose behalf Gardiner explained that the letters had been intercepted by the rebels, from whom they had been taken by the Government, but had been destroyed or lost in the sack of his library. This plausible story seemed to satisfy the ambassador, but a few days later he told the Council that his King had been informed that the letters had been given to Renard to decipher. This they denied, "for that they took the King to be her Majesty's friend, and besides, if they would, they could not decipher his letters"! [6]

Courtenay was sent to the Tower February 12. Elizabeth arrived at Westminster February 22. She was lodged in the palace, carefully guarded. It was determined early in March that Gardiner, Arundel, Paget, and Petre should examine her, but no steps to this end appear to have been taken till after Wyatt's trial on March 15. Meanwhile Renard complained of the delay in bringing Elizabeth and Courtenay to justice, which, he said, was due entirely to Gardiner, who had the management of the whole matter in his hands, and who was thus endeavoring to save them. Indeed, it seemed to Renard that Gardiner was generally remiss in not pushing the prosecutions of political offenders with more vigour.[7]

Wyatt at his trial confessed that he had sent a letter to Elizabeth, urging her to get as far from the city as she could, and said that she had sent him thanks for his good will, but not in writing.[8] The next day, March 16, Gardiner and several other Councillors visited her and charged her with complicity in the rising of both Wyatt and Carew. She protested her entire innocence and on the morrow wrote to the Queen saying: "As for that traitor Wyatt, he might, peradventure, write me a letter, but on my faith I never received any from him." She was taken to the Tower Palm Sunday, March 18, and within five days Gardiner, Arundel, and others of the Council confronted her with Sir James Crofts, who had brought her a message to remove from Ashbridge to her house at Donnington. She admitted having heard her officers and Crofts talk about going thither, but said she did not see that this was much to the purpose, as she might go to her own houses at any time. Nor does it appear that her examiners were able to get any more damaging admission either from her or from Crofts.

The truth of the case would seem to be, as Mr. Gairdner suggests, that Wyatt sent her a letter which she refused to receive, returning him a non-committal verbal message of thanks for his good will.[9] She remained none the less the hope of the malcontents and a peril to the throne. Mary summed up the case against her thus:

> "When it appeared that copies of her secret letters to us were found in the packet of the French ambassador, and that divers of the most notable traitors made their chief account upon her, we can hardly be brought to think they would have presumed to do so, except they had more certain knowledge of her favour towards their unnatural conspiracy than is yet confessed by her." [10]

Gardiner, when urged by Renard early in April to make preparations for her trial, answered "that as long as Elizabeth lived he had no hope of seeing the Kingdom at peace," adding that if everyone worked as hard as he did himself things would go better[11]—words which were undoubtedly intended to put Renard off by seeming to agree with him; for it is clear that Gardiner strained every faculty to save Courtenay, and in so doing he inevitably shielded Elizabeth, much as he may have desired her out of the way. His plan for her was exclusion from the succession by statute.[12]

As no incriminating evidence was forthcoming, Elizabeth was liberated from the Tower May 19, 1554, and removed to Woodstock, where she remained under surveillance until April 1555.[13] Courtenay had been more clearly implicated in the rebellion than she, but Gardiner succeeded in saving him. He was released from the Tower May 28, removed to Fotheringay, and next year sent abroad.[14]

Wyatt, on the scaffold, exonerated Elizabeth and Courtenay from the charge of being privy to his rebellion, which naturally started a rumour in London that his previous confession implicating them had been forced from him by the Government. Gardiner, hearing of a certain London apprentice who had spoken of this, sent immediately, not for the apprentice, but for the Lord Mayor, Sir Thomas White, to appear in the Star Chamber and bring the apprentice with him. On their arrival he laid aside all other business, explained to everyone present that Wyatt's first confession had not been constrained, and censured the Lord Mayor for neglecting his duty in not punishing those who said the contrary.

"The party is here," said the Mayor.

"Take him with you and punish him according to his desert," replied the Chancellor, adding this admonition: "My Lord, take heed to your charge! The city of London is a whirlpool and sink of all evil rumours, where they be bred, and from thence spread into all parts of this realm."[15]

Another summary disposal by the Chancellor of a difficulty in which the Government found itself as an aftermath of Wyatt's rising, was the case of Sir Nicholas Throgmorton, who was charged with complicity in the rebellion but was unanimously acquitted by a jury at the Guildhall in April 1554. The jury was immediately haled to the Star Chamber (April 25), two of them sent to the Tower, and ten to the Fleet. Four of the ten were set free on confession that they had done wrong, but the eight who manfully maintained the justice of their doings were kept in jail till December, and then only released upon payment of a heavy fine. Throgmorton was kept in the Tower until January of the next year.[16]

Mary's Government had come dangerously near overthrow by Wyatt, so near that the determination to prevent at all hazards another such rising explains, if it does not excuse, this high-handed interference with the courts.

Meanwhile, on February 17, every foreign-born "preacher, printer, bookseller, or other artificer, . . . not being denizen or merchant known," was warned by a proclamation, doubtless of Gardiner's penning, to avoid the realm within twenty-four days, since it was "assuredly known unto her Majesty" that such persons not only incited her subjects "to this most unnatural rebellion," but also "desist not still to practise with her people eftsoons to rebell." [17] On February 24, the Chancellor was empowered by the Queen to receive as denizens whatever strangers seemed to his discretion convenient.[18]

On March 4 a set of articles, probably also of Gardiner's composition, was sent to the bishops, commanding them to put into execution with speed and diligence all ecclesiastical laws of the time of Henry VIII, not expressly opposed to the laws of the realm. They were no longer, in any ecclesiastical process, to use the clause *Regia auctoritate fulcitus,* nor to exact from anyone admitted to an office in the Church "any oath touching the primacy or succession." Heretical preachers and school teachers were to be removed, and clergy who, "contrary to the state of our order and the laudable custom of the Church," had married were to be deprived. Clemency was to be shown those who, with the consent of their wives, promised to abstain; but any who had, as members of a religious order, once solemnly professed chastity, were to be deprived, divorced, and punished. Touching persons who had been "promoted to any orders after the new sort, . . . considering they were not ordered in very deed," the bishop of the diocese was empowered to "supply that thing which wanted in them before, and then, according to his discretion, admit them to minister." [19]

In Gardiner's own diocese, which in his day contained some four hundred and eighty parishes, there were, from November 26, 1553 to September 10, 1554 (the only part of Mary's reign for which his register is extant), fifty-four vacancies caused by resignation, deprivation, and churches *de jure vacante.*[20] This was over four times the number of similar vacancies in the diocese in the opening years of Edward VI's reign, and six times that recorded in Ponet's register—a difference which may be due to the fact that Gardiner, early in Edward's reign, counselled his clergy to conform to established changes and that Ponet's register is incomplete. But it may, on the other hand, indicate, as Mr. Malden suggests, that many of the Winchester clergy had availed themselves of the Edwardine permission to marry and were unwilling now to put away their wives.

It was in the latter part of March, 1554, that Gardiner undertook to let the dowager Duchess of Suffolk know that her religion was suspect. The Duchess was the daughter of a Spanish lady who had come to England as maid of honour to Queen Catherine, and hence had in her as much Spanish blood as Queen Mary herself; yet, strange to say, she had adopted the new teachings in religion. After the death of the Duke of Suffolk she had married Richard Bertie, Esq., who was summoned to appear before the Chancellor just before

Easter 1554. Following some talk about a debt due the crown from
the late Duke, the Chancellor proceeded to the question of religion,
recalling, not, it seems, without amusement at the memory of his own
discomfiture, certain previous passages with the Duchess which
justify Fuller's characterization of her as "a lady of sharp wit and
sure hand to thrust it home."

> "If I may ask the question of my Lady your wife," said
> Gardiner, "is she now as ready to set up the Mass, as she was
> lately to pull it down, when she caused in her progress a dog in
> a rochet to be carried and called by my name? or doth she
> think her lambs now safe enough, which said to me, when I vailed
> my bonnet to her out of my chamber window in the Tower, that
> it was merry with the lambs now the wolf was shut up? An-
> other time, my Lord her husband, having invited me and divers
> ladies to dinner, desired every lady to choose him whom she
> loved best, and so place themselves. My Lady your wife, taking
> me by the hand, for that my Lord would not have her to take
> himself, said, that forasmuch as she could not sit down with my
> Lord whom she loved best, she had chosen him whom she loved
> worst."

Bertie made excuses for his sharp-witted lady and said that if
she were to be won again to the old religion it must be by persuasion
rather than by force. Gardiner then exhorted him to persuade her,
adding:

> "It will be a marvellous grief to the Prince of Spain, and
> to all the nobility that shall come with him, when they shall
> find but two noble personages of the Spanish race within this
> land, the Queen and my Lady your wife; and one of them gone
> from the faith."

When the Prince of Spain arrived, the Duchess was gone not
only from the faith but from the realm.[21]

The Prince's marriage treaty was ratified and sworn to March
6, 1554, by Mary and Count Egmont, Philip's proctor, Gardiner
presiding at the ceremony.[22]

A week later Gardiner, Tunstall, Bonner, and three others were
commissioned to deprive seven reforming bishops—four who were
married, and three who had been appointed by letters patent from
Edward VI "during good behaviour."[23] Five of the sees thus
vacated, as well as that of Barlow who had fled to the Continent,
were filled Sunday, April 1, at St. Mary Overies, in Southwark,
when Gardiner, assisted by Tunstall and Bonner, consecrated John
White, Warden of Winchester College, as Bishop of Lincoln, James
Brooks as Bishop of Gloucester, Gilbert Bourne (whose sermon at
Paul's Cross had caused the riot the preceding August) as Bishop

of Bath, Henry Morgan as Bishop of St. David's, and George Cotes as Bishop of Chester.[24] After the ceremony there was, says Machyn, "as great a dinner as you have seen," at Gardiner's house. It is said that both White and Brooks had, as young men, been members of Gardiner's household.[25]

These bishops were consecrated just in time to strengthen the Chancellor's party in the House of Lords, for Parliament opened the next day, April 2. This Parliament, said the Chancellor in his opening speech, was called "for the corroboration of true religion, and touching the Queen's Highness' most noble marriage."[26]

As early as February 23, the Council had appointed a committee consisting of Gardiner, Tunstall, Paulet, Paget, Petre, Baker, and Hare "to consider what laws shall be established in this Parliament,"[27] but it appears that the recommendations of this commitee, as might have been expected from its composition, were not unanimous. Renard tells us that when Gardiner laid the legislative programme before the Council in March, Paget and Pembroke purposely absented themselves that they might not be included in any pledge to support the religious proposals of the Government. A week or two later Paget assured Renard that although he was now convinced that it was vain to think of remedying the affairs of the kingdom without the re-establishment of religion, there would be difficulty if this were done according to the plans of Gardiner, "who was anxious to carry through the matter by fire and blood"—a remark which, made to Renard, was superfluous, for Renard had recently expressed his own opinion that although Gardiner was remiss in proceeding against rebels he was "most ardent and hot-headed in the affairs of religion."[28] The truth of the case was that Gardiner, as he had frankly told Renard some months before, believed the reunion of Christendom of much more importance than the consummation of the Spanish match. He knew that the latter would hinder rather than help the former, for if the reunion of England with continental Catholicism were to be effected under the ægis of Philip, it would appear as a Spanish project, doubly foreign and un-English. Hence Gardiner's desire to force certain ecclesiastical measures through this Parliament which would be the last before the arrival of the Spaniards. Renard, on the other hand felt that this would stir Protestant resentment and thus place obstacles in the way of Philip's coming. Paget, who had staked his fortunes on the success of the Spanish marriage, took the same view.

Gardiner's legislative programme included parliamentary sanction of the Queen's marriage and of the proposition that her authority was equal to that of any of her male predecessors; the restoration of the bishopric of Durham, which in Edward's last Parliament had been divided into two dioceses and its temporalities confiscated; the exclusion of Elizabeth from the throne, in the form of a law giving

Mary the right to name her successors; the punishment of heretics; the suspension of the title of Supreme Head; and a guarantee that the holders of Church lands would be undisturbed in return for their support of the Supreme Head measure. He had persuaded the Queen, probably not without difficulty, to assent to this compromise,[29] and had suggested, in a letter, to Cardinal Pole that he write to Parliament urging unity of religion, but not with too much insistance on the rights of the Pope, and promising that no attempt would be made to recover monastic property.[30]

There was no opposition to the ratification of the Queen's marriage, for the suppression of Wyatt's rebellion had settled that question in her favour. All factions in the Council had agreed to support it, and, as Soranzo, the Venetian Ambassador, tells us, considerable effort had been made to secure the election of members "known to be of the Queen's mind" on this matter.[31] The act asserting her authority to be as great as that of her predecessors passed with equal ease. This settled all doubts as to whether a woman could reign in her own right, and forestalled any claim Philip might make either in right of his Queen or his own descent.[32]

The bill for the restoration of the see of Durham also passed, but not without vigorous opposition.[33] This was a notable achievement for the Chancellor's party since it dealt with the dread subject of Church property. It was, to be sure, property but recently confiscated and for the benefit of Northumberland, but it caused alarm, for a bill, manifestly not a Government measure, passed Commons providing that "no bishop shall convent any man for abbey lands." This went no further than a second reading in the Lords, for the Chancellor's supporters were unwilling thus to insure the holders of Church lands without a *quid pro quo,* which, by previous agreement, was the suspension of the title of Supreme Head. No bill suspending this title appears even to have been introduced, undoubtedly because Renard and Paget so played upon the Queen's fears for Philip's safety, that she abandoned it. Nor is there record of the introduction of any bill empowering Mary to name her successors, although Noailles tells us that Gardiner urged the need for such a measure in his opening speech.[34] Paget, moreover, succeeded in killing in the Lords a "bill against heretics and erroneous preaching," and a "bill for the punishment of Lollards," both of which had been sent up from Commons.

The Lords had little objection to the punishment of heretics. They voted in the negative because Paget persuaded them that these bills, if passed, would enable the bishops to recover Church property by prosecuting its holders for heresy. Although this consideration may have had some weight with Paget himself, his compelling motive appears to have been one of personal pique. Owing to his support of the Spanish marriage he had won the backing of Renard

and the confidence of the Queen to such an extent that his faction,
up to this time, had been in the ascendant in the Council; but now
Gardiner and his followers had succeeded in persuading Mary that
Paget's chief support came from the heretics, and he was losing
ground with her. He was, moreover, wholly ignored by Gardiner in
the preparation of his ecclesiastical programme. He therefore acted
as he did, said Renard, out of spite for Gardiner because he had not
been consulted about these measures.[35]

Such was his alarm at the ease with which these bills had gone
through the lower house that he wrote frantically to Renard:

> "For the love of God, Sir, persuade the Queen to dissolve
> Parliament at once. . . . The weather is beginning to be
> warm, and men's tempers will wax warm too; and I see that
> this man's [Gardiner's] private leanings will cause him to bring
> forward proposals that will heat the people too much, for he
> proceeds without considering the present times, his Highness'
> coming, or the danger ahead." [36]

Renard persuaded the Queen "to proceed gently in the reformation
of religion" lest some new obstacle to Philip's coming arise. Parliament was dissolved May 5.

The Queen, however, was thoroughly angry at Paget because of
his opposition, not only to these ecclesiastical measures, but also to
a bill giving Philip the benefit of the treason laws, approval of which
he had previously expressed to her. After the dissolution he came
to her and asked forgiveness, which she granted, but she confided
to Renard that she could never trust him again. When, shortly after,
he asked her permission to go home for a few days, she tartly told
him he could go and come as he pleased, but warned him that he had
been guilty, to her detriment, of inconstancy, that he had followed
evil counsels, which she would not put up with, and that if he did
wrong he would suffer for it.[37]

Although he had succeeded in quashing Gardiner's entire ecclesiastical programme with the exception of the restoration of the see of
Durham, he had nevertheless got himself into the Queen's disfavour
as effectively as his bitterest enemies could have desired.

The struggle between him and the Chancellor had become inter-
necine during the spring of 1554. In March he had complained that
Gardiner was endeavouring to play the part of a Northumberland;
and such was the spirit of faction in the Council that Renard, in
consultation with Paget and Petre, devised a plan to secure harmony
and efficiency. According to this, the affairs of state were to be
conducted by an inner council composed of Gardiner, Arundel,
Thirlby, Paget, Rochester, and Petre. Gardiner was to confine his
attention to the business of the chancellorship and attend Council
meetings only when he desired to do so, or when his presence was

necessary. A reconciliation of Paget and Arundel with Gardiner was to be effected, all three binding themselves by oath "to fraternity, loyalty, duty, and diligence." This was more easily said than done. Moreover, as Paget seconded the scheme he clearly expected to have the best of it; and it assigned to Gardiner a departmental rôle he was not likely to accept without protest. Finally, it provided that the principal nobles might be permitted to attend meetings of the Council when they were at court, but otherwise all but the six inner councillors were to be excluded. This naturally raised an outcry from men like Walgrave and Englefield, whom Mary could not but recognize as her unquestionably loyal servitors. Their protest was backed by Gardiner, and although Renard seems to have succeeded in inducing the Queen to attempt some such reduction of her Council, the plan was soon abandoned. By the middle of the session of Parliament factional strife became so acute that Renard wrote that he saw no other end to it but "arms and tumult." Gardiner, he said, was supported by Rochester, Walgrave, Englefield, Southwell, Sir John Gage, Sir Henry Jerningham, and Sir John Bourne; Paget by Arundel, Pembroke, Sussex, Petre, Sir Edward Hastings, Sir Thomas Cornwallis, and Lord William Howard. Mary complained that "she spent her days in shouting at her Council, but all with no result." [38]

After the dissolution of Parliament both parties feared their opponents were plotting their destruction. In order to discover Gardiner's plans, Paget forcibly detained in his house a friend of the Bishop and had him examined as if he were a spy. This convinced Gardiner that Paget's party was designing to seize him, clap him in the Tower, and then compel the Queen to submit to their wishes. Nor were Gardiner's fears groundless, if we may believe Noailles who wrote, May 18, that the greater part of the Council had sworn to ruin the Chancellor, and would have done so had it not been for the Queen, who commanded the captain of the guard not to lay hands on him, and the Lieutenant of the Tower not to receive him as a prisoner unless he were accompanied by a ring sent from her.

Gardiner's supporters, on the other hand, urged the Queen to imprison Paget, Arundel, and Pembroke, but after a consultation with Gardiner, Rochester, and Paulet she decided that this might precipitate an outbreak; it was better to watch them carefully, take all possible measures of defence, and send doubtfully loyal nobles who, if permitted to stay in Paget's proximity, might be tampered with, to various parts of the realm on special business. [39]

The result of all this was to put into Gardiner's hands the undisputed direction of affairs. When the ambassador of Ferrara arrived in London in June 1554, he described Gardiner as the ruler of the kingdom, and when Soranzo wrote his description of England later in the summer of the same year, he said that although the Council met early every morning for the discussion of affairs, Gardiner, "the present Prime Minister," had the management of everything. Paget, he said, had for a while taken precedence of all the councillors because of his advocacy of the Spanish marriage, but he was now out of favour, while Gardiner, "who at the commencement opposed the marriage and ran great risk of disgrace, until being convinced of the Queen's firm intention he diligently aided its accomplishment, is now paramount to everybody." [40]

Thus had the Chancellor succeeded in cutting off, at least from dominant influence, another "hurtful member" of the commonwealth—mort hurtful, doubtless in his view, than Wyatt, Jane Grey, Elizabeth, the piquant Duchess of Suffolk, or the reforming Churchmen.

XXXI

THE KING AND THE CARDINAL

"The usurped government of an affectionate woman is a rage without reason." "Had she [Queen Mary], I say, and such as now be of her pestilent Council been sent to hell before these days, then should not their iniquity and cruelty so manifestly have appeared to the world."

This was John Knox's "faithful admonition . . . unto the professors of God's truth in England," not written, as the vehemency of its language would suggest, after the fires of Smithfield had been lighted, but as a protest against the Spanish marriage.

"O thou beast!" continued the Scotsman, "I speak to you, Winchester, more cruel than any tiger, . . . ashamest thou not, bloody beast, to betray thy native country . . .? Fearest thou not to open such a door to all iniquity that the whole England shall be made a common stew to Spaniards?" "O thou son of Satan! . . . Thou art brother to Cain and fellow to Judas the traitor." [1]

With such words coming from the pens of the refugees it would be small wonder if Gardiner actually said what one of these refugees later wrote that he said—that he would "bring all such runagates to such need that they would eat their fingers for hunger." [2]

Knox's *Faithful Admonition* was issued from the press July 20, 1554. On that day Philip landed at Southampton. With him were the lords of Flanders and the flower of the Spanish nobility. The nobility of England was there to welcome them, and on the morrow in the rain came the Lord Chancellor with a diamond for Philip from the Queen. [3]

On the 23d the Prince "with a white feather in his hat, very fair," was received at the door of Winchester Cathedral by Gardiner and five other bishops in procession, and led to the choir, where the *Te Deum* was sung. He was lodged at the dean's house, not more than "a pair of but-lengths" from the Bishop's palace, where Mary had taken up her residence. That night in the presence of the Bishop and a few of the nobles he saw and talked with his bride for the first time, "each of them merrily smiling on other, to the great comfort and rejoicing of the beholders."

Arras and cloth of gold made splendid the grey aisles of the cathedral on the wedding day, July 25, Feast of St. James, patron of Spain. So gorgeous were the "rich and sundry apparels" of the

nobility that, in the words of Darnley's tutor, the Scotch John
Elder, who was present, it "were but a phantasy and loss of paper
and ink" to describe them. At ten o'clock Philip arrived at the
cathedral and waited half an hour for his bride. Before the wedding
began Gardiner declared to the people that the Emperor had given
his son the Kingdom of Naples, so that Mary would marry, not a
prince, but a king. The Bishop then, in the phrase of the Scotchman, "solemnizated" the marriage, having declared "the biddings
and the banns thereof" in both Latin and English. After this he
celebrated high Mass, "the King's Highness at the *Agnus Dei* kiss-
ing the celebrator."

The wedding over, Philip and Mary walked to the Bishop's palace, "above the inner port" of which were two verses, written, as
Elder was informed, "by my Lord Bishop of Winchester . . .
whose exact learning is well known everywhere, yea and he to be
of most exact judgement in all kind of good letters." The verses
were:

> "*O domus es felix nimium, nimiumque beata,*
> *Hospito tales nunc habitura tuo.*"

which Elder translates:

> "Thou art happy house, right blest and blest again,
> That shortly shalt such noble guests retain."

For the next five or six days there was, in the words of the en-
thusiastic Elder, "such triumphing, banqueting, singing, masking,
and dancing" in the Bishop's house "as was never in England heretofore." "To behold the dukes and noblemen of Spain dance with
the fair ladies and the most beautiful nymphs of England, it should
seem to him that never see such to be another world." [4]

On July 31 the royal party left Winchester for Windsor, stopping
at Paulet's house at Basing for a few days on the way. While passing through Reading, August 2, Gardiner heard of a certain John
Bolton who was in jail for unseemly words on the Mass, and, following his usual custom of trying to convert heretics by persuasion,
sent for him; but as Bolton "most boldly reproved the said Bishop
to his face," there was nothing to do but send him back to jail
again. [5]

They arrived at Windsor August 3, and on Sunday the 5th
Philip was installed by Gardiner in the order of the Garter. Going
on to Richmond August 11, they came the following Friday afternoon, August 17, by water to Southwark, "and there had a banquet
in the Lord Chancellor's house." The next day they "rode through
Southwark, over the bridge and so through London." [6]

As at the coronation procession, so now, there were verses and
pageants, this time applicable to Philip. There were acrobatic feats

also at St. Paul's, where "a fellow came slipping upon a cord . . .
from Paul's steeple to the ground, and lighted with his head foreward on a great sort of feather beds." [7] The people were amused
and fêted and displayed little if any ill-feeling toward the new King.

In one of the pageants Henry VIII's picture had appeared with
a book marked *Verbum Dei* in his hand. This so offended Mary
that Gardiner summoned the painter and sharply rebuked him, saying
that he should rather have put the book in the Queen's hand, for
she indeed had reformed religion according to the word of God. [8]

Six weeks after Philip's reception in London, on Sunday, September 30, Gardiner "made a goodly sermon" at Paul's Cross, to "as
great a audience," says Machyn, "as ever I saw in my life." He
expounded the Gospel for the day (Matthew xxii. 34-46), in which
the Scribes and Pharisees test Christ with questions, one asking him
what the greatest commandment is. "In these Scribes and Pharisees," said the Bishop, "is the nature of many men described, that
is, to search and know high things, and to reason and dispute of that
whereof they have no understanding." The possible application of
this to the new teachers is obvious. After exhorting his hearers,
according to Christ's answer, to the love of God and their neighbour, and alluding to the opposite—the licence, deceit, and dissension—resulting from the heresy preached in Edward's days, he
concluded with a eulogy of "the King and his dominions and riches,
and willed all so obediently to behave themselves that he might
tarry still with us." [9]

Two days later the Bishop's conclusion was re-enforced by twenty
cartloads of Spanish gold, drawn through the streets of London to
fill the impoverished treasury of the Queen.

It may well have seemed, even to him who had so vigorously
opposed the marriage, that, after all, it might prove a blessing to
the realm. Philip was genuinely trying to conform to English ways
and to observe the terms of the treaty. He was, said Gardiner in
his sermon, "as wise, sober, gentle, and temperate a prince as ever
was in England." The prospect of lightened taxation, restored currency, protection against France at the cost of Spain, and, if an heir
were born, an end to the disputes over the succession and the union
under one government of England and her Flemish markets, were
blessings for which he might well exhort the people "obediently to
behave themselves."

In the months following Philip's coming, Gardiner found time
again to attend to things academic. By virtue of his position as
Lord Chancellor, he was "visitor" of Christ Church, Oxford, the
college of his old masters Wolsey and Henry VIII. Hearing that
the students there were practising "such factious stubbornness" as
impaired the "good and decent order of that whole university," he

wrote them, September 1, 1554, a sharp letter, bidding them obey the injunctions of their dean, and assuring them that if the offense were repeated, the offender would "have cause continually to abstain from like presumption." [10] To Cambridge he sent orders "that every scholar should wear his apparel according to his degree in the schools," that his former decrees on the pronunciation of Greek be observed, and that every preacher there should declare the whole style of the King and Queen in his sermons. [11]

Meanwhile, on August 25, death had claimed his long-time political ally, the Duke of Norfolk. An obsequy of "dirge and Mass on the morrow" was held at St. Mary Overies, October 5 and 6, with the Bishop himself as "chief mourner." [12]

Strangely enough, the passing of this stout champion of the old order, who had declared that "it was merry in England before this new learning came up," and was not ashamed to say he had "never read the Scriptures nor ever would," [13] was almost coincident with the return of that old order which he had so stoutly championed. For now that Philip was safely on the throne of England, the Emperor deemed it safe to put no more obstacles in the way of the coming of Cardinal Pole and the consummation of Mary's hopes.

Early in August Renard, at the request of the Queen, had discussed with Gardiner the question of Pole's coming. Gardiner said he thought it would be safe for Pole to come about the end of September, if the door were opened to him by dexterity and authority. That is, he should be represented as coming to congratulate Philip and Mary on their marriage, to take possession of the see of Canterbury (to which he had been appointed), and to induce the Queen to mediate peace between France and the Empire; and he should be permitted to come by the royal authority, which could be exercised for this purpose without waiting for the Council to take action or for Parliament to meet. If Council or Parliament were permitted to dictate in the matter, said Gardiner, they might not consent to Pole's coming at all. The Chancellor evidently thought the surest way to win parliamentary sanction to reunion with Rome was to bring Pole in on an errand which would not rouse anti-Papal feeling, and thus give him a chance to approve himself to nobility and commons, to study English sentiment at first-hand, and, above all, to learn the necessity of guaranteeing the tenure of the holders of erstwhile Church property, full authority for which he must, Gardiner insisted, bring with him.

Gardiner went on to assure Renard that Pole's coming on royal invitation would not cause trouble, since Mary had already created bishops by the Pope's power, had obtained a Papal dispensation for her marriage, and had asked the Pope's advice on several matters of conscience, without any regrettable consequences, although the fact that she had done all this had been made public by Paget, who found it out when he was in favour.

Philip disagreed with Gardiner. He thought it not possible to explain Pole's coming on any other ground than the real one, and decided that this coming must be put off till Parliament met, for his Spanish advisers—Renard and de Courrieres—assured him that recognition of Papal authority "is far more objectionable to the people here than the Mass ever was."

The Chancellor, however, remained firm in his opinion, and at the beginning of September strongly urged the Queen to lay the question before the Council. That he did so seems to indicate that the Council was now in agreement with him. The immediate coming of Pole was undoubtedly what Mary herself desired, which was, perhaps, the chief reason the Chancellor urged it. But Philip was determined to proceed with the utmost caution.[14]

Early in October letters were sent out to men of prominence asking their influence in the election of members "of the wise, grave, and Catholic sort" to the coming Parliament, and protesting that the Queen intended nothing for "the alteration of any particular man's possession."[15]

Since Pole, despite Gardiner's warnings, had expressed a hope that some of the Church property now in private hands might be recovered, lest it look as if the Pope were buying back his authority in England, Renard was dispatched to Brussels in the middle of October to impress upon the Cardinal the absolute necessity of guaranteeing the titles of the possessors of all such property.[16] Some weeks before this, Renard had put the matter in a nutshell:

> "It is my duty to inform your Majesty that the Catholics hold more Church property than do the heretics, and unless they obtain a general dispensation to satisfy them that their titles will never be contested, they will not allow the Cardinal to execute his commission."[17]

On November 3, after the return of Renard, the question of the Cardinal's coming was finally submitted to the Council. It was their unanimous decision "that, provided the holders of Church property were not molested in their possessions," the Cardinal should be welcomed; and Paget and Sir Edward Hastings were dispatched so to inform him and to accompany him to England.[18]

This mission was an indication of the political rehabilitation of Paget. After his discomfiture of the previous May, he had, with Arundel, become the centre of a group of malcontents too powerful for the Government to touch and too wary to give the Government an excuse for touching them. Philip felt it to be the course of wisdom to conciliate rather than antagonize them further, hence this appointment of Paget, which, according to Renard, made Gardiner and his supporters so jealous they were unable to contain themselves.[19]

At Brussels Paget was received by the Emperor, and at a private interview spoke freely of English affairs. His recent fall into the Queen's disfavour was, he plausibly explained, entirely the fault of Gardiner, of whose "self-sufficiency and asperity" he went on to speak, "saying frankly that he was a better hand at stopping up a dangerous hole than at preventing the hole from being pierced." Petre, Arundel, and Clinton he praised; the management of English finances he censured; Philip, he said, should govern the kingdom with a small council of expert councillors.

The Emperor sent a report of Paget's observations to Philip, and urged the reduction of the Council, suggesting that among the councillors retained, Gardiner, Paget, Thirlby, and Petre should find a place.

Renard, who received and presented to Philip this account of Paget's interview, replied to the Emperor that the reduction of the Council was a thorny matter, as he had learned from experience. As for Paget's censure of the financial administration—his chief supporter, Arundel, wanted the post of Lord High Treasurer! Paget himself, said Renard, sought the chancellorship, and although affairs really ought to be better managed than they are, "it is considered to be dangerous to raise Paget to such an office." [20] This was a significant admission from one who had, half a year previous, been one of Paget's allies.

Parliament met November 12. In the bidding prayer before the sermon at the Mass of the Holy Ghost in the Abbey, preceding the opening of the session, the Pope was prayed for. It was a brilliant procession to the Parliament house, "all the bishops and the lords in their Parliament robes, with trumpeters blowing, and all the heralds in their coat armours, and the judges in their robes;" the King was mounted, the Queen, gowned in crimson velvet, in an open chariot beside him, and "afore them rode together my Lord Chancellor and my Lord Treasurer." [21] In his opening speech the Chancellor declared that Parliament had been "called for confirmation of true religion." [22]

Cardinal Pole, having assured Paget and Hastings that the matter of Church property would be so handled by the Pope that everyone in England would be contented,[23] landed at Dover November 20. Two days later, while he was journeying slowly toward London, Mary and Philip went to the Parliament house to give final assent to the bill repealing his attainder. On November 24 he came by water from Gravesend to London, where Gardiner met him in his barge near the Stilyard and accompanied him to Whitehall. After a joyous reception by Mary and Philip, he was conducted by Gardiner to Lambeth. Then followed daily conferences between Legate, King, and Chancellor.

On the afternoon of the 28th—the day *Te Deum* was sung at St. Paul's upon the report that the Queen was with child [24]—Parliament assembled at Whitehall, where, before King and Queen, the Chancellor introduced the Cardinal, saying that he had come "upon one of the most weightiest causes that ever happened in this realm." Pole then delivered a long oration, which, in the pithy phrase of the Commons' Journal was "to move us to come again to the unity of the Church." Gardiner thanked him in the name of the assembly, and said that Parliament would deliberate on his proposal. When Pole had withdrawn, he exclaimed, in a paraphrase of Scripture, "The Lord hath raised up a prophet from among our brethren that he might save us." He endorsed Pole's words, acknowledged himself to be of the number of those who had erred, and urged Parliament to proceed to a reconciliation.

The next day the Lords appointed a committee headed by the Chancellor to confer with a similar body from Commons. Together they devised a supplication to Philip and Mary, asking that the realm might be reunited to the Church by means of the Cardinal. In it they professed repentance for their schism and promised the repeal of all laws against the See Apostolic. This met with unanimous approval in the Lords and lacked but two votes of unanimity in Commons.

The following afternoon, November 30, the Feast of St. Andrew, Parliament again assembled at the Palace. Gardiner announced the decision to which they had come and asked whether they continued in the same mind. Upon their affirmative acclamation he presented the supplication to King and Queen, who opened it and delivered it again to him to read aloud. The Queen, in her own name and the King's, interceded for the pardon of the realm, and the Cardinal, after expressing his joy, pronounced the absolution, Lords and Commons, in the words of John Elder, "sitting all on their knees." [25]

That Pole would, from now on, have an increasing share in the government of Church and State and in the confidence of the Queen, was clear. Over a year before his coming, Renard said that Mary had more regard for him than for all her Council put together,[26] and there was much truth in his observation. Gardiner must have known this as well as Renard. Had he been jealous of Pole, as both the Imperial and the French ambassadors said he was,[27] he would have been no more than human; but the Imperial ambassador was, at the time he said this, receiving most of his information about Gardiner from the most unreliable of all sources of such information; namely, Paget; and the French ambassador was ready to believe or conjecture anything about one so unfavourable to France as was the Chancellor. Indeed, the French ambassador's chief reason for attributing jealousy to Gardiner was Gardiner's remark to him that he did not believe the Cardinal's abilities sufficient for effecting a peace between France and the Empire unless he were aided by men more capable than himself—an observation which was not only true but, in the light of the devious diplomacy of the period, to the Cardinal's credit as a religious leader. If Gardiner were jealous of Pole, it is all the more to his praise that he smoothed the way for his coming and acted with him in such loyal and hearty accord.

The Sunday after the reconciliation to Rome, December 2, 1554, was a festival day at St. Paul's. "All the crafts in their livery, and my Lord Mayor and the aldermen" were there an hour before service time, "against my Lord Cardinal's coming." My Lord Cardinal came from Lambeth by water, and, landing at Paul's wharf, proceeded to the cathedral with his cross and his pillars and pole-axes before him. A procession of bishops and clergy, headed by Gardiner, met him at the church door; they entered and sang *Te Deum,* then returned to meet the King, who came by land from Westminster with a company of nobles and gentry and four hundred of the guard. Mass was sung by Bonner, and after the benediction King and Cardinal repaired to a window overlooking the church yard, where gathered "such an audience of people as was never seen in that place." The Lord Chancellor ascended the outdoor pulpit; "and after that the people ceased, that so much as a whispering could not be heard amongst them." [28]

It was the first Sunday in Advent, and in the Epistle for the day, Romans xiii. 8-14, the Bishop found words peculiarly appropriate to his theme. "Now," wrote the Apostle to the Gentiles, "it is time to awake out of sleep."

> "Now also," said the Bishop, "it is time that we awake out of our sleep, who have slept or rather dreamed these twenty years past. For as men intending to sleep do separate themselves from company and desire to be alone, even so we have separated ourselves from the See of Rome, and have been alone, no realm in Christendom like us; as in sleep men dream of killing, maiming, burning, and such beastliness as I dare not name, so among us one brother has destroyed another, half our money has been wiped away at one time,[29] those who would defend their conscience have been slain or troubled; as in sleep all senses are stopped, so the ceremonies of the Church, which were instituted to move our senses, were taken away; as the candle is put out when a man would sleep, so such writers as did hold with the See Apostolic have been condemned, and images, laymen's books, cast down and broken."

So graphic was the Bishop's description of the late "ruin and decay" of the realm that, according to John Elder, it "moved a great number of the audience with sorrowful sighs and weeping tears to change their cheer."

"During these twenty years," continued the preacher, "we have been without a head. When King Henry was head perhaps there was something to be said for it, but what a head was Edward, to whom they had to give a protector! He was but a shadow. Nor could the Queen, being a woman, be head of the Church. Thus while we desired to have a Supreme Head among us, it came to pass that we had no head at all, no, not so much as our two Archbishops, who were both rightfully put forth from their sees.

When the tumult was in the north, in the time of King Henry VIII, I am sure the King was determined to have given over the supremacy again to the Pope, but the hour was not yet then come, and therefore it went not forward, lest some would have said that he did it for fear. After this, Master Knyvet and I were sent ambassadors unto the Emperor to desire him that he would be a mean between the Pope's Holiness and the King, to bring the King to the obedience to the See of Rome, but the time was neither then come, for it might have been said that it had been done for a civil policy. Again in the beginning of King Edward's reign the matter was moved,[30] but the time was not yet. Neither in the beginning of the Queen's reign was the hour come, for it would have been said that it was done in a time of weakness. Likewise when the King first came, if it had been done, they might have said it had been done by force and violence. But now, even now, *hora est,* the hour is come, when nothing can be objected, but that it is the mere mercy and providence of God.

Now the realm is at peace. Now the Queen is with child. Now there is sure hope of an heir. Even now hath the Pope's Holiness sent unto us this most reverend father, the Cardinal, not to revenge injuries done by us against his Holiness, but to give his benediction to those that defamed and persecuted him. Rejoice in this day, that such a noble birth is come, yea, such a holy father, which can speak unto us as unto brethren. The King and Queen's Majesties have already restored our holy Father the Pope to his supremacy; the estates assembled in Parliament have also submitted themselves to his Holiness. Wherefore let us not any longer stay. It is time for us also to awake—not for the Queen, nor the King, nor my Lord Cardinal, who have never fallen asleep—but for us, us—I do not exclude myself forth from the number. I acknowledge my fault, and exhort all who have fallen into this sleep through me or with me, with me to awake!"[31]

The sermon, wrote one of Philip's attendants, lasted two hours, and at the end the preacher announced that he had been empowered by the Legate to absolve his hearers and admit them once more into the fold of the Church. Whereupon, "all those present, over fifteen thousand persons, knelt down. A sight to be seen it was; and the silence was such that not a cough was heard."[32] Cardinal Pole declared that he had never heard a sermon which pleased him better.[33] James Haddon, an English refugee at Strassburg, on receiving an account of it, exclaimed against the "subtle and versatile talent" of the preacher, whom he dubbed a turncoat, a monster, a pest of the state.[34]

"Since the day of which sermon," wrote John Elder at the opening of the next year, "all such things as were amiss and out of order here begin now to come to rule and square, and occupy their ancient and accustomed places."

Four days after the sermon both houses of Convocation went to Lambeth to receive pardon from the Cardinal. The next day, December 7, they decided that, notwithstanding the desirability of recovering Church property, "the manifold unavoidable contracts, sales, and alienations which have been made about the same," made any attempt at such recovery dangerous to the peace of the realm and the unity of the Church. They therefore petitioned the King and Queen to request the Legate to confirm the titles of the present possessors. They also asked that their former ecclesiastical rights, liberties, and jurisdictions, without which they were not able to perform their duties, be restored. As this petition was presented to their Majesties by Gardiner and a committee from the lower house,[35] it presumably expressed the policy which he himself sponsored.

This declaration of the willingness of the Church to forego its claims on its lost lands undoubtedly facilitated the adoption of Gardiner's ecclesiastical programme in the Parliament then in session. The heresy laws of Richard II, Henry IV, and Henry V, repealed in the reign of Edward, were re-enacted, although the severer Act of the Six Articles was not revived. The treasons acts of Henry VIII were emulated in statutes making it treason to "pray or desire" that God would shorten the Queen's days, or to affirm that anyone had a better right to the throne than she. All laws against the See of Rome made since the 20th year of Henry VIII were repealed, thus restoring Papal and episcopal authority to its former state, but in this repeal it was provided that no ecclesiastical court had any power to call in question the title of holders of Church lands. That the Church, however, might regain what property it could by an appeal to conscience, the mortmain acts, which prohibited legacies to the Church, were suspended for twenty years.[36] Gardiner again desired to have Elizabeth excluded from the throne by statute, but it was feared that such a proposal would redound to Philip's unpopularity.[37]

The Chancellor, in his speech at the closing of the session, January 16, 1555, contrasted with satisfaction the parliamentary dissension over the measures which had separated England from Rome, with the unanimity shown in accomplishing reunion. Such was the felicity of the times, he said, that he felt he might properly describe them in the words of David: "Mercy and truth are met together, righteousness and peace have kissed each other." [38]

XXXII

THE MARTYRS

"I take heresies in the Church to be like boils in a man's body, which oversoon lanced wax sorer and in time putrify their matter," but "heal of their own self with a little cleansing plaster of the chief surgeon." [1] So wrote Gardiner in 1545. Ten years later it became his task as chief surgeon to apply the cleansing plaster.

On January 18, 1555, two days after the dissolution of Parliament, he went to the Tower with other lords of the Council to release, by royal pardon, Holgate, late Archbishop of York, the four sons of Northumberland, Sir Nicholas Throgmorton, Sir James Crofts, and other political offenders. [2] On January 22, two days after the recently re-enacted heresy laws had become effective, another group of offenders were brought from the London prisons to his house in Southwark. To them also, in the presence of bishops and councillors, he offered the Queen's pardon, but on a condition which few of them were willing to accept. Among them were some of the foremost Edwardine preachers—Bishops Hooper and Ferrar, Prebendaries Rogers and Bradford, Drs. Rowland Taylor and Edward Crome, Lawrence Saunders and John Cardmaker. The condition of their pardon was a return to the Church. [3]

Those who refused to conform were remanded to jail and subsequently given each a second and third chance to do so, at more formal proceedings in the Church of St. Mary Overies, January 28, 29, and 30. [4] The purpose of these examinations was not to discover what the opinions of these men were. That was well known. Indeed, in the previous May and again during the late Parliament, they had issued from prison joint declarations of faith, offering to give themselves "to the halter or stake" in defence of the same. [5] They were now examined to see if they meant to maintain these opinions despite the reconciliation to Rome and the re-enacted laws against heresy.

Cardmaker recanted (although he later recanted his recantation); decision in the case of Crome was deferred; Ferrar was returned to prison and subsequently sent to St. David's for trial. Rogers, Hooper, Bradford, Saunders, and Taylor were condemned as heretics and burned.

These were the first examinations under the revived heresy laws. They were the last conducted by Gardiner. Of the almost three hundred Marian martyrs, on these five only did he pass judgement.

Foxe is without doubt correct when he says that these men were condemned in the hope "that all the rest would soon be quailed by their example." Gardiner had seen both Romanists and extreme Protestants quailed by a few such examples in Henry's reign. He had seen Anglo-Catholics silenced by less rigorous measures in the days of Edward. Indeed it is highly probable that he and many another Englishmen supposed that the mere re-enactment of the heresy laws would be sufficient to bring the adherents of the new theology to conformity. Sir Robert Southwell must have given expression to what many a courtier thought, when he said to Rogers at his first examination, "Thou wilt not burn in this gear, when it cometh to the purpose; I know well that." The convictions, courage, and constancy of the reformers were underestimated.

As soon, however, as the Chancellor saw the futility of these methods he refused to be a party to further proceedings of a similar nature. Even Foxe admits that "Gardiner, seeing thus his device disappointed, and that cruelty in this case would not serve to his expectation, gave over the matter as utterly discouraged, and from that day meddled no more in such kind of condemnations;" [6] and he relates how, later in this year, when an officious informer haled a preacher of Edwardine doctrines to Winchester House, he

"was highly checked and rated of the Bishop, asking if there were no man unto whom he might bring such rascals but to him. 'Hence,' quoth he, 'out of my sight, thou varlet! What dost thou trouble me with such matters?' " [7]

To use Gardiner's own simile, the boils of heresy on the body politic had been lanced oversoon.

Of the five men condemned, four have left us some report of the proceedings against them.[8] Since the Chancellor had presided at the Council when they had originally been committed to ward, since they felt that they had been thus already unjustly and excessively punished by him, and since they looked upon his theology as the doctrine of Antichrist, they can hardly be expected to give a sympathetic interpretation of his words and manner at their examinations. Two weeks before these examinations, Hooper spoke of him as "God's enemy and mine;" both Rogers and Bradford openly accused him of having sent them to prison without law and against law; and Rogers, writing after condemnation, called him the "bloody, butcherly Bishop of Winchester."[9] Yet it is obvious that they attempted to give a true relation of what was said at their examinations, and their statements can on the whole be trusted.

From their accounts it is clear, in the first place, that the Chancellor desired to win them to conformity. This is also the impression which he made on the brother of one of them, Sir Edward

Saunders, soon to become Chief Justice of the Queen's Bench, who wrote to his brother Lawrence, during the latter's imprisonment:

> "I send you . . . hearty commendation, being sorry for your fault and your disobedient handling of yourself toward my Lord Chancellor, who, I assure you, mindeth your good and preservation." [10]

It is, however, no less clear from the accounts of the examinations that when the accused maintained their opinions with a constancy which seemed to the Bishop sheer obstinacy, he lost his patience and his temper and descended to a roughness of speech and a vehemence of manner which, though often matched by the words and demeanour of the prisoners, ill accorded with the dignity of his position.

When Taylor asserted that Gardiner's book on the Sacrament contained many things "far wide from the truth," the Bishop exclaimed, "Thou art a very varlet."

"That," said Taylor, "is as ill as *raca* or *fatue*."

"Thou art an ignorant beetle-brow," retorted Gardiner.

Said Taylor, "My Lord, ye did write one book, *De Vera Obedientia;* I would you had been constant in that, for indeed you never did declare a good conscience that I heard of, but in that one book." [11]

"Tut, tut, tut," ejaculated the Bishop, "I wrote against Bucer in priests' marriages, but such books please not such wretches as thou art, which hast been married many years."

Taylor said he thanked God he was married, and denounced the proceedings against priests' marriages as "the maintenance of the doctrine of devils."

This was not the first time Taylor had come before the Chancellor. In the spring of 1554 he had been summoned for withstanding an attempt to set up the Mass at Hadleigh. His examination at that time had been quite as tempestuous, though perhaps the account of it has been in some degree dramatized by Foxe, according to whom the Chancellor exclaimed:

"Art thou come, thou villain? How darest thou look me in the face for shame?"

"How dare ye," demanded Taylor, "for shame look any Christian man in the face, seeing ye have forsaken the truth, denied our Saviour Christ and his word, and done contrary to your own oath and writing?"

"Tush, tush," answered the Bishop, "that was Herod's oath, unlawful and therefore worthy to be broken; . . . our holy Father the Pope hath discharged me of it."

"You shall not be so discharged before Christ," retorted Taylor.

"I see," quoth the Bishop, "thou art an arrogant knave and a very fool."

"Leave your unseemly railing at me," said Taylor, "He that saith, Thou Fool, is in danger of hell fire."

"Ye are false," countered the Bishop, "and liars, all the sort of you." [12]

At his examinations in 1555 Taylor declared, as he tells us himself, the "papistical doctrine" of the Sacrament "most wicked idolatry, blasphemy, and heresy," and "desired the bishops to repent for bringing the realm from Christ to Antichrist."

The same calmly irritating assumption of the infallibility of their own position, the same blunt denial of what Gardiner held to be the central truth of religion, the same thrusts—"privy nips," Foxe calls them—at his previous support of the breach with Rome, marked the defence of the other prisoners. The Chancellor, on the other hand, accused them all of pride and arrogancy, called Bradford "altogether ignorant and vainglorious," dubbed him out of hand a liar on three occasions, and denounced him as "a churlish heretic."

Rogers gives a vivid reproduction of one altercation with the Chancellor. After permitting Rogers to speak for some time on the superiority of Scripture to the decrees of general councils and of parliaments, Gardiner finally bade him sit down, saying he was there to be instructed, not to instruct.

"My Lord," said Rogers, "I stand and sit not. Shall I not be suffered to speak for my life?"

"Shall we suffer thee to tell a tale and to prate?" quoth the Bishop, and then, says Rogers, he

> "stood up and began to deface me, after his old arrogant proud fashion, marking that I was in a way to have touched them somewhat, which thing he would hinder, and dash me out of my tale; and so he did, for I could never be suffered to come to my tale again, no, not to one word of it, but he had much like communication with me as he had the day before, and as is accustomable to him, taunt for taunt, and check for check." [13]

With unnecessary harshness the Chancellor refused Rogers' request, after condemnation, that the woman to whom he had been married for eighteen years might visit him in prison, asserting that she was not his wife.

Hooper has left us no account of his examination, but judging from what we know of his resolute nonconformity, and from a few hints given us by Foxe, his hearings appear to have been as stormy as any. Foxe says that when Gardiner earnestly moved him to return to the Church and acknowledge the Pope as its head, he replied that the Pope "was not worthy to be accounted as a member of Christ's Church, much less to be head thereof."

"I wonder," said the sheriff who conducted him back to prison after his second examination, "that ye were so hasty and quick with my Lord Chancellor and did use no more patience." [14]

Besides the regrettable lack of good temper on the part of both examiner and examined, much else of significance to the biography of Gardiner is to be found in the accounts of these examinations.

There is his retrospect on the royal supremacy and the breach with Rome:

When Rogers said that he knew no other head of the Church than Christ, Gardiner asked him why he had acknowledged Henry VIII as head of it.

"I never granted him," answered Rogers, "to have any supremacy in spiritual things, as are the forgiveness of sins, giving of the Holy Ghost, authority to be a judge above the word of God, etc."

"Yea," said the Bishop, "if thou hadst said so in his days thou hadst not been alive now."

Tunstall and Heath heartily concurred in this, and all three, says Rogers, "nodded on me with a laughter," and "looked and laughed one upon another and made a business at it, so that I was constrained to let it pass."

Gardiner then turned to Lord William Howard and explained that it was no inconvenience "to have Christ to be Supreme Head, and the Bishop of Rome thereto." To which Rogers rejoined that he could not believe his examiners really thought this, since they had preached and written the contrary for twenty years, and since Parliament had also approved the same.

> "Tush, man!" exclaimed the Chancellor, "that Parliament was, of most great cruelty, constrained to abolish and put away the primacy of the Bishop of Rome. . . . They were so often and so cruelly called upon in that Parliament to let that act go foreward, yea, and even with force driven thereunto; whereas in this Parliament it was so uniformly received . . ."

Rogers did not gainsay this. Indeed, in the account he wrote of what he would have said at a subsequent hearing, had he been given the opportunity, he makes some amazing admissions:

> "As in Henry VIII's days ye in your Parliaments followed only his will and pleasure, even to grant the Queen's Majesty to be a bastard (God it well knoweth, against your wills, and, as ye well know, against the wills of the whole realm . . .)— likewise the taking away of the supremacy of the Bishop of Rome, with other things not a few—even so in King Edward's days did the most of the learned of the clergy (against their wills as it doth now appear) set their hands to the marriage of priests, . . . and the most part of the bishops to the alteration of the service into English, and to the taking away of the

positive laws which before had prohibited the said marriage—
this I say they did for the Duke of Somerset's and others of the
King's executors' pleasure. . . ."

"And in like manner," continues Rogers, since the Queen has committed the Government "to the cure of the Bishop of Winchester
. . . the consent of the whole Parliament followeth his head and
his will . . . and what he cannot do in one Parliament that he doth
in another." [15]

Such an explanation of the religious changes of these three reigns
is far too easy, but it contains the probable truth that in each reign
they were accomplished by a resolute minority.

When Rogers taxed Gardiner with having led the Queen Rome-
ward—to Antichrist, as he called it—Gardiner made the reply already quoted [16] that "the Queen went before him, and that it was her
own motion," to the truth of which his associates bore witness.

Another significant passage occurs in Bradford's account of his
second examination. Gardiner had asked him what he believed
concerning the Sacrament.

> "I have been now a year and almost three quarters in prison,"
> quoth Bradford, "and of all this time you never questioned with
> me hereabouts, when I might have spoken my conscience
> frankly without peril; but now you have a law to hang up and
> put to death if a man answer freely. . . . Ah, my Lord,
> Christ used not this way to bring men to faith. . . ."
>
> "Here the Chancellor was apaused, as it seemed, and spake
> most gently that he used not this means. 'It was not my doing
> although some there be,' quoth he, 'that think this to be the
> best way. I, for my part,' quoth he, 'have been challenged for
> being too gentle oftentimes.' The which thing the Bishop of
> London confirmed, and so did almost all the audience, that he
> 'had been ever too mild and too gentle.' " [17]

It is hard to see why Gardiner should have said this of himself,
or the bishops and councillors present affirmed it of him, unless it
were true, for they all, even the prisoners themselves, shared the
belief that heretics were rightly to be put to death. The question
was: Who are the heretics? John Knox, in his *Faithful Admonition* of 1554, declared that Gardiner, Tunstall, and Bonner justly deserved death "for their false doctrine and traitorous acts;" and in
his *Appellation* of 1558 he roundly asserted that "it is not only lawful
to punish to the death such as labour to subvert the true religion, but
the magistrates and people are bound so to do." [18] Even the mild
and tolerant Cranmer had, in Edward's reign, condemned Joan
Bocher to the stake for denying the humanity of Christ; and in his
scheme for the revision of the Canon Law the obstinate heretic was

in the last resort to be handed over to the secular arm. Philpot, one of the Marian martyrs, at his examination before Bonner and others, later in 1555, avowed that Joan Bocher was "a heretic indeed, well worthy to be burnt, because she stood against one of the manifest articles of our faith, contrary to the Scriptures."[19] Indeed, much of the discussion between the Chancellor and the prisoners he examined hinged on whether Scripture or the Church were to be the judge of heresy.

If there must be a judge of heresy the reformers certainly had the weaker side of the argument.

"By whom will you be judged in matters of controversy?" asked Bishop Brooks of Philpot in October 1555.

"By the word of God," said Philpot.

"What if you take the word one way and I another way; who shall be judge then?"

"The primitive Church."

"I know you mean the Doctors that wrote thereof."

"I mean verily so."

"What if you take the Doctors in one sense and I in another?"

"Then let that be taken which is most agreeable to God's word."[20]

Which brought the argument back to precisely where it started.

The case for the Church was pithily put by Gardiner in one sentence to Rogers: "Thou canst prove nothing by the Scripture; the Scripture is dead and must have a lively exposition."[21]

But Gardiner's practical statesmanship would not let him rest here. Heresy to him was evil not merely because the Church said so, but because of what he believed to be its outcome in the body politic. He declared, says Bradford,

"that the doctrine taught in King Edward's days was heresy, using for probation and demonstration thereof, no Scripture nor reason, but this, that it ended with treason and rebellion, 'so that,' quoth he, 'the very end were enough to improve that doctrine to be naught.'"[22]

This was the position which Gardiner had ever maintained, and was almost exactly that taken by Cecil, when he became Elizabeth's chief minister. No state, said Cecil, could be in safety where there was toleration of two religions, for they that differ in the service of their God can never agree in the service of their country.[23] Cecil discreetly conformed under Mary.

Another article of Gardiner's political creed was stated during the second examination of Rogers. The Bishop had again asked Rogers if he would accept mercy and arise with the whole realm from schism.

Rogers tartly replied that "the arising which he spake of was a very fall into error and false doctrine," and offered to prove the soundness of his own views by Scripture and the early Fathers. Gardiner's answer is thus recorded:

> "That should not, nor might, nor ought to be granted me, quod he, for I was but a private man and might not be heard against the determination of the whole realm. Should, when a Parliament had concluded a thing, one or any private person have authority to discuss whether that they had done right or wrong? No, that may not be." [24]

Canon Dixon calls this an "astounding thesis," but it represents the attitude normally taken in Tudor times. Gardiner himself, we recall, had said, in connection with the breach with Rome, that he felt that an act of Parliament discharged his conscience, and that of all Englishmen. In 1547 he had written to Cranmer advocating the principle that "living in a commonwealth men must conform themselves to the more part in authority," avowing his own determination to honour laws passed by Parliament even if "they be passed without my knowledge or against my mind." [25] Later in Edward's reign he had promised to set forth in his diocese whatever had been enacted by Parliament, despite his disapproval of it.

One line of defence which the prisoners delighted to take was that they had been taught to deny the power of the Bishop of Rome by the very men who were now urging them to acknowledge it. This Gardiner admitted. He, with the whole realm, had, he said, fallen into error; but

> "if they had erred through his authority when he was not so well learned and grounded, they should much more repent and recant through his authority, being now better learned through longer study and better grounded through larger experience." [26]

If, as they maintained, their examiners had been their preceptors, how, asked Gardiner, had they learned their heresies on the Sacrament? [27]

The Sacrament, at the mere mention of which the Bishop ever rose and put off his cap, was indeed the crucial point, and the one to which the examiner's questions always led; yet we have no record that he required any of the prisoners to subscribe specifically to the doctrine of transubstantiation.

> "Dost thou not believe," he asked Bradford, "that Christ's body naturally and really is there, under the form of bread and wine?"
>
> "My Lord," quoth Bradford, "I believe Christ is present

there to the faith of the due receiver. As for transubstantiation, I plainly and flatly tell you I believe it not. . . ."

"We ask no question," said Gardiner, "of transubstantiation, but of Christ's bodily presence." [28]

This they all denied.

It is one of the ironies of history that one of the chief counts against Bradford and his fellows was the denial of what a host of their successors in the Anglican Communion find no difficulty in accepting. Nay, more—if we may believe a contemporary Wesleyan, the Rev. W. G. Peck—what many a Methodist and other free Churchman feels to be the central truth of religion. "The metaphysical theory of transubstantiation," says this writer, "may depend upon categories of a philosophy no longer generally accepted; but there is nothing inherently absurd or superstitious in it;" and he goes on to point out that the sacramental faith expressed in some of Wesley's hymns

"must surely be seen to require almost a philosophical equivalent of that doctrine, if the faith is to be theologically interpreted at all. What we are concerned to deny is that there is anything irreligious or materialistic in the Roman doctrine, or anything to vex or offend the souls of those who have really entered into the great sacramental experience." [29]

As Chesterton has well said, persecution does not prove either side to be right; it proves that both sides are in desperate earnest.

It is difficult for the modern man to understand the attitude of mind which in the sixteenth century deemed persecution for religion needful. It is difficult because, on the one hand, the modern man is indifferent to most of the dogmas for which his forefathers were ready to kill or to die, and, on the other, he has long lived in a world where it has become clear that the holding of such dogmas does not seriously endanger the unity and stability of the commonwealth. Yet, as we have learned during the late war, the persecuting spirit is even now easily aroused against those whose tenets are believed to be dangerous to the State. The pacifist in the modern nation as war is as near a counterpart as our century has produced to the Protestant of the sixteenth. He is a rebel against the policy of his Government and the social judgement of his fellows; he justifies his rebellion by an appeal to the sovereignty of the individual conscience, and defends it, usually, on the ground of religious conviction. The Government, the Churches, the law-abiding, respectable citizens look on him at first as a lamentable aberration and endeavour to persuade him to recant. When he refuses, and, moreover, becomes numerous and vociferous, he is regarded as a menace to the commonwealth and rigorously repressed. He is often as cocksure, as irritating, as steadfast, as heroic as the Tudor heretic, and modern governmental, social, and religious opinion as intolerant and as zealous for the public safety as Tudor orthodoxy. We do not, indeed, burn the pacifist at the stake; but then we no longer hang thieves nor decapitate fallen premiers.

XXXIII

GOOD-NATURED PROTESTANTS

The Jesuit Parsons, in his attempt in Elizabeth's latter days to portray Gardiner as "a most tender-hearted and mild man," says that he believes that if one should ask "any good-natured Protestant that lived in Queen Mary's time," he would confess that no one in the Government was further from bloodshed and cruelty than the Chancellor.[1] Strype retorts that this Protestant would have had to be very good-natured indeed.

It happens, however, that one such Protestant—Gardiner's most distinguished contemporary in the history of English letters—has left us much the sort of testimony to which Parsons appeals. This is Roger Ascham.

Gardiner had long been his patron. When, in 1545, Ascham, then a Fellow of St. John's, Cambridge, had completed his treatise on archery, the *Toxophilus,* and desired recognition therefor at court, it was Gardiner who commended the book to the Council and helped to secure him access to the King.

> "No time since I was born," wrote Ascham to Gardiner in 1554, "so sticketh in my memory as that when I, unfriended and unknown, came first to your Lordship with my Book of Shooting, and what, since that time, you have done for me, both with King Henry, King Edward, and Queen Mary, I never shall forget, nor hitherto have hidden either in England or abroad."

Gardiner's favour to Ascham in Mary's reign took the substantial form of an appointment as Latin Secretary to the Queen, and an increase from ten to twenty pounds of a yearly pension first granted by Henry VIII in recognition of Ascham's writing. Ascham, in 1567, described to Queen Elizabeth the way in which he had secured the increase: Since the grant had become void at the death of Edward VI, Ascham was told by Gardiner to have a new copy of it made. This he did, instructing the writer to leave out the sum. When Gardiner asked why the sum was omitted, Ascham replied that it was the fault of the writer who had done ill "to leave the vacant place so great, for the old word ten will not fill up half the room," adding that unless Gardiner inserted the word "twenty," which would fill both the place and his purse, he would be put to new charges to have the patent rewritten; at which he says:

"the Bishop fell in a laughter, and forthwith went to Queen Mary and told her what I had said, who . . . made my patent twenty pounds by year during my life."

The Bishop, moreover, shielded him from an inquiry into his religious opinions. Over a decade later, Ascham wrote to the Earl of Leicester that although Gardiner, Heath, and Pole

"knew perfectly that in religion, by open writing and privy talk, I was contrary unto them, yet that where Sir Francis Englefield by name did note me specially at the Council Board, Gardiner would not suffer me to be called thither, nor touched elsewhere."

"Winchester's good will," he adds, "stood not in speaking fair and wishing well, but he did indeed that for me whereby my wife and children shall live the better when I am gone."

To his friend Johan Sturm, the Strasburg humanist, he wrote, in September 1555:

"There have not been wanting some who have endeavoured to hinder the flow of his [Gardiner's] benevolence towards me on account of my religion, but they have not succeeded. I owe much therefore to the kindness of Winchester, and I willingly owe it. Not only I but many others have experienced his goodness." [2]

One of these others was Sir Thomas Smith, who has come into our narrative as the courteous opponent of Gardiner on the question of Greek at Cambridge, and the friendly envoy to him from Somerset's Council. At Mary's accession he retired from public activity and, according to his biographer Strype, "his life was saved, though he were a Protestant, and had £100 per annum allowed him for his subsistence." His safety, says Strype,

"was in a great measure owing to that deference that that stern and cruel Bishop Gardiner . . . had to his exemplary virtue and learning. . . .

This must be remembered to this Bishop's commendation, among the many evil things that asperse and blacken his name to this day. Nor must a like favour, or a greater, be forgotten, by him shown to such another learned and grave Protestant, friend and contemporary with Smith, I mean Roger Ascham. . . .

Thus lived two excellent Protestants, under the wings, as it were, of the sworn enemy and the destroyer of Protestants." [3]

The "excellent Protestantism" of Smith and Ascham in Mary's reign is, however, open to question. Both men doubtless remained

Protestants at heart, and were probably known by Gardiner to be such, but there is every indication that in outward observances they conformed,⁴ as did Cecil, to the religion established. This does not, however, detract from the credit due to Gardiner for shielding them from inquisition into their private views.

Another formerly Protestant man of letters whom Gardiner assisted, was Nicholas Udal, reporter of his St. Peter's Day sermon, who became, as we learn from the Bishop's will, his "schoolmaster." ⁵

Nor is it out of place here to record the testimony of Sir John Harington, whose father Gardiner imprisoned for complicity in Wyatt's rebellion:

> "My father, only for carrying a letter to the Lady Elizabeth and professing to wish her well, he [Gardiner] kept in the Tower twelve months and made him spend a thousand pounds ere he could be free of that trouble. My mother, that then served the said Lady Elizabeth, he caused to be sequestered from her as an heretic. . . . So as I may say, in some sort, this Bishop persecuted me before I was born.
>
> Yet that I speak not all in a passion, I must confess I have heard some as partially [i.e. favourably] praise his clemency and good conscience, and, namely, that he was cause of restoring many honourable houses, overthrown by King Henry VIII, and in King Edward's minority. The Duke of Norfolk . . . and those descended of him were beholding to him, with the house of Stanhope and the Lord Arundell of Warder; and I have heard old Sir Matthew Arundell say that Bonner was more faulty than he, and that Gardiner would rate at him for it, and call him ass for using poor men so bloodily; and when I would maintain the contrary, he would say that my father was worthy to have lain in prison a year longer for the saucy sonnet he wrote to him out of the Tower."

The truth of old Sir Matthew's observation on Harington, Senior, is attested by such lines from the "saucy sonnet" as these:

> "And better were that all your kind
> Like hounds in hell with shame were shrined." ⁶

Still another Protestant, Edward Underhill, known as "the hot gospeller," and reported to Gardiner as an arch heretic, was, as a member of the Gentlemen Pensioners, permitted by him to attend the Queen's wedding. That he had fought for the Queen against Wyatt seems to have been sufficient extenuation, in the Bishop's eyes, for his heresy.⁷

In the seventeenth century, Thomas Fuller, the historian, after venturing the opinion that Gardiner "had an head if not an hand in the death of every prominent Protestant," adds this paragraph, not without humour:

"However (as bloody as he was), for mine own part I have particular gratitude to pay to the memory of this Stephen Gardiner, and here I solemnly tender the same. It is on the account of Mrs. Clarke, my great-grandmother by my mother's side, whose husband rented Farnham Castle, a place whither Bishop Gardiner retired, in Surrey, as belonging to his see. This bishop, sensible of the consumptionous state of his body, and finding physic out of the kitchen more beneficial for him than that out of the apothecary's shop, and special comfort from the cordials she provided him, did not only himself connive at her 'heresy' as he termed it, but also protected her during his life from the fury of others. Some will say this his courtesy to her was founded on his kindness to himself, but, however, I am so far from detaining thanks from any deserving on just cause, that I am ready to pay them where they are but pretended due on any colour." [8]

Rogers, the first to suffer of the five condemned by Gardiner, was burned February 4, 1555. Saunders, Hooper, and Taylor followed in quick succession. Then there was a lull. The effect on the people was the reverse of what had been expected. The unflinching courage of the martyrs stirred the admiration of all who saw them die. There were ugly murmurings, robbings of London churches of the tabernacles of the Sacrament, acts of contempt such as the twice repeated mutilation of the new statue of Becket over the door of the Mercers' Chapel in Cheapside, and, more serious still, threats of rising in Norfolk and conspiracy in Cambridgeshire. On March 19 Michiele wrote that the Government was not displaying becoming rigour, in the hope that leniency and time would mitigate the fury of the people, but from Renard's letters it would seem that renewed dissensions in the Council accounted, in part at least, for the Government's inaction.

Before the end of March, however, the Council was proceeding vigorously with the arrest and examination of the Cambridgeshire conspirators and preparing for further execution of already condemned heretics. During the last days of March there were eight burnings. Only the presence of the Earl of Oxford and Lord Riche, with armed retainers, prevented a riot at those in Essex. [9]

On Easter, April 14, a priest at St. Margaret's, Westminster, in the act of communicating the people, was struck on the head with a wood knife so that his blood ran down on the consecrated wafers. The offender was condemned as a heretic, and the Council decreed that since his offence "was so enorme and heinous," his right hand, "for the more terrible example," should be stricken off before his

execution. He was burned April 24.[10] Two days later a citizen
of London, hanged for robbery at Charing Cross, harangued the
crowd before his execution on the evils of Popery, and bade them
say *Amen* to the petition from the Henrician Litany, "From the
tyranny of the Bishop of Rome and all his detestable enormities,
Good Lord deliver us"—to which some three hundred responded
heartily. The Council wrote to Bonner that it was "not convenient
that such a matter should be overpassed without some example to the
world." Whereupon the thief was exhumed, condemned, and burned
as a heretic.[11]

As a leading member of the Council, Gardiner certainly concurred
in, if he did not originate these measures. Meanwhile, on March
24, as Chancellor of Cambridge, he had instructed the vice-chancellor
that hereafter none were to vote at elections or upon graces or be
admitted to degrees who had not

> "openly in the congregation house detested particularly and by
> articles the heresies lately spread in this realm, and professed
> by articles the Catholic doctrine now received, and subscribed
> the same with their hands."[12]

The international situation, however, appears to have taken most
of the Chancellor's attention during the spring of 1555. By the
treaty of Passau, 1552, hostilities between Charles and the German
Protestants had practically come to an end, and all their differences
seemed in a fair way of settlement at the Diet meeting at Augsburg in 1555. At neither Passau or Augsburg was France—ally of
the Protestants—included. Now that England had become so closely
connected with the Empire, it was to her interest to work for peace
on the Continent. If the dominions of Philip and his father were
at peace, Mary's position in England would be strengthened; if war
continued, Mary might be drawn into it. Accordingly it was proposed that representatives of France and the Empire meet on neutral ground and, through English mediation, come to terms. The
plan seems to have originated in a correspondence between Montmorency, Constable of France, and Gardiner.[13]

Gardiner, Arundel, and Paget were to act as mediators. Pole as
representative of the Papacy, was to preside. The spot chosen for
the negotiations was a plain near Marck, a village in the Calais pale
equally distant from the French and Imperial borders. Here, at the
cost of England, a wooden conference hall was erected, with four
smaller buildings—one for the Cardinal, and one each for the French,
Imperial, and English delegations. Gardiner left London May 13.
His retinue and that of his colleagues made such a fine show that
Michiele said that many persons would "wish themselves present at
so noble and renowned a congress."[14]

The conference opened Ascension Day, May 23, with great ceremony, "the English omitting nothing that became their grandeur,"
but despite the "fruitful exhortations" of Pole and the diplomacy
of Gardiner the gathering broke up June 7, having accomplished
nothing. Gardiner made every effort to hold it together, but neither
side was willing to concede anything of importance. There is some
reason to believe that Paget, no longer in Mary's favour, played
for the approval of Charles and Philip by siding with the Imperialists
against Gardiner's moderate proposals for compromise.[15] Gardiner,
however, hoped that a way had been opened for further negotiation
in the near future.[16]

During even this brief absence from London the Chancellor was
not free from the problem of religious dissent. He found Calais a
haven for heretics, and quarreled with the Deputy, Lord Wentworth,
about it;[17] and at Canterbury, on his homeward journey, hearing
that a layman, Nicholas Sheterden, was under examination for erroneous opinions, sent for him and endeavoured to persuade him to
recant. Sheterden said he had been imprisoned before the re-enactment of the heresy laws and therefore refused to answer to anything
thing but the charge on which he was arrested, which was not, he
said, forthcoming. Gardiner suggested that he first clear himself
of suspicion of heresy and then get a writ of false imprisonment.
Sheterden replied that his doctrine had been "openly taught and
received by authority of the realm." No, said the Bishop, it had
never been received that one might speak against the Sacrament.

"Against some opinion of the Sacrament," replied Sheterden, "it
was openly taught."

"By no law," said Gardiner, adding that "it was notable to consider that God preserved that, so that no law could pass against it."

"He made many words, but very gently, of the Sacrament . . ."
wrote Sheterden, "but I let him alone and said nothing."[18]

On his arrival at Hampton Court, June 16,[19] the Chancellor once
again found threat of insurrection to be dealt with. During his
absence the Queen had decided to push the persecution with increased vigour. On May 24 she and Philip had admonished Bonner
to proceed zealously against the heretics.[20] On May 30 Cardmaker
and another had gone to the stake, and seven more suffered before
the middle of June. There was local tumult and conspiracy in Kent,
Cornwall, Sussex, Essex, and Suffolk, which gave the Council, and
especially the Chancellor, much to do during the coming weeks. It
was found that some of this disturbance was due to the wet summer
and the high price of wheat.[21]

Bradford, after innumerable attempts had been made to win him to
conformity, was burned July 1; eleven more suffered during the

month, eighteen in August, eleven in September, and eight in October, which, with Philpot in December, make up the tale of seventy-four victims during the first year of the persecution.[22]

It is difficult to appraise Gardiner's responsibility for all this. That none of these burnings occurred in the diocese of Winchester [23] may prove no more than the orthodoxy of that diocese. As late as 1564 it was reported that almost all who bore authority in Winchester city were "addict to the old superstition and earnest fautors thereof." [24] Gardiner believed that a heretic deserved death, not only for his heresy but also for the disruption it effected in the commonwealth. Moreover, he had sponsored the revival of the heresy laws, had begun the examinations under them, and, as a leading member of the Council, must surely have given formal consent to many of the orders given by that body to proceed with the burning of men condemned by Bonner and other bishops. What evidence we have tends to show that he believed that the revival of the heresy laws and the prompt and vigorous application of them to a few of the leading reformers would frighten the rest into conformity; and that when this hope proved vain he gave his consent to subsequent burnings with reluctance.

His position was a difficult one. From both principle and interest he was bound to further the Queen's projects. And the Queen sincerely believed she was doing God service in burning heretics. Moreover, he agreed with her that heretics ought to die; but he disliked the rôle of persecutor, and he differed with her as to the political wisdom of continued execution. The burning of Protestant leaders, for the most part of irreproachable life and unexcelled courage, had failed of its purpose; it served only to arouse the sympathy of the people. Yet it was the Chancellor's duty to carry out the royal policy.

"A new order," he had written to Somerset in 1547, "engendereth a new cause of punishment against them that offend; and punishments be not pleasant to them that have the execution, and yet they must be; for nothing may be contemned." [25]

To Cranmer, in the same year, he had described the method he had hitherto used with heretical preachers:

"If I had ever charged any man with anything by him uttered contrary to the true doctrine, and then he would deny it and forswear it, as I have known them accustomed to do, I would never use pains ne further trouble him. But such a cruel mind have I had, I would go to the place of public audience myself and show them how the man had been sore defamed to me, and then show how he denied such matter stoutly and stiffly, and so dismiss him." [26]

The difficulty, from Gardiner's point of view, with the Marian martyrs was that so few of them were willing to forswear or even to remain silent about their convictions. His relation to such "good-natured Protestants" as Ascham and Smith indicates that as long as they were good-natured enough to conform outwardly and to refrain from propagating their doctrines, he not only had no desire to molest them but was ready to shield them from inquisition into their beliefs. That he was not the driving force behind the persecution is obvious from the fact that over twice as many burnings occurred after his death as before, and that his old enemy Bucer, who had been called to the chair of divinity at Cambridge in Edward's reign and had died there, remained quietly in his grave until Cardinal Pole had him dug up, condemned, and burned in 1557.

How far the policy of the Government toward the three most notable martyrs, Cranmer, Latimer, and Ridley, may be attributed to Gardiner it is impossible to say. Ridley, because of a vehement sermon against Mary, had been sent to the Tower before Gardiner was released from it, but when Latimer and Cranmer first appeared before the Council, Gardiner was present and undoubtedly concurred in their imprisonment. Latimer, however, had been given, as we recall, what amounted to an official warning to flee rather than appear, and Cranmer, despite his connection with Northumberland's conspiracy, had been left at liberty till his manifesto on the Mass forced the Government to deal with him. It may have been at Gardiner's suggestion that the three bishops were sent to dispute at Oxford; certainly he was present in Council when it was decided to send them thither.[27] We do not know what influence he exercised on the selection of the representatives of Convocation and of the universities to dispute with them, nor is there evidence that he interfered with the course of the disputation. He had no voice in the condemnation of any of the three. The deaths of Latimer and Ridley occurred almost a month after he had ceased, because of illness, to attend the Council, and Cranmer was not brought to the stake till he had been four months in his grave.

That he took delight in persecution is farthest from the evidence. He appears to have been speaking in all sincerity when he said to George Joye: "Howsoever ye diffame me of cruelty I know it [*i.e.* cruelty] is not my fault, and yet I am a sinner and have many other faults."[28]

The fact that no burnings occurred in his diocese may, as we have remarked, prove only that no heresy flourished there; yet when we ask the question why a diocese, contiguous to London, remained so free from the new teachings, part at least of the answer may be the "vigilant and diligent eye" of the Bishop. That he had accomplished this without undue severity in one diocese, and that as exposed as any to influences from the Continent, gives rise to the speculation as to what might have happened throughout the realm had his policies been earlier and more thoroughly followed.

XXXIV

"THE FALL OF SENNACHERIB"

On August 26, 1555 Philip rode through London, on his journey to the Low Countries for a conference with his father. It was perhaps at this time that Thomas Mowntayne, whose none too flattering description of the Chancellor on another occasion we have read, stood in Cheapside and watched the royal procession pass. The Chancellor, he says,

> "rid on the one side before King Philip, and the great seal afore him; and on the other side there rid the Queen, and the Cardinal afore her with a cross carried afore him, he being all in scarlet and blessing the people as he rid through the city, for the which he was greatly laughed to scorn; and Gardiner being sore offended on the other side because the people did not put off their caps and make curtsy to the cross that was carried afore the Cardinal, saying to his servants, 'Mark that house;' 'Take this knave and have him to the Counter;' 'Such a sort of heretics who ever saw, that will neither reverence the cross of Christ nor yet once say so much as, God save the King and Queen! I will teach them to do both and I live.' This did I hear him say, I standing at Sopar Lane end." [1]

Before departing, Philip, following the advice of the Emperor, committed the administration of the realm to an inner Council, composed of Pole, "whenever he would or conveniently could attend," Gardiner, Paulet, Arundel, Pembroke, Thirlby, Paget, Rochester, and Petre.[2] Nothing of importance was to be done without reference to the Cardinal, but as he took little part in the civil administration, that remained primarily under Gardiner's direction. This, indeed, appears to have been Philip's intention, for on October 15, on hearing that Gardiner was ill, he wrote to him, expressing his deepest concern, "because," he said, "on thy health, the health of that Kingdom seemeth in great part to depend." He urged the Bishop to take care of himself, yet, as far as possible to continue, with his "invariable prudence," to "preside over all affairs." [3] The chief of these at the moment, were the finances;[4] but Gardiner was not long permitted to give his attention to them.

As early as September 16, Michiele wrote that the Chancellor, after his return from Calais, fell into such a state of "oppilation" that, besides having become jaundiced, he by degrees got confirmed dropsy. Had it not been for his robust constitution, said the Venetian, he would have been in a bad way, "his physiognomy being so changed as to astound all who see him." Nothing prescribed by the physicians had benefited him, but if the remedy recently sent by the Emperor were efficacious, it would be "very advantageous for England, he being considered one of the most consummate chancellors who have filled the post for many years." [5]

Despite the increasing seriousness of his illness, Gardiner continued to attend the meetings of the Council,[6] then with the court at Greenwich, until his physicians, early in October, forbade him to leave his house. He then retired to Southwark, whither, sometime in the first week of October, Pole and the whole Council made a special trip to consult him, presumably on matters connected with the coming Parliament.[7]

The day after this consultation, Noailles, the French ambassador, conferred with him for two hours and wrote thereafter to Montmorency that although the Bishop was suffering so from jaundice and dropsy that he could not live till Christmas, he had never been so calm, gracious, and attentive as on this occasion. He insisted, when Noailles departed, on escorting him out, according to his usual custom. When the ambassador protested, he prayed him to permit it, that he might show himself to the people who, he said, thought him dead. So, leaning on Noailles' arm, he traversed three salons filled with onlookers.[8]

On October 14 Michiele reported that the Chancellor was losing ground daily, being then hardly able to go up and down stairs. He rallied, however, at the beginning of Parliament, October 21, mounted his mule, rode to Westminster, although he had to be held in the saddle by four of his servants, and made the opening speech.[9] The sheer determination shown in thus overcoming his malady stirred the amazement and admiration of his hearers.

During the opening days of Parliament he literally lived on his nerve. Not only was his body broken with disease, but the political situation was such as might well have driven a less resolute spirit to despair. In the Commons sat many an influential opponent of the Government; in the country were failing crops, high prices, growing distrust of the Spaniard, increasing sympathy for the martyrs. The conservative cause was put in jeopardy by its best friends, notably the Queen herself, who roused dissent by her restoration of Church lands, by her willingness to crown her Spanish consort, by her eagerness for the persecution. Above all, the supreme disappointment of the reign had come in the recent assurance that her hope of issue was utterly vain. This was more than a blow to Mary's maternal desires; it shook the foundations of the Government, for it laid open once again the old vexed question of the succession, with the likelihood that Elizabeth, who, despite her outward conformity, was known to be at heart an adherent of the new learning, would, in some not distant day, topple over the whole fabric which the Chancellor had so laboriously been building.

Though his body was at death's door, his mind was vigorous and alert, his will unshaken, His programme, as appears from the letters of the Venetian ambassador, was clear and definite—assurances from the Government that the crown would not be given to the Spaniard, and that no one's title to Church lands would be questioned; in return, a demand for financial support and for the exclusion of Elizabeth from the throne. As for the crowning of Philip and the restoration of Church lands, Parliament indeed needed reassurance. Both Philip and Charles deemed such coronation essential, and had brought every pressure to bear on Mary to secure it; she herself was all too ready to place the crown on Philip's head, but the nation, as she well knew, would have none of it. Many of the Church lands held by the crown she had voluntarily returned, and obviously thought it the duty of every Christian to follow her example. Moreover, the new Pope, Paul IV, had recently issued a bull condemning the alienation of ecclesiastical property.

The Chancellor, in his opening speech, treated of the finances, enumerating at length the expenses of the crown and appealing for the necessary grants. He was careful to point out that Philip while in England had spent, of his own money, more than the Queen; that her Majesty's debts were largely inherited from Henry and Edward; that she had generously refused the subsidy granted by the last of her brother's Parliaments; and that she had not confiscated the estates of rebels, but shown clemency by returning to them their lands with their lives. Moreover, writes Michiele, he

"gave it publicly to be understood that they must not be disturbed by false reports, as nothing would be said about the King's authority or of his Majesty personally, thus alluding to the coronation without specifying it distinctly." [10]

Two days later, October 23, he again appeared in Parliament, and, in the Queen's name, replied to the address from the Speaker of the House of Commons. Then after a letter from Philip, lamenting his inability to be present, was read, the Chancellor enlarged upon it in behalf of the Queen, and went on to speak

"at great length to remove any doubt or suspicion of its being intended to make any motion about Church revenues or property, certain persons having disseminated a malicious report to the effect that her Majesty insisted on everybody surrendering them as she herself had done, saying that this had never been thought of, and assuring the House that no one would ever receive injury or molestation on this account; and he ordered the reading of the bull made by the most illustrious Legate about the cession of the said revenues, and the confirmation of the bull, lately received from Rome." [11]

In all this the Chancellor, who a fortnight before had been thought dead by the people, manifested a vigour of will and spirit which completely triumphed over his bodily weakness. His energy, said Michiele, was unexpected.[12] He seemed, wrote Pole to Philip,

"not only to surpass himself in ability, eloquence, discretion, and piety, in which he is wont to excell all men, but to surpass his own physical strength, for whilst serving his sovereigns and his country by word of mouth, he so subdued his malady as to show no sign of corporal infirmity." [13]

"My Lord Chancellor," wrote Basset to Courtenay, "never did better in his life than he did these two days at the Parliament." [14]

The effort left him exhausted. He was lodged in the royal palace, Whitehall, to be near Parliament, but he never appeared in Parliament again. Basset, however, writing October 27, said the physicians were in "marvellous good hope of his recovery," and went on to tell how the Queen used him "with exceeding great gentleness." "It is impossible to show more gentleness, kindness, care, and love than her Majesty hath showed divers ways unto him." [15] Pole, writing to Cardinal Caraffa about the opening of the national synod into which Convocation was merged November 4, said that one reason why it was held at Whitehall was that Gardiner who was lodged there might attend it,[16] but it does not seem likely that he did.

It must have soon become clear to him that the end was not distant, for on November 8 he made his will.[17] It begins with the same formula as does his father's, written half a century before:

"In the name of God, Amen.

I Steven, Bishop of Winchester, of perfect memory, make and ordain my last will and testament in manner and form following:

First, I commit my soul to the infinite mercy of Almighty God, and recommend my wretched estate unto the great mercy of our Saviour, Jesus Christ, by mediation of whose blood and passion I trust to be saved, and by the intercession of all the company of heaven. . . .

Secondly, I will my wretched body to be conveyed to the earth from whence it came with such convenient ceremonies as to mine executors shall be thought meet.

Thirdly, partly to recognize the great benefits and special favour that I have received of my most gracious and Sovereign Lady, the Queen's most excellent Majesty, which I can in no part recompense if I should live many lives, I have and do for witness thereof leave unto her a cup of gold with a sapphire in the top, as worthy to have precious stones and gold as ever was a princess.

Item, I bequeath to my Lord Legate's Grace a ring with a diamond, not so big as he is worthy to have, but such as his poor orator is able to give.

Item, I will £200 to be bestowed upon liveries at mine interment.

Item, I bequeath to Trinity Hall in Cambridge £100."

Then follows the bequest of his "chapel stuff," vestments, and hangings to his cathedral church and his successors, and the specification of moneys, in addition to the £200 for liveries, to be spent in connection with his burial—£500 for his interment, £400 "for the erection of a chantry that I may be prayed for," and £300 for a tomb. £40 is "to be bestowed upon rings to give to my especial good lords and friends to remember me withal, at the discretion of mine executors;" £40 "to my godson Cheston of Bury;"[18] "my spoon of gold" to one Mistress Longe; "all my humanity and law books" to Thomas Worliche; "to Christopher Newman, because he hath done me so long service and spent his time with me, I bequeath him a hundred marks."

There are some seventy persons named in the will, most of them evidently members of the Bishop's household, to whom are left small bequests, varying in amount from 40s. to 100 marks (£66 13s. 4d.). Among them are the names of such faithful servitors as Master Jacques Wingfield, who bombarded Somerset with petitions for the Bishop's release from prison; Robert Massie, who rode across Europe with his dispatches from Rome in the days of Wolsey; William Coppinger, Thomas Growte, and John Davy, who lived in the Tower as yeomen of his chamber. These and others who had been in his employ for a score of years and more are pleasant reminders of an age when men spent a lifetime in the service of one master. Lest any be passed over, he bequeathed "to every of my yeomen and grooms whom I have not otherwise specially remembered 20s." Among the seventy particular bequests perhaps the most worthy of remark is that "to Master Nicholas Udal, my schoolmaster, forty marks."

Eight executors are named, among whom we are doubtless justified in recognizing some of the Bishop's best friends. There is Sir Anthony Browne, recently created Viscount Montague, son to that Sir Anthony who, at the bedside of Henry VIII, dared suggest that Gardiner's name had been mistakenly omitted from the royal testament; there is Bishop Thirlby, Gardiner's old college mate; John White, successively scholar, master, and Warden of Winchester

College, now Bishop of Lincoln; Rochester and Englefield, the Chancellor's colleagues and supporters in Council; James Basset, son of Lady Lisle, now Chamberlain to the Queen; Master Harding, the Bishop's Chaplain, and Master Thomas Thwaites, his comptroller.[19] Each of the executors was to have £20.

The money bequests in the will amount to almost £2,400, in a time when money had perhaps ten times its present purchasing power. £700 of this was to go for chantry and tomb, £700 for the funeral. These seemingly excessive funeral expenses were typical of the sixteenth century.[20]

On November 9, the day after making the will, the Bishop wrote a codicil providing that if anything remained after the payment of his debts and bequests, his executors should devote it either to the relief of his poorest servants, or to an almshouse, or to building a religious house, or some other godly purpose as they saw fit. Michiele tells us that shortly before his death Gardiner had given 4,000 ducats ready money to the see of Winchester.[21]

Two days after the completion of the will it was known that he was *in extremis.*

> "The Lord Chancellor," wrote Michiele, November 11, "is now in such a state that his life can last but for hours. The loss is most important at the present moment, it being freely admitted that for the service of a sovereign, whether as Chancellor or for the performance of any other office, no better or more sufficient minister could be desired, as neither here nor elsewhere could his like have been found." [22]

At the same time Pole wrote to Cardinal Morone that in Gardiner's approaching death there would be lost, to the exceeding sorrow of the Queen and all good men, a truly powerful instrument for the safety and welfare of the realm.[23]

Between eleven o'clock and midnight, Tuesday, November 12, 1555, death came. The Bishop died where he had been lodged near Parliament, at Whitehall, the palace of his old master Wolsey, "in the gallery there on the right hand the gate going into the court." [24]

Foxe tells us that he heard from one who was present, that during Gardiner's last illness Bishop Day came to him and began to comfort him with words of Scripture concerning free justification.

> "What, my Lord," exclaimed Gardiner, "will you open that gap now? . . . To me and such others in my case you may speak it; but open this window to the people, then farewell altogether!" [25]

Another story, told by Thomas Stapleton, would seem to indicate that, up to the time of his death, Gardiner had had no profound regrets for his part in the breach with Rome. The Bishop, says Stapleton,

> "lying in his deathbed, caused the passion of Christ to be readen unto him, and when he heard it readen that Peter, after the denying of his master, went out and wept bitterly, he, causing the reader to stay, wept himself full bitterly, and said *Ego exivi, sed non dum flevi amare:* I have gone out, but as yet, I have not wept bitterly." [26]

Ponet, who was on the Continent at the time, heard—or at any rate wrote—that Gardiner, when he came to die,

> "did not lament his sins but sent for the Queen and wept to her that he could no longer live to serve her Grace, . . . but he desired her to proceed as he had counselled her by his word and writing." [27]

What Ponet regarded as sins in Gardiner worthy repentance, were looked on by Stapleton as virtues.

Michiele, in London, wrote that the Chancellor "made a very Christian and a Catholic end." [28] The faithful Basset had watched with him day and night. [29] Courtenay, then on the Continent, but in correspondence with Basset and other friends of Gardiner, heard that he died reconciled to Paget. [30]

By three of the clock on the morning of November 13 his body had been brought by water to his house in Southwark, by five his bowels had been buried before the high altar of St. Mary Overies. [31] Then, after the vestments "which he was vested withal when he was first consecrate bishop" were put upon him, he was "chested and wrapped in lead, wherein was cast epitaphs graven on copper, . . . and so set in his chapel with lights about him burning day and night, and continual service till his remove." The knell rang all that day and the next, in the afternoon of which (November 14) there was dirge in every parish in London. Bonner sang it at St. Mary Overies, where, next morning, he celebrated Mass of requiem. Bishop White preached the sermon "which lasted an hour and a half," the whole Parliament, or as Machyn puts it, "all bishops and lords and knights and gentlemen" attending. Then followed dinner at Winchester House "where was great fare, and after dinner a great dole both of meat and money given to the poor." [32]

The body was to be interred in the cathedral at Winchester, but owing, says Wriothesley, to "the great waters that have fallen this winter it could not conveniently be carried." Hence on the afternoon of November 21, when the knell rang again, executors and mourners "with great company of priests and clerks and all the bishops," brought the body to St. Mary Overies for solemn dirge.

> "My Lord of London did execute the office and wear his

mitre; and there were two goodly white branches burning, and the hearse with arms and tapers burning, and four dozen of staffs [torches]; and all the choir with black, and his arms; and afore the corpse the king of heralds with his coat, and with five banners—[one] of his arms, and four of images wrought with fine gold and in oil." [33]

The next morning Bonner again celebrated requiem Mass; White preached the sermon; and, at the service of burial, the body was placed "on the left hand the high altar," in a vault of brick "covered with the pall of black velvet with a cross of white satin, two candlesticks with tapers set thereon, and the crucifix between."

The morrow after, the executors brake up the Bishop's household, "and paid both gentlemen and yeomen their year's wages; that is to say, to every gentleman twenty nobles and to every yeoman four marks." [34]

The Chancellor's death was an irreparable loss to the Government, an occasion of exultation to its adversaries. "I cannot but joy with you, my heartily beloved in Christ, of the fall of Sennacherib," wrote Philpot, the troublesome Archdeacon of Winchester, from his London prison to Lady Vane, November 19. He was not, however, able to share the Lady's hope of better days, "for although the cockatrice be dead, yet his pestilent chickens, with the whore of Babylon, still live." [35]

Parliamentary opposition to Government measures increased immediately. On November 18 Michiele wrote that the Queen found "the loss of the Chancellor more and more serious and important daily." The licentiousness of the Commons, he said.

"grows every day worse, especially as the death of the Chancellor, who had been feared and respected in an extraordinary degree by everybody, induces them, so to say, to feel secure. For it seems to them as though there remains no longer any one who knows how to exercise authority in such a way as he did, nor with knowledge so extensive and minute, both of the business and of all the persons of any account in this kingdom, and also of the time and means by which to please and flatter, or to overawe and punish them, and thereby to keep them always in hand, and to suppress the insolence towards which they are naturally inclined." [36]

Pole, at about the same time, wrote to Philip that since Gardiner's death, England had experienced "the increasing audacity of all reprobates." [37] Indeed, the day before his death, the Cardinal had written to the King that he felt that religion and justice were expiring with the Bishop of Winchester, and added that from the time his malady commenced both the one and the other had sadly degenerated. He could wish, he said, the new Chancellor somewhat less harsh and stern but no less firm and ardent.[38]

Paget coveted the vacant office, but it was finally given to Heath, Archbishop of York. Pole succeeded as Chancellor of Cambridge, Dr. Mowse as Master of Trinity. The see of Winchester, after a vacancy of over half a year, went to Gardiner's old friend and executor, John White, Bishop of Lincoln, while Lincoln was given to his former chaplain, Thomas Watson.

On Sunday the 23rd of February, 1556, there was solemn dirge for the late Chancellor at St. Mary Overies, and the next morning, after Mass of requiem and sermon by Bishop White, began the journey to Winchester. Five horses "trapped with black cloth garnished with scutcheons" drew the chariot in which the corpse rested. Upon the white and sable pall which covered the coffin lay a "picture" or effigy of the Bishop, in mitre and cope of gold, hands gloved, crozier staff in the left, and on the middle finger of the right "a ring of gold wherein was a sapphire." In front of the chariot was borne the banner of the Bishop's arms and at the four corners the banners of St. Stephen, St. George, Our Lady, and the Trinity. Fifty gentlemen, two and two on horseback, chaplains, executors, heralds in their coat armour—Rouge Croix pursuivant and Garter Principal King-at-Arms—went before; on either side four and twenty black-coated yeomen riding, with torches burning all the way; Sir Anthony Browne, Viscount Montague, chief mourner, following the corpse; then other mourners, and at the end the servants of the Bishop's house. In all "above two hundred horse of gentlemen and yeomen all in black." [39]

Through twenty-nine parishes they passed, and in every parish curate and clerks "stood in the way in their best ornaments . . . bidding their orisons . . . and devoutly censed the corpse as it proceeded." The first night's halt was made at Kingston, the second at Farnham, at Arlsford the third; and at every lodging there was dirge and Mass.

The fourth day brought them to Winchester,

> "and at the town's end the Mayor and all his brethren stood on the one side and the priests and clerks on the other side, which proceeded in their order through the town of Winchester with seven crosses of sundry parish churches that went before till they came before the west door of St. Swithen's, where the chariot rested. . . . Then came the Bishop [White] of Lincoln *in pontificalibus* and censed the corpse and cast holy water."

Entering they found "the high altar hung with black, and around about the chancel from the steps upward garnished with scutcheons." Rouge Croix pursuivant "bad the bedes:"

"Of your charity pray for the soul of the Right Reverend Father in God, Stephen Gardiner, late Bishop of Winchester, Lord Chancellor of England, Prelate of the most noble Order of the Garter, and late Counsellor of the King and Queen's most excellent Majesty."

Dirge was sung by Bishop White; then all departed for the night, and next morning, Februray 28, after Lauds and the customary early Masses, the company returned to the cathedral at nine o'clock. Bishop White again preached the sermon, and thereafter sang Mass of requiem, "for that it was the custom there the sermon to be preached before the Mass of requiem begin."

"Then was taken up the body by eight tall yeomen assisted with gentlemen at every corner, and brought up on the left hand the high altar and there set above the ground between two walls made of brick a yard of height. The Bishop of Lincoln *in pontificalibus* with his assistants standing at the head, and about the same the gentlemen holding the banners of saints, proceeded in the service of the burial; the officers of the household, the two gentlemen ushers, and the two porters standing by, with their staves and rods in their hands. And when the mold was cast upon the coffin by the prelate executing, at the words *pulverem pulveri et sinerem sineri,* they brake their staves and rods on their heads and cast them into the place where the body lay, which was all done with exceeding sorrow and heaviness, not only of them but of many other standers by. Then after *de profundis* said, was laid over a board covered with a rich pall, so that there was no ground broke for him, but lay there in manner as he did at St. Mary Overies till such time as a chapel should be made for him as was appointed by his executors. After which ceremonies was done, every man avoided the church and went to Wolvesey to dinner where was great cheer."

"Thus," concludes the nameless recorder of these events, "ended the funeral of the holy Bishop, on whose soul God have mercy. Amen." [40]

At what date the chapel, or chantry, provided for by the Bishop in his will, and erected by his executors, was completed, is not certain; possibly within the year 1556. Nor do we have record of the ceremonies with which he was laid therein.

The head of his recumbent stone figure, in the long niche in the chantry's outer side, has been hacked from the body by zealots of a later day, but his bones rest undisturbed,[41] near those of a notable company—Richard Foxe, William Waynfleet, Henry Beaufort, and William of Wykeham.

XXXV

WHAT MANNER OF MAN?

The portrait of Gardiner at Trinity Hall[1] shows him in his bishop's rochet, almuce, and square cap, with face shaven, direct piercing eyes, well-formed lips, straight, strong nose and chin—the face of a thoughtful, determined man, not unkindly, nor without some slightest twinkle of humour lurking in corners of the eyes and mouth. It might have been, says Canon Dixon, "the face of a courtier or of an ascetic; perchance of an inquisitor; of a martyr perhaps."[2]

It was certainly the face of a lawyer. We have seen how from early youth to manhood the law had been his principal study, how he achieved note at Cambridge as a teacher of it, how his rise in the royal favour resulted from his thorough knowledge of the law touching Henry's first divorce, and his skilful advocacy of the case at Rome and in England. There was no question among his contemporaries that he was the foremost civilian and canonist in the land. His learning, his memory, his eloquence, his power of subtle and incisive argument were acknowledged by all. He is, said a member of the reforming party, "the wittiest, the boldest, and the best learned in his faculty that is in England, and a great rhetorician."[3]

Much as this specialization had to do in determining the temper of his thinking, he was no mere specialist. The humanities claimed his attention in only a degree less than did the law. He spoke French and Latin with the fluency of his mother tongue; he translated a part of the New Testament from the original Greek; he composed in Latin a learned discourse on Greek pronunciation; he acted in the comedies of Plautus; he delighted in the poetry of Virgil, the satires of Juvenal, the epigrams of Martial; he wrote Latin verses for diversion. In youth he was the admirer of Erasmus, in maturity the patron of Nicholas Udal and Roger Ascham. He was an author of no little reputation, although it must be said that his Latin prose is as far surpassed in clarity and simplicity by that of Erasmus, as is his English by that of Ascham and Cranmer. As Ascham himself put it:

> "Ready speakers generally be not the best, plainest, and wisest writers. . . . Stephen Gardiner had a quick head and a ready tongue, and yet was not the best writer in England."[4]

Law and letters did not complete the sphere of his interests. Theology, as he grew older, claimed his increasing attention. "I professed the civil laws, as your Lordship did," said Dr. Rowland Taylor, at his examination before Gardiner in 1555. "Touching my profession," replied the Bishop, "it is divinity, in which I have written divers books."[5] In his dozen divers books of divinity he treated the whole range of subjects in controversy in his day. His partisans looked upon his work as the ablest exposition and defence of the faith then written, his opponents as that most worth answering.

Legist, humanist, theologian—Gardiner was all these. He was also a bishop in the Church, a diplomat of unrivalled knowledge of continental politics and continental personages, and a party chief skilled in all the Tudor methods of marshalling majorities.

In his statecraft, in his diplomacy, in his leadership in the Church, in his theology, he was predisposed by his legal training to take his stand upon established ways, to defend the existing order, to look askance upon innovation. In this he was confirmed by his observations on the Continent, for already in his young manhood the Lutheran movement had been accompanied by the beginnings of that social and political upheaval which was to devastate Germany for a century. The Knights' War, the Peasants' Revolt, the struggle of the princes against the Emperor, were object-lessons sufficient to confirm in him his dread of the new theology. "In these matters of religion," he said, in May 1547, "I have been long exercised, and have, thanks be to God, lived so long as I have seen them thoroughly tried."[6] In a similar manner did the excesses of the French Revolution blind many an Englishman to the value of the reforms which preceded the period of violence and which would last after it was gone.

"I will withstand fancies even in pronunciation, and fight with the enemy of quiet at the first entry," said Gardiner as Chancellor of Cambridge in 1543.[7] "Ye will remain quiet and contented to follow and allow such laudable customs and rules as have always been, time out of mind, used amongst you," was his peremptory direction, as Chancellor of the Realm, in 1555, to the Mayor and aldermen of Leicester who, he had heard, were "desirous of newfangleness."[8] Perhaps the most revealing sentence he ever wrote was that to Somerset, describing a conference with Cranmer in October 1547:

> "My Lord of Canterbury charged me that I like nothing unless I do it myself; whereof I am not guilty. I was never author of any one thing, either spiritual or temporal, I thank God for it."[9]

"Very loth to condescend to any innovations,"[10] was Thirlby's pithy characterization of his lifelong friend.

His training not only inclined him to the conservative side in
matters of Church and State, it gave him that respect for law which
constrained him to insist that the actions of his sovereigns have at
least the form of legality. This may not have been very high
ground to take, but in an age when Machiavelli was the mirror for
monarchs, when Cromwell held up the Sultan as a model for Christian princes, Gardiner rendered no little service to the continuance
of constitutional government in England when he threw the weight
of his learning and the strength of his personality on the side of
parliamentary right and judicial custom. He told Henry VIII that
he had "read indeed of kings that had their will always received for
a law," but warned him that "to make the laws his will was more
sure and quiet." "By this form of government ye be established,"
said Gardiner, "and it is agreeable with the nature of your people." [11]

His legal temper is evident in his theological writings. They are
polemic or expository, not creative. He would have scouted the
idea that theological writing might be creative. He confessed frankly
that he had never been so bold as to discover any meaning in Scripture which he had not already found in some approved author.

So high was his esteem for the law that it tended to become, in
his view, a safe guide for conscience. Such he deemed the act of
Parliament abolishing Papal jurisdiction. He appears to have had
little if any doubt of his own or Henry's actions in the divorces of
Catherine and Anne of Cleves, since both cases had been legally
conducted. He declared himself ready, in 1550, to set forth religious
changes established by law, though he disapproved of many of them.
"Living in a commonwealth, men must," he said, "conform themselves to the more part in authority." [12] He lost patience with the
prisoners for religion in 1555 because they refused to subordinate
their convictions to the act of Parliament reuniting England to Rome.

It is a matter of speculation as to what ground he would have
taken had he been asked to conform to the second Prayer Book of
Edward VI; or had Parliament, in Edward's reign, touched what
he believed to be of the essence of religion, namely the doctrine of
Christ's bodily presence in the Sacrament. He deemed it a stroke
of divine providence that no law was passed expressly declaring
that doctrine heretical. Had such a law been passed it seems almost
certain that he would have resisted it, thereby, perhaps, becoming as
heroic as the Marian martyrs and, from his own standpoint, as illog-
ical and obstinate as he thought them to be. For Gardiner, as well
as the reformers, recognized a law in matters of religion ultimately
superior to the law of the land. This they both called "God's law,"
but by it they meant different things. With the reformers it was
Scripture interpreted by the enlightened individual; with Gardiner
it was Catholic tradition. The one tended to be uncertain because
variable with the individual, or with differing groups of like-minded

individuals (though few reformers would admit the validity of any great variation from their own norm) ; the other was, on the whole, constant, known, and ratified by the age-long acceptance of Christendom. That it was the latter sort of ultimate authority on which Gardiner took his stand is again characteristic of the legal mind. It should be noted, however, that Gardiner had, like the reformers, exercised the right of private judgement when he distinguished between those elements of the Catholic tradition which the state might rightfully alter and those which it might not.

He was a man of marked reserve, of circumspection, caution, prudence—"a man of great forecast," as Thirlby said of him in the days of Cromwell's ascendancy; one who had often said to Thirlby that "he would not be compassed to enter into dangerous things by any man, before the King, but . . . he would go with and follow." [13] When Thomas Smith was urging the disuse of the customary pronunciation of Greek, Gardiner reminded him how, when Melancthon suggested to Erasmus the abandonment of Scotus and of all scholastic theology, Erasmus, like a wise man, answered that he would consider giving up scholastic theology when there was a better to substitute for it. [14]

To say that Gardiner's statecraft and theology were not creative does not mean that they lacked either individuality or consistency. Despite the entire accuracy of his disclaimer of innovation, there was no little truth in Cranmer's charge that he liked nothing unless he did it himself. His aims were clear, his pursuance of them determined, and his confidence in his own judgement of men and policies firm. "A man of great pertinacity in all his doings," was the phrase applied to him at the French court. [15] "God taught me to be importunate when the request is good," he wrote to the Council in protest against the Homilies of 1547. [16] "Marry, I myself could use him, and rule him to all manner of purposes, as seemed good unto me; but so shall you never do," are the words said to have been uttered by the dying Henry VIII to his executors. [17] Whether they were Henry's words or not, they certainly express the view of the executors, and the prophecy contained in them was fulfilled. The statement of the King's ability to rule the Bishop, however, might well have been supplemented by one concerning the Bishop's ability to influence the King. Few, if any, of Henry's advisers so well understood him as did Gardiner; few knew so precisely when to oppose, to yield, or to flatter; few were better able so to suggest a plan as to make the King think it had been wholly a matter of his own initiative. In so far as Gardiner may have complied against his own judgement or conscience with Henry's desires, he was an opportunist, but his career as a whole indicates that not many a Tudor statesman pursued so consistent a policy as he. There is doubtless truth in Ponet's assertion that one of Gardiner's precepts to his pupils was to give back two foot with the ram that they might win the third.[18]

While far from averse to the reform of ecclesiastical abuses and the abolition of superstitious practices, Gardiner's aim in things ecclesiastical was to keep the English Church Catholic in doctrine and practice and to preserve in both Church and Realm the prerogative and power of the episcopate. In this his motive was as truly national as it was ecclesiastical, for it was his conviction that only by preserving at once the Catholicity and the power of the Church could the Realm be saved from such civil strife as was making a shambles of Germany. He was willing to support the royal supremacy as long as it promised the realization of this aim. When, under Northumberland, that supremacy tended to the denial of the faith as he conceived it, and the reduction of the episcopate to a mere department of the State, dependent on the pleasure of the Council for its tenure and salary, he was driven to reconsider the claims of the Pope. He can hardly be blamed for concluding that the religious innovations of Somerset and Northumberland had some connection with the arrant misgovernment, the extreme economic distress, and the final treason of the reign. He had before his eyes, in the words of the last Parliament he attended, "the dolorous experience of the inconstant government during the time of the reign of the late King."[19] The royal supremacy seemed to have failed to preserve either peace, faith, prosperity, or loyalty. There was nothing left for one of his training and temperament but to look to the Papacy as the one hope for both Church and Realm, especially when his sovereign led the way thither.

His support of the royal supremacy under Henry, and his return to Rome under Mary cannot, therefore, be regarded as the acts of apostacy which Romanists and Anglicans are wont, respectively, to regard them. It does not appear that he ever believed the Papal supremacy to be of the essence of the Church, although he came to look upon it as the bulwark of episcopal power and of orthodoxy. Had he lived to see the impotence and utter subordination of the episcopate effected by the Council of Trent he might have judged otherwise.

In matters secular his object was to maintain peace and prosperity by economy of administration, rehabilitation of the currency, the avoidance of war, and the prevention of civil strife. "Like as in a natural body, rest without trouble doth confirm and strengthen it, so it is in a commonwealth,"[20] was his admonition to the Protector. Essential to the attainment of such "rest without trouble" was, he believed, the eradication of that most fruitful of all roots of civil discord in his day, religious dissention. It was his fear of

anarchy which made him suspicious of the slightest doctrinal innovation. For the prevention of such anarchy, if for no other purpose, Churchmen, he believed, must have a prominent part in the
counsels of the Realm, and if the Churchmen who served the Realm
were to serve it with independence of spirit, their lands and revenues
must enable them to rank with dukes and earls. With the opinion,
soon to become current after his time, that it was better for both
Church and State if ecclesiastics kept out of politics, he would have
utterly disagreed.

In advocating enforced conformity to the religious standards
adopted by the State he was neither behind nor in advance of his
times. Such conformity had been exacted by Henry VIII, and was
to be exacted by Cecil and Elizabeth. It is indeed a question whether
any other policy would have preserved England from the century
of civil strife which, in the name of religion, turned Germany into
a desert. That the immoderate use of the stake in enforcing this
conformity was a tactical mistake, Gardiner came soon to see, but
he appears to have been powerless to remedy it.

In the realm of foreign relations he strove to revive and maintain
the Spanish alliance, thus abandoning the brilliant but unstable
diplomacy of Wolsey and reverting to the more solidly advantageous
policy of Henry VII, by which England would have one assured
friend on the Continent, and that friend the ruler of Flanders—
England's wool market. But well disposed as he was to Spain, he
did everything to prevent such Spanish domination as he feared
might result from the marriage of Mary and Philip. It was better,
he said, for England and Spain to remain friends than to seek a
closer union. Although some people, he said to Somerset, think
me "not a good Christian man," I have been "no evil civil man, and
your Grace, at our being with the Emperor, had ever experience of
me that I was a good Englishman." [21]

He was a man of extraordinary activity, his body, until his latter
years, answering in vigour and alertness to the restless energy of his
mind. Confinement daunted him nothing; from five years in the
Tower came forth six volumes of no small compass. John Harington, Senior, author of the "saucy sonnet," previously quoted,[22] aptly
characterized him in the opening line of a mock epitaph:

"Here lie the bones of *busy Gardiner* dead." [23]

In his early years ambition seems often to have been the sole motive of his career, but after attaining eminence he became the devoted
servitor of Church and Commonwealth, ambitious for their welfare
rather than his own, displaying, in the difficult days of Edward VI, a
courage and a constancy in defence of what he believed to be the
truth, surpassed only by the constancy and courage of those whom

he in turn condemned to suffer in the next reign. His sudden elevation to power under Mary came unasked; he used it with single-hearted devotion to England and its Queen.

In the exercise of authority he was often peremptory and stern, his manner brusque and threatening. He had, moreover, a violent temper which all too easily slipped beyond control, especially if he were irritated by the words or actions of those with whom he dealt. This aspect of his character impressed his opponents. Warwick (Northumberland) called him "the arrogant Bishop;"[24] Marillac, French ambassador at Henry's court, spoke of his accustomed insolence;[25] Rogers, the martyr, of "his old arrogant proud fashion."[26] Bale has him roaring and raging "as it were great Cerebus of hell."[27] In Foxe's "proud and glorious spirit of that man" we have the reformers' composite picture of him. "He was," says Foxe, "of a proud stomach, . . . toward his superiors flattering and fair spoken, to his inferiors fierce, against his equal stout and envious."[28]

From Gardiner's own letters it appears that he was well aware of his failing in the matter of temper, and strove to overcome it. Nor is it by any means clear that his imperious bearing and roughness of speech were not occasionally put on in the hope of alarming offenders into conformity that they might thereby escape the extremity of the law. He could, when not provoked to anger, be gentle and persuasive, and there are not a few first-hand testimonies to his courtesy and patience in dealing with those who thought differently than he.

Some of his enemies charged him with vindictiveness. The most serious indictment on this score is that in a letter from Paget to Petre, November 1, 1544—a date when Paget was still, ostensibly, Gardiner's friend and follower. He infers that the Bishop had excluded Dr. Nicholas Wotton, resident ambassador at Brussels, from certain diplomatic conferences there in order to bring him into discredit at the Imperial court, adding:

> "My lord of Winchester hath certain affectioñs in his head many times towards such men as he greatly favoureth not (amongst whom I account Mr. Wotton . . .), and when he seeth time can lay on load to nip a man; which fashion I like not and think it devilish. God amend all our faults."[29]

It is hard to tell whether this pious observation was written by one who was in reality still a friend of the Bishop, or by one who was already preparing to turn against him. Certain is it that Gardiner did not hesitate to "nip" Cromwell when his chance came. On the other hand, Northumberland, from whom he had suffered infinitely more than from Cromwell, appears to have looked to him as the one man at Mary's court from whom in the day of his necessity he might hope for kindness. Philip Paris, Esq., of Linton, who had once been farmer to the Bishop, deposed at his trial that the Bishop had never permitted legal action to be taken against any of his own tenants or against "any other that had done wrong or injury to him." [30]

Another charge not infrequently brought against Gardiner was that of craft and subtlety. He was popularly known as "Wily Winchester." [31] The epithet was not inapt in so far as it portrayed his proficiency in all the arts of legist and diplomat. He was not, on occasion, averse to giving the diplomatic lie, nor to the use of indirect means to attain a desired end. Yet there can be little doubt that much of his reputation for subtlety arose from his natural reticence and reserve. But among those who knew him well, he was noted for his plain speaking. His dispatches from foreign courts were wont to picture conditions less favourable to England than they were, lest too great hopes be raised at home. "Very wilful to write the truth," is the way Norfolk described him.[32] Nor did he mince words when giving advice to his sovereigns. He pictured himself correctly when he said to Somerset:

> "In writing I do speak as the matter leads, continuing mine old manner, to be earnest; which as some men have dispraised, so some have commended it. And therefore in a good honest matter I follow rather mine own inclination, than to take the pains to speak as butter would not melt in my mouth."
>
> "If I show not your Grace such proof as cannot be denied," he exclaimed, "let me . . . be accounted a liar, which I abhor above all faults." [33]

"If he promiseth a little, he will perform that with more," said Philip Paris of him at his trial; and many another bore witness that he was "a man of just promise, duly observing the same."

He was the last to claim perfection for himself. "I go not about to prove myself a saint," he wrote, "for I have made no such outward visage of hypocrisy." [34] At the same time he was convinced of the rightness of the cause for which he stood:

> "I, for myself, boast not my works to the world, but do the office of an hand at a cross to say this is the right way; and whether I steer or no to enter the way myself, I have God to my judge to whom I stand or fall." [35]

Like Wolsey, Gardiner loved pomp, delighted in ceremony, and entertained lavishly. Although incessantly occupied in affairs of State and Church he was a genial companion, with such a saving sense of humour that even in the Tower he regaled the councillors who there visited him, with "merry tales" of his imprisonment. Indeed it shows no small quality of personal attraction that among his friends he counted such diverse persons as Peter Vannes, Ed-

ward Fox, Lord and Lady Lisle, Thomas Thirlby, the Duke of
Norfolk, the Anthony Brownes, father and son, Thomas Wriothesley, John White, Roger Ascham, Thomas Watson, Thomas Smith,
Cuthbert Tunstall, and Edward Courtenay.[36] He won the confidence of Wolsey, Henry VIII, Mary, Philip, and Pole. Somerset
never ceased to respect him.

The most striking of all his personal relationships is that with
the members of his household. It must have been clear to them
at the time of his trial that his conviction was a foregone conclusion,
that no possible profit could come to them for appearing in his
behalf; yet servants and ex-servants rose up and testified for him,
and the chief of them gave not only good words, but time and zeal
and energy in the conduct of his case. A significant bit of testimony
was given incidentally by Jacques Wingfield, a gentleman who in
1551 had been in Gardiner's service above a score of years. He was
deposing as to his master's expectation of release from the Tower in
June 1550. The Bishop, he said, then asked him to summon two
servants from Farnham to prepare his chamber in Southwark "and
to keep it privy from the rest of his household, for fear lest they,
being stricken with gladness thereof, would come straggling up." [37]

There must have been something unnoticed by his enemies in
character of this "proud and glorious" prelate to inspire such affection
in those who served him that he had to keep from them the news of
his possible release, lest from Farnham and Winchester they come
straggling up to London, "stricken with gladness thereof."

APPENDIX I

ON GARDINER'S BIRTH AND PARENTAGE

John Bale tells us that Gardiner was born at Bury St. Edmunds (*Scriptorum*, 685). Bale was a contemporary of Gardiner and studied at Cambridge while Gardiner was there. His statement has never been questioned. He also speaks of Gardiner's obscure parents, *"obscuris parentibus ortus,"* but neither names them nor dates his birth. Soranzo, Venetian ambassador in England early in Mary's reign, said that Gardiner's father had been a man of "very middling station" (*Ven. Cal.*, V, p. 558).

A generation after Gardiner's death, the story grew up that he was the illegitimate son of Lionel Woodville, Bishop of Salisbury, brother of Elizabeth, Queen of Edward IV. This seems to have been first made current by Francis Godwin (1562-1633), Bishop of Hereford, in his *Catalogue of the Bishops of England* (p. 283, ed. 1601). He gives the information on hearsay, telling us that a near kinsman of Woodville assured him that Gardiner was the son of that Bishop, who, to cover his fault, married the mother to one of his followers named Gardiner. Godwin endeavoured, says Anthony Wood, "out of a puritanical pique," to bring a scandal on the Catholic bishops (*Ath. Ox.*, I, 581). Richard Parker, writing about 1622, repeats the Woodville story, suggesting that the name "Stevens," by which Gardiner was familiarly known, was that of his mother. (*Sceletos Cantab.*, in Leland, *Antiq.*, V. 212). The story is accepted with more or less confidence by most editors of biographical collections, and the historians Strype and Collier. Gardiner's connection with royalty is an easy explanation of his rapid rise in the favour of Henry VIII.

Lionel Woodville died in 1484, hence Gardiner's birth has been usually given as 1483.

Apart from the positive evidence which the publication of John Gardiner's will has brought to this question, we have negative evidence, first, against Gardiner's being the illegitimate son of anyone, and second, against his being the illegitimate son of Lionel Woodville. The first is the silence of his enemies; the second is the date of Woodville's death.

His enemies, Bale, Jewell, and Joye, all of whom refer to his origin, suggest neither illegitimacy, on the one hand, nor noble connection, on the other. Bale has already been cited. Jewell, in answer to a Papal bull calling Elizabeth's councillors obscure and beggarly, asks, "may not princes have any other councillors than dukes and earls?" and refers, among others, to Wolsey and Gardiner as cases in point. "Of what honourable parentage, of what noble blood came they? . . . Who was their father, grandfather? What duke, earl, lord, baron, or knight?" (*Works*, IV, 1146). The worst that Joye has to say is that Henry promoted Gardiner "out of the dunghill to sit fellowlike with lords and dukes" (*Refutation*, f. cxxxi). Neither Foxe nor Ponet (who excells in abuse of Gardiner) say anything, so far as I have been able to discover, about his parentage. Burnet (II, 515) says that in one of the books written in defence of the married clergy Gardiner and Bonner were said to be enemies of marriage because they were born in adultery. Burnet's editor, Pocock, notes in the margin, "Poynet, *Treatise of Politic Power*, p. 29," but this is a reference to Bonner only. I have examined several of the early books in defence of clerical marriage but have been unable to find the one referred to by Burnet.

Thomas Fuller (1608-61) refused to believe in the Woodville story, first, because Salisbury, of which Woodville was bishop, is six score miles from St. Edmund's Bury; second, because "time herein is harder to be reconciled than place. For, it being granted an error of youth in that Bishop, . . . Gardiner . . . must be allowed of greater age than he was at his death" (*Worthies*, III, 168), which occurred, says Fuller, when he was past sixty (*Ch. Hist.*, Bk. VIII, *Sect.* 3, § 42). Fuller does not say where he learned that Gardiner was past sixty at his death.

I have found no contemporary statement of Gardiner's age. We know, however, that he entered Cambridge in 1511 and received the degree of Bachelor of Civil Law in 1518, that the usual age of boys entering the university in his day was thirteen or fourteen, that of bachelors of law, twenty. We also know that his course had not been lengthened by taking a previous degree in arts. Moreover, he later referred to himself as having been a little boy, "*puellum*," in 1511 (*see* above, Chapters I and II). All this would suggest about 1597 as the year of his birth.

Unfortunately there are no baptismal registers at St. James' Church, Bury, before 1558, nor Trinity Hall matriculation registers before 1557. Matriculation by the university authorities at Cambridge was not practised till 1515. We can reach only an approximate date. One thing, however, is clear, his birth a year before, or even a year after, the death of Lionel Woodville is out of the question. James Gairdner suggests that 1483 may have been a mistaken reading for 1493. It was more likely a consequence of the Woodville story.

The use of the titles "Doctor Stevyn," "Master Stevens," "Master Stehpynis," have nothing whatever to do with the name of Gardiner's mother. It was a common custom to address secretaries and ambassadors by their first names. The state papers abound in references to "Master Gregory," for Gregory Casale, "Master Vincentius," for his brother Vincent, and "Master Peter," for Peter Vannes. "Master Stevens," the most frequent of the many spellings of Gardiner's first name, is merely the anglicization of "Magister Stephanus." The statement, sometimes met with, that he was not known by the name of Gardiner until he assumed it in 1531, on becoming Bishop of Winchester, is wholly false. On his embassy to the Pope in 1528, he regularly signed his letters "Steven Gardyner." His first appearance in any public record, March 3, 1525, is as "Stephanus Gardyner" (Hearne, *Adam de Domerham*, cii). In the years 1517 to 1521 there are no less than five entries in the Cambridge *Grace Books* concerning "Stephanus Gardyner" (*B*, II, 88, 95, 97; Γ, 159, 196).

Beside all this negative evidence we have the positive evidence of John Gardiner's will, in which there appears a Stephen Gardiner, lawful son of John, of Bury St. Edmunds, of schoolboy age at the beginning of 1507, and destined for the university. The place, the date, the intended career all fit the future Bishop of Winchester. This was sufficient to persuade C. H. Cooper and James Gairdner that the Stephen of the will and the Stephen of Winchester were the same. Additional evidence for this identity follows:

1. There is but one Stephen Gardiner upon the university lists of the period.

2. The will mentions a brother, William. We know, on the testimony of one of Bishop Gardiner's body servants, that the Bishop had a brother William who died in 1550 (Foxe, VI, 194).

3. Thomas and Richard Eden are named several times in the will as trustees for the money bequests to John Gardiner's children. Stephen Gardiner, in a letter to Erasmus, mentions that as a boy in Paris he lived in the household of an Englishman named Eden (*see* above, Chapter I), and in his own will he leaves bequests to a John and a Thomas Eden, perhaps sons or nephews or grandsons of the Edens in his father's will.

4. Two articles bequeathed to the Stephen of the will, a silver salt-cellar and a mazer or drinking-bowl, which he was to receive on coming of age, correspond to those given by the Stephen at Cambridge as cautions or pledges that he would fulfil certain requirements of the university. In the academic year 1521-22 his pledge is *unum salinum argenteum* (*B,* II, 100). In 1522-23 it is *una mirra* (*B,* II, 111).

If we accept this evidence, the will in its turn presents a further reason for the late date of Stephen Gardiner's birth.

It need excite no wonder that Gardiner does not, in his writings, mention his parents. His father died in less than a year after his will was made. We do not know how long his mother lived, but in any case he was not likely, when called to be the peer of dukes and earls, to vaunt his plebian origin.

The will of John Gardiner was published in 1853. C. H. Cooper, in the *Gentleman's Magazine* of May, 1855, p. 495, quoted it in part, summed up the statements concerning Gardiner's birth made by biographical editors and historians since the seventeenth century, and indicated his inclination to accept the will as that of Gardiner's father. He placed the date of his birth at about 1495 (*Ath. Cantab.,* I, 139). J. B. Mullinger in the *Dictionary of National Biography* accepted John Gardiner as the father of Stephen but retained the old date with a question mark (1483 ?). This he corrected in his *History of the University of Cambridge* (II, 36), by saying that Gardiner in 1540 was in his forty-sixth year. Joseph Foster in *Alumni Oxonienses* (Early Ser., II, 548) also followed Cooper in making John Gardiner, Stephen's father. James Gairdner selected, as I have pointed out, 1493 as the birth date, and was convinced of John Gardiner's fatherhood (*Typical Eng. Churchmen,* Ser. II; *Dict. Eng. Ch. Hist.,* "Gardiner"; *Ency. Brit.,* "Gardiner").

The Woodville tradition is still current in encyclopaedias and guide books. Only in its latest edition has the Britannica discarded it. H. E. Malden, in his excellent chapter on Gardiner in *Trinity Hall* (1902), makes no mention of John Gardiner's will. Though doubting the Woodville story, he dates Gardiner's birth at 1483, which leads him to the conclusion that Gardiner entered the university late, probably because of poverty in early life. In fact Gardiner neither entered late, nor was he poor.

Variants of the Woodville tradition are found in Burnet (II, 515) and Rapin de Thoyras (II, 44) who, not without hesitation, name Lionel Woodville's brother Richard as Gardiner's father. Edmund Lodge (*Illust. of Brit. Hist.*, I, 125) tells us that one of the Rawlinson MSS. in the Bodleian makes him a younger son of Sir Thomas Gardiner, Knight, of Lancashire. The confident assertions of *The Complete Peerage* have given some recent currency to the view that he was the son of William Gardiner, citizen of London, and his wife Helen, illegitimate daughter of Jasper Tudor, uncle to Henry VII. This appears in V. Gibbs' new edition of the *Complete Peerage* (II, 73, ed. 1912), and in R. Davey's *The Sisters of Lady Jane Grey* (p. xxix, 1911). Both evidently take their information from G. E. Cokayne's *Complete Peerage* (I, 295, ed. 1887), which in turn seems to go back to William Betham's *Genealogical Tables*, DCX (1795). At this point the story vanishes into thin air.

APPENDIX II

GARDINER'S WORKS

A. PUBLISHED VOLUMES.

B. VOLUMES STILL IN MANUSCRIPT.

C. SERMONS AND SPEECHES.

D. BOOKS ATTRIBUTED IN PART TO GARDINER.

A. ' PUBLISHED VOLUMES
(In the order of their publication)

Note: After each of the early editions of Gardiner's works I have indicated libraries in which copies are to be found, using the following abbreviations:

Advoc.: Advocates' Library, Edinburgh.
B.M.: British Museum.
Bibl.Nat.: Bibliotheque National.
Bodl.: The Bodleian.
Camb.: Cambridge University Library.
Cong.: Library of Congress.
Dubl.: Trinity College, Dublin.
Emman.: Emmanuel College, Cambridge.
Gen.: General Theological Seminary, N. Y.
Harv.: Harvard University.
Hunt.: Library of H. E. Huntington, Los Angeles, Cal.
Lamb.: Lambeth Palace.
Marsh: Archbishop Marsh's Library, Dublin.
Ryl.: John Ryland's Library, Manchester.
Sion: Sion College, London.
Temp.: Middle Temple Library, London.
Trin.: Trinity College, Cambridge.
Union: Union Theological Seminary, N. Y.

i. *De Vera Obedientia Oratio.*

The writing of this was completed by Sept. 26, 1535. See *L. P.,* IX, 442. It has been the most frequently reprinted of Gardiner's works.

For title pages of some of the early editions *see* Maitland, *Essays,* XVII.

Editions and reprints in Latin:

1) London, 1535. First edition. (B.M., Bodl., Harv.)

2) Hamburg, 1536. Preface by Bonner. (B.M. 2 cop., Dubl., Lamb. ?)

3) *Argentinae* (Strassburg), 1536. Preface by Capito, Hedio, and Bucer. (B.M.)

4) Reprint of Strassburg edition in Goldastus, *Monarchia S. Rom. Imp.*, I, 716. Hanover, 1611.

5) Reprint of the same in the same. Hanover, 1612.

6) Reprint of the same in the same. Frankfurt, 1621.

7) Reprint of the same in the same. Frankfurt, 1668.

8) Reprint of Hamburg edition in Edward Brown, *Fasciculus Rerum*, II, 800. London, 1690. *Cf.* Maitland, *Essays*, 360.

An English translation, probably by John Bale (*cf. Athenae Cant.*, III, 87), of the Hamburg edition was issued in 1553, without Gardiner's approval.

Editions and reprints of the English translation:

1) "Roane," Oct. 26, 1553.

2) Another edition of the same place, date, and form. Copies of one or the other of these "Roane" editions are in B.M. (2 cop.), Bodl., Camb., Dubl. (2 cop.), Gen., Harv., Hunt., Lamb., Trin., Union.

3) "Rome," Nov. 1553. (B.M. 2 cop., Bodl., Camb., Dubl., Emman., Hunt., Lamb., Marsh.)

> The places "Rome" and "Roane" are probably fictitious, but there is no reason to doubt that the dates are approximately correct. The *Chronicle of Queen Jane,* 33, tells us that a translation of the *De Vera* appeared about Christmas Eve, 1553. Both the "Rome" and the "Roane" editions contain introductions by the translator, slightly varying, but equally scurrilous. The "Roane" edition also contains a translator's conclusion.

4) Reprint of the "Rome" edition in Wm. Stevens, *Memoirs of the Life and Martyrdom of John Bradford* . . . London, 1832. A very careless reprint, several of whose mistakes are pointed out by Maitland, *Essays,* 364-6.

5) Reprint of the "Rome" edition, omitting translator's introduction, in B. A. Heywood, *The Royal Supremacy in Matters Ecclesiastical in Pre-Reformation Times. Bishop Gardiner's Oration on True Obedience with Bishop Bonner's Preface,* . . . London, 1870.

A careful reprint, but seemingly as rare as the editions of 1553. I know of but four copies of it (Advoc., B.M., Dubl., and Public Library, Boston, Mass.)

> Maitland (Essay XVIII) expresses a doubt that Bonner wrote the preface attributed to him in the Hamburg edition. Maitland's chief reason for this doubt is that as Bonner in 1536 was not nearly so prominent as Gardiner, he was not likely to bestow prefatory patronage upon him; but Bonner's preface was to an edition published in Germany where Bonner was better known than Gardiner, being ambassador there at the time. It does not appear that Bonner or any of his contemporaries ever denied his authorship of the preface, an authorship not only proclaimed on the title page of the edition of 1536 and of the English translations of 1553, but referred to several times as an evident matter by the contemporaries Hooper

(*Later Writings*, 267-8, 557, 567) and Jewell (I, 34; IV, 848, 1074, 1080). Maitland himself gives us a contemporary record of Bonner's own acknowledgement of it.

Moreover, Maitland's argument against Hamburg as the place, and 1536 as the date, of this edition is weakened by a sentence in a letter from Bonner and Candish, ambassadors at Hamburg in 1536: "They have printed the Bishop of Winchester's book" ("They" apparently referring to the Protestant princes of North Germany). *L. P.*, X, p. 112.

D. N. B. lists, among Gardiner's works, a *Palinodia Libri de Vera Obedientia*. It does not appear that Gardiner ever published anything under this title, which probably rests on Pits' inaccurate list of Gardiner's works (*Relationum Historicarum de Rebus Anglicis*, 748-9, Paris, 1619), in which there is noted a *De vera & falsa obedientia*, followed by *Palinodiam dicti libri*, which seems to be Pits' descriptive title for Gardiner's Advent sermon of 1554, a Latin version of which was published at Rome, 1555, under the title *Concio* etc., as given below, C, i.

ii. *Stephani VVinton. Episcopi Angli ad Martinum Bucerum De Impudenti eiusdem Pseudologia Conquestio.* *Lovanii*, August 1544. 4to. Dated at end by Gardiner, July 27, 1544. (B.M. 2 cop., Bodl., Dubl. 2 cop., Sion, Trin.)

Another edition. *Coloniae*, 1545. 4to. (B.M. 2 cop., Temp., Union.)

iii. *Stephani VVinton. Episcopi Angli, ad Martinum Bucerum Epistola, qua cessantem hactenus & cunctantem, ac frustratoria responsionis pollicitatione, orbis de se iudicia callide sustinentem, vrget ad respondendū de impudētissima eiusdē psuedologia iustissimae conquestioni ante annū aeditae.* *Louanii*, Mar. 1546. 4to. Dated at end by Gardiner, *Traiecti* [Utrecht], Dec. 12, 1545. (Advoc., B.M., Bodl., Dubl. 2 cop.)

Another edition. *Ingolstadii*, 1546. 4to. (B.M., Union.)

These two books (Nos. ii and iii) were called forth by a reference to Gardiner made by Bucer in:

Scripta duo adversaria D. Bartholomaei Latomi LL. Doctoris, et Matrini Buceri theologi . . . Argentorati, 1544.

They were answered by Bucer in:

Gratulatio Martini Buceri ad ecclesiam Anglicanam . . . Et Responsio eiusdem ad duas Stephani episcopi Vintoniensis Angli cōuiciatrices Epistolas, De coelibatu sacerdotum . . . [Basle?] 1548.

This was translated by Sir Thomas Hoby:

The gratulation of . . . Martin Bucer . . . unto the churche of Englande . . . And Hys answere unto the two raylinge epistles of Stevē, Bisshoppe of Winchester . . . London, [1548 or 1549.] *Cf.* Hoby's autobiography, 5-6, in *Camden Miscel.*, X.

Gardiner replied in No. ix below. *See also* B, ii.

To Gardiner's books against Bucer here listed, *D. N. B.* erroneously adds another: *Contra Convitia Martini Buceri.* This is merely a descriptive title used by Pits for No. iii above. Bale lists the same book under the title *Convicia in Bucerum.* Both identify the book by quoting its first line.

iv. *The Examination of the Hunter.*

William Turner (under pseudonym of William Wraghton) published:

The huntyng and fyndyng out of the Romyshe foxe, which more then seuen yeares hath bene hyd among the bisshoppes of Englonde . . . Basle, Sept. 14, 1543.

Gardiner replied, probably in 1543 or 1544, in a book or pamphlet evidently called:

The Examination of the Hunter, no copy of which appears to be extant; but about 40 pages of it are quoted in Turner's reply to it (again under pseudonym of Wm. Wraghton), entitled:

The Rescvynge of the romishe fox othervvyse called the examination of the hunter deuised by steuen gardiner. The seconde covrse of the hvnter at the romishe fox & hys aduocate, & sworne patrone steuen gardiner doctor & defender of the pope's canon law and hys ungodly ceremonies. "Winchester," Mar. 4, 1545 [*i.e.,* 1546]. (Advoc., B.M., Bodl., Camb., Ryl.)

Nine years later Turner again attacked Gardiner in:

The Huntyng of the Romyshe Vuolfe, made by Vuylliam Turner doctor of Phisik. [Basle ? 1555 ?]

v. *A Declaration of suche true articles as George Joye hath gone about to confute as false.* London, 1546. 4to. (B.M., Bodl., Camb., Dubl., Lamb.)

Another edition. London, 1546. 8vo. (B. M. 2 cop., Camb., Cong., Emman., Harv., Hunt., Lamb., Ryl., Union.)

The 4to edition has at the end a list of "Fautes escaped in the printynge," which are corrected in the 8vo edition. This seems to indicate that the 4to was the first edition. Both were printed by Jn. Herford at the charges of Robt. Toye. Gardiner finished writing the book by Nov. 5, 1545 (*L. P.,* XX, ii, 732). It must have been published before Easter 1546, for Joye says he received a copy at that time (*Refutation,* f. cxci). It was an answer to an attack by Joye entitled:

George Joye confuteth Winchesters false Articles. Wesill in Cliefe Lande, 1543.

Joye replied to Gardiner in:

The refutation of the byshop of Winchesters derke declaratiō of his false articles, once before confuted by George Ioye. [London,] 1546.

vi. *A Detection of the Devils Sophistrie, wherewith he robbeth the unlearned people, of the true byleef, in the most blessed Sacrament of the aulter.* London, 1546. 8vo.

Another edition of the same place, date, and form. Copies of both in B.M. Copies of one or the other in Bodl., Camb. 2 cop., Emman., Hunt., Lamb., Marsh, Ryl., Sion., Trin., Union.

This was answered in:

An Answer to the devillish detection of Stephane Gardiner . . . Compiled by A.G. [Anthony Gilby] [London,] 1547,

and:

An Answer unto my lord of wynchesters booke intytlyd a detection of the devyls Sophistrye . . . made by Johann Hoper. Zurich, 1547. (Reprinted in Parker Soc. ed. of Hooper.)

vii. *An explicatiō and assertion of the true Catholique fayth, touchyng the moost blessed Sacrament of the aulter with confutacion of a booke written agaynst the same. Made by Steven Byshop of Wynchester, and exhibited by his owne hande for his defence to the Kynges maiesties Commissioners at Lambeth.* [Roan ?] 1551. (B.M. 2 cop., Bodl., Camb., Lamb., Trin., Union.)

This must have been written in 1550, for Gardiner refers to it in his book against Hooper of that year, f. 22. Cranmer says it was printed in France (*Lord's Supper,* Parker Soc., 48). The Bodleian Catalogue gives Roan as place of printing.

Reprinted in all editions of Cranmer's reply to it; namely,

a) 1551.

b) 1580.

c) 1833, ed. Jenkyns.

d) 1844, Parker Soc.

Gardiner's book was an answer to Cranmer's:

A Defence of the true & catholike Doctrine of the sacrament of the body & bloud of our Saviour Christ . . . London, 1550. Reprinted, London, 1807, 1817, 1825; Oxford, 1833.

Cranmer replied to Gardiner in:

An Avnsvver . . . Vnto a craftie and Sophisticall cauillation, deuised by Stephen Gardiner . . . London, 1551; London, 1580; Jenkyns' *Remains of Thomas Cranmer,* Oxford, 1833; Parker Soc., Cambridge, 1844.

Gardiner thereupon composed an answer not only to Cranmer but to all objections to the Catholic doctrine of the Sacrament. *See* No. viii.

viii. *Confvtatio Cavillationvm, Quibus Sacrosanctvm Evcharistiae Sacramentum, ab impiis Capernaitis, impeti solet, Authore Marco Antonio Constantio, Theologo Louaniensi.* Parisiis, 1552. Dated by printer at end, July 20, 1552. (B.M., Bibl.Nat., Union.)

Another edition: *Confvtatio Cavillationvm, Quibus Sacrosanctū Evcharistiae Sacramentum, ab impiis Capharnaitis impeti solet, Authore Stephano Winton. Episcop. Angliae Cancellario. Editio Altera, Cui Index accessit locupletissimus. Lovanii, 1554.* (B.M., Bibl.Nat., Bodl., Dubl., Lamb., Trin., Union.)

> (Mr. A. F. Pollard, in his *Cranmer,* 357, n., makes the astonishing statement that no copy of this book of Gardiner's appears to be known.)

Peter Martyr replied to this in:

Defensio doctrinae veteris et apostolicae de sacrosancto Eucharistiae sacramento, D. Petri Martyris Vermilii . . . adversus Stephani Gardineri . . . librum . . . Confutatio cavillationum . . . [Zurich, 1559]. (Erroneously dated 1551 in *D. N. B.,* "Vermigli." *See* Martyr's letter of Jan. 7, 1559, in Gorham, 406.)

Ridley also considered some of M. Antonius' [Gardiner's] answers to objections to the Sacrament in his little book:

A brief declaration of the Lordes Supper, written by . . . Nicholas Ridley . . . a litel before he suffered deathe . . . 1555. (Reprinted in Parker Soc.)

ix. *Exetasis testimoniorvm, qvae M. Bucerus ex sanctis patribus non sancte edidit, vt partrocinetur opinioni de caelibatus dono, quam sine dono spiritus, contra ecclesiam defendit orthodoxam. Lovanii, 1554.* 4to. (B.M. 2 cop., Bodl., Dubl.)

Gardiner's preface is dated May 7, 1548. The printer, in a preface dated Apr. 4, 1554, says he received the manuscript almost six years previous, but withheld it from publication lest it cause trouble for the author (who had just been committed to the Fleet). Page Ai, containing printer's preface, is lacking in one of the B.M. copies.

x. *De Pronuntiatione Graecae.*

Both Gardiner's and Cheke's treatises (written 1542) were published without their knowledge, by Coelius Secundus Curio to whom Cheke had lent the manuscripts, under the title:

J. Cheki . . . de Pronuntiatione Graecae potissimum linguae disputationes cum Stephano Wintoniensi Episcopo. Basileae, 1555. 8vo. (B.M.) Reprinted in Havercamp, *Sylloge Altera. Lugduni Batavorum, 1740.*

Thomas Smith's treatise was published under the title:

De recta & emendata Linguae Graecae pronuntiatione . . . ad Vintoniensem Episcopum epistola. Lutetiae, 1568. (Reprinted in Havercamp.)

xi. *Responsio Venerabilium Sacerdotum Henrici Ioliffi & Roberti Ionson, sub protestatione facta, ad illos articulos Ioānis Hoperi, Episcopi Vigorniae nomen gerentis, in quibus à Catholica fide dissentiebat: Vna cum Cōfutationibus eiusdē Hoperi, & Replicationibus reuendiss. in Christo patris, bonae memoriae, Stephani Gardineri, Episcopi Vin-*

*toniensis, tunc temporis pro confessione fidei in carcere detenti. Antver-
piae, 1564.*

This volume, with an introduction by Henry Joliffe, contains 19
articles ministered by Bp. Hooper to the clergy of the diocese of
Worcester in 1552. They are different from the set of 50 articles
ministered to the clergy of Gloucester, printed in Hooper's *Later
Writings,* 120 ff. Each article is followed by the answer made to
it by Henry Joliffe and Robert Jonson, canons of Worcester. Eleven
of these answers are followed by replies by Hooper, which are in
turn answered by Gardiner. The major portion of the volume is
by Gardiner. Joliffe says that Gardiner wrote it with incredible
diligence as soon as the Hooper-Joliffe-Jonson material came to his
hands. This must have been in the latter part of 1552. (*Cf.* Hooper's letter to Cecil, Oct. 25, 1552, in Strype, *Cranmer,* App. No.
xlviii.) Gardiner's answers deal with various phases of the Sacrament, with purgatory, invocation of saints, good works done before
justification, the sinlessness of the Virgin Mary, works of supererer-
gation, and clerical celibacy.

B. Volumes Still in Manuscript

i. A pamphlet in defence of Bishop Fisher's execution, in answer to
Paul III's brief deposing Henry VIII. Latin. Written Sept. 1535.
(*Cf. L. P.,* IX, 442). Calendared in *L. P.,* VIII, 1118, where, however,
Gardiner's authorship is not noted. *See* Chapter X, n. 26.

ii. *Contemptum humanae legis justa autoritate latae gravius et severius
vindicandum quam divinae legis qualemcunque transgressionem.* MSS.
C.C.C.C. 113, No. 34. A neatly written tract of 20 pages, against Bucer.
Probably written in the latter part of Henry VIII's reign. *Cf.* Gardiner's *Exetasis,* 155-8.

iii. *In Petrū Martyrem florentinum malae tractaconis querela Sanctis-
simae Eucharistiae nōīe edita, authore Stephano Winton.* B.M., Arundel MS. 100. A volume of 264 pages, very clearly written in a clerk's
hand, a few passages in Greek filled in in another (Gardiner's?) hand.
Initials decorated. Marginal references to authorities, and indications
of content.

Written 1549 or 1550. It is mentioned by Gardiner in his book
against Hooper of 1550, f. 22. It could not have been written
before 1549 since it is a reply to Peter Martyr's:

Tractatio de Sacramento Evcharistiae . . . London, 1549.

iv. *A Discussion of Mr. Hopers oversight where he entreateth amonge
his other Sermons the matter of the Sacrament of the Bodye and Bloode
of Christe, 1550.* R.O., St. P. Dom. Ed. VI, Vol. XII. A volume of 132
pages, neatly written in a clerk's hand. Signed at the beginning and the
end by Sir Thomas Pope, in whose possession it must have been.

This was a reply to the portion on the Sacrament of Hooper's:

An oversight, and deliberacion upon the holy Prophete Jonas . . .
London, 1550. (Preface dated Sept. 6.)

v. *Annotacones in Dialogum Johannis Oecolampadii cum suo Nathanaele de mysterio Eucharistico Disceptantis.* Lambeth MSS. Vol. 140, ff. 225-333. A volume of 218 pages, neatly written in a clerk's hand, passages in Greek filled in in the same hand as in No. iii above. Anonymous and without date. Identified as Gardiner's probably by Archbishop Sancroft. Probably written while Gardiner was in the Tower; and, as he says in the opening paragraph, at the request of someone who asked his opinion of Oecolampadius':

> *Quid de Evcharistia Veteres tum Graeci, tum Latini senserint, Dialogus . . .* 1530. No place.

vi. A note-book, or rather two note-books bound together, kept by Gardiner while he was in the Tower. MSS. C.C.C.C. 127, pp. 167-190 and 191-342. The first is filled with Latin proverbs, the first 58 pages of the second with extracts from Martial, Juvenal, and Virgil, the remaining 93 pages with original Latin verses (elegiacs), in a running hand, frequently corrected. On pp. 298-9, which seem to have been inserted into the book, is a neatly written poem of 79 lines on the name of Jesus. *See* James, *Catalogue,* I, 298.

A copy of a single poem by Gardiner is preserved in B.M., Egerton MS. 2642, f. 241. *See* Chapter XXVI, n. 2.

C. Sermons and Speeches
(Including the communication with Judge Hales)

i. *Concio reveren. d. stephani, episcopi vintonien. angliae cancellarii, habita dominica prima adventvs, praesentibvs sereniss. rege et reverendiss. legato apost. in maxima popvli freqventia. Romae,* 1555. 4to. (B.M., Bibl. Nat.)

Reprinted in Quirini, *Epistolae Poli,* V. 293. *Brixiae,* 1757.

> This is a Latin version of Gardiner's Advent sermon of 1554, made by Nicholas Harpsfield, Archdeacon of Canterbury, and is probably the book referred to in some lists of Gardiner's works as *Palinodia Libri de Vera Obedientia.* It was a palinode or retraction of his earlier position on the royal supremacy. He does not appear to have published anything under the title *Palinodia* etc.

English notes of this sermon are printed in Foxe, VI, 577.

John Elder's version is printed in *Chron. of Queen Jane,* 161.

ii. Udal's report of Gardiner's St. Peter's Day sermon of 1548 is printed in Foxe, VI, 87.

Another account of this sermon, preserved in MSS. C.C.C.C. 127, pp. 15-29, probably by John Redman, is printed with some condensation in Foxe, VI, 236.

iii. Brief reports in Latin of two English speeches by Gardiner at the close of Parliament, Jan. 16, 1555, are printed in a rare anonymous pamphlet entitled *Acta Postrema conclvsionis proximi anglicani conventvs.* [Dillingen ?] 1555. (B.M.) Of its ten pages, over five are given to Gardiner's speeches. The same appears in ms. in B.M., Add. MS. 15,388, f. 336 ff., *"ex Regesto liter. Card. Poli, Tom. 19, pag. 103."*

iv. *The Commvnication betweene my Lord Chauncelor and judge Hales,
being among other judges to take his oth in VVestminster hall Anno
M.D.Liii. Vi of October.* [Roane, 1553.] 8vo. (B.M., Bodl., Camb.)
A pamphlet published as a score against Gardiner.

Reprinted in *Harleian Miscellany,* III, 174 (London, 1808); Foxe, VI,
712; and Howell, *State Trials,* I, 713.

D. Books Attributed in Part to Gardiner

i. *The King's Book (A Necessary Doctrine and Erudition for any
Christian Man).* For the degree to which this may be attributed to
Gardiner, *see* above, p. 106.

ii. Gardiner has been credited with some part in the authorship of a
book by Thomas Martin on clerical celibacy. The facts in the case are
as follows:

In 1549 John Ponet (who became Bishop of Winchester on Gardiner's deprivation in 1551) published:

*A Defence for Mariage of Priestes, by Scripture and aunciente
Wryters.* London, 1549.

Five years later there appeared:

*A Traictise declaryng and plainly prouyng, that the pretensed mar-
riage of Priestes, and professed persones, is no mariage, but allto-
gether unlawful, and in all ages, and al countreies of Christendome,
both forbidden, and also punyshed.*
*Herewith is comprised in the later chapitres, a full confutacion of
Doctour Poynettes boke entitled a defens for the marriage of
Priestes. By Thomas Martin, Doctour of the Civile Lavves.* London, 1554.

Two years later Ponet replied to this in:

*An apologie fully aunsweringe . . . a blasphemose Book gatherid
by D. Steph. Gardiner of late Lord Chauncelar/ D. Smyth of Ox-
ford/ Pighius/ and other Papists as by their books appeareth & of
late set forth under the name of Thomas Martin . . . against
the . . . mariadge of priests . . . 1556.* No place.

Burnet (II, 446) claims to have seen proof sheets of a great part
of Martin's book "dashed and altered in many places by Gardiner's
hand." Martin was Chancellor of Winchester, and it is altogether
probable that he received material and help from Gardiner. He
must surely have been familiar with Gardiner's books on the subject. Moreover, chapters XI-XIII, comprising the confutation of
Ponet, resemble Gardiner's English works in diction, style and
manner of argument.

APPENDIX III

A CALENDAR OF GARDINER'S LETTERS

Almost all of Gardiner's letters in the reign of Henry VIII are calendared in *L. P.* Hence, for this reign, only those which are not in *L. P.*, together with a few corrections of those which are, are here given. For the reigns of Edward VI and Mary all Gardiner's letters known to me are here calendared. When they are in print or when the nature of their contents has been indicated in this volume no further description of their contents is given in the calendar.

IN THE REIGN OF HENRY VIII

Letters and other Gardiner material not in *L. P.*:

Gardiner to Erasmus, Feb. 28 [1526 or 1527]. *See* Chapter I, p. 4 and n. 10.

Gardiner's Papal safe-conduct to Venice, June 17, 1528. In Ehses, No. 27.

Gardiner's oath to the King for the temporalities of his bishopric, renouncing all grants from the Pope which are or may be prejudicial to the King. In B.M., Add. MS. 34,319, f. 21b. Copy. No date, but possibly of Dec. 1531. Certainly before the middle of Apr. 1534, for Gardiner is called therein Principal Secretary to the King. The oath is similar, but not identical, to Cranmer's in Strype, *Cranmer*, App. vii. *Cf. L. P.*, VI, 291, 292.

Articles concerning the valuation of the see of Winchester, 1535. Said by Strype to be in Gardiner's hand. Printed in Strype, *Mem.*, I, i, 329.

Decision of Gardiner and Thirlby in a disputed election to the proctorship at Cambridge, 1542. In MSS. C.C.C.C. 106, No. 14; and a note by Matthew Parker concerning the same, *ib.*, No. 13. A copy of the decision is in *ib.*, 127, No. 6.

Gardiner to Dr. Edmonds, Vice-Chancellor of Cambridge, May 15, 1543. In MSS. C.C.C.C. 106, No. 57. Copies in B.M., Add. MS. 5843, p. 419; Bennet's Register of Emm. Col. Camb., p. 244. Printed in Lamb, 43; Strype, *Mem.*, I, ii, 481; Ellis, 2nd Ser., II, 206; Cooper, *Annals*, I, 405.

Privy Council to Cambridge University, signed by Wriothesley, Gardiner, Russell, and Paget, May 16, 1545. In MSS. C.C.C.C. 106, No. 162. Printed in Lamb, 57; Parker, *Corresp.*, 29; Cooper, *Annals*, I, 427.

Gardiner to Parker and the Regents *etc.* of Cambridge, May 18, 1545. Latin. In MSS. C.C.C.C. 119, No. 12. (It is not clear why the rest of the Gardiner-Parker correspondence of this year is relegated to a foot note in *L. P.*, XX, i, p. 379, and not regularly entered in the calendar. *See* Chapter XVII, n. 7.)

Privy Council to the Mayor and Aldermen of Chester, signed by Wriothesley and Gardiner, Sept. 24, 1546. In the Great Letter-Book of the Corporation of Chester. *See Hist. MSS. Com.*, Report 8, p. 373b.

Gardiner's tract against Bucer, probably written in latter part of Henry VIII's reign. *See* App. II, B, ii.

Corrections and additional information concerning Gardiner's Letters in *L. P.*:

L. P., IV, 4078. A considerable portion of this is printed in *St. P.*, VII, 60.

L. P., IV, 4090 is printed in full in Pocock, I, 88, in large part in *St. P.*, VII, 63.

L. P., IV, 4103 makes Gardiner write: "except there be some change of the inhabitants soon it will be of little consequence who are lords of this country." What he said was that unless the pestilential weather soon changed it would be of little consequence *etc.*

L. P., IV, 5476, 5518 are printed in full in Burnet, V, 448; VI, 23.

L. P., IV, 5798, 5819, 5821 are printed in full in Pocock, I, 265, 248, 266.

L. P., IV, 5819 should be dated July 28, 1529. *See* Chapter VI, n. 5.

L. P., IV, 6112. For correction, *see* Chapter VI, n. 23.

L. P., V, 1016(5). For Gardiner's authorship of this and collections in which it is printed, *see* Chapter VIII, p. 46 and n. 3.

L. P., V, 1019. Holograph original is in B.M., Cleop. E. VI, 200 (new p. no. 203). Printed in full in Atterbury, 528 (as well as in Wilkins, III, 752).

L. P., VII, 858 is printed in full above, p. 56.

L. P., VIII, 654 is printed in full in Strype, *Mem.*, I, i, 327.

L. P., VIII, 1118 is of Gardiner's composition. *See* Chapter X, n. 26.

L. P., X, 256. A holograph draft is in B.M., Harl. 283, 137 ff. Printed in full in Collier, *Records,* ii, No. 34 (as well as in Strype, *Mem.*, I, ii, 236).

L. P., XXI, ii, 487, 488 are printed in full in Maitland, *Essays,* 330 ff. (as well as in *St. P.*, I, 883).

IN THE REIGN OF EDWARD VI

1547

Feb. 5, Southwark. To Paget.
> R.O., St. P. Dom. Ed. VI, Vol I, No. 5. Original signed. Printed in Tytler, I, 21.

[Between Feb. 23-38, Southwark.] To Ridley.
> In Foxe, VI, 58-63. From Foxe in Ridley's *Works,* Parker Soc., 495, and Tierney's Dodd, II, App. i.

Feb. 28, Southwark. To Somerset.
> In Foxe, VI, 24-6. From Foxe in Howell, *State Trials,* I, 560, and Tierney's Dodd, II, App. i.

Mar. 1, Southwark. To Paget.
> R.O., St. P. Dom. Ed. VI, Vol. I, No. 25. Original, signed. Unpublished; *see* above, p. 146. (A small part is quoted in Gasquet and Bishop, 44-5, where it is incorrectly cited as St. P. Dom. Ed. VI, Vol. I, No. 24.)

May 3, Winchester. To Capt. Edward Vaughan.
> In Foxe, VI, 26-28. From Foxe in Howell, I, 554, and Tierney's Dodd, II, App. i. (An answer to this by Somerset, undated, but referred to by Gardiner as of May 27, is in Foxe, VI, 28-30.)

May 21, Winchester. To Somerset.
> In Foxe, VI, 30-4. From Foxe in Howell, I, 563, and Tierney's Dodd, II, App. i. A ms. copy of the last twelve lines is in B.M., Add. MS. 28,571, f. 21. (An answer by Somerset, undated but apparently about the end of May, is in Foxe, VI, 34-6.)

June 6, Winchester. To Somerset.
> In Foxe, VI, 36-41. From Foxe in Howell, I, 573, and Tierney's Dodd, II, App. i.

June 10, Winchester. To Somerset.
> In Foxe, VI, 41. From Foxe in Howell, I, 580.

[Shortly after June 12,] Winchester. To Cranmer.
> ("your letters of the 12th came to my hands the [blank] of the same.") B.M., Add. MS. 29,546, ff. 1-9b. Copy. Unpublished. *See* above, pp. 154-7. Some pages of a draft of this (less than one third of the whole) in Gardiner's hand is in B.M., Harl. 417, ff. 79-83b. This is printed with some inaccurate conjectural emendations in Strype, *Cranmer,* App. xxxv.

[Shortly after June 12, Winchester.] To Somerset.
> In Foxe, VI, 41-2. From Foxe in Howell, I, 581.

[Shortly after July 1, Waltham ?] To Cranmer.
> ("I have received your letters of the 1st of July.") B.M., Add. MS. 29,546, ff. 9b-24b. Copy. Another copy in Bibl. Nat., Latin 6051, ff. 30-46. Unpublished. *See* above, pp. 157-9.

[Shortly before Aug. 30,] Waltham. To Privy Council.
> B.M., Add. MS. 28,571, ff. 16b-20b and 6a. Copy. Unpublished. *See* above, p. 162.

[Aug. 30, Waltham.] To Privy Council.
> B.M., Add. MS. 28,571, ff. 6a-9a. Copy. Unpublished. *See* above, pp. 162-3.

Aug. 30, Waltham. To [Sir John] Mason.
> B.M., Add. MS. 32,091, ff. 142-143a. Original, signed. Unpublished. *See* above, p. 163.

[Before Sept. 25, Waltham.] To Sir John Godsalve.
> MSS. C.C.C.C. 127, No. 3. Printed in Burnet, V, 163.

Oct. 14, the Fleet. To Somerset.

In Foxe, VI, 42-6, where, however, at p. 42 a long passage is omitted, which is supplied in Strype, *Cranmer,* App. xxxvi, from an imperfect copy in B.M., Cotton, Vesp. D. 18, f. 138 ff. Burnet, V, 166 prints a portion from the same source, which is clearly not the source used by Foxe. Howell, I, 582 reprints what is given in Foxe. In Tierney's Dodd, II, App. iv the whole letter is reprinted from Foxe and Strype. Some pages of a draft in Gardiner's hand are in B.M., Harl. 417, f. 84; an imperfect copy, in Bibl. Nat., Latin 6051, ff. 46-7; a copy, in Bodleian, Cod. MSS. Tho. Tanneri lxxxvii, 61. (I have not examined the last and therefore cannot say what relation it bears to the source used by Foxe.)

[Oct. 27,] the Fleet. To Somerset.

(Written twenty days after Gardiner's conference with Cranmer on Oct. 7.) In Foxe, VI, 46-50. From Foxe in Howell, I, 588.

[Shortly after Nov. 4, the Fleet.] To Somerset.

(Written soon after opening of Parliament, Nov. 4.) In Foxe, VI, 53b. From Foxe in Howell, I, 599.

[Nov. 12, the Fleet.] To Somerset.

("Seven weeks saving one day I have been here.") In Foxe, VI, 54-5. From Foxe in Howell, I, 600. A copy of the first eleven lines is in B.M., Add. MS. 28,571, f. 14b.

[Between Nov. 12 and 20, the Fleet.] To Somerset.

In Foxe, VI, 53a. From Foxe in Howell, I, 598.

[Between Nov. 12 and 20,] the Fleet. To Somerset.

In Foxe, VI, 140-2. Imperfect copies are in B.M., Add. MS. 28,571, ff. 13a-14b; and Bibl. Nat., Latin 6051, f. 48.

[About Nov. 20,] the Fleet. To Somerset.

("here I have remained this viii weeks.") In Foxe, VI, 51-3. From Foxe in Howell, I, 595.

[After Nov. 20 ?] the Fleet. To Somerset.

In Foxe, VI, 53c-54. From Foxe in Howell, I, 599.

[About Dec. 4, the Fleet.] To Somerset.

("here I have continued x weeks.") Camb. Univ. Lib., Ee II. 12, No. 24, where it is erroneously said to have been written from the Tower. Copy. Unpublished. Gardiner requests a hearing by the Protector in the presence of the bishops.

1548

[Between Jan. 19-Feb. 20, Southwark.] To Somerset.

(Written while Gardiner was a prisoner in his own house.) B.M., Add. MS. 28,571, ff. 15b-16b. Copy. Unpublished. Desires to have Scripture and the Fathers shown him [for the position on justification taken in the articles given him for subscription. *See* above, pp. 170-1].

[Between Jan. 19-Feb. 20,] Southwark. To Somerset.

(Written while Gardiner was a prisoner in his own house.) B.M., Add. MS. 28,571, ff. 9b-10b. Copy. Unpublished. Refers to treating with Ridley [on justification], and desires permission to go to his house in Hampshire.

Mar. [no day,] Winchester. To Somerset.

B.M., Add. MS. 28,571, ff. 10b-12a. Copy. Unpublished. Complains of Philpot's untrue report of one of his sermons and says he never suffers his servants to brawl.

[Early in Apr., Winchester.] To Somerset.

B.M., Add. MS. 28,571, ff. 9a-9b. Copy. Unpublished. Thanks Somerset for accepting his illness as an excuse for not answering summons [of Privy Council, Apr. 1. *See* above, p. 172], and affirms that he has done nothing contrary to any proclamation or commandment.

[About Nov. 3, the Tower.] To Somerset.

In Gardiner's *Long Matter,* in Foxe, VI, 111. (Perhaps a summary by Gardiner of a longer letter.)

In Bp. Kennett's ms. collections (B.M., Lansdowne 980, ff. 154-5) there are two sentences headed "Admonitions written by Stephen Gardiner, prisoner in the Tower, to the Duke of Somerset, Protector." They are: "I. Take not all that you can nor do all that you may, for there is no greater danger in a nobleman than to let slip the reins of his lust and not to be able to refrain them with the strong bit of reason. II. Let not ambition entangle your mind, for her nature is to overthrow herself etc." A marginal note refers to the ms. collections of Dr. N[athaniel] Johnston. I have been unable to trace further the source of these admonitions. If authentic, they are more likely to have been written from the Fleet than from the Tower.

There is in B.M., Add. MS. 28,571, ff. 4b-5b, 15a, a copy of a letter from Somerset to Gardiner, Mar. [no day, but before the 25th] 1548, in answer to Gardiner's refusal to surrender Trinity Hall. From it we learn something of the position taken by Gardiner in his letter of refusal which is lost. *See* above, p. 171.

1549

Oct. 18, the Tower. To Warwick.

MSS. C.C.C.C. 127, p. 117, with postscript on p. 121. Unpublished. *See* above, p. 185.

Oct. 30, the Tower. To Privy Council.

In Stow, 600. From Stow in Tytler, I, 108-9. (Either a very brief note or a paragraph of, or a condensation of, a longer one.)

[Nov., the Tower.] To Privy Council.

In Stow, 600; and in *Egerton Papers,* 25-7, where the editor is unaware that Gardiner is the author.

In the Reign of Queen Mary

1553

Aug. 25, Southwark. To Vice-Chancellor and Senate of Cambridge University.

> (Latin. Dated 8 Kal. Sept. Londini ex aedibus meis.) MSS. C.C.C.C. 106, No. 326. Original. Copies in Camb. Univ. Lib., Baker MS. xxxiv, p. 328; R.O., St. P. Dom. Mary, I, No. 12; B.M., Sloane MS. 3562, f. 57 (No. 49); B.M., Add. MS. 5843, p. 426. Printed in Lamb, 169; Parker, Corresp., 56; Strype, Parker, I, 85.

Oct. 18, Southwark. To Vice-Chancellor and Senate of Cambridge University.

> B.M., Add. MS. 5843, pp. 427-8. Copy. Unpublished. See Chapter XXVIII, n. 23.

1554

Jan. 13, [no place.]. To the President and Fellows of St. Catharine's, Cambridge.

> St. Catharine's Col. Register, p. 41. Copy. Another copy in MSS. C.C.C.C. 106, No. 327. Printed in Browne, St. Catharine's College, 70-1; and Lamb, 169.

Jan. 27, Southwark. To Sir Wm. Petre.

> R.O., St. P. Dom. Mary, II, No. 20. Original, signed. Printed in Chron. Qu. Jane, 184.

Jan. 31, Southwark. To Sir Wm. Petre.

> R.O., St. P. Dom. Mary, II, No. 32. Original, signed. Unpublished. See Chapter XXIX, n. 27.

Feb. 11, Southwark. To Sir Wm. Petre.

> R.O., St. P. Dom. Mary, III, No. 22. Original, signed. Unpublished. See Chapter XXX, n. 7.

Apr. 4, Southwark. To the Masters and Presidents of the colleges at Cambridge.

> Camb. Univ. Lib., Baker MS. xxxiv, pp. 328-9. Copy. Another copy in B.M., Add. MS. 5843, p. 428. Unpublished. (Summarized in Cooper, Annals, II, 85.)

Apr. 5, Southwark. To Pole.

> B.M., Add. MS. 25,245, f. 241. Copy in Italian. Unpublished. See above, p. 253.

[Before May 1, no place.] To the President and Fellows of Peter House in Cambridge.

> Printed in Heywood, Early Camb. Statutes, II, 79-80, from the Register of the College of St. Peter.

May 1, St. James. To the Fellows and Company of Peter House.

> Printed in Heywood, Early Camb. Statutes, II, 80, from the Register of the College of St. Peter.

June 17, The Court. To Dr. Yonge, Vice-Chancellor of Cambridge.

> Camb. Univ. Lib., Baker MS. xxxiv, p. 330. Copy. Another copy in B.M., Add. MS. 5843, pp. 429-30. Unpublished. *See* Chapter XXVIII, n. 23.

Sept. 1, The Court. To the Students of Christ Church, Oxford.

> R.O., St. P. Dom. Mary, IX, No. 14. A certified copy made by a notary public in 1556. Another copy in B.M., Harl. 7001, f. 233. Printed in Thompson, *Christ Church,* 39-40.

Nov. 16, London. To [Montemorency] Constable of France.

> In Noailles, III, 321-2, and again, with slight verbal changes and dated Nov. 15, in Noailles, IV, 17-18. French.

Letters from the Privy Council signed by Gardiner and others in 1554:

Apr. 7, St. James. To Vice-Chancellor of Cambridge.

> Camb. Univ. Lib., Baker MS. xxxiv, p. 328. Copy. Unpublished. Dr. Edwin Sandys is released from Tower. All his goods at Cambridge are to be restored to him.

Nov. 27, Westminster. To Bonner.

> In Wilkins, IV, 109; and Foxe, VI, 567, where it is said to have been printed by John Cawod.

1555

Jan. 8, Southwark. To the Mayor and his brethren of Leicester.

> Borough of Leicester, Book of Acts, p. 19. Copy. Printed in Bateson, *Records of the Borough of Leicester,* III, p. 82; and, less carefully, in Nichols, *Hist. and Antiq. of Leicester,* I, ii, p. 395.

Feb. 18, Southwark. No address.

> B.M., Add. MS. 6668, p. 761 (= f. 399). Original, signed. Unpublished. The recipient is advised to reform himself rather than be ordered at Gardiner's hands as justice shall require.

Feb. 19, Southwark. To Vice-Chancellor and others of the Council of the University of Cambridge.

> Camb. Univ. Lib., Baker MS. xxxiv, p. 334. Copy. Another copy in *ib.,* xxxi, p. 241. Unpublished. (Summarized in Cooper, *Annals,* II, 94, where Baker MS. is incorrectly cited as xxxiv, 324.)

Mar. 22, Southwark. To Sir John Shelton.

> B.M., Harl. 6989, f. 159. Original, signed. Unpublished. Assures Shelton that his servant has delivered certain examinations of felons.

Mar 24, Southwark. To Vice-Chancellor of Cambridge.

> MSS. C.C.C.C. 106, No. 328. Copy. Another copy in Camb. Univ. Lib., Baker MS. xxxiv, pp. 334-5. Printed in Lamb, 170; and Cooper, *Annals,* II, 94-5.

Apr. 10, Esher. To Bonner.

> Camb. Univ. Lib., Baumgarten Papers (Strype Correspondence) II, No. 45. Copy *"ex Registro Ecclesia Christi Cant."* Another copy in

B.M., Add. MS. 5853, p. 439. Printed in Holinshed, III, 1128; and Foxe, VII, 37, where the editor says it is from Reg. Bonner, f. 358. (It is accompanied by Latin prayers for use during vacancy in Papacy.)

Letters from the Privy Council signed by Gardiner and others in 1555:

Apr. 28, Hampton Court. To Bonner.

In Foxe, VII, 92.

End of May, Hampton Court. To Wotton.

R.O., St. P. For. Mary. *See Cal.* No. 379, p. 173.

June 26, Hampton Court. To Earl of Shrewsbury.

Coll. Arm., Talbot MSS. B. p. 71. Original. Unpublished. The Greames have submitted to Dacres. The question of their redress to the Scots is committed to Shrewsbury. Copy of 'a letter to Dacres (*ib.*, pp. 67-9) is enclosed, informing him that the Greames' case is committed to Shrewsbury.

June 27. [no place.] To Sir Thos. Gresham.

(Signed by Gardiner and Paulet only.) R.O., St. P. For. Mary, VI, p. 167. *See Cal.* p. 177.

July 11, Hampton Court. To Earl of Shrewsbury.

Coll. Arm., Talbot MSS. B. p. 83. Original. Unpublished. Good news of Imperial success in Italy and "India," whence three millions of gold have lately arrived. Is there truth in the rumour of the coming of the Danish fleet to Scotland?

Aug. 24, Greenwich. To the Corporation of the City of Cambridge.

In Cooper, *Annals*, II, 98, from MS. Metcalfe, 174b.

Gardiner must also have signed many of the letters from the Privy Council of which only drafts or minutes remain in the R.O.; it is probable that he was the author of some of them as well as of some sent out in the name of the Queen, drafts of which are in the R.O.

Latin prayers for the safe delivery of the Queen, for use at Mass, are attributed to him. *See* Chapter XXXI, n. 24.

For Mary's proclamations during his chancellorship, many of which must have been of his composition, *see* R. Steele, *Tudor and Stuart Proclamations*, I, pp. 44-9. Only one, No. 463, is there listed as signed by him.

For records of his trial *see* Chapter XXIV, n. 12, and Chapter XXV, n. 2.

For his will and the ms. account of his funeral *see* Chapter XXXIV, and *ib.*, notes 17 and 31.

His episcopal register is now being edited by Mr. H. E. Malden.

LIST OF PRINTED BOOKS CITED IN THIS VOLUME

(On manuscript citations see p. 338.)

Acta Postrema conclvsionis proximi anglicani conventvs. [Dillingen ?] 1555.

Allen, P. S. A letter containing Gardiner-Erasmus correspondence in *The Academy*, XLVIII, 317. London, Oct. 19, 1895.

Archaeologia. Vols. XVIII, XXIII, XXXVIII. London, 1817, 1831, 1860.

Ascham, R. *The Scholemaster.* Ed. J. E. B. Mayor. London, 1863.

Works. Ed. J. A. Giles. 3 vols. in 4. London, 1864-5.

Askew, A. *Examinations. See* Bale, J. *Select Works.*

Athenae Cantabrigienses. See Cooper, C. H.

Atterbury, F. *The Rights, Powers, and Privileges of an English Convocation.* London, 1701.

Baker, T. *History of the College of St. John the Evangelist, Cambridge.* Ed. J. E. B. Mayor. 2 vols. Cambridge, 1869.

Bale, J. *Scriptorum Illustrium maioris Brytanniae.* 2 vols. in 1. Basle, 1557, 1559.

Select Works [containing *Examinations of Anne Askew*]. Ed. H. Christmas. Parker Soc. Cambridge, 1849.

Bannatyne Miscellany. Vol. I (Bannatyne Club Pub. Vol. 19). Edinburg, 1827.

Barnes, R. *Supplication.* In *The Whole Works of W. Tyndall, John Frith, and Doctor Barnes.* London, 1573.

Works. Ib.

Sentenciae ex Doctoribus collectae . . . Per Anto. Anglum. Wittenberg, 1530.

Bateson, M. *Records of the Borough of Leicester.* Vol. III. Cambridge, 1905.

Betham, W. *Geneological Tables.* London, 1795.

Besant, W. *London in the Time of the Tudors.* London, 1904.

Biographia Britannica. Vol. III. London, 1750.

Blass, F. *Pronunciation of Ancient Greek.* Tr. W. J. Purton. Cambridge, 1890.

Bradford, J. *Writings.* Ed. A. Townsend. Parker Soc. Vol. I. Cambridge, 1848.

326

Brevis Narratio eorvm, qvae in proximo Anglicano conuentu . . . de Religione pristina restituenda, acta sunt . . . [Compiled by S. Solidus.] *Dilingae,* 1554.

Brewer, J. S. *The Reign of Henry VIII.* 2 vols. London, 1884.

Brinklow, H. *Complaynt of Roderyck Mors.* Early English Text Soc. Extra Series, XXII. Ed. J. M. Cowper. London, 1874. *The Lamentacyon of a Christen Agaynst the Cytye of London, made by Roderigo Mors.* In the same.

Browne, G. F. *St. Catharine's College.* London, 1902.

Bucer, M. *Gratulatio. See* App. II, A, iii.

Burgon, J. W. *The Life and Times of Sir Thomas Gresham.* 2 vols. London, 1839.

Burnet, G. *The History of the Reformation of the Church of England.* Ed. N. Pocock. 7 vols. Oxford, 1865.

Busch, W. *Der Sturz des Cardinals Wolsey.* Historisches Taschenbuch, Sechste Folge. Leipsig, 1890.

Bywater, I. *The Erasmian Pronunciation of Greek.* London, 1908.

Caius, J. *Historiae Cantabrigiensis Academiae.* In *Works.* Ed. E. S. Roberts. Cambridge, 1912.

Calendar of Letters, Dispatches, and State Papers Relating to the Negotiations between England and Spain. 11 vols. Ed. G. A. Bergenroth, P. de Gayangos, M. A. S. Hume, and R. Tyler. London, 1862-1916. [Cited as *Sp. Cal.*]

Calendar of State Papers and Manuscripts Existing in the Archives and Collections of Milan. Ed. A. B. Hinds. London, 1913. [Cited as *Milan. Cal.*]

Calendar of State Papers and Manuscripts Relating to English Affairs, Preserved in the Archives of Venice. Vols. I-VI. Ed. R. Brown. London, 1864-84. [Cited as *Ven. Cal.*]

Calendar of State Papers, Domestic Series, of the Reigns of Edward VI, Mary, Elizabeth, 1547-1580. Ed. R. Lemon. London, 1856.

Calendar of State Papers, Domestic Series, of the Reign of Elizabeth, 1601-1603; with Addenda 1547-1565. Ed. M. A. E. Green. London, 1870.

Calendar of State Papers, Foreign Series, Edward VI. Ed. W. B. Turnbull. London, 1861.

Calendar of State Papers, Foreign Series, Mary. Ed. W. B. Turnbull. London, 1861.

Cambridge Modern History, The. Vols. I and II. London and New York, 1902, 1904. [Cited as *C. M. H.*]

Camden Miscellany. Vols. X, XII. Camden Soc. London, 1902, 1910.

Cardwell, E. *Documentary Annals of the Reformed Church of England.* 2 vols. New Edition. Oxford, 1844.

Cavendish, G. *The Life and Death of Cardinal Wolsey.* Boston and New York, 1905.

Cheke, J. *De Pronunciatione.* See App. II, A, x.

Chester, J. L. *John Rogers.* London, 1861.

Chronicle of Calais, The. Ed. J. G. Nichols. Camden Soc. London, 1846.

Chronicle of Queen Jane and of Two Years of Queen Mary, The. Ed. J. G. Nichols. Camden Soc. London, 1850. [Cited as *Chron. Qu. Jane.*]

C. M. H. See Cambridge Modern History.

Collier, J. "A Collection of Records"; *Ecclesiastical History,* Vol. IX. Ed. F. Barham. London, 1841.

Commons' Journals. See Journals.

Complete Peerage. Ed. G. E. C[okayne]. Vol. I. London, 1887. New Edition. Ed. V. Gibbs. Vol. II. London, 1912.

Cooper, C. H. *Annals of Cambridge.* 5 vols. Cambridge, 1842-1908.
  Athenae Cantabrigienses. Vol. I. (C. H. and T. Cooper.) Cambridge, 1858. Vol. III. Ed. G. J. Gray. Cambridge, 1913.
  A letter on the parentage of Stephen Gardiner, in *The Gentleman's Magazine,* London, May, 1855, p. 495.

Coverdale, M. *A Confutacion of that treatise which one John Standish made agaynst the protestacion of D. Barnes in the yeare M.D.XL.* [1541?] No place.

Cranmer, T. *A Defence of the True and Catholic Doctrine of the Sacrament.* In *The Remains of Thomas Cranmer.* Vol. II. Ed. H. Jenkyns. Oxford, 1833.
  Miscellaneous Writings and Letters. Ed. J. E. Cox. Parker Soc. Cambridge, 1846. [Cited as Cranmer, *Letters.*]
  A Short Instruction into Christian Religion: Being a Catechism set forth by Archbishop Cranmer in 1548. Ed. E. Burton. Oxford, 1829.
  Writings and Disputations . . . Relative to the Sacrament of the Lord's Supper. Ed. J. E. Cox. Parker Soc. Cambridge, 1844. [Cited as Cranmer, *Lord's Supper.*]

Dasent, J. R. *Acts of the Privy Council.* Vols. I-V. London, 1890-2.

Davey, R. *The Sisters of Lady Jane Grey.* London, 1911.

Davis, E. J. "Ecclesiastical History"; *V. C. H., London,* I. London, 1909.

De Antiq. Brit. Eccl. See Parker, M.

Declaration. See App. II, A, v.

Description of the Ancient and Present State of the Town and Abbey of Bury St. Edmunds, A. Anon. Printed by W. Green. Bury, 1768.

De Selve, O. *Correspondence Politique.* Ed. G. Lefèvre-Pontalis. Paris, 1888.

De Vera. See App. II, A, i.

Dictionary of National Biography. Ed. L. Stephen and S. Lee. 63 vols. London, 1885-1900. [Cited as *D. N. B.*]

Dixon, R. W. *History of the Church of England.* 6 vols. London, 1878-1902.

D. N. B. See Dictionary of National Biography.

Documents Relating to the University and Colleges of Cambridge: Published by Direction of the Commissioners Appointed by the Queen. 3 vols. London, 1852.

Dodds, M. H. and R. *The Pilgrimage of Grace 1536-37 and the Exeter Conspiracy 1538.* 2 vols. Cambridge, 1915.

Dollman, F. T. *The Priory of St. Mary Overie, Southwark.* London, 1881.

Edward VI. *Literary Remains.* Ed. J. G. Nichols. Roxburghe Club. 2 vols. London, 1857. [Cited as Ed. VI, *Lit. Remains.*]

Egerton Papers. Ed. J. P. Collier. Camden Soc. London, 1840.

Ehses, S. *Römische Dokumente zur Geschichte der Ehescheidung Heinrichs VIII.* Görres Gesellschaft. Paderborn, 1893.

Ellis, H. *Original Letters.* 3 series. 11 vols. London, 1825-46.

Ellis, A. J. *The English, Dionysian, and Hellenic Pronunciation of Greek.* London, 1876.

Encomia. See Leland, J.

English Historical Review. Articles cited are:
M. A. S. Hume, "The Visit of Philip II." VII, 253. London, 1892.
J. Gairdner, "New Lights on the Divorce of Henry VIII." XI, 673; XII, 1, 237. London, 1896, 1897.
A. F. Pollard, Review of Dasent's *Acts of the Privy Council.* XVIII, 567. London, 1903.
A. F. Pollard, "Council, Star Chamber, and Privy Council under the Tudors. I. The Council." XXXVII, 337. London, 1922.

Enthoven, L. K. *Briefe and Desiderius Erasmus.* Strassburg, 1906.

Epistolae Reginaldi Poli. Ed. Quirini. 5 vols. *Brixiae,* 1744-57. [Cited as *Ep. Poli.*]

Epistolae Tigurinae. Parker Soc. Cambridge, 1848.

Erasmus. *See* Enthoven, L. K.; Förstemann and Günther; and Nichols, F. M.

Evans, F. M. G. *The Principal Secretary of State.* Manchester, London, and New York, 1923.

Exetasis. See App. II, A, ix.

Förstemann, J. and Günther, O.　*Briefe an Desiderius Erasmus.*　Leipsig, 1904.

Foster, J. *Alumni Oxonienses.*　Early Series, 4 vols. London, 1891-2.
　The Register of Admissions to Gray's Inn, 1521-1889.　London, 1889.

Fowler, T.　*The History of Corpus Christi College.*　Oxford, 1893.

Foxe, J.　*Acts and Monuments.*　The Church Historians of England, Reformation Period.　[Ed. J. Pratt.] 8 vols. in 16. London, 1853-70. (When earlier editions of Foxe are cited the date is given with the citation.)

Friedmann, P.　*Anne Boleyn.*　2 vols. London, 1884.
　"Some New Facts in the History of Queen Mary"; *Macmillan's Magazine,* XIX, 1. Cambridge, Nov. 1868.

Frith, J.　*A boke made by John Fryth prysoner in the Tower of London, answerynge unto M. Mores letter.*　[London,] 1548.

Froude, J. A.　*History of England.*　12 vols. London, 1898-1901.

Fuller, T.　*The Church History of Britain.*　Ed. J. S. Brewer. 6 vols. Oxford, 1845.
　The History of the University of Cambridge.　Ed. J. Nichols. London, 1840.
　The History of the Worthies of England.　Ed. P. A. Nuttall. Vol. III. London, 1840.

Gairdner, J.　*The English Church in the Sixteenth Century.*　London, 1902.
　"The Fall of Cardinal Wolsey"; *Transactions of the Royal Historical Soc.*　New Series, XIII, 75. London, 1899.
　"Gardiner, Stephen"; *A Dictionary of English Church History.*　Ed. S. L. Ollard and G. Crosse.　London and Milwaukee, 1912.
　"Gardiner, Stephen"; *Encyclopaedia Britannica,* 11th ed.　Cambridge, 1910.
　Lollardy and the Reformation in England.　4 vols. London, 1908-13.
　"New Lights on the Divorce of Henry VIII."　*See English Historical Review.*
　"Stephen Gardiner"; *Typical English Churchmen.*　Series II. Church Historical Soc.　London, 1909.

Gardiner, S.　*See* App. II.

Gardiner, G.　*A letter of a yonge gentylman named mayster Germen Gardynare . . . wherein men may se the demeanor & heresy of John Fryth.*　London, 1534.

Gasquet, F. A.　*Henry VIII and the English Monasteries.*　2 vols. London, 1889-90.

Gasquet, F. A. and Bishop, E.　*Edward VI and the Book of Common Prayer.*　3d ed. London, 1891.

Gee, H. and Hardy, W. J. *Documents Illustrative of English Church History.* London, 1896.

Gilby, A. *See* App. II, A, vi.

Giles, J. A. *See* Ascham.

Godwin, F. *A Catalogue of the Bishops of England.* London, 1601.

Gorham, G. C. *Gleanings of a Few Scattered Eras During the Period of the Reformation in England.* London, 1857.

Grace Book A (1454-1488). Ed. S. M. Leathes, Cambridge, 1897.

Grace Book B, Part I (1488-1511), Part II (1511-1544). Ed. M. Bateson, Cambridge, 1903, 1905.

Grace Book Γ (1501-1542). Ed. W. G. Searle. Cambridge, 1908.

Grace Book Δ (1542-1589). Ed. J. Venn. Cambridge, 1910.

Granvelle, Cardinal de. *Papieres D'État.* Ed. C. Weiss. Collection de Documents Inédits. Vol. IV. Paris, 1843.

Grey Friars' Chronicle. See Monumenta Franciscana.

Griffet, H. *Nouveaux Éclaircissements sur l'histoire de Marie, Reine d'Angleterre.* Amsterdam, 1766.

Guaras, A. de. *The Accession of Queen Mary.* Ed. R. Garnett. London, 1892.

Hacket, J. *Scrinia Reserata, a Memorial . . . of John Williams.* London, 1693.

Haile, M. *Life of Reginald Pole.* New York, 1910.

Hale, W. H. *A Series of Precedents.* London, 1847.

Hall, E. *Henry VIII* [from Hall's Chronicle]. Ed. C. Whibley. 2 vols. London and Edinburg, 1904.

Hamilton Papers. Ed. J. Bain. 2 vols. Edinburg, 1890-2.

Harington, J. *A Briefe View of the State of the Church of England, as it stood in Q. Elizabeths and King James his Reigne, to the Yeare 1608.* London, 1653.
Nugae Antiquae. Ed. T. Park. 2 vols. London, 1804.
A Tract on the Succession to the Crown. Ed. C. R. Markham. Roxburghe Club. London, 1880.

Harleian Miscellany. Ed. W. Oldys and T. Park. 10 vols. London, 1808-13.

Havercamp, S. *See* App. II, A, x.

Haynes, S. *State Papers.* 2 vols. London, 1740.

Hearne, T. *A Collection of Curious Discourses.* Vol. II. London, 1773.
Adami de Domerham Historia. Oxford, 1727.

Herbert, E. *The History of England under Henry VIII.* London, 1870.

Heylyn, P. *Ecclesia Restaurata.* Ed. J. C. Robertson. 2 vols. Cambridge, 1849.

Heywood, J. *Early Cambridge University and College Statutes.* London, 1855.

Historical Account of Sturbridge, Bury, and the Most Famous Fairs, An. Anon. Cambridge, [1773.]

Historical Manuscripts Commission. Sixth Report. London, 1877-8.
Eighth Report. London, 1881.
Ninth Report, Part I. London, 1883.
Cecil MSS. (Calendar of MSS. preserved at Hatfield House), Parts I and II. London, 1883, 1888.

Hoby, T. *The gratulation of . . . Martin Bucer. See* App. II, A, iii.

Holinshed, R. *Chronicles of England, Scotland, and Ireland,* 6 vols. London, 1807-8.

Hooper, J. *Early Writings.* Ed. S. Carr. Parker Soc. Cambridge, 1843.
Later Writings. Ed. C. Nevinson. Parker Soc. Cambridge, 1852.
An oversight, and deliberacion upon the holy Prophete Jonas. London (Daye and Seres), 1550.

Howell, T. B. *A Complete Collection of State Trials.* Vol. I. London, 1816.

Hume, M. A. S. *The Wives of Henry the Eighth.* New York, 1905.
"The Visit of Philip II." *See English Historical Review.*

James, M. R. *A Descriptive Catalogue of the Manuscripts in the Library of Corpus Christi College, Cambridge.* 2 vols. Cambridge, 1912.
On the Abbey Church of S. Edmund at Bury. Publications of the Cambridge Antiquarian Soc. No. 28. Cambridge, 1895.

Jewell, J. *Works.* Ed. J. Ayre. Parker Soc. 4 vols. Cambridge, 1845-50.

Journals of the House of Commons. Vol. I. London, n. d.

Journals of the House of Lords. Vol. I. London, n. d.

Joye Confuteth etc. *See* App. II, A, v.

Joye, G. *Refutation. See ib.*

Katterfeld, A. *Roger Ascham, Sein Leben und Seine Werke.* Strassburg and London, 1879.

Kaulek, J., Farges, L., and Lefèvre, G. *Correspondence politique de MM. de Castillon et de Marillac.* Paris, 1885. [Cited at Kaulek.]

King's Book, The. Ed. T. A. Lacy. London, 1895.

Knox, J. *Works.* Ed. D. Laing. 6 vols. Edinburg, 1846-64.

Laemmer, H. *Monumenta Vaticana.* Freiburg, 1861.

Lamb, J. *A Collection of Letters, Statutes, and Other Documents from the Manuscript Library of Corpus Christi College.* London, 1838.

Latimer, H. *Sermons and Remains.* Ed. G. E. Corrie. Parker Soc. Cambridge, 1844.

Leach, A. F. *A History of Winchester College.* New York, 1899.
The Schools of Mediaeval England. New York, 1915.
"Schools"; *V. C. H., Suffolk,* II; *Surrey,* II. London, 1907, 1902.
"Udal, Nicholas"; *Encyclopaedia Britannica,* 11th ed. Cambridge, 1910.

Leland, J. *Antiquarii de Rebus Britannicis Collectanea.* Ed. T. Hearn. 6 vols. London, 1770. [Cited as Leland, *Antiq.*]
Principium, ac illustrium aliquot & eruditorum in Anglia virorum Encomia, Trophaea, Genethliaca, et Epithalamia. London, 1589. [Cited as Leland, *Encomia.*]

Le Neve, J. *Fasti Ecclesiae Anglicanae.* Ed. T. D. Hardy. 3 vols. Oxford, 1854.

Letters and Papers, Foreign and Domestic, of the Reign of Henry VIII. Ed. J. S. Brewer, J. Gairdner, and R. H. Brodie. 21 vols. London, 1862-1910. [Cited as *L. P.*] 2d. ed. Ed. R. H. Brodie. Vol. I. London, 1920. [Cited as *L. P., New Ed.*]

Lingard, J. *A History of England.* 3d. ed. 14 vols. London, 1825-31.

Lloyd, C. *Formularies of the Faith put forth by Authority During the Reign of Henry VIII.* Oxford, 1825.

Lodge, E. *Illustrations of British History.* Vol. I. London, 1838.

Lollardy. See Gairdner, J.

Lords' Journals. See Journals.

Lord's Supper. See Cranmer, T.

Love Letters of Henry VIII. Ed. L. Black. London, 1907.

L. P. See Letters and Papers.

McGiffert, A. C. *Martin Luther.* New York, 1914.

Machyn, H. *Diary.* Ed. J. G. Nichols. Camden Soc. London, 1848.

Maitland, F. W. *English Law and the Renaissance.* Cambridge, 1901.
Roman Canon Law in the Church of England. London, 1898.

Maitland, S. R. *Essays on Subjects Connected with the Reformation.* London, 1849.

Malden, H. E. *Trinity Hall.* London, 1902.

Merriman, R. B. *Life and Letters of Thomas Cromwell.* 2 vols. Oxford, 1902.

Meyer, A. O. *Die Englische Diplomatie in Deutschland zur Zeit Edwards VI und Mariens.* Breslau, 1900.

Milan. Cal. See Calendar of State Papers . . . Milan.

Monumenta Francisana. Vol. II (containing *Grey Friars' Chronicle*). Ed. R. Howlett. London, 1882. [Cited as *Mon. Fr.*]

Mullinger, J. B. "Gardiner, Stephen"; *Dictionary of National Biography.*
St. John's College. London, 1901.
The University of Cambridge. Vol. II. Cambridge, 1884.

Mumby, F. A. *The Girlhood of Queen Elizabeth.* Boston and New York, 1909.

Narratives of the Reformation. Ed. J. G. Nichols. Camden Soc. London, 1859. [Cited as *Nar. of the Ref.*]

Nichols, F. M. *The Epistles of Erasmus.* 2 vols. London and New York, 1901-4.

Nichols, J. G. "Some Additions to the Biographies of Sir John Cheke and Sir Thomas Smith"; *Archaeologia,* XXXVIII, 98. London, 1860.

Nichols, J. *The History and Antiquities of the County of Leicester.* Vol. I, Part ii. London, 1815.

Nicolas, H. *Proceedings and Ordinances of the Privy Council.* Vol. VII. London, 1837.

Noailles, A. de and F. de. *Ambassades de Messieurs De Noailles en Angleterre.* Ed. l'Abbe de Vertot. 5 vols. Leyden, 1763.

Nott, G. F. *The Works of Henry Howard, Earl of Surrey, and of Sir Thomas Wyatt the Elder.* 2 vols. London, 1815-16. [Cited as Nott's *Wyatt.*]

Nugae Antiquae. See Harington, J.

O. L. See Original Letters.

Oman, C. W. C. "The Tudors and the Currency"; *Transactions of the Royal Historical Soc.* New Series, IX, 167. London, 1895.

Original Letters Relative to the English Reformation. Ed. H. Robinson. Parker Soc. 2 vols., continuously paged. Cambridge, 1846-7. [Cited as *O. L.*]

Panorama of London, Westminster, and Southwark in 1543. By A. Van den Wyngaerde. In Besant, *London in the Time of the Tudors.* London, 1904.

Parker, M. *Correspondence.* Ed. J. Bruce and T. T. Perowne. Parker Soc. Cambridge, 1853.
De Antiquitate Britannicae Ecclesiae. [By Parker and his secretaries.] London, 1572.

Parsons (or Persons), R. *A Storie of Domesticall Difficulties in the English Catholike cause.* Catholic Record Soc. *Miscellanea,* II. London, 1906.
A Temperate Ward-Word to the Turbulent and Seditious Watch-Word of Sir Francis Hastings. 1599. No place.

Peacock, G. *Observations of the Statutes of the University of Cambridge.* London, 1841.

Peck, W. G. *From Chaos to Catholicism.* London, 1920.

P. H. E. See Political History of England.

Philpot, J. *Examinations and Writings.* Ed. R. Eden. Parker Soc. Cambridge, 1842.
The Trew report of the dysputacyon had & begōne in the Convocacyō hows. Basle, [1554.]

Pilkington, J. *Works.* Ed. J. Scholefield. Parker Soc. Cambridge, 1842.

Pits, J. *Relationum Historicarum de Rebus Anglicis.* Paris, 1619.

Planche, J. R. *Regal Records.* London, 1838.

Pocock, N. *Records of the Reformation.* 2 vols. Oxford, 1870.

Political History of England, The. Ed. W. Hunt and R. L. Poole. 12 vols. London, 1906, *etc.* [Cited as *P. H. E.*]

Pollard, A. F. "Bonner"; *Encyclopaedia Britannica,* 11th ed. Cambridge, 1910.
"Council, Star Chamber, and Privy Council under the Tudors." *See English Historical Review.*
England under Protector Somerset. London, 1900.
Henry VIII. London and New York, 1905.
Political History of England, Vol. VI. *From the Accession of Edward VI to the Death of Elizabeth.* London and New York, 1910.
Review of Dasent's *Acts of the Privy Council. See English Historical Review.*
Thomas Cranmer and the English Reformation. London and New York, 1904.
Tudor Tracts. London, 1903.

Ponet (or Poynet), J. *A Shorte Treatise of politike pouuer.* 1556. No place.

Poole, R. L. *Catalogue of Oxford Portraits.* Vol. I. Oxford, 1912.

Proceedings of the Bury and West Suffolk Archaeological Institute. John Gardiner's Will, in Vol. I, 329. Bury St. Edmunds, May, 1853.

Rapin de Thoyras. *History of England.* Tr. N. Tyndall. 5 vols. London, 1739.

Rashdall, H. *The Universities of Europe in the Middle Ages.* 2 vols. Oxford, 1895.

Raumer, F. von. *History of the Sixteenth and Seventeenth Centuries.* Translated from the German. 2 vols. London, 1835.

Ridley, N. *Works.* Ed. H. Christmas. Parker Soc. Cambridge, 1841.

Rymer, T. *Foedera.* 10 vols. The Hague, 1739-45.

Rose-Troup, F. *The Western Rebellion of 1549.* London, 1913.

Sanders, N. *Rise and Growth of the Anglican Schism.* Tr. D. Lewis. London, 1877.

Sawtry, J. *The defence of the Mariage of Preistes.* Auryk, 1541.

Secretan, E. *Catalogue of . . . Paintings.* 2d ed. 2 vols. Paris, 1889.

Smith, T. *De recta . . . pronuntiatione. See* App. II, A, x.

Sp. Cal. See Calendar of Letters . . . Spain.

Stapleton, T. *A Counterblast to M. Hornes Vayne Blaste Against M. Fekenham. Lovanii,* 1567.

State Papers during the reign of Henry VIII. 11 vols. London, 1830-52. [Cited as *St. P.*]

Statutes of the Realm. Vols. 3, and 4, part i. Ed. T. E. Tomlins and W. E. Taunton. London, 1817, 1819.

Steele, R. *Tudor and Stuart Proclamations.* Vol. I. Oxford, 1910.

Stevens, W. *Memoirs of the Life and Martyrdom of John Bradford.* London, 1832.

Stone, J. M. *The History of Mary I, Queen of England.* London, 1901.

Stow, J. *The Annales or Generall Chronicle of England.* London, 1615.

St. P. See State Papers.

Strype, J. *Ecclesiastical Memorials.* 3 vols. in 6. Oxford, 1822. [Cited as Strype, *Mem.*]
The Life and Acts of Matthew Parker. 3 vols. Oxford, 1821.
The Life of the Learned Sir John Cheke. London, 1705.
The Life of the Learned Sir Thomas Smith. Oxford, 1820.
Memorials of the Most Reverend Father in God, Thomas Cranmer. 2 vols. Ed. P. E. Barnes. London, 1853.

Stubbs, W.   *Registrum Sacrum Anglicanum.* 2d ed. Oxford, 1897.

Supplication. See Barnes, R.

Thompson, H. L. *Christ Church.* London, 1900.

Thompson, W. *Southwark Cathedral.* London, 1910.

Tierney, M. A. *Dodd's Church History of England.* 5 vols. London, 1839-43. [Cited as Tierney's Dodd.]

Transactions of the Royal Historical Society. See Gairdner, J., and Oman, C. W. C.

Tudor Tracts. See Pollard, A. F.

Turner, W. *See* App. II, A, iv.

Two London Chronicles: From the Collections of John Stow. Ed. C. L. Kingsford. *Camden Miscellany,* Vol. XII. Camden Soc. London, 1910.

Tytler, P. F. *England under the Reigns of Edward VI and Mary.* 2 vols. London, 1839.

Valor Ecclesiasticus. Vol. II. London, 1814.

Vaughan, J. *Winchester Cathedral.* London, 1919.

V. C. H. See Victoria History.

Ven. Cal. See Calendar of State Papers . . . Venice.

Victoria History of the Counties of England, The.
Hampshire, Vols. II, V. London, 1903, 1912.
London, Vol. I. London, 1909.
Suffolk, Vol. II. London, 1907.
Surrey, Vols. II, III, IV. London, 1902, 1911, 1912.

Visitation Articles and Injunctions. 3 vols. Ed. W. H. Frere and W. McC. Kennedy. Alcuin Club. London, 1910.

Walker, T. A. *Peterhouse.* London, 1906.

Warren's Book [a history of Trinity Hall by W. Warren]. Ed. A. W. W. Dale. Cambridge, 1911.

Wilkins, D. *Concilia Magnae Brittaniae.* 4 vols. London, 1737.

Wilkinson, R. *Londina Illustrata.* London, 1819.

Wills from Doctors' Commons [containing Gardiner's will]. Ed. J. G. Nichols and J. Bruce. Camden Soc. London, 1863.

Wilson, H. A. *Magdalen College.* London, 1889.

Winchester Cathedral Documents, 1541-1547. Ed. G. W. Kitchen and F. T. Madge. Hampshire Record Soc. London, 1889.

Wood, A. *Athenae Oxonienses.* London, 1721.

Wordsworth, C. *Scholae Academicae.* Cambridge, 1877.

Wriothlesley, C. *A Chronicle of England.* Ed. W. D. Hamilton. 2 vols. Camden Soc. London, 1875, 1877.

NOTES

ABBREVIATIONS USED IN NOTES AND APPENDICES

Manuscripts are cited under their usual designations, in each case the place where they are to be found being indicated thus:

B. M.—British Museum.
Bibl. Nat.—Bibliotheque National, Paris.
Camb. Univ. Lib.—Library of Cambridge University.
C. C. C. C.—Corpus Christi College, Cambridge.
Coll. Arm.—College of Arms, London.
Lambeth—Lambeth Palace Library.
R. O.—Public Record Office.

The abstracts prepared by Mr. Royal Tyler for the yet unpublished vol. XII of the *Spanish Calendar,* and now in the Public Record Office, are cited as:
R. O., Tyler abstracts.

In the citation of printed books the following abbreviations are used:

Cal. St. P. Dom.—Calendar of State Papers, Domestic Series.
Cal. St. P. For.—Calendar of State Papers, Foreign Series.
Chron. Qu. Jane—The Chronicle of Queen Jane and Two Years of Queen Mary. Camden Soc.
C. M. H.—The Cambridge Modern History.
Commons' Journ.—Journals of the House of Commons.
D. N. B.—Dictionary of National Biography.
Ep. Poli—Epistolae Reginaldi Poli.
Lords' Journ.—Journals of the House of Lords.
L. P.—Letters and Papers, Foreign and Domestic of the Reign of Henry VIII.
Milan. Cal.—Calendar of State Papers . . . in the Archives . . . of Milan.
Mon. Fr.—Monumenta Franciscana (containing *Grey Friars' Chronicle*).
Nar. of the Ref.—Narratives of the Reformation. Camden Soc.
O. L.—Original Letters Relative to the English Reformation. Parker Soc.
P. H. E.—The Political History of England.
Sp. Cal.—Calendar of Letters . . . Relating to the Negotiations between England and Spain.
St. P.—State Papers during the Reign of Henry VIII.
Strype, *Mem.*—Strype, *Ecclesiastical Memorials.*
V. C. H.—The Victoria History of the Counties of England.
Ven. Cal.—Calendar of State Papers . . . Preserved in the Archives of Venice.

Fuller titles, names of editors, and dates of editions of these, as well as of other books cited, may be found in the list of printed books beginning at p. 326.

Several well known histories and collections of documents, such as those of Burnet, Dixon, Ehses, Foxe, Pocock, *etc.,* are cited under the names of author or editor only. Titles and editions used may be found in the list of printed books beginning at p. 326.

In citations from printed books, Roman numerals, unless otherwise indicated, refer to volumes, Arabic numerals to pages; except that in references to the *Letters and Papers . . . of the Reign of Henry VIII* (cited as *L. P.*) Arabic numerals refer to the numbers of the entries in that collection.

338

NOTES TO CHAPTER I

[1] The baptismal registers of St. James', Bury, do not commence till 1558.

[2] A mark was worth ⅔ of a pound.

[3] The will is published in part in the *Proceedings of the Bury and West Suffolk Archaeological Institute*, I, 329 (May 1853), from the original in Reg. of Wills, Bury, Lib. Pye, f. 196. It was proved Nov. 20, 1507. In it the children are named in this order: Stephen, Rose, Joan, John, William. William is clearly an adult, the others minors. Mr. J. Gairdner, in *Typical Eng. Churchmen*, Ser. II, 188, suggests that William was the child of a former marriage, and that Stephen was the first born of Agnes, second wife of the testator. William died 1550. Foxe, VI, 194. One sister, doubtless Joan, married a certain Frances, and her son, Henry Frances, was made bailiff of the Clink in Southwark by her brother Stephen, then Bishop of Winchester. *Nar. of the Ref.*, 48.

[4] See App. I for discussion of birth date and parentage.

[5] Quoted in M. R. James, *On the Abbey Church of S. Edmund at Bury*, 126, 166. For Bury and its abbey see also *V. C. H.*, *Suffolk*, II, 56-72, and *A Description of the Ancient and Present State of the Town and Abbey of Bury St. Edmunds*, printed by Wm. Green, 1768.

[6] *An Historical Account of Sturbridge, Bury, and the Most Famous Fairs*. Camb. [1773].

[7] For evidence that this school was still existing in the time of Gardiner's youth, see *V. C. H.*, *Suffolk*, II, 306 ff.

[8] Gerardus to Erasmus, June 8, 1533. *Briefe an Erasmus*, ed. Förstemann and Günther, 222. Gardiner is here called *"vir qui et litteras et natare didicit."*

[9] Richard Eden was granted the clerkship of the King's Council for life, June 14, 1512. *L. P.*, I, i, 1462 (26), new ed. Wolsey appears later to have intruded two others into this office, but shortly after Wolsey's disgrace, when Gardiner was in high favor at court, the clerkship of the council was granted, Apr. 20, 1530, to Richard and Thomas Eden in survivorship, on surrender of Richard's patent of 1512. *L. P.*, IV, 6490 (1). See A. F. Pollard in *Eng. Hist. Rev.* XXXVII, 347-9. Gardiner, in his will, left small bequests to a John and Thomas Eden, perhaps children or grandchildren of the trustees named in his father's will.

[10] This letter, written in Latin, was first printed by P. S. Allen in the *Academy*, XLVIII, 318. It has since appeared in L. K. Enthoven, *Briefe an Desiderius Erasmus*, 73. The original is in the Stadtbibliothek, Breslau. It is dated at the house of Cardinal Wolsey, Feb. 28, but is without year date. It is, however, certain that Gardiner's meeting Erasmus occurred in 1511, for the following reasons: a) Gardiner was in Wolsey's service 1524-9; a meeting with Erasmus in Paris sixteen years before could only have happened in 1511, for the only time Erasmus was in Paris between 1506 and 1517 was Apr. 1511. See F. M. Nichols, *Ep. Eras.*, II, 10, 11, 16, and Chronological Register. b) The *Folly* almost certainly appeared in 1511. c) The reply of Erasmus, which must have been in the same year as Gardiner's letter, else he would have apologized for delay, was in 1526 or 1527. Contemporary editions of Erasmus give the former, Le Clerk the latter date. Mr. Nichols, who gives a partial translation of Gardiner's letter in *Ep. Eras.*, II, 12, says that it was one of a batch of letters sent to Basel in August 1526, but the date is clearly Feb. 28, and Mr. P. S. Allen tells me there is no indication of any letters to Erasmus from England in August of that year.

[11] Erasmus to Gardiner, Basle, Sept. 3, [1526 or 1527]. Cf. Gairdner, *Typical Eng. Churchmen*, Ser. II, 170; *L. P.*, IV, 3399. This letter has long been known, but the ignorance of Gardiner's letter to which it is a reply has led to speculation as to when Gardiner and Erasmus first met. It has been erroneously suggested that they were fellow students at Paris (Brewer, *Hen. VIII*, II, 245), or that they met while Gardiner was abroad as tutor to the

Duke of Norfolk's children (*D. N. B.* and *Athenae Cantab.*). It does not appear that Gardiner ever acted as tutor to the Duke of Norfolk's children; but according to a ms. note in the front of the 1563 ed. of Foxe in the B. M. (copy c. 37. h. 2), Thomas, grandson of the Duke of Norfolk, became Gardiner's pupil early in Mary's reign, which may be the basis for the other statement. See below, Chapter XXVIII, n. 49.

[12] *De Vera,* "Roane" ed. f. xliiii.

NOTES TO CHAPTER II

[1] Nichols, *Ep. Eras.,* II, 224, 331, 375.

[2] There is no record of Gardiner's matriculation, since matriculation by the university authorities was not practiced before 1515. There are no extant Trinity Hall registers earlier than 1557. However, the Grace granting Gardiner the degree of Bachelor of Law in 1518, says he had studied seven years in the university. *Grace Book Γ,* 159.

[3] 35 H. VIII, c. 15.

[4] Translation by Brewer, *Hen. VIII,* I, 239.

[5] 1513, 1518, 1521, 1524. *Grace Book B,* II, 29; *Grace Book Γ,* xxxv.

[6] Made in 1688, before the old buildings had been much altered. Reproduced in Malden, frontispiece, and *Warren's Book,* 62.

[7] Caius, *Hist. Cant. Acad.,* I, 63; Survey of 1546 in *Documents relating to Cambridge,* I, 157.

[8] *Warren's Book,* 85.

[9] MSS. C. C. C. C., Vol. 127, pp. 167-342. Cf. Giles, *Ascham,* I, ii, 385.

[10] *St. P.,* I, 430.

[11] There is no record in the *Grace Books* of his taking either a B.A. or an M.A. degree. Moreover he paid "commons," *i.e.,* a fee of 20*d.,* on admission to incept in Civil Law. *Grace Book B,* II, 88. Those who paid commons in the higher faculties had not taken an arts course. *Grace Book B,* I, xx.

[12] Candidates for the degree of D. J. Can. had to hear lectures on the Bible during two years. *Documents relating to Cambridge,* I, Statute 122.

[13] Gerardus to Erasmus, June 8, 1533, in Förstemann and Günther, 222.

[14] *George Joye confuteth Winchester's false Articles,* f. viii.

[15] Leland, *Encomia,* 48.

[16] Burnet, V, 352.

[17] Malden, 18.

[18] *Grace Book B,* II, 63, 65; *Grace Book Γ,* 159.

[19] *Grace Book Γ,* 196; *Grace Book B,* II, 88, 95. During seventeen years, 1512-28 inclusive, only sixteen doctor's degrees in Civil Law were granted. In the same period twenty-eight D. J. Can. *Grace Book B,* II, vi (tables of degrees).

[20] *Grace Book B,* II, 98. In biographical dictionaries the dates of Gardiner's doctor's degrees are given usually as 1520 D. J. Civ., and 1521 D. J. Can. In the *Grace Books* the first is entered for the college year 1520-1, the second 1521-2. The year represented is from Michaelmas (Sept. 29) to Michaelmas, and it was customary to grant these degrees at the great commencement on the first Tuesday in July. Unless there was something exceptional in Gardiner's case, he would have become D. J. Civ. in July 1521, and D. J. Can. July 1522. In the list of Cambridge Doctors appended to the *De Antiq. Brit. Eccl.* his degrees are dated 1521 and 1522.

[21] For the study and teaching of Canon and Civil Law see *Grace Book A,* xxv-xxviii, xxxviii; Peacock, *Observations on the Statutes,* 34-5; *Documents relating to Cambridge,* I, Statutes 104, 120-1, 152, 156-7.

[22] For the statement in *D. N. B.* that Gardiner was a Fellow of Trinity

Hall, I have been unable to find contemporary authority, but it is altogether probable. He may have been Fellow successively in Civil and Canon Law, for vacant fellowships in Civil Law were filled by bachelors in that faculty, and vacant fellowships in Canon Law were filled by Civil Law Fellows if they were willing to become canonists and, within a year, priests. A Fellow not in priest's orders received £4 13s. 4d. annually, one in priest's orders £5 6s. 8d. Malden, 16, 36-9; *Documents relating to Cambridge*, I, 157. The date of Gardiner's ordination is unknown. He was probably not a priest when he became D. J. Civ. in 1521, for priests were forbidden to study Civil Law. Rashdall, *Universities*, I, 260, 323. If he held a Canon Law Fellowship he was doubtless ordained to the priesthood before leaving Cambridge.

[23] A lecturer was required to place an article of value in the hands of the proctors as a "caution" or pledge that he would pay the rental of the "schools" or university lecture halls. It was customary to give the caution for the Chairs of Civil and Canon Law in the year before the chairs were to be used. In 1520-1 Gardiner gave *"unum antiquum nobile et duo ducketes"* as a caution for the chair of Civil Law. In 1521-2 he paid 20s. rental for the same, and gave *"unum salinum argenteum"* as a caution for the chair of Canon Law. In 1522-3 he gave a caution for the chair of Civil Law, not described, and *"una mirra, annulus aureus, unus ducatus, et una corona aurea"* as caution for the chair of Canon Law. 1523-4 he again paid 20s. rental for the chair of Civil Law. *Grace Book B*, II, 96, 100, 111, 117.

[24] *Encomia*, 48. John Cheke also bears testimony to Gardiner's reform of the study of Civil Law, but he probably refers to a later period when Gardiner as Chancellor of the university seconded the new ideas which Thomas Smith brought from the Continent in 1541. *See* Mullinger, *Univ. of Camb.*, II, 126.

[25] *Grace Book B*, II, 97, 110, 114; *Grace Book Γ*, 209. *D. N. B.*, "Gardiner," erroneously makes him "one of Sir Robert Rede's lecturers,"—a mistake repeated by F. W. Maitland in *English Law and the Renaissance*, 62.

[26] There is an item in *Grace Book B*, II, 119, entered after the audit of July 13, and before that of Nov. 16, 1524, for the expenses of one of the proctors on a journey, on university business, to Wolsey and certain members of his household, including Gardiner. This makes it reasonably certain that Gardiner entered Wolsey's service sometime before the latter date. Moreover, the proctor's item speaks of "the costs in the law for my declaration by the space of a month now and a fortnight before Sturbridge Fair," which seems to indicate that the entry was made a month after Sturbridge Fair, which was held Sept. 4. If this interpretation be correct, Gardiner must have been in Wolsey's service at the beginning of October 1524, if not before.

[27] *Grace Book B*, II, 119, 135, 144, 153, 157.

[28] *Warren's Book*, 11, 13, 152.

[29] See above, p. 171 and n.

[30] Hacket, *Scrinia Reserata*, I, 62.

[31] Malden, 81, 95-7. Gardiner left Trinity Hall £100 (in 1555), which would mean perhaps more than 1,000 in present values.

[32] R. O., Nov. 13, 1545 (*L. P.*, XX, ii, 788).

[33] *Encomia*, 49.

[34] Neither Wriothesley nor Paget took a degree at Cambridge. Ponet tells us they were brought up by Gardiner at Cambridge. *Treatise of politike pouuer*, f. Iiii. Leland speaks of both as members of Gardiner's household. *Encomia*, 100-1. Gardiner himself says that he was Paget's "teacher and tutor, afterward his master." Foxe, VI, 259.

[35] Foxe, IV, 620-1.

[36] Except Coverdale, Paget, and Wriothesley, these names, with dates of degrees and often the number of years spent in study may be found in the *Grace Books*. For this period the index of *Grace Book Γ* should be first consulted, as it includes and rectifies that of *B*, II. The index of *Athenae Cantab.*,

III, is helpful in using the *Grace Books*. Coverdale lived at the Austin Friars in Cambridge 1514-26 (*D. N. B.*). For Paget and Wriothesley see above, n. 34.
[37] Gardiner's *Declaration*, f. 4.

NOTES TO CHAPTER III

[1] Hearne, *Adam de Domerham*, xcvii-ciii. Gardiner is here called *utriusque juris Doctor, Norwicen.* His home, Bury St. Edmunds, was at that time in the diocese of Norwich.

[2] Bp. Tunstall's testimony at Gardiner's trial in 1550. Foxe, VI, 188. Tunstall went so far as to say that Henry took Gardiner into his service because of his work on this treaty, but this must have been an imperfect memory, for Gardiner did not enter the King's service till 1529.

[3] *L. P.*, IV, 1962. An archdeacon was an ecclesiastical judge. The importance of the office both judicially and financially in the sixteenth century may be gathered from the cases cited from archdeaconal courts in Hale, *A Series of Precedents.*

[4] Barnes' *Supplication*, 201a, 215b.

[5] *The cause of my condemnation,* and *The hole disputation between the byshops and doctour Barnes,* in *The Supplication of doctour Barnes unto the moost gracyous Kynge Henrye the eight.* [1532?] The citations here made are from the edition of 1573 in the collected works of Tyndall, Frith, and Barnes. The text of this is the same as that of the first edition, but most of the marginal headings are additions.

[6] Gardiner's introduction to *A Declaration of suche true articles as George Joye hath gone about to confute as false.* 4to and 8vo editions in 1546. The latter is here cited.

[7] Foxe, V, 414 ff. Though agreeing in the main with Barnes and Gardiner, this contains details not given by either, especially of Gardiner's assistance to Barnes. Foxe is the last person conceivable to invent stories in Gardiner's favour.

[8] These articles, with Barnes' explanation of them, are in his *Supplication,* 205.

[9] *Ib.*, 221.

[10] Foxe, V, 416.

[11] *Supplication*, 215.

[12] Foxe, V, 417.

[13] *Supplication*, 206.

[14] Foxe, V, 418. Cf. *Supplication,* 225; Hall; Stow; *Mon. Fr.* II, 192; *Camden Miscel.,* XII, 2. On purple as the colour for cardinals see Brewer, *Hen. VIII,* I, 271, n.

[15] Arthur, as we learn from the *Grace Books,* had been a contemporary of Gardiner at Cambridge. It is said that he was a Trinity Hall man (Malden, 93) but the fact that he proceeded B.A., M.A., and B.D., and took no law degree, casts doubt on this. He recanted in 1527, and died in 1532. Bilney also recanted in 1527, later repented his recantation, and was burned 1531, after condemnation by the Bishop of Norwich.

[16] Joye's account of Gardiner's relations to himself, Stafford, and Chikes, is in his *Refutation of the byshop of Winchesters derke declaration,* 1546, f. lxxxi. Most of the passage is reprinted in Foxe, IV, 754.

[17] Gardiner, *Declaration,* f. 4

NOTES TO CHAPTER IV

[1] *L. P.*, IV, 6748 (7) (11).

[2] *L. P.*, IV, 3138.

[3] *Ib.*, 3140; *Sp. Cal.*, III, ii, p. 193; cf. Friedmann, I, 51 ff.

[4] *L. P.,* IV, 3216; Cavendish, 45; *Chronicle of Calais,* 38. They landed at Calais July 11.

[5] *L. P.,* IV, 3231. All of Wolsey's important letters at this time were dictated to or copied by Gardiner.

[6] *L. P.,* IV, 3289; *St. P.,* I, 222.

[7] For the custom of addressing secretaries by their first name, see App. I, p. 306. In *L. P.,* IV, 2576 "Master Stephyns," chaplain to the Marquis of Exeter, is John Stephyns, not Gardiner. See *ib.,* 6748(14).

[8] *L. P.,* IV, 3335; *St. P.,* I, 255. This correspondence is misread in *D. N. B.,* "Gardiner."

It must have been about this time that Wolsey, according to Cavendish, worked, one day, on dispatches from 4 A.M. till 4 P.M., his chaplain vested all the while, awaiting him at mass. Mr. Brewer suggests that the chaplain may have been Gardiner (*Hen. VIII,* II, 215), but Wolsey would not have kept Gardiner idle for twelve hours.

[9] *St. P.,* I, 260, 264, 280.

[10] *Eng. Hist. Rev.,* XI, 685, 689; Ehses, No. 19; *Sp. Cal.,* VIII, p. 577. Cf. Sanders, *Ang. Schism,* 56.

[11] *L. P.,* IV, 3913, 3918-20.

[12] *Mei dimidium. Ib.,* 3912. Wolsey doubtless had in mind the words in which Horace spoke of Virgil: *animae dimidium meae.*

[13] For contemporary instances see Pollard, *Hen. VIII,* 212.

[14] *St. P.,* VII, 51.

[15] Pocock, I, 74.

[16] *L. P.,* IV, 5391.

[17] *Love Letters of Hen. VIII,* ed. Black, 52.

[18] Pocock I, 73, 75; *St. P.,* VII, 52. Most of the letters sent by Gardiner and Fox on this embassy are in Gardiner's hand and, in all probability, of his authorship.

[19] Pocock, I, 78; *L. P.,* IV, 3958. Cf. *ib.,* 3611, 3865.

[20] *Ib.,* 3955.

[21] *Ib.,* 3954, 3977-80.

[22] *L. P.,* IV, 4003, 4078; Pocock, I, 83, 86; *St. P.,* VII, 59, 60.

[23] Pocock, I, 88, 90; *St. P.,* VII, 63.

[24] *Ib.*

[25] *L. P.,* IV, 3913. The desire for a male heir seems, in truth, to have been Henry's prime motive for seeking divorce and remarriage. He might have enjoyed the charms of Anne Boleyn without either. For a discussion of the whole matter see Pollard, *Hen. VIII,* Chapter VII.

[26] Conferences with the Pope, Mar. 22-31, are described in a letter of the latter date. Pocock, I, 95. Cf. *Sp. Cal.,* VIII, p. 577.

[27] Gardiner's letter reporting negotiations Apr. 1-13, is in Pocock, I, 120.

[28] Ehses, No. 22; *Eng. Hist. Rev.,* XI, 701; XII, 6.

[29] Joye's *Refutation,* f. cxxvi.

[30] Pocock, I, 141-155.

[31] *Ib.,* I, 156-9.

[32] *St. P.,* VII, 78.

[33] *St. P.,* VII, 87. He held a Papal safe-conduct for the journey, dated June 17, 1528. Ehses, No. 27.

[34] *St. P.,* VII, 88.

[35] *Ib.,* 90; *L. P.,* IV, App. 200.

NOTES TO CHAPTER V

[1] Pocock, I, 113, 135; *L. P.,* IV, 4460, 4696, 4755, 4778. In Nov. Gardiner upheld the privileges of Cambridge University against the Bishop of Ely, whose Chancellor had attempted to infringe them. *L. P.,* IV, 4885; *Grace Book B,* II, 153; Lamb, 12.

[2] *L. P.*, IV, 4736-37.

[3] *Ib.*, 5178-9, 5195. Gardiner replaced Knight and Benet, who, owing to unfavourable news from Italy, had gone no farther than Lyons. He was given £100 for preparation toward his journey, and 26s. 8d. a day for expenses. *L. P.*, V, p. 308.

[4] *L. P.*, IV, 5184.

[5] *Ib.*, 5237, 5294; Pocock, I, 205.

[6] Pocock, II, 590, 607.

[7] *L. P.*, IV, 5391, 5393, 5417. He must have written a gracious if not encouraging note to Anne Boleyn, for early in April she replied, thanking him for his letter in which, she said, she perceived his "willing and faithful mind" to do her service. *Ib.*, 5422.

[8] Burnet, IV, 79; *L. P.*, IV, 5474.

[9] Burnet, V, 448-51. "If my Lord Campegius would promise your Majesty to give sentence frankly and apertly, having *propitium judicem*, I would trust, being there with such consultations as I should bring from hence, to say something in this breve there, *apud illos et ista est sacra anchora majestatis vestrae*, for from hence shall come nothing but delays; desiring your Highness not to show this to my Lord Campegius, ne my Lord's Grace." *Ib.*, 450. "My Lord's Grace" is undoubtedly Wolsey, and the suggestion that something in the letter be kept from him has been taken as an indication of Gardiner's faithlessness to him. It is, however, plain that it was Campeggio especially who Gardiner thought should not be told of what he wrote. What his motive was in asking that it be also kept from Wolsey is, from this shred of evidence, impossible to say.

[10] Burnet, IV, 98-9; *Eng. Hist. Rev.* XII, 245. The promise as given in Burnet, VI, 26, seems to be this second form devised by Gardiner. The first is in Ehes, No. 23, and *Eng. Hist. Rev.*, XII, 8. The promise or "polliciatation" is confused with the commission in Brewer, *Hen. VIII*, II, 335-6.

[11] *L. P.*, IV, 5417, 5440, 5529; *St. P.*, VII, 169.

[12] Burnet, VI, 23-4. Gardiner concludes the sentence quoted thus: "which is all that can be said after my poor wit herein, considering that your Highness hath been not well handled, ne according to your merits by the Pope or some other; it becometh not me to arrecte the blame certainly to any man." This has been interpreted as a covert thrust at Wolsey, but Campeggio is the person aimed at.

[13] Burnet, IV, 95.

[14] He left Rome early in June. *L. P.*, IV, 5606, 5649, 5712.

[15] Cavendish, 80.

[16] *L. P.*, IV, 5181, 5733, 5742. As Mr. Pollard remarks, Clement "did not mind what his legates did so long as he was free to repudiate their action when convenient." *Hen. VIII*, 220, n.

[17] *L. P.*, IV, 5798. For the nature of the post at this time see Evans, *The Principal Secretary of State*, Chapter II.

[18] *Encomia*, 48; also in Leland, *Antiq.*, V, 117.

NOTES ON CHAPTER VI

[1] Pocock, I, 265.

[2] *St. P.*, VII, 190.

[3] For the King's itinerary, see *L. P.*, IV, 5965. He stayed at Wolsey's place at Tittenhanger Aug. 14-15. Ellis, 3 Ser., I, 345. If Sanders' account of Wolsey's meeting the King "in a place near St. Albans" is to be trusted, it must have occurred at this time. *Ang. Schism*, 74. See *L. P.*, IV, 5865, where Wolsey's language contains a hint of having met the King at Tittenhanger. Sanders' further account of this meeting, however, lacks versimilitude.

He says that Gardiner, "knowing himself to be suspected of having been the cause of the divorce, asked Wolsey openly to declare . . . who they were who had been the first movers in the matter. 'I will never deny,' said Wolsey, 'that I alone have done it.'" It is unlikely that anyone suspected Gardiner of having been the cause of the divorce, or if they did, that he should have taken pains to have it denied. There may be this germ of truth in the story—that Gardiner desired to have it made clear that it was not he who had insisted on submitting the case to a Papal rather than an English court. See J. Gairdner in *Transactions of the Royal Historical Soc.*, New Series, XIII, 80.

[4] These are given in abstract in *L. P.*, IV, 5816-5993 *passim*. Eight of them have been printed in full in *St. P.*, one in Ellis, two in Pocock.

[5] Pocock, I, 248, where it is erroneously dated June 30, 1529. In *L. P.*, IV, 5819 it is placed after Aug. 1, 1529. The letter is dated "From Greenwich this Wednesday" which is clearly July 28, 1529, for on that day Gardiner wrote to Vannes "*hodie primum aulam ingredior.*" Pocock, I, 265. The first Wednesday in August (Aug. 4) Gardiner was at Waltham. *L. P.*, IV, 5825.

[6] *L. P.*, IV, 5802.

[7] *St. P.*, I, 339.

[8] R. O., Aug. 6, 1529 (*L. P.*, IV, 5831).

[9] R. O., Sept. 3, 1529 (*L. P.*, IV, 5918). Cf *St. P.*, I, 342.

[10] Cavendish, 95, 97-8. Cavendish makes Wolsey greet Gardiner as if he had not seen him since his return from Rome, a month before. This is an imperfect recollection of Cavendish, who wrote some years after the occurrence. Gardiner had been home for three months, during one of which he had been in Wolsey's service.

[11] Ellis, 1 Ser., I, 307-10.

[12] Gardiner to Somerset, Oct. 14, 1547. Foxe, VI, 43. Mr. Mullinger, *D. N. D.*, "Gardiner," referring to this letter (Harleian MS. 417, f. 85) makes the surprising statement that Gardiner professed to believe that Wolsey merited his fate.

[13] *L. P.*, IV, 5945. In a contemporary French account of Wolsey's fall, in Raumer, II, 64-5, the writer accuses Gardiner of duplicity, but his information is admittedly based on hearsay. "I was told," he says, thus and so about Gardiner.

[14] *Hen. VIII*, II, 369.

[15] *Der Sturz des Cardinals Wolsey*, 62-3, 71-2, 99.

[16] *Anne Boleyn*, I, 95.

[17] Rymer, VI, ii, 138. In this memorandum Gardiner is called clerk of the King's Council.

[18] Friedmann (I, 99) says that Gardiner preferred the promise of the see of Winchester to the office of Chancellor. But there is no evidence that such a promise was made him. The see was kept open for two years after the indictment of the Cardinal and for ten months after his death in the hope that Pole would accept it. See Haile, *Pole*, 77, citing Becatelli, and Gairdner, *Eng. Church in the Sixteenth Cent.*, 102.

[19] *L. P.*, IV, 6019.

[20] Hall, II, 156.

[21] *L. P.*, IV, 6098, 6181, 6224, 6545.

[22] *Ib.*, 6098, 6299.

[23] B. M., Titus B. 1, 370. The abstract of this letter in *L. P.*, IV, 6112 is, in one phrase, misleading. It reads, "went to Mr. Secretary who said he knew nothing at all about my Lord's Grace." This is quoted in Brewer, *Hen. VIII*, II, 404, as if it were the exact words of the writer. The phrase leaves the impression that Gardiner washed his hands of all connection with Wolsey, while in reality it was neither the Cardinal nor his affairs, but recent tidings of the King's pleasure concerning him, of which Gardiner disclaimed knowledge. Sadler asked him if he "knew any news touching my Lord his Grace, who answered that he knew nothing at all."

[24] R. O., Oct. 17, 1530 (*L. P.*, IV, 6688).

[25] *St. P.*, I, 357.

[26] *L. P.*, IV, 6213-14, 6220.

[27] *Ib.*, 6076, 6181-2, 6295. We have nine letters from Wolsey to Gardiner, Dec. 1529-Aug. 1530. Gardiner's letters to Wolsey at this time seem no longer to exist.

[28] *L. P.*, IV, 6261, 6529; V, 1453.

[29] *Ib.*, IV, 6224, 6261, 6529.

[30] R. O., Aug. 1, 1530 (*L. P.*, IV, 6545).

[31] *Hen. VIII*, II, 412.

[32] Strype, *Mem.*, I, ii, No. 33.

[33] R. O., July 20, 1530 (*L. P.*, IV, 6523).

[34] *L. P.*, IV, 6579, 6679.

[35] R. O., Oct. 11, 1530 (*L. P.*, IV, 6679).

[36] R. O., Oct. 17, 1530 (*L. P.*, IV, 6688).   Henry announced his intention of having a college at Oxford, and, in 1532, having suppressed the Cardinal's college, he established, on the same site, a small religious house known as "King Henry VIII's College," which he replaced in 1546 by his grander foundation, Christ Church. See Thompson, *Christ Church*, 10-11.

NOTES TO CHAPTER VII

[1] *L. P.*, IV, 5806.

[2] *Ib.*, 6016. "Copie of a letter sent to the Cardinal Campegius," is written in Gardiner's hand on the back of the copy in the R. O. Cf. Brewer, *Hen. VIII*, II, 377.

[3] *L. P.*, IV, 6043. 31 H. VIII, c. 10 (1539), provided that when the King's Chief Secretary was neither a bishop nor a baron he should "sit and be placed at the uppermost part of the sacks, in the midst of the said Parliament Chamber," which doubtless legalized an already existing custom.

[4] *L. P.*, IV, 6047. According to Le Neve, II, 484, citing Reg. Nyx, Gardiner was admitted Mar. 1, 1529, to the archdeaconry of Norfolk, void by the resignation of Thomas Winter (Wolsey's son); but in the Convocation list of Nov. 1529, Winter still holds that title. *L. P.*, IV, 6047.

[5] Morice's account of Cranmer, in *Nar. of the Ref.*, 241-2. It is upon this that Foxe (VIII, 6) based his version of the same incident. Foxe's statement that Gardiner was displeased because Fox did not tell Henry that the device was of their own invention, is not in Morice. Morice's account was not used by Foxe till his edition of 1570. In his earlier editions he credits Gardiner with having first brought Cranmer to the King's attention for persuading five doctors of Cambridge to change their opinion on the divorce Cf. *ib.*, VIII, 805.

[6] *Nar. of the Ref.*, 242; *L. P.*, IV, 6218; Pollard, *Cranmer*, 41-2.

[7] Burnet, IV, 130-3; *L. P.*, IV, 6247, 6259, 6325.

[8] *L. P.*, IV, 6513. For the importance attached to university opinions see Pollard, *Cranmer*, 39-40.

[9] See above, pp. 37-8.

[10] *L. P.*, IV, 6227. Cf. *ib.*, 5853.

[11] *L. P.*, IV, 6402; Wilkins, III, 727; Foxe V, 599; VII, 505; cf. *Lollardy*, II, 241, ff.

[12] *L. P.*, IV, 6618, 6755; V. 40, 45. In Aug. 1530, Scarpinello, Milanese ambassador in England, wrote that the persons having influence with Henry were Norfolk, Wiltshire (Thomas Boleyn), and Gardiner, but added that Henry desired to know and superintend everything himself. *Milan, Cal.*, p. 521.

[13] *L. P.*, V, 287. Chapuys, who describes the scene, names Gardiner as one who had begun to favour Catherine and who was now much suspected by

Anne Boleyn; but Chapuys was perhaps too prone to see signs of favour in the actions of Catherine's opponents.

[14] *Ib.*, 361.

[15] *Ib.*, 368. Mr. Mullinger, *D. N. B.*, "Gardiner," says that at this time, the summer of 1531, Gardiner, though still advocating a middle course in relation to the divorce, had altogether lost Catherine's confidence. There is no indication that up to this time he had ever had her confidence, or advocated anything less than the annulment of her marriage.

[16] Merriman, I, 344.

[17] See above, n. 4.

[18] *L. P.*, IV, 6447. The grant is dated July 23, 1530. He enjoyed the revenues for two years, surrendering his rights June 13, 1532. *Ib.*, 6542(23). Hanworth was then given to Anne Boleyn. *Ib.*, V, 1139(32), 1207(7).

[19] Collated Mar. 25, installed Mar. 31. Le Neve, II, 61, citing Reg. Linc. Upon accepting Leicester he gave up Norfolk, for his successor at Norfolk was collated Apr. 2, 1531. Le Neve II, 484 (Reg. Nyx.). He must have given up Worcester at the same time, for Wm. Claybrooke was collated to Worcester Apr. 4, 1531. Le Neve, III, 75 (no register cited). He gave up Leicester on becoming Bishop of Winchester, Edward Fox succeeding him. Le Neve, II, 61 (Reg. Linc.). Cranmer appears to have succeeded him at Taunton. See Pollard, *Cranmer*, 47.

[20] Henry asked the Pope to promote Gardiner to Winchester Sept. (no day) 1531. *L. P.*, V, 419. Chapuys writing Sept. 26, says that York has been given to Lee and Winchester to Gardiner, and that Catherine fears this has been done to get two more votes in the Lords in Henry's favor. *Ib.*, 432.

[21] Oct. 12, 1531. Foster, *Alumni Oxon.*, Early Series, II, 548.

[22] *L. P.*, V, 627 (8. ii) ; Reg. Gardiner, f. 2.

[23] Stubbs, 99; Reg. Gardiner. License, Nov. 27, 1531. *Ib.* Neither the consecrators nor the place of consecration are named.

[24] Reg. Gardiner, f. 3; *L. P.* V, 627(8). Grant dated Hampton Court, 29 Nov.; Del. Chelsea, 5 Dec.

[25] Reg. Gardiner, f. 4. The Papal procurators at the installation were Robert Sherborne, Bp. of Chichester, and Edmund Steward, whom Gardiner had made his Vicar General Dec. 8, 1531. Steward had been a fellow student of Gardiner's at Cambridge, becoming Bachelor of Civil Law there in 1515. *Grace Book* Γ, 125. He became Dean of Winchester in 1554. Nicholas Harpsfield was a witness at the installation.

[26] £4,095 16s. 5¾d. in 1529, according to Loseley MSS., cited in *V. C. H. Surrey*, II, 17. The revenues in 1535 amounted, after deducting certain alms and fees to officials, to £3,885. *Valor Eccl.*, II, 2.

[27] *L. P.*, V, 657.

[28] B. M., Titus B. 1, 373 (*L. P.* V, 1138).

[29] *L. P.*, V, 886, 1285(iv) ; VI, 841.

[30] *I.e.*, St. Mary's over the river.

[31] *St. P.*, I, 328.

[32] *Encomia*, 100-1. For description and views of Winchester House, see *V. C. H., Surrey*, IV, 147; for St. Mary's Church, see Dollman, *The Priory of St. Mary Overie;* for Southwark and London in Gardiner's day, see the *Panorama of London, Westminster, and Southwark in 1543*, by Anthony Van den Wyngaerde, reprinted in Besant, *London in the Time of the Tudors.* The bishop of Winchester was lord of the manor of Southwark; he had a manor court and jail, rights of wharfage at the dock, and other feudal rights and dues.

[33] *Joye confuteth Winchester*, f. viii.

[34] Wm. Turner, *The Huntyng of the Romyshe Vuolfe*, Eiiii.

[35] Foxe, VI, 250.

[36] *Ib.* 36.

[37] *L. P.*, V, 614, 620, 686, 711. He arrived in Abbeville before Jan. 7, 1532. *Milan. Cal.*, p. 548.

[38] *L. P.,* V, 756, 807.
[39] The terms are given in Friedmann, I, 153, summarizing Camusat, *Meslanges historiques,* II, ff. 84-88.
[40] *L. P.,* V, 742, 755, 791.

NOTES TO CHAPTER VIII

[1] *L. P.,* V, 850.
[2] Gee and Hardy, 145; Merriman, I, 104.
[3] Hall, II, 209-10, 212; *L. P.,* V, 1013, 1025. The fullest version of the first answer of the ordinaries is printed in Gee and Hardy, 154. For records of Convocation, shorter version of first answer, second answer, an offer of compromise, final submission, and the King's demands of May 10, see Wilkins, III, 748-55, and Atterbury, 86-95, 521-48. On Apr. 15 Gardiner read in the upper house of Convocation an answer to the preface and first portion of the Supplication. It passed there immediately, and in the lower house Apr. 19. As this dealt with the matter of most importance, the legislative power of Convocation, it may, as Canon Dixon (I, 92-3) suggests, have been the answer submitted to the King and the one given in Wilkins, the extended form being composed at more leisure. Canon Dixon is probably in error when he says that Gardiner merely corrected answers conceived in the lower house. It is true that the lower house considered the matter, since many ordinaries (bishop's deputies *etc.*) sat there, but the upper house also considered it. The lower house was asked to prepare the *second* answer. Even in this Gardiner may have had a hand. Certainly Henry deemed him responsible for the answers, and Gardiner did not hesitate to avow his adherence to the principles embodied in them.
[4] Wilkins, III, 752; Atterbury, 528.
[5] *L. P.,* V, 1058 (May 31). Gardiner's presence is recorded, perhaps erroneously, at Greenwich, May 20, when the King gave the great seal to Thomas Audley. *Ib.,* 1075.
Mr. Mullinger, *D. N. B.,* "Gardiner," says that in 1532 Volusenus, the Scotch scholar, dedicated to Gardiner a commentary on Psalm 1, praising his energy and example in diocesan activities. A similar statement concerning a commentary on Psalm li, is made in *V. C. H., Hampshire,* II, 52. I have been unable to verify either of these statements. That Volusenus was acquainted with Gardiner is clear from his wish to be remembered to him, expressed in a letter to John Starkey [1535], printed in *The Bannatyne Miscellany,* I, 336.
[6] Aug. 23, 1532.

NOTES TO CHAPTER IX

[1] *L. P.,* V, 738, 834, 1058, 1291.
[2] *Ib.,* 1109, 1274, 1292.
[3] *Chronicle of Calais,* 41. He landed at Calais Oct. 11.
[4] *L. P.,* V, 1256, 1523, App. 33; *Tudor Tracts,* 4 ff.
[5] He reached Eltham Nov. 24. *L. P.,* V, 1579.
[6] *Ib.,* VI, 180; Friedmann, I, 188-9.
[7] Pocock, II, 442-459. On Palm Sunday, Apr. 6, the day after this business was finished, Bishop Fisher, who had led the opposition to the King in Convocation, was arrested and put in Gardiner's care, but three days later was sent to one of his own places where he remained in confinement till after Anne Boleyn's coronation. *Ven. Cal.,* IV, No. 870; *L. P.,* VI, 324, 653.

[8] *L. P.*, VI, 366, 461, 469; Cranmer's *Letters,* 244. Mr. Mullinger, *D. N. B.,* "Gardiner," says Gardiner "was one of the assessors in the court which . . . pronounced Catherine's marriage null." Mr. Gairdner, *Ency. Brit.,* 11 ed., "Gardiner," says, "he was not exactly, as is often said, one of Cranmer's assessors, but according to Cranmer's own expression, 'assistant' to him as counsel for the King." Both these statements are inaccurate. It is the Bishop of Lincoln whom Cranmer calls his assistant, not however as counsel for the King, but as judge; he names Gardiner as King's Counsel. In the anonymous and often inaccurate *Life and Death of Archbishop Cranmer,* Gardiner is erroneously spoken of as a judge in this trial. *Nar. of the Ref.,* 222.

[9] *St. P.,* I, 395.

[10] *Typical Eng. Churchmen,* Ser. II, 174.

[11] Foxe, VI, 45-6. Cf. *L. P.,* VII, 1554, for Cromwell's advocacy of the Sultan as a model for Christian princes.

[12] *L. P.,* VI, p. 208.

[13] *Ib.,* 737(7). The date of the marriage was kept secret. Cranmer said it was about Jan. 25, 1533. *Ib.,* 661.

[14] *L. P.,* VI, 563, 601; Cranmer, *Letters,* 245; Hall, II, 238.

[15] *L. P.,* VII, 807; cf. *ib.,* 1166. It seems that Gardiner and others had some apprehension that the Papal censures might become effective in England, for Benet, the English ambassador at Rome, secured a dispensation dated Aug. 20, 1533, for himself, Gardiner, the Archbishop of York, the Marquis of Exeter, and Lord Sandes, to have Mass celebrated four times during life, even when their country was under an interdict. *Ib.,* App. 6.

[16] *L. P.,* VI, 1069, 1071, 1164, 1424.

[17] R. O., Oct. 5, 1533 (*L. P.,* VI, 1218).

[18] Burnet, VI, 56. Cf. Friedmann, I, 249-56.

[19] *L. P.,* VI, 1426-7, 1572. The date of Gardiner's return is not recorded.

[20] Wilkins, III, 747-8; Foxe, VII, App. VI, VII. Foxe (IV, 682) says that Stokesley "with the assistance of Winchester and other bishops" judged Richard Bayfield, who was condemned for heresy Nov. 20, 1531; but Bayfield's sentence, printed by Foxe from Stokesley's register, names as Stokesley's assistants the Abbots of Westminster and Waltham, and the Prior of Christ Church, London. Moreover, Gardiner was not consecrated to the see of Winchester until two weeks after Bayfield's condemnation.

[21] Cranmer, *Letters,* 246.

[22] The only extant copy, it seems, of Germain Gardiner's account, printed in 1534, is that in the Grenville Library, B. M. It is summarized in *L. P.,* VII, 1606. See also *Lollardy,* I, 405 ff. Germain also tells how, after Frith's condemnation, Bishop Gardiner continued to endeavour to convert him by sending to him passages from the Fathers. Foxe has two accounts of Frith (V, 3; VIII, 695) slightly discrepant in the parts assigned to Gardiner in his examination. See also Hall, II, 261, and Bale, 657. For Frith's views see Foxe, V, 7-14, and *A boke made by John Frith . . . answerynge unto M. Mores letter. . . .* 1548.

Germain Gardiner makes passing mention of a Thomas Philippes, examined for heresy "the Thursday next ensuing," presumably by Stokesley, Gardiner, and Longland, though he does not say so. This may be the Thomas Philips whom Foxe (IV, 585) lists among those who abjured in Hen. VIII's days. Cf. Strype, *Mem.,* I, i, 116; Dixon, I, 198.

NOTES TO CHAPTER X

[1] Herbert, who appears to have used Convocation records no longer extant, tells us this. *Hen. VIII,* 467.

[2] See above, p. 47.

[3] *Lords' Journ.*, I, 82.

[4] *L. P.*, IX, 547. Abbot Gasquet in *Hen. VIII and the Monasteries*, I, 460, citing *L. P.*, VII, 146, erroneously quotes Gardiner as saying that he regards the breach with Rome as a temporary measure; the words to which the Abbot refers are those of Dr. John London. The abstract in *L. P.* is somewhat ambiguous. See R. O., Theological Tracts, VI, No. 6.

[5] Foxe, VI, 190.

[6] In *L. P.*, VII his name appears in but thirty-nine documents; Cromwell's in almost a thousand.

[7] *L. P.*, VII, 441, 483, 522.

[8] *L. P.*, VII, 425. Cf. *ib.*, VIII, 453(2); XV, 722; *V. C. H., London*, I, 247-51.

[9] Cranmer, *Letters*, 283. The conference was held about Easter time. Easter in 1534 was Apr. 5.

[10] Pocock, II, 536.

[11] Gardiner to Richmond, R. O., June 30, 1534 (*L. P.*, VII, 905). Cf. *Nar. of the Ref.*, 49.

[12] R. O., July 6, 1534 (*L. P.*, VII, App. 31).

[13] *L. P.*, VII, 1031, 1332, 1601(11).

[14] R. O., June 20, 1534 (*L. P.*, VII, 858).

[15] Foxe, V, 69, 71; *L. P.*, VIII, 190.

[16] *L. P.*, VIII, 121.

[17] Ellis, 2 Ser., II, 85; *L. P.*, VIII, 592. Cf. *St. P.*, I, 423. The phrase "coloured doubleness" is quoted in *D. N. B.*, "Gardiner," as if it expressed Henry's appraisement of Gardiner's character or habitual conduct. It is clear from the context that Henry uses it in reference to a particular incident and then with a doubt as to whether it applied to Gardiner or Mores.

[18] *L. P.*, VIII, 129, 149(74)(77); IX, 4, 450; Strype, *Mem.*, I, i, 328. *Valor Eccl.*, II, 2. For a correction of Canon Dixon's interpretation of Gardiner's words concerning the valuation of Winchester College, see Leach, *Hist. of Win. Col.*, 239-40, and *Schools of Mediaeval Eng.*, 231-2.

[19] *L. P.*, IX, 472.

[20] Pollard, *Cranmer*, 95.

[21] Cranmer, *Letters*, 304. Cf. *V. C. H., Hampshire*, II, 52.

[22] Commissions which dealt with land drainage and sea defence.

[23] Written at his house at Bishop's Waltham. *St. P.*, I, 430; Foxe, V, 69; VI, 223; *L. P.*, VIII, 149 (33). Gardiner's translations are not now known to exist. Mr. Gairdner suggests that they were destroyed when the rebels under Wyatt sacked Gardiner's library. *Lollardy*, I, 368, n.

[24] During this period occurred the only recorded instance of Gardiner's ordaining to the ministry. At Winchester, Mar. 28, 1535, he ordained two priests, two deacons, seven subdeacons, and one acolyte. Reg. Gardiner, f. 23b. Other ordinations recorded in his register were performed by his suffragan, John Draper, Prior of Christchurch, Hants, and titular *Episcopus Neopolitanus*, and by John Salcot, Bishop of Bangor. *Ib.*, f. 24.

[25] *L. P.*, VIII, 1117. Owing to the Pope's failure to secure either French or Imperial support against England, the bull depriving Henry of his kingdom was never published. Cf. Pollard, *Hen. VIII*, 302, 334.

[26] *L. P.*, IX, 442, 594, p. 198; cf. *ib.*, 213(1)(5), 218. The answer does not appear to have been published, a few copies for diplomatic use only being necessary. Gardiner's Latin draft of it, a fair copy, and an English translation are in the R. O. In *L. P.*, VIII, 1118, the draft is said to be in Wriothesley's hand, but Mr. Brodie has identified it as Gardiner's.

[27] *L. P.*, IX, 442. At about this time the bishops were required to take out new commissions for the exercise of episcopal authority from the King, as the fountain of all jurisdiction, ecclesiastical as well as secular. Gardiner's is dated Oct. 20, 1535. Reg. Gardiner, f. 25. Cf. Dixon, II, 167.

NOTES ON CHAPTER XI

[1] For editions of the *De Vera Obedientia* see Appendix II, A, i.
[2] *De Vera,* "Roane" ed. ff. xvi-xxiii.
[3] *Ib.,* ff. xviii-xxxi.
[4] *Ib.,* ff. xxxviii-xliiii.
[5] *Ib.,* ff. xlvi-lii.
[6] *Ib.,* f. xvi.
[7] *Ib.,* ff. liiii-lx.
[8] *L. P.,* IX, 442.
[9] *Ib.,* IX, 848, 964, p. 324, 965; X, 7; cf. XII, ii, 620.
[10] *Ib.,* X, 7, 276.
[11] *Ib.,* IX, 548, 873, 947; Friedmann, II, 208.
[12] *L. P.,* X, 570. Cf. *ib.,* 956.
[13] *Ib.,* X, 374-5, 576, 823.
[14] *Ib.,* IX, 1000.
[15] *Ib.,* X, 1089. The reason for attributing this suggestion to Gardiner is a note in Cromwell's hand, "My Lord of Wynch. The Staple," at the end of the ms. containing it. At about the same time, June 1536, Campeggio asked his brother to go to England to persuade Henry VIII to restore the first-fruits of the bishopric of Salisbury, and be reconciled to Rome; Campeggio mentioned as friends in whom he chiefly trusted, the Dukes of Norfolk and Suffolk, and Bishops Clerk, Tunstal, and Gardiner. *Ib.,* X, 1077. Mr. Mullinger, *D. N. B.,* "Gardiner," assumes that this, in connection with Gardiner's suggestion about Papal bulls, is evidence of "a certain disingenuousness" on Gardiner's part; but there is no evidence that Gardiner ever heard anything of Campeggio's scheme. It was natural that Campeggio should express the hope that conservatives rather than reformers might favour reconciliation to Rome.

NOTES TO CHAPTER XII

[1] *Chronicle of Calais,* 46; *L. P.,* IX, 443, 676. Cf. *ib.,* 878. His pay as ambassador began Oct. 1, 1535; it ended Sept. 28, 1538. *Ib.,* XIII, ii, 444. A letter from Gardiner from Antwerp, Nov. 30, printed in *Chronicle of Calais,* 165, and there dated 1535, should be 1545. See *L. P.,* XX, ii, 905.
[2] Stubbs, 99. Hugh Latimer was consecrated Bishop of Worcester, and John Hilsey, Bishop of Rochester, at the same time and place, and presumably by the same consecrators. *Ib.*
[3] Fox died May 8, 1538.
[4] *L. P.,* XI, 445; XII, i, 59, 274, 626; XII, ii, 78.
[5] *L. P.,* XII, i, 960.
[6] Burnet, VI, 150; Merriman, II, 3.
[7] Strype, *Mem.,* I, ii, 236; Collier, *Records,* ii, No. 34.
[8] *Ib.*
[9] Latimer, *Sermons,* Parker Soc., 33-57.
[10] *L. P.,* XII, i, 953; *St. P.,* I, 849.
[11] Dodds, *Pilgrimage of Grace,* I, 347-8, 374-5.
[12] B. M. Add. MS. 25,114, f. 247 (*L. P.,* XII, i, 445). In answering the charge of the rebels that noblemen were no longer employed as royal counsellors, Henry pointed out that while at his accession the Council contained two laymen of noble birth and two bishops, in 1536 it contained nine lay nobles and three bishops, Fox, Sampson, and Gardiner. *St. P.,* I, 508. This is in no sense a commendation of Gardiner as worthy to be called noble, though in *D. N. B.* it is cited as such.
[13] Foxe, VI, 578. See above, p. 265.

[14] Gardiner to Cranmer, July —, 1547. B. M., Add. MS. 29,546, ff. 20-1.
[15] L. P., IX, 765, 857; XII, i, 599; ii, 790; XIII, i, 538, 984, 1090-1, 1272; ii, 446; App. 42; XIV, i, 973. At Gardiner's trial, 1550-1, Basset, then twenty-four years old, testified that he had been in Gardiner's service for twelve years. Foxe, VI, 231. Honor Grenville, Lady Lisle, was the widow of Sir John Basset (d. 1528). In 1528 she became the second wife of Arthur Plantagenet, Viscount Lisle, Deputy of Calais 1533-40. Lisle's first wife was Elizabeth, widow of Edmund Dudley and mother of John Dudley, who, after his step-father's death in 1542, became Viscount Lisle, later Earl of Warwick, and finally Duke of Northumberland.
[16] L. P., IX, 868, 887, App. 7. Gardiner kept no copies of his correspondence on this embassy; ib., XIII, ii, p. 53; the originals of most of his letters are lost.
[17] Ib., XIII, ii, p. 54; cf. Foxe, V, 162.
[18] L. P., IX, 148, 205; XIII, i, 386.
[19] L. P., IX, 443, 838, App. 7; X, 760. Gardiner was, incidentally, to secure the release of certain English merchant ships detained by the French at Bordeaux. Ib., IX, 714 848, 861, App. 8, 9; X, 16, 25, 235, 410.
[20] Ib., X, 235; cf. ib., IX, 1038.
[21] Merriman, II, 2; L. P., X, 374-5.
[22] R. O. (L. P., X, 446.)
[23] L. P., X, 575, 666, 688, 699, 1069.
[24] Ib., X, 760, 2; cf. ib., XI, 28.
[25] Ib., XI-XIII passim. The negotiations are summed up by Gardiner in his instructions to Bonner, ib., XIII, ii, p. 53.
[26] Ib., XI, 1242.
[27] L. P., XI, 1353, XII, i, 123, 367-8, 463, 625, 779, 988.
[28] L. P., XII, i, 760, 817, 865, 931.
[29] The French Ambassador in England told Henry that Gardiner had said to Francis that he would be satisfied if Pole were driven out of France; Henry demanded of Gardiner a denial of this; Gardiner replied evasively. L. P., XII, i, 939, 1032; cf. Foxe, VI, 189. Seven years later Gardiner incidentally mentioned in a letter to Paget that he had exhorted Francis to deliver Pole as he was bound to do in honour by his treaty, in spite of Pole's safe-conduct; to which Francis replied that Gardiner "could no skill of princes' honours, with such a fashion and gesture as I was fain to hold my peace; and so I did, and left that word and entered with him in the matter another way; but yet I spake truth." St. P., X, 665. It would thus seem that Gardiner first complied with his instructions, and thereafter made the admission which the French Ambassador reported to Henry.
[30] L. P., XI, 656, 1130, 1305, XII, i, 12, 53; St. P., VII, 669.
[31] Merriman, II, 96; L. P., XII, ii, 1004, 1125; XIII, i, 1405, 1496; ii, 77, 143, p. 53. Cromwell's letter to Gardiner telling of Jane Seymour's death is mistakenly attributed to Gardiner in Stone, Mary I, 153.
[32] L. P., XII, ii, 46.
[33] Ib., XII, ii, 832, 868-9, 1249, 1253, 1290; XIII, i, 63, 69, 117, 132, 279, 281, 328, 351, 386-7; XIII ii, 143.
[34] L. P., XIII, i, 131, 205.
[35] Ib., XIII, i, 458.
[36] Ib., XIII, i, 712, 900, 1063, 1071.
[37] Ib., XIII, i, 117; ii, 77, 1163; XIV, i, 37.
[38] Ib., X, 952; XI, 28, 151; XIII, i, 778; ii, 444; Merriman, II, 12, 16, 19-21, 23, 97-8, 136; Friedmann, II, 308. See below, Chapter XXVII, n. 4.
[39] L. P., XIII, i, 1440; ii, 8.
[40] Foxe, V, 154-8. Cf. L. P., XIII, i, 1441; ii, 59, 60, 130-1, 144.
[41] Foxe, V, 152.
[42] L. P., XIII, ii, 143.
[43] Foxe, V, 159. There were at this time at least twelve young gentlemen

about the age of nineteen in the Bishop's household. *L. P.,* XIII, i, 327. Beside these were chaplains, secretaries, guards, couriers, and other servants. Gardiner's allowance from the English treasury of 56*s.* 4*d.* a day and post money seems to have come far short of meeting the expenses of his household. He protested against granting a £100 pension to Brian on the ground that he was in need of money himself; and in Aug. 1537 he asked a loan of £2,000 from the King. *L. P.,* XII, i, 770; ii, 586; XIII, ii, 444. See A. O. Meyer, *Die Englische Diplomatie,* for discussion of expenses and households of English ambassadors in Tudor times.

⁴⁴ *St. P.* VIII, 51. If the "doing at Canterbury" refers to the dismantling of Becket's shrine, Gardiner's wish to have the same done at Winchester was already fulfilled, for one week previous Wriothesley and Richard Pollard had "made an end of the shrine" of St. Swithen, in the cathedral at Winchester. They had been disappointed in finding the shrine jewels all counterfeits, but were somewhat compensated by 2,000 marks worth of silver, some jeweled crosses and gold chalices. *L. P.,* XIII, ii, 401.

⁴⁵ Nott's *Wyatt,* 306 (*L. P.,* XVI, p. 310). Cf. *L. P.,* XIII, ii, 270, and Foxe, V, 154.

⁴⁶ Foxe, VI, 66.

⁴⁷ *L. P.,* XIII, ii, 444, 446.

⁴⁸ Foxe, V, 231. Lambert, who denied the corporeal presence in the Sacrament, had appealed from Cranmer to the King, who with great pomp, exercised "the very office of a Supreme Head of his Church," and "benignly . . . assayed to convert the miserable man." Lambert was burned Nov. 22. *L. P.,* XIII, ii, 851-2, 899, 924; Foxe, V, 227 ff. Foxe's assertion that Gardiner was at this time in high authority, and therefore the real author of the whole proceeding is without foundation. Cf. Dixon, II, 91, n. Indeed Foxe himself admits that Robert Barnes persuaded Dr. John Taylor (both of whom favoured the New Learning, but did not go so far as Lambert) to report Lambert's heresies to Cranmer. Foxe also erroneously attributed to Gardiner's influence the Injunctions of 1538. Foxe, V, 258.

⁴⁹ *L. P.,* XIV, i, 5. Ed. VI, *Lit. Remains,* cclxiv. At the next New Year another cup from Gardiner is recorded. *Ib.,* cclxv.

⁵⁰ *L. P.,* XIV, i, 662.

NOTES TO CHAPTER XIII

¹ *L. P.,* XIV, i, 120, 206, 412, 775, 890.

² *Ib.,* 520, 573, 634, 662.

³ Although Anne's brother William, who succeeded to the duchy Feb. 7, 1539, was not a Protestant, he was sympathetic to reforming ideas, at enmity with the Emperor over the possession of Gelderland, and brother-in-law of the Elector of Saxony, Protestant leader.

⁴ 31 H. VIII, c. 14 (in Gee and Hardy, 303). Cf. *Lords' Journ.,* I, 105 ff.

⁵ *L. P.,* XIV, i, 1003, 1015, 1040; *Lollardy,* II, 195.

⁶ *L. P.,* XIV, i, 1063, 1065. Cf. Pollard, *Cranmer,* 130.

⁷ *L. P.,* XIV, i, 1092.

⁸ Geo. Constantyne, in *Archaelogia,* XXIII, 59.

⁹ Brinklow's *Lamentacyon,* 79, 82. See also Coverdale's letters in *L. P.,* XIV, i, 253, 444.

¹⁰ Foxe, V, 261.

¹¹ *Lords' Journ.,* I, 109.

¹² Turner, *Rescvynge of the romishe fox,* f. A[vii]. Burchart, Vice Chancellor of Saxony, who was in London while the act was under discussion in the House of Lords, names Stokesley and Gardiner as its especial sponsors. *L. P.,* XIV, ii, 423. For other contemporaries who believed Gardiner in some

degree responsible for the act, see Brinklow, *Complaynt of Roderyck Mors,* 64; Foxe, V, 260-1, 264; Bucer and Melancthon in *L. P.,* XIV, ii, 186, 444. Cf. *ib.* i, 631. In a joint letter from Luther, Jonas, Bugenhagen, and Melancthon to the Elector of Saxony, Oct. 23, 1539, the articles are denounced, and Gardiner is characterized as a tyrant who has burnt two men for their views on transubtantiation, and who travels about with two lewd women in men's clothing. *L. P.,* XIV, ii, 379. I find no record of the two heretics with whose death these reformers credit Gardiner, unless they refer to Frith and Hewet, whom Stokesley condemned in 1533, Gardiner acting as one of his assistants, and Lambert, in whose examination in 1538, Gardiner had a distinctly minor part. The evidence for the two lewd women is equally cogent. Beside the writers of this letter, none of whom were in a position to have first-hand knowledge of the matter, I find only two among the many contemporary detractors of Gardiner who charge him with immoral relations with women. One is Bale, whose unrestrained abuse of Gardiner on all counts is such as to render of doubtful verity his sweeping statements that Gardiner supported many loose women and was much given to harlotry. *Script.,* 685-6. The other is Henry Brinklow, an ex-friar who wrote satires on social and religious conditions, 1542-5. He says: "Stevyn Gardiner, which was the chief causer of that wicked act [Six Articles], is it not manifest and openly known that he keepeth other men's wives, which I could name and will do hereafter if he leave not his shameless whoredom." *Complaynt of Roderyck Mors,* 64; cf. his *Lamentacyon,* 110. If Gardiner's immoralities were as flagrant as Bale and Brinklow suggest, it is surprising that his many other opponents did not refer to them. It is, of course, possible that, in the light of the frequently irregular relations between women and the clergy of the period, such relations were not referred to in Gardiner's case, because they were taken for granted. Strype, *Mem.,* III, i, 173, names "one Mrs. Godsalve," "among other women," kept by Gardiner, but I find no contemporary source for this statement.

[13] Burnet, VI, 233. In the discussion of the last article, Gardiner, Tunstall, and Lee maintained that auricular confession was of divine institution, but were refuted by Cranmer and the King; hence the 6th article merely asserted "that auricular confession was expedient and necessary to be retained." *Ib.,* IV, 400, 405. Cf. *ib.,* VI, 248.

[14] A conclusion drawn from the composition of the committees. One consisted of Cranmer, Goodrich, Barlow, and Dr. Petre; the other of Lee, Tunstall, Gardiner, and Dr. Tregonwell. *Lords' Journ.,* I, 113.

[15] Yet Foxe (V, 498, 506-13) names Gardiner as their chief persecutor. For references to contemporary letters relating to the Calais heretics see *L. P.,* XIV, ii, p. xliv, n. Gardiner's assurance that Hare would yet do the King good service proved true. In 1542 he received a grant of 9d. a day for his services in Ireland. *Ib.,* XXI, i, 717(8).

Foxe records a curious discussion at Hare's examination over the phrase used by Hare, "The Lord is my witness." This, said Gardiner, was a sure sign of heresy, for the faithful said "Our Lord" [as they said "Our Father" and "Our Lady"] while heretics said "the Lord" [literally translating ὁ κύριος]. The question was deemed important enough for discussion in Convocation in 1542, when all but three of the bishops declared for "Our Lord." Wilkins, III, 862. According to Gardiner "Our Lord" was put in the *King's Book* at the instance of Henry himself. Foxe, VI, 61. Cf. *ib.,* V, 856; *Nar. of the Ref.,* 180.

[16] *L. P.,* XIV, i, 1217, 1219; XXI, i, 823. The resignations were probably forced.

[17] Hall, II, 285. Cf. *Lollardy,* II, 200.

[18] *L. P.,* XIV, ii, 423, 750, pp. 279-80.

[19] Foxe, V, 418-9; *L. P.,* XVI, 106.

[20] Barnes' *Works,* 183-205.

[21] Foxe, V, 419. Cf. *L. P.,* V, 532-3, 593.

[22] *Declaration,* f. 6.

[23] Wilkins, III, 836; Wriothesley, I, 81; see "Barnes" in index of *L. P.,* VII, VIII, IX, X, XIV.

[24] Barnes' *Works,* 226 ff.; and his *Sentenciae ex Doctoribus.*

[25] *L. P.,* XIV, i, 441-3, 955-8, 982, 1156, 1273, 1278; ii, 59, 400; *Archaelogia,* XXIII, 57. Foxe (V, 420) erroneously says Barnes was ambassador to Cleves.

[26] *L. P.,* XIV, ii, 107, 688; *O. L.,* 627. Cf. *ib.,* 614.

[27] *L. P.,* XV, 145.

[28] Barnes later admitted that he had been deceived as to the condition of affairs, and warned Melancthon not to come to England. The letter in which he did so, and in which he also spoke of the controversy going on between Gardiner and himself, bears the date (as printed by the Parker Soc., *O. L.,* 616) London, May 21, 1540, "from the house of Thomas Parnell." But Barnes was in the Tower at this time, nor could the date be May 21, 1539, since he was then on the Continent. Perhaps it should be Mar. 21, 1540. Canon Dixon's (II, 254, n.) quotation from Wriothesley, I, 114, in support of 1539, is a misreading of the chronicle.

[29] Wriothesley, I, 113. Gardiner says he was asked the Sunday before Lent, Feb. 8, to preach the following Friday, and implies that he was not appointed for the succeeding weeks until after the first sermon. *Declaration,* f. 7.

[30] *Declaration,* ff. 8-11. Cf. *L. P.,* XV, 306, 334-5, 383.

[31] Probably Richard Cox, royal chaplain, later tutor to Ed. VI, and Bishop of Ely under Elizabeth; and Thomas Robinson or Robertson, chaplain to the Bishop of Durham, and Dean of Durham under Mary.

[32] *Declaration,* ff. 11-16.

[33] For Jerome and Garret, see Foxe, V, 421-38, 830, 833, App. VI, VII, VIII, XXI; Wriothesley, I, 114; *L. P.,* XV, index.

[34] *L. P.,* XV, 289.

[35] *Ib.,* 429.

[36] *Mon. Fr.,* II, 203; *L. P.,* XV, 414, 425.

[37] *Declaration,* ff. 16-18. Gardiner's statement that Barnes and his fellows first recanted and then preached the contrary, is attested by Foxe, V, 433; cf. Wriothesley, I, 114, and Marillac, in *L. P.,* XV, 485.

[38] Merriman, I, 288-9. Mr. Merriman erroneously dates this dinner Mar. 30. Norfolk's account of it is quoted in a letter from Wallop written at Abbeville Mar. 31. Norfolk must have written to Wallop some days before. *L. P.,* XV, 429.

[39] *Ib.*

[40] Wriothesley, I, 114.

[41] Stubbs, 102. Bonner was elected Bishop of Hereford while in France, 1538; he was translated to London before consecration.

[42] Nott's *Wyatt,* 306 (*L. P.* XVI, p. 310). Cf. Foxe, V, 413.

[43] *L. P.,* XV, 486.

[44] *Ib.,* 804. See Gardiner's own statement above, p. 89.

[45] *L. P.,* XV, 472, 480, 529, 543.

[46] *Ib.,* 567.

[47] A French groom of the Queen's, named Maundevild, an Italian painter, and an Englishman, both unnamed, were, according to Wriothesley, I, 118, burnt in Southwark for heresy on the Sacrament, May 3, 1540. July 7, one Collins was burnt in the same place for the same offence. *Ib.,* 119. Marillac, on May 8, said three persons of low condition, two Flemings and an Englishman, had recently been executed for speaking irreverently of the Sacrament. *L. P.,* XV, 651. Richard Hilles mentions "three persons" burnt in Southwark at this time, saying, "as these things took place in the diocese of Winchester, it was remarked by many persons that these men were brought to the stake by the procurement of the Bishop; just as he burned, shortly after, a crazed

man of the name of Collins." *O. L.*, 200. Stow, 579, says that the three burned May 3, were examined in St. Margaret's Church, Apr. 29, and condemned as Anabaptists, but he names, erroneously it would seem, Collins as one of these three. Foxe does not mention the three burned May 3, and wrongly dates the death of Collins 1538. He says Collins was mad, tells how he lifted a puppy above his head in church in mockery of the elevation of the host, says that he was burnt at Smithfield, but makes no mention of Gardiner in connection with him (V, 251). Hilles tells us that Collins shot an arrow at a crucifix, but adds that some people thought he was punished for applying to the the great men of the kingdom texts from the prophets about unrighteous judgements. He also adds that on occasions he acted in a sane manner.

We learn from Wriothesley, I, 115, that a priest "of the new sect," who was awaiting examination by Gardiner, committed suicide by hanging, Apr. 12, 1540. It is evidently to this that Brinklow refers in his *Complaynt of Mors,* 29, written 1542 or 1543: "Was not one within these two years murdered in the Bishop of Winchester's lodge? and then the matter was forged that he hanged himself." Foxe (V, 530) elaborates the incident, misdating it: "Coming now to the year of our Lord 1545, first passing over the priest, whose name was Saxy, who was hanged in the porter's lodge of Stephen Gardiner, Bishop of Winchester, and that, as it is supposed, not without the consent of the said Bishop, and the secret conspiracy of that bloody generation." The reader, as Mr. Gairdner remarks, is expected to regard murder by a prominent bishop "as a thing so evidently credible in itself that it may be suggested in a parenthesis." *Typical Eng. Churchmen,* II, 190.

[48] Foxe, V, 515-6. Lisle died March 1542 from excitement at the news of his release and restoration to the King's favour. See *D. N. B.,* "Arthur Plantagenet."

[49] Hall, II, 306; *L. P.,* XV, 719, 736-7, 747, 758; Strype, *Mem.,* I, ii, 381. Sampson was taxed with undue affection for ancient ceremonies, and replied that Tunstall and Gardiner had encouraged him in this. Both he and Wilson were later pardoned by the King. Hall, II, 311; *O. L.,* 211.

[50] *L. P.,* XV, 737. Cf. *ib.,* 792 (ii).

[51] *Ib.,* 735.

[52] *O. L.,* 202; *L. P.,* XVI, 269.

[53] *Ib.,* XV, 765-7; *St. P.,* VIII, 349; Burnet, IV, 415; *Lords' Journ.,* I, 145-9. The attainder was passed June 29.

[54] *L. P.,* XV, 804. Cf. *ib.,* XVI, 308; *Ven. Cal.,* V, 219; *Epistolae Tigurinae,* 154.

[55] *L. P.,* XIV, i, 662.

[56] *L. P.,* XV, 821-4, 845, 860-1, 898(5), 908, 976; XVI, 12; Wilkins, III, 851. For discussion of Canon Law involved in the case, see Pollard, *Cranmer,* 140.

[57] The date of the marriage was probably July 28. Cf. Pollard, *Hen. VIII,* 398, n.

[58] *Lords' Journ.,* I, 159, 160. Cf. *L. P.,* XV, pp. 215, 217.

[59] Wriothesley, I, 120; *Mon. Fr.,* II, 203. Foxe charges Gardiner with Barnes' death (V, 434). Barnes at the stake mentioned Gardiner, saying that if he or any of the Council or any other "have sought or wrought this my death . . . I pray God forgive him." *Ib.,* 435. Hall says that "most men said" that Gardiner chiefly procured Barnes' death (II. 304, 309). Among those who said so were Bale (*Script.,* 667), Hooper (*Later Writings,* 376), Wm. Turner (*Romyshe Vuolfe,* Ei), and Joye, in his book against Gardiner. Gardiner in his *Declaration against Joye,* from which I have quoted at some length, gives a circumstantial account of his dealings with Barnes, and appeals to men who knew the circumstances to witness the truth of his statements. Foxe thought Gardiner's account sufficiently trustworthy to follow. John Standish, who wrote a refutation of Barnes' *Protestation,* implied that Barnes'

forgiveness of Gardiner at the stake was "feigned charity," intended to discredit Gardiner. Miles Coverdale, the reformer, answered Standish, saying, "As touching any contentious manner between my Lord of Winchester and Dr. Barnes though you and I both, as I suppose, be ignorant what direction the King's Highness did take therein, yet seeing the one was reconciled to the other openly at the Spital, ye should now not take the matter so hot." *A Confutacion,* Miii. It is noteworthy that Coverdale makes no charge against Gardiner. Hilles does not even mention him, but conjectures that the King ordered the burning of Barnes and his companions in order to gain popularity for financial reasons. *O. L.,* 210. This admission, from an adherent of the new theology, of the unpopularity of the three preachers is, as Miss E. Jeffries Davis remarks, significant. *V. C. H., London,* I, 277.

[60] The practise of attainting a man in Parliament without giving him a chance to defend himself was begun in the previous year. *L. P.,* XIV, i, p. xlvi. Foxe commenting on the "fatal destiny" by which Cromwell, the initiator of the practice, was brought to his own death by it, says, "It is said (which I also do easily credit), that he made this violent law . . . for a certain secret purpose, to have entangled the Bishop of Winchester." V, 402.

[61] McGiffert, *Luther,* Chapter XXV; Cardwell, No. x, p. 61.

[62] For this and an earlier instance of Papal licence for bigamy, see Pollard, *Hen. VIII,* 207.

[63] Gardiner's *Declaration,* ff. 151-3.

[64] *Ib.,* ff. 39, 141.

[65] Barnes *Works,* 294.

[66] Foxe, V, App. VIII; *L. P.,* XV, 345.

[67] Foxe, V, App. VII; Burnet, IV, 498.

NOTES TO CHAPTER XIV

[1] On Aug. 10, 1540, Gardiner's protégé, Paget, was appointed clerk of the Privy Council, and from that date we have brief minutes of its proceedings. It then consisted of nineteen members, of whom three, Cranmer, Tunstall, and Gardiner, were Churchmen. When the King left London, part of it accompanied him; part stayed behind; hence the term "the Council at court" and "the Council in London." As the clerk went with the court, no minutes of the meetings of the councillors in London were kept. Our knowledge of their activities comes from correspondence between them and the councillors at court, and other contemporary references. Gardiner was with the Council at court at Windsor and Reading, Aug. 17-23; then the court moved to Grafton and Ampthill and Gardiner remained in London. He was again with the Council at court at Windsor Oct. 23, Nov. 1, 7, 14, 15. Nicolas, VII. For his business in London, see *L. P.,* XV, 902, 995; XVI, 12, 100, 112, 157, 168, 173, 181, 223, 347. His work on the commission for the collection of the subsidy began Oct. 9, and brought with it heated discussions with the French ambassador over the right to tax Frenchmen in London, in which, says Marillac "The Bishop of Winchester answered me with intolerable insolence and impudence." Kaulek, 238.

[2] *L. P.,* XVI, 269, 319; *St. P.,* VIII, 486; *Ven. Cal.* V, No. 231. Gardiner was paid 10 marks (£6 13*s.* 4*d.*) a day, which was over twice as much as he had received on any previous embassy. *L. P.,* XVI, 745, f. 50; XVII, 258, ff. 50-3; XVIII, ii, p. 125.

[3] *L. P.,* XVI, 295, 308, 311, 336, 358; *Ven. Cal.,* V, Nos. 233-40. Gardiner arrived in Calais on or before Nov. 28, and in Mons before Dec. 18.

[4] Osiander may refer to something similar to the swelling of Gardiner's cheek, described by Bonner (Above, p. 75). See also Bucer's remark about the veins in Gardiner's hand (Above, p. 99). Osiander's sentence reads,

"Est autem homo alioqui aulicissimus et sophisticissimus, sed quales juris-consulti sophistae sunt, non theologi aut philosophi, virulentiam quandam in colore preferens, alioqui justae ac vivacis staturae." L. P., XVI, 667; cf. *ib.*, 669.

[5] Laemmer, *Monumenta Vaticana*, 355. The last line on p. 260, L. P., XVI, 548, in the abstract of this letter is a misleading translation.

[6] *L. P.*, XVI, 676, 870. Cf. Burnet, VI, 275.

[7] *L. P.*, XVI, 711, 733.

[8] Cf. *L. P.*, XVI, 1291; XVII, App. B, 13; *Lollardy*, II, 348.

[9] Foxe, VI, 578. See above, p. 265.

[10] Foxe, VI, 165-8.

[11] *Ib.*, VII, 588-91. Cf. Brinklow, *Complaynt*, 58.

[12] *Ven. Cal.*, V, Nos. 244, 257.

[13] Gardiner's account of the discussion in his book against Turner, preserved in Turner's *Rescvynge of the romishe fox*, f. L ff. See also Gardiner's books against Bucer.

[14] Bucer, *Gratulatio*, 53 ff; Hoby's translation, f. Giiii ff. Gardiner retorted that if his veins did swell, as Bucer said, it was not with anger, but with inordinate mirth at the stupidity of Alesius. *Exetasis*, 2-3.

[15] *Exetasis*, 3.

[16] See above, pp. 125, 173.

[17] *L. P.*, XVI, 749.

[18] *Ven. Cal.*, V, Nos. 257-8.

[19] *L. P.*, XVI, 910; Cf. *ib.*, XVII, p. 172.

[20] *Ven. Cal.*, V, 267.

[21] *L. P.*, XVI, 968, 1073. Archdeacon Pate, whom Knyvet came to replace, had feared for his life and fled to Rome.

[22] Francis Driander to Edm. Crispin, Sept. 22, 1541. Foxe, VI, 139. See also the account given by Wm. Medowe, Gardiner's chaplain, *ib.*, VI, 202 Cf. *ib.*, 106, 185, 190, 223.

[23] *L. P.*, XVI, 1243, 1266, 1292.

[24] *L. P.*, XVIII, ii, p. 339; see above, p. 110.

[25] St. Swithin's had been dissolved, upon voluntary surrender, Nov. 14, 1539, and reconstituted as a cathedral chapter of twelve prebendaries and a dean. The dean, William Kingsmill, had been prior of the monastery, and most of the monks found places on the cathedral staff. The letters patent formally establishing the chapter are dated Mar. 28, 1541. It received new statutes in 1544. See *Winchester Cathedral Documents*, and *L. P.*, XIV, ii, 429-30, 520; XV, 139; XVI, 91, 678(53), 878(1).

[26] Wriothesley, I, 108, 113; *L. P.*, XV, 498(64); XVIII, i, p. 553; Dollman, *The Priory of St. Mary Overie*, 8. Gardiner gave £24 13s. 11d., and obtained subscriptions from others. *V. C. H., London*, I, 275. Cf. *V. C. H., Surrey*, II, 174. The words "bought of the King" seem to refer to the church goods such as bells, plate, vestments, *etc.* and not to the building which was leased, a yearly rent being paid to the crown until it was purchased from James I. W. Thompson, *Southwark Cathedral*, 13-14.

NOTES TO CHAPTER XV

[1] *L. P.*, XVI, 1454.

[2] *Ib.*, 1328.

[3] B. M., Add. MS., 29,546, f. 22b.

[4] *L. P.*, XVI, 1457.

[5] *L. P.*, XVII, 143, 145, and English-French correspondence throughout the volume.

[6] *St. P.*, IX, 293, 301-2.

[7] Foxe, VI, 26.

[8] *L. P.*, XVII, 291; cf. *ib.*, p. xv.

[9] *St. P.*, IX, 23.

[10] *Sp. Cal.*, VI, ii, p. 24; *L. P.*, XVII, App. B, 22. Gardiner added that Henry was aware of the advantages of the alliance, but would not like to hear Chapuys urge it on that score. Chapuys wrote to Granvelle, June 30, 1542, that if anyone were to be sent from England to the Emperor in this matter, they should try to see that it was Gardiner, because of his knowledge of Henry's character. *Sp. Cal.*, VI, ii, p. 44.

[11] *L. P.*, XVII, 319-60 (*passim*), 949, App. B, 22-3.

[12] B. M., Add. MS. 29,546, f. 22b. Ecclesiastics, in proportion to their revenues, contributed wages of soldiers. According to *L. P.*, XVII, 631, Cranmer paid for 300, Gardiner for 200, but the text, as printed in Kaulek, 451, reads "*l'arcevesque de Cantuberry de trois cens hommes, l'evesque de Hoincester d'aultant.*" Gardiner took an active part in the collection of a large "loan" to the King early in the year. Wriothesley, I, 136; *L. P.*, XVII, 193, 286, App. B, pp. 721, 729.

[13] *L. P.*, XVIII, i, 144. The treaty was almost wrecked on the eve of final agreement by the English insisting on styling Henry Supreme Head of the English Church in the preface. If this were omitted, they said, he would refuse to hear any more of the alliance. It was settled that the title should be omitted in the copy of the treaty signed and sealed by Chapuys, and retained in the one signed and sealed by Gardiner and Wriothesley. When Chapuys said that he could, on receiving their copy, cancel the title, they replied that he might then do as he pleased, their duty had been done. *L. P.*, XVIII, i, 150.

[14] *L. P.*, XVII, 1212; XVIII, i, 873, 894, 955. It is probable that, as Mr. Hume points out, Catherine was at this time regarded as a member of the Catholic party. *Wives of Hen. VIII*, 404.

[15] *L. P.*, XVIII, i, 719, 746, 795, 804-5. Gardiner drafted for the King a letter dated Apr. 4, 1543, to Ralph Sadler, then at the Scotch court, telling him how to advise the Earl of Arran to reform the Scotch Church. Two methods are commended: publication of the Bible in the vernacular and dissolution of the monasteries. Care must be taken to prevent seditious persons from using the Bible to raise evil opinions in the heads of the unlearned against the Government and the Church. The dissolution of the monasteries "requireth politic handling." Commissions, ostensibly to reform them, can gather damaging evidence against them; the nobles can be won over by promises of grants of monastic land, and the bishops by the prospect of "some such small houses as lie conveniently for them." Though drafted by Gardiner, this was corrected by Henry himself. It is this letter which contains the statement that Henry is about to "establish such a certain doctrine as is maintainable by mere truth, and such as no man shall be able to impugn,"—a reference to the *King's Book*. *Hamilton Papers*, I, No. 348; *L. P.*, XVIII, i, 364.

[16] *L. P.*, XVIII, ii, 526.

[17] According to the injunctions of 1538, a copy of the "great Bible" was to be in every church. This Bible, which was not through the press till 1539, was an edition of "Matthew's" [John Rogers'] Bible, which in turn was a combination of Tyndale's translations of the N. T. and of the O. T. as far as II Chron., and Coverdale's translation of the rest of the O. T., the controversial prefatory and marginal material of the earlier versions being omitted.

[18] The complete list is printed by Fuller who copied it from records of Convocation now lost. *Church Hist.*, III, 199. It has been reprinted in Wilkins, III, 861, *Lollardy*, II, 296, and Dixon, II, 287 (with one omission). In this Convocation Gardiner served with Thirlby and Bell on a committee to consider a statute against simony, and was appointed to draft a decree against leasing benefices for more than 20 years. *L. P.* XVII, 176.

[19] Foxe, VI, 37.

[20] Gardiner to Cranmer, June —, 1547. B. M., Add. MS. 29,546, f. 8a.

[21] *L. P.*, XVI, 783; XVII, 220(45); *Lollardy*, II, 290-9.

[22] *Ib.*

[23] 34 & 35 H. VIII, c. 1; cf. *Lollardy*, II, 301-2. One of the abuses of the Bible was the reading aloud or expounding of it by contentious persons in church during service time. See Maitland, *Essays*, 278 ff., and Cranmer, *Letters*, 390.

[24] *Sp. Cal.*, VI, ii, p. 303.

[25] Dasent, I, 97-128 *passim*.

[26] Adam Damplip, one of the Calais heretics who had fled from an examination before Cranmer in 1538, and who had been attainted for treason 1540, was later apprehended and, at this time, sent back to Calais for execution. Foxe attributes his death to Gardiner. Foxe, V, 400, 498-501, 520-2. See Cranmer, *Letters*, 372-3, 375; *L. P.*, XV, 498(58). Foxe also says that Gardiner assisted in the examination of Damplip in 1538, but Gardiner did not return from his three years residence in France until four months after Damplip had fled from his examiners. Foxe adds that Gardiner also condemned one George Eagles as a traitor. But from Foxe's own account it appears that Eagles was condemned 1557, two years after Gardiner's death! (V, 400; VIII, 393.)

[27] There is little beside internal evidence to enable us to say what part Gardiner took in the preparation of the book. He, as well as Cranmer, was a member of the committee of twenty divines to revise the *Bishops' Book*, appointed by the King, and named by Cromwell in Parliament, 1540. *Lords' Journ.*, I, 129. He was at the Imperial court in the latter part of 1540 when questions on the Sacrament and Church government were submitted to these divines, which doubtless accounts for our failure to have answers from him. Burnet, IV, 443; VI, 241-8. Cf. Dixon, II, 303, n; Cranmer, *Letters*, 83. He took a prominent part in the meetings of Convocation in Apr. 1543, when the clergy gave their approval of the book. Wilkins, III, 868. In a letter to the Privy Council in 1547 he denied that he had had a hand in the portion on justification which, he said, was the work of Bishops Heath, Thirlby, and Day and Doctors Cox, Robinson, and Redman, B. M., Add. MS. 28,571, f. 19a. Burnet, I, 462, says that Gardiner was for shortening the Second Commandment and casting it into the first, but when Cranmer objected a compromise was reached by which it was shortened but kept separate. No authority for this is given.

[28] *Refutation*, f. cxxx.

[29] *Recvynge of the romishe fox*, f. Nv.

[30] *Nar. of the Ref.*, 248.

[31] Strype, *Cranmer*, App. No. xxxv.

[32] B. M., Add. MS. 29,546, f. 21b. The *King's Book* has been reprinted by a modern Anglican who recommends it as "the calm deliberate teaching of the Church of England, pure and uncontaminated." *The King's Book*, with Introd., by T. A. Lacy, London, 1895. It is also available in Lloyd's *Formularies of Faith in the Reign of Henry VIII*, Oxford, 1825; second ed. 1856.

[33] Foxe, V, 486.

[34] "Sir Thomas Parson" of the Council minutes appears to have been the same man. Dasent, I, 97-8.

[35] Hall, II, 342-4; Foxe, V, 464-97; *L. P.*, XVIII, ii, 327 (9).

[36] In his *Declaration against Joye*, f. lxvii, Gardiner speaks of the "marvellous celerity" with which a musician deviseth "the descant that he playeth upon his instrument, which is a wonderful swiftness and agility of the powers of the soul."

[37] Foxe, V, 475, 478-9. We only have Marbeck's account as used by Foxe.

[38] *L. P.*, XVIII ii, 241(6). The best known of these are Thomas Sternhold, author of a metrical version of the Psalms, and Thomas Cawarden

and Philip Hoby, both knighted 1544. Hoby was a diplomat of some note, and brother to Sir Thomas Hoby who translated into English Bucer's book against Gardiner.

[39] Wriothesley, I, 142; Foxe, V, App. XII, XXII.* Cf. Strype, *Mem.*, I, ii, 463. Wriothesley dates the recantation July 8; the title page of Wisdom's account says July 14, but this may not have been written by him. Cf. *Lollardy*, II, 380, n.

[40] *L. P.*, XVIII, ii, p. 339.

[41] The ms. record of these examinations in Corpus Christi College has been printed, with slight condensation, in *L. P.*, XVIII, ii, pp. 291-378. From this is taken the account of the situation at Canterbury and the attempts to gather evidence concerning it, given in this chapter. Some of the utterances of John Scory, a cathedral preacher, who became a bishop under Ed. VI, were too much even for Cranmer, who noted them as "error," "slanderous," or "seditious." *Ib.*, p. 305. The examinations seem to have lasted at least from the latter part of Sept. to the beginning of Nov. 1543. See also *ib.*, p. xxxiv ff; *Lollardy* II, 357 ff; Pollard, *Cranmer*, 145 ff.

NOTES TO CHAPTER XVI

[1] *Nar. of the Ref.*, 250.

[2] *Ib.*, 252-3.

[3] *L. P.*, XVIII, ii, pp. 328-9, 340, 358, 370-1.

[4] This appears also in the treatment of Richard Turner, preacher at Chartham, Kent, who was summoned before the Council by Gardiner in July, committed to ward, and, later, when Cranmer was himself present at the examination of the prebendaries, sent to him to recant. He was indicted in Kent, Sept. 27, and probably released by the general pardon of 1544. In a letter from Morice to friends at court in Turner's behalf, Nov. 2, 1543, it appears that Cranmer, over six weeks after the examination of the prebendaries had been committed to him, did not feel himself safe. Says Morice, "As for my Lord of Canterbury, he dare do nothing for the poor man's delivery, he hath done so much already. And his Grace hath told me plainly that it is put into the King's head that he is the maintainer and supporter of all the heretics within the realm." Foxe, VIII, 31-4; *L. P.*, XVIII, ii, pp. l-lii. See *ib.*, index, under "Turner"; Dasent, I, 156.

[5] *Nar. of the Ref.*, 253.

[6] Foxe, V, 494-6; VI, 179; Hall, II, 344; *L. P.*, XVIII iii, 241(6).

[7] *Mon. Fr.*, II, 206. On Mar. 19 another was hanged, presumably for the same offense. *Ib.* Practically nothing is known of the circumstances leading to Germain Gardiner's execution. He was indicted for treason by jury Feb. 15, 1544. *Lollardy*, II, 411. He appears also to have been attainted. *L. P.*, XIX, i, 442(10), 444(6), 812(53). Cf. *ib.*, XVIII, ii, 479. Foxe calls him a near kinsman to the Bishop; John Dudley (Warwick) spoke of him as one 'nearest about the said Bishop, of his own bringing up." Foxe, V, 526; VI, 179. Modern writers call him a nephew (*Lollardy*, I, 408; II, 411) and a cousin (*Ath. Cantab.*, I, 83) of the Bishop. His sister or half-sister seems to have married Wriothesley. *L. P.*, XII, i, 1209; ii, 47; cf. *D. N. B.*, "Wriothesley."

[8] Foxe, V, 690. Suffolk's description of the attempt to send Gardiner to the Tower, as reported by Foxe, though containing several impossibilities, must have some basis in fact. Chapuys, ambassador to England, 1540-5, writing early in 1547, said. "When I was last in England Winchester would have been sent to the Tower by the orders of the Earl [of Hertford, Edward Seymour] and the Admiral [John Dudley], if the Duke of Norfolk had not interceded and informed the King, to whom Winchester justified himself

and escaped." *Sp. Cal.*, VIII, p. 556 (where the editor confuses Paulet with Gardiner).

[9] Foxe, V, 526.

[10] B. M., Add. MS. 29,546, f. 3a. For his activities in this post, see *L. P.*, XIX-XXI *passim; Sp. Cal.*, VII, p. 223; Foxe, VI, 32. He was assisted at first by Sir. Wm. Paulet, and later by Sir John Gage and Sir Richard Riche.

[11] Foxe, VI, 34.

[12] Turner, *Rescvynge of the romishe fox*, f. Nvi.

[13] *L. P.*, XIX, i, 273, 1032(5).

[14] *Ib.*, 819.

[15] *Ib.*, ii, 216, 235, 276-7, 424, 546.

[16] *Ib.*, 336, 344.

[17] *Ib.*, 374, 509.

[18] *Ib.*, 383, 391. For negotiations at Calais see *ib.*, 354-470 *passim*, and 542-6.

[19] *Ib.*, 456, 462-3, 479, 492.

[20] For negotiations at Brussels see *L. P.*, XIX, ii, 479-661 *passim; St. P.* 147-220. All the letters from Hertford and Gardiner are in Gardiner's handwriting, and, evidently, of his composition.

[21] *L. P.*, XX, i, 7, 12, 261, 345.

[22] On June 12, 1545, Gardiner sat on the commission for the collection of the subsidy in the Guildhall. Wriothesley, I, 155. He headed the commission to collect the benevolence of 1545 in Surrey, and acted on that for Hants. *L. P.*, XX, i, pp. 325-6. In 1546 he was appointed one of the assessors for the "contribution" from London, *L. P.*, XXI, i, 970(33), and was named on a commission to take the account of the treasurer of the mints. *Ib.*, 1166(53). In the same year he appeared on a commission to examine the state of the revenues and command the treasurers to gather up all debts. *Ib.*, 1166(71). In Feb. 1546 he was named at the head of two commissions for the survey of chantries, hospitals, *etc.;* one for Berks, Hants, Winchester, Southampton, New Windsor, and the Isle of Wight; the other for Surr., Suss., and Southwark. *Ib.*, 302(30) How far he acted on these commissions is not known. He was abroad at the time and did not return till Mar. 21, 1546. On Jan. 17, 1546 he wrote to Paget expressing his solicitude for the hospitals of St. Cross beside Winchester, and Mary Magdalene "wherein poor folks be relieved," "for the country is poor and very poor, and these two houses somewhat garnish the town, which by reason of friars, monks, and nuns, whose houses stand all to-torne, with the decay of the inhabitants, is now much defaced." No man, he says, will give more for St. Cross than he will give to have it stand. *Ib.*, 74. Both houses continued to stand.

[23] *Treatise of politike pouuer*, f. Fiii.

[24] Foxe, VI, 32.

[25] Strype, *Cranmer*, App. xxxv.

[26] *L. P.*, XX, ii, 586 589, 604, 625, 639, 714, 737; Foxe, VI, 190.

[27] He sailed from Dover Oct. 21, tarried at Nieuport, arrived at Bruges Oct. 31. *L. P.*, XX, ii, 610, 627, 668-70, 724; *St. P.*, X, 649.

[28] Chapter XVIII.

[29] *L. P.*, XX, ii, 714.

[30] *Ib.*, 732, 788, 871.

[31] *L. P.*, XX, ii, 772. On Nov. 7 he had written to Paget of the preliminaries for the conference, describing his feelings about it in the vivid phrase: "We be fearful as a doe is that stayeth hearkening to every crash of a bough." *St. P.*, X, 664.

[32] *L. P.*, XX, ii, 774; *St. P.*, X, 675.

[33] *Ib.*, 656-7.

[34] *L. P.*, XX, ii, 788, 794, 803.

[35] *St. P.*, X, 664.

[36] *L. P.*, XX, ii, 831.

[17] *Ib.*, 802-3, 821, 870-2. Gardiner left Bruges early Nov. 17, arriving at Antwerp Nov. 18 at night.

[38] *Ib.*, 903, 977.

[39] *L. P.*, XXI, i, 8, 71, 212. Gardiner left Maastricht, whither the court had moved, Mar. 2, and travelled to Calais via Antwerp. *Ib.*, 315 ff.

[40] *Ib.*, 432, 439.

[41] Many of these are printed in *St. P.*, X, and XI. Full abstracts of all are given in *L. P.*, XX, ii, and XXI, i.

[42] Foxe, VI, 51.

[43] *St. P.*, XI, 9.

[44] *L. P.*, XXI, i, 610.

[45] They left London June 1 or 2; were at Boulogne on or before June 6; left June 10; were in London again on or before June 14. *L. P.*, XXI, i, 972, 987, 1016-7, 1028, 1058.

In the minutes of the Privy Council Gardiner and Browne are recorded as present May 30; the attendance thereafter, through June 9, is indicated by the words *"ut supra,"* which accounts for the erroneous entries in *L. P.*, XXI, i, in which Gardiner and Browne are listed as present in Council during their trip to Boulogne.

[46] *Sp. Cal.*, VIII, pp. 235, 265, 425, 451.

NOTES TO CHAPTER XVII

[1] Gardiner was amused by the tales told of these soldiers. He wrote to Paget, "The report of their conceits has some mirth in it. He that had no money would go into the town showing a borrowed groat and saying, 'Will no man give me four pence?' And when some simple body, thinking to change the groat, gave fourpence, he put off his cap with a great many thanks, and, being asked for the groat, laid his hand on his breast and swore that it was not his, but he would remember her kindness." *L. P.*, XX, ii, 627.

[2] *Grace Book B*, II, 227; *Grace Book Γ*, 349.

[3] *L. P.* XVI, 27.

[4] Translated in Strype, *Smith*, 49-50. For Ascham's letter, see his *Works*, ed. Giles, I, 26; cf. *ib.*, p. xxxvii. Cheke's letters and treatises and Gardiner's letters and decree were published under the title *De Pronunciatione Graecae* . . ., at Basle, 1555, without Cheke's knowledge, by Coelius Secundus Curio, to whom Cheke had lent the manuscripts. Smith's treatise was published at Paris, 1568, as *De recta & emendata Linguae Graecae Pronunciatione.* . . . All this material from Gardiner, Cheke, and Smith, together with Erasmus' dialogue, may be found in Havercamp, *Sylloge Altera Scriptorum*, 1740. Gardiner's decree is also printed in Strype, *Mem.*, I, ii, 479, and Cooper, *Annals*, I, 402. Brief English abstracts of Gardiner, Cheke, and Smith, as well as of an additional letter from Gardiner to Smith, are given in *L. P.*, XVII, 327, 482-3, 611, 742, 803, 891-2. See also Mullinger, *Univ. of Camb.*, II, 54 ff; Wordsworth, *Scholae Academicae*, 106 ff; *Grace Book B*, II, 239; Katterfeld, *Ascham*, 36-40; C. M. H., I, 580; Blass, *Pronunciation of Ancient Greek*, 1-18; Ellis, *The English, Dionysian, and Hellenic Pronunciation of Greek*, 4-6; Bywater, *The Erasmian Pronunciation of Greek;* Strype, *Cheke*, 15-24; Strype, *Smith*, 10-26, 49-50; *D. N. B.*, "Smith" and "Cheke." For Smith's and Cheke's relations to Gardiner in Mary's reign see Chapter XXXIII, p. 279 and n. 3.

[5] Lamb, 43.

[6] The play was translated into English by Bale. It is described in Mullinger, *Univ. of Camb.*, II, 73 ff.

[7] The Gardiner-Parker correspondence of 1545 was as follows: G. to P. Mar. 27; P. to G. Good Friday (Apr. 3); G. to P. Apr. 23; P. to G.

May 8; G. to P. May 12; Privy Council to the university May 16; G. to P. and the regents, *etc.* May 18. The last is in MSS. C. C. C. C. 119, No. 12. The others are printed from MSS. C. C. C. C. 106, Nos. 157-162, in Parker, *Corresp.*, 20-30; Cooper, *Annals*, I, 422-7; and, except a part of the first, in Lamb, 49-57. James, Cat. MSS. C. C. C. C. I, p. 213, follows a ms. note at the top of the first letter erroneously dating it 1544. Cf. Dasent, I, 162. In this letter Gardiner also writes concerning provision for "decayed cooks" at Cambridge. For other matters relating to Cambridge in which Gardiner had a hand in Hen. VIII's reign, see *Grace Book* △, 9; *L. P.*, XXI, i, 822, 824; ii, 333, 334; MSS. C. C. C. C. 106, Nos. 13, 14; and 127, No. 6; Mullinger, *Univ. of Camb.*, II, 39; Giles, *Ascham*, I, i.

In Foxe, I, i, App. XVIII there is an undated Latin letter from John Foxe, written presumably while in residence at Magdalen College, Oxford, to Gardiner, who, by virtue of his bishopric, was visitor of that College.

   [8] Foxe, VI, 566.

NOTES TO CHAPTER XVIII

   [1] Referred to by both Gardiner and Bucer in their books against each other. See also App. II, B, ii. For titles of books by Gardiner, Bucer, Turner, Joye, Gilby, and Hooper mentioned in this chapter see App. II, A, ii-vi.
   [2] *L. P.*, XXI, i, 661.
   [3] *Exetasis*, 2.
   [4] See above, p. 173.
   [5] Gardiner's *Examination of the Hunter*, in Turner's *Rescvynge of the romishe fox*, ff. Cvi-vii, Dvi-vii, G, Kvii. Gardiner's book must have been written after Sept. 14, 1543, the date of publication of Turner's book to which it was a reply.
   [6] Gardiner's *Declaration*, f. i.
   [7] *Complaynt of Roderyck Mors . . . unto the parliament howse of Ingland . . .* and *The Lamentacyon of a Christen Agaynst the Cytye of London. . . .* The first appears to have been written in 1543, the second not long after. It was printed 1545. Both have been edited by J. M. Cowper, Early Eng. Text Soc., Extra Series, XXII. Cf. *L. P.*, XX, ii, 733.
   [8] *L. P.*, XX, ii, 732; Joye, *Refutation*, preface to reader, and ff. xxxi, cxci. Cf. Joye *Confuteth* etc. f. xxii.
   [9] *L. P.*, XX, ii, 732.
   [10] The 8vo. ed. of Gardiner's *Declaration* is here used. The pages from which quotations are made are, in the order in which they here occur, ff. xxxviii-xxxix, cxxxiiii, xlii-lxxxvi, cvii-cx, cxxxi, xxi-xxii, cxi-cxx, clx, clxxix, clxxvii. Passages from this book on justification and predestination have been quoted in Chapter XIII.
   [11] There is relatively much more space given to the Sacrament of the Altar in this book than is indicated in this summary of its contents. Gardiner's views on the Sacrament will be considered more fully in Chapter XXVI. The three long passages here quoted are from ff. xcii, cxii, cxvii.
   [12] Gilby, ff. ii, v.

NOTES TO CHAPTER XIX

   [1] Foxe, V, 561-3; *Nar. of the Ref.*, 342; Cranmer, *Letters*, 414-5. It is possible that the attempt of the Council to send Cranmer to the Tower, from which he was saved by the King's ring, occurred while Gardiner was at

the Imperial court. The story is told by Morice (*Nar. of the Ref.*, 254-8), and dramatized in Shakespere's *Henry VIII.* Mr. Gairdner concludes that what evidence we have of its date points either to May or Nov. 1545, and he is inclined to believe Nov. the more likely. *Lollardy*, II, 415 ff. Gardiner was away from England Oct. 1545—Mar. 1546. He is nowhere mentioned by Morice as having anything to do with this "plot" against Cranmer.

[2] Dasent, I, 400-509 *passim; St. P.*, I, 842-78 *passim; Sp. Cal.*, VIII, pp. 394, 398, 426.

[3] Foxe, V, App. XVI; *Mon. Fr.*, II, 210-11; Ellis, 2 ser., ii, 176; *Lollardy*, II, 436 ff, 465.

[4] Shaxton may have been summoned on other grounds. The Council minutes are not clear. Dasent, I, 417.

[5] *St. P., I,* 849. For the sermon Gardiner objected to, see above, pp. 67-8.

[6] Foxe, V, App. XVII, and references in n. 9, below.

[7] *L. P.*, XXI, i, 898, 1491; Dasent, I, 467; *St. P.*, I, 866, 875, 878.

[8] Published by Bale 1547; accessible in Parker Soc. ed. of Bale, and, in part, in Foxe, V, 543 ff. Gardiner saw it in 1547 and said the examination was "utterly misreported." Foxe, VI, 31. See also *ib.*, V, 538 ff; *Lollardy*, II, 426 ff.

[9] Foxe, V, 546-50; Wriothesley, I, 167-70 (cf. *Lollardy*, II, 449, n. on correction of date in Wriothesley); Ellis, 2 ser., ii, 177; Mon. Fr., II, 211. According to the Six Articles all who denied transubstantiation were to suffer death even if they recanted, but the act was no longer interpreted strictly and pardon was offered to all who would recant.

[10] Foxe, VI, 30-1.

[11] *L. P.*, XXI, i, 836, 845.

[12] Foxe, V, 565, App. XVIII; Wriothesley, I, 168, 175; Mon. Fr., II, 212; *L. P.*, XXI, i, 1233; ii, 321. *Lollardy*, II, 461, n. Among the prohibited books were those of Gardiner's assailants, Joye, Barnes, Turner, Bale.

[13] *O. L.*, 36.

[14] Cranmer, *Letters*, 415.

[15] Wyatt died 1542, Audley and Baynton 1544, the others 1545.

[16] *L. P.*, XXI, i, 1094.

[17] Foxe, V, 547. See *Lollardy*, II, 451, for some speculations concerning Anne's relations with the court, based on sub-contemporary writings.

[18] Foxe, V, 553-61. See Maitland, *Essays*, 315 ff., and *Lollardy*, II, 455 ff., for discussion of this story. See *L. P.*, XXI, i, 289, 346, 552, for rumours early in 1546 that Henry was about to change queens again.

[19] "One has, however, some reason to wonder that when John Bale wrote his article of Queen Catherine Parr . . . he should say nothing of this iniquitous contrivance. Nor is it less strange that . . . this should not be remembered in the proceedings at his [Gardiner's] deprivation." *Biographia Britannica*, "Gardiner."

[20] *St. P.*, I, 851-82 *passim; L. P.*, XXI, ii, 14-416 *passim.*

[21] *Sp. Cal.*, VIII, pp. 464, 467; *St. P.*, I, 851-61.

[22] Sp. Cal., VIII, pp. 485, 488.

[23] *Ib.*, pp. 465, 469-70, 534.

[24] *L. P.*, XXI, ii, 347; *Dasent*, I, 546.

[25] *L. P.*, XXI, ii, 756.

[26] *St. P.*, I, 883-4; Foxe, VI, 138; *L. P.*, XXI, ii, 487-8, 493, 647(10); Maitland, *Essays*, 330 ff.

[27] Burnet, VI, 275. D. Lewis, in his edition of Sander's *Ang. Schism*, 153, n., so quotes Norfolk as to make him say something quite different.

[28] *Sp. Cal.*, VIII, p. 534.

[29] *O. L.*, 639.

[30] *L. P.*, XXI, ii, 634. Cf. Pollard, *Sommerset*, 3 ff.

[31] Foxe, V, 691. On the same page Foxe relates two other incidents

concerning Gardiner in the latter days of Henry VIII which appear to be apocryphal.

[32] Foxe, VI, 163, 170, 177, 180-1. Testimony of Somerset (Hertford), Warwick (Lisle), Bedford (Russell), and Paget, who at that time had shamelessly turned against his old patron.

[33] *Ib.*, 36.

[34] There is official record of his attendance in the Privy Council as late as Jan. 16, 1547. Dasent, I, 564. How frequently he attended during the two months previous is uncertain. He was present Nov. 11, but after that the attendance is noted so irregularly that it is impossible to know whether he were there or not. He himself said later that he had been a member of the Privy Council until Henry's death. Foxe, VI, 106; cf. *ib.*, 189.

[35] *Lords' Journ.*, I, 283-91.

[36] A contemporary account of Henry's funeral, signed J. S., printed in Strype, *Mem.*, Repository A.

NOTES TO CHAPTER XX

[1] A marginal comment by Foxe on Gardiner's letter to Somerset, May 21, 1547.

[2] *L. P.*, XX, ii, 732, 788.

[3] Foxe, VI, 126; Dasent, II, 7, 30; Leland, *Antiq.*, IV, 327.

[4] Foxe, VI, 24, 26, 58. He retired to Winchester early in March. *Sp. Cal.*, IX, 50, 52.

[5] Foxe, VI, 25-6, 106.

[6] *Ib.*, 31, 106.

[7] Tytler, I, 21.

[8] *Ib.*

[9] Dasent, II, 13.

[10] Burnet, V, 127.

[11] Reg. Gardiner, f. 52.

[12] R. O., St. P. Dom. Ed. VI, Vol. I, No. 25.

[13] Tytler, I, 24; Maitland, *Essays,* 335.

[14] *Treatise of politike pouuer,* f. Iv.

[15] Foxe, VI, 24-6.

[16] *Ib.*, 58-63.

[17] *Ib.*, 26-28.

[18] *Ib.*, 28-30, undated, but referred to by Gardiner as of May 27. In this letter Somerset takes Gardiner to task for a misinterpretation of the figures on the great seal, which Gardiner explains in his reply, *ib.*, 37.

[19] *Ib.*, 36-41.

[20] *The true hystorie of the Christen departynge of* . . . *Martyne Luther* . . . *translated* . . . *by* J. Bale [1546]; *The first examinacyon of A. Askewe* . . . *with the elucydacyon of* J. B. 1546; *The lattre Examinacyon of A. Askewe* . . . *with the elucydacyon of* J. B. 1547. The last two have been reprinted by the Parker Soc. Gardiner characterized these books as "very pernicious, seditious, and slanderous."

[21] Foxe, VI, 30-4.

[22] *Ib.*, 34-6. In this letter Somerset taxes Gardiner with not having opposed the pro-Papal writings of Dr. Richard Smith, who had recently recanted. Gardiner replied that he never had been a friend of Smith, had not seen him in three years, nor heard of his book until he was in trouble over it. Foxe, VI, 39-40; cf. *ib.*, 34.

[23] Foxe, VI, 36, 42; cf. Gasquet and Bishop, 51.

NOTES TO CHAPTER XXI

[1] Dixon (II, 314, n.) dates this 1543, but Gardiner mentions his negotiations with the Imperial ambassador at Stepney in May 1542, and other happenings in that year, as subsequent to the proposal of the homilies. B. M., Add. MS. 29,546, f. 22b.

[2] All the quotations in this chapter up to this point are from Gardiner's letter to Cranmer, B. M., Add. MS. 29,546, ff. 1-9. A fragment of this letter, with some inaccurate conjectural emendations, is printed in Strype, *Cranmer*, App. xxxv, from an imperfect draft in B. M., Harl., 417, ff. 79-83b.

[3] Gardiner to Cranmer, early in July, 1547. B. M., Add. MS. 29,546, ff. 9-24. There were at least three letters from Cranmer to Gardiner and three from Gardiner to Cranmer concerning the proposed homilies. The two from Gardiner which we have, are his second and third.

[4] *Ib.*, f. 15.

[5] *Ib.*, f. 21.

[6] *Ib.*, f. 23.

[7] *Ib.*, f. 24.

[8] Foxe, VI, 41-2.

[9] De Selve, 140; *Lollardy*, III, 28.

[10] *Nar. of the Ref.*, 247; Foxe, VIII, 15.

[11] Foxe, V, 563. In Edward VI's will was the provision "that during the young years of any my heirs or successors my executors . . . shall not suffer any piece of religion to be altered." Strype, *Mem.*, II, ii. 120.

NOTES TO CHAPTER XXII

[1] B. M., Add. MS. 29,546, ff. 4-5 (Strype, *Cranmer*, App. xxxv).

[2] In anticipation of the visitation, the power of the bishops had been suspended in May. This suspension was relaxed in June, but renewed in August. The first inhibition of Gardiner is dated May 16, the relaxation June (no day), the renewed inhibition Aug. 23, the day Somerset left for Scotland. Reg. Gardiner, ff. 56, 57. At this time Gardiner was at his house at Waltham, in Hampshire, where he seems to have remained until he came up to London Sept. 25. Foxe, VI, 245, 254.

[3] *Ib.*, 42-3.

[4] B. M., Add. MS. 28,571, ff. 16b-20b and 6a.

[5] B. M., Add. MS. 28,571, ff. 6a-9a. The law referred to is 34 & 35 H. VIII, c. 1.

[6] B. M., Add. MS. 32,091, ff. 142-143a.

[7] Foxe, VI, 43-4. "Common lawyers" is erroneously given in Foxe as "commons." See Gardiner's draft in B. M., Harl. 417, ff. 84-9. For Voysey's praemunire see Rose-Troup. *Western Rebellion*, Chapter IV.

[8] *P. H. E.*, VI, 15; *Cranmer*, 197.

[9] 31 H. VIII, c. 8.

[10] Repeal of 34 & 35 H. VIII, c. 1, by 1 Ed. VI, c. 12.

[11] Burnet, II, 87.

[12] Burnet, V, 163. The letter is undated. When Gardiner says he writes it on the sixteenth anniversary of his attaining his bishopric he evidently refers to his election, which occurred in Sept. 1531 (day not recorded), not his consecration, which was Dec. 3.

[13] Dasent, II, 517; Foxe, VI, 127.

[14] Dasent, II, 131; Foxe, VI, 44, 47, 246.

[15] Foxe, VI, 45-51. Paget, in a confidential conversation in Oct. 1547 with Van Der Delft, Imperial ambassador in England, declared with much unction

that he doubted if there were a man living more grieved at Gardiner's misfortune than himself, adding that in several long discussions with him he had found him quite intractable and entirely different from what he used to be. *Sp. Cal.*, IX, p. 187. This was meant for consumption at the Imperial court.

[16] Foxe, VI, 45, 48, 141; Dasent, II, 131.

[17] Foxe, VI, 106, 127-8, 209-28, 248-54 *passim*. See also B. M., Add. MS. 28,571, f. 15, for letter from the visitors thanking Dr. Steward, Gardiner's chancellor, for his diligence in assisting them.

[18] Foxe, VI, 41, 48.

[19] Strype, *Cranmer*, App. xxxvi. Foxe, VI, 42, 47-55, 141-2. Somerset, excusing some of the errors in translation, said, "in a long work a slumber is pardonable." Gardiner replied, "this translator was asleep when he began." *Ib.*, 142. Nicholas Udal, Miles Coverdale, and John Olde are all credited with a part in the translation. Udal edited a 2nd ed. "thoroly corrected" in 1551-2.

[20] Foxe, VI, 48-55, 128, 141, 244-53 *passim*.

[21] *Ib.*, 51-3, 140-1; Camb. Univ., MS. Ee. II, 12, No. 24.

[22] Foxe, VI, 202, 231, 249-50, 253. Medowe, now about 58 years old, was Master of Holy Cross Hospital, and had been one of Gardiner's chaplains from the beginning of his episcopate. He had accompanied him to the Continent on five embassies. *Ib.*, 202. He seems to have been Gardiner's confessor. *Ib.*, 192. For Basset, see above, p. 69.

[23] Foxe, VI, 53-4.

[24] I Ed. VI, c. 11 and 12. 28 H. VIII, c. 17, had given the King, on coming of age, the right to repeal laws passed in his minority, *any act or acts hereafter to be made to the contrary notwithstanding*. It was perhaps on the strength of this clause that Gardiner—if Warwick's testimony be accurate—said to Warwick in 1550 that although the King was "as much a king at a day's age as at forty years," yet if anything were passed in his minority which he later saw to be "prejudicial to him," he might "use therein the benefit of his young years." At the same time Gardiner said that he, Wriothesley, and Riche had been appointed by Henry VIII to consider this whole matter. Foxe, VI, 178.

[25] Dasent, II, 157-8. Gardiner was brought from the Fleet to Hampton Court Jan. 7, and came before the Council the next day. Foxe, VI, 65, 107, 128, 246. The warden of the Fleet later testified that twice during his imprisonment Gardiner had been brought before the Protector "at his house at the Strand." *Ib.*, 246. If this be correct, it probably occurred shortly before his release.

[26] Foxe, VI, 65, arts. xi, xii on pp. 107, 206, 228, 231; art. xiii on pp. 128, 248. See also letter from Cecil to Gardiner, Feb. 20, 1548, B. M., Add. MS. 28,571, f. 15, and two letters from Gardiner to Somerset, written sometime during the preceding four weeks, *ib.*, ff. 9b-10b, 15b-16b.

We learn from a remark of Ridley's that at this time he and Gardiner "had to do with two Anabaptists in Kent," which is all we know of the circumstance. Foxe, VII, 523.

[27] Foxe, VI, art. xiv on pp. 107, 206-15, 232. Testimony concerning this sermon speaks of it as on "St. Matthew's Day in February." St. Mathias is clearly meant, which, in 1548, being leap year, came Feb. 25.

[28] Foxe, VI, 67, art. xiv on pp. 128, 249-54. While Gardiner was still at Southwark the Council ordered no candles to be borne on Candlemas, Feb. 2. The order was sent out Jan. 28, which was rather short notice, but so expeditious was Gardiner in sending word to his chancellor at Winchester, that no candles were used there or in the churches within five miles thereof. Foxe, V, 716; VI, 219, 223.

[29] Somerset was elected Nov. 14, 1547; his letter of acceptance is dated Dec. 9. Lamb, 80-2; Cooper, *Annals*, II, 6.

[30] Gardiner's letter of refusal is lost. See Somerset's reply, in B. M., Add. MS. 28,571, ff. 4b-5b and 15a: "You do very much mistrust our doings, and are

in too great a fear of the surrender, betwixt the which and the establishing of a new college we had thought to have had no mean time in the which the college should be put in adventure, as you write." See also Foxe, VI, 65, art. xiii on pp. 107, 221. Fuller, who may have seen letters from Gardiner now lost, says that Gardiner told Somerset that Trinity Hall "could alone breed more civilians than all England did prefer according to their deserts." *Hist. of Camb.,* 180. F. W. Maitland erroneously conjectures that Gardiner opposed Somerset's plan because the Civil Law exalted the power of the King over the Church. *Roman Canon Law in the Church of England,* 93-4. But Trinity Hall had, since the abolition of the study of Canon Law, itself become a Civil Law College.

[31] We do not know the date on which Gardiner was ousted from the mastership. Possibly not until he was deprived of his bishopric in 1551. Dr. Walter Haddon became master Feb. 1552.

[32] The plan appears to have been presented to Commons sometime during the session of Nov. 1548-Mar. 1549, but was rejected (Foxe, VI, art. xiii on pp. 107, 221). Yet the commissioners, who were appointed Nov. 12, 1548, to visit the university, went on with their work and, on May 15, 1549, Gardiner being then in the Tower, reported the consent of the fellows of Trinity to the union. The Master and fellows of Clare opposed it, and Ridley, who was one of the commissioners, expressed conscientious objections to the dissolution of that college. His objections were finally overcome, but he was recalled. This was June 15, 1549. The visitation ended July 4, without having effected the union. See *Cal. St. P. Dom. Ed. VI,* pp. 11-18 *passim;* Burnet, V, 347-52; Malden, 81-4; Cooper, *Annals,* II, 23-36, 58; V, 280-6; Ridley's *Works,* 327; Lamb, 102 ff.

[33] Dasent, II, 550; Foxe, VI, 65; B. M., Add. MS. 28,571, f. 9.

[34] Foxe, VI, art. xv. on pp. 107, 199-223. Mr. Gairdner says Gardiner had received commands to preach on obedience. *Lollardy,* III, 235. The only reference I can find to such commands is that one Wm. Lawrence, a weaver of Winchester, said he *supposed* the Bishop had been so commanded. Foxe, VI, 209. Of those who later testified concerning this sermon most thought it was delivered Palm Sunday, some, Low Sunday. Gardiner said it was in April or May. Easter 1548 came Apr. 1.

[35] Foxe, VI, 65-6, 78, art. vi on pp. 150, 154, arts. xvii, xviii on pp. 129, 249-55; Dasent, II, 209.

[36] Foxe, VI, 65; art. xvi on pp. 107, 197, 206, 220-1, 232.

[37] *I.e.,* burying the Sacrament in a structure in the church prepared for the purpose on Maundy Thursday and resurrecting it on Easter.

[38] Foxe, VI, 65-6; art. xvii on pp. 107, 169, 171, 186; art. xix on pp. 129; arts. i-iv on pp. 133, 164; art. xxxvi on pp. 207, 228, 233. The date of Gardiner's appearance at court is given by his chaplain Watson as Saturday in Whitsunweek, *i.e.,* May 26. *Ib.,* 207. Gardiner forgot the date when he spoke of it later. His statement that he afterward sent a letter on ceremonies to Somerset is omitted by Foxe, but found in B. M., Harl. 304, No. 14, art. 6; and Add. MS. 31,824, ff. 1-15, art. 6. The letter itself is not extant.

Canon Dixon (II, 517) says, "the charges against Gardiner were concocted chiefly, as the Bishop himself declared, by Philpot, the Archdeacon of Winchester, a man whom he affirmed to be altered in his wits." But Gardiner declared that it was not Philpot's charges he was called on to answer: "One Philpot in Winchester, whom I accounted altered in his wits (as I have heard), devised tales of me, the specialties whereof I never was called to answer unto." Foxe, VI, 66 (where Winchester is incorrectly given as Westminster; cf. B. M., Harl. 304, No. 14, and Add. MS. 31,824, ff. 3a). Gardiner wrote to Somerset in March, 1548, complaining of Philpot's captious behaviour. B. M., Add. MS. 28,571 ff. 10b-12a. For Gardiner's further dealings with Philpot see above, p. 230 and *Nar. of the Ref.,* 48. Philpot became Archdeacon under Bishop Ponet.

[39] *Gratulatio*, Hoby translation, f. Biiii.

[40] *Exetasis*, 1.

[41] *Exetasis testimoniorum, quae M. Bucerus ex sanctis patribus non sancte edidit*, etc. See App. II, A, ix.

[42] The printer, in a special preface, says that although Gardiner desired its publication his friends were against it, lest it increase his difficulties. The printer therefore took it on himself to postpone publication. Of the two copies of the *Exetasis* in the B. M. only one (that in the Grenville collection) contains the printer's preface.

NOTES TO CHAPTER XXIII

[1] Now about thirty-two years old; chaplain to Gardiner since 1545.

[2] Foxe, VI, 67, 102, 107-8, 152, 207.

[3] A copy of these articles does not appear to be extant, but a summary of them in Article VIII of the articles ministered to Gardiner at the first session of his trial is printed in two slightly varying versions in Foxe, VI, 67, 96. The second contains a clause, not in the first, concerning general and particular councils which does not seem to have been in the original articles. Gardiner accepted the summary given in Foxe, VI, 67, as a fair statement of the contents of the original articles, with two exceptions: (1) the summary contained a clause on the King's authority during his minority, of which, said Gardiner, there was no word in the original; (2) the summary omitted all reference to the Sacrament, whereas, said Gardiner, in the original there was specific "mention of the Mass and of the Sacrament." He cited "Masses satisfactory," and his chaplain, Medowe, said that he showed him that he was to speak on certain articles among which was communion in both kinds. *Ib.*, 68-9, 108-9 (xxvii, xxx), 203 (xxxiv), 112 (xlviii); cf. 159 (top), 223 (xxix). Sir Thomas Smith said later that he visited Gardiner at this time to persuade him to repeat the articles, *ib.*, 149; but Gardiner said Smith confused Feb. with June. *Ib.*, 260. See above, p. 171.

[4] *Ib.*, 108.

[5] Much testimony was taken at Gardiner's trial concerning the circumstances of this visit of his to court, the prosecution asserting that he had been called before the Council, had by them been commanded to preach, and before them had given his promise to do so. This point was evidently made in order to give a more official character to the proceedings than could be attributed to an informal conference with Somerset, Paulet, and Smith. Gardiner, however, asserted definitely that he was not brought before the Council on this occasion, nor spoken to by any but these three. It appears from a careful examination of the evidence that Gardiner's account is the correct one. It is given in Foxe, VI, 67-8, 108-9; that of the members of his household, *ib.*, 152, 197-8, 207, 228, 234-5. See also that of Smith, *ib.*, 149-50, 186-8, and of Sir Thomas Chaloner, clerk of the Council, *ib.*, 147.

[6] Foxe, VI, 68-70, 109, 126 (vii), 145, 159, 206 (xxxi), 260.

[7] Somerset's letter is printed in Burnet, V, 226; Wilkins, IV, 28; and Foxe, VI, 86; Somerset's and Cecil's testimony concerning it, *ib.*, 170(8), 145(x); Gardiner's comments on it, *ib.*, 69-71, 109-10, 118; the testimony of his household, *ib.*, 153, and art. xxxiii on pp. 197, 203, 207, 232.

[8] Stow, 595. See engraving in Foxe, VII, of Latimer preaching before Edward. This gives the setting of Gardiner's sermon.

[9] Contemporary accounts of the sermon speak of it as delivered at Whitehall in Westminster. John Redman's testimony makes it clear that it was in the King's garden there. Foxe, VI, 239.

[10] Dasent, II, 209.

[11] Foxe, VI, 157. Udal's report is printed *ib.,* 87-93. The accuracy of it is shown by the many depositions concerning the contents of the sermon given at Gardiner's trial, the longest of which are those of John Redman, Robert Willanton, George Bullocke, and James Basset, *ib.,* 204, 225, 232, 236. Redman's account as given in Foxe appears to be a slight condensation of the account preserved in MSS. C. C. C. C. 127, pp. 15-29.

[12] The sermon as here given is, with minor omissions, from Udal's report; parts not in quotation are condensations. The concluding remark about subjects who rule like kings and obedience to the King only, is not in Udal, but other auditors reported it, and Gardiner himself tells of his pointing to the King and saying he only should be obeyed. The saying about the monastic vows of obedience and poverty is from Dr. Cox's summary of the sermon, not Udal. Foxe, VI, 68-9, 151, 226, 233.

Odet de Selve wrote to the French King that he had been informed that Gardiner said in his sermon that he would rather be burnt a hundred times than deviate from the Church's teachings on the Mass, and that he told the King he ought not usurp the title of Supreme Head. De Selve, 397-8. This may have been popular rumour, or what de Selve was told in court circles in order to justify Gardiner's imprisonment. It was certainly not what he said.

[13] Foxe, VI, art. xx on p. 129; xxix on pp. 109, 199, 203, 206; xxxviii on pp. 110, 198, 200, 203, 228, 235; liv on p. 113.

[14] *Ib.,* 71, 111.

[15] Dasent, II, 208-10. The record of the Council's determination to commit Gardiner to the Tower is signed by Somerset, Cranmer, Paulet, Russell, and Cheyne. At least two, if not all, of these signatures were not written before Jan. 1550, and probably not before Gardiner's trial, Dec. 1550; for Paulet and Russell, who were created Earls of Wiltshire and Bedford, Jan. 1550, first signed under these styles, then crossed them out and signed St. John and Russell, in order, evidently, to make it appear that they had signed in 1548. See A. F. Pollard, *Eng. Hist. Rev.,* XVIII, 567-8.

[16] *Cal. St. P. Dom. Ed. VI,* IV, No. 20.

[17] Wriothesley, II, 4; Foxe, V, 763.

[18] *Mon. Fr.,* II, 216.

NOTES TO CHAPTER XXIV

[1] John Davy and Thomas Growte, both of whom had attended him in the Fleet. The latter fell sick in the Tower and was replaced by Wm. Coppinger.

[2] Foxe, VI, 72, 111, 169, 175, 191-6, 198, 229, 235.

[3] *Ib.,* art. xi on pp. 72, 160; arts. xlvi-lvi on pp. 112-3, 171-2, 176, 195. John Ab Ulmis, writing to Bullinger Mar. 2, 1549, of the discussions on the Prayer Book in the recent Parliament, mistakenly names the Bishop of Winchester as Cranmer's opponent on the Sacrament. *O. L.,* 388. He may mean the Bishop of Worcester (Heath).

[4] MSS. C. C. C. C. 127, p. 117. On the anticipated conservative reaction and probable release of Gardiner see *Sp. Cal.,* IX, p. 458. Cf. *O. L.,* 69, 464.

[5] Stow, 600.

[6] Stow, 600-1.

[7] The sees were not actually reunited till Apr. 1, the day on which Ridley received the bishopric and Thirlby was translated.

[8] *O. L.,* 79-81, 87, 559. It should be said to Hooper's credit that he did not want the bishopric and that only after a fortnight in the Fleet were his objections to vestments, *etc.,* overcome.

[9] Foxe, VI, 637.

[10] *O. L.*, 80.

[11] Tytler, II, 21-4 (June 26, 1550, not 1551 as in Tytler).

[12] Dasent, III, 43. In *Lollardy*, III, 209, Lord Wentworth is named in place of Parr, an error due to mistaking the Lord Chamberlain (Wentworth) for the Lord Great Chamberlain (Parr).

Most of the Privy Council's dealings with Gardiner from this point to the end of his trial, cited here from Dasent, are also printed in Foxe, VI, 79 ff., and *Archaeologia*, XVIII, 135 ff.

[13] Gardiner's *Long Matter*, in Foxe, VI, 113-4.

[14] Dasent, III, 44. The Council minute (*ib.*, 48) to the effect that the Lieutenant of the Tower, who brought the Prayer Book to Gardiner, reported, June 13, that he had read it, but said "he could make no direct answer unless he were at liberty," seems to have been a deliberate falsification, made in order to give colour to the subsequent treatment of the Bishop.

[15] For documents relating to Heath, see *Lollardy*, III, 178 ff.

[16] An account of Gardiner's conferences on the Prayer Book and Ordinal is given in Gardiner's *Long Matter*, arts. lvii-lxvii (Foxe, VI, 113-5), the truth of which is attested by the depositions of Somerset, Paulet, Parr, Russell, and Cobham (*ib.*, 169, 172, 174, 181-2), and the Journal of Ed. VI (*Lit. Remains*, 276, 278).

It is singular that the conference on the Prayer Book and Ordinal of June 14 is overlooked by Mr. Gairdner in his account of Gardiner's relations with the Council at this time (*Lollardy*, III, 209 ff.). This oversight, coupled with his printing the Council minutes for June 13 and July 8 together, leads the reader erroneously to suppose that Gardiner persisted in his refusal to give an opinion on the Prayer Book while in the Tower. Gasquet and Bishop, in their account of Gardiner's relations to the Prayer Book (*Ed. VI and the Book of Common Prayer*, 277 ff.) also seem unaware of this conference, and make several errors in the chronology of Gardiner's imprisonment.

[17] Foxe, VI, art. lxvii on p. 114; art. lxviii on pp. 115, 191-3, 195, 198, 207, 220, 236. Cf. *Sp. Cal.*, X, 109; *O. L.*, 269; Gorham, 157.

[18] Richard Whalley to Cecil, June 26, 1550, in Tytler, II, 21-4, misdated 1551.

[19] Dasent, III, 65. Edward, however, records in his Journal that on June 9 Gardiner "made answer that he would obey, and set forth all things set forth by me and my Parliament; and if he were troubled in conscience, he would reveal it to the council and not reason openly against it," and on June 14 that "the Duke of Somerset with five other of the Council went to the Bishop of Winchester to whom he made this answer: 'I, having deliberately seen the Book of Common Prayer, although I would not have made it myself, yet I find such things in it as satisfieth my conscience, and therefore both I will execute it myself, and also see other my parishioners to do it.' This was subscribed by the foresaid councillors that they heard him saying these words." *Lit. Remains*, II, 276, 278.

[20] Dasent, III, 65-9.

[21] Foxe, VI, art. xii on pp. 73-4; arts. lxix-lxxiii on pp. 115-6, 172, 177-9, 183.

[22] *Ib.*, 179.

[23] Dasent, III, 70.

[24] Foxe, VI, art. xiii on p. 74; art. lxxiv on pp. 116, 183; cf. Dasent, III, 72, and Ed. VI, *Lit. Remains*, II, 283-4.

[25] Dasent, III, 73-7. Ridley, Petre, Cecil, and Goodrick were appointed to draw up these articles. Ed. VI, *Lit. Remains*, II, 284.

[26] Foxe, VI, art. xiv on p. 75; art. lxxv on pp. 116, 184; Dasent, III, 78.

[27] Foxe, VI, 170.

[28] The phrase "humbly suffer" appears in Foxe, VI, 76, as "humbly stand to his conscience." The former is found in two ms. copies of Gardiner's defence, B. M., Add. MS. 31,824, ff. 1-15, art. 16, and B. M., Harl. 304,

No. 14, art. 16. Gardiner may have used both phrases, one in the final version of his defence, the other in a draft. Foxe remarks that this was an excuse which would not serve the reformers in Mary's reign. There is, however, this distinction to be observed: Conscience was urged by the reformers as an excuse for refusal to obey the law; Gardiner here urged conscience as an excuse for refusal to obey commands which he maintained were not in accord with the law.

²⁹ For the instrument of sequestration and records of the Council see Dasent, III, 84-7. Gardiner's account is in Foxe, VI, 75-6 (arts. xv-xvii) and 116-7 (arts. lxxvi-lxxviii); testimony on latter articles, *ib.*, 169-184 *passim*. One week after the decree of sequestration was delivered, Gardiner protested its nullity before his two servants in the Tower, and declared that, if it were law, he would intimate an appeal at the first opportunity. This opportunity did not come till after the opening of his trial in Dec. 1550, when the appeal was intimated to the commissioners at Lambeth. Foxe, VI, 76, 100, 117-8, 193-4, 196. Mr. Gairdner says that the Council did not take further proceedings at the end of three months because they were stopped by Gardiner's appeal (*Lollardy*, III, 223); but it does not appear that the Council was aware of the appeal until his trial began. When Gardiner says, "which time of three months ran not, because it was suspended by his appellation made from the sequestration" (Foxe, VI, 132), he is merely making a counter claim in law to that of the commissioners "that the said three months are now thoroughly expired and run" (*ib.*, 76).

³⁰ *Lollardy*, III, 223.

³¹ Foxe, VI, 76, 117-8, 191, 193, 196. On Nov. 23, 1550 the Council appointed Bishop Holbeach, Secretary Petre, Drs. May and Glynne, all learned in the Civil Laws, to decide how to deal with Gardiner "duly by the order of the law." On Nov. 26, Dr. Edmund Steward, Gardiner's chancellor, was committed to the Marshalsea for refusing to sign "a recantation of certain things wherein he had offended contrary to the King's Majesty's proceedings." On Dec. 4, William Watson, Gardiner's chaplain, was summoned to appear before the Council. On Dec. 14 (Sunday), the Council notified the Lieutenant of the Tower to bring Gardiner on Monday to Lambeth. Dasent, III, 161, 163, 174, 179.

NOTES TO CHAPTER XXV

¹ Foxe, VI, 94-5.

² The records of the trial are preserved in Foxe, VI, 24-266. This is a mine of material on Gardiner, to which frequent reference has been made in the previous pages. A few of the documents are reprinted from Foxe in Howell, *State Trials*, I. In MSS. C. C. C. C. 127, No. 9 are copies of the testimony of Somerset, Warwick, Russell, Herbert, Parr, Paulet, and Cobham, certified by W. Say, notary at the trial, as "*concordat cum registro.*" In the same collection are documents and drafts of documents presented by Gardiner in his defence: Nos. 11 and 14, two drafts, of which No. 14 is earlier and incomplete, of his answers to the Council's reason's for his imprisonment = Foxe, VI, 127-30 (No. 14 is incorrectly catalogued in James, I, 297, as "other articles of defence"); No. 12, Gardiner's protestation against his sequestration = Foxe, VI, 100; No. 13, a draft of his Articles Additional = Foxe, VI, 125-7; No. 15, his reply to a request for fuller answers to certain articles = Foxe, VI, 132, where it is printed in the past tense. B. M., Add. MS. 31,824, ff. 1-15, a copy of the nineteen articles of indictment and Gardiner's answers thereto, = Foxe, VI, 64-77. Another copy of the same, omitting Gardiner's first five answers and his concluding paragraph, is in B. M., Harl. 304, Nos. 13 and 14. A comparison of Foxe with these mss. in C. C. C. C. and B. M.

shows that the records of the trial in Foxe are printed with a high degree of accuracy.

[3] Sessions at Lambeth Dec. 15, 18, 23; Jan. 8, 12, 26; Feb. 3, 13, 14. Session in the Tower Jan. 27. Foxe, VI, 93-143, 258-66; *Mon. Fr.*, II, 230; Wriothesley, II, 45-6. In *Lollardy*, III, 232, it is said that at the first session Gardiner protested that he did not by his presence intend to acknowledge the jurisdiction of the commissioners. This is inaccurate. Gardiner said he did not "admit their jurisdiction any otherwise, or further, than by the law he was bound to do." Foxe, VI, 96.

On the day of, or the day before, the second session, "the Thames beneath the bridge did ebb and flow three times in nine hours," which was regarded as a portent in some way connected with the Bishop. *Two London Chronicles,* 22; *Mon. Fr.*, II, 230.

[4] Wriothesley, II, 45-6.

[5] Foxe, VI, 99, 120, 134. Two proctors of the Arches, Thos. Dockwray and Jn. Clerk, are also named as Gardiner's proctors, but they seem to have played a rôle subordinate to those named in the text. Wingfield had been in Gardiner's service over twenty years, Basset, twelve. *Ib.,* 197, 231. Little is known of Thos. Somerset. He bore the banner of Gardiner's arms at his funeral. MSS. Coll. Arm., I, 11, 121, ff. A Sir Jn. Morgan seems to have acted as Gardiner's temporal counsel. Foxe, VI, 134. The promoters, *i.e.* prosecutors, were David Clapham and Jn. Lewis, proctors of the Arches. *Ib.,* 95.

[6] *Ib.,* 64-77.

[7] Dasent, II, 208.

[8] Foxe, VI, 97-8.

[9] His *Long Matter justificatory,* in Foxe, VI, 105-19; see also his answers to the 19 articles ministered to him at the 1st session, *ib.,* 64-77; his further answers, *ib.,* 101-3; his articles additional, *ib.,* 125-127; his answers to the Council's reasons for his imprisonment, *ib.,* 127-130; his interrogatories, *ib.,* 99, 133. Cf. Summary of matters on which he agreed in the reform of the Church, *ib.,* 255, 261.

[10] See above, p. 176; also Cecil's deposition and Gardiner's rejoinder, Foxe, VI, 145, 260.

[11] "When Christ taketh bread and sayeth, 'Take, eat, this is my body,' we ought not to doubt but we eat his very body. And when he taketh the cup . . . we ought to think assuredly that we drink his very blood." These were the words of Cranmer's catechism of 1548 (reprinted Oxford, 1829, p. 208). Gardiner again appealed to this in his book against Cranmer on the Sacrament. See Cranmer, *Lord's Supper,* 13, 20, 55, 106, 188, 227. Cranmer somewhat disingenuously replied, "if it may please you to add or understand this word 'spiritually,' then is the doctrine of my catechism sound and good." *Ib.,* 227.

[12] A contemporary report of this discussion is printed in Gasquet and Bishop, App. v. See also depositions of four of these bishops, Foxe, VI, 240-1.

[13] "Interrogatories ministered by the Office" at the 8th session, Foxe, VI, 123.

[14] See above Chapter XIV. Gardiner presented as evidence a copy of a letter he had written to Henry from Ratisbon, but this has been lost. Foxe, VI, 142.

[15] *Ib.,* 162-5; cf. *ib.,* 259. See Maitland, *Essays,* XV, XVI; *Lollardy,* III, 238 ff.

[16] Foxe, VI, 168, 173, 174, 177, 181.

[17] *Ib.,* 189-91. In order to prove Henry's misliking for Gardiner the prosecution also brought forward the omission of his name from the committee appointed to compile the book "last set forth by his Majesty touching a uniformity in matters of religion." Thirlby testified that he himself, "being one of the six that were appointed to the framing of that book, knew divers

that the late King favoured left out, and never heard of any such cause."
Ib. The book referred to is probably the Primer of 1545.

[18] Paget Paulet, Russell, Somerset, and Warwick, being unable to deny this, tried to make it appear that he had been so employed merely because he was a good linguist. Foxe, VI, 165, 168, 171, 177, 181.

[19] This was the granting to Secretary Petre of an annuity from his revenues, formerly paid to Norfolk. According to Paget, the King made the request "after the attainder of the Duke of Norfolk in the upper and nether house of Parliament." The bill of attainder was first read in the Lords Jan. 18, 1547, referred to Commons Jan. 20, returned from Commons Jan. 24. Henry died Jan. 28. Paget, who had brought Gardiner both the request and the King's thanks, now tried to explain it away by saying that "it may be" he used "another form of request to the said Bishop than the said King would have liked," and "it might be that he used such comfortable words of the King's favourable and thankful acceptation of the thing . . . rather for quiet of the said Bishop than for that it was a thing indeed"! Foxe, VI, 133, 165.

[20] *Ib.*, 258.
[21] See above, Chapter XIV, p. 99.
[22] *Sp. Cal.*, X, pp. 214, 226.
[23] Foxe, VI, 259-61. Since the trial was conducted under the rules of Canon not Common Law, the burden was laid on Gardiner to disprove the charges against him; hence no less than seventy-eight witnesses were called by the defence, only twenty-seven by the prosecution, of whom eleven were also among those called by the defence. The depositions of eighty-eight of these ninety-four witnesses are given by Foxe. It is not likely that those of the six not preserved contained anything of importance, except perhaps that of Dr. Edmund Steward, Gardiner's chancellor at Winchester, who was called by the defence to testify as to how the injunctions *etc.* had been carried out in the diocese, and how the Bishop had conducted himself there after his release from the Fleet.

[24] *Ib.*, 262-4.
[25] *Ib.*, 264-5.
[26] Dasent, III, 213.
[27] *Cal. St. P. For. Ed. VI*, 73-4.
[28] *Ven. Cal.*, V, p. 349.
[29] Dasent, III, 231; Patent dated Mar. 23. *Cal. St. P. Dom. Ed. VI*, p. 32.
[30] *Sp. Cal.*, X, 261; Dasent, III, 358-9, 497; Strype, *Mem.*, II, i, 483-5; ii. 263-4.
[31] *Machyn*, 8; *Mon. Fr.*, II, 232.
[32] Sanders, *Ang. Schism*, 209.

NOTES TO CHAPTER XXVI

[1] See App. II, A, vii, viii, xi; B, iii, iv, v.
[2] See App. II, B, vi. A specimen of his verse, from B. M., Egerton MS. 2642, f. 241, follows:

> *Certam que faciunt mortem mihi facta minantur*
> *Interea verbis praedia sola petunt.*
> *Facta nihil terrent, an par sit cedere verbis?*
> *Vitaque cui vilis, praedia cara fient*
> *Quem res non moveat, sonus hunc terrebit inanis?*
> *Nihil homini gravius, morte minetur homo.*
> *Vivere non liceat, quid vitae ludicra curem?*
> *Vita alia est melior, que meditanda mihi est*

Ista perhennis erit, nullis obnoxia dampnis
Cetera cuncta abeant, nec remorentur eam
Mors veniat faelix eternae Janua vitae
Vita peracta modo hoc, tota beata foret.
Hinc mihi tota salus, deus hanc det quod reliquum sit
Dixero nunc proprie vana salus hominis.

³ He also seems to have been accustomed to say Mass in the Tower. *Ven. Cal.,* V, p. 400.

⁴ See above, p. 186.

⁵ Hooper's *Oversight,* Sermons 5 and 6.

⁶ Gardiner's volume was not printed. The quotations here given are from the ms. copy, dated 1550, in the R. O., ff. 53, 61, 64, 65, 66. See App. II, B, iv.

⁷ Foxe, VI, 134.

⁸ Cranmer's *Defence of . . . the Sacrament,* in Vol. II of Jenkyn's *Remains of Thomas Cranmer.* The pages from which quotations are made are: 308-9, 401, 403, 422, 425, 427, 437-8.

⁹ See App. II, A, vii. The edition here cited is that in the Parker Soc. ed. of Cranmer, *On the Lord's Supper.* The pages from which quotations and citations are here made are, in the order in which they here occur, as follows: 10, 195, 19-20, 239, 59, 200, 22-3, 116, 162, 189, 139, 155, 233, 175, 214, 217, 360, 358, 193, 229, 16, 63, 37, 70, 201, 251-2, 239, 300, 256-7, 325, 333. Dr. Richard Smith, Peter Martyr's predecessor in the chair of divinity at Oxford, had also written a book against Cranmer on the Sacrament. Cranmer said he was informed by Smith that Gardiner received from him all the authorities he had gathered. *Ib.,* 163. Foxe (V, 9) says Cranmer got most of his material from Frith's writings on the Sacrament.

¹⁰ Cranmer, *Letters,* 455-8; cf. Foxe, VIII, 35.

¹¹ See App. II, A, viii.

¹² Gardiner, *Explication* (in Parker Soc. Cranmer, *Lord's Supper*), 51, 55, 62, 79, 83, 84 bis, 92, 229, 325.

¹³ A phrase used in A. F. Pollard's "Bonner," in *Ency. Brit.*

NOTES TO CHAPTER XXVII

¹ Foxe, VI, 350, 352.

² *Sp. Cal.,* XI, 80.

³ *Ib.,* 114.

⁴ *Ib.,* 120. Cf. *Camden Miscel.,* X, 75. On Aug. 6 the Privy Council ordered Parr's officers to leave the house and give Gardiner's folk immediate entry. Dasent, IV, 312. The lordship of the manor of Southwark, which had gone to the crown on Gardiner's deprivation, was restored to the see by Mary. Wilkinson, *Londina Illustrata,* I. She also restored to the see the estate of Esher, which Gardiner had been required to cede to Hen. VIII in 1537. *V. C. H., Surrey,* III, 448.

⁵ Stow, 613; *Chron. Qu. Jane,* 14; Wriothesley, II, 93-5; *Sp. Cal.,* XI, 150-2. Cf. *Camden Miscel.,* XII, 29.

⁶ Wriothesley, II, 96, says the night of Aug. 4; the Council minutes, Aug. 5. Dasent, IV, 311.

⁷ Machyn, 40, says that Gardiner came out of the Tower Aug. 9, and was conducted by the Earl of Arundel "to his own parish of St. Mary Overies, and form thence with my Lord of Arundel to dinner at Bath Place," but Aug. 11 is the date given in Wriothesley, II, 97, and *Chron. Qu. Jane,* 15.

⁸ His deprivation was assumed to have been illegal. The Venetian ambassador says that Mary authorized Gardiner to reimburse himself from

the revenues derived by the crown from the first-fruits, for the revenues of his see which he had not received during his imprisonment. *Ven. Cal.*, VI, p. 245.

[9] Date of restoration to Trinity Hall uncertain. The university wrote to him as their chancellor a letter of congratulation, Aug. 13, 1553. Lamb, 167; Cooper, *Annals*, II, 78.

[10] Dasent, IV, 329; Wriothesley, II, 101; Stow, 616. Burnet (III, 384) citing pat. 1 Mar. Reg. m. 37, gives "the appointments of the Lord Chancellor," granted Sept. 21, to commence from Aug. 23: £542 15s. yearly for wages, diets, and for the masters in chancery; £50 every term for attending the Star Chamber; £300 salary; £64 for twelve tun of wine; and £16 for wax.

[11] Four laymen, the first of whom was Sir Robert Bourchier in 1340, held the office under Ed. III, and five others in subsequent reigns before that of Hen. VIII. The combined terms of these lay chancellors cover a period of only about four years more than that of the five lay chancellors of Hen. VIII and Ed. VI.

[12] d. 1544.

[13] Goodrich conformed in Mary's reign and retained his bishopric till his death, 1554.

[14] Burnet, II, 405; Strype, *Mem.*, Cat. Nos. v, vi; Stow, 616; *Transactions of Royal Hist. Soc.*, New Ser., IX, 184-5; *Sp. Cal.*, XI, 192, 210, 214-5; Dasent, IV, 387; *Lollardy*, IV, 34-5. For Royal proclamations during Gardiner's Chancellorship concerning coinage *etc.* see Steele, I, Nos. 428-9, 447-8, 452, 458. Sir Thomas Gresham, the financier, later questioned the wisdom of one of Gardiner's financial measures. In 1558 he addressed a communication to Elizabeth recounting his services to Edward and Mary, saying that in Henry VIII's days the exchange fell from 26s. 8d. to 13s. 4d., and that, owing to his exertions, it rose under Edward to 23s. 4d; he goes on to say, "I did cause all foreign coins to be unvalued, whereby it might be brought into the mint to his Majesty's most fordle; at which time the King your brother died, and for my reward of service the Bishop of Winchester sought to undo me, and whatsoever I said in these matters I should not be credited; and against all wisdom the said Bishop went and valued the French crown at 6s. 4d. and the pistolet at 6s. 2d. and the silver rial at 6s. ob. Whereupon, immediately, the exchange fell to 20s. 6d. and 21s., and there hath kept ever sithence." Burgon's *Gresham*, App. XXI, 485. On the basis of this paragraph Gresham's biographer speaks of Gardiner's bitter enmity to Gresham on religious grounds, *ib.*, 114; but it would seem rather that there was merely a difference between them as to financial policy.

[15] *Sp. Cal.*, XI, 132.

[16] *Ib.*, 216, 327-8, 343. Tunstall also was regarded as belonging to this inner group, *ib.*, 270, but he does not appear to have been very active in it.

[17] *Ib.*, 200-1, 205, 252.

[18] *Ib.*, 130, 154, 205, 228, 252, 292, 309; Noailles, II, 308.

NOTES TO CHAPTER XXVIII

[1] *Sp. Cal.*, XI, 156, 168, 215. Cf. *Ven. Cal.*, V, 533.

[2] Parsons, *Ward-Word*, 43-4.

[3] Raumer, II, 79-80. Cf. *P. H. E.*, VI, 63, n.

[4] *Sp. Cal.*, XI, 186.

[5] *Ib.*, 122, 168, 179, 196.

[6] *Ven. Cal.*, V, Nos. 766, 776. He wrote similarly to Gardiner, *ib.*, 777. Cf. B.M., Add. MS. 25,425, f. 204b.

[7] *Sp. Cal.*, XI, 218-9; *Ven. Cal.*, V, 557.

[8] *Sp. Cal.*, XI, 110-1, 122, 130, 287.

[9] Chester, *Rogers,* 307.

[10] Foxe, VI, 537; *Sp. Cal.,* XI, 116-9, 131, 134, 156-7, 210; *O. L.,* 367-8; Noailles, II, 108-9; *Camden Miscel.,* XII, 29; *Mon. Fr.,* II, 245. Gardiner led the dirge in Latin the evening before.

[11] *Sp. Cal.,* XI, 156-7; *Chron. Qu. Jane,* 16.

[12] Noailles, II, 110-1; *Chron. Qu. Jane,* 16; *Sp. Cal.,* XI, 169; Foxe, VI, 767.

[13] *Sp. Cal.,* XI, 170.

[14] Machyn; Wriothesley; Stow; Guaras; *O. L.,* 368; *Sp. Cal.,* XI, 169; Foxe, VI, 391; VI, 144.

[15] Dasent, IV, 317, 319-22; Wriothesley, II, 98.

[16] *Sp. Cal.,* XI, 173-4.

[17] In full in Gee and Hardy, 373; Guaras, 145; Cardwell, No. xxviii; Foxe, VI, 390. Cf. Steele, I, No. 427.

[18] Machyn; Wriothesley; *Chron. Qu. Jane; Mon. Fr.,* II, 245.

[19] In full in Lamb, 165; Cooper, *Annals,* II, 78; Parker, *Corresp.,* 54; Ellis, 2 ser., II, 244; Strype, *Parker,* I, 83. A similar letter was sent to Sir John Mason, Chancellor of Oxford. R. O., St. P. Dom. Mary, I, 11.

[20] Parker, *Corresp.,* 54, 56.

[21] *Scholemaster,* 71; Baker, *St. John's Col.,* 137; Mullinger, *St. John's Col.,* 45. Within a year Watson was promoted to the deanery of Durham, and soon after Gardiner's death raised to the see of Lincoln.

[22] Heywood, *Early Camb. Stat.,* II, 79; Lamb, 169.

[23] There were such changes at Cambridge in all but Gonville, Jesus, and Magdalen. Mullinger, *Univ. of Camb.,* II, 150. Gardiner nominated Edmund Cosyn for St. Catharine's, Rowland Swynbourne, for Clare, Thomas Segiswicke, and later Andrew Perne, for Peterhouse. Foxe VI, 541; Heywood, *Early Camb. Stat.,* II, 79-80; Walker, *Peterhouse,* 83; Browne, *St. Catherine's,* 70; Lamb, 169. On Oct. 18, 1553 he decided a disputed election to the proctorship in favour of Henry Barleye. B.M., Add. MS. 5843, pp. 427-8. On Apr. 4, 1554 he ordered all the colleges to contribute to a new university processional cross. *Ib.,* 428; Cooper, *Annals,* II, 85; Lamb, 101. On June 17, 1554 he instructed the Vice-Chancellor to favour John Bullocke, newly elected Master of St. John's, in a suit against John Meres which seems to have been for "the recovery of those ornaments whereof the college is shamefully spoiled." B.M., Add. MS. 5843, pp. 429-30. For Gardiner's subsequent activities in connection with Cambridge, see above, pp. 260, 282, and below, p. 387. In 1559 Parker wrote to Cecil saying some doubt is made if Cecil's authority as Chancellor extends to college statutes, and adding that Gardiner would not be so restrained in his doings (whether upon warrant of the Queen's letters of commission or by authority of his office he leaves Cecil to determine). *Hist. MSS. Com.,* Report 6, p. 452. At Oxford Gardiner instituted, in Oct. 1553, a visitation of Magdalen, Corpus, and New College, which were under his jurisdiction as Bishop of Winchester. For the resulting changes at Magdalen see Wilson, *Magdalen Col.,* 101 ff.

[24] Inferred from record in *Grace Book* Δ, 105, of a degree in this subject granted 1554-5.

[25] Wriothesley, II, 101-2; *Camden Miscel.,* XII, 29. Renard says Mass was sung at St. Paul's Aug. 24. *Sp. Cal.,* XI, 188.

[26] Aug. 29. Rymer, VI, iv, 4; Dixon, IV, 23.

[27] *Sp. Cal.,* XI, 199.

[28] Lansd. MSS. 1236, f. 25, quoted in Rose-Troup, *Western Rebellion,* 227. See also Mary's letters in Foxe, VI, 7 ff.

[29] Foxe, VIII, 570.

[30] Chester, *Rogers,* 306. Canon Dixon (IV, 317-8) makes the inexplicable mistake of saying that Gardiner on this occasion called Henry VIII an usurper.

[31] Burnet, II, 448-9.
[32] See App. II, C, iv.
[33] Foxe, VI, 543, 710 ff; cf. *ib.*, 395.
[34] Printed in Strype, *Mem.*, III, ii, No. xxiv, and Hooper *Later Writings*, 374; cf. *ib.*, 592.
[35] Dixon, IV, 61, n.
[36] Philpot's book, *The trew report of the dysputacyon* . . . is reprinted without the preface in Foxe, VI, 395 ff, and in Parker Soc. ed. of Philpot. His accounts of his examinations in 1555 are in Foxe, VII, 606 ff. and Parker Soc. ed. On Oct. 2, 1555 he said he had been imprisoned by Gardiner eighteen months before. Bonner said his book was the chiefest matter laid to his charge. Foxe, VII, 660. For his remark about Geneva see *ib.*, 680.
[37] In *Nar. of the Ref.*, 175 ff.
[38] For his violation of the tomb of Richard Whittington see *Lollardy*, IV, 331-2.
[39] Dasent, IV, 341, 349; *O. L.*, 512.
[40] *O. L.*, 372, 506.
[41] Heylyn, II, 102. Heylyn gives no authority for this statement.
[42] *Sp. Cal.*, XI, 217.
[43] Foxe, VI, 592; Dasent, IV, 321; Chester, *Rogers*, 114, 118, 120. Thomas Becon, arrested the same day as Rogers, escaped Mar. 22, 1554, and went abroad. Becon's *Works*, III, 221; Foxe, V, 696.
[44] Foxe, VI, 645.
[45] *Ib.*, VII, 464; Dasent, IV, 340, 345.
[46] Dasent, IV, 347; *Sp. Cal.*, XI, 240; Foxe, VI, 539; Cranmer, *Lord's Supper*, 428.
[47] He was then sent by Gardiner to the Marshalsea. Foxe, VI, 541, 612-6.
[48] *Ib.*, 678-81; Dasent, V, 3.
[49] Dr. Edwin Sandys, sent to the Tower with Northumberland, was released on warrant from Gardiner and fled to the Continent, although Foxe says Gardiner sought his reapprehension. *Ib.*, VIII, 599 ff. Foxe himself was one who fled. A ms. note in the front of the 1563 ed. of Foxe in the B. M. (copy c. 37. h. 2), says that Foxe, early in Mary's reign, used secretly to visit his former pupil, Thomas Howard (b. 1536), grandson of the Duke of Norfolk, then a pupil of Gardiner's at Winchester House, Southwark; and Gardiner "having notice of it by a false brother might once or twice have instantly apprehended him, if the circumstances of person and place of recourse had not dissuaded." (This note follows one dated 1578 and is in a similar though perhaps not the same hand. It is signed but the signature is so rubbed as to be almost illegible. Mr. J. P. Gilson conjectures it to be "P(?)— Scott.") In the trustworthy life of Foxe, prefixed to Vol. II of the 1641 ed. of Foxe, young Howard is not said to have been a pupil of Gardiner's nor to have resided in his house; but Gardiner, on a visit to him in his own house, is said to have found Foxe with him, and on Foxe's withdrawal, asked who he was. "My physician," replied Howard. "I like his appearance," said Gardiner, "and will on occasion employ him"—words which Foxe thought ominous and thereupon fled to the Continent. Either or both of these traditions may have some basis in fact, but neither is very well attested. They are combined to make a pleasant anecdote in modern accounts of Foxe. Cf. *D. N. B.*, "Foxe," and Foxe, I, 13.
From Basle in 1554 Foxe sent an address to Parliament expostulating against the revival of the Six Articles, in which he spoke of Gardiner as a Chancellor well learned and of no bad disposition, were it not for the counsels of some. Strype, *Cranmer*, App. lxxvi.
[50] *Sp. Cal.*, XI, 238, 240, 253, 256; Noailles, II, 167.
[51] Planche, *Regal Records*, 1-32; *Camden Miscel.*, X, 96-7; Noailles, II, 200; Foxe, VI, 540; *Chron. Qu. Jane*, 27-31; Stow, 616-7; *Sp. Cal.*, XI, 259, 262; Guaras, 117-23; *Mon. Fr.*, II, 246; Wriothesley, II, 103. At the corona-

tion banquet Gardiner sat on the Queen's right, Elizabeth and Anne of Cleves on her left.

[52] *Sp. Cal.*, XI, 220, 231, 237, 240, 243, 252, 273; *Ven. Cal.*, V, 430-2.
[53] *Ven. Cal.*, V. 431.
[54] *Sp. Cal.*, XI, 310.
[55] *Ib.*, 324.
[56] Gardiner told Renard that on the final vote in Commons, Nov. 8, there were 80 nays out of 350 votes. *Sp. Cal.*, XI, 349. This statement has been misread in *P. H. E.*, VI, 102, n. We learn from Noailles, II, 247, of eight days opposition to the measure before its passage. There had been disturbances in two London churches in the middle of October, and Gardiner had taken up his residence in the palace, to be under the Queen's protection. *Sp. Cal.*, XI, 307.

NOTES TO CHAPTER XXIX

[1] *Sp.*, XI, 223, 386; cf. *ib.*, 165, 178, and Guaras, 113.
[2] *Sp. Cal.*, XI, 132.
[3] Noailles, II, 247. Cf. *Lollardy*, IV, 110-3.
[4] *Sp. Cal.*, XI, 242.
[5] *Ib.*, 207.
[6] *Ib.*, 154, 265 ff., 396.
[7] *Ib.*, 202, 206-7, 236, 254.
[8] *Ib.*, 238-9, 254, 288-97, 310-3, 317, 319-20, 328, 332-4.
[9] *Ib.*, 337-9. For criticism of Froude's erroneous account of Gardiner's views as expressed in this interview, see *Lollardy*, IV, 118-9.
[10] *Sp. Cal.*, XI, 331.
[11] *Ib.*, 339-43. The accuracy of Gardiner's forecast concerning Spanish promises appears in the protestation made by Philip two months later at Valladolid, that since he had known nothing of the terms of the marriage treaty till they had been granted by the Emperor, and since he would swear to observe them not of his own free will but that the marriage might take place, he did not regard them as binding. R. O., Tyler abstracts, Jan. 4, 1554.
[12] *Sp. Cal.*, XI, 347-9, 357.
[13] *Ib.*, 363-5, 372; cf. *Ven. Cal.*, V, 560.
[14] *Sp. Cal.*, XI, 365, 372, 387-433 *passim*. Paget also foresaw the necessity of having the treaty in as favourable a form as possible, and took pains to have Renard understand all the objections which might be raised to it. *Ib.*, 266-71, 381-2.
[15] *Ib.*, 382, 416.
[16] Noailles, II, 169-70, 233. On Noailles' mistaken suspicions concerning Gardiner, and Froude's unwarranted treatment of them as matters of fact, See *Lollardy*, IV, 119, n., 128-9.
[17] *Chron. Qu. Jane*, 34; *Cal. St. P. For. Mary*, 45; Machyn, 50; R. O., Tyler abstracts, Jan. 7, 9, 12. The articles were signed and sealed Jan. 12. The Imperial ambassadors were, beside Renard, Counts Egmont and Lalaing, Jean de Montmorency (Sieur de Courrieres) and Philip de Nigri (Chancellor of the Order of the Golden Fleece).
[18] Rymer, VI, iv, 20. This became the model for the proposed marriage treaty of Elizabeth and the Duke of Anjou. See *Hist. MSS. Com., Cecil MSS.*, II, 241, 243, 288, 291-3, 544-6.
[19] *Chron. Qu. Jane*, 34-5; *Camden Miscel.*, XII, 31; *Sp. Cal.*, XI, 447; Stow, 617; Wriothesley, II, 106.
[20] Jan. 3; *Chron. Qu. Jane*, 34.
[21] "Roane" ed., f. Aiiii.
[22] *Chron. Qu. Jane*, 33.
[23] Dixon, IV, 114. Canon Dixon is in error in agreeing with Maitland

that Bonner did not write the preface. On this and the editions of this translation see Appendix II, A.

²⁴ *Sp. Cal.*, XI, 411.

²⁵ Tytler, II, 320.

²⁶ Noailles, III, 31; Renard to Emperor, Jan. 23, in *Lollardy*, IV, 216, and R. O., Tyler abstracts. See *ib.*, Renard to Philip, Feb. 19.

²⁷ R. O., Tyler abstracts Jan. 31, Feb. 3, Feb. 5. The Imperial ambassadors, alarmed at Wyatt's proximity, anxiously asked Gardiner what they should do. He suggested (in a note to Petre of Jan. 31, 1554) that they might take ship in the river that night, or "if they tarry tomorrow, they would send their stuff first to my chamber or some other place in the Queen's court, with order to convoy the same by barge as it were to the Tower and thence to their ships, whereby all suspicion of their departure by water should be avoided." R. O., St. P. Dom. Mary, II, 32. All except Renard left London Feb. 1.

²⁸ Foxe, VI, 415.

²⁹ Stow, 619; cf. *Tudor Tracts*, 243; *O. L.*, 513-4; *Cal. St. P. For. Mary*, 60.

³⁰ R. O., Tyler abstracts, Renard to Emperor, Feb. 8. A large part of the government force under Norfolk had gone over to Wyatt, Jan. 28, at Strood, and Norfolk had to retire. Pembroke (Wm. Herbert), one of the new nobility and no friend of Gardiner, was in command of the forces in London. Mary and Gardiner met him on their way to the Guildhall, Feb. 1. Mary "bowed herself partly low," and Gardiner "bowed himself beneath the pommel of his saddle." *Chron. Qu. Jane*, 40. With the fiasco of Norfolk, Pembroke had become the Queen's chief hope of safety. That the event proved the soundness of Renard's advice enabled him to crow over Gardiner. When, in the middle of February, Gardiner assured the Queen that Philip might come in safety, Renard told her that he "trusted the Chancellor not at all, for if she had followed his advice she would be in a sorry plight." A month later he observed that "the Chancellor behaved so timorously in the recent troubles that no one believes him capable of conducting all the affairs of State by himself." R. O., Tyler abstracts, Feb. 17, Mar. 14.

NOTES TO CHAPTER XXX

¹ *Chron. Qu. Jane*, 54.

² *Lollardy*, IV, 259: R. O., Tyler abstracts, Feb. 8.

³ *Sp. Cal.*, XI, 335.

⁴ *Chron. Qu. Jane*, 184. Cf. Noailles, III, 43, and *Lollardy*, IV, 278 ff.

⁵ *Tytler*, II, 383-4; Renard to Emperor, Feb. 5, in *Lollardy*, IV, 292, and R. O., Tyler abstracts. Cf. Noailles, III, 60. Because of Gardiner's efforts to shield Courtenay, Renard concluded that Gardiner approved of Wyatt's undertaking. This so obviously mistaken surmise shows us with what caution much of Renard's unfavourable comment on Gardiner must be taken.

⁶ *Cal. St. P. For. Mary*, II, 60-1, 80.

⁷ R. O., Tyler abstracts, Renard to Emperor, Mar. 14, Mar. 22, Mar. 24. Tytler, II, 321, 337-9, 346. In a note from Gardiner to Petre of Feb. 11, 1554, concerning certain examinations following Wyatt's rising, occurs this paragraph:

"Tomorrow at your going to the Tower it shall be good ye be earnest with one little Wyat there prisoner, who by all lightlywode [*i.e.* likelihood] can tell all. He is but a bastard and hath no substance. And [*i.e.* if] it might stand with the Queen's Highness' pleasure, there were no great accompt to be made whether ye pressed him to say truth by sharp punishment or promise of life." R. O., St. P. Dom. Mary III, 22. It is not clear to whom the phrase "one little Wyat" refers.

⁸ Howell, I, 863; *Lollardy*, IV, 298; cf. Tytler, II, 313.

[9] *Lollardy,* IV, 304. For Elizabeth's coming to court and her examination, with several sources bearing thereon printed in full, see *ib.,* 278-304; also Mumby, *Girlhood of Queen Elizabeth,* Chapter V. Cf. Foxe, VIII, 607 ff. According to *Chron. Qu. Jane,* 75, Gardiner and others of the Council were again at the Tower with Elizabeth Apr. 12.

[10] Mary to Sir. Hen. Bedingfield, June 25, 1554, in Mumby, 153.

[11] R. O., Tyler abstracts, Renard to Emperor, Apr. 3; Tytler, II, 365.

[12] R. O., Tyler abstracts, Renard to Emperor, Dec. 21; Tytler, II, 382; Granvelle, IV, 348; *Van. Cal.,* VI, p. 199. Griffet, 168-72, using French and Imperial correspondence, says that Gardiner, on Elizabeth's arrival at court, insisted on sending her to the Tower, but after examining the evidence against her and Courtenay, declared that neither of them could be executed, not because they were innocent, but because there was not sufficient evidence for a conviction.

[13] Mumby, 184-7; *Ven. Cal.,* VI, pp. 57, 61. According to Foxe, VIII, 620-1, Gardiner had two interviews with her on her coming to court [early in May 1555—not July, as in *Tudor Tracts,* 361], urging her to confess her fault; she so steadfastly maintained her innocence that he finally kneeled down and said, "Then your Grace hath the vantage of me and other the lords for your wrong and long imprisonment." She was shortly after set at liberty. Cf. *Ven. Cal.,* VI, p. 82. Mr. Mumby finds no evidence to support the tales of alleged attempts on Elizabeth's life at Woodstock. Foxe's connection of Gardiner with such attempts is, on Foxe's own admission, made on the basis of hearsay and supposition.

[14] Tytler, II, 375, 397. He died suddenly at Padua, Sept. 1556.

[15] Foxe, VI, 431-2.

[16] Holinshed, IV, 31 ff.; Wriothesley, II, 115; *Camden Miscel.,* XII, 39-41; Tytler, II, 374; Foxe, VI, 549, 561-2, 579, 587; *Cal. St. P. Dom. Addenda, Mary,* p. 434. Cf. *D. N. B.,* "Throckmorton."

[17] Foxe, VI, 429-30. For date, see Steele, I, No. 445.

[18] Rymer, VI, iv, 16.

[19] Cardwell, No. xxx; *Visitation Articles and Injunctions,* II, 322; Foxe VI, 426: Burnet, V, 382; Gee and Hardy, 380. A commission was issued to Gardiner, Mar. 29, 1554, to remove married prebendaries at Westminster (that being exempt from the Bishop of London's jurisdiction). Rymer, VI, iv, 20.

[20] Reg. Gardiner.

[21] Foxe, VIII, 569 ff. Cf. Dasent, V, 180; *D. N. B.,* "Richard Bertie" and "Catherine Bertie"; B. M., Add. MS. 33,271, f. 9b.

[22] R. O., Tyler abstracts, Egmont and Renard to Emperor, Mar. 8; Griffet, 162.

[23] The commission to deprive Holgate of York, Ferrar of St. David's, Bird of Chester, and Bush of Bristol, was issued Mar. 13; that to deprive Taylor of Lincoln, Hooper of Gloucester, and Harley of Hereford, on Mar. 15. Burnet, V, 386. According to Machyn, 58, the commissioners sat Mar. 16 and 17. Foxe, VI, 645, gives an account of the examination of Hooper by the commissioners, dating it Mar. 19. It appears to have been a stormy session.

[24] *Hist. MSS. Com.,* Rep. 9, pt. I, p. 101a, a memorandum of the consecration; Machyn, 58; Wriothesley, II, 114. Stubbs, 104, makes Bonner the chief consecrator, assisted by Gardiner and Tunstall.

[25] Strype, *Mem.,* III, i, 466. No authority for the statement is given. White certainly must have been a very old friend. He had been Headmaster of Winchester College 1534-41, and Warden since 1541.

[26] *Commons' Journ.,* I, 33; cf. Tytler, II, 368; Noailles, III, 151.

[27] Dasent, IV, 397-8. Gardiner also headed two committees on financial matters.

[28] Tytler, II, 345-6, 366.

[29] Noailles, III, 151-3; Tytler, II, 373; see Paget's version of this, *ib.*, 382. Mr. Gairdner says that in summoning Parliament Gardiner, in spite of the opposition of some of the Council, insisted that the Queen be styled Supreme Head of the Church. *Lollardy*, IV, 374. This seems to be a misinterpretation of Renard's statement that Gardiner, in spite of the opposition of some of the Council, insisted that the title of Supreme Head be debated in Parliament with a view to its abolition. See Tytler, II, 302.

[30] Gardiner to Pole, Apr. 5, 1554. B. M., Add. MS. 25,245, f. 241.

[31] *Ven. Cal.*, V, p. 561.

[32] Tytler, II, 390; *P. H. E.*, VI, 118. Gardiner, at about this time, produced a genealogy of Philip showing his relation to the House of Lancaster, which, as Mr. A. F. Pollard suggests, may not have been an entirely friendly act. *Ib.*

[33] *Commons' Journ.*, I, 34; R. O., Tyler abstracts, Renard to Emperor, Apr. 22; Tytler, II, 373.

[34] Noailles, III, 153.

[35] R. O., Tyler abstracts, Renard to Emperor, Apr. 22, May 6. Two other bills against heresy were introduced in Commons, one of which was a "Bill to revive the Statute of Six Articles," but there is no record of it in the Journals after its first reading. In *P. H. E.*, VI, 119, it seems to be identified, wrongly, with the "Bill against heretics and erroneous preaching." In Dixon, IV, 169-70, it is erroneously stated that all four anti-heresy bills got as far as the Lords.

[36] R. O., Tyler abstracts, Paget to Renard Apr. [19]. Cf. Tytler, II, 382.

[37] R. O., Tyler abstracts, May 13, May 22-25; Tytler, II, 379, 385-6, 389-92.

[38] R. O., Tyler abstracts, Renard to Emperor, Mar. 22, Apr. 3, Apr. 22; Tytler, II, 345-7, 350, 371-3.

[39] R. O., Tyler abstracts, May 13, May 22-5; Tytler, II, 392-401; Granvelle, IV, 244; Noailles, III, 218-9, 225.

[40] *Ven. Cal.*, VI, p. 1643; V, p. 559. Soranzo believed that Gardiner's favour with the Queen was "caused principally by his having been an excellent agent for restoring the religion to its present state." *Ib.*

NOTES TO CHAPTER XXXI

[1] Knox, *Works*, 293, 296, 298-9.

[2] Pilkington, *Works*, 252; Bullinger attributed a like saying to Gardiner. Gorham, 336.

[3] Granvelle, IV, 277; *Cal. St. P. For. Mary*, 106; *Ven. Cal.*, V, 524; *Eng. Hist. Rev.*, VII, 268.

[4] Elder's letter in *Chron. Qu. Jane*, App. x; English Herald's account, *ib.*, App. xi; Tytler, II, 430-2; Wriothesley, II, 118-21; *Eng. Hist. Rev.*, VII, 253-280; R. O., Tyler abstracts, end of July. At the wedding banquet Gardiner alone, of all the notables present, sat at the table with King and Queen.

[5] Foxe, VI, 575; cf. Strype, *Mem.*, III, ii, No. 58.

[6] Wriothesley, II, 121-2; *Camden Miscel.*, XII, 37; *Chron. Qu. Jane*, 77, 78, 144-5. Stow and *Grey Friars' Chron.* misdate the entry of Philip and Mary into London.

[7] *Chron. Qu. Jane*, 145-51; cf. *ib.*, 78-81.

[8] *Chron. Qu. Jane*, 79, and note. Cf. Foxe, VI, 557-8, and Stone, *Mary I*, 330.

[9] Machyn, 69; *Chron. Qu. Jane*, 82-3 and note; Foxe, VI, 559-60; Wriothesley, II, 122. B. M., Add. MS. 15,388, f. 246; R. O., Tyler abstracts, Langosco to Bp. of Arras, Oct. 6. Renard said that more than ten thousand

were present in the audience. Granvelle, IV, 324. The Gospel on which Gardiner preached is that assigned to the 18th Sunday after Trinity in the Anglican calendar (the 19th after Pentecost in the Latin). This Sunday in 1554 should have come on Sept. 23, but Gardiner preached on Sept. 30. Mr. W. H. Frere writes me that the apparent discrepancy is doubtless due to the insertion of a Sunday in the octave of Corpus Christi which put off the beginning of the Pentecost series one week.

[10] The letter is printed in Thompson, *Christ Church*, 39. See B. M., Harl. 7001, f. 233, for two later letters of the same tenor from subsequent Chancellors (1556, 1581). Another instance of Gardiner's influence at Oxford occurred in Oct. 1555, when Pole communicated to him a report he had received of the neglect of theological study there, and, on Gardiner's advice, had the Queen replace the Hebrew lectureship by a lectureship in theology. *Ep. Poli*, V, 47.

[11] Foxe, VI, 566.

[12] Machyn, 70.

[13] *L. P.*, XVI, 101.

[14] R. O., Tyler abstracts, Renard and de Courrieres to Emperor, Aug. 5 and Aug. 8; the same to Philip, undated [middle of August]; Renard to Emperor, Sept. 3.

[15] Burnet, VI, 313.

[16] R. O., Tyler abstracts, Emperor to Renard and de Courrieres, Aug. 2; Mary to Emperor, Oct. 16; *Ven. Cal.*, V, No. 960.

[17] R. O., Tyler abstracts, Renard to Emperor, Sept. 3.

[18] *Ib.*, Nov. 6.

[19] *Ib.*, Nov. 23.

[20] *Ib.*, Nov. 14, account of Paget's negotiations at Brussels; and Renard to Emperor, Nov. 23.

[21] *Mon. Fr.*, II, 254; Machyn, 74.

[22] *Commons' Journ.*, I, 37. See also a rare pamphlet in B. M.. Grenville Collection, entitled: *Brevis Narratio eorum quae in proximo Anglicano conventu . . . de Religione pristina restituenda, acta sunt . . . 1554.*

[23] Tytler, II, 445-7, 460. Pole appears to have regarded his assurances as containing loopholes through which lost property might still be recovered. See *Ven. Cal.* VI, No. 14.

[24] Prayers for the safe delivery of the Queen were thereafter offered at the Mass in all churches. They were, wrote Antonio Maria di Savoia to the Bp. of Arras, composed by Gardiner. R. O., Tyler abstracts, Dec. 25, 1554. They are printed in Foxe, VI, 774-5, from a broadside by John Cawod.

[25] Elder, in *Chron. Qu. Jane*, 153 ff; Foxe, VI, 568; Machyn, 75; *Commons' Journ.*, I, 38; *Descritio Reductionis Angliae ad Catholicam Unitatem*, in *Ep. Poli*, V, 303 ff.; Haile, *Pole*, 446 ff.; *Nar. of the Ref.*, 290; *P. H. E.*, VI, 128. See also pamphlet mentioned in note 22, and R. O., Tyler abstracts, Account of Pole's arrival, enclosed in letter of Dec. 10.

[26] *Sp. Cal.*, XI, 314.

[27] *Ib.*, 202; Noailles, II, 169-70; IV, 121. The statements in Burnet and Godwin that Gardiner later sent secret information to Rome against Pole, and kept Cranmer alive to keep Pole out of the archbishopric, go back to the *De Antiq. Brit. Eccl.*, by Matthew Parker and his secretaries, 1572, p. 402, where they appear to be based on conjecture.

[28] Elder, in *Chron. Qu. Jane*, 161; Machyn, 77; *Mon. Fr.*, II, 255; Wriothesley, II, 124; R. O., Tyler abstracts, Di Stroppiana to Bp. of Arras, Dec. 3, and De Cordova to King of the Romans, Dec. 10.

[29] By debasement of the coinage.

[30] This may be a reference to Pole's letters to Somerset or to the rising in Cornwall. For the occasions referred to in Hen. VIII's reign see above, pp. 68, 96.

[31] There are three contemporary accounts of this sermon, one in Foxe,

VI, 577, one in Elder's Letter (*Chron. Qu. Jane,* 161), and one by Nicholas Harpsfield, in Latin, published at Rome 1555. See App. II, c, i. The three accounts agree in general. In the sermon as here given the first paragraph is a condensation from Foxe, the second mostly from Harpsfield, the third an almost verbatim quotation from Foxe, the last a condensation from Foxe and Harpsfield. As Canon Dixon points out, the most significant differences in these accounts are: (1) in Foxe, "when King Henry did first take upon him to be head of the Church, it was then no Church at all." In Harpsfield, *"In persona Henrici regis prima facie aliquid fortasse videbatur posse dici,"* which is probably nearer to what Gardiner said. Elder omits this passage. (2) Foxe and Elder omit the mention of the Queen's pregnancy.

There are some notes on the sermon in *Camden Miscel.,* XII, 40; and brief summaries by Renard, in Granvelle, IV, 346, and by Count di Stroppiana, in R. O., Tyler abstracts, Dec. 3. Noailles (IV, 38) says he asked Gardiner for a seat at the sermon but was told there would be no room for ambassadors. From the window of his lodgings in Paul's Churchyard he noted that the Venetian ambassador sat near the King. After the sermon Gardiner went to dinner with the Lord Mayor. Wriothesley, II, 125.

[32] R. O., Tyler abstracts, De Cordova to King of Romans, Dec. 10. Count di Stroppiana also estimated the audience at 15,000. *Ib.,* Dec. 3.

[33] Haile, *Pole,* 452, quoting the Abbot of San Saluto.

[34] *O. L.,* 298.

[35] Heylin, II, 138; Wilkins, IV, 94.

[36] 1 & 2 Ph. & M. c. 8. The Commons objected to certain clauses "containing nineteen lines," as passed by the Lords, and on the day of the final passage of the act, Jan. 4, 1555, "the said nineteen lines were not razed nor taken out of the act, but the Chancellor, in the sight of all the Lords, with a knife cut them out, saying these words, 'I now do rightly the office of a chancellor.'" *Lords' Journ.,* I, 484.

Mary determined to restore Church property in the possession of the crown and appointed Gardiner chief of a committee to determine the amount which might be restored without damage to the crown. See *Ven. Cal.,* VI, Nos. 14, 32 p. 27.

[37] R. O., Tyler abstracts, Renard to Emperor, Dec. 21.

[38] See App. II, C, iii.

NOTES ON CHAPTER XXXII

[1] *Declaration,* f. 7.

[2] Machyn, 80; Foxe, VI, 587; Stow, 626.

[3] *P. H. E.* (VI, 135) errs in saying that even before the day on which the heresy acts became effective Gardiner held a preliminary examination of the principal prisoners for religion.

[4] Foxe (VI, 588) says that these examinations were held under commission from Pole, but the process against Hooper reads *"Coram . . . Wintoniensi episcopo, auctoritate sua ordinaria illic judicaliter sedente,"* and Gardiner himself said to Bradford, Jan. 29, "Dost not thou know that I sit here as Bishop of Winchester in mine own diocese, and therefore may do this which I do and more too?" Bradford, I, 476. This need not imply, however, that Pole issued no commission, but merely that Gardiner thought it unnecessary. Tunstall, in 1527, protested against Wolsey's commission for the examination of Bilney and Arthur, saying he wished to deal with them in his own diocese by his ordinary jurisdiction. See *V. C. H., London,* I, 255.

From Hooper's process we learn that on Jan. 28 Gardiner was assisted by twelve, and on Jan. 29 by thirteen other bishops. The same document gives the names of nobles and others present. Processes against Hooper, Cardmaker, Rogers, Taylor, Bradford, Saunders, and Crome, and sentences on

Bradford and Hooper, are in B. M., Harl. 421, f. 36 ff. Hooper's process is printed in Burnet, VI, 370 (cf. *ib.,* III, 415), his sentence in Strype, *Mem.,* Cat. No. xxviii (cf. *ib.,* III, i, 286); Bradford's process and sentence in Foxe, VII, App. X, and Bradford, I, 585 (misdated); Rogers' process in Chester's *Rogers,* 423, his sentence *ib.,* 418, from Foxe, ed. 1563, pp. 1029-30 (in English in later editions, VI, 601).

[5] Foxe, VI, 550, 589; Strype, *Cranmer,* App. No. lxxxiv.

[6] Foxe adds that Gardiner "referred the whole doing thereof to Bonner," VI, 704. Burnet, II, 506, cites an instance of Gardiner's turning over to Bonner a heretic from the diocese of Winchester, but Burnet seems here to confuse the Marquis of Winchester (Paulet) with the Bishop of Winchester. See Foxe, VII, 322.

[7] *Ib.,* VII, 718.

[8] Saunders in Foxe, VI, 625, 630. Taylor, *ib.,* 685. Bradford, *ib.,* VII, 149 ff. Also in Parker Soc. ed. of Bradford, and Stevens' *Memoirs of Bradford.* Rogers in Chester's *Rogers,* and, inaccurately, in Foxe, VI, 593 ff. In App. XII of the Church Historians ed. of Foxe, Rogers' examinations have been carefully reprinted from the Lansdowne MSS. What appears to be a first-hand account of Ferrar's examination, probably of Jan. 22, is in Foxe, VII, 22.

[9] Which disproves Miss Stone's observation that "Gardiner was not hated, even by the reformers, with the exception of Foxe." *Mary I,* 310.

[10] Foxe, VI, 636.

[11] The *De Vera* was also cited against Gardiner by Bradford, and, earlier, in this month, by Thomas Rose who, with a congregation of some thirty, was apprehended on the night of New Year's Day, 1555, holding a secret service in English at a house in Bow-church-yard. "I have long looked for thee and at length have caught thee," said Gardiner to Rose, Jan. 3, "I will know who be thy maintainers or else I will make thee a foot longer." Rose was sent to the Tower where Gardiner saw him twice again, on which occasions, says Rose, "the Bishop had no great talk with me, but spake friendly." In May he was sent to Norwich and there examined. He escaped to the Continent. See Foxe, VI, 579, 585, 775; VIII, 584 ff; Maitland *Essays,* 434; Machyn, 79; Dasent, V, 88.

[12] Foxe, VI, 682. Foxe errs when he says that Taylor had, in Jan. 1555, been in prison a year and three-quarters, for he was not summoned by the Council till Mar. 26, 1554. Dasent, V, 3.

[13] Chester, *Rogers,* 316.

[14] Foxe, VI, 648-9. The Council, Gardiner presiding, committed Hooper to the Fleet, Sept. 1, 1553. Dasent, IV, 337. Foxe says he was charged with debt to the Queen. He was deprived of his bishopric by a commission headed by Gardiner in Mar. 1554. Foxe, VI, 645. Cf. Dixon, IV, 50, n., 138.

[15] Chester, *Rogers,* 296-7, 319-21.

[16] See above, p. 223.

[17] Bradford, I, 481. For the emendation of "apaused" *i.e.* checked, for "appalled" or "appeased," see addenda to Foxe, VII, 157.

[18] *Works,* III, 293-4; VI, 507.

[19] Foxe, VII, 631. Cf. *ib.,* 619, for a similar statement by Saunders. George Paris, a Dutch physician, was also burned in England under Edward, for denying the divinity of Christ. Stow, 605.

[20] Foxe, VII, 619.

[21] Chester, *Rogers,* 302.

[22] Bradford, I, 471.

[23] *P. H. E.,* VI, 69, citing Peck, *Desiderata Curiosa,* 1732, I, 44.

[24] Chester, *Rogers,* 306.

[25] B. M., Add. MS. 29,546, f. 20b.

[26] Gardiner's words, as summarized in T. Stapleton, *A Counterblast to M. Horne's Vayne Blaste,* 1567, p. 367.

[27] See Saunder's examination, Foxe, VI, 626. (Saunders was sent to jail by Gardiner, Oct. 15, 1553, for preaching without license. *Ib.*, 614-6.)
[28] Bradford, I, 488.
[29] *From Chaos to Catholicism*, 1920, pp. 43 ff., 201 ff.

NOTES TO CHAPTER XXXIII

[1] *Ward-word*, 42.
[2] Giles, *Ascham's Works*, I, ii, 418, 445; II, 129, 154; cf. *ib.*, I, i, p. lxxxvii; Katterfeld, *Ascham*, 59-61, and Chapter IV. Early in Mary's reign Ascham sent Gardiner a copy of the Psalms in Greek, and in the accompanying letter likened him to Socrates in having composed poems in prison. Giles, I, ii, 385.
[3] Strype, *Smith*, 50. Cheke, Gardiner's other opponent on Greek pronunciation, was Secretary of State to Queen Jane, committed to the Tower, pardoned, and permitted to travel abroad. In Dec. 1554 he appealed to Gardiner for financial aid, with what result we do not know. *Nugae Antiquae*, I, 56. For Cheke and Smith, see, in addition to Strype, *Archaeologia*, XXXVIII, 98-127.
[4] Katterfeld, *Ascham*, 301 ff. Even under Edward, Smith was thought by some to be "neutral" in religion. *Archaelogia*, XXXVIII, 126. Cf. Maitland, *Essays*, 452.
[5] *Wills from Doctors' Commons*, 43. Udal may have been instructor to the youth in Gardiner's household or Master of the Winchester Grammar School, to which the Bishop had the appointment. See Leach, "Udal"; *Ency. Brit.*
[6] Harington, *Briefe View*, 45-6; reprinted in *Nugae Antiquae*, II, 67. Cf. *ib.*, I, 363. The elder Harington's share in the rebellion appears to have been larger than his son admits. See *Chron. Qu. Jane*, 182-4. Fuller adds the family of the Hungerfords to Harington's list of those whom Gardiner restored. *Worthies*, III, 169.
[7] Underhill's autobiography in *Nar. of the Ref.*
[8] *Church Hist.*, Cent. XVI, Bk. viii, Sect. ii.
[9] Granvelle, IV, 400, 404; *Ven. Cal.*, VI, pp. 28, 31, 37, 45; Dasent, V, 97, 104; Machyn, 82-3; Foxe, VI, 705; Maitland, List of Martyrs, in *Essays*, 576.
[10] Foxe, VII, 70 ff; Machyn, 84; Dasent, V, 115, 118; *Ven. Cal.* VI, p. 50.
[11] Foxe, VII, 92 ff.
[12] Cooper, *Annals*, II, 94. On Feb. 19 he had requested the election of Wm. Muryell, his old servant and scholar, to the office of one of the bedells, vacated by death. Muryell failed of election even on the third scrutiny, which Gardiner attributed to religious opposition, hence his letter of Mar. 24. The Senate thereupon chose four doctors who drew up fifteen articles for subscription. *Ib.*, 95; Mullinger, *Univ. of Camb.*, II, 154-5. On Feb. 22, 1555, Pole had empowered Gardiner, as Chancellor of Cambridge, to receive all who were willing to be reconciled to the Church. B. M., Add. MS. 5843, p. 430. For Gardiner's action in a dispute between the university and the town, and in the disputed election of Mayor, 1555, see Cooper, *Annals*, II, 97-8.
[13] *Ven. Cal.*, VI, No. 76; Granvelle, IV, 343; cf. Noailles, III and IV *passim*.
[14] *Ven. Cal.*, VI, No. 80. The chief French representatives were Anne de Montmorency, Grand Constable, and Cardinal Louis de Guise; among the Imperialists were Antoine de Granvelle, Bishop of Arras, and the Duke of Medina Celi. Cecil accompanied Pole, unofficially.
[15] *Ven. Cal.*, VI, p. 328; cf. *ib.*, p. 162, and Friedmann in *Macmillan's*

Magazine, XIX, 12. For accounts of the congress see *Ven. Cal.,* VI, pp. 20-125 *passim;* Tytler, II, 476-9; Noailles, IV, 318 ff.

[16] *Ven. Cal.* VI, pp. 112, 119.

[17] The Venetian ambassador with the Emperor heard that Gardiner ran great risk of personal injury by attempting to examine one of Wentworth's gentlemen. *Ven. Cal.,* VI, p. 102. Parsons later wrote that Gardiner found so many heretics in Calais that he said that if Wentworth were not removed, Calais would not be English one year together. *Domestical Difficulties,* in Cath. Record Soc. *Miscel.,* II, 57.

[18] Foxe, VII, 310. William Tyms, a deacon, was another heretic with whom Gardiner later talked, but all we know of the conversation is that upon Gardiner's remark that Tyms was not dressed like a deacon, Tyms retorted that he was dressed more like a deacon than Gardiner like an apostle. *Ib.,* VIII, 108.

[19] *Ven. Cal.,* VI, pp. 102, 112. He was delayed by a storm at Calais.

[20] Burnet, V, 429; Foxe, VII, 86, 286; *Ven. Cal.,* VI, p. 94; cf. *ib.,* App. No. 136, and Dasent, V, May, June.

[21] Dasent, V, 151-81 *passim; Ven. Cal.* VI, pp. 144, 148. In July Gardiner warned the Dudleys and other released participants in Wyatt's rising that their meetings in London were suspect. *Ib.,* p. 137; Granvelle, IV, 447.

[22] Maitland's List of Martyrs, *Essays,* 576.

[23] Gardiner's register contains only one process against a heretic, dated Mar. 21, 1534. The accused was an obscure person who readily submitted to Gardiner's Vicar General, Edmund Steward. There were, however, four burnings in the diocese of Winchester in 1540. See above, Chapter XIII, n. 47.

[24] *Hist. MSS. Com., Cecil MSS.,* I, 310.

[25] Foxe, VI, 42.

[26] B. M., Add. MS. 29,546, f. 3b.

[27] Dasent, IV, 345-7, 406. Renard, writing to the Emperor, Mar. 14, 1554, said that Gardiner had insisted that the Queen hold Parliament at Oxford "on account of the three deposed bishops whom he means to have burnt unless they will recant." R. O., Tyler abstracts. But Renard is seldom trustworthy in his interpretation of Gardiner's motives.

[28] *Declaration,* f. clxxvii.

NOTES TO CHAPTER XXXIV

[1] *Nar. of the Ref.,* 209-10.

[2] Burnet, VI, 386. Cf. *Ven. Cal.,* VI, pp. 178-9, 183; Granelle, IV, 340, 396.

[3] *Ven. Cal.,* VI, No. 247. How much of Gardiner's time was given to the judicial duties of the chancellorship it is hard to say. There are incidental references to his sitting in the Star Chamber (see above, pp. 229, 249), and an elegy written at his death praises his administration of justice (in Hearne's *Curious Discourses,* II, 416 ff.); but he was so engrossed in affairs of State that he must have delegated much of his judicial work to the judges in the Star Chamber and the masters in Chancery.

That his legal attainments were not unrecognized by the practitioners of the Common Law may perhaps be indicated by his admission to Gray's Inn sometime in 1555. Foster, *Register of Admissions to Gray's Inn,* 25.

[4] Cf. Burnet, VI, 384-5.

[5] *Ven. Cal.,* VI, p. 189.

[6] The last specific mention of his presence in the Council minutes is on Sept. 18, 1555, but as the attendance at subsequent meetings through Sept. 25 is indicated by the words, "The appearance as before," it would seem

that he attended these meetings as well. There are no entries between Sept. 25 and Oct. 7. He was not present on or after Oct. 7.

[7] *Ven. Cal.*, VI, Nos. 237, 240, p. 208; Noailles, V, 150.

[8] *Ib.*, Oct. 6, 1555.

[9] *Ib.*, 173; *Ven. Cal.*, VI, Nos. 246, 251.

[10] *Ven. Cal.*, VI, Nos. 251, 258, p. 229.

[11] *Ib.*, pp. 228-9.

[12] *Ib.*, p. 217.

[13] *Ib.*, p. 225; *Ep. Poli*, V, 46.

[14] *Ven. Cal.*, VI, No. 259.

[15] *Ib.*

[16] *Ib.*, p. 240. Canon Dixon (IV, 455) conjectures that the issuing of the letters patent (dated Nov. 2. Wilkins, IV, 130) enabling Pole to call this synod, was Gardiner's last official act; but we learn from Michiele that owing to Gardiner's illness the great seal had been put in the hands of Thirlby at least as early as Oct. 14. *Ven. Cal.*, VI, No. 246.

[17] In full in *Wills from Doctors' Commons*, Camden Soc. It was proved Jan. 28, 1557.

[18] Two other Chestons are remembered, John, with £66 13*s.* 4*d.*, and Alice with £40 "towards her marriage."

[19] Cf. *Ven. Cal.*, VI, p. 255. Thwaites was a young man in Gardiner's service in 1538. *L. P.*, XIII, i, 327. Thos. Harding, former chaplain to the father of Lady Jane Grey, was converted to Catholicism after Mary's accession and later, as a refugee on the Continent, wrote interminably against Jewell. That Gardiner's former chaplain Watson was not remembered in the will was doubtless due to the fact that he was now well provided for as Dean of Durham and on the road to further preferment.

[20] See J. G. Nichols' Note on Funerals in Machyn, p. xx ff.

[21] *Ven. Cal.*, VI, p. 252.

[22] *Ib.*, p. 245.

[23] *Ib.*, p. 247.

[24] Heralds' account of his burial, in MSS. Coll. Arm. I, 11, 121.

[25] Foxe, VII, 593. The absurdity of Foxe's hearsay tale (*ib.*, 592) of Gardiner's last dinner, with the old Duke of Norfolk (then two months in his grave!) has been shown in Lingard, VII, 496, and Stone, *Mary I*, 378.

[26] *A Counterblast to M. Horne's Vayne Blast Against M. Fekenham*, 1567, p. 368. Slightly varying versions of this story appear in Foxe, VIII, 635 (first in the ed. of 1570, p. 2300); *De Antiq. Brit. Eccl.*, 402 (1572); Parsons' *Ward-Word*, 48 (1599).

[27] *Politike pouuer*, f. L.

[28] *Ven. Cal.*, VI, p. 252.

[29] *Ib.*, p. 255. Wriothesley II, 132, says that some supposed Gardiner "had been poisoned when he went over seas to intreat a peace between the Emperor and the French King," but Michiele tells us that he died "of dropsy, as seen by outward and inward signs, the body having been opened to clear up the suspicion of those who attributed his death to poison." *Ven. Cal.*, VI, p. 252. Bale, 686, adds what appears to be a bit of gratuitous slander, saying, *"ex arido enim hydropi, qui morbus est subcutaneus & prodigiosa quadam scabie, emortuus esse fertur."* Pilkington, who, like Bale, was on the Continent at the time of Gardiner's death, said, five years later, that Gardiner "rotted alive; and ere he died such a rank savour steamed from all his body that none of his friends were able to come at him, but that they were ready to vomit." *Works*, 655. Bale makes similar statements and may be Pilkington's source. They are repeated in *De Antiq. Brit. Eccl.*, 402, and Strype *Mem.*, III, i, 465. Perhaps the earliest version of divine retribution shown in the manner of Gardiner's death is that of Philpot who, late in 1555, said to Bonner that God had judged Gardiner "who by report died miserably." *Examinations*, 86.

[30] *Cal. St. P. Dom. Mary,* p. 72.

[31] Machyn, 96-7. Gardiner's obsequies are described at length in the Heralds' account in MSS. Coll. Arm., I, 11, 121-4, continued *ib.*, 127-33. Some details not given by the Heralds are found in the brief accounts in Wriothesley, II, 132-3; and Machyn, 96-7, 100-1. See also Stow, 627. The Heralds' account tells us that when Gardiner died his barge was "lying in a readiness under the Queen's privy stairs," and at break of day he was "conveyed therein, and from thence brought to his place at St. Mary's Overies, where, in the great chamber, he was laid and opened, his entrails taken forth and closed up in two pots of a gallon and a half apiece; and the water within his body reserved in a great kettle. The quantity of the water was seven gallons. And after that had into a little close house at the further end of the same chamber on the left hand, where he was dried and put into his winding sheet, and upon that sered, and after that his albe and other vestments put upon him."

[32] Heralds' account, and Machyn. Dixon, IV, 451, erroneously places Bonner's requiem Mass in St. Paul's.

[33] Machyn, 97. Gardiner's arms were argent a cross sable between four griffins' heads razed azure with a garden lily argent upon the cross. See *V. C. H., Hampshire,* V, 56.

[34] Heralds' account.

[35] Philpot, *Examinations and Writings,* 269.

[36] Michiele to the Doge, Nov. 18, 1555, translated by Friedmann in *Macmillan's Magazine,* XIX, 12. Cf. *Ven. Cal.,* VI, No. 282.

[37] *Ib.,* No. 287; *Ep. Poli,* V, 53-4.

[38] *Ib.,* V, 52. Cf. *Ven. Cal.,* VI, p. 246.

[39] Heralds' account, with some details from Wriothesley and Machyn.

[40] Heralds' account. This makes it clear that Gardiner's chantry was not erected till after his death, and that he was not, in all probability, responsible for its inferior design.

[41] Mr. John Vaughan in his *Winchester Cathedral,* 1919, p. 65, tells us that at the beginning of the last century, Dr. G. F. Knott, prebendary of the cathedral 1810-41, "opened the coffin of Bishop Gardiner, and, just lifting the lid, he took the episcopal ring from the Bishop's finger. At the same time one of his assistants put his hand into the coffin and drew out a handful of black hair." This is given "on the authority of the late Mr. F. J. Baigent." The ring is of gold with an intaglio of the profile head of Minerva. It is preserved in the Cathedral Library.

NOTES TO CHAPTER XXXV

[1] There are two portraits of Gardiner at Trinity Hall, one a replica of the other, but there is a difference of opinion as to which is the original, which was probably done by a painter of Holbein's school. A similar small portrait is in Gray's Inn, London. The ms. catalog of paintings in the Master's Lodge at Trinity College, Cambridge, lists a portrait of Gardiner. I have been unable to find it or anyone at Trinity College who knows what has become of it. Poole's *Cat. of Oxford Portraits* (I, No. 33) lists one of Gardiner in the Bodleian. There is in the Museum at Berlin a portrait, purchased from the Secretan collection, said to be of Gardiner, and attributed to Jan Matsys. The features are so very different from those of Gardiner's portraits at Trinity Hall that it is doubtful if it be a picture of him. A good reproduction of it may be seen in Secretan, *Cat. of Paintings,* II, 33. There is a tiny picture of Gardiner in an illumination on a document at Winchester, which is reproduced as frontispiece and described on p. 67 of *Winchester Cathedral Documents.*

[2] Dixon, II, 418.

[3] George Constantyne, in *L. P.*, XIV, ii, 400.

[4] *Scholemaster*, 133-4.

[5] Foxe, VI, 686.

[6] *Ib.*, 30.

[7] Lamb, 43.

[8] Bateson, *Records of the Borough of Leicister*, III, p. 82.

[9] Foxe, VI, 45.

[10] *Ib.*, 190.

[11] *Ib.*, 46.

[12] B. M., Add. MS. 29,546 f. 20b.

[13] *St. P.*, VIII, 51.

[14] *L. P.*, XVII, 803.

[15] *For. Cal. Ed. VI*, p. 81.

[16] B. M., Add. MS. 28,571, f. 6a.

[17] Foxe, V, 692.

[18] *Politike Pouuer*, f. Iiiii.

[19] 1 & 2 Ph. & M. c. 10.

[20] Foxe, VI, 42.

[21] *Ib.*, 141.

[22] See above, p. 280.

[23] Harington, *A Tract on the Succession*, 101. Harington, in his *Briefe View*, 49 ff. (cf. *Nugae Antiq.*, 72 ff.) has also preserved for us two "elegies" on Gardiner, one an encomium by a certain Mr. Prideaux, the other an answer, verse by verse, by "an ill-wisher" of the Bishop. One of Mr. Prideaux's quatrains is a sufficient specimen:

> The Prince main plaine his death,
> the realm his lack may rue;
> All men may say, O Winchester,
> most worthy wight adue!

The Latin elegy by John Morwen, chaplain to Bonner and Greek scholar from Corpus Christi College, Oxford, published 1555, has been reprinted in Hearne's *Curious Discourses*, II, 416. According to Foxe, VIII, 208, this was answered by Julins Palmer, former fellow of Magdalen, Oxford. Bale, 687, preserves Latin verses in dispraise of Gardiner.

[24] Warwick to Cecil, June 14, 1548, in Tytler, I, 108.

[25] *L. P.*, XVI, 223, 467.

[26] See above, p. 271.

[27] Translator's preface to "Rome" ed. of *De Vera*.

[28] Foxe, VI, 24, 585.

[29] *L. P.*, XIX, ii, 532.

[30] Foxe, VI, 230.

[31] This epithet was not confined to Foxe. Warwick spoke of Gardiner's "accustomed wiliness." Tytler, I, 108. Gardiner himself protested to the Council in 1547, "I am not Wily Winchester, but plain, humble and obedient," etc. B. M., Add. MS. 28,571, f. 8b.

[32] *L. P.*, XI, 1242.

[33] Foxe, VI, 37, 47.

[34] *L. P.*, XX, ii, 732.

[35] *Declaration*, f. xxvii.

[36] Among friends living at his death and mourning it, the following are mentioned in Morwen's epitaph (see n. 23): Archbishop Heath, Bishops Bonner, Day, Tunstall, and White, Dr. (later Bishop) Watson, Dean (later Abbot) Feckenham, Drs. William Chedsey and Thomas Martin, William Roper, son-in-law of Sir Thomas More, James Basset, and William Coppinger.

[37] Foxe, VI, 199.

INDEX

Abbeville, 347, 355.
Abbreviations used in this volume, 338.
Ab Ulmis, John, 371.
Acrobats, 234, 258-59.
Act asserting Mary's authority to be as great as her predecessors', 253.
Act concerning laws passed during minority, 165, 170, 368.
Act concerning royal proclamations, 164.
Act forbidding teaching contrary to *King's Book,* 162-63; in conflict with injunctions of *1547, ib.,* repealed, 164, 170.
Act giving royal proclamations force of law, 164.
Act legitimizing marriage of Henry VIII and Catherine of Aragon, 235.
Act of Six Articles, passed, 80; expresses dominant contemporary views, 80-1; Gardiner probable author, 81; enforced, 82; enforcement stayed, *ib.*; checks negotiations with Protestant powers, 84; enforced, 90; convictions under, *1543,* 108; amended, 113; convictions under, *1546,* 136-37; repealed, 170; mentioned, 92, 104, 105, 107, 125, 186, 190, 266, 354, 365, 379, 383.
Act of Succession, 54, 55, 58, 60.
Act of Supremacy, 57, 58, 163, 164, 298; repealed, 263.
Act of Uniformity, *1549,* 183-84.
Act of Uniformity, *1552,* 226, 228.
Act repealing ecclesiastical legislation of Edward VI, 240.
Act restricting use of Bible, 105.
Act reuniting England and Rome, 298.
Ad Martinum Bucerum De Impudente, etc., 125, 311.
Ad Martinum Bucerum Epistola, 125, 311.
Aigues Mortes, 74.
Aix, 74.
Aldrich, Robert, Bishop of Carlisle, *1537-56,* 223.
Alesius, Alexander, 97-99, 358.
Alessandria, 29.
Allen, Francis, gentleman servant of Gardiner, 183.

Allen, P. S., 339.
Alliances. *See* Treaties.
Altars, 126, 204-6, 216.
Alterations in religion. *See* Innovation in religion; Reform of English Church.
Alward, Thomas, 35.
Ambrogio, Signor, Papal secretary, 65.
America, 21, 108.
Amiens, 20, 34.
Ampthill, 357.
Anabaptists, 16, 17, 84, 93, 133, 356, 368.
Anarchy, feared as result of religious reform, 17, 53, 92-93, 139, 276, 300-1.
Anglicans, 276, 300, 360. *See also* Anglo-Catholics; Anti-Papal Catholicism; Reformers.
Anglo-Catholics, 269. *See also* Anti-Papal Catholicism.
Anjou, Duke of, 380.
Annates, 42, 54, 58.
Anne Boleyn. *See* Boleyn, Anne.
Anne of Cleves, 95, 101, 353, 380; marriage, 79, 84; Henry VIII's aversion for, 85, 91; divorce, 91.
Annebaut, Claude d', Admiral of France, 116-17.
Annotaciones in Dialogum J. Oecolampadii, etc., 215, 316.
Anti-Papal Catholicism, 80, 98, 107, 148, 216, 219, 223, 235, 243, 244. *See also* Catholic doctrine and practice, under Henry VIII.
Anti-Papal feeling, 57, 80, 219, 243-44, 260-61.
Anti-reforming party. *See* Conservative party.
Antwerp, 118, 127, 351, 363.
Apostles, 14, 61, 62, 172, 388; Canons of the, 112.
Appeals to Rome, forbidden, 49, 54.
Aragon, Catherine of. *See* Catherine.
Archbishop's Court. *See* Court.
Archdeacon, office of, 8, 146, 342.
Ardres, 90, 91.
Arlsford, 294.
Arran, Earl of, 359.
Arras, Bishop of. *See* Granvelle, Antoine de.